International Investment Law and Dispute Resolution in the Western Balkans

Nijhoff International Investment Law Series

Series Editors

Prof. Eric De Brabandere (*Leiden University*)
Prof. Tarcisio Gazzini (*University of Padua*)
Prof. Stephan W. Schill (*University of Amsterdam*)
Prof. Attila Tanzi (*University of Bologna*)

VOLUME 27

The titles published in this series are listed at *brill.com/iils*

International Investment Law and Dispute Resolution in the Western Balkans

Regional Prospects for a European Future

Edited by

Fahira Brodlija
Armela Ramić

BRILL | NIJHOFF

LEIDEN | BOSTON

Library of Congress Cataloging-in-Publication Data

Names: Brodlija, Fahira, editor. | Ramić, Armela, editor.
Title: International investment law and dispute resolution in the Western balkans : regional prospects for a European future / edited by Fahira Brodlija, Armela Ramić.
Description: Leiden ; Boston : Brill/Nijhoff, 2025. | Series: Nijhoff international investment law series ; volume 27 | Includes index.
Identifiers: LCCN 2025002737 (print) | LCCN 2025002738 (ebook) | ISBN 9789004729872 (paperback) | ISBN 9789004729889 (ebook)
Subjects: LCSH: Investments, Foreign–Law and legislation–Balkan Peninsula. | Dispute resolution (Law)–Balkan Peninsula. | Investments, Foreign (International law)
Classification: LCC KJC6433 .I57 2025 (print) | LCC KJC6433 (ebook) | DDC 346.496/092–dc23/eng/20250118
LC record available at https://lccn.loc.gov/2025002737
LC ebook record available at https://lccn.loc.gov/2025002738

Typeface for the Latin, Greek, and Cyrillic scripts: "Brill". See and download: brill.com/brill-typeface.

ISSN 2351-9542
ISBN 978-90-04-72987-2 (hardback)
ISBN 978-90-04-72988-9 (e-book)
DOI 10.1163/9789004729889

Contents

Foreword

Against the background of global economics and law, the Western Balkans stands out as a region of profound transformation and potential. The dissolution of Yugoslavia set the stage for a complex journey towards market-based economies, a path marked by political and industrial reforms that have re-shaped the region's economic landscape. Yet despite these advances, the Western Balkans' foreign direct investment (FDI) has trailed behind its Central and Eastern European neighbors, often channeled into service sectors with limited industrial spillover.

"Investment Protection and Investor-State Dispute Resolution in the Western Balkans: Regional Prospects for a European Future" fills an important void in our understanding the dynamics that have shaped FDI trends in the region. Its specific contribution is a dissection of the legal and institutional frameworks that underpin investment protection and dispute resolution, and the role they serve in attracting and retaining foreign investment. Drawing on insights from government officials, legal experts, practitioners, academics, and representatives from international organizations, the book provides unparalleled insights into the region's complex investment and dispute settlement architecture, with chapters focused both on specific cross-cutting topics and on individual countries in the region.

Within the country-specific chapters, readers will find a detailed examination of each Western Balkans economy, their legal systems, FDI trends, treaty practices, empirical data on investment dispute resolution cases, and related policy reforms. Cross-cutting chapters discuss the importance of regional approaches to investment policy reform, bilateral investment treaty protections and model provisions, and modernization attempts, including implications of EU accession on investment policies and treaties.

The institution that I represent—the International Centre for Settlement of Investment Disputes (ICSID)—serves an important role in this space. Established in 1966 by the Executive Directors of the World Bank Group, ICSID is the only organization that is specifically dedicated to the resolution of international investment disputes to promote foreign investment. As my colleague Frauke Nitschke explains in her contribution to the book, countries of the Western Balkans have accounted for a relatively small portion of ICSID's overall caseload (about 4% at the time of publication). These cases have nonetheless played an important role in the evolution of ICSID caselaw. Furthermore, as members of ICSID, the states of the Western Balkans have contributed to the governance of ICSID. For that I am grateful, and ICSID stands ready to support the region in its continued economic development.

Finally, to the editors and contributors of this important book, I extend a heartfelt congratulations. You have produced an indispensable resource for policymakers, legal practitioners, and scholars with an interest in how the region's economic and regulatory environment intersects with investment promotion and protection.

Martina Polasek
Secretary-General, ICSID

Illustrations

Figures

Tables

Notes on Co-editors

Fahira Brodlija
is the Rule of Law Advisor for a regional GIZ legal reform project focusing on the legal framework for investment protection and investor-state dispute settlement in the Western Balkans. Her work includes advisory support for the governments in the Western Balkans and abroad on the procedural and substantive provisions of (model) investment treatises, support in designing and developing dispute prevention and management mechanisms, and capacity development, including practical training and simulations.

Fahira is an adjunct lecturer at the International University of Sarajevo, where she initiated the Annual IUS Summer School in international arbitration, taking place since 2021. She frequently writes and speaks on topics related to ISDS reform, investment law and international dispute resolution more broadly.

Fahira is a tutor for the CiArb Diploma program, and appeared as guest lecturer at esteemed universities, such as Columbia University in New York, Bocconi University in Italy and College of Law, Chrisland University in Nigeria. She is also a lecturer for the Africa Arbitration Academy program.

Fahira has authored over 50 articles, most recently published in the Penn State Law journal and European Investment Law and Arbitration Review, with others published in university journals and online platforms such as the Kluwer Arbitration Blog. In addition, Fahira has co-edited two Kluwer books on international commercial and investment arbitration, while contributing chapters to others.

Fahira is a former Vis Moot participant and a coach of law faculties from Bosnia and Herzegovina and the region since 2016. Fahira is a member of Association ARBITRI, and founder of the GEM diversity and mentorship program supporting young academics and practitioners in the field of international arbitration.

Armela Ramić
is a bar-certified Attorney at Law and a legal practitioner with over twelve (12) years of professional experience. She is the lead attorney for the development and execution of complex foreign direct investment projects in Bosnia and Herzegovina (BiH), with a focus on construction and infrastructure projects. Armela regularly demonstrates her capabilities in handling complex legal matters in an extremely challenging local legal environment. Armela specializes construction and energy law (with focus on FIDIC based projects),

international transactions and dispute resolution (litigation and arbitration proceedings).

Furthermore, Armela is a co-founder and the president of the ARBITRI Association, established in 2013. The association's primary goal is to develop a robust arbitration system in Bosnia and Herzegovina and attract foreign investors to the country. Armela has designed and implemented numerous training programs for the business community, in-house lawyers, judges of commercial departments and government institutions in the field of arbitration. Armela is listed as an arbitrator at the Arbitration Court of the Foreign Trade Chamber of Bosnia and Herzegovina and is included in the list of individuals qualified to serve as arbitrators at the Permanent Arbitration at the Chamber of Commerce and Industry of Serbia.

She regularly speaks at conferences and seminars dedicated to dispute resolution, arbitration and international contract law, contributes to various international publications, as well as informs the government's legislative efforts to enhance the regulatory framework in Bosnia and Herzegovina.

Notes on Authors

Irena Alajbeg
is Director General for Economic Affairs and Development Cooperation at Ministry of Foreign and European Affairs. Her responsibilities include EU trade and investment policy issues, bilateral and multilateral economic affairs, development cooperation and humanitarian aid. Prior to that she served as Director for Trade and Investment Policy in charge of WTO issues, bilateral investment treaties and investor to state dispute settlement.

She is a member of Trade Policy Committee of the Council of EU and she represents Croatia in OECD Trade Committee, Investment Committee and UNCITRAL WG III (Reform of Investor to State Dispute Settlement System).

Previously she held various positions in ministries of economy and finance, mainly dealing with issues of international agreements (economic cooperation, double taxation agreements) and foreign investment policies.

She holds a master law degree from Faculty of Law, Zagreb University.

Filip Balcerzak
LL.M. (2011, Canada), Ph.D. (2016, Poland), Ph.D. (2024, Spain), FCIArb, is a lecturer in law at Brunel University of London (United Kingdom), an associate professor at Adam Mickiewicz University in Poznań (Poland), an attorney-at-law (Poland, Spain) and a partner at SSW law firm (Poland).

He has served as an arbitrator in over fifty arbitration cases, in all capacities: as a presiding arbitrator, side arbitrator, sole arbitrator and an emergency arbitrator. The European Commission nominated him as a candidate arbitrator and expert on trade and sustainability in disputes regarding trade agreements between the EU and third countries.

Fahira Brodlija
is the Rule of Law Advisor for a regional GIZ legal reform project focusing on the legal framework for investment protection and investor-state dispute settlement in the Western Balkans. Her work includes advisory support for the governments in the Western Balkans and abroad on the procedural and substantive provisions of (model) investment treatises, support in designing and developing dispute prevention and management mechanisms, and capacity development, including practical training and simulations.

Fahira is an adjunct lecturer at the International University of Sarajevo, where she initiated the Annual IUS Summer School in international arbitration, taking place since 2021. She frequently writes and speaks on topics related to ISDS reform, investment law and international dispute resolution more broadly.

Fahira is a tutor for the CiArb Diploma program, and appeared as guest lecturer at esteemed universities, such as Columbia University in New York, Bocconi University in Italy and College of Law, Chrisland University in Nigeria. She is also a lecturer for the Africa Arbitration Academy program.

Fahira has authored over 50 articles, most recently published in the Penn State Law journal and European Investment Law and Arbitration Review, with others published in university journals and online platforms such as the Kluwer Arbitration Blog. In addition, Fahira has co-edited two Kluwer books on international commercial and investment arbitration, while contributing chapters to others.

Fahira is a former Vis Moot participant and a coach of law faculties from Bosnia and Herzegovina and the region since 2016. Fahira is a member of Association ARBITRI, and founder of the GEM diversity and mentorship program supporting young academics and practitioners in the field of international arbitration.

Lyra Cela

is currently a doctoral candidate at Bocconi University in Milan, Italy. Ms. Çela completed her basic legal studies at the Faculty of Law of the University of Prishtina and holds an LLM in International Civil and Commercial Law from Leiden University in the Netherlands. Her research interests lie in the intersection between private international law and international arbitration with international human rights law. She has completed fellowships/research stays at Oslo University's Norwegian Center for Human Rights and at the European Court of Human Rights in Strasbourg. Additionally, she has coached the University of Prishtina's team for the Willem C. Vis International Commercial Arbitration Moot in Vienna.

Ms. Çela has an extensive experience within the rule of law institutions in the Republic of Kosovo. Most recently, she served as Chief of Cabinet and Senior Legal Advisor to the President of the Constitutional Court of the Republic Kosovo. Prior to this role, she has directed the Division for Bilateral and International Treaties at Kosovo's Ministry of Justice Department for International Cooperation and served as Deputy Chairperson of Kosovo's Agency for Free Legal Aid.

Silvana Cinari

holds a PhD from the University of Tirana, Faculty of Law, where she defended a thesis concerning provisional measures in civil litigation and arbitration proceedings. She is also a graduate of the University of Geneva and the Graduate Institute of International and Development Studies (IHEID) with a Master of Laws in International Dispute Settlement (MIDS, 2020). Silvana has fourteen years of academic experience.

She is a lecturer in the courses of Civil Procedure Law, ADR and International Arbitration at the Faculty of Law, University of Tirana. She is the co-author of a textbook on Alternative Dispute Resolution and has authored several other publications focused mainly on dispute resolution. She has also attended several international summer programs, mainly concerning international arbitration and private international law in France, Netherlands, etc., and conducted research at the Max Planck Institute of Comparative and International Private Law, Hamburg, Germany. She has also been engaged as a legal expert in various national, regional, and international projects related to her areas of expertise and research. Silvana is also a senior associate at "Kola & Associates" Law Firm providing counseling and legal representation in litigation and arbitration proceedings mainly on Commercial, Tax, IP, Administrative, Labor, Construction, Mining, and Energy Law disputes.

Vangel Dokovski

is an Associate Professor of Private International Law at the University Ss. Cyril and Methodius, Iustinianus Primus Law Faculty in Skopje. He has held this position since 2016. Dr. Dokovski earned his PhD in Law from the Iustinianus Primus Faculty of Law in Skopje in 2015, with a dissertation focused on "Party autonomy in non-contractual obligations."

Throughout his career, Dr. Dokovski has pursued extensive additional education and training in private international law and arbitration, including:

- Attending the Summer session of the Hague Academy of International Law in Private International Law, The Hague (2011)
- Participating in the Paris International Academy for Arbitration Law, Paris (2011)
- Engaging with the Fondation pour le droit continental, Paris (2012)
- Completing the Law & Business in Europe program at Collegio Carlo Alberto, Turin, Italy (2012)
- Studying at the Istituto Universitario di Studi Europei, Turin, Italy (2014)
- Attending Vienna University of Economics and Business, Vienna (2015)
- Participating in the Xiamen Academy for International Law, Xiamen, China (2018)

Dr. Dokovski has co-authored two books: "Private International Law" (a textbook) and "Private International Law: Cases and Materials." Additionally, he has written more 30 articles in his field. Alongside Professor Toni Deskoski, Dr. Dokovski coaches the teams for the Willem C. Vis International Arbitration

Moot and the Frankfurt Investment Arbitration Moot, contributing significantly to the development of future legal professionals in international arbitration.

Kabir Duggal
is an attorney in Arnold and Porter's New York office focusing on international arbitration and public international law matters, serving both as arbitrator and mediator. He is recognized as a "Chartered Arbitrator" (the highest ranking for arbitrators) by both the Chartered Institute of Arbitrators and the Asian Institute of Alternative Dispute Resolution. He also frequently serves as an expert on international arbitration and public international law matters. Dr. Duggal is also a Lecturer-in-Law at Columbia Law School, an adjunct Professor at Fordham Law School, and a Course Director and a Faculty Member for the Columbia Law School-Chartered Institute of Arbitrators Comprehensive Course on International Arbitration. He also acts as a Consultant for the United Nations Office of the High Representative for Least Developed Countries (UN-OHRLLS) on the creation of a novel "Investment Support Program." Dr. Duggal works closely with the U.S. Department of Commerce's Commercial Law Development Program (CLDP) as an expert.

He has also conducted training and capacity-building sessions for several Governments on public international law and dispute resolution matters. He has published over 60 articles and has spoken at over 300 arbitration events all over the world. He is also a passionate advocate for diversity, equity, and inclusion issues and frequently writes and speaks on these issues. He is the Co-Founder of REAL (Racial Equality for Arbitration Lawyers), a non-profit seeking to create greater representation in international arbitration. He is a graduate of the University of Mumbai, University of Oxford (DHL-Times of India Scholar), NYU School of Law (Hauser Global Scholar), Leiden Law School (2019 CEPANI Academic Prize), and is currently pursuing an SJD Degree from Harvard Law School. Dr. Duggal is admitted to practice law in New York, District of Columbia, England & Wales (as a Barrister), and in India.

Ivana Gardašević
is a results-driven professional with a steadfast commitment to promoting investments and economic development. She has recognized expertise in investment-related activities and fiscal reforms. Ivana boasts a proven track record of cultivating strategic partnerships and implementing innovative strategies to drive sustainable development.

Currently, Ivana serves at the United Nations Development Programme (UNDP) within the field of Public Finance for Development and Integrated

Local Development. She is particularly focused on advancing sustainable finance and public finance management, working closely with government ministries and bodies to implement crucial public finance reforms and foster fiscal sustainability.

From 2016 to 2023, Ivana led the Competitiveness division within the Regional Cooperation Council, overseeing finance and investment initiatives, including FDI screening, ISDS, and both investment policy and promotion. She coordinated with domestic, regional, and international stakeholders, mobilized resources, and negotiated new projects, enhancing financial and investment integration.

Ms. Gardašević's earlier career includes serving at the Ministry of Economy – Government of Montenegro from 2007 to 2016. During her tenure, Ivana played a pivotal role in negotiating International Investment Agreements (IIAs) and served as the Deputy Chief Negotiator for Chapter 30 – External Relations, integral to Montenegro's EU accession. She spearheaded the Economic Reform Program, focusing on investment and competitiveness. Ivana also managed bilateral economic cooperation and donation packages from countries like Norway and Japan, enhancing Montenegro's investment climate and economic growth through strategic negotiations, policy formulation, and direct engagement with investors and international entities.

Samiha Gopal
is an attorney admitted to practice in India. She holds an LL.M. from Columbia University and earned her first law degree at NALSAR University, Hyderabad.

Kevin W. Gray
is assistant professor of law at Peking University – School of Transnational Law. He holds law degrees from Canada and the United States, as well as graduate degrees in philosophy.

Flutura Kola Tafaj
graduated from the Faculty of Law, University of Tirana in 1995 and completed her master's studies at the same faculty in 2004. In 2009, she defended the scientific degree "Doctor" at the Faculty of Law, University of Tirana with a thesis concerning arbitral awards, their challenge, and enforcement. Since 2012, she holds the academic title "Associate Professor". Assoc. Prof. Flutura Kola Tafaj has twenty-nine years of experience as an academic and practitioner. She is a professor of Civil Procedure Law, ADR, Legal Clinics, and International Arbitration at the Faculty of Law University of Tirana and a partner at the "Kola & Associates" law firm.

She has participated in numerous national and international conferences and has conducted research in different countries such as Suffolk University,

Boston, Massachusetts, USA; University "Montesquieu Bordeaux IV", Bordo, France; Max Planck Institute for Comparative and International Private Law, Hamburg, Germany; IDLI and UNIDROIT, Rome, Italy, etc. She co-authored textbooks and commentaries on Civil Procedure Law, ADR, and Private International Law and has published several research papers. She is also a training expert at the School of Magistrates and has been engaged as a legal expert in many regional and international projects.

Marialena Komi
is a Greek-qualified dispute resolution lawyer with extensive experience in international arbitration and investment law. She holds an LLB from the National and Kapodistrian University of Athens and an LLM in Transnational Arbitration and Dispute Settlement from Sciences Po Law School, in Paris.

Marialena has worked in top-tier law firms both in Athens and in Paris. She has advised on significant energy and construction projects and participated in several commercial arbitrations under the ICC, LCIA and SCC Rules. She also has a strong focus on investment arbitration. She has participated in several investment cases under the ICSID and UNCITRAL Rules.

In parallel, she acts as a research assistant to Professor Nikos Lavranos, assisting with comprehensive research on investment law and arbitration.

Nikos Lavranos
is the first Secretary-General of the European Federation for Investment Law and Arbitration (EFILA). He is founder & owner of NL-Investmentconsulting, external Legal Advisor for numerous law firms. He is also Partner at Herreveld van der Hurk & Partners, Senior Advisor at Grayston & Company (Brussels) and Of Counsel at Wöss & Partners (Vienna). He specializes in international investment law & arbitration, EU law, WTO law and public international law. Nikos has advised in numerous disputes involving in particular Dutch BIT s, intra-EU BIT s and the ECT initiated under various rules such as ICSID, UNCITRAL and SCC rules. He is listed as Arbitrator by the EU regarding EU free trade and investment agreements, as Arbitrator and/or Mediator at CIETAC, VIAC, AIAC, Energy Disputes Arbitration Centre (EDAC) and Energy Community.

In addition, he is Visiting Professor International Arbitration at Leiden University and Guest Professor at several other universities in Europe.

Vlora Maxhuni
is a Rule of Law Adviser at Deutsche Gesellschaft für Internationale Zusammenarbeit (GIZ) in the Regional Project "Legal Reform for Economic Development in the Western Balkans," based in Prishtina, Kosovo. With extensive

experience in legal advisory roles, she has contributed to drafting strategic documents and primary and secondary legislation and provided comprehensive legal advice in the area of Rule of Law in Kosovo. She holds an LL.M. in International Trade and Investment Law from Maastricht University (2019) and a Bachelor's degree in Law from the University of Prishtina (2018). Additionally, she has passed the Kosovo bar exam in 2023.

Maja Menard
is managing partner of Fatur Menard (Slovenia). She represents clients before the European Commission, the EU courts and the ECHR, advises clients and acts as arbitrator in proceedings under the auspices and rules of the Ljubljana Arbitration Centre, the International Court of Arbitration of the ICC, the LCIA, the SCC Arbitration Institute, UNCITRAL and ICSID.

Maja is a member of the International Court of Arbitration of the ICC, the ICC Commission on Arbitration and ADR, the LCIA and the ILA, is admitted to the Paris and Slovenian Bars and lectures and publishes on her areas of expertise.

Ilija Mitrev Penushliski
is a partner in Three Crowns' Paris office. He extensive experience representing and advising States, corporations and individuals in both investor-State and commercial disputes, particularly in the energy sector.

Ilija has advised and trained companies and States on arbitration and public international law matters, including in the Western Balkans. He is a Member of the ICC Court of Arbitration and an Ambassador for VIAC. He has regularly featured in Who's Who Legal, including as a Global Elite Thought Leader.

Ilija teaches international arbitration at the Université de Fribourg, Switzerland. He holds degrees from Harvard Law School, the University of Oxford and the Ss. Cyril and Methodius University. He is admitted to practice law in New York and Paris.

Dragana Nikolić
is a qualified Serbian attorney-at-law specializing in dispute resolution, investment law and public international law. She assisted in representing companies, individuals and governments in numerous high-stake investment and commercial arbitrations under all major sets of arbitration rules, including ICSID, UNCITRAL, ICC, SIAC, LCIA and VIAC rules. Additionally, she handles civil lawsuits and has expertise in the energy, construction, and banking sectors.

Dragana holds master's degrees in international law from the University of Cambridge and the University of Belgrade, completing her undergraduate studies at the latter. Her academic excellence has been recognized with various merit-based scholarships, awards, and honors, including the prestigious Pegasus Trust Scholarship Award from the Honourable Society of the Inner Temple. Dragana worked at leading law firms specializing in international arbitration in London and Paris and is currently collaborating with a premier Austrian law firm. Recognized as a 'Rising Star' in Dispute Resolution in Serbia by Legal 500, Dragana serves as the regional representative for the Young ICCA association and as an ambassador for the Arbitrator Intelligence organization in the CEE. She regularly lectures and writes on all aspects of international arbitration.

Frauke Nitschke

is a Senior Counsel at the International Centre for Settlement of Investment Disputes (ICSID). Frauke serves as the team lead for ICSID staff handling proceedings in English. Frauke also serves as Secretary of tribunals, conciliation commissions and *ad hoc* committees in investor-State proceedings conducted pursuant to the ICSID Convention and the ICSID Additional Facility Rules involving a variety of economic sectors and legal instruments. Frauke further leads ICSID's investor-State mediation activities, including the drafting of the ICSID Mediation Rules and amendments to ICSID's conciliation frameworks. Frauke has conducted investment mediation skills trainings for mediators and government officials. Frauke regularly speaks at international conferences on investment mediation and recently chaired ICSID's Investment Mediation Insights seminars. Prior to joining ICSID, Frauke served in the World Bank's Legal Vice Presidency and the Inspection Panel. Frauke is an accredited mediator and admitted to the D.C. and New York State Bar. She holds a law degree from the Freie Universität Berlin, an LLM from Georgetown University Law Center, and a master's degree in psychology from the Fern Universität Hagen.

Milana Ranković

is a Teaching Assistant at the University of Montenegro, Faculty of Law, for the subjects Private International Law and Arbitration Law and a Ph.D. student of Private International Law at Faculty of Law, University of Novi Sad.

She graduated from the Faculty of Law, University of Montenegro, with an average grade 9.00 in Bachelor studies and 10.00 in Specialist studies. She continued her education in Great Britain, at the University of Swansea, as a Chevening scholar, where she obtained a Masters degree with "distinction", for which the equivalent grade in Montenegro is 9.4. Due to the achieved results, the Faculty awarded her with the recognition that she is one of the best 10% of students at the Institute of International Shipping and Trade Law for 2019/2020, and the law firm "HFW" from London presented her with an award because she achieved the highest grade in the module carriage of goods by sea, air and road. She is coordinating coach of the Vis Moot Court Team from University of Montenegro, in charge of the preparation of students for Willem C. Vis International Commercial Arbitration Moot in Vienna. She has four years of work experience in legal practice. She participated in numerous projects, and professional and scientific conferences in Montenegro and abroad and is the author of several scientific and research articles. She is fluent in English and has good knowledge of Italian and German.

Armela Ramić
is a bar-certified Attorney at Law and a legal practitioner with over twelve (12) years of professional experience. She is the lead attorney for the development and execution of complex foreign direct investment projects in Bosnia and Herzegovina (BiH), with a focus on construction and infrastructure projects. Armela regularly demonstrates her capabilities in handling complex legal matters in an extremely challenging local legal environment. Armela specializes construction and energy law (with focus on FIDIC based projects), international transactions and dispute resolution (litigation and arbitration proceedings).

Furthermore, Armela is a co-founder and the president of the ARBITRI Association, established in 2013. The association's primary goal is to develop a robust arbitration system in Bosnia and Herzegovina and attract foreign investors to the country. Armela has designed and implemented numerous training programs for the business community, in-house lawyers, judges of commercial departments and government institutions in the field of arbitration. Armela is listed as an arbitrator at the Arbitration Court of the Foreign Trade Chamber of Bosnia and Herzegovina and is included in the list of individuals qualified to serve as arbitrators at the Permanent Arbitration at the Chamber of Commerce and Industry of Serbia.

She regularly speaks at conferences and seminars dedicated to dispute resolution, arbitration and international contract law, contributes to various international publications, as well as informs the government's legislative efforts to enhance the regulatory framework in Bosnia and Herzegovina.

Peter Rižnik
is an arbitrator in independent practice based in Vienna, Austria. As a Slovenian national he has particular expertise in the Central-European and Central-Eastern European markets. With extensive experience serving as arbitrator, tribunal secretary, and counsel, Peter has participated in commercial

and investment arbitrations conducted under the rules of the ICC, LCIA, VIAC, SCC, Ljubljana Arbitration Centre, Finnish Arbitration Institute and the UNCITRAL Arbitration Rules.

Peter is a founding member and board member of ArbCEE, a member of the ICC Commission on Arbitration and ADR and its taskforce on combating corruption. He is also active in academia and regularly lectures on arbitration.

Diana Rosert

is Economic Affairs Officer at the United Nations trade and development body (UNCTAD) in Geneva. She holds a Master of Arts from the University of Warwick and a Postgraduate Diploma in Laws from the University of London. She has over 12 years of experience in policy research focused on investment treaties and investor–State arbitration, and is responsible for UNCTAD data on investment dispute settlement cases. She also contributes to capacity-building activities for governments focusing on investment treaty reform options.

Ajla Serdarević

is a graduated law student from Sarajevo, Bosnia and Herzegovina. She pursued her BA in law at the International University of Sarajevo (IUS) and at the Faculty of Law of the University of Sarajevo. She is currently pursuing the Geneva LL.M. in International Dispute Settlement (MIDS), a joint program of the University of Geneva, Faculty of Law, and the Graduate Institute of International and Development Studies.

Ajla successfully completed the Harvardx course called HLS4X: Bioethics: The Law, Medicine, and Ethics of Reproductive Technologies and Genetics. She successfully completed Summer School of International Arbitration in 2021 and 2022 at the International University of Sarajevo. In 2024 she successfully completed the International Winter school on Energy transition at the School of Economics and Business of the University of Sarajevo. She participated in the International Investment Arbitration Moot Competition Mediateguru competition, in which her team won third place, and Ajla Serdarević won the Best Speaker title. Ajla participated in the 29th and the 30th Willem C. Vis International Commercial Arbitration Moot competition. After winning the Western Balkans Arbitration Writing Competition she published her article on Energy Charter Treaty- In Search for Balance and Clarity in Austrian Yearbook on International Arbitration 2023. As a member of Association ARBITRI, Ajla supports the activities and work of the Association, including conducting the Sarajevo Arbitration Day conference and the Girl Empowerment and Mentorship Program.

Aneta Spaić
is the Dean of Faculty of Law, University of Montenegro, elected in two mandates (2019-2022; 2022-2025).

At the Faculty of Law, she was elected to all University positions, from Assistant in 2005, to Full Professor in 2020. Currently, she teaches at the Faculty of Law and the Faculty of Political Sciences of the University of Montenegro, at the following subjects: Business Law clinic, Fundamentals of Law, International Business Law, Media Law and EU Law. She was also engaged as a visiting professor – researcher at American University, Washington College of Law, USA and as visiting professor at Washington and Lee Law School, Virginia. Since 2010, she has been the national correspondent of Montenegro at UNCITRAL. She is a member of the Legal and Political Sciences Committee of CANU, and since 2014 she has been a member of the Academy of Young Scientists in Berlin. Since 2005, she has been an arbitrator of the Foreign Trade Arbitration of Montenegro, she is on the list of mediators of the Mediation Centre of Montenegro, and she was also a member Prosecutor's Council of Montenegro for a period of three years. Also, she is VIAC Ambassador for Montenegro. She has been the president of the Montenegrin branch of the International Legal Association, based in London, since 2019.

As a national and international expert, she is engaged in numerous projects of the Council of Europe, GIZ, OSCE, UNESCO, UNDP. She participated at a large number of conferences and symposiums and is the author of several monographs by renowned publishers (Cambridge, Oxford Press and Kluwer) and a significant number of texts published in indexed international journals.

Samira Sulejmanović
is a Head of the Department for Bilateral Trade Relations in the Ministry of Foreign Trade and Economic Relations of Bosnia and Herzegovina. In her portfolio, she deals with overall bilateral trade and economic relations of the country, including negotiation and implementation of the International Investment Agreements (IIAs), preferential trade agreements and economic cooperation agreements.

The IIAs became part of her portfolio ever since she had taken over Department at the end of 2010. She has been very active in the IIAs' reform process by advocating the need to rethink the national policy objectives, working to establishing a critical level of awareness and pursuing joint action among countries in the Western Balkan's region and contributing multilateral work and debate under the auspices of various international fora, primarily UNCTAD, UNCITRAL and OECD.

The reform of IIAs' regime in Bosnia and Herzegovina is among her major professional achievements in the recent time. The whole reform was phased in over almost a decade and consisted of different yet related parts, i.e., reform of the investment policy reflected in the IIAs, drafting new model agreement text, creating a governmental body for peaceful resolution of investment disputes, creating mechanism for early detection and prevention of investment disputes.

She has published a number of professional articles, co-authored studies/ commentaries, and delivered lectures to postgraduate students on trade negotiations from the perspective of Bosnia and Herzegovina. She graduated in economics from the School of Economics and Business, University of Sarajevo.

CHAPTER 1

Introduction: Investment Protection and Investor-State Dispute Resolution in the Western Balkans

Mapping the Path of Regional Reform

Fahira Brodlija

The Western Balkans region slowly entered a stage of transition to market-based economy following the dissolution of former Yugoslavia,[1] with newly independent countries developing at a pace affected by a number of factors, primarily political instability, deindustrialization and inward-facing privatization.[2] The region has seen economic growth in the first decade of the 21st century, but the foreign direct investment flows have lagged far behind the levels of other transitioning countries in Central and Eastern Europe (CEE).[3]

Foreign Direct Investment (FDI) was not a high priority for the regional governments, and even when investment flows increased, they were directed at non-tradeable markets in service sectors.[4] This has resulted in a disproportionately low level of FDI in productive industries, compared to other transitioning countries in the CEE region, and a lagging spillover of know-how and technologies into the Western Balkans.[5]

As the European Union (EU) ambitions of the region intensified, the EU started setting reform standards for economic development and restructuring,

1 Christopher Cviić and Peter Sanfey, *In Search of the Balkan Recovery: The Political and Economic Reemergence of South-Eastern Europe*, New York: Columbia University Press (2010).

2 Saul Estrin and Milica Uvalic, 'Foreign direct investment in the Western Balkans: what role has it played during transition?' Comparative Economic Studies, London School of Economics and Political Sciences, ISSN 0888-7233 DOI: 10.1057, 2016) https://eprints.lse.ac.uk/67004/1/ESTRIN.pdf, accessed 10 June 2023.

3 Ibid.

4 Saul Estrin and Milica Uvalic, FDI into transition economies: Are the Balkans different? (Economics of Transition, 10.1111/ecot.12040, vol 22, 2014), https://www.researchgate.net/publication/260802571_FDI_into_transition_economies_Are_the_Balkans_different/citation/download, accessed 10 June 2023.

5 Ibid.

 DOI:10.1163/9789004729889_002

backed up by generous financial support and incentives.[6] As a result, the Western Balkans economies (WB economies) have engaged in a series of reforms which largely affect the legal, institutional and economic approach to investment protection.[7] Very soon, this will inevitably include the pivot from investment arbitration, which is now declared contrary to EU law, to a more judicialized form of dispute resolution with foreign investors (as proposed by the EU Commission).[8] Over the years, the region is gradually shedding its reputation as the Wild, Wild West(ern) Balkans, and coming into its own as an increasingly important player on the European and global marketplace. Today, the region is at the center of attention as an appealing destination for robust renewable energy projects, given its wealth of natural resources and strategic geographic positioning in Europe.

The visible results of regional efforts for integration into the EU and global markets, coupled with the sustained regulatory action towards improving transparency and legal certainty, have made the Western Balkans a more attractive terrain for foreign investors seeking lucrative opportunities, international development organizations interested in accelerating reforms, and the legal community at large seeking to offer their services in the process.[9] The region recognized international investment protection treaties as a tool to demonstrate its openness to foreign investment, protected by norms of international law. As a result, Western Balkans economies entered into a robust network

6 The reform and collaboration framework of the EU with the Western Balkans includes an Economic and Investment Plan, with a special focus on energy and roaming, as well as a separate Western Balkans Investment Framework (WBIF). Information and updates about the EU policies and initiatives for the region are available on the website of the European Commission here: https://neighbourhood-enlargement.ec.europa.eu/enlargement-policy/enhanced-eu-engagement-western-balkans_en, accessed 10 June 2023.

7 Bosnia and Herzegovina, Montenegro and North Macedonia are in the final stages of developing new Model BITs, aligned with EU policies, almost all countries are deliberating dispute prevention frameworks and there are efforts to create a robust investment screening mechanism. All of these activities are taking place under the broader framework of the Common Regional Market for the Western Balkans as well as the related Action Plan.

8 The new model BITs in the region provide that the dispute resolution mechanism for investor-State disputes provided in the treaty will be replaced with the mechanism established by the EU (possibly the multilateral investment court) upon their accession to the EU.

9 The EU is the largest donor and trade partner in the region, and EU companies account for over 60% of the overall FDI stock in the region. Almost 70% of the region's total trade in 2021 was within the EU and EU companies are by far the leading investors, accounting for 61% of FDI stock in the region in 2021 relations. the EU views the socio-economic prosperity of the Western Balkans as a staple of stability in Europe, which explains the EU Commission's pledge to dedicate technical, financial and political support for the region on its path to EU accession https://neighbourhood-enlargement.ec.europa.eu/system/files/2022-12/eu_wb_relations.pdf, accessed 10 June 2023.

of bilateral investment treaties and other international agreements offering generous protections to foreign investors, including the ability to pursue their rights against the host States directly in investment arbitration proceedings.

Naturally, there are still lingering issues of slow and large bureaucracy, political instability and risk which are at the front of mind for the stakeholders interested in investing in the WB economies. All these concerns can be mitigated and navigated with the proper information and engagement with the local institutions and experts in the field.

In a very short period of time, a wide spectrum of stakeholders became interested in understanding the region and participating in its development and related opportunities.[10] This includes policy makers, international organizations, development banks, foreign investors from around the world, business enterprises from a variety of sectors, lawyers and legal experts, scholars and educators, etc.

However, since most foreign (and even domestic) stakeholders do not have direct access to the sources of key information, there is an imminent need for a reliable navigation tool which will inform them about the risks and opportunities in the investment protection landscape in the Western Balkans region. This means, in particular, the legal and institutional infrastructure at their disposal in each jurisdiction, as well as the existing trends and ongoing reform efforts which will shape the region in the years to come.

The book, „Investment Protection and Investor State Dispute Resolution in the Western Balkans: Regional Reforms for a European Future“ will be the first resource of this kind, providing comprehensive, systemic and well-rounded analysis of all the key issues of interest for stakeholders in the field of investment protection and dispute resolution. In addition to the clear and precise analysis of the legal and institutional frameworks, the book will also provide a "glance behind the curtain" shedding light on the context and background of the emerging trends, as well as the realities "on the ground" within the investment protection framework in the Western Balkans. Each chapter will be carefully curated and crafted by select experts, including government representatives, legal practitioners, academics and representatives of international development organizations. Thus, the book will open new avenues for

10 Naida Taso, 'It is high time to empower Western Balkan citizens to go green with renewables self-consumption'(Energy Community, 2022) https://sustainable-energy-week.ec.europa.eu/news/it-high-time-empower-western-balkan-citizens-go-green-renewables-self-consumption-2022-09-06_en, accessed 30 June 2023; Western Balkans Investment framework, Clean Energy (WBIF) https://www.wbif.eu/sectors/energy, 30 June 2023; European Union, 'The EU and the Western Balkans: towards a common future' https://www.eeas.europa.eu/eeas/eu-and-western-balkans-towards-common-future_en, accessed 30 June 2023.

understanding the regional dynamics, and planning for any type of engagement in the region.

While there are many moving parts and developments within the Western Balkans region, there is very little accessible and cohesive literature providing insights into the investment protection framework and investment disputes related to the region. There is certainly no publication providing a comprehensive and in-depth analysis of all the regional economies, placing them in the broader context of the global dynamics and reform processes. There is notoriously little information about the past and pending investment arbitrations against the WB economies, and most news reports or government documents addressing these issues are only available in the local languages.[11] Many of the primary sources of regulation in the investment protection realm (such as national laws, bylaws, and decisions) are also not translated to English, or easily accessible online in all instances.

This sends any interested stakeholder on a scavenger hunt for information which is in high demand, whether in the exploratory phase for a potential investment in the region, or in preparation for an investment dispute involving a government institution or entity in the region. This includes the identification of the competent institution at different stages of the investment cycle, the applicable rules and procedures at different levels of government, and the domestic grievance mechanisms, administrative and judicial remedies available to foreign investors. With fragmented and often outdated information, the interested parties may not fully appreciate certain risks, or in other cases, may reinforce negative stereotypes about the WB economies which could affect their decision to invest or practice law in the region.

This book will provide a wealth of accumulated institutional and scholarly knowledge, packaged into a well-structured and comprehensive publication. As such, it can help bridge the information gap and serve as a one-stop window into the most recent, accurate and contextualized analysis, available for national, regional, and international stakeholders. At the national level, the book will be helpful to domestic policymakers in assessing past and present trends which can inform their future policy direction for sustainable reform and development. It will be particularly useful to understand the dynamics in the other WB economies and to learn about their challenges and best

11 General information can be found on the UNCTAD Investment Policy Hub, the ICSID Website, the website of the Permanent Court of Arbitration, while news reports about the cases are usually hidden behind a paywall in subscription-based platforms, such as Global Arbitration Review, International Investment Arbitration Reporter or Jus Mundi. Therefore, reliable and comprehensive information is difficult to find.

practices - for example to observe the differences between the situation in Croatia one decade after EU accession, and the other aspiring EU members in the region. For the institutions competent for treaty negotiations, the book will provide important context and highlight risks that emerge from the existing body of investment jurisprudence so that they can be avoided or mitigated in new treaties. State attorney's offices (or other bodies in charge of representing the WB economies in investment disputes) can equally benefit from understanding the broader framework for investment protection in the region, and their experiences in investment arbitrations.

Legal practitioners, particularly external counsel for the foreign investors or WB economies involved in investment disputes, will benefit from the book as a valuable resource for preliminary research and as a lighthouse for the relevant primary sources underlying the investment protection and dispute resolution frameworks in the region.

For international development organizations, the book will highlight the key areas of concern and facilitate the identification of future areas of intervention and tracking of the effects of previous projects and activities in this area. By analyzing the common features and divergencies between the regional economies, the international actors operating in foreign trade and investment can conduct their own cost-benefit analysis for various project options and activities. This can be particularly useful to determine whether certain issues should be addressed at the national or regional level, and whether there is a need to modify the tools and modalities of international technical support.

From the perspective of scholars and academics, within the region and beyond, the book can serve as a steppingstone and baseline capturing the *status quo* at this period of development, from which further areas of research and analysis can proliferate. It will also be a benchmark for periodical assessments and comparative analysis at the national and regional levels, particularly once the WB economies accede to the EU (one by one or simultaneously). For university students in the region, the book can be used as regular course material (textbook) in the courses related to international law, international dispute resolution, public international law, private international law, international arbitration (commercial and investment), as well as for legal clinics and student competitions (such as the Frankfurt Investment Moot).[12] The same potential exists for universities outside the region, where the relevant legal fields are studied from an international or comparative perspective.

12 An overview of the framework and history of the Frankfurt Investment Moot is available here: https://www.investmentmoot.org/, accessed 10 June 2023.

1 Overview of the Content of the Book

1.1 *Section 1: International Perspectives and Reforms*

The book will open with a set of chapters providing the bird's eye view of the global discourse surrounding international investment law and dispute resolution, providing a primer on the various reform efforts undertaken at the international level. At the same time, these chapters will place the Western Balkans' current and prospective legal and institutional framework into the international matrix and assess the ongoing reforms against this broader backdrop.

1. The dynamics and benefits of regional reform efforts, as opposed to fragmented, individual reforms will be analyzed in the chapter on "The Importance of a Regional Approach to International Investment Policies, Dispute Resolution and Reform" authored by Kiran Nasir Gore. This chapter will assess the contemporary dynamics of regional reforms of investment policies and investment treaties on different continents to highlight the most prominent movements. Further, the chapter will address the results of the regional reform efforts in the Western Balkans to date, in the broader context of the procedural and substantive reforms pursued at the international level.[13] Through this analysis, the readers will be provided with insights about the specific drivers of regional reform and its effects on the ability of the region to harness its full potential and become more attractive to foreign investors.
2. In the context of EU accession Samira Sulejmanović and Ivana Gardašević will explore the features and viability of the proposal to replace the network of bilateral investment treaties between Western Balkans economies and the EU member states with bilateral treaties between the EU and each Western Balkans Economy. This proposal is part of a unique strategy for trade and investment integration within the region, through the so-called Common Regional Market and related Action Plan for the region.[14] It raises complex issues of public and private international law, adaptation to the EU investment protection framework, and the challenges of dealing with pending ISDS cases in the transition to the EU (in light of the *Achmea* and *Komstroy* decisions). This chapter will explain

---

13 Conducted at the UNCITRAL Working Group III, as well as through the activities of UNCTAD, World Bank Group, ICSID, etc.

14 Common Regional Market for the Western Balkans Action Plan, overview available at: https://neighbourhood-enlargement.ec.europa.eu/enlargement-policy/policy-highlights/common-regional-market_enandhttps://www.rcc.int/pages/143/common-regional-market, accessed 10 June 2023.

the scope and nature of these proposals, and the feasibility of such a treaty regime in the WB economies.

3. In the chapter on "The EU Model Clauses for Member States' BITs with Third Countries – Implications for EU Candidate States" Nikos Lavranos and Marialena Komi will take a deeper dive into the EU investment protection policies towards third states, as reflected in the recently published model clauses. The chapter will analyze the key substantive and procedural clauses, comparing them to the recent EU treaty practice and positions taken at the international stage in the context of ISDS reform. As the Western Balkans economies are working towards EU accession, the chapter will address the implications of the model clauses on their BITs with EU Member States, prior to and after joining the EU.[15]
4. With the additional pressures towards energy transition and climate change mitigation, the region will be in dire need for extensive investments in infrastructure and technology to replace the existing bulk of fossil fuel and carbon-reliant energy production systems.[16] Aside from the Paris Agreement,[17] the Western Balkans region has also committed to the Western Balkans Green Agenda,[18] which is an extension of the EU Green

15 Note by the UNCITRAL Secretariat, *Possible reform of investor-State dispute settlement (ISDS) Appellate and multilateral court mechanisms* (UNCITRAL, 29 November 2019) https://documents-dds-ny.un.org/doc/UNDOC/LTD/V19/113/57/PDF/V1911357.pdf?OpenElement; European Parliamentary Research Service Briefing, *Multilateral Investment Court Overview of the reform proposals and prospects* (published 20 January 2020) https://www.europarl.europa.eu/RegData/etudes/BRIE/2020/646147/EPRS_BRI(2020)646147_EN.pdf, accessed 10 June 2023.

16 European Commission, *Guidelines for the Implementation of the Green Agenda for the Western Balkans* (European Commission, 06 October 2020) https://neighbourhood-enlargement.ec.europa.eu/system/files/2020-10/green_agenda_for_the_western_balkans_en.pdf, accessed 10 June 2023, pp. 37– ; "The Regional Cooperation Council (RCC) published a Study on climate change in the Western Balkans, showing an alarming increase of temperature over the whole territory, predicting an temperature increase of 1.2°C in the near future, destined to warm further by 1.7 – 4.0°C and even exceeding 5.0°C by the end of the century, depending on the global effort in greenhouse gas (GHG) emission reduction." Regional Cooperation Council, *Study on Climate Change in the Western Balkans Region* (RCC, 2020) https://www.rcc.int/pubs/62/study-on-climate-change-in-the-western-balkans-region, accessed 10 June 2023.

17 An overview of the features and goals of the Paris Agreement is available here: https://unfccc.int/process-and-meetings/the-paris-agreement, accessed 10 June 2023.

18 European Commission, *Guidelines for the Implementation of the Green Agenda for the Western Balkans* (European Commission, 06 October 2020) https://neighbourhood-enlargement.ec.europa.eu/system/files/2020-10/green_agenda_for_the_western_balkans_en.pdf, accessed 10 June 2023.

Deal.[19] The accomplishment of these goals under their ambitious timelines will be a demanding balancing act for the region: attracting robust investments in the renewable energy sector, preventing and mitigating large-scale investment claims by fossil fuel investors facing phase-out regulations, establishing and maintaining a stable regulatory framework for renewable energy (to avoid the Spanish scenario), all while ensuring a continued and affordable energy supply for consumers.[20]

The success of the energy transition process around the world will largely depend on the scale of investments in the renewable energy sector, which in turn requires government incentives and legal stability. The Western Balkans region will be no exception. While the large potential of the region to accommodate and operate a robust renewable energy framework is well established, there are concerns about the legal framework and infrastructural capacities to realize the ambitious energy transition goals. The Spanish "renewables saga" has demonstrated the risks and vulnerabilities created by regulatory reforms in the renewables sector, and the resulting exposure to massive investment claims, even for strong economies such as Spain.[21]

In his chapter, Ilija Mitrev Penushliski will analyze the lessons learned from the most prominent ISDS jurisprudence in the renewable energy sector, to highlight the substantive and procedural reforms that should be undertaken in the Western Balkans and other regions to successfully navigate the legal and economic aspects of the energy transition process. The chapter will also provide insights on the anticipated risks, treaty mechanisms and governmental measures that could help mitigate the risks of the transition and facilitate the inflow of much needed investments in the renewable energy sector.

---

19 EU Commission, *A European Green Deal* (European Commission, 2019) https://commission.europa.eu/strategy-and-policy/priorities-2019-2024/european-green-deal_en, accessed 10 June 2023.

20 There are estimates that the annual cost of ensuring low-carbon energy suppy to meet the market demands will be 3,5 trillion USD. International Energy Agency, *Perspectives for the Energy Transition – Investment Needs for a Low Carbon Energy System* (Bonn: iea/irena, 2017), https://www.iea.org/publications/ insights/insightpublications/PerspectivesfortheEnergyTransition.pdf, accessed 10 June 2023, p. 8.

21 Anette Magnusson and Michel McIlwrath, Energy Disputes and Climate Targets: Survey Reveals How to Plan (Kluwer Arbitration Blog, 29 May 2023) https://arbitrationblog.kluwerarbitration.com/2023/05/29/energy-disputes-and-climate-targets-survey-reveals-how-to-plan/, accessed 10 June 2023; Queen Mary University of London (QMUL) and Pinsent Masons, The Future of International Energy Arbitration Survey Report (QUML, 2022) https://arbitration.qmul.ac.uk/media/arbitration/docs/Future-of-International-Energy-Arbitration-Survey-Report.pdf, accessed 10 June 2023.

5. When planning and preparing for potential future disputes, it is important to understand and internalize the lessons from the previous body of investment claims raised against the WB economies under the existing regime.

The Chapter "Western Balkans Investment Disputes within the Broader Landscape of ISDS: Facts, Figures and Trends" authored by Diana Rosert, will provide an empirical analysis of the known investment cases against the WB economies, revealing the most frequent nationalities of the claimant investors, the most affected sectors, most frequently challenged state measures, the investment protection standards which served as the basis of the claims, and the outcomes of these cases. After dissecting the causes and effects of past cases, the author places the WB cases in the EU context, in the aftermath of the *Achmea* decision of the Court of Justice of the EU, and the Agreement to Terminate Intra-EU BITs.

6. In recognition of the effects of the previous experience with ISDS based on old-generation investment treaties, the Western Balkans economies have also engaged in redesigning and modernizing their international investment agreements, primarily BITs. The regional delegations have been active participants in the ongoing reform process conducted by the UNCITRAL Working Group III (ISDS Reform), OECDD and UNCTAD, in order to align their policy direction with the international best practices.[22]

In their chapter, Kabir Duggal, Kevin W. Gray and Samiha Gopal reflect on the recent Model BITs developed by WB economies as the first fruits of their efforts to modernize their investment treaty network. The chapter will provide a nuanced comparative analysis of the North Macedonian, Serbian and BiH Model BITs, to showcase their common features and specificities. This analysis will provide insights into the policy priorities of the different economies, as well as their treaty design preferences for modern investment treaties. In

22 The Western Balkans Economies have made three joint submissions to the UNCITRAL WGIII (two in writing, and one at the UNCITRAL Forum on alternative dispute resolution in 2021). UNCITRAL Secretariat, *Draft Code of Conduct, Comments by State/Commenter as of January 14, 2021* (UNCITRAL, 2021) https://uncitral.un.org/sites/uncitral.un.org/files/media-documents/uncitral/en/code_of_conduct_comments_by_state_commenter_updated.pdf, accessed 10 June 2023, pp. 818–6; UNCITRAL Secretariat, *Dispute prevention and alternative dispute settlement, Submission of the Western Balkans region*, (UNCITRAL, 2021) https://uncitral.un.org/sites/uncitral.un.org/files/media-documents/uncitral/uncitral_wg_iii_submission_western_balkans_-_mediation.pdf, accessed 10 June 2023. In addition, some economies participated in pilot programs for the assessment of the international investment treaty networks by UNCTAD, and early dispute prevention by the World Bank Group.

their analysis, the authors will consider how the new Model BITs in the region respond to past ISDS experiences in the region, and how they may lower the risks of future claims for the WB economies.

In addition to the big picture issues related to the investment treaty regime and investor-State disputes, it is important to zoom in to address some of the key substantive investment protection standards, which are covered in two chapters of this book. 7. Vlora Maxhuni first analyzes in depth the key conceptual issue of defining the investor and investment, as provided in the existing BITs concluded by the WB economies, highlighting their strengths and risks factors for investor-state disputes. These are threshold issues which determine whether an investor and their investment qualify for treaty protection, and relatedly, play a crucial role at the jurisdictional stage of investment disputes.

7. Filip Balcerzak, in turn, considers the existing Fair and Equitable Treatment (FET) clauses in the BITs concluded by WB economies, which is the most frequent and most successful claim raised by investors in investment arbitration (as confirmed in chapter 5). On the basis of the modern treaty practices in the EU and beyond, the author proposes the features of improved FET clauses for future investment treaties in the WB region. Such clauses should protect the states' right to regulate and narrow the interpretive space for arbitral tribunals in future cases, to more closely reflect the policy intentions of the treaty parties behind the FET standard, in line with the interpretive standards under the Vienna Convention (VCLT)

Finally, the book will look beyond the standard and widespread practice of adversarial dispute resolution, typically through investment arbitration (and possibly a standing investment court in the future).

8. In her chapter, Fahira Brodlija will explore the potential of dispute prevention mechanisms as tools to reduce the likelihood and scope of investment disputes against the Western Balkans economies. While there are already some coordination bodies and agencies established in the region (as described in detail in Section 2 chapters), the chapter will assess their effectiveness and propose models for their enhancement, based on the regional structures and in light of the international best practices.[23] Several international development organizations have already supported and piloted the establishment of dispute prevention mechanisms in

23 UNCITRAL Secretariat, *Compilation of International Best Practices on Dispute Prevention and Mitigation* (UNCITRAL, March 2023), https://uncitral.un.org/sites/uncitral.un.org/files/media-documents/uncitral/wg_iii_compilation_on_dispute_prevention_and_summary.pdf, accessed 10 June 2023.

the region, including the German Development Organization (GIZ), the Regional Cooperation Council (RCC) and the World Bank Group.[24] This chapter will draw directly from the previous experiences proposing ways to improve communication channels and inter-ministerial coordination bodies which should enable a seamless flow of information and prompt reactions by the competent institutions before the emergence of a legal dispute.

9. In situations where the early responses to the investor complaints cannot be resolved proactively at the technical level, there are also viable options in the so-called „cooling-off" period (and beyond) for the parties to amicably resolve the dispute and avoid lengthy and expensive arbitrations. In her chapter on "Investment Mediation in the Western Balkans: Uncharted but Promising Waters" Frauke Nitschke will analyze the legal and institutional framework for investment mediation, primarily from the perspective of the ICSID Mediation Rules. As mediation is still underutilized in investment disputes, the chapter will reveal the real and perceived obstacles, concerns expressed by the states and the normative and procedural safeguards which can help overcome these issues. This chapter will also shed light on the general features and benefits of the mediation process within the ICSID framework, and its advantages for both parties.

The Section 2 chapters will analyze the legal and institutional frameworks of each Western Balkans economy, unlocking key perspectives on treaty practice, investment disputes, emerging trends, special features and ongoing reform efforts. Through each chapter, esteemed experts from academia and practice will explain the key features of the investment protection landscape in the region, giving unique insights into the complexities of each economy, including the nuanced comparative perspectives from two EU Member States, Croatia and Slovenia.

24 The World Bank Group piloted its model early grievance mechanism (SIRM) in Bosnia and Herzegovina, starting from 2017. World Bank Group, *Retention and Expansion of Foreign Direct Investment – Political Risk and Policy Responses* (The World Bank Group, 2019), https://documents1.worldbank.org/curated/en/387801576142339003/pdf/Political-Risk-and-Policy-Responses.pdf, accessed 10 June 2023, p. 46; The GIZ project „Legal Reform for Economic Development in the Western Balkans" has developed model „Communication Roadmaps for Investment Dispute Prevention" for wach WB Economy in 2022; In 2023, the RCC has supported the development of „Standard Operating Procedures for ISDS" for Montenegro, which are meant to serve as a starting point and model that each WB economy can adapt and use in designing its own mechanisms and infrastructure for each stage of an investment dispute.

The authors in this section are renowned regional experts, including Silvana Cinari and Flutura Kola (Albania), Armela Ramić and Ajla Serdarević (Bosnia and Herzegovina), Irena Alajbeg (Croatia), Lyra Cela (Kosovo), prof. Aneta Spaić (Montenegro), prof. Toni Deskoski and prof. Vangel Dokoski (North Macedonia), Dragana Nikolić (Serbia) and Peter Rižnik and dr. Maja Menard (Slovenia). The economy-level chapters will cover a common core of topics, outlining the key legal and institutional features of each legal system in a cohesive and unified manner. However, the scope of analysis per topic will depend on the availability of the relevant information for each economy. Thus, each economy-level chapter will cover the following: FDI trends, key sectors for foreign investments, legal framework for foreign investment protection, international investment treaty framework, ISDS cases and outcomes, ongoing reforms, and special features.

In aggregate, the economy-level and regional perspectives provided in the book should help interested parties understand the *status quo* of investment protection and dispute resolution in the Western Balkans, as well as their causes and effects. More importantly, they will enable information-based policy and business decisions, which should propel the region in a more prosperous and sustainable future. At a more academic level, the book will be a touchstone for the analysis of the investment protection framework in the Western Balkans at a crucial period of its journey towards EU accession.

PART 1

International Perspectives on International Investment Law and Investor-State Disputes in the Western Balkans

CHAPTER 2

The Reform of Investment Protection Treaties in the Western Balkans

Samira Sulejmanović and Ivana Gardašević

1 Introduction*

Since the beginning of the 1990's, there has been a track record of Western Balkans[1] effort to create an attractive and investor-friendly business environment and to facilitate greater inflow of fresh capital. This was particularly significant and important considering the recent past of the economies considered at present as part of the Western Balkans region. Nearly overnight dramatic changes of their investment policies were important signs of their true intentions to become open and friendly environments for foreign direct investments.

Investment protection treaties, along with other policy measures, were intended to create and offer additional assurances for foreign investors. Combined with measures at the national level, these efforts were meant to facilitate and contribute to inflows of fresh capital into the economies of the Western Balkans. What once was seen as positive and progressive practice, i.e. conclusion of a great number of investment protection treaties, turned into a spaghetti bowl of treaties which are now obsolete and lack precision and modernity.

Implementing much needed reform in an effective and practical manner turned out to be quite a challenge. As the analysis in the following sections will demonstrate, the economies of the Western Balkans have seriously considered their options and have decided their best course of action.

Thus, the chapter will begin with a short overview of the evolution of investment regimes in the Western Balkans economies, followed by a historic review of investment protection treaties concluded by them. Since most of those treaties were concluded with EU Member States, the third section is

* The views expressed in this paper reflect those of the authors and do not necessarily reflect the views of the institutions with which they are affiliated.

1 For the purpose of this paper, the Western Balkans refers to 6 economies: Albania, Bosnia and Herzegovina, Kosovo, Montenegro, North Macedonia and Serbia.

 | DOI:10.1163/9789004729889_003

dedicated to analysis of those investment protection treaties. The application of the treaties had exposed Western Balkans economies to significant claims before international arbitration *fora*, some with extreme requests for monetary compensation of the investor. The fourth section is therefore dedicated to analysis of investment claims, patterns and costs indicating high need for reform. The fifth and sixth section explain reform options discussed by the Western Balkans economies and analyse positive aspects and challenges of the selected reform policy options. In the final section, it is explained that despite the Western Balkans economies aim is to enhance legal consistency and reduce the vulnerability to legal disputes, balancing between attracting foreign investment and maintaining the regulatory autonomy needed to address local economic issues remains a delicate endeavour. The emerging policy framework therefore must navigate between adapting to EU norms and responding to the unique developmental needs of the Western Balkans.

2 Evolution of Investment Regime in the Western Balkans in 1990's to Present

To understand the substance and evolution of investment regime reform that has taken place in the last decade of the twentieth century, it is important to take a brief glance at context. What was happening in this little piece of the world, prior to regime reforms, matters in understanding how and why those reforms took place. Unlike many developed countries in the western hemisphere, the end of the century in the Western Balkans spelled sharp changes in whole political and economic systems. The 1992–1995 war in Bosnia and Herzegovina further delayed necessary reforms.

The Socialist Federal Republic of Yugoslavia (SFRY) had been experimenting with a combination of self-management and mixed planned/market economy since the mid-fifties.[2] The first law permitting foreign capital in the SFRY economy was enacted on 27 July 1967.[3] Over the next five years, the investment of foreign capital had changed in three phases. In the initial phase, foreign companies established contacts and gathered information on the provisions of the law. The second phase was marked by the hesitation of foreign investors due to the serious economic situation in the country and imposition of special

---

2 David D. Nagler, *Yugoslavia: Law on Foreign Investments*, American Society of International Law (1989).

3 Mirodrag Sukijasovic, *Legal Aspects of Foreign Investment in Yugoslavia*, Duke L. Sch. Repository, at 474.

stabilization measures. The third phase began with introduction of a stabilization program (late 1970–early 1971).

New elements have been introduced to the foreign capital investment regime to make conditions more favourable for foreign investors. For example, the SFRY adopted constitutional amendments that strengthened the position and the economic power of unified labour and provided for foreign capital investment. They supplemented and amended the Law on Resources and Assets of the Economic Organizations.[4]

At the dawn of the SFRY's dissolution process in January 1989, the state promulgated a new Law on Foreign Investment.[5] The SFRY Government had already been working on the reform of its economic system. This law, along with others (such as the Law on Business Organizations and Law on Yugoslav Bank for International Economic Cooperation), was part of that process. The key objective of the reform was to de-bureaucratize the economy, give greater independence and flexibility to businesses, and stimulate foreign trade.[2]

According to David D. Nagler, some of the relevant features of the new law related to investment were the following:

1. Yugoslav citizens residing abroad were deemed foreign investors for the purposes of the Law;
2. There was no limit on foreign equity – unlike before, businesses could be wholly-owned by foreign investors;
3. An investment contract would be deemed approved by federal authorities unless rejected within 30 days of the submission of the contract to the proper agency (45-days in 1989);
4. An investment could be for an unlimited term;
5. Investors participated in profits (and losses) in proportion to their investment;
6. Investors' voting and management rights and powers were proportionate to their share of the business;
7. Investments were transferrable and could be repatriated;
8. Tax incentives may have been available;
9. Foreign investors could obtain concessions for the extraction of certain natural resources;
10. Investors could invest in a greater variety of businesses; and
11. Investments could be made in different forms (cash, exchange of debt, etc.).[1]

4 The Law on Resources and Assets of the Economic Organizations was enacted on 28 July and came into effect on 13 August 1970.

5 Law on Foreign Investments, (no. 77, item 1023), (1989) (SRFY).

Albania was not part of SFRY, yet also had a restrictive investment regime in the twentieth century. Due to its recent history and the closure of the country to the rest of the world, there is very little reliable information available on what was happening in Albania before 1990's. According to the International Monetary Fund, practically no economic reforms were introduced in Albania before 1990.[6] External sector reforms had focused on removing legal impediments to foreign credit and foreign investment and on partially liberalizing foreign trade and exchange restrictions. In July 1990, Decree No. 7406, "On the protection of foreign investments in the People's Socialist Republic of Albania," and Decree No. 7407 "On the economic activity of enterprises with participation of foreign capital in the People's Socialist Republic of Albania" were approved by the Albanian Parliament, lifting the constitutional ban on foreign borrowing which was introduced in 1976.[7]

The decrees allowed foreign direct investment, established legal protections against arbitrary expropriation and nationalization, and permitted joint ventures of foreign firms with Albanian enterprises and the remittance of profits abroad. Bilateral investment treaties (BITS) were subsequently signed with various partner countries, and in August 1991, a foreign investment agency was established under the Ministry of Foreign Economic Relations. It was made responsible for investment promotion and the review of investment proposals.[5]

After a decade of serious political and economic instability in the Western Balkans region, the 2000's brought a number of positive developments, including improved macroeconomic performance and acceleration of transition-related economic reforms.[8] Even after three decades of reforms, none of the six economies has completed the transition process. Much of it was disrupted or slowed down by global economic and financial crises. The key reasons though, were internal systemic deficiencies aggravated by the reluctance of political leadership to conduct deep reforms, remnants of the socialist ownership system, deindustrialisation etc. The Investment Policy Review of South-East Europe (SEE)[9] confirmed this, noting that despite economic reforms centred on the privatization of State-owned industries (SOES), competition, and

6 Mario I. Bléjer, Toward Economic Reform V (IMF eLibrary) (1992) (ebook).

7 The entire 1976 Constitution was subsequently abrogated on 29 April 1991, and pending the adoption of a new constitution, which is currently being drafted, Parliament (elected in March 1991) adopted Law No. 7491, entitled "Principal Constitutional Provisions," which confirmed the liberalization measures introduced in these decrees.

8 Saul Estrin & Milica Uvalic, Foreign direct investment in the Western Balkans: what role has it played during transition? 58 Comp Econ Stud 58, pp.455–483 (2016).

9 The SEE region in this publication included all Western Balkans economies plus Moldova.

labour markets, the transition to a market economy was incomplete – which affected investment.[10] Even though certain reforms have been implemented with regard to State-owned enterprises, the weight of SOEs and public monopolies remained high, which created barriers to foreign investments.

The same publication summarized the FDI legal framework in the SEE as follows: "The SEE economies are fairly open to foreign investment, with relatively few formal ownership restrictions. Nevertheless, de facto barriers to both domestic and foreign investors exist in most SEE economies, as certain sectors are dominated by government monopolies and/or SOEs. Investor protection standards are high throughout the region. All SEE economies guarantee non-discriminatory treatment between domestic and foreign investors in the post-establishment phase. Furthermore, all SEE economies protect investors' rights in case of expropriation; they allow investors to transfer proceeds resulting from their investments abroad in freely convertible currency, proceeds resulting from their investment. All economies bring investor – State disputes under the jurisdiction of local courts, and several explicitly provide investors with the option to settle such disputes through international arbitration proceedings. In terms of promoting responsible investment, SEE economies are split between those that actively promote corporate social responsibility (CSR) standards and those which have not undertaken any active measures in this direction." Several sectors remained under the control of state or SOEs, such as defence, media, gambling, and air transport.

3 History of Investment Protection Treaties in the Western Balkans

Since the beginning of the 1990's, there has been a track record of Western Balkans effort to create an attractive and investor-friendly business environment, and to facilitate greater inflow of fresh capital.

Once part of a single country, i.e., the SFRY, the economies of the Western Balkans[11] inherited a number of investment treaties after the state dissolved. While it is difficult to establish the exact number of such treaties, it can be stated with great certainty that the majority of them, unless replaced with new ones, are still in force (at least in Serbia, being the legal successor of the SFRY).

10 UNCTAD, Investment Policy Review of the South-East Europe (2017).

11 Currently six economies of which only Albania was not a part of the SFRY, i.e., Bosnia and Herzegovina, Kosovo (which declared its independence from Serbia on 17 Feb. 2008 but disputed with Serbia over it and not member of the UN), Montenegro, the Republic of North Macedonia, and the Republic of Serbia.

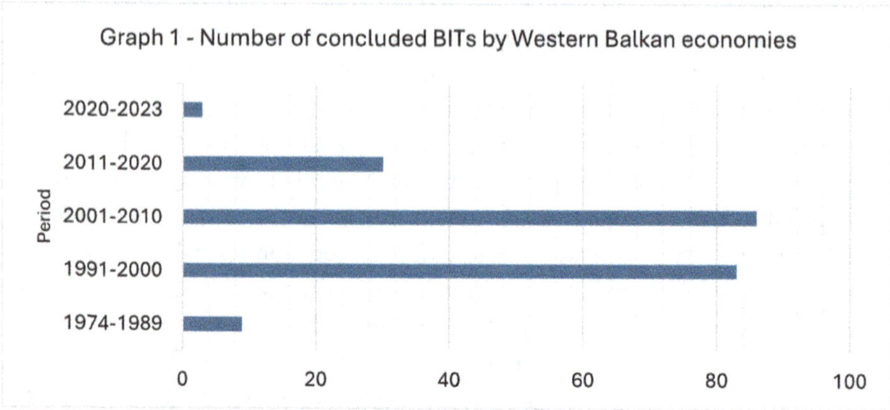

GRAPH 1 Number of concluded BITs with Western Balkans
SOURCE: AUTHORS' CREATION BASED ON AVAILABLE DATA

Others have decided in succession processes whether to keep them or not, and generally have replaced them with more recent treaties.

The majority of BITs (80%, 169 treaties) were concluded in two decades time, i.e., from 1991 to 2010 (*see* Graph 1). The number of treaties concluded by a former joint state is small. Even though there is no easily available data for treaties concluded by SFRY, it is pretty certain that their number was greater than number of treaties in the UNCTAD database for period 1974–1989, for at least two reasons. First, some of them were terminated and second, the majority were superseded by new treaties concluded between individual Western Balkans economies and states which were originally contracting parties in treaties with SFRY. Some very old treaties still remain in force and pose a great threat for potential investor-state disputes (e.g., Serbia–Germany BIT from 1989).

In concluding their BITs, all Western Balkans economies largely followed the European 'post-establishment' BIT model[12] and contained standard clauses, such as the most-favoured-nation (MFN) treatment, national treatment (NT), fair and equitable treatment (FET), free transfers, and fair compensation in the

12 The BIT model based on the Abs-Shawcross Draft Convention model endorsed by the OECD Council in 1962. In comparison to the 'North American Model', the main distinction is that the former mainly applies to the post-entry phase, while the latter also covers investment at the pre-establishment phase. Among different variations, two emerged as the basic ones, as described in M. Houde & K. Yannaca-Small, Relationships between International Investment Agreements, OECD Working Papers on International Investment, (2004/01).

case of expropriation. This model BIT also contained the 'investor-state' and 'state-to-state' dispute settlement mechanisms.

The most representative example of these old treaties are those of Serbia which inherited all treaties concluded by a former state (SFRY).

According to the analysis of the Serbian law firm BDK Advokati, "the existing treaty regimes [of Serbia] on investment protection vary significantly: from quasi-investment-protection treaties (United States), to an ancient type of BITs (France), to usual type of BITs with more or less restrictive provisions (China, Russia, Germany), to BITs that have never entered into force (Italy). Investors from the United States and Italy currently do not have access to international arbitration; those from China do, but only regarding disputes 'involving the amount of compensation for expropriation' (which is open to several interpretations), while investors from Russia and Germany can refer all investment disputes to arbitration. Presumably, investors from France can also refer all investment disputes to arbitration; however, given the ambiguous formulation used in that BIT [with France], it remains to be tested whether it contains advance state consent. The regimes that recognition and enforcement of court decisions apply to are less diverse: most countries analysed do not have judgment recognition and enforcement treaties with Serbia (United States, China, Germany, Italy). There are such treaties with Russia and France, making recognition/enforcement of their court decisions significantly easier than if the judgment creditors had to rely only on Serbian national law."[13]

4 Investment Protection Treaties between Western Balkan Economies and the EU

According to available data,[14] a total of 211 International Investment Agreements,[15] mostly BITs are concluded by the six economies of the Western Balkans. Over half of that number (53%, 107 treaties) were concluded with member states of the European Union.

The greatest number of BITs concluded by the Western Balkan economies either with EU member states or third states can be qualified as "old

13 Relja Radovic, Investment Protection Between Serbia and Major Economies: France, BDK Advokati (2022), <https://www.bdkadvokati.com> accessed 12 April 2024).

14 UNCTAD, Investment Policy Hub, www.investmentpolicy.unctad.org (last visited Apr. 12, 2024); EDIT, www.edit.wti.org (last visited Apr. 12 2024).

15 International investment agreements (IIAs) include bilateral investment treaties and other Treaties with Investment Provisions (TIPs).

European model BITs" (*See* Title 3 for more details) with some, minor, or greater differences.

For example, as mapped the structure of specific provisions of the existing BITs is as follows:

- *Definition of investment:* Most treaties opt for a broad, asset-based definition of investment, and most include a legality requirement – which means that to be covered by the treaty, the investment needs to be made in accordance with host economy laws and regulations. Such an open-ended definition may cover investments not originally envisioned, potentially exposing economies to unexpected investor claims and financial liabilities.
- *National Treatment (NT) and Most Favoured Nation (MFN)* provisions: Most treaties offer non-discrimination guarantees vis-à-vis national competitors and investors from third economies. However, few of them specify that investors must be 'in like circumstances,' which may expand the scope of the clauses and make them difficult to implement.
- *Fair and Equitable Treatment (FET)*: While most of the treaties include provisions granting FET, only few qualify the standard. This can lead to lack of clarity on interpretation of the provision and opens the door for an expansive approach to interpretation. Recent treaties have increasingly started including a qualified standard and providing illustrations of the scope of the provision.
- *Expropriation:* The majority of the treaties have a provision covering both indirect and direct expropriation. At the same time, indirect expropriation is rarely defined, failing to distinguish between indirect expropriation which compensates the investors, and legitimate public policymaking which does not entail a duty to pay. This can also lead to lack of clarity and disputes.
- *Transfer and convertibility of funds:* All the treaties reviewed by UNCTAD grant the right to freely transfer any investment-related funds into and out of the economy. Yet only few define exceptions to this general right, making it difficult for the economies to deal with balance of payment difficulties or other macroeconomic problems that lead to sudden and massive outflows or inflows of capital.
- *Investor-State Dispute Settlement (ISDS):* Although most treaties include ISDS provisions, very few circumscribe the scope of the provision. For example, by listing those issues to which ISDS applies, excluding certain policy areas from the scope, providing for a limitations period, or providing for more transparency by granting public access to arbitration.

The available case law establishes that vague and imprecise provisions were among the main reasons for arbitration tribunals to interpret these treaties more broadly than was ever intended by the negotiating parties. Therefore, their revision or replacement with treaties having more precision and including modern provisions, e.g., right to regulate, MFN carve-outs, climate, or energy transition provisions, etc., is ever more important for the Western Balkans economies.

Nonetheless, as the Western Balkans had gradually positioned itself as a viable destination for foreign investments, this transformation exposed the region to investment disputes based on the provisions of these old treaties. The surge of investments progressively emphasized the need for a robust dispute settlement mechanism to address such disputes.

5 State of Play of Investment Arbitration Cases in the Western Balkans

The Western Balkans, a dynamic region at the crossroads of Europe, has witnessed significant evolution in its investment landscape over recent years. While positively this evolvement meant substantial change and opening of the investment policy, it also made them vulnerable (yet unprepared) to be challenged before international investment arbitration. Drawing upon data from ICSID and UNCTAD, a snapshot of the state of play of investment arbitration cases in the Western Balkans can be made, shedding light on prevalent trends, challenges, and implications for both investors and host states.

All six economies of the Western Balkans wish to become members of the European Union (EU). They have signed the Stabilisation and Association Agreement with the EU and have started to garner increased attention of foreign investors, primarily those from the EU member states. In the last decade of the twentieth century, the conclusion of investment treaties (along with avoidance of double taxation treaties) was part of package offers of the Western Balkans economies to capital exporting countries.

Investment treaties were considered a pivotal tool in attracting investment, and little attention or concern was attributed to their potential effects. The great majority of concluded treaties were very much alike, with minor differences at the later stage (*See* Title 4). Until investors started using provisions of these treaties to challenge the action or non-action of the home state(s) of their investment, these treaties served as a goodwill declaration which, at the same time, presented an excellent photo opportunity for political leaders.

The first case against a Western Balkans economy (Albania) was registered in 1994, and was one of the two cases in total brought against the home state of an investor in that year in the world. This small part of the world was among the first to feel the teeth of these (initially considered) toothless treaties. As the number of claims was rising in the world, the same trend followed in the Western Balkans. Yet, it took a long time for the governments to wake up and acknowledge what was going on.

The data of investment disputes brought against Western Balkans economies up to September 2024[16] are very indicative and set clear guidance for policymakers on where pressing reform should be made, if not already completed. A total number of fifty-three investment dispute cases were registered in the region. Arbitrations are still held under the veil of secrecy and non-transparency, so even when the case is registered before ICSID, and, as such, publicly known, there is little further information about a case during and at the end of the procedure.

According to the data available, half of arbitration cases initiated by investors from EU member states have no data on the amount of monetary compensation claimed. Nevertheless, for the other half, where data available, the EU member states investors claimed 6.053 billion USD compensation from Western Balkans economies home of their investment. In comparison to total requested monetary compensation (7.077 billion USD), the EU member states investors claims made 85.5%. Since there is no data available for half of the arbitration cases brought by EU member state investors, it can be stated with great certainty that this amount is even higher. Over half of all cases (52%) were initiated in three major sectors; mining and quarrying, electricity and gas, and manufacturing.[17]

The costs for respondents in legal disputes are quite high. The average cost of a dispute proceeding in the Western Balkans is about 3.4 million USD.[18] This average is found by adding up all the costs and dividing by the number of cases. The median cost, which helps show what most people might pay without extreme high or low cases affecting the average, is 1.2 million USD. These figures tell us that being involved in a legal case as a respondent in the Western Balkans can be very expensive.

The compensation requests registered in specific cases additionally call for action as such amounts pertain to a small percentage of high-value cases in the work. For example, in a significant arbitration case registered with ICSID

16 *See* ICSID Case Database, <https://icsid.worldbank.org/cases/case-database> accessed 3 September 2024). ; *see also* UNCTAD, *supra* (n 13).

17 Authors' calculation based on available data of UNCTAD database – Investment Policy Hub (February 2024).

18 Lucia Raimanova, Partner at Allen & Overy, panelist, VIAC CAN Congress, Vienna, (9 February 2024).

in June 2014,[19] a Slovenian investor, Elektrogospodarstvo Slovenije – razvoj in inženiring (EGS), took legal action against Bosnia and Herzegovina. The dispute arose from alleged treaty violations related to an investment in a thermal power plant managed by the local entity Rudnik i termoelektrana Ugljevik (RiTE Ugljevik). EGS's claim, citing breaches of the bilateral investment treaty with the Republic of Slovenia and the Energy Charter Treaty (ECT), totalled an astonishing 750 million USD. This includes compensation for the initial funds invested and losses due to undelivered electricity.

A similar case was brought against Montenegro in 2016 by Russian oligarch Oleg Deripaska, who personally filed an UNCITRAL claim[20] in a long-running dispute over his investments in the state that had already led to an unsuccessful ICSID claim. Deripaska alleged that Montenegro unlawfully expropriated his investments in former state-owned aluminium smelting company KAP and bauxite mining company Rudnici Boksita, as well as breaching the fair and equitable treatment provisions of the treaty between the Russian Federation and Yugoslavia.[21] Prior to that, in 2014, CEAC (the company through which Deripaska made his investment) filed an ICSID claim[22] against Montenegro in relation to KAP for a reported 600 million euros, alleging that the state had breached the Montenegro-Cyprus BIT by failing to obtain its consent before initiating insolvency proceedings.

This case highlights the substantial financial risks and potential high costs associated with arbitration in the Western Balkans, reflecting the hefty economic burdens that can emerge from such legal disputes. Investors from EU member states such as Austria, Greece, and the Netherlands, are frequently involved in arbitration cases against the Western Balkans, indicating specific national investment policies or market conditions affecting these disputes. Even though many are still pending, the current distribution of case outcomes is in favour of the host state of investment. It can, however, be noted that 71.7% of all the arbitration cases initiated against Western Balkans were those initiated by investors from EU member states.

This updated framework offers a detailed look into the investment arbitration landscape in the Western Balkans, highlighting the challenges and opportunities for both investors and host states in the context of evolving legal and geopolitical environments. For foreign investors, challenges include

19 Elektrogospodarstvo Slovenije – razvoj in inzeniring d.o.o. v. Bosn.&Herz., ICSID Case No. ARB/14/13, Decision on Jurisiditicion, (May 18, 2020).

20 Oleg Vladimirovich Deripaska v. Montenegro, PCA Case No. 2017-07 Award (Oct. 15, 2019).

21 Applied by Montenegro by succession.

22 CEAC v. Montenegro, ICSID Case No. ARB/14/8, Award (Jul. 26, 2016).

navigating diverse legal systems and potentially facing broad and undefined treaty provisions. Understanding regional nuances and geopolitical risks is crucial as well. For host states, challenges include managing broad definitions in treaties and risks associated with outdated treaties, legal complexity with clear need to deal with potential claims and financial liabilities due to broad asset-based definitions in treaties.

6 Reform Options – Challenges and Advantages

Crafting robust, clear, and balanced investment treaties is more than just a legal necessity for the Western Balkans. It is a strategic imperative. These treaties send a message to the international community about the Western Balkans economies' readiness for enhanced global economic participation. Furthermore, as EU accession talks progress, the Western Balkans will be under increased scrutiny regarding their investment frameworks. The EU, with its rigorous standards, will undoubtedly consider the clarity and fairness of the Western Balkans investment treaties as a reflection of their broader commitment to a rules-based international system.

The journey of the Western Balkans towards EU membership is intertwined with their approach to international investment law. As they stand at this crucial juncture, the significance of astute treaty drafting and diligent treaty implementation becomes paramount. It is not just about attracting investment, but about shaping the future of the region in the global economic landscape. As the region continues to evolve, so will its approach to investment and the mechanisms to safeguard it.

Investment reform is a narrative of evolving economies and geopolitical shifts. With the aim of aligning with international benchmarks and EU standards, the Western Balkans economies embarked on a collaborative venture, setting the stage for a comprehensive investment policy overhaul. This drive was crystallized in the formative phase of the Multi-annual Action Plan for a Regional Economic Area (MAP REA), a beacon of the region's commitment to economic integration and coherence, which was then followed by the Common Regional Market Action Plan for the period 2021–2024 (CRM AP).[23]

The impetus for continuation of reform in this direction was multi-fold, i.e., the need to modernize investment framework(s) in the region, the desire to

23 Regional Cooperation Council, Common Regional Market Action Plan, 09 November 2020. <https://www.rcc.int/docs/543/common-regional-market-action-plan> accessed 12 April 2024).

streamline disparate national policies into a cohesive regional strategy, and, crucially, the aspiration to forge a path towards EU accession. The collective action reflected in these initiatives signify more than policy alignment, it represents a regional renaissance, underscoring a unified vision for economic progress and stability.

6.1 *Charting the Options: Navigating the Reform Agenda*

Within the framework of this concerted effort, the Western Balkans economies have considered various strategic avenues, each with distinct blueprint, merits, and challenges. These options were not just routes on a map but symbolized the region's adaptability, ambition, and foresight. They encompassed the following:

1. *The Regional Investment Treaty:* This option presented a legal mosaic that offered uniform investment rules across the six Western Balkans economies. This tapestry of regulations stood as a testament to regional unity and legal coherency, promising a new era of investment certainty.
2. *CEFTA Additional Protocol or Chapter on Investment*: Building on the solid foundations of the Central European Free Trade Agreement (CEFTA[24]), this option represented an evolutionary step in regional economic cooperation. It was akin to adding a new chapter to an ongoing success story, enhancing the narrative of regional integration.
3. *Western Balkans Ministerial Decision on Regional Investment Policy*: This approach echoed a symphony of flexibility and pragmatism. It was a political commitment, a soft but significant step forward, reflecting the harmonious tune of collaborative decision-making.
4. *Regional Standards for the Negotiation of International Investment Agreements ('Regional Standards')*: Imagine a compass guiding the individual voyages of the Western Balkans economies in the sea of international investment. These standards were intended to serve as the North Star for negotiation of investment protection treaties, ensuring each economy sails confidently, backed by a collective regional consensus.
5. *Regional Investment Policy Statement*: This statement option was akin to a collective declaration of intent, a beacon illuminating the Western Balkans aspirations on the global investment map. It was seen as a flexible, yet impactful testament to the region's dedication to fostering a unified investment environment.

---

24 Regional free trade agreement which covers Moldova, in addition to the Western Balkans six economies.

In exploring these options, the Western Balkans were not just navigating the complexities of investment reform, but also charting a course towards a future of economic prosperity and integration. The path forward required a blend of pragmatism and ambition, an understanding that the journey is as important as the destination. As the Western Balkans economies continue to weave this narrative of reform and growth, the regional investment agenda stands not just as a policy framework but as a testament to the power of collective vision and action.

6.2 *Embracing Change – the Tapestry of Commitment and Cooperation*

Even though each option had something specific to offer, Regional Standards[25] were chosen at the time as the most viable one. Namely, complex relations in the region implied that certain options were considered too ambitious and thus probably difficult to implement. On the other hand, opting for the least demanding proposal would keep regional cooperation stalled.

The Regional Standards, however, served multiple causes. First, they represented mutual understanding among the Western Balkans economies of the standards to be included in future investment protection treaties. Second, they promoted modern solutions and policies which were painfully absent in the existing treaties, such as principles of fairness, equity, and sustainable growth. Third, they indirectly included alignment of regional policy to that of the EU.

In the realm of economic cooperation, the Western Balkans transcend the role of isolated actors to emerge as integral players in a collective orchestration of regional integration. Each nation contributed its distinct strengths and insights, harmonizing within a framework that acknowledges diverse national interests and priorities. Yet, amidst this diversity, a shared commitment to forging a dynamic investment environment emerged as the unifying beat. The Western Balkans, once characterized by disparate economic narratives, were to march to a synchronized rhythm.

The Regional Standards offered a harmonized approach of the region to investment policies, crucial for fostering a predictable and stable legal environment. By aligning with EU standards, they paved the way for smoother integration into the European economic framework, thereby enhancing the region's appeal to global investors and potentially boosting economic growth. The emphasis on sustainability and equity within these standards heralded a commitment to balanced economic development, mindful of both environmental

25 Regional Cooperation Council, Regionally Accepted Standards for Negotiating IIAs, adopted 10 November 2020.

and social impacts. It should not be neglected that this option strengthened regional cooperation, promoting stability and collective progress across the Western Balkans.

The implementation of the Regional Standards was left to the economies to decide whether to implement them into relevant national legislation or solely in the future investment protection treaties (or both). The adherence to the Regional Standards in the negotiation of future investment protection treaties served not only to consolidate the policies in the Western Balkans region and align with EU policy, but also created a firm shield in the negotiation of investment protection treaties with non-EU countries which could insist on different solutions.

6.3 *Way Forward from Regional Standards*

The adoption of Regional Standards was only the first step in the economic transformation of the Western Balkans, which later evolved further through the adoption of the CRM AP. This pivotal plan was more than a growth strategy. In essence, it was a declaration of a new era in the region offering the potential for greater unity and prosperity. While the initial versions of this document were far more ambitious, the final text was still comprehensive in scope, covering trade, investment, mobility, and digital transformation.

The investment pillar was particularly important, as it encompassed the most pressing issues in the region in this area. The overarching objective was to increase the attractiveness of the region for foreign investors and facilitate higher investment inflows through joint investment retention and promotion of activities to foster sustainable industrial activity, trade and, ultimately, jobs. The policymakers in the region recognised that " ... international investors increasingly operate regionally, basing investment decisions on market size, regional production and supply networks, availability of talent in Western Balkans, and infrastructure linkages."[22] To achieve potential, it was concluded that greater regional alignment of investment policies and better-coordinated investment promotion, particularly in the most promising value chains, is needed. To that end, specific actions were agreed in the priority area of a Regional Investment Area of CRM AP to:

- Conduct a regional investment promotion campaign;
- Develop regional guidance criteria and procedures for FDI screening mechanisms in the economy;
- Attract new investment leading to sustainable regional value chains; and
- Conclude economy-specific International Investment Agreement between the EU and each economy of the Western Balkans.

Having in mind all the complexities of the network of investment protection treaties in the region, the importance and effects of the last point are elaborated in the next section.

7 Alternative Approach to the Reform of Investment Protection Treaties' Concluded with EU Member States by the Western Balkans

Huge number of existing, old investment protection treaties concluded by the Western Balkans economies with EU member states (107 BITs) is all but simple to reform in a short or even medium term. Even if individual EU member states would immediately positively respond to initiative for renegotiation of existing treaty(s), the whole process would take a long time, – likely a decade, or potentially even longer. At the same time, while trying to reform old treaties, it would remain unclear to what extent Western Balkans economies could maintain consistency of negotiated provisions across the board.

Having all these and many other arguments in mind, the economies of the Western Balkans tried to come up with an approach which would meet at least two key criteria: (1) to have the set of old treaties concluded with EU member states replaced in the shortest possible time, and (2) to do so in a procedural and legal manner as simply as possible. The conclusion of economy-specific treaties between EU states and each economy of the Western Balkans, i.e. having six instead of 107 treaties, proved to be the approach to meet both criteria.

7.1 *Benefits and Positive Aspects of this Policy Option*

The advantages of this policy option are multiple. Immportantly the benefits are mutual for Western Balkans economies and EU states. The following is identified among the most important benefits and positive aspects.

Modernization – Based on the mapping of content and the analysis, it can be stated that existing BITs concluded by the Western Balkans economies are obsolete. They suffer from ill-defined definitions and a lack of policy space (i.e. the right to regulate), as well as little regard for a sustainable development dimension. At the same time, these treaties include standards that are not aligned with recent EU standards and pose a significant risk for the economies in the region, as well as EU member states, to be sued under the investor-State dispute settlement mechanism (ISDS). Considering the fact that the majority of these treaties are those concluded with EU member states (107 – 53% of all treaties concluded), replacing them with single treaty per Western Balkans economy would enable comprehensive modernisation.

Alignment with EU policy – The economies of the Western Balkans are obliged to comply with EU standards and EU investment policy. The EU Regulation 1219/2012 established transitional arrangements for bilateral investment treaties between EU member states and third countries, and specified the terms, conditions, and procedures under which the member states are authorised to amend existing (or conclude) new bilateral investment treaties with third countries. In that regard, aiming to avoid the negotiation procedure with each EU member state, which would take decades to replace, and in accordance with the Lisbon Treaty and the competences of the European Commission, it would be the easiest to replace all existing BITs with the new economy-specific treaty concluded between each economy and the EU.

Mitigation of risks – According to the *Achmea* judgment of the European Court of Justice,[26] EU Member States concluded the *Agreement for the termination of Bilateral Investment Treaties between the Member States of the European Union*[27] by which all intra-EU BITs were terminated. This would also be applied to BITs concluded between the Western Balkans economies and EU member states upon the accession of the former to the EU. Replacing the existing BITs with economy-specific treaties negotiated with the EU would be an opportunity to solve all potential issues linked to these treaties, especially by integrating a clause foreseeing their termination upon EU accession. From an EU perspective, this would facilitate the accession process. In the future, it would also unburden both EU member states as well as the EU as whole from having to ensure that intra-EU BITs created through the accession of the Western Balkans economies need to be terminated. Also, termination of intra-EU BITs has prompted some law offices and investors to consider potentials of using ISDS mechanism contained in existing BITs with EU member states against EU member states. This may not be an imminent threat, but can surely be explored by EU investors as an option to avoid implications of the *Achmea* judgment.

Inclusiveness – By having an economy-specific treaty between each Western Balkans economy and the EU, the same level of legal protection would be provided to all EU investors irrelevant of their origin, which currently is not the case. Only investors of EU member states with which there is already a BIT in place are protected. Currently, none of the regional economies have a BIT concluded with all EU member states (Albania – 23; Bosnia and Herzegovina – 20, Kosovo* – 5, Montenegro – 16, North Macedonia – 19, and Serbia – 24).

---

26 *Achmea B.V. v. Slovak Republic*, Case C-284/16, Judgment, CJEU (06 March 2018).

27 Agreement for the Termination of Bilateral Investment Treaties between the Member States of the European Union, 2020 O.J. (L 169), pp. 1–41.

Practicality and effectiveness – Signing economy-specific investment protection treaties with the EU would allow the termination, at once, of all the old generation BITs with EU member states and include protections for unprotected EU investors. With relatively little effort, it would be possible to modernize the existing treaties and ensure alignment with standards promoted by the EU in recent trade and investment agreements.

Consistency in Policy Towards Third Countries – Having replaced old BITs with economy-specific investment treaties with the EU would give negotiators from the Western Balkans economies additional power to request from third parties in negotiations provisions that are in line with EU standards.

From the very practical point of view, and taking into account the New EU Growth Plan for the Western Balkans building on the 30 billion euros Economic and Investment Plan (EIP) launched back in 2020, it would be of utmost importance for the Western Balkans economies and to the benefit of both sides to implement the activity 6.2.1 of the CRM AP as planned.[22]

7.2 *Challenges of this Policy Option*

The initiative to consolidate the network of existing investment protection treaties between each economy of the Western Balkans and the EU into a single treaty represents an ambitious step towards regional economic modernization and integration. However, this approach introduced several challenges that warranted careful attention.

Sovereignty and Policy Flexibility – a major concern is the potential reduction in national sovereignty. Harmonizing treaties to conform to EU standards could significantly restrict each Western Balkans economy's ability to implement policies tailored to their specific economic conditions. This could hinder their responsiveness to local economic challenges and their capacity to support local industries or pursue particular developmental goals.

Economic Dependence on the EU – aligning closely with the EU means the Western Balkans economies might become overly dependent on the economic health of the EU. If the EU experiences economic downturns or political instability, the Western Balkans could face unintended economic setbacks. This dependence could also limit the Western Balkans opportunities to diversify their economic and investment relationships with other global regions.

Legal and Regulatory Alignment – aligning national laws and regulations with a comprehensive EU-centric investment protection policy (via concluding treaty) involves complex legal revisions and regulatory updates. This alignment is resource-intensive and requires ongoing efforts to stay current with EU legislation, adding a continuous administrative burden.

Imbalances in Economic and Political Power – the economic and political differences between Western Balkans and the EU could lead to a power imbalance in negotiations, potentially resulting in terms more favourable to EU. This might disadvantage smaller or economically weaker nations within the Western Balkans, affecting their economic equity and negotiating capacities.

Increase in Litigation and Disputes – switching to a new investment policy framework may lead to more disputes as businesses and governments adjust to new regulations. This could increase legal costs and the administrative workload of managing these disputes. Also, relying on EU dispute resolution mechanisms may conflict with local legal practices and philosophies in the Western Balkans, at least for those who are not yet fully complying with EU regulations.

Costs of Transition – although the single investment protection treaty could bring long-term economic stability and growth, the immediate costs, and logistical challenges of implementing this new policy framework are substantial. The transition requires significant investment in legal and administrative processes and might disrupt existing investment flows temporarily, representing a high upfront cost against future benefits.

Delay in Ratification – an additional significant concern is the potential delay in the ratification of the single treaty by all EU member states. This process can be lengthy, as seen in cases like Croatia, which experienced a prolonged period of uncertainty while it worked to terminate all intra-EU BITs during its accession to the EU. Such delays could leave the Western Balkans economies in a similar state of limbo, impacting economic stability and prolonging the period of legal uncertainty regarding investment protections.

In sum, while aligning the Western Balkans with EU investment standards through a single treaty could stabilize investment flows and foster economic integration, it also brings different challenges. A careful and well-balanced approach is therefore essential to ensure that the benefits of integration with the EU do not come at the expense of the Western Balkans economic autonomy and developmental objectives.

8 Conclusion – the Way Forward

The journey of investment protection treaties' reform in the Western Balkans revealed a focused attempt to cultivate a robust and attractive business environment, crucial for attracting significant foreign investment. Since the early 1990's, the region has strived to transition from outdated bilateral investment treaties to a more refined framework that aligns with EU standards, as underscored by the challenges these older treaties present, such as vague definitions and insufficient regard for sustainable development.

The drive for modernization has evolved through various phases, reflecting the region's complex historical and economic landscape. Starting with tentative reforms in the former SFRY era, to more structured reforms post-2000, the Western Balkans have slowly but steadily worked towards creating a conducive environment for foreign capital. This evolution is characterized by attempts to reduce bureaucratic constraints, ensure greater business flexibility, and integrate with global economic practices.

Today, after establishing a set of Regional Standards, focus is on transitioning from numerous bilateral investment treaties to a single investment protection treaty with the EU. The proposed single investment protection treaty seeks to streamline and update the legal framework, offering a consistent and modern approach to investment across the region. This move towards harmonization with EU standards is not just a strategic alignment but also a practical response to the complexities and inefficiencies of negotiating separate treaties with individual EU member states. By consolidating these treaties into a single treaty framework, the Western Balkans economies aim to enhance legal consistency and reduce the vulnerability to legal disputes that have historically burdened the region.

The insights gleaned from the ICSID and UNCTAD data and the evolving dynamics of the Western Balkans paint a vivid picture of a region at a critical inflection point. The challenge for the Western Balkans economies is not just to attract investment, but to craft an investment landscape that is resilient, fair, and conducive to long-term growth.

While legal clarity in treaty terms is crucial to prevent disputes and ensure investor confidence, these treaties must also be perceived as legitimate and beneficial by the domestic population. Balancing investor interests with public policy objectives, especially in sensitive sectors such as the environment and public health, is key to maintaining a social license to operate.

However, this journey is not devoid of challenges. There remains a delicate balance to be struck between attracting foreign investment and maintaining the regulatory autonomy needed to address local economic issues. The emerging policy framework must navigate between the dual pressures of adapting to EU norms and responding to the unique developmental needs of the Western Balkans. The region's approach to these reforms will be important in determining its future economic landscape, highlighting the importance of strategic, inclusive, and legally coherent policymaking in fostering a stable and prosperous investment climate.

The way forward for the Western Balkans is paved with challenges but is also brimming with opportunities and should be pursued with optimism. By crafting well-thought-out investment treaties and aligning them with a broader vision for the region, the Western Balkans economies can attract the right kind of investment, i.e. investments that are not just financially lucrative, but also socially and environmentally responsible. As the region continues to integrate more closely with the EU and the global economy, its approach to investment treaties and arbitration will be a litmus test of its commitment to a prosperous, stable, and equitable future.

CHAPTER 3

Western Balkans Investment Treaty Disputes within the Global Landscape of ISDS Trends

Diana Rosert

1 Introduction

This chapter examines trends in investment treaty disputes involving Western Balkan economies, including Albania, Bosnia and Herzegovina, Kosovo (United Nations Administrative Region, Security Council resolution 1244 (1999)), Montenegro, North Macedonia and Serbia, as well as Croatia and Slovenia as European Union (EU) comparator countries.[1]

At least 78 investment treaty arbitrations have been encountered by these eight economies, counting the publicly known investor-State dispute settlement (ISDS) cases pursuant to international investment agreements (IIAs) that have progressed to the arbitration stage.[2]

Claimants from EU member States brought about 80 per cent of the 78 publicly known cases, mostly based on investment treaties signed in the 1990s. The large majority of these cases relied on bilateral investment treaties (BITs). Aside from various BITs, the most frequently used legal basis was the Energy Charter Treaty (ECT, 1994) with 12 cases.

The financial implications of ISDS cases can be significant. In past cases against the eight economies, the maximum claimed compensation reached 1.1 billion US dollars in a single case.

This chapter also discusses the dynamics at play for intra-EU ISDS cases as well as policy developments related to intra-EU BITs such as the termination agreement, which can provide insights for Western Balkan economies.

---

1 The views expressed in this chapter are those of the author and do not necessarily represent those of UN Trade and Development (UNCTAD) or the United Nations.

2 This includes ISDS cases based on bilateral investment treaties and other economic treaties with investment provisions, as well as mixed cases invoking both an investment treaty and another legal basis such as a domestic investment law or a contract. Disputes that have not progressed to arbitration proceedings (i.e. those at the notice of dispute or notice of intent stage) are not covered in this chapter, nor are arbitrations that are based exclusively on national investment laws or investor-State contracts.

 | DOI:10.1163/9789004729889_004

2 Western Balkans and Global Trends in Known Treaty-based ISDS Cases

At the global level, claimants have brought a total of 1,332 known treaty-based ISDS cases from 1987 to 2023 according to UNCTAD data. These ISDS cases have involved over 130 economies and one economic grouping – the EU – as defendants.

All eight economies examined in this chapter have faced investment treaty cases:

- Albania (with 14 known ISDS cases)
- Bosnia and Herzegovina (5 cases)
- Croatia (19 cases)
- Kosovo[3] (2 cases)
- Montenegro (6 cases)
- North Macedonia (11 cases)
- Serbia (15 cases)
- Slovenia (6 cases)

The first known treaty-based case against one of the eight economies was brought in 1994, *Tradex Hellas v. Albania*.[4] All but two of the 78 known ISDS cases were initiated after 2000, with a regular occurrence of several new cases each year after 2010 (figure 3.1). Most cases – about 85 per cent – were launched between 2011 and 2023. As some arbitrations can be kept fully confidential, the actual number of cases for the eight economies could be higher. Investment arbitrations based on domestic laws or contracts are not covered in this chapter.

3 Western Balkan Economies as ISDS Respondents

Looking at home States of ISDS claimants, claimants from EU member States turn out to be the largest group. They initiated 62 of the 78 cases against these eight economies.

3 Kosovo, United Nations Administrative Region, Security Council resolution 1244 (1999).

4 *Tradex Hellas S.A. v. Republic of Albania* (ICSID Case No. ARB/94/2).

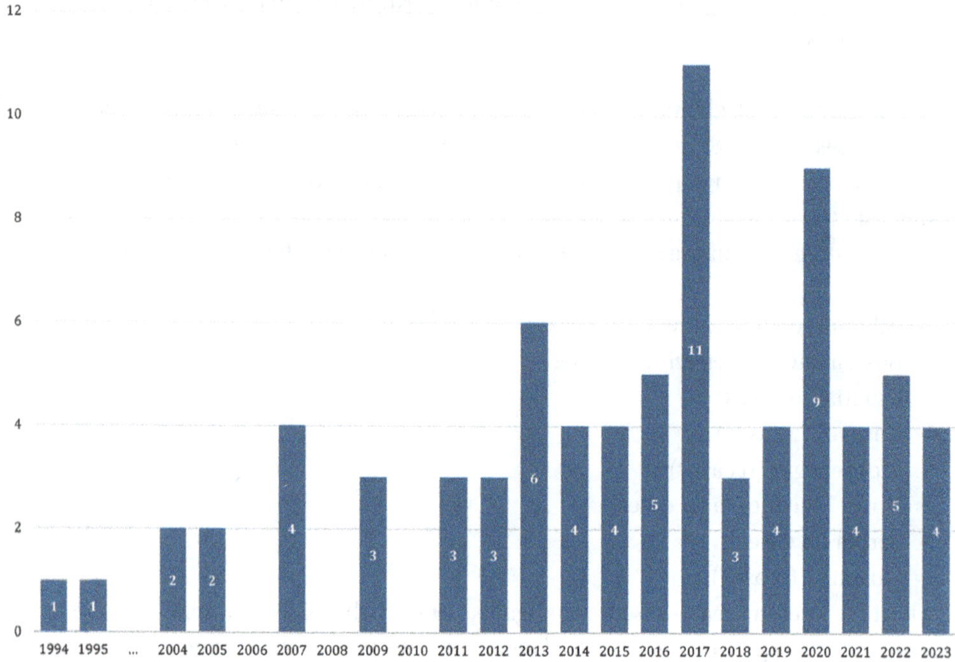

FIGURE 3.1 Annual number of known treaty-based ISDS cases for eight respondents, 1994–2023 (by date of initiation)
SOURCE: UNCTAD INVESTMENT DISPUTE SETTLEMENT NAVIGATOR AND PUBLIC SOURCES
Note: This data covers investor-State arbitration cases based on investment treaties involving the following respondents: Albania, Bosnia and Herzegovina, Croatia, Kosovo (United Nations Administrative Region, Security Council resolution 1244 (1999)), Montenegro, North Macedonia, Serbia and Slovenia.

In terms of individual home States, examining ISDS cases against Croatia and Slovenia separately is useful here since they are EU member States and could be subject to a different ISDS pattern:[5]

- For Croatia and Slovenia, the most frequent home States of ISDS claimants are Austria (8 cases), the Netherlands (5 cases), followed by Canada and Hungary with 2 cases each.
- For the six other economies, claimants from Greece (with 7 cases) and Austria (6 cases) are followed by Cyprus, Italy and the Netherlands with 5 cases each.

5 Taken together, the most frequent home States of ISDS claimants are Austria with 14 cases, followed by the Netherlands (10 cases), Greece (7), Italy (6) and Cyprus (5).

Noticeable by their relative absence are cases brought by claimants from the United States and the United Kingdom (3 cases taken together).[6] At the global level, claimants from the United States and the United Kingdom figure prominently as the ones bringing the largest numbers of ISDS claims.

Intra-group cases for the eight economies have also occurred. Six cases are between a claimant from the eight economies and a respondent from the same group:

- One case involved an Albanian claimant against North Macedonia.[7]
- Two cases involved Croatian claimants against Slovenia (1 case) and Serbia (1 case).[8]
- Three cases involved Slovenian claimants against Bosnia and Herzegovina (2 cases) and North Macedonia (1 case).[9]

Virtually all cases invoked investment treaties concluded between 1989 and 2010. About 70 per cent of the known ISDS cases relied on investment treaties signed in the 1990s. Only one ISDS case relied on a BIT signed in 2011,[10] and two cases on a 2014 BIT in conjunction with a 2005 BIT.[11] The most frequently used legal basis was the ECT (1994) in 12 of the 78 known cases.[12] This makes a share of 15 per cent for ECT-based cases,[13] which is broadly in line with the global share of ISDS cases initiated based on the ECT (12 per cent, i.e. 162 out of 1,332).

---

6 One of the cases involves claimants from the United Kingdom and the United States: *Durres Kurum Shipping SH. P.K., Durres Container Terminal SH.A, Metal Commodities Foreign Trade Corp. and Altberg Developments LP v. Republic of Albania* (ICSID Case No. ARB/20/37). The other two cases are: *Ascent Resources Plc and Ascent Slovenia Ltd v. Republic of Slovenia* (ICSID Case No. ARB/22/21); *Medusa (Montenegro) Limited v. Montenegro* (PCA Case No. 2015-39).

7 *Amadeus Group and Amadeus Development DOOEL v. Republic of North Macedonia* (ICSID Case No. ARB/23/35).

8 *Hrvatska Elektroprivreda d.d. v. Republic of Slovenia* (ICSID Case No. ARB/05/24); *Tvornica* Šećera *Osijek d.o.o. v. Republic of Serbia* (ICC).

9 *Elektrogospodarstvo Slovenije – razvoj ininzeniring d.o.o. v. Bosnia and Herzegovina* (ICSID Case No. ARB/14/13); *Boris Goljevšček, Viaduct d.o.o. Portorož and Vladimir Zevnik v. Bosnia and Herzegovina* (ICSID Case No. ARB/16/36); *Blazo Tasev v. Republic of North Macedonia* (PCA Case No. 2019-09).

10 *Mabco Constructions SA v. Republic of Kosovo* (ICSID Case No. ARB/17/25).

11 *Rand Investments Ltd. and others v. Republic of Serbia* (ICSID Case No. ARB/18/8); *Coropi Holdings Limited, Kalemegdan Investments Limited and Erinn Bernard Broshko v. Republic of Serbia* (ICSID Case No. ARB/22/14).

12 This includes four cases against Albania, three against Slovenia, two cases against Bosnia and Herzegovina, two cases against Croatia, and one against North Macedonia. In four of the 12 cases, the ECT and a BIT were invoked at the same time.

13 In contrast to this, for EU member States as respondents, ECT cases account for about 40 per cent of all cases brought against them.

4 Outcomes of ISDS Cases Involving Western Balkan Economies as Respondents

About two thirds of the 78 ISDS cases involving the eight economies as respondents have been concluded, while the remaining ones are currently pending (25 cases). The outcomes of the concluded 53 ISDS cases are as follows (figure 3.2):

- 22 cases were decided in favour of the respondent (41 per cent)
- 10 cases were decided in favour of the claimant(s) (19 per cent)
- 10 cases were settled (19 per cent)
- 5 cases were discontinued for reasons other than settlement (9 per cent)
- 3 cases were decided in favour of neither party (liability found but no damages awarded) (6 per cent)
- 3 cases were concluded but the precise outcome is not public (data not available) (6 per cent)

Due to the smaller size of this data set, a comparison with global ISDS outcomes offers only limited insights. Broadly, a comparison shows that, as on the global level, respondents are successful in defending about 40 per cent of cases (41 per cent in figure 3.2 and 38 per cent globally). In the global data set of 1,332 ISDS cases, cases decided in favour of the claimant(s) or settled, taken together, account for about 46 per cent – higher than the combined 38 per cent for such outcomes here (figure 3.2).

Looking at the cases decided in favour of the respondent, about 60 per cent were dismissed for lack of jurisdiction or admissibility, and 40 per cent failed on the merits.

In cases decided in favour of the investor with compensation being awarded, the tribunal most frequently found the respondent liable for breaches of the fair and equitable treatment standards (7 cases), sometimes alongside other breaches (table 3.1).

In the three cases decided in favour of neither party (breaches found but not damages awarded), the tribunal determined that the respondent had violated the fair and equitable treatment provision (2 cases), and full protection and security (1 case).

In almost all the cases with relevant available information, breaches of fair and equitable treatment were alleged,[14] usually in combination with alleged breaches of other provisions (table 1).

---

14 The exception is *Kornikom v. Serbia.* In this ISDS case only breaches of the expropriation provision were claimed. See *Kornikom EOOD v. Republic of Serbia* (ICSID Case No. ARB/19/12), Award, 20 September 2023.

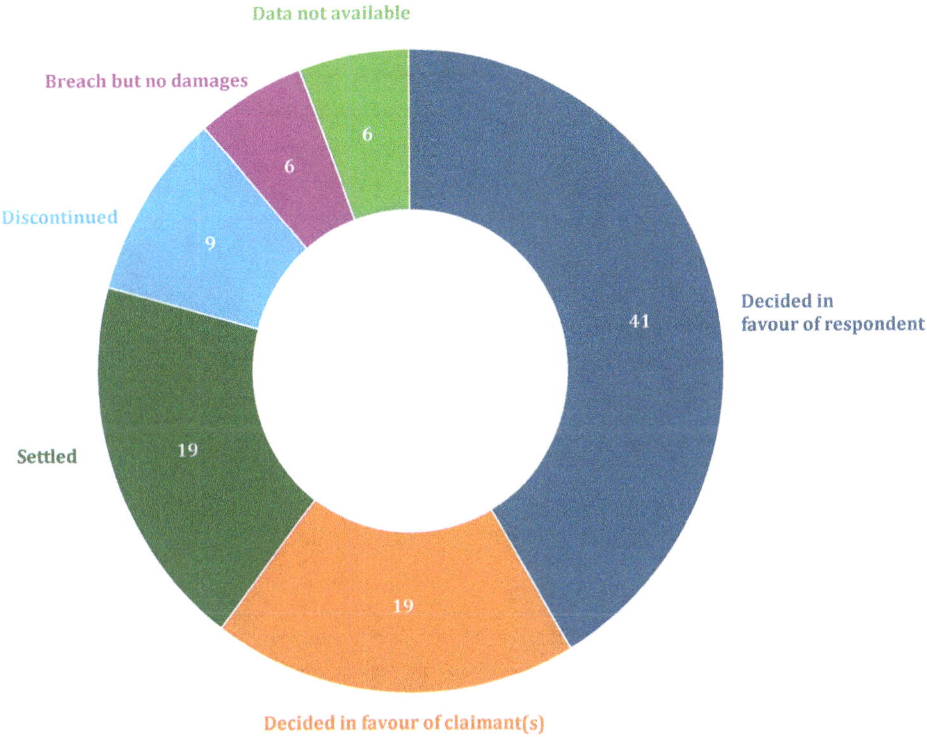

FIGURE 3.2 Results of concluded treaty-based ISDS cases for eight respondents, 1994–2023 (per cent)
SOURCE: UNCTAD INVESTMENT DISPUTE SETTLEMENT NAVIGATOR AND PUBLIC SOURCES
Note: This data covers concluded cases for the following respondents: Albania, Bosnia and Herzegovina, Croatia, Kosovo (United Nations Administrative Region, Security Council resolution 1244 (1999)), Montenegro, North Macedonia, Serbia and Slovenia. "Breach but no damages" refers to cases decided in favour of neither party (liability found but no damages awarded). The data on outcomes concerns original proceedings only and the outcomes do not take into account subsequent annulment or set-aside proceedings.

5 Selected Issues in ISDS Awards and Decisions

Respondents' objections surrounding corporate nationality, (dual) nationality of natural persons, and abuse of process allegations featured prominently in awards and decisions rendered in treaty-based ISDS cases against the eight economies. Corporate restructuring, nationality planning and treaty shopping have also emerged as pertinent concerns to be addressed through the

TABLE 3.1 Breaches alleged and found in concluded ISDS cases for eight respondents (number of cases)

	Breaches alleged	Breaches found
	(*N* = 27)	(*N* = 12)
National treatment	4	0
Most-favoured-nation treatment	5	0
Fair and equitable treatment, or similar	26	9
Full protection and security, or similar	8	1
Arbitrary, unreasonable or discriminatory measures	7	0
Direct expropriation	6	2
Indirect expropriation	19	1
Transfer of funds	2	0
Umbrella clause	6	1

SOURCE: UNCTAD INVESTMENT DISPUTE SETTLEMENT NAVIGATOR
Note: This data includes cases in which decisions (awards) on jurisdiction and awards on liability were rendered. It excludes pending cases as well as cases that were discontinued, settled or for which information on the exact outcome is not available.

clause-by-clause reform of old-generation investment treaties;[15] they surfaced in broader discussions on the future of the IIA regime and the ISDS mechanism,[16] as well as in the stocktaking of major policy challenges for international investment governance.[17]

Examples of ISDS tribunals' findings on corporate nationality, nationality of natural persons and abuse of process include the following:

15 See, for example, "Definition of investor" in UNCTAD (2020a). *International Investment Agreements Reform Accelerator.* Geneva: United Nations.

16 UNCTAD (2018). *UNCTAD's Reform Package for the International Investment Regime.* Geneva: United Nations.

17 For a discussion of complex ownership structures and policy implications, see UNCTAD (2016). *World Investment Report 2016 – Investor Nationality: Policy Challenges.* Geneva: United Nations.

- In CEAC *v. Montenegro*, the tribunal's majority decided that the claimant did not have a "seat" in Cyprus (the purported home State) and did not qualify as an "investor" under the Cyprus–Montenegro BIT (2005).[18]
- In *Mera Investment v. Serbia*, the respondent had alleged that the claimant – a company incorporated in Cyprus – was fully owned and controlled by nationals of Serbia (the host State), arguing that this should leave the tribunal without jurisdiction under the Cyprus–Serbia BIT (2005). The tribunal dismissed the respondent's jurisdictional objection.[19]
- In *Mihaljevic v. Croatia*, the tribunal ruled that the claimant was a national of Croatia (the host State) on the date the Request for Arbitration was registered and declined jurisdiction under the Croatia–Germany BIT (1997) on this basis.[20]
- In *Guardian Fiduciary v. North Macedonia*, the tribunal concluded that the claimant had failed to prove that it qualified as a national of the Netherlands, the alleged home State of the claimant, under the North Macedonia–Netherlands BIT (1998).[21] The claimant was an entity organized under New Zealand law and it had argued in the proceedings that it was indirectly controlled by a foundation organized under the law of the Netherlands.
- In *Rand Investments and others v. Serbia*, the tribunal's majority dismissed the respondent's objection that the claimants' conduct amounted to abuse of process.[22] The respondent had argued that the dispute primarily related to a domestic investment, which involved a national of Serbia (the host State), and that the main Canadian claimant had "fabricated" his beneficial ownership over the investment.[23]
- In BRIF *v. Serbia*, the respondent prevailed in its jurisdictional objection on abuse of process. The tribunal's majority determined that the restructuring

---

18 CEAC *Holdings Limited v. Montenegro* (ICSID Case No. ARB/14/8), Award, 26 July 2016, with Separate Opinion of William W. Park.

19 *Mera Investment Fund Limited v. Republic of Serbia* (ICSID Case No. ARB/17/2), Decision on Jurisdiction, 30 November 2018.

20 *Marko Mihaljevic v. Republic of Croatia* (ICSID Case No. ARB/19/35), Award, 19 May 2023, with Concurring Opinion by Maria Vicien-Milburn.

21 *Guardian Fiduciary Trust, Ltd, f/k/a Capital Conservator Savings & Loan, Ltd v. North Macedonia* (ICSID Case No. ARB/12/31), Award, 22 September 2015.

22 *Rand Investments Ltd., Allison Ruth Rand, Kathleen Elizabeth Rand and others v. Republic of Serbia* (ICSID Case No. ARB/18/8), Award, 29 June 2023, with Dissenting Opinion by Marcelo G. Kohen.

23 *Ibid.*, paras. 455–459.

of the investment took place after the dispute had become foreseeable and was "aimed at acquiring a previously crystalised ICSID claim without an independent economic purpose".[24]

- In *Swisslion v. North Macedonia*, the respondent alleged that the claimant was not under the control of an entity of Switzerland (the alleged home State) but under the control of a Serbian national (a third country). Without regard to the nationality of the ultimate owner, the tribunal affirmed jurisdiction since more than 50% of the investment was beneficially owned by a Swiss company.[25]

Other recurring issues of jurisdiction, admissibility and the merits concerned the legality of investment and domestic law compliance, the scope of fair and equitable treatment and legitimate expectations, the full protection and security standard, obligations under umbrella clauses, and access to ISDS (notice periods, local litigation, consent in intra-EU disputes). These contentious topics are also mirrored in ISDS awards and decisions at the global level.[26]

6 Economic Activities Involved

Most of the 78 ISDS claims against the eight economies related to the following economic activities:
- Mining and quarrying (14 cases)
- Financial and insurance activities (13 cases)
- Manufacturing (12 cases)
- Supply of electricity, gas, steam and air conditioning (12 cases)
- Construction (7 cases)
- Real estate activities (6 cases)
- Arts, entertainment and recreation (5 cases)
- Information and communication (5 cases)

24 *BRIF TRES d.o.o. Beograd and BRIF-TC d.o.o. Beograd v. Republic of Serbia* (ICSID Case No. ARB/20/12), Award, 30 January 2023, para. 222, with Dissenting Opinion by Samaa Haridi.

25 *Swisslion DOO Skopje v. North Macedonia* (ICSID Case No. ARB/09/16), Award, 6 June 2012, para. 132.

26 *See*, for example, UNCTAD (2023a). "Review of 2021 Investor–State Arbitration Decisions: Insights for IIA Reform". IIA Issues Note, No. 1.

At least nine cases related to fossil fuel industries[27] and at least five cases involved renewable energy investments.[28] In light of the climate emergency and global climate goals, energy-related ISDS cases have increasingly been under the spotlight, and have served as evidence for the need to accelerate the reform of the IIA regime and the ISDS mechanism.[29]

7 Challenged Measures

The following types of measures taken by the government or public authorities were most commonly challenged by ISDS claimants in the 78 examined cases:

- Legislation pertaining to currency conversion for Swiss franc-denominated loans
- Interference with contracts and concessions, or failure to fulfill contractual obligations
- Termination of concessions
- Restructuring, temporary administration and bankruptcy proceedings
- Privatization processes or their reversal
- Disputes regarding land ownership and land use
- Measures relating to environmental issues and concerns
- Decisions rendered by domestic courts
- Investigations into money laundering or corruption
- Tax-related measures (e.g. audits and investigations)

27 *Ascent Resources Plc and Ascent Slovenia Ltd v. Republic of Slovenia* (ICSID Case No. ARB/22/21); *Elektrogospodarstvo Slovenije – razvoj ininzeniring d.o.o. v. Bosnia and Herzegovina* (ICSID Case No. ARB/14/13); *Ivicom Holding GmbH v. Republic of Albania* (SCC Case No. 2021/155); *Kornikom EOOD v. Republic of Serbia* (ICSID Case No. ARB/19/12); *Mamidoil Jetoil Greek Petroleum Products Societe Anonyme S.A. v. Republic of Albania* (ICSID Case No. ARB/11/24); *Medusa (Montenegro) Limited v. Montenegro* (PCA Case No. 2015-39); *MOL Hungarian Oil and Gas Company Plc v. Republic of Croatia* (ICSID Case No. ARB/13/32); *Pramod Mittal, Sangeeta Mittal, Vartika Mittal, Shristi Mittal and Divyesh Mittal v. Bosnia and Herzegovina* (UNCITRAL); *Towra SA-SPF v. Republic of Slovenia* (ICSID Case No. ARB/22/33).

28 *Albaniabeg Ambient Sh.p.k, M. Angelo Novelli and Costruzioni S.r.l. v. Republic of Albania* (ICSID Case No. ARB/14/26); *Amlyn Holding B.V. v. Republic of Croatia* (ICSID Case No. ARB/16/28); *Arka Energy B.V. v. Republic of Albania* (ICSID Case No. ARB/20/54); *Boris Goljevšček, Viaduct d.o.o. Portorož and Vladimir Zevnik v. Bosnia and Herzegovina* (ICSID Case No. ARB/16/36); *Hydro S.r.l. and others v. Republic of Albania* (ICSID Case No. ARB/15/28).

29 *See* further UNCTAD (2023b). "Trends in the Investment Treaty Regime and a Reform Toolbox for the Energy Transition". IIA Issues Note, No. 2; UNCTAD (2022a). "The international investment treaty regime and climate action". IIA Issues Note, No. 3; UNCTAD (2022b). "Treaty-based investor–State dispute cases and climate action". IIA Issues Note, No. 4.

– Alleged failure to implement EU laws (in the context of EU accession)
Laws that mandated the conversion of loans denominated in Swiss Francs into Euros gave rise to at least seven cases brought against Croatia, Montenegro and Slovenia.[30]

At least five cases stemmed from alleged interference of the government or local authority with contracts and concessions, or from failures to fulfill contractual obligations.[31] Similarly, termination of concessions by the government or public authorities was central in five cases.[32] In four cases, claims were brought regarding the restructuring, temporary administration and bankruptcy proceedings instituted by public authorities.[33] Disputes over privatization processes or reversals prompted at least five cases.[34]

Disputes over land ownership and land use led to four cases. The cases involved a contested land lease for a shopping center project, the alleged

---

30 The seven cases are: *Addiko Bank AG and Addiko Bank d.d. v. Republic of Croatia* (ICSID Case No. ARB/17/37); *Addiko Bank AG v. Montenegro* (ICSID Case No. ARB/17/35); *Addiko Bank AG v. Republic of Slovenia* (ICSID Case No. ARB/22/9); *Erste & Steiermärkische Bank d.d., Erste Group Bank AG, and Steiermärkische Bank und Sparkassen AG v. Republic of Croatia* (ICSID Case No. ARB/17/49); *OTP Bank Plc v. Republic of Croatia* (ICSID Case No. ARB/20/43); *Raiffeisen Bank International AG and Raiffeisenbank Austria d.d. v. Republic of Croatia* (I) (ICSID Case No. ARB/17/34); *UniCredit Bank Austria AG and Zagrebačka Banka d.d. v. Republic of Croatia* (ICSID Case No. ARB/16/31).

31 *APG SGA SA and D.O.O. za promet i usluge Alma Quattro Beograd v. Republic of Serbia* (ICSID Case No. ARB/21/13); *Boris Goljevšček, Viaduct d.o.o. Portorož and Vladimir Zevnik v. Bosnia and Herzegovina* (ICSID Case No. ARB/16/36); *Kunsttrans Holding GmbH and Kunsttrans d.o.o. Beograd v. Republic of Serbia* (ICSID Case No. ARB/16/10); *Mamidoil Jetoil Greek Petroleum Products Societe Anonyme S.A. v. Republic of Albania* (ICSID Case No. ARB/11/24); *Pantechniki S.A. Contractors & Engineers v. Republic of Albania* (ICSID Case No. ARB/07/21).

32 *Artem Skubenko and others v. Republic of North Macedonia* (ICSID Case No. ARB/19/9); *Durres Kurum Shipping SH. P.K., Durres Container Terminal SH.A, Metal Commodities Foreign Trade Corp. and Altberg Developments LP v. Republic of Albania* (ICSID Case No. ARB/20/37); *Gokul Das Binani and Madhu Binani v. Republic of North Macedonia* (I) (PCA Case No. 2018-38); *Gokul Das Binani and Madhu Binani v. Republic of North Macedonia* (II); *Kornikom EOOD v. Republic of Serbia* (ICSID Case No. ARB/19/12).

33 *Adria Group B.V. and Adria Group Holding B.V. v. Republic of Croatia* (ICSID Case No. ARB/20/6); *Atlas Group and Duško Knežević v. Montenegro* (UNCITRAL); *Oleg Vladimirovich Deripaska v. the State of Montenegro* (PCA Case No. 2017-07); *Raiffeisen Bank International AG and Raiffeisen Bank Austria d.d. v. Republic of Croatia* (II) (PCA Case No. 2020-15).

34 *ACP Axos Capital GmbH v. Republic of Kosovo* (ICSID Case No. ARB/15/22); *Kornikom EOOD v. Republic of Serbia* (ICSID Case No. ARB/19/12); *Mabco Constructions SA v. Republic of Kosovo* (ICSID Case No. ARB/17/25); *Mytilineos Holdings v. Serbia* (II) (PCA Case No. 2014-30); *Rand Investments Ltd., Allison Ruth Rand, Kathleen Elizabeth Rand and others v. Republic of Serbia* (ICSID Case No. ARB/18/8).

expropriation of agricultural and grazing land, authorities' alleged misrepresentation of the construction zone for a luxury resort development, and alleged obstruction of the acquisition for real estate properties located on the Adriatic coast.[35]

Measures relating to environmental issues and concerns played a role in three cases,[36] notably including a high-profile dispute, *Ascent v. Slovenia*, related to Slovenia's 2022 mining law amendment that banned the use of hydraulic stimulation for the exploration and exploitation of hydrocarbons.

At least three cases concerned domestic court decisions, with varied backgrounds such as a golf resort construction, debts allegedly due following the acquisition of a national electricity distributor, and a real estate transaction which was considered not in conformity with local law.[37]

Three claims arose out of government measures against money laundering and corruption.[38] In two of the three cases, claimants also challenged tax audits and investigations.[39]

One claim related to Croatia's alleged failure to liberalize its postal services market according to EU law, following its accession to the EU in 2013.[40]

8 Amounts at Stake in Investment Treaty Cases

The amounts at stake in investment treaty cases can be significant, particularly for small economies (table 3.2). In the 44 cases involving the eight economies for which relevant information was publicly available, the average amount

35 *BRIF TRES d.o.o. Beograd and BRIF-TC d.o.o. Beograd v. Republic of Serbia* (ICSID Case No. ARB/20/12); *Chantal C. van Riet, Christopher van Riet and Lieven J. van Riet v. Republic of Croatia* (ICSID Case No. ARB/13/12); *Georg Gavrilovic and Gavrilovic d.o.o. v. Republic of Croatia* (ICSID Case No. ARB/12/39); *Haakon Korsgaard v. Croatia* (PCA Case No. 2019-02).

36 *Artem Skubenko and others v. Republic of North Macedonia* (ICSID Case No. ARB/19/9); *Ascent Resources Plc and Ascent Slovenia Ltd v. Republic of Slovenia* (ICSID Case No. ARB/22/21); *Elitech B.V. and Razvoj Golf D.O.O. v. Republic of Croatia* (ICSID Case No. ARB/17/32).

37 *Elitech B.V. and Razvoj Golf D.O.O. v. Republic of Croatia* (ICSID Case No. ARB/17/32); *EVN AG v. North Macedonia* (ICSID Case No. ARB/09/10); *Marko Mihaljevic v. Republic of Croatia* (ICSID Case No. ARB/19/35).

38 *Guardian Fiduciary Trust, Ltd, f/k/a Capital Conservator Savings & Loan, Ltd v. North Macedonia* (ICSID Case No. ARB/12/31); *Hydro S.r.l. and others v. Republic of Albania* (ICSID Case No. ARB/15/28); *Mera Investment Fund Limited v. Republic of Serbia* (ICSID Case No. ARB/17/2).

39 *Hydro S.r.l. and others v. Republic of Albania* (ICSID Case No. ARB/15/28); *Mera Investment Fund Limited v. Republic of Serbia* (ICSID Case No. ARB/17/2).

40 *B3 Croatian Courier Coöperatief U.A. v. Republic of Croatia* (ICSID Case No. ARB/15/5).

TABLE 3.2 Amounts claimed and awarded in known treaty-based ISDS cases, 1987–2023 (in United States dollars, USD)

	Selected eight economies	Global
Amounts claimed	(*N* = *44*)	(*N* = *902*)
Highest	1.1 billion	200 billion
Average	220 million	1.1 billion
Median	109 million	143.1 million
Lowest	2 million	40,000
Amounts awarded	(*N* = *9*)	(*N* = *259*)
Highest	183.9 million	40 billion[41]
Average	45 million	384.6 million
Median	16 million	32.5 million
Lowest	430,000	30,000

SOURCE: BASED ON UNCTAD INVESTMENT DISPUTE SETTLEMENT NAVIGATOR AND PUBLIC SOURCES

Note: The eight economies covered are Albania, Bosnia and Herzegovina, Croatia, Kosovo (United Nations Administrative Region, Security Council resolution 1244 (1999)), Montenegro, North Macedonia, Serbia and Slovenia. The data for amounts awarded consists of damages, without interest, awarded as part of the original proceedings. It does not include settlements. It does not take into account subsequent annulment or set-aside proceedings.

claimed was USD 220 million. In *MOL v. Croatia*, the amount claimed was the largest with USD 1.1 billion, while the lowest amount was about USD 2 million (in *Pantechniki v. Albania*). In comparison, at the global scale, the maximum damages claimed in one single case are as high as USD 200 billion (table 3.2).[42]

In this data set of only 9 known damages figures for eight economies, the average amount awarded was USD 45 million. The lowest amount of approx. USD 430,000 excluding applicable interest was awarded in *Swisslion v. North Macedonia* in 2012, which is the oldest damages award in this data set.[43] The

41 This amount was awarded in Hulley Enterprises v. Russia. A combined USD 50 billion was awarded in three cases related to the Yukos company: Hulley Enterprises Ltd. v. Russ*ian Federation* (*PCA Case No. 2005-03/AA226*); *Veteran Petroleum Li*mited v. The *Russian Federation* (*PCA Case No. 2005-05/AA228*); *Yukos Universal Limited* (*Isle of Man*) *v. The Russian Federation* (PCA Case No. 2005-04/AA227).

42 *Zeph Investments Pte. Ltd. v. The Commonwealth of Australia* (I) (PCA Case No. 2023-40), Procedural Order No. 2, 17 November 2023, para. 20.

43 *Swisslion DOO Skopje v. North Macedonia* (ICSID Case No. ARB/09/16), Award, 6 June 2012.

highest damages were the USD 183.9 million, excluding interest, awarded a decade later in *MOL v. Croatia* in 2022.[44] This is anecdotal evidence of the rising figures in amounts awarded over the past 10 years or so. At the global level, this trend is confirmed by a 2021 study which showed that "investors are claiming, and are being awarded, larger amounts".[45]

The awarded interest, not included in the above figures, can also be substantial. In addition, costs for the legal representation of each party, tribunal costs and administrative fees apply. The costs for respondents' legal representation range from hundreds of thousands to millions of US dollars, including for economies in the Western Balkans.

Examples of the legal representation costs for Western Balkan economies include:[46]

- *ACP Axos v. Kosovo*: "Totals Incurred 2,060,138.68 USD and 132,446.2 Euro"[47]
- *Burimi v. Albania*: "Legal representation costs EUR 348,856"[48]
- *CEAC v. Montenegro:* "Montenegro requests that it be awarded EUR 865,678.51 as legal fees and expenses."[49]
- *Guardian Fiduciary v. North Macedonia*: "Total 1,515,885 USD and £40,999.50"[50]
- *Mamidoil v. Albania*: "On 22 April 2014, Respondent likewise submitted its final statement of costs and expenses. They amount to 528,453.40 Euro, including fees and expenses of external and internal counsel, expert fees and costs of travel and translation."[51]

---

44 *MOL Hungarian Oil and Gas Company Plc v. Republic of Croatia* (ICSID Case No. ARB/13/32), Award, 5 July 2022.

45 Hodgson, M. (2021). "Costs, damages and duration in investor-State arbitration" < > accessed 12 April 2024. See further Hodgson, M., Y. Kryvoi and D. Hrcka (2021). "2021 Empirical Study: Costs, Damages and Duration in Investor-State Arbitration". London: Allen & Overy, and British Institute of International and Comparative Law.

46 Examples collected and verified based on Hodgson, M., and D. Hrcka (2021). "Study of Cost Awards in Investment Treaty Arbitrations up to 31 May 2020, Master Table" < accessed 12 April 2024.

47 Including 400,000 USD arbitration costs. *ACP Axos Capital GmbH v. Republic of Kosovo* (ICSID Case No. ARB/15/22), Award, 3 May 2018, para. 262. Case decided in favour of the respondent.

48 *Burimi SRL and Eagle Games SH.A v. Republic of Albania* (ICSID Case No. ARB/11/18), Award, 29 May 2013, para. 155. Case decided in favour of the respondent.

49 *CEAC Holdings Limited v. Montenegro* (ICSID Case No. ARB/14/8), Award, 26 July 2016, para. 219. Case decided in favour of the respondent.

50 Costs including ICSID and tribunal fees and expenses. *Guardian Fiduciary Trust, Ltd, f/k/a Capital Conservator Savings & Loan, Ltd v. North Macedonia* (ICSID Case No. ARB/12/31), Award, 22 September 2015, para. 141. Case decided in favour of the respondent.

51 *Mamidoil Jetoil Greek Petroleum Products Societe Anonyme S.A. v. Republic of Albania* (ICSID Case No. ARB/11/24), Award, 30 March 2015, para. 831. Case decided in favour of the respondent.

- *Pantechniki v. Albania*: "Albania's corresponding claim is EUR 269,657"[52]
- *Swisslion v. North Macedonia*: "The Respondent has quantified its costs, inclusive of advance ICSID fees and expenses, in the amount of USD 3,675,211.23."[53]

At the global level, average legal costs for respondents in investor-State arbitration stand at around USD 4.7 million.[54] In a share of cases, costs are partly or fully shifted onto the other (losing) party. In case of a win on the merits for the claimant, the respondent would usually have to bear its own costs and, at times, a portion of the claimant's costs.[55]

9 Insights from Intra-EU ISDS Cases

Claimants from EU member States have initiated 40 investment treaty arbitrations against the six Western Balkan economies, accounting for 75 per cent of their caseload (table 3.3). Since the six Western Balkan economies have embarked on EU accession paths as candidates and potential candidates, examining the ISDS dynamics at play for the 13 countries that joined the EU in 2004, 2007, and 2013 can offer some insights.

By the end of 2023, a total of 223 ISDS cases based on BITs and the ECT were brought by a claimant from one EU member State against another EU member State. This includes one case against the EU by claimants from Germany, Denmark and the United Kingdom.[56] The largest share of these intra-EU ISDS cases was directed at the 13 new EU member States (figure 3.3). New EU member States, which had joined the EU in 2004 or thereafter, were respondents to twice as many known cases (149) as the "old" EU-15 countries (73 cases).

Among the new EU member States, Czechia and Poland received the highest number of intra-EU cases (table 3.3). The majority of the cases brought against the EU-15 were against Spain (46 cases) and Italy (13 cases). Legislative

52 *Pantechniki S.A. Contractors & Engineers v. Republic of Albania* (ICSID Case No. ARB/07/21), Award, 30 July 2009, para. 103. Case decided in favour of the respondent.

53 *Swisslion DOO Skopje v. North Macedonia* (ICSID Case No. ARB/09/16), Award, 6 June 2012, para. 353. Case decided in favour of the claimant.

54 Hodgson, M., Y. Kryvoi and D. Hrcka (2021). "2021 Empirical Study: Costs, Damages and Duration in Investor-State Arbitration". London: Allen & Overy, and British Institute of International and Comparative Law.

55 *Ibid.*

56 *Klesch Group Holdings Limited & others v. European Union* (ICSID Case No. ARB(AF)/23/1).

TABLE 3.3 Known ISDS cases brought by claimants from EU home countries and total caseload for eight economies as respondents

Respondents	Known ISDS cases brought by claimants from EU home countries against respondent	Total number of known ISDS cases against respondent
Albania	13	14
Bosnia and Herzegovina	3	5
Kosovo (United Nations Administrative Region, Security Council resolution 1244 (1999))	1	2
Montenegro	4	6
North Macedonia	5	11
Serbia	14	15
SUB-TOTAL (6 economies)	40	53
Croatia	16	19
Slovenia	6	6
TOTAL (8 economies)	62	78

SOURCE: UNCTAD INVESTMENT DISPUTE SETTLEMENT NAVIGATOR AND PUBLIC SOURCES

acts concerning the renewable energy sector continue to be the most frequently challenged measures in intra-EU ISDS proceedings.[57]

A distinct pattern of intra-EU cases is that the ECT served as the legal basis in almost half of them (figure 3.4). The large number of intra-EU cases pursuant to the ECT together with the prominent fact that the ECT has been the most frequently invoked IIA worldwide probably gave an impetus to the modernisation process of the ECT's investment protection chapter.

Since a large number of BITs – more than 90 – are in force between EU member States and the six Western Balkan economies,[58] lessons can be drawn from policy developments surrounding intra-EU BITs.

57 See also UNCTAD (2018). "Fact Sheet on Intra-European Union Investor-State Arbitration Cases". IIA Issues Note, No. 3.

58 Based on data from UNCTAD's International Investment Agreements Navigator and public sources.

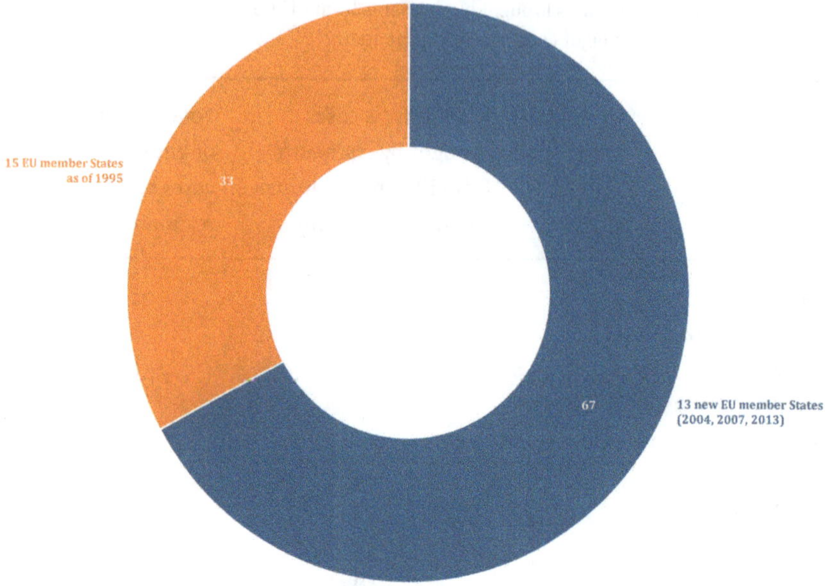

FIGURE 3.3 Respondents in known intra-EU ISDS cases based on BITs and the ECT, 1994–2023 (per cent)
SOURCE: UNCTAD INVESTMENT DISPUTE SETTLEMENT NAVIGATOR
Note: This data covers 222 known treaty-based ISDS cases, aside from *Klesch v. EU*, between the EU 28 member States with the United Kingdom, i.e. taking into account cases brought by claimants from the United Kingdom prior to withdrawal. It also includes cases brought against EU member States prior to their accession date.

The intra-EU BIT issue has long been on the agenda of the European Commission.[59] The so-called intra-EU BITs were in large part pre-existing investment treaties between the 15 EU member States (as of 1995) and the "new" EU member States which acceded in 2004, 2007 and 2013.[60] After rounds of infringement proceedings and a 2019 joint declaration on the legal consequences of the *Achmea* judgment and on investment protection, the EU

59 See, for example, European Commission (2015a). "Commission asks Member States to terminate their intra-EU bilateral investment treaties". Press Release < accessed 12 April 2024.

60 European Commission (2015b). "Get the facts: Intra-EU bilateral investment treaties". Press Release < accessed 12 April 2024.

TABLE 3.4 Most frequent respondents in intra-EU ISDS cases, 1994–2023

Respondents	No. of intra-EU ISDS cases
Spain	46
Czechia	33
Poland	26
Romania	19
Croatia	16
Hungary	15
Italy	13
Bulgaria	10
Slovakia	10
Slovenia	6
Germany	5
Latvia	5
Cyprus	3
Estonia	3
Greece	3
Lithuania	3
Denmark	2
Netherlands	2
Austria	1
EU	1
France	1
TOTAL	223

SOURCE: UNCTAD INVESTMENT DISPUTE SETTLEMENT NAVIGATOR
Note: This data covers known treaty-based ISDS cases between the EU 28 member States with the United Kingdom, i.e. taking into account cases brought by claimants from the United Kingdom prior to withdrawal. It also includes cases brought against EU member States prior to their accession date.

agreement for the termination of intra-EU BITs was signed by 23 EU member States in 2020.[61]

The EU termination agreement for intra-EU BITs offers a practical example of how to cease legal commitments under investment treaties between

61 European Commission (2020). "EU Member States sign an agreement for the termination of intra-EU bilateral investment treaties". Press Release < accessed 12 April 2024.

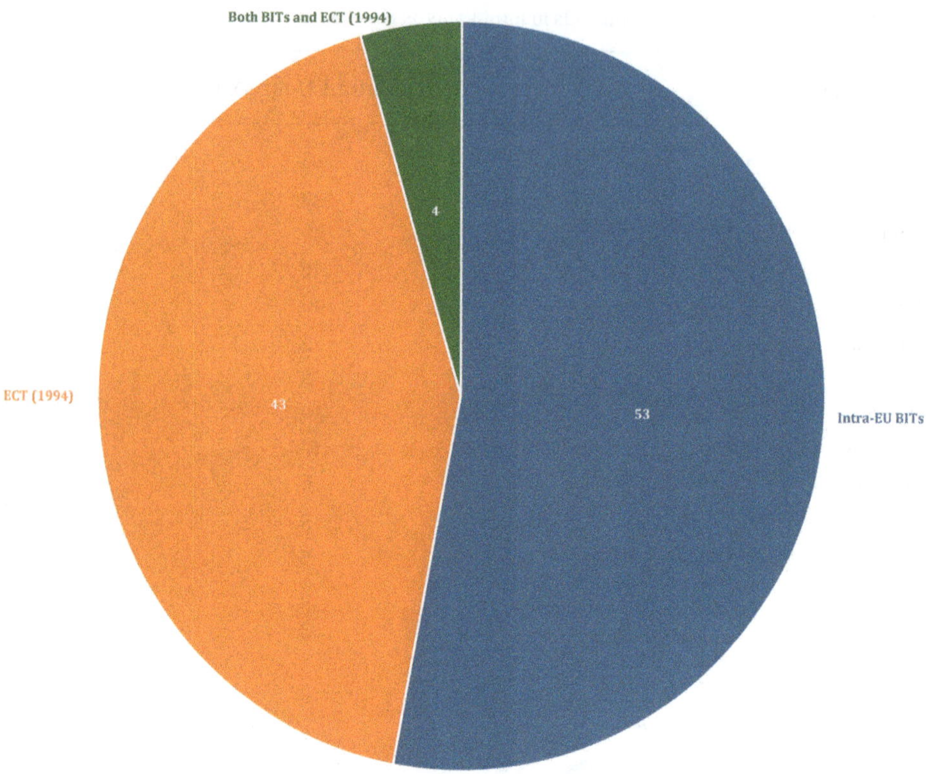

FIGURE 3.4 Invoked legal basis in intra-EU ISDS cases, 1994–2023 (per cent)
SOURCE: UNCTAD INVESTMENT DISPUTE SETTLEMENT NAVIGATOR

like-minded countries on a large scale. The agreement has resulted in the effective termination of about 150 intra-EU BITs within less than 3 years since its conclusion. Two features of the termination agreement stand out:

1. The "for greater certainty" provision to neutralize the legal effects of survival clauses in listed BITs upon termination through the EU termination agreement (Article 2).
2. The explicit "termination of possible effects" of survival clauses in listed BITs which had already been terminated, on a unilateral or joint basis, prior to the conclusion of the intra-EU termination agreement (Article 3).

As the EU's approach to intra-EU BITs (termination) is different from the EU's approach to BITs with third countries (reformed clauses), it remains to be seen which specific solution will be implemented for EU member States' BITs with the six Western Balkan economies. Meanwhile, the Western Balkan economies have already initiated processes to align their existing and future BITs with EU standards.[62]

10 Western Balkans Economies' Past ISDS Exposure and Global Reform Issues

Considering Western Balkan economies' past exposure to ISDS cases based on IIAs, three facts are noteworthy:

1. A high number of BITs are in force between EU member States and the six Western Balkan economies, which gave rise to 40 ISDS cases against them (table 3.2).
2. Four of the six economies are contracting parties of the ECT (1994), which was invoked in seven ISDS cases (table 3.4).
3. Only one of the six economies has an investment protection agreement with the United States (the most frequent home State of ISDS claimants globally), and there is only one known ISDS case invoking that BIT.[63]

The modernisation process of the ECT's investment chapter was started in 2020. The ECT (1994) creates legal commitments between 50 countries and EU/Euratom,[64] and is the "world's largest existing agreement that contains BIT-like investment protection provisions and ISDS".[65] At the time of writing the future of the modernization process is uncertain in light of the recently notified withdrawals of several individual EU member States and the United Kingdom from the ECT, and pending decisions at EU level concerning a potential coordinated withdrawal. The developments concerning the ECT could have wider implications for the investment treaty regime, including for Western Balkan economies.

62 See, for example, Regional Cooperation Council (2018). "Regional Investment Reform Agenda for the Western Balkans Six" < accessed 12 April 2024. Regional Cooperation Council (2020). "Western Balkans Six: Regionally Accepted Standards for Negotiating International Investment Agreements (IIAs)" < accessed 12 April 2024.

63 Albania–United States of America BIT (signed in 1995, entered into force in 1998). For the eight economies that are the subject of this article, the only other BIT with the United States is the Croatia–United States of America BIT (signed in 1996, entered into force in 2001).

64 This is the number of contracting parties prior to recent withdrawals.

65 UNCTAD (2022a). "The international investment treaty regime and climate action". IIA Issues Note, No. 3.

TABLE 3.5 Energy Charter Treaty membership and known ISDS cases for eight economies as respondents

	Energy Charter Treaty (ECT, 1994) membership	No. of known ISDS cases under the ECT (1994) as respondent
Albania	YES	4
Bosnia and Herzegovina	YES	2
Croatia	YES	2
Kosovo (United Nations Administrative Region, Security Council resolution 1244 (1999))	NO	Not applicable
Montenegro	YES	0
North Macedonia	YES	1
Serbia	NO	0
Slovenia	YES (notification of withdrawal on 13 October 2023, effective on 14 October 2024)	3

SOURCE: ENERGY CHARTER SECRETARIAT; UNCTAD INVESTMENT DISPUTE SETTLEMENT NAVIGATOR

Various agencies and international organizations, including UNCTAD, provide technical assistance and capacity-building activities to government officials for the reform of IIAs, including with aim of minimizing the risks of ISDS. The ISDS reform outputs emerging from deliberations at UNCITRAL Working Group III could also influence countries' ISDS exposure and their capacity to manage disputes. For example, a future advisory centre on international investment dispute resolution could potentially provide access to more affordable legal services in this respect.[66]

In the past 10 years, countries and regions have moved ahead and implemented different ISDS approaches in their IIAs and related investment

66 United Nations (2024). "UNCITRAL Working Group III concludes its work on the draft statute of an advisory centre on international investment dispute resolution" < accessed 12 April 2024.

instruments.[67] By now, there is a clear trend towards ISDS reform across the globe: Over half of the IIAs signed between 2020 and 2023 contain improved ISDS procedures, limit ISDS access or omit ISDS.[68] Countries and regions have also pursued reforms of older existing IIAs, through their amendment, replacement and termination.[69] However, the current depth and speed of reform actions worldwide is not yet sufficient to effectively address the global risks arising from investment treaties, for instance for climate action policies. The global increase in ISDS cases, coupled with the high financial stakes and the inherent litigation risks for public policy measures, underscore the need to accelerate the reform of the investment treaty regime and the ISDS mechanism.

67 For instance, the "no ISDS"-approach was advanced by Brazil and its treaty partners in 14 investment cooperation and facilitation agreements concluded since 2015. UNCTAD (2020b). *World Investment Report 2020: International Production Beyond the Pandemic.* Geneva: United Nations. For the prevalence of ISDS reform features in recent IIAs (2020–2023), see UNCTAD (2023). "Trends in the Investment Treaty Regime and a Reform Toolbox for the Energy Transition". IIA Issues Note, No. 2 (2023).

68 See figure 4 in UNCTAD (2023). "Trends in the Investment Treaty Regime and a Reform Toolbox for the Energy Transition". IIA Issues Note, No. 2 (2023).

69 UNCTAD (2019). "Taking Stock of IIA Reform: Recent Developments". IIA Issues Note, No. 3 (2019).

CHAPTER 4

Arbitrating Disputes in the Renewable Energy Sector in the Western Balkans

Ilija Mitrev Penushliski

1 Introduction[1]

The share of renewable energy in global energy production has been rapidly growing. For example, renewable energies accounted for 83% of all new energy generation capacity added in 2022.[2]

That rapid growth is likely to continue. The Intergovernmental Panel on Climate Change concluded that increases in global temperature need to be kept to 1.5 degree Celsius below pre-industrial levels to avoid serious consequences.[3] Investment in clean energy projects and infrastructure will need to surpass USD 4 trillion by 2030 to meet that target.[4] International investment is critical to the transition to clean energy, particularly for renewable power generation.[5]

This need for investment in renewables is felt strongly across the six Western Balkans States (the ***WB6***). The World Bank estimates that the most cost effective method for the WB6 to reach net zero carbon emissions by 2050 requires increasing their share of solar and wind energy to 61% of power generation and 68% of installed capacity.[6] On 10 November 2020, the WB6 issued the Sofia Declaration which committed the WB6 States to work with the EU to implement the Green Agenda for the Western Balkans.[7] In the declaration,

1 Partner, Three Crowns LLP, Paris, ilija.mitrev-penushliski@threecrownsllp.com. I wish to thank Mr Mitchell Dorbyk, Associate at Three Crowns LLP, for his valuable research assistance.

2 International Renewable Energy Agency, 'Renewable Power Generation Costs in 2022' (2023) p. 27.

3 Intergovernmental Panel on Climate Change, 'An IPCC Special Report on the impacts of global warming of 1.5°C above pre-industrial levels and related global greenhouse gas emission pathways, in the context of strengthening the global response to the threat of climate change, sustainable development, and efforts to eradicate poverty' (2018).

4 International Energy Agency, 'World Energy Outlook' (2021) p. 18.

5 UNCTAD, 'World Investment Report 2023' (2023) p. 143.

6 World Bank Group, 'Western Balkans 6: Country and Climate Development Report' (2024) 5.

7 Sofia Declaration on the Green Agenda for the Western Balkans (10 November 2020).

 | DOI:10.1163/9789004729889_005

the six governments committed to "increase the share of renewable energy sources and provide the necessary investment conditions, in line with the EU and Energy Community *acquis* and target".[8] The EU's investments in the WB6 include substantial investment in renewable energy, for example, wind farms in Bosnia and Herzegovina and a solar plant in Albania as part of the EU's December 2023 EUR 680 million package for the region.[9]

At the same time, the incentivisation and regulation of renewable energy entails significant State involvement. State intervention in turn can lead to disputes with foreign investors. A popular avenue for such disputes is arbitration under bilateral or multilateral treaties for the promotion and protection of foreign investment. Such arbitration is the main form of investor-State dispute settlement (ISDS).

In recent times, ISDS has become particularly relevant for renewable energy disputes. In September 2022, UNCTAD found that at least 80 ISDS cases concerning investments in the renewables sector had been reported, compared with 192 fossil fuel ISDS cases in the same period.[10] In 60% of those renewables arbitrations Spain was the respondent and in 90% the relevant investment agreement was the Energy Charter Treaty (ECT).[11]

This chapter examines the types of State support and involvement that is typical in the renewable energy sector, both generally and in the WB6, and then discusses different species of ISDS disputes that have arisen from such involvement. The focus is on wind and solar projects, given the rise of investment in these sectors in recent years. The aim is to understand where arbitration risks may arise for the WB6 with respect to renewables. In what follows, Section 2 explains the economics of renewables and how States incentivise projects, Section 3 provides an overview of renewables regimes in the WB6, Section 4 examines the arbitration risks for the WB6 based on examples from other renewables disputes, and Section 5 concludes.

---

8 *Ibid*, p. 2.

9 European Commission, 'European Commission announces additional €680 million investment package for the Western Balkans under the Economic and Investment Plan' (13 December 2023) <https://neighbourhood-enlargement.ec.europa.eu/news/european-commission-announces-additional-eu680-million-investment-package-western-balkans-under-2023-12-13_en> accessed 27 June 2024.

10 UNCTAD, 'Treaty-Based Investor-State Dispute Settlement Cases and Climate Action' (Issue 4, September 2022) 13–21.

11 UNCTAD, 'Treaty-Based Investor-State Dispute Settlement Cases and Climate Action' (Issue 4, September 2022) 5–6.

2 Economics of Renewable Energy Projects

Renewable energy companies, like all for-profit companies, are designed to generate returns for their investors. Private enterprise will not construct new capacity unless there is a sufficient business case to do so. Renewables projects have high up-front sunk costs, but once the enterprise is operational, it generally requires minimal financial spend.

Historically, many renewable energy companies relied on government incentives to be competitive in their electricity markets.[12] While renewable energy projects have become relatively robust and financially independent in recent times,[13] producers still look to government incentives for various reasons. One major reason is for renewable energy producers to be able to properly compete with traditional energy producers.

In addition, commercial and operational issues can impact renewable energy producers differently. For instance, supply chain constraints and rising interest rates imperilled most offshore wind developments between 2017 and 2022.[14] Given the debt renewables investors must shoulder before sunk costs can be recovered in these projects, disruptions of this nature may be more difficult for them to weather. That debt may also come at a higher cost because financial institutions often perceive financing renewables investments as riskier than conventional investments, resulting in a higher cost of capital for renewables projects.[15]

There are also non-economic factors pushing States to adopt measures to accelerate the adoption of renewable energy production. Globally there is increasing pressure to cut back on fossil fuel emissions to combat climate change.[16] Regionally, many European States are searching for alternative

12 See generally, International Renewable Energy Agency, 'Renewable Power Generation Costs in 2022' (2023).

13 International Renewable Energy Agency, 'Renewable Power Generation Costs in 2022' (2023) 69 ("In 2022, around 59 gigawatts (GW) of the new onshore wind projects commissioned had an LCOE lower than the weighted average cost of new fossil fuel-fired power by country/region. This was 87% of the new onshore wind capacity additions in 2022").

14 Richard Millard, 'The struggles of the offshore wind industry' *Financial Times* (London, 30 October 2023) <https://www.ft.com/content/00e8af58-f2b4-4d91-9c6e-bd2045c22c20> accessed 27 June 2024.

15 World Bank Group, 'Western Balkans 6: Country and Climate Development Report' (2024) 82.

16 International Renewable Energy Agency, 'Renewable Power Generation Costs in 2022' (2023) p. 34.

energy sources to reduce dependence on Russian fossil fuels.[17] Even outside the region, renewables allow States without easy access to oil, gas, or other energy sources to secure their own domestic electricity.[18]

All of these factors have led States to create incentive structures to promote investment into renewables.

2.1 *The Types of Incentives States Offer to Renewables Investors*

There are several types of measures that governments deploy – individually or in conjunction with each other – to attract investments in the renewables sector.[19] Some of the prominent types of incentives are briefly addressed here. These can be divided generally into tariff-, tax – and volume-based incentives.

The most common tariff incentive is a **feed-in tariff** (*FiT*), which is a commitment from the government or operator to purchase electricity generated from a renewable energy plant at a fixed rate. A FiT will allow prospective investors to calculate potential returns based on a consistent revenue stream.[20] A FiT is usually combined with a further commitment by the government to offtake the electricity generated, thus alleviating both the investor's price and volume risk.[21]

Closely related to the FiT is the **feed-in premium** (*FiP*). A premium rate offers investors a fixed bonus above the market price for every unit of electricity sold.[22] A FiP thus allocates some of the electricity market risk to the investor. It is, in part, designed to avoid over – or under-compensation that may arise where a FiT is set too high or low as compared to the going rate in the market.

States also incentivise renewable energy through **tax advantages.**[23] This can be by offering reductions in corporate tax rates, exempting or limiting value added tax on components of renewable energy projects like wind turbines

17 International Renewable Energy Agency, 'Renewable Power Generation Costs in 2022' (2023) p. 18.

18 International Energy Agency, 'Renewables 2022: Analysis and forecast to 2027' (2022) 10.

19 See Peter Meier, Maria Vagliasindi, & Mudassar Imran, 'The Design and Sustainability of Renewable Energy Incentives: An Economic Analysis' (World Bank Group 2015) pp. 8–11.

20 Yuehong Lu *et al*, 'A Critical Review of Sustainable Energy Policies for the Promotion of Renewable Energy Sources' (2020) 12 Sustainability 5078, Section 4.2.

21 National Renewable Energy Laboratory, 'A Policymaker's Guide to Feed-in Tariff Policy Design' (1 July 2010) p. 6.

22 National Renewable Energy Laboratory, 'A Policymaker's Guide to Feed-in Tariff Policy Design' (1 July 2010) p. 50.

23 Sikandar Abdul Qadir *et al*, 'Incentives and strategies for financing the renewable energy transition: A review' (2021) p. 7 Energy Reports 3590, 3598 "Fiscal and tax incentives".

and photovoltaic cells, or other methods to lower the company's tax burden.[24] Investment itself might also be subsidized through favourable loans or grants.

Volume-based incentives are the last category. They oblige a State, for example, via the electrical grid operator or another State entity, to secure a certain volume of its electricity from renewable sources.[25] For example, renewable energy producers may be issued certificates or credits in addition to compensation for the value of their electricity sold. The grid operator is then required to purchase a certain number of certificates. That way, renewables producers are guaranteed a certain offtake from the State.

2.2 *How States Offer Incentives to Would-Be Investors*

Generally, incentives are offered through legislation or regulations, or through auctions. Offering incentives through legislation entitles qualifying investors to access subsidies without the need to enter into any agreement with the State or may entitle the investor to a standard form incentive contract. Auctioning is the practice of offering incentives to new investors through a competitive bidding process. States typically invite bids for certain quantities of renewable energy and investors will offer to produce and supply electricity for a certain price over a certain period.[26] Successful bidders enter into a contract with the State, which memorialises the rights and obligations of both the State and the investor.[27]

Many EU Member States have transitioned from using general legislation to employing auctions to increase government control and predictability in the market.[28] Between 2005 and 2015 the number of countries auctioning

24 *Ibid.*

25 Philippe Menanteau, Dominique Finon, & Marie-Laure Lamy, 'Prices versus quantities: choosing policies for promoting the development of renewable energy' (2003) 31(8) Energy Policy 799, 803.

26 International Renewable Energy Agency and Clean Energy Ministerial, 'Renewable Energy Auction: A Guide to Design' (2015) pp. 17–20.

27 International Renewable Energy Agency and Clean Energy Ministerial, 'Renewable Energy Auction: A Guide to Design' (2015) p. 15.

28 See, e.g., Merethe Dotterud Leiren & Inken Reimer, 'Historical institutionalist perspective on the shift from feed-in tariffs towards auctioning in German renewable energy policy' (2018) p. 43 Energy Research & Social Science pp. 33, 38–39 (discussing the rise of renewables auctions within the Germany and the EU, more generally); and Union Renewable Development Platform, 'RES Auctions Platform: Member States overview' (EC) <https://union-renewables-development-platform.ec.europa.eu/auctions/auctions-table-overview?overview=chart&country=eu&year=2026> accessed 27 June 2024 (containing the renewables auctions planned by EU Member States).

renewable energy incentives increased from 6 to 60.[29] This trend towards auctions is also prevalent in the WB6.

3 The Renewables Framework in the Western Balkans

The Western Balkans is a region with strong potential for renewable energy.[30] Some of that potential has been realised but, for the most part, the WB6 are working to improve their capacity for renewable energy generation.

Like most of the world, the States of the WB6 are investing in their renewable energy capacities. The impetus for this investment is partially fuelled by policy goals shared around the world, namely, fighting climate change or securing domestic energy supply. There are also region-specific motivations. Coal reliance is high in the WB6,[31] affecting air quality across many of the region's cities, to take one effect only.[32] EU membership is also a driving force, with the EU establishing funding mechanisms to bring energy infrastructure up to union standards.[33]

Within the WB6, the current renewable energy generation capabilities are primarily in hydroelectricity and/or biomass.[34] However, data from the International Renewable Energy Agency (*IRENA*) indicates that recent investments have primarily been focused on wind and solar generation.[35]

Each WB6 member State has its own bespoke regime for incentives in the renewable energy sector that employs a mixture of FiTs, FiPs, tax incentives, and the like. This chapter is written at a time when many of the governments

---

29 International Renewable Energy Agency, 'Renewable Energy Auction: A Guide to Design' (2015) p. 38.

30 OECD, 'Clean energy transition in the Western Balkans' (October 2022) p. 3.

31 Jakov Milatovic & Damin Chung, 'How can Western Balkans electricity mix be made sustainable?' (European Bank for Reconstruction and Development 2018) p. 1.

32 OECD, 'Air Quality Management in the Western Balkans' (21 January 2020) <https://www.worldbank.org/en/region/eca/publication/air-quality-management-in-western-balkans> accessed 27 June 2024.

33 Western Balkans Investment Framework, 'About the WBIF' <https://www.wbif.eu/about/about-wbif> accessed 27 June 2024.

34 International Renewable Energy Agency, 'Energy Profile (Serbia)' (8 August 2023) p. 1; International Renewable Energy Agency, 'Energy Profile (Bosnia & Herzegovina)' (8 August 2023) p. 1; International Renewable Energy Agency, 'Energy Profile (Albania)' (8 August 2023) p. 1; International Renewable Energy Agency, 'Energy Profile (North Macedonia)' (8 August 2023) p.1; International Renewable Energy Agency, 'Energy Profile (Montenegro)' (8 August 2023) p. 1; Energy Community Secretariat, 'Kosovo: Annual Implementation Report' (1 November 2023) p. 2.

35 *Ibid.*

in the region have recently revised their incentive regimes or are in the process of doing so. These new regimes in each of those States are briefly examined in turn.

3.1 *Albania*

Albania's energy generation is distinct from the other WB6 States in that, as of 2020, it acquires most of its energy from renewable sources.[36] The reason for this are Albania's hydroelectric capabilities.

In 2023, Albania adopted the Law on the Promotion of the Use of Energy from Renewable Sources.[37] Whereas its previous renewables regime focused primarily on hydropower, the new law expressly covers wind and solar energy.[38] Additionally, the law provides that projects in the energy sector must be awarded through a competitive process.[39] The law allows for support in the form of an energy purchase agreement, a so-called contract for difference,[40] or a FiP contract – the specific incentive offered must be indicated at the start of a tender process.[41] Plants previously operating on the FiTs were moved to contracts for difference that allowed the plants to continue to be paid the difference they would have made under the old scheme in the interim.[42]

Since enacting the new law, Albania has been busy auctioning off solar and wind projects to pursue its goal of becoming a net energy exporter by 2030. In July 2023, it held its first wind power auction where three investors were awarded the total of 222.5 MW in capacity.[43] Albania commissioned the largest solar plant in the Western Balkans in December 2023, in Karavasta, planned to have a capacity of 140 MW. The French investor, Voltalia, won a long-term power purchase agreement for this contract in a State sponsored auction in

36 International Renewable Energy Agency, 'Energy Profile (Albania)' (8 August 2023) p. 1.

37 Law No 24/2023 (Albania).

38 *Ibid*, Article 10(4).

39 *Ibid*, Articles 10(3) and 13.

40 A Contract for Difference commits the State to pay to the investor the difference between the price for electricity offered in the contract and the average price of electricity in the market at the time it is sold. See Vitaliy Radchenko, 'Contracts for Difference: Experiences made in Albania' (Energy Community 13 March 2018) 10.

41 Law No 24/2023 (Albania), Article 12(1).

42 Pippa Gallop & Lira Hakani, 'Albania's draft renewables law must support small producers and end incentives for hydropower' *Bankwatch Network* (Prague, 21 October 2022) <https://bankwatch.org/blog/albania-s-draft-renewables-law-must-support-small-producers-and-end-incentives-for-hydropower> accessed 27 June 2024.

43 Igor Todorović, 'Albania selects winners of its first wind power auction' *Balkan Green Energy* (Belgrade, 26 July 2023) <https://balkangreenenergynews.com/voltalia-completing-its-140-mw-solar-power-plant-karavasta-in-albania> accessed 27 June 2024.

TOTAL ENERGY SUPPLY (TES)

Total Energy Supply (TES)	2015	2020
Non-renewable (TJ)	53 955	48 297
Renewable (TJ)	43 354	51 329
Total (TJ)	97 309	99 626
Renewable share (%)	45	52

Growth in TES	2015-20	2019-20
Non-renewable (%)	-10.5	-7.5
Renewable (%)	+18.4	+29.5
Total (%)	+2.4	+8.5

Primary energy trade	2015	2020
Imports (TJ)	62 828	63 114
Exports (TJ)	52 652	32 513
Net trade (TJ)	- 10 176	- 30 601
Imports (% of supply)	65	63
Exports (% of production)	56	43
Energy self-sufficiency (%)	96	76

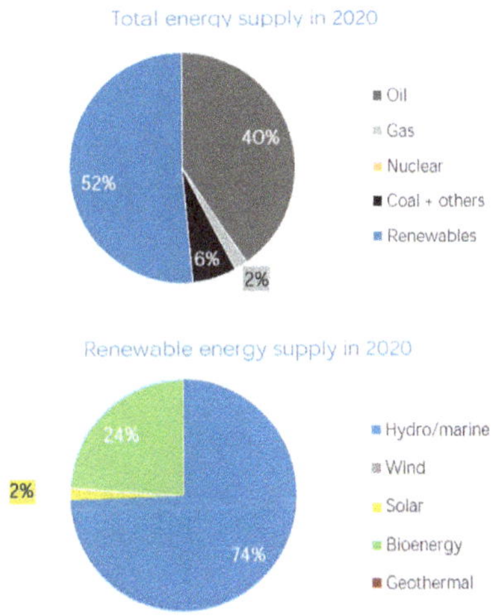

FIGURE 4.1 IRENA energy profile (Albania), 8 August 2023

2021.[44] Albania launched its fifth renewable energy auction in January 2024, offering 15-year Contracts for Difference for wind and solar projects totalling 300 MW.[45]

3.2 *Bosnia and Herzegovina*

Bosnia and Herzegovina is a unique case amongst the WB6 in that its different subdivisions – the Federation of Bosnia and Herzegovina and the Republic of Srpska – have different renewable energy laws. As a result, investors will be faced with different incentives depending on where within the territory they invest. Between 2015 and 2020, Bosnia and Herzegovina had the greatest increase in the share of its energy from renewable sources of all the WB6 States.[46] Like Serbia, most of this renewable supply comes from hydropower and biomass.

44 Igor Todorović, 'Voltalia completing its 140 MW solar power plant Karavasta in Albania' *Balkan Green Energy* (Belgrade, 5 October 2023) <https://balkangreenenergynews.com/voltalia-completing-its-140-mw-solar-power-plant-karavasta-in-albania/> accessed 27 June 2024.

45 Igor Todorović, 'Albania kicks off qualifications for 300 MW solar power auction' *Balkan Green Energy News* (Belgrade, 15 January 2024) <https://balkangreenenergynews.com/albania-kicks-off-qualifications-for-300-mw-solar-power-auction/> accessed 27 June 2024.

46 International Renewable Energy Agency, 'Energy Profile (Bosnia & Herzegovina)' (8 August 2023).

TOTAL ENERGY SUPPLY (TES)

Total Energy Supply (TES)	2015	2020
Non-renewable (TJ)	209 123	229 421
Renewable (TJ)	41 242	76 388
Total (TJ)	250 365	305 808
Renewable share (%)	16	25

Growth in TES	2015-20	2019-20
Non-renewable (%)	+9.7	-1.4
Renewable (%)	+85.2	+17.8
Total (%)	+22.1	+2.7

Primary energy trade	2015	2020
Imports (TJ)	140 376	122 285
Exports (TJ)	51 934	46 344
Net trade (TJ)	- 88 442	- 75 941
Imports (% of supply)	56	40
Exports (% of production)	30	20
Energy self-sufficiency (%)	69	74

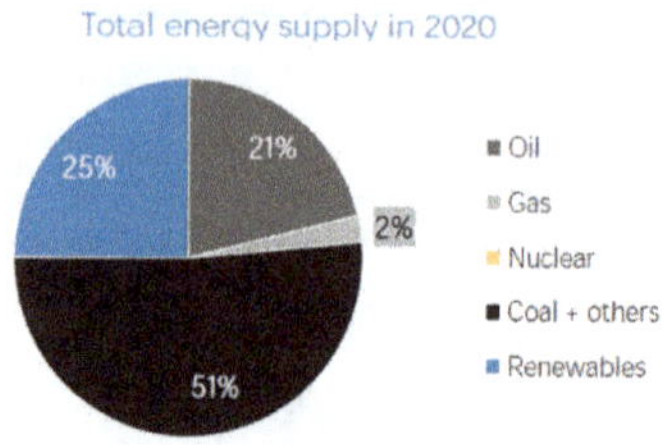

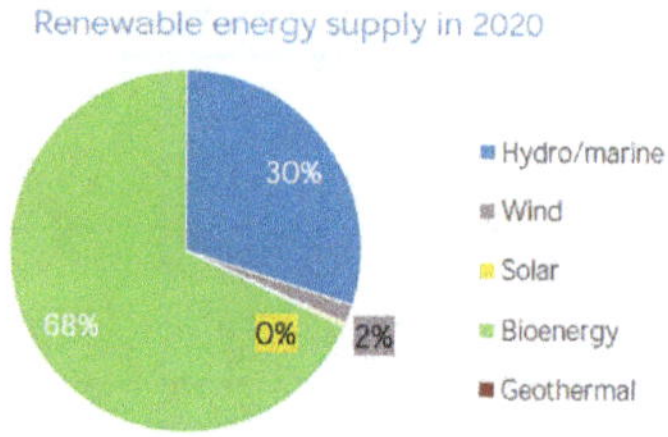

FIGURE 4.2 IRENA energy profile (Bosnia & Herzegovina), 8 August 2023

In August 2023, the Parliament of the Federation of Bosnia and Herzegovina passed the Law on the Usage of Renewable Energy and Efficient Co-generation. The legislation provides for energy auctions where small players can compete to receive a FiT and large players can compete for fixed FiPs.[47] Producers of renewables also receive priority on the delivery of their energy to the grid.[48] Under this regime, the FiTs and FiPs are determined for 12-year periods.[49] The amount of the FiT and FiP depends on the form of primary energy (i.e., solar or wind), the agreed period of energy purchase or allocation premiums, the technology used, and installed capacity of the plant.[50]Bosnia and Herzegovina is currently in the process of reviewing a draft decree which would see it auction off 240 MW of capacity from 2025–2030.[51]

Additional measures, such as providing incentives for domestic production and procurement of equipment which is used to produce renewable energy

47 Law on the Use of Renewable Energy and Efficient Co-generation 2023 (Bosnia & Herzegovina).

48 *Ibid*, Article 26.

49 *Ibid*.

50 *Ibid*, Article 42.

51 Vladimir Spasić, 'Federation of BiH drafts 2025–2030 renewable energy auctions plan' *Balkan Green Energy News* (Belgrade, 16 April 2024) < https://balkangreenenergynews.com/federation-of-bih-drafts-2025–2030-renewable-energy-auctions-plan/> accessed 27 June 2024.

(solar collectors, etc), are envisaged.[52] The law also aims to reduce administrative barriers and construction procedures for wind and solar plants and allows for natural persons to produce electricity on equal foot with legal persons.[53]

The Republic of Srpska has its own regime: the Law on the Renewable Energy Resources, enacted in February 2022. The law aims to increase the share of energy produced from renewable sources.[54]

For larger renewables producers (above 150 kW or 500 kW if the solar panels are on a roof) the Republic of Srpska offers FiTs and FiPs for 15-year periods (compared to 12 years in the Federation).[55] Contracts are awarded through auctions.[56] Wind and solar producers with capacities below 150 kW (or below 500 kW if the solar panels are on a roof) can receive incentives without an auction, namely FiTs or FiPs.[57]

3.3 *Kosovo*

Data on Kosovo's energy market is less readily available compared with the rest of the WB6, but it shows that Kosovo's energy generation is similar to most of the WB6: high amounts of energy produced by coal with a growing fraction of renewable production.[58]

Kosovo is the most recent jurisdiction to update its renewable energy regime at the date of writing. On 17 May 2024, the Law on the Promotion of the Use of Renewable Energy Sources entered into force.[59] This law resulted from public consultations that began as far back as 2022.[60]

---

52 Law on the Use of Renewable Energy and Efficient Co-generation 2023 (Bosnia & Herzegovina) Article 30.

53 Tatjana Drljić, 'The House of Peoples of the FBiH Parliament adopted a set of reform energy laws' *N1* (Sarajevo, 31 July 2023) <https://n1info.ba/vijesti/dom-naroda-parlamenta-fbih-usvojio-set-reformskih-energetskih-zakona/> accessed 27 June 2024.

54 Vladimir Spasić, 'Republika Srpska received a new Law on Renewable Energy Sources' *Balkan Green Energy News* (Belgrade, 11 February 2022) <https://balkangreenenergynews.com/rs/republika-srpska-dobila-novi-zakon-o-obnovljivim-izvorima-energije/> accessed 27 June 2024.

55 Law on the Renewable Energy Resources 2022 (Republic of Srpska) Articles 35, 39, and 40.

56 Law on the Renewable Energy Resources 2022 (Republic of Srpska) Articles 36–38.

57 Law on the Renewable Energy Resources 2022 (Republic of Srpska) Articles 8 and 31.

58 Energy Community Secretariat, 'Kosovo: Annual Implementation Report' (Energy Community 1 November 2023), p. 2.

59 Law on the Promotion of the Use of Renewable Energy Sources, Law No 08/L258 2024 (Kosovo).

60 Ministry of Economy of Kosovo, 'Law on Renewable Energy Resources out for public consultations' (8 December 2022) <https://me.rks-gov.net/en/blog/law-on-renewable-energy-sources-out-for-public-consultations/> accessed 27 June 2024.

Incentives for renewables under the new framework include FiTs and FiPs.[61] Privileged producers are selected through competitive auctions with the winning bids contracting with the Renewable Energy Operator.[62] The Renewable Energy Operator will be created by Kosovo within the 2024 calendar year and will be the counterparty for all of the State's renewable energy contracts.[63]

The Kosovo Government was already experimenting with auctions before the new law. A solar power auction in Kosovo launched in 2023 saw more than 140 companies express interest in a 15-year power purchase agreement for 90 to 105 MW in connection capacity. That was the first renewable energy auction in Kosovo.[64] In February 2024, Kosovo announced that it received six applications in this auction. After the evaluation, qualified bidders are set to proceed to electronic bidding or e-auction.[65] After the pilot auction for the solar power, Kosovo is planning to conduct a competitive bidding process in 2024 for 150 MW of wind power. The call is set to be issued by mid-2024 in what will be the first wind power auction in Kosovo.[66]

With its new Energy Strategy, Kosovo aims to reach 1.6 GW worth of renewable electricity capacity and introduce batteries of 340 MW in total by 2031.[67] In line with this energy strategy, Kosovo plans to auction 950 MW in the next two years with investments worth EUR 1.2 billion in total.[68]

---

61 Law on the Promotion of the Use of Renewable Energy Sources, Law No 08/L258 2024 (Kosovo) Article 10(4).

62 *Ibid*, Article 10(5).

63 *Ibid*, Article 23.

64 Igor Todorović, 'Solar power auction in Kosovo* draws interest from over 140 companies' *Balkan Green Energy News* (Belgrade, 31 July 2023) <https://balkangreenenergynews.com/solar-power-auction-in-kosovo-draws-interest-from-over-140-companies/> accessed 27 June 2024.

65 Igor Todorović, ‹Kosovo* receives six applications for its first solar power auction› *Balkan Green Energy News* (Belgrade, 1 February 2024) <https://balkangreenenergynews.com/kosovo-receives-six-applications-for-its-first-solar-power-auction/> accessed 27 June 2024.

66 Igor Todorović, 'Kosovo* to hold its first wind power auction in 2024' *Balkan Green Energy News* (Belgrade, 17 October 2023) <https://balkangreenenergynews.com/kosovo-to-hold-its-first-wind-power-auction-in-2024/> accessed 27 June 2024.

67 Igor Todorović, 'Kosovo outlines energy transition until 2031 in strategic document' *Balkan Green Energy News* (Belgrade, 24 March 2023) <https://balkangreenenergynews.com/kosovo-outlines-energy-transition-until-2031-in-strategic-document/> accessed 27 June 2024.

68 'Kosovo to auction 950 MW of renewables, energy storage by 2025' *Balkan Green Energy News* (Belgrade, 6 February 2024), <https://balkangreenenergynews.com/kosovo-to-auction-950-mw-of-renewables-energy-storage-by-2025/> accessed 27 June 2024.

3.4 *Montenegro*

Montenegro's share of energy from renewables is above average for the region, with most of that coming from hydropower and biomass.[69]

The legal framework of renewable energy resources in Montenegro is regulated by the Energy Law and the decrees made thereunder. Since 2010, producers in the renewable energy sector received an annually adjusted FiT.[70] In 2019, the government unveiled regulations which would gradually phase out the FiT.[71] Montenegro's current energy law provides that renewable energy companies who acquire the status of a privileged producer can still receive a FiT.[72] This, however, only applies to small projects with an installed capacity up to 1 MW.[73]

Without any promotion of larger projects, Montenegro has been left with a hole in its legislation. To patch this, in February 2024, the Government published a draft Law on the Use of Energy from Renewable Sources, which

TOTAL ENERGY SUPPLY (TES)

Total Energy Supply (TES)	2015	2020
Non-renewable (TJ)	28 531	30 070
Renewable (TJ)	14 967	15 855
Total (TJ)	43 498	45 925
Renewable share (%)	34	35

Growth in TES	2015-20	2019-20
Non-renewable (%)	+5.4	-6.5
Renewable (%)	+5.9	+11.4
Total (%)	+5.6	-1.0

Primary energy trade	2015	2020
Imports (TJ)	16 787	35 346
Exports (TJ)	4 061	23 320
Net trade (TJ)	- 12 726	- 12 026
Imports (% of supply)	39	77
Exports (% of production)	13	70
Energy self-sufficiency (%)	72	73

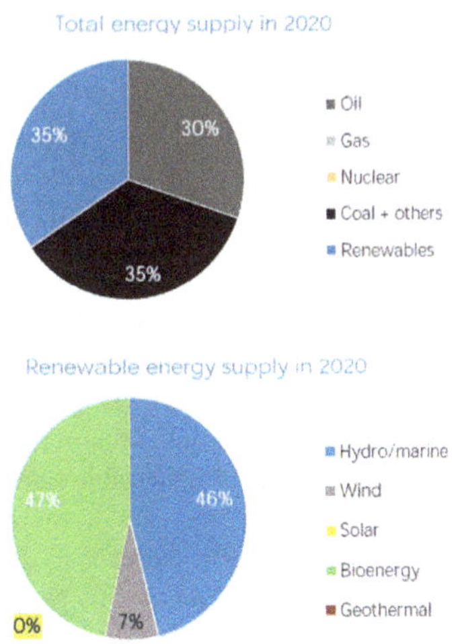

FIGURE 4.3 IRENA energy profile (Montenegro), 8 August 2023

69 International Renewable Energy Agency, 'Energy Profile (Montenegro)' (8 August 2023).

70 Montenegro Fifth Progress Report on promotion and use of energy from renewable sources for the period 2020–2021 (8 August 2023) p. 6.

71 Regulation on the Method of Achieving and the Amount of Incentive Prices for Electricity Energy Produced from Renewable Sources and Highly Efficient Cogeneration 2019 (Montenegro).

72 Energy Law 2022 (Montenegro) Articles 104 and 107.

73 *Ibid*, Article 104.

introduces auctions for FiPs and FiTs.[74] The Government is making efforts to enact the law swiftly to unlock access to EU funds and loans from the World Bank.[75]

3.5 *North Macedonia*

Despite increasing its total renewable energy capacity between 2015 and 2020, North Macedonia is the only member of the WB6 whose share of energy generated from renewables dropped during that timeframe.[76]

The renewable energy market in North Macedonia nevertheless posted a growth of 160% in 2023, maintaining the top spot in the WB6.[77] Notable projects include solar power plants in Pehčevo and Stip, a cogeneration facility in Skopje, and a photovoltaic plant with gas engines.[78] All these investments are part of North Macedonia's "Just Transition Investment Platform", launched in December 2023, which aims to phase out coal usage.[79]

While some of the investment is from the government, much of it is driven by external capital. North Macedonia's Energy Law provides for incentives for private renewables projects including FiTs and FiPs.[80] North Macedonia determines who can apply for each incentive, based on the size of the plant and the type of renewable energy.[81] For example, once capacity is met, solar producers could only apply for an FiP and not the FiT.[82]

---

74 Draft Law on the Use of Energy from Renewable Sources 2024 (Montenegro).

75 Vladimir Spasić, 'Montenegro drafts first renewables law, sets rules for auctions' *Balkan Green Energy News* (Belgrade, 19 February 2024) <https://balkangreenenergynews.com/montenegro-drafts-first-renewables-law-sets-rules-for-auctions/> accessed 27 June 2024.

76 International Renewable Energy Agency, 'Energy Profile (North Macedonia)' (8 August 2023).

77 Igor Todorović, 'North Macedonia posts 160% growth in 2023 in new renewables capacity' *Balkan Green Energy News* (Belgrade, 29 January 2024) <https://balkangreenenergynews.com/north-macedonia-posts-160-growth-in-2023-in-new-renewables-capacity/> accessed 27 June 2024.

78 Vladimir Spasić, 'UPDATE: North Macedonia prepares first agreements with strategic investors for solar power plants, cogeneration' (Belgrade, 5 February 2024) <https://balkangreenenergynews.com/update-north-macedonia-prepares-first-agreements-with-strategic-investors-for-solar-power-plants-cogeneration/> accessed 27 June 2024.

79 Vanora Bennett, 'North Macedonia launches just energy transition investment platform at COP28' *European Bank for Reconstruction and Development* (3 December 2023) <https://www.ebrd.com/news/2023/north-macedonia-launches-just-energy-transition-investment-platform-at-cop28.html> accessed 27 June 2024.

80 Energy Law No 08-3424/1 2018 (North Macedonia) Article 186.

81 Energy Community, 'Annual Implementation Report' (2023) 103.

82 Energy Community, 'Annual Implementation Report' (2023) 103.

TOTAL ENERGY SUPPLY (TES)

Total Energy Supply (TES)	2015	2020
Non-renewable (TJ)	90 681	95 248
Renewable (TJ)	25 640	22 542
Total (TJ)	116 321	117 790
Renewable share (%)	22	19

Growth in TES	2015-20	2019-20
Non-renewable (%)	+5.0	-7.4
Renewable (%)	-12.1	+20.4
Total (%)	+1.3	-3.1

Primary energy trade	2015	2020
Imports (TJ)	66 012	74 699
Exports (TJ)	7 538	6 474
Net trade (TJ)	- 58 474	- 68 225
Imports (% of supply)	57	63
Exports (% of production)	13	13
Energy self-sufficiency (%)	50	43

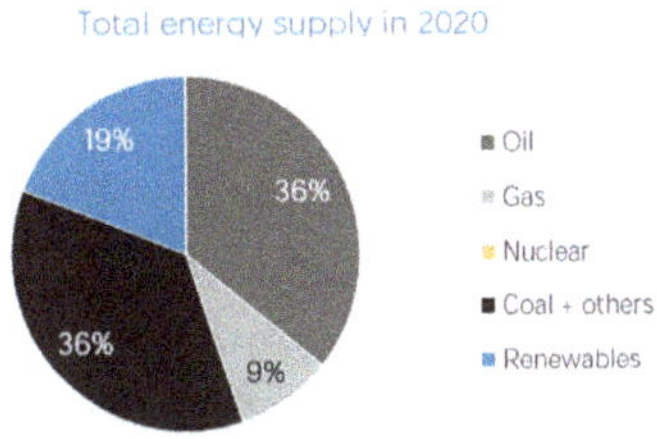

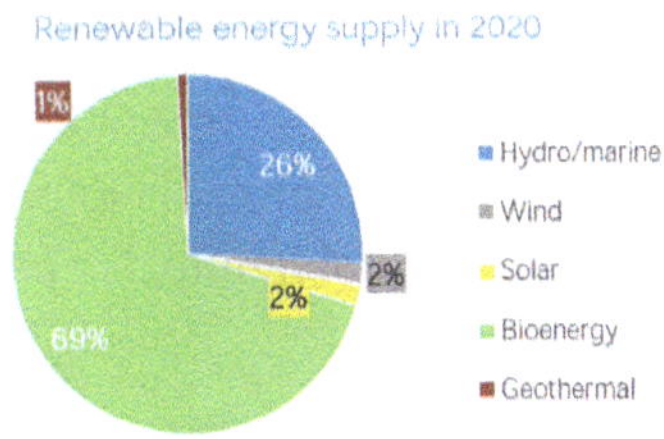

FIGURE 4.4 IRENA energy profile (North Macedonia), 8 August 2023

North Macedonia's law on Strategic Investments has also encouraged foreign investment in its renewable energy market.[83] The law provides that investors with larger project proposals, including in energy, are eligible to participate in open tenders and receive State benefits.[84] An example strategic investment is Virovi – North Macedonia's largest wind farm at the time it was announced – constructed by German investor, WPD.[85]

In March 2024, the government adopted the draft Law on Renewable Energy Sources together with the draft Law on Energy, separating the green segment for the first time.[86] The Ministry of Economy stated that the move is aligned

83 Claudia Patricolo, 'Western Balkans aim to attract foreign investment to foster renewable projects' *CeeEnergy News* (Budapest, 5 September 2022) <https://ceenergynews.com/renewables/western-balkans-aim-to-attract-foreign-investment-to-foster-renewable-projects/ > accessed 27 June 2024.

84 The Law on Strategic Investment 2020 (North Macedonia).

85 Igor Todorović, 'German wind farm investment in North Macedonia to top EUR 500 million' *Balkan Green Energy News* (Belgrade, 13 October 2021) <https://balkangreenenergynews.com/german-wind-farm-investment-in-north-macedonia-to-top-eur-500-million/> accessed 27 June 2024.

86 Igor Todorović, 'Government of North Macedonia sends two energy bills to parliament' *Balkan Green Energy News* (Belgrade, 13 March 2024) <https://balkangreenenergynews.com/government-of-north-macedonia-sends-two-energy-bills-to-parliament/> accessed 27 June 2024.

with the cabinet's commitment to encourage investments in renewables as well as with the European Union's policies and regulations.[87]

3.6 *Serbia*

Serbia is the largest WB6 State in both population and area. It is also the largest consumer of electricity in the region.[88] As of 2020, Serbia obtained most of its energy from non-renewable sources, with biomass being the largest contributor to its share of renewables production.[89]

Since 2009, Serbia has offered a FiT for renewable energy sources.[90] Following amendments in 2016, FiT rates were guaranteed for 12 years in Power Purchase Agreements.[91] This system led to the adoption of the Law on the Use of Renewable Energy Resources in 2021.[92] Serbia's FiT regime had the opposite problem to, for example, Spain's (discussed later in this chapter): it

TOTAL ENERGY SUPPLY (TES)

Total Energy Supply (TES)	2015	2020
Non-renewable (TJ)	531 780	553 034
Renewable (TJ)	82 681	112 804
Total (TJ)	614 461	665 838
Renewable share (%)	13	17

Growth in TES	2015-20	2019-20
Non-renewable (%)	+4.0	+1.0
Renewable (%)	+36.4	+33.8
Total (%)	+8.4	+5.3

Primary energy trade	2015	2020
Imports (TJ)	229 476	256 531
Exports (TJ)	61 388	60 537
Net trade (TJ)	- 168 088	- 195 994
Imports (% of supply)	37	39
Exports (% of production)	14	13
Energy self-sufficiency (%)	73	70

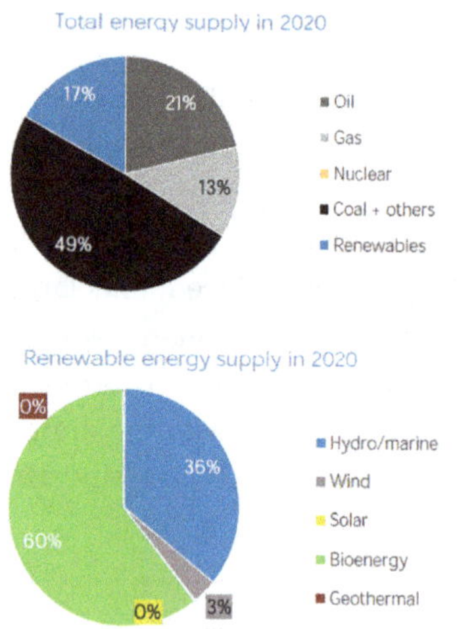

FIGURE 4.5 IRENA energy profile (Serbia), 8 August 2023

87 *Ibid.*

88 International Renewable Energy Agency, 'Energy Profile (Serbia)' (8 August 2023) p. 1.

89 International Renewable Energy Agency, 'Energy Profile (Serbia)' (8 August 2023) p. 1.

90 Ministry of Mining and Energy, 'Progress Report on the Implementation of the National Renewable Energy Action Plan of the Republic of Serbia' (December 2016) p. 5.

91 Decree on Incentive Measures for Electricity Generation from Renewable Energy Sources and High-Efficiency Cogeneration of Electricity and Heat 2016 (Serbia) Article 45.

92 Law on the Use of Renewable Energy Sources 2021 (Serbia).

became unattractive because the market offered a better rate, which led many companies to terminate their FiT contracts.[93]

To modernise its incentive structure, Serbia amended its renewable energy regime in April 2023. The primary change was that it started offering FiTs and FiPs using auctions.[94] FiT rates earned in these auctions are adjusted each calendar year in line with inflation within the Eurozone.[95] Power purchase agreements at preferential prices are now concluded for 15-year periods.[96]

Serbia inaugurated this new scheme with a June 2023 auction for solar and wind projects. This auction resulted in the allocation of capacity to eight projects: four wind and four solar.[97] In total, these projects will produce 400 MW of wind power and 50 MW of solar power once online.[98]

Shortly after, in July 2023, Serbia opened bids for a much larger project: solar plants with a net capacity of 1 GW.[99] There were three bidders, of which two, from China and a Hyundai-led consortium of companies from both South Korea and the United States, met the criteria.[100] In November 2023, the government selected the Hyundai consortium.[101] As of January 2024, Serbia's Energy Minister reported that the State was in talks with the consortium for the construction of the project.[102]

Most recently, the Ministry of Mining and Energy announced that EUR 400 million would be invested in the reconstruction of four hydropower plants run

93 Vladimir Spasic, 'Renewable energy producers in Croatia, Serbia terminate feed-in tariff contracts' *Balkan Green Energy News* (Belgrade, 11 October 2022) <https://balkangreenenergynews.com/renewable-energy-producers-in-croatia-serbia-terminate-feed-in-tariff-contracts/> accessed 27 June 2024.

94 Law on the Use of Renewable Energy Resources 2023 (Serbia) Articles 16 and 35.

95 *Ibid*, Article 38.

96 Law on the Use of Renewable Energy Resources 2023 (Serbia) Articles 32 and 45.

97 Energy Community, 'Serbia: Annual Implementation Report' (1 November 2023) p. 7.

98 Energy Community, 'Serbia: Annual Implementation Report' (1 November 2023) p. 7.

99 Vladimir Spasic, 'Three bids for strategic partner for 1 GW of solar in Serbia' *Balkan Green Energy News* (Belgrade, 21 September 2023) <https://balkangreenenergynews.com/three-bids-for-strategic-partner-for-1-gw-of-solar-in-serbia/> accessed 27 June 2024.

100 *Ibid.*

101 Igor Todorović, 'Serbia selects Hyundai Engineering, UGTR consortium as strategic partner for solar power plants of 1 GW in total' *Balkan Green Energy News* (Belgrade, 6 November 2023) <https://balkangreenenergynews.com/serbia-selects-hyundai-engineering-ugtr-consortium-as-strategic-partner-for-solar-power-plants-of-1-gw-in-total/> accessed 27 June 2024.

102 Iskra Pavlova, 'Serbia in talks with Hyundai Engineering on 1 GW solar power project' *See* News (Belgrade, 23 January 2024) <https://seenews.com/news/serbia-in-talks-with-hyundai-engineering-on-1-gw-solar-power-project-846312> accessed 27 June 2024.

by State-owned power utility EPS.[103] Serbia is the only WB6 State, amongst those who IRENA monitors, that brought new hydro capacity online in 2023.[104]

4 Potential Renewables Disputes in the Western Balkans

States are exposed to claims from foreign investors wherever there are investment treaties, investment agreements, or statutes that provide for dispute resolution with the State. That risk is particularly pronounced in the renewables area, given the burgeoning investment and regulatory activity in the sector. Indeed, solar and hydro investors have brought claims against Albania and Bosnia,[105] whereas nearby Bulgaria was ordered to pay EUR 61 million to a Maltese investor for breaches of the ECT relating to an investment in solar energy.[106]

The WB6 are also exposed to arbitration claims regarding investments in renewable energy. This section examines ISDS case law in the renewable energy sector to identify common themes that have, in the past, given rise to disputes relating to renewables, and how those may be relevant for the WB6.

4.1 *Claims Arising out of Changing Regulations*

The principal State obligation on which investors rely when they allege their rights have been breached under international law is the obligation to provide fair and equitable treatment (*FET*), which is common across nearly all investment treaties.[107] It has been described as "the most important standard in investment disputes" given that it is invoked by claimants in nearly all investor-State arbitrations.[108] FET provides a broad range of protections to the investor, and they have been held to include the requirements that the State

103 Igor Todorović, 'Serbia to invest EUR 400 million in reconstruction of hydropower plants' *Balkan Green Energy News* (Belgrade, 18 March 2024) <https://balkangreenenergynews.com/serbia-to-invest-eur-400-million-in-reconstruction-of-hydropower-plants/> accessed 27 June 2024.

104 International Renewable Energy Agency, 'Energy Profile (Serbia)' (8 August 2023) p. 2.

105 *Arka Energy B.V. v Republic of Albania*, ICSID Case No ARB/20/54; *Boris Goljevšček, Viaduct d.o.o. Portorož and Vladimir Zevnik v Bosnia and Herzegovina*, ICSID Case No ARB/16/36; *Hydro S.r.l. and others v Republic of Albania*, ICSID Case No ARB/15/28.

106 *ACF Renewable Energy Limited v Bulgaria*, ICSID Case No ARB/18/1, Award, 5 January 2024, para 1843.

107 Only 126 out of the 2592 investments treaties mapped by UNCTAD do not contain an FET provision. See UNCTAD, 'Mapping of IIA Content' <https://investmentpolicy.unctad.org/international-investment-agreements/iia-mapping#> accessed 9 June 2024.

108 Christoph Schreuer, 'Fair and Equitable Treatment in Arbitral Practice' (2005) 6:3 Journal of World Trade and Investment 357, 357.

act reasonably,[109] in a transparent manner,[110] in accordance with due process,[111] and in a non-discriminatory fashion.[112]

A key element of FET is the State obligation not to frustrate the investor's legitimate expectations.[113] To prove that the State has breached international law in this respect, investors must show that the State made representations to the investor which it had reasonably relied upon in deciding to invest.[114] Some tribunals have held that relevant representations can be found in legislation and may create expectations in a degree of legislative stability.[115] On this basis, investors in the renewable energy sector have alleged that, based on representations made by the host State at the time when they invested, they reasonably and legitimately expected that the relevant regulatory framework, on which the investor relied to commit capital, would not be altered to the detriment of the investor. At the same time, tribunals recognise that, in the absence of a clear promise not to change its laws in a way that negatively affects the investor, the State enjoys the prerogative to amend its legal framework.[116] Accordingly, changes to regulatory regimes are likely to breach legitimate expectations only

---

109 *Saluka Investments BV v The Czech Republic, PCA Case No 2001-04*, Partial Award, 17 March 2006, para 460.

110 Lucy Reed and Simon Consedine, 'Fair and Equitable Treatment: Legitimate Expectations and Transparency' in Meg Kinnear *et al* (eds), *Building International Investment Law: The First 50 Years of ICSID* (Kluwer 2016) 11; *Rumeli Telekom A.S. and Telsim Mobil Telekomunikasyon Hizmetleri A.S. v, Republic of Kazakhstan*, ICSID Case No ARB/05/16, Award, 29 July 2008, para 609.

111 *GPF GP S.à.r.l v Poland*, SCC Case No 2014/168, Final Award, 29 April 2020, para 543.

112 *Electrabel S.A. v The Republic of Hungary*, ICSID Case No ARB/07/19, Decision on Jurisdiction, Applicable Law and Liability, 30 November 2012, para 7.74.

113 Elizabeth Snodgrass, 'Protecting Investors' Legitimate Expectations: Recognizing and Delimiting a General Principle' (2006) 21 ICSID Review 1, 56; *RENERGY S.à r.l. v Kingdom of Spain*, ICSID Case No ARB/14/18, Award, 6 May 2022, para 611; *FREIF Eurowind Holdings Ltd v Kingdom of Spain*, SCC Case No 2017/060, Final Award, 8 March 2021, para 534.

114 Martin Paparinskis, *The International Minimum Standard and Fair and Equitable Treatment* (OUP 2013) 238 citing to *Waste Management v United Mexican States (II)*, ICSID Case No ARB(AF)/00/3, Award, 30 April 2004, para 98. See also *Addiko Bank AG v Montenegro*, ICSID Case No ARB/17/35, Award, 24 November 2021, para 629; *9REN Holding S.a.r.l v Kingdom of Spain*, ICSID Case No ARB/15/15, Award, 31 May 2019, para 295.

115 Jack Biggs, 'The Scope of Investors' Legitimate Expectations under the FET Standard in European Renewable Energy Cases' (2021) 36 ICSID Review pp. 99, 109; Filip Balcerzak, 'Renewable Energy Arbitration – Quo Vadis?' (Brill 2023) p. 196. Although some authorities reject that general regulations can ever form a stabilisation guarantee. *See* for example *Oxus Gold plc v Republic of Uzbekistan*, UNCITRAL, Final Award, 17 December 2015, para 823.

116 See, e.g., *Alejandro Diego Díaz Gaspar v Republic of Costa Rica*, ICSID Case No ARB/19/13, Award, 29 June 2022, para 368.

where the State has expressly guaranteed the stability of its law or where the change is drastic or discriminatory.[117]

This section explores some of the ways in which the WB6 may risk frustrating the legitimate expectations of investors in the renewables sector.

4.1.1 Amendments to the Tariff System

Investors have brought a number of claims against States based on the State's alteration of the tariff system. The key argument has been that the legislative changes were contrary to investors' legitimate expectations.

Spain has been sued by many investors for having altered its tariff incentives offered to renewable energy investors. Spain first enacted decrees to incentivize investment, most notably Royal Decree 661/2007. That decree provided investors the option to choose between a FiT or FiP, either of which would last the entire lifetime of the investment and could not be revised except in accordance with Spain's consumer price index.[118] The regime also guaranteed that Spain would purchase all energy generated by renewable energy companies.

Shortly after, Spain reversed course in light of, among other things, the global financial crisis and a decline in the price of solar cells in the market which led to a glut of renewables investments that the State could not afford to support. Starting in 2008, Spain issued Royal Decrees (i) reducing the lifetime duration of FiTs and FiPs to 25 years, (ii) introducing a cap on the volumes for which a plant would be entitled to receive FiT/FiP, and (iii) ultimately doing away with the special regime for renewable energy altogether, instead guaranteeing investors a "reasonable rate of return" that would be recalculated every six years.[119]

---

117 *Sevilla Beheer B.V. and others v Kingdom of Spain*, ICSID Case No ARB/16/27, Decision on Jurisdiction, Liability and the Principles of Quantum, 11 February 2022, para 799; *Horthel Systems BV, Poland Gaming Holding BV and Tesa Beheer BV v Republic of Poland*, PCA Case No 2014-31, Final Award, 16 February 2017, paras 255 and 259; *Toto Costruzioni Generali S.p.A. v The Republic of Lebanon*, ICSID Case No ARB/07/12, Award, 7 June 2012, para 244; *Parkerings-Compagniet AS v Republic of Lithuania*, ICSID Case No ARB/05/8, Award, 11 September 2007, para 332.

118 Royal Decree 661/2007 (Spain) Annex VII.

119 The key measures taken by Spain in this regard are summarised in (*1*) *Foresight Luxembourg Solar 1 S.À.R.L.*, (*2*) *Foresight Luxembourg Solar 2 S.À.R.L.*, (*3*) *Greentech Energy Systems A/S*, (*4*) *GWM Renewable Energy I S.P.A.*, (*5*) *GWM Renewable Energy II S.P.A. v Kingdom of Spain*, SCC Case No 2015/150, Final Award, 14 November 2018, para 58.

This led investors to commence arbitrations against Spain. While most disputes concern the solar sector,[120] Spain also faced claims from wind[121] and hydro producers.[122] Different tribunals have arrived at different decisions, including as to whether general legislation could create legitimate expectations.

One group of tribunals found that Spain had effectively offered stabilization guarantees through Royal Decree 661/2007 and that the subsequent amendments frustrated the investors' legitimate expectations.[123] For example, the *Cube* Tribunal held that a regulatory regime established to attract investors by holding out that investments would be subject to regulatory principles that would be maintained for a finite length of time, could give rise to legitimate expectations when investments are made in reliance upon such expectations.[124] It also held that the State's obligation could be met either by maintaining the regulatory regime for the length of time guaranteed, or by adjusting the regime in a manner that would not "significantly alter the fundamental economic basis of investments made in reliance" on Spain's representation.[125]

Another group of tribunals found that, based on the law, investors could only form legitimate expectations in respect of a "reasonable rate of return", that Spain's amended legal regime continued to offer such a return, and that Spain therefore had not breached its international obligations.[126] In this regard, the

---

120 See for example *JGC Holdings Corporation (formerly JGC Corporation) v Kingdom of Spain*, ICSID Case No ARB/15/27; *Mitsui & Co., Ltd. v Kingdom of Spain*, ICSID Case No ARB/20/47; *Sapec, S.A. v Kingdom of Spain*, ICSID Case No ARB/19/23; *European Solar Farms A/S v Kingdom of Spain*, ICSID Case No ARB/18/45; *Portigon AG v Kingdom of Spain*, ICSID Case No ARB/17/15.

121 *Watkins Holdings S.à r.l. and others v Kingdom of Spain*, ICSID Case No ARB/15/44; *FREIF Eurowind Holdings Ltd v Kingdom of Spain*, SCC Case No 2017/060.

122 *Hydro Energy 1 S.à r.l. and Hydroxana Sweden AB v Kingdom of Spain*, ICSID Case No ARB/15/42; *E.ON SE, E.ON Finanzanlagen GmbH and E.ON Iberia Holding GmbH v Kingdom of Spain*, ICSID Case No ARB/15/35.

123 *OperaFund Eco-Invest SICAV PLC and Schwab Holding AG v Kingdom of Spain*, ICSID Case No ARB/15/36, Award, 6 September 2019, para 485; *9REN Holding S.a.r.l v Kingdom of Spain*, ICSID Case No ARB/15/15, Award, 31 May 2019, paras 297 and 301; *Novenergia II – Energy & Environment (SCA) (Grand Duchy of Luxembourg), SICAR v The Kingdom of Spain*, SCC Case No 2015/063, Final Award, 15 February 2018, para 681.

124 *Cube Infrastructure Fund SICAV and others v Kingdom of Spain*, ICSID Case No ARB/15/20, Decision on Jurisdiction, Liability and Partial Decision on Quantum, 19 February 2019, para 388.

125 *Ibid*, para 412.

126 *Stadtwerke München GmbH, RWE Innogy GmbH, and others v Kingdom of Spain*, ICSID Case No ARB/15/1, Award, 2 December 2019, para 282; *BayWa r.e. Renewable Energy GmbH and BayWa r.e. Asset Holding GmbH v Spain*, ICSID Case No ARB/15/16, Decision on Jurisdiction, Liability and Directions on Quantum, para 473; *Isolux Infrastructure Netherlands BV v Kingdom of Spain*, SCC Case No V2013/153, Award, 12 July 2016, para 787; *Eurus Energy*

Kruck Tribunal held that investors could not expect laws to be "petrified" and that Spain could amend its regulations "in the face of changing circumstances and changing policies" so long as the modification is "reasonable" meaning it is not an "abandonment of the fundamentals of that regime".[127] This led tribunals – like the one in *Infracapital* – to find no breach of the relevant investment treaty because the Claimant should have known that changes to the system were a possibility.[128] Even though this group concluded that the investors did not have expectations in absolute regulatory stability, some tribunals did find that Spain's legislative amendments were unreasonable and frustrated the investors' legitimate expectations.[129] In *Antin* the Tribunal recognized that the investor could not expect absolute regulatory stability.[130] It viewed that the investor only had a legitimate expectation that the "essential features" of the renewables regime would remain in force.[131] The Tribunal went on to find a breach of the ECT's FET provision on the basis that Spain's measures had dismantled the "essential features" of the renewables regime – that had guaranteed a FiT and priority grid access – by eliminating those elements.[132]

In 2005, **Czechia** adopted an Act for the promotion of electricity production from renewable energy sources offering similar incentives, namely, a 15-year FiT or Green Bonus (essentially an FiP).[133] The FiT could be adjusted by the Energy Regulatory Office but could not be the subject of a decrease of more than 5% each year.[134]

The same market factors present in Spain, including decreasing costs for investors to purchase equipment leading to a larger than expected quantity of investments, affected Czechia. This led to Czechia adopting a tax on revenues

Holdings Corporation v Kingdom of Spain, ICSID Case No ARB/16/4, Decision on Jurisdiction and Liability, 17 March 2021, para 332; *Cavalum SGPS, S.A. v Kingdom of Spain*, ICSID Case No ARB/15/34, Decision on Jurisdiction, Liability and Directions on Quantum, 31 August 2020, para 515.

127 *Mathias Kruck, Frank Schumm, Joachim Kruck, Jürgen Reiss and others v Kingdom of Spain*, ICSID Case No ARB/15/23, Decision on Jurisdiction, Liability and Principles of Quantum, 14 September 2022, paras 198 and 211.

128 *Infracapital F1 S.à r.l. and Infracapital Solar B.V. v Kingdom of Spain*, ICSID Case No ARB/16/18, Decision on Jurisdiction, Liability and Directions on Quantum, 13 September 2021, para 602.

129 See for example *Infrastructure Services Luxembourg S.à.r.l. and Energia Termosolar B.V. (formerly Antin Infrastructure Services Luxembourg S.à.r.l. and Antin Energia Termosolar B.V.) v Kingdom of Spain*, ICSID Case No ARB/13/31, Award, 15 June 2018, paras 553–555.

130 *Ibid*, para 553.

131 *Ibid*, para 556.

132 *Ibid*, para 560.

133 Act No 180/2005 (Czechia) Articles 4 and 6.

134 *Ibid*, Article 6.

generated by solar companies in 2010, known as the solar levy, to mitigate the State's financial liabilities.[135] This levy applied only to power plants that began operating in 2009 or 2010 and taxed revenues for the 2011–2013 period of operation. The tax was not directly paid by the company, but instead the grid operator – who would pay out the FiT or Green Bonus – would decrease its payment to the investor by the amount of the solar levy. In essence, the State used the tax lever to modify the tariff scheme without formally amending its Renewable Energy Sources Act.

Czechia's decision to implement a levy instead of directly altering the FiT was subsequently found by the *Antaris* Tribunal to have been deliberately introduced to protect it against investment claims.[136] The Tribunal nevertheless rejected the investors' claims on the basis that "the market which the Claimants were entering was a bubble and that the Czech Government considered that the FiT regime was out of balance and that would have been obvious to anyone who participated in industry discussions, or paid attention to warnings by specialist professionals, or read the local press".[137] In essence, it determined that at the time the investor invested in Czechia, it should have expected impending changes to the regime for promoting renewable energy. Nearly all tribunals that evaluated Czechia's conduct found that the solar levy was not a violation of FET or the investors' legitimate expectations because Czech law did not guarantee fixed returns and the State was entitled to enact the new tariff in the form of the solar levy.[138] Tribunals did not view Czech law as offering a stabilisation guarantee, which meant that the State was free to amend its laws so long as changes did not "significantly undermine" the support framework.[139] Only one tribunal, in *Natland*, found in favour of the investor.[140] The *Natland* Tribunal reasoned that the retroactive effect of the law breached FET because

---

135 Act No 402/2010 (Czechia).

136 *Antaris Solar GmbH and Dr. Michael Göde v Czech Republic*, PCA Case No 2014-01, Award, 2 May 2018, para 420.

137 *Ibid*, para 434.

138 *Jürgen Wirtgen, Stefan Wirtgen, Gisela Wirtgen and JSW Solar (zwei) GmbH & Co. KG v Czech Republic*, PCA Case No 2014-03, Final Award, 11 October 2017, para 425; *Antaris Solar GmbH and Dr. Michael Göde v Czech Republic*, PCA Case No 2014-01, Award, 2 May 2018, para 430; *Voltaic Network GmbH v Czech Republic*, PCA Case No 2014-20, Award, 15 May 2019, paras 502 and 503.

139 *I.C.W. Europe Investments Limited v Czech Republic*, PCA Case No 2014-22 Award, 15 May 2019, para 586; *Photovoltaik Knopf Betriebs-GmbH v The Czech Republic*, PCA Case No 2014-21, Award, 15 May 2019, para 499.

140 *Natland Investment Group NV, Natland Group Limited, G.I.H.G. Limited, and Radiance Energy Holding S.A.R.L. v The Czech Republic*, PCA Case No 2013-35, paras 421 and 508(d).

the investor had invested under the premise that the State was committing to a fixed rate of return.[141]

While the WB6 have uniformly expressed their commitment towards supporting investment in renewables and have codified this in their laws, they have so far avoided stipulating directly in their legislation that investors would be guaranteed certain rates of return. In that way, in theory, the risk of the Spanish scenario is more limited in the WB6. But some States – for example North Macedonia – do offer FiTs to smaller scale plants through legislation. And, so, the withdrawal of such incentives by amendment could be inconsistent with the BITs, depending on the circumstances.

More generally, any radical or drastic changes to the legislative framework that withdraw the support for renewable energy producers could pose risks of international claims and damages awards. Likewise, multiple legislative changes in different directions – so-called "roller-coaster" legislation[142] – may also lead to claims.

Moreover, regulatory changes that affect an investor might occur even without a change in the law. As a leading commentator has observed, in practice, legitimate expectations may be violated, not only by a change in law, but by different positions taken on the interpretation of a law by different levels of government, as identified above.[143] The WB6 are vulnerable to this insofar as changes of government in the region are sometimes followed by reversal of prior policies or practices.

Finally, as discussed below, where the State or State-owned entities enter into long-term contracts with investors, the contractual provisions guaranteeing an FiP or FiT may be a basis for legitimate expectations, such that a breach or repudiation of a contract by the State could lead to a FET breach.

4.1.2 Amendments to Volume-based Incentives

As explained earlier, volume-based measures provide producers with a guarantee that a certain volume of energy will be purchased by the State (via the grid operator or otherwise).

An example of a State that has employed volume-based measures is Romania. Romanian law initially required the government entity Transelectrica to

141 *Ibid*, para 416.

142 Rudolf Dolzer, 'Fair and Equitable Treatment: Today's Contours' (2014) 12 Santa Clara Journal of International Law pp. 7, 22 citing to *PSEG Global Inc. and Konya Ilgin Elektrik Üretim ve Ticaret Limited Sirketi v Republic of Turkey*, ICSID Case No ARB/02/5, Award, 19 June 2007, para 250.

143 Christoph Schreuer, 'Fair and Equitable Treatment in Arbitral Practice' (2005) 6(3) Journal of World Trade and Investment pp. 357, 375.

award renewables producers a certain quantity of green certificates for the volume of electricity they produced and required the utility companies to purchase a mandated number of those certificates proportionate to the volume of electricity sold. The value of a certificate was determined by the market although Romania set a minimum and maximum value adjusted annually with the consumer price index.[144]

Companies began establishing solar plants in Romania basing their financial calculations for the profitability of their investments with revenue not only on the sale of electricity, but from the sale of green certificates.[145] The costs for this system were passed onto consumers and their electricity bills began to rise, prompting Romania to amend the system. Initially it deferred some of the green certificates owed to investors to later years.[146] Romania then adjusted the number of certificates the utility companies had to purchase from producers, which led to a decrease in the value of the certificates.[147] Finally, Romania deferred the green certificates further, again decreasing the number of certificates to be purchased by the utility companies, and lowered the minimum and maximum values the certificates could be traded at.[148]

While there are reportedly multiple pending arbitrations concerning these measures,[149] there is only one public decision: *LSG Building Solutions & others v Romania*. Investors from different European countries alleged that Romania had breached the Energy Charter Treaty (*ECT*) by frustrating their legitimate expectations and violating other obligations of fair and equitable treatment.[150] The majority held that while States may amend their legal and regulatory frameworks in the public interest investors are "entitled to expect that the essential characteristics of the legal and regulatory regime on which they are reasonably relying upon will remain stable".[151] The tribunal decided

144 Law No 220/2008 (Romania) Article 10.

145 Pavel Atănăsoae & Eugen Hopulele, 'The impact of the support scheme on the installed capacity in renewable energy sources in Romania' (2014) EPE 1148, Figure 1.

146 Emergency Government Ordinance No 57/2013 (Romania).

147 Law No 23/2014 (Romania).

148 Emergency Government Ordinance No 24/2017 (Romania).

149 See 'Another Renewable Energy Investor Lodges ICSID Arbitration Against Romania' *IAReporter* (4 May 2022) <https://www.iareporter.com/articles/another-renewable-energy-investor-lodges-icsid-arbitration-against-romania/> accessed 10 June 2024, referring to *KELAG-Kärntner Elektrizitäts-Aktiengesellschaft and others v Romania*, ICSID Case No ARB/21/54, *EP Wind Project (Rom) Six Ltd. v Romania*, ICSID Case No ARB/20/15, and *Fin. Doc S.r.l. and others v Romania*, ICSID Case No ARB/20/35.

150 *LSG Building Solutions GmbH and others v Romania*, ICSID Case No ARB/18/19, Decision on Jurisdiction, Liability and Principles of Quantum, 11 July 2022, para 811.

151 *Ibid*, para 1064.

in favour of the investors. The majority concluded that Romania had unreasonably altered the "essential characteristics" of the legislation that caused the Claimants to invest in Romania.[152]

Consistent with the lessons from the Spanish and Czech tribunals, it is a warning to States that they must be aware of what their legislation is designed to do. Renewables incentives – which are inherently designed to create favourable economics to induce investment – risk creating legitimate expectations for investors.

4.1.3 Amendments to Renewable Energy Legislation and the Right to Regulate

Just as States have the regulatory authority to enact laws to promote the adoption of renewable energy generation, they too retain that same power to regulate the industry. The line in the sand where otherwise legitimate regulations run afoul of the State's obligation to provide FET can shift depending on the circumstances, treaty, sector, and other factors.

As States have had increasing experience with dispute settlement under investment treaties, there has been a growing call by States and commentators that any investor expectations regarding regulatory stability must be weighed against the State's right to regulate matters for the general welfare.[153] Tribunals have recognised this.[154] Of course, there will be outer bounds to the right to regulate, such as that the State must not act discriminatorily, arbitrarily, and without according due process.[155]

---

152 *Ibid*, para 1068.

153 See for example Crina Baltag, Riddhi Joshi, and Kabir Duggal, 'Recent Trends in Investment Arbitration on the Right to Regulate, Environment, Health and Corporate Social Responsibility: Too Much or Too Little?' (2023) 38(2) ICSID Review 381, 382 (referring to States' efforts to increase their power to regulate without owing compensation to investors as part of the ongoing UNCITRAL Working Group III investor-State arbitration reform process). See also Federico Ortino, 'The Obligation of Regulatory Stability in the Fair and Equitable Treatment Standard: How Far Have We Come?' (2018) 4 Journal of International Economic Law pp. 845, 865; Aikaterini Titi, *The Right to Regulate in International Investment Law* (Hart 2014) p. 52.

154 *Perenco Ecuador Ltd. v The Republic of Ecuador and Empresa Estatal Petróleos del Ecuador (Petroecuador)*, Decision on Remaining Issues of Jurisdiction and Liability, 12 September 2014, para 560; *WCV Capital Ventures Cyprus Limited and Channel Crossings Limited v Czech Republic*, Final Award, 26 July 2023, para 262; *Plama Consortium Limited v Republic of Bulgaria*, ICSID Case No ARB/03/24, Award, 27 August 2008, para 177.

155 *WCV Capital Ventures Cyprus Limited and Channel Crossings Limited v Czech Republic*, Final Award, 26 July 2023, para 263; *Rusoro Mining Ltd. v Bolivarian Republic of Venezuela*, ICSID Case No ARB(AF)/12/5, Award, 22 August 2016, para 525.

In the context of the energy transition, the call for the respect of the right to regulate has been most strongly made against claims by fossil fuel companies.[156] Nonetheless it is also invoked by States in defending claims by investors in renewables,[157] despite the prevailing view that further investment in renewables benefits society at large.[158] It is natural to assume that States would be entitled to, among other things, fight the evolving circumstances of climate change by way of evolving regulation. Tribunals recognize that States will need to regulate to meet environmental commitments and that expectations in regulatory stability should be couched accordingly in industries where regulations are actively changing.[159] Again, such deference would not extend to politically motivated, discriminatory, or otherwise arbitrary regulation that substantially affects foreign investment.[160]

The language of an investment treaty can affect the latitude given to a State for what otherwise would be a treaty breach. In the WB6, many of the treaties are old Yugoslavia BITs that are still in force.[161] A result of the reliance on those treaties is that many of the 'modern' provisions found in more recent treaties – including the right to regulate or environmental carve outs – are absent from

---

156 The Working Group on climate change has highlighted the use of investment arbitration by fossil fuel companies as a chilling effect on environmental policy IPCC, 'Climate Change 2022: Mitigation of Climate Change', Working Group III Contribution to the IPCC Sixth Assessment Report (AR6) (2022), Chapter 14, 1499–1501. *See* also Joshua Paine & Elizabeth Sheargold, 'A Climate Change Carve-Out for Investment Treaties' (2023) 26 Journal of International Economic Law 285, 288.

157 *AES Solar and others (PV Investors) v The Kingdom of Spain*, PCA Case No 2012-14, Final Award, 28 February 2020, para 215; *LSG Building Solutions GmbH and others v Romania*, ICSID Case No ARB/18/19, Decision on Jurisdiction, Liability and Principles of Reparation, 11 July 2022, para 789; *SunReserve Luxco Holdings SRL v Italy*, SCC Case No 132/2016, Final Award, 25 March 2020, para 687.

158 Jorge Viñuales, *The International Law of Energy* (CUP 2022) p. 422.

159 Jorge Viñuales, 'The Environmental Regulation of Foreign Investment Schemes under International Law', in Pierre Dupuy & Jorge Viñuales (eds.), *Harnessing Foreign Investment to Promote Environmental Protection: Incentives and Safeguards* (CUP 2012) Chapter 11 citing *Chemtura Corporation v Government of Canada*, UNCITRAL, Award, 2 August 2010, para 149 ("a sophisticated registrant experienced in a highly-regulated industry, the Claimant could not reasonably ignore the PMRA's practices and the importance of the evaluation of exposure risks within such practices"). See also *Philip Morris Brand SARL, Philip Morris Products S.A. and Abal Hermanos S.A. v Oriental Republic of Uruguay*, ICSID Case No ARB/10/7, Award, 8 July 2016, para 430.

160 See generally Fernando Dias Simoes, 'When Green Incentives Go Pale: Investment Arbitration and Renewable Energy Policymaking' (2017) 45 Denv J Int'l L & Pol'y 251.

161 See for example Germany – Yugoslavia BIT (1989) (Signed on 10 July 1989, entered into force on 25 October 1990) 1707 UNTS 605; France – Yugoslavia BIT (1974) (Signed on 28 March 1974, entered into force on 3 March 1975).

treaties in force with the WB6.[162] In line with global trends, it can be expected that this may change as WB6 members revise their investment agreements in the future.

4.2 *Claims Regarding the Design and Conduct of Auctions*

As discussed, the trend across the WB6 is towards auctions. While auctions give States a degree of control over the electricity market and allow States to screen investors and investments, the State's involvement in the auction process may also give rise to investment claims. In particular, the State may set the terms of the auction or manage it in a manner that favours one investor over another.

Auctions are issued with criteria to allow the decision maker – usually the State or a State entity – to sort different bids.[163] How the State goes about fixing the auction criteria may lead to investment claims.

One such example is *Mesa Power v. Canada*. Ontario introduced legislation authorising its Ministry of Energy to direct the electricity operator to establish a FiT program.[164] Participants could apply for either 20-year or 40-year fixed rate FiT contracts and had to meet certain eligibility requirements, for example, for solar projects to have a capacity above 10 MW.[165] A points system was established whereby eligible projects with the highest points would receive contracts.[166]

Mesa Power, an American company, applied for six FiT contracts, but was unsuccessful each time.[167] It scored low point totals for its projects, largely due to the proposed location of the solar farms and the difficulty of connecting

162 Michail Dekastros & Marios Tokas, 'Promoting and Protecting Green Investment in Western Balkans BITs: Existing Limitations and Future Opportunities' in Ben Beaumont *et al* (eds) *The Future of Investor-State Dispute Settlement: Reforming Law, Practice and Perspectives for a Fast-Changing World* (Kluwer 2024) pp. 225–227.

163 Vasilios Anatolitis, Alina Azanbayev, & Ann-Katrin Fleck, 'How to design efficient renewable energy auctions? Empirical insights from Europe' (2022) 166 Energy Policy, 2; David Toke, 'Renewable Energy Auctions and Tenders: How good are they?' (2015) 8 International Journal of Sustainable Energy Planning and Management 43, 53.

164 Green Energy Act 2009 (Ontario) Schedule A.

165 See Ontario Power Authority, Feed-In Tariff Program: FIT Rules, Version 1.3.0; Ontario Power Authority, Feed-In Tariff Contract, Version 1.3.0. 40-year contracts were offered for hydropower projects and 20-year contracts for project utilising all other sources of renewable energy, see Ontario Power Authority, Feed-In Tariff Program: FIT Rules, Version 1.3.0, Clause 6.3(a).

166 Ontario Power Authority, Feed-In Tariff Program: FIT Rules, Version 1.3.0, see the use of "Criteria Score".

167 *Mesa Power Group, LLC v Government of Canada*, UNCITRAL, PCA Case No 2012-17, Award, 24 March 2016.

them to the electrical grid, among other factors.[168] Mesa Power challenged Ontario's FiT program alleging its design and implementation were "arbitrary and unfair".[169] In terms of design, the investor alleged two main defects both of which were amendments to the procedure once the tender had started. First, it alleged that Ontario reserved some of the auction capacity for a Korean consortium after having already requested bids.[170] Second, it alleged that when the province decided later in the process to auction off capacity in the region where Mesa Power operated – the Bruce Peninsula – the authorities departed from the original FiT rules.[171] Mesa Power alleged that this change was intended to benefit its competitors who scored higher as a result of the amended procedure.[172]

The Tribunal rejected both allegations related to the program's design. It found that reserving capacity for the Korean consortium served a legitimate policy objective because, unlike other investors, the consortium had agreed to build manufacturing capabilities in the province.[173] Discussing the amended design for the Bruce Peninsula, the Tribunal concluded that Ontario was not bound to implement a particular process and that its choice of auction method was, in any event, not crafted to benefit a competing investor.[174] While the rules were amended in this later round of bidding – Ontario had auctioned off capacity in three phases and this change was made for the third – the amendments were a legitimate response to ensure that renewables capacity would be allocated to the Bruce Peninsula without risking over-allocation at the end of the auction.[175] The tribunal held that, in choosing this amended tender process, the auctioneers had run an auction that was close to the tender documents and, as a result, "respect[ed] the expectations of FiT Applicants".[176]

As regards the implementation of the auction, the Tribunal found that the incentive scheme was "unobjectionable" and that there was no evidence of collusion or unfair preference on the part of the authorities that had led to Mesa Power receiving a lower score than it ought to have.[177] The Tribunal

168 *Ibid*, paras 27–37.
169 *Ibid*, para 37.
170 *Ibid*, paras 544–545.
171 *Ibid*, para 616.
172 *Ibid*, para 637.
173 *Ibid*, paras 566, 574, and 579.
174 *Ibid*, paras 670 and 682.
175 *Ibid*, paras 630 and 670.
176 *Ibid*, para 636.
177 *Ibid*, paras 530 and 541.

held that the claimant's case for collusion relied on "conjecture" and was not substantiated.[178]

Although the claim here was dismissed, the fact that Mesa Power felt sufficiently aggrieved to start an international proceeding indicates that investors will be sensitive to the design and management of auctions. *A fortiori*, where auctions are conducted in an arbitrary manner, this may entice further claims.

At the same time, where the design of an auction is such to exclude a certain category of bidders, it could be said that this is a question of access to the host State market or the process preceding the making of the investment. In that respect, treaties may set out no more than best-efforts obligations, requiring States to strive or endeavour to provide a certain kind of treatment at that stage of the investment lifecycle, for example, non-discriminatory treatment.[179] In such circumstances, where an investment has not been made or where the State has made no representation to the investor that it would be eligible for an auction, an investor may face a difficult task to show a violation of international law. Whereas some treaties provide protection to activities in the establishment of an investment,[180] absent an express provision that the treaty applies to pre-investment activity, the basis for an investment claim prior to the making of its investment may be questionable.[181]

One can imagine, however, situations where personal interests may prevail over public ones and accordingly affect how auctions are carried out and who is given preferential treatment. Accordingly, where an investor has already established an investment in the renewable energy sector, but a law or regulation is adopted excluding it from participating in auctions and it is shown that

178 *Ibid*, para 673.

179 *See* The Energy Charter Treaty (signed on 17 December 1994, entered into force on 16 April 1998) 2080 UNTS 95, Article 10(2)-(3) ("[e]ach Contracting Party shall endeavour to accord to Investors of other Contracting Parties, as regards the Making of Investments in its Area … [treatment] no less favourable than that which it accords to its own Investors or to Investors of any other Contracting Party or any third state, whichever is the most favourable.").

180 For example, *see* the definition of investor in the China-Nicaragua FTA (2023) (signed on 31 August 2023, entered into force on 1 January 2024) Article 9.21 "*investor of a Party* means a Party, or a national or an enterprise of a Party, *that attempts to make … an investment* …" (emphasis added). See also USMCA (2018) (signed on 30 November 2018, entered into force on 1 July 2020) Article 14.1; Australia-Peru FTA (2018) (signed on 12 February 2018, entered into force on 11 February 2020) Article 8.1.

181 *Generation Ukraine Inc. v Ukraine*, ICSID Case No ARB/00/9, Award, 16 September 2003, para 8.6; *Nordzucker AG v Republic of Poland*, UNCITRAL, Partial Award (Jurisdiction), 10 December 2008, para 189.

this is due to the economic interests of local politicians or businesses, the State would likely be exposed to claims of discrimination and arbitrariness.

4.3 *Claims Arising out of Failure to Enter into a Contract*

As discussed above, the result of a successful auction bid is that the investor is entitled to enter into an investment contract with the State. Before the contract is finalised or before it enters into force, there will be additional steps or conditions precedent for the renewables investor to acquire its contractual incentives. This can include, for example, negotiating the terms of the agreement or obtaining permits for construction. At this stage, too, the State can interfere with the investor's rights.

Such an interference occurred in a different Ontario-related dispute. A US company, Windstream, was awarded a FiT contract through an auction,[182] and obtained the right to connect to the grid.[183] However, thereafter, the Government of Ontario enacted a moratorium on all offshore wind development pending further studies of environmental consequences.[184] Windstream's project, which was offshore wind, was unable to proceed.

Windstream brought a claim under the North America Free Trade Agreement (NAFTA). The Tribunal found that imposing the moratorium was itself not a violation of the treaty because the Government was driven by a "genuine policy concern" due to the uncertain environmental impact of offshore wind farms.[185] Nevertheless, the Tribunal did find a breach of FET on the basis that the State had acted in a non-transparent fashion after the moratorium was enacted, and had not taken scientific studies necessary to solve the purported uncertainty of the effects of offshore wind.[186]

Ontario has maintained the moratorium and Windstream brought a fresh NAFTA claim following the eventual termination of its FiT contract in February 2020.[187] That claim is ongoing.

---

182 *Windstream Energy* LLC *v Government of Canada* (*I*), PCA Case No 2013-22, Award, 27 September 2016, para 137.

183 *Ibid*, para 140.

184 Ontario Newsroom, 'Ontario Rules Out Offshore Wind Projects' (11 February 2011) <https://news.ontario.ca/en/release/16973/ontario-rules-out-offshore-wind-projects> accessed 27 June 2024.

185 *Windstream Energy* LLC *v Government of Canada* (*I*), PCA Case No 2013-22, Award, 27 September 2016, para 376.

186 *Ibid*, para 379.

187 *Windstream Energy* LLC (*USA*) *v The Government of Canada* (*II*), PCA Case No 2021-26, Claimant's Memorial, 18 February 2022.

One claim based on post-auction conduct has already been brought against a WB6 State. While the details are not public, Albania faced a now terminated investment claim under the Albania-Netherlands BIT from the investor Arka Energy.[188] The investment was in the construction of the Arkeni solar farm, won in a 2018 tender commissioned by Albania's Ministry of Infrastructure and Energy.[189] Reportedly, Albania pulled out of the contract or otherwise interfered before the project could be brought online.[190] The case was reportedly discontinued.[191]

Albania is not the only WB6 State that requires additional steps to perfect an investment beyond just winning a tender process. In choosing regimes for promoting renewables that rely on auctions, the WB6 have crafted systems that inherently rely on additional conditions to perfect an investment agreement including regulatory permits, government sign off, etc. In circumstances where those additional approvals are unreasonably or discriminatorily withheld or denied, a disgruntled investor may decide to pursue their rights in arbitration.

4.4 *Claims Arising out of Breach of Contract*

Given the nature of the WB6's present incentive structure focused on auctions, the States have – and will continue to accrue – a plethora of contractual commitments to various investors. Both international law and the legal systems in the Western Balkans recognise the sanctity of contracts and, accordingly, an investor that has concluded a long-term agreement (here, for the offtake of electricity) will have acquired rights and developed expectations on the basis of which it will plan and carry out its investment project.

Reneging on such contractual commitments risks exposing the State to two types of arbitration claims: (i) claims for breach or termination of contract under the agreements themselves[192] and (ii) investment treaty claims. Such proceedings could take place in parallel.

---

188 *Arka Energy B.V. v Republic of Albania*, ICSID Case No ARB/20/54.

189 Investment Policy Hub, 'Arka Energy v Albania' (UNCTAD) <https://investmentpolicy.unctad.org/investment-dispute-settlement/cases/1072/arka-energy-v-albania> accessed 27 June 2024.

190 'Arbitration Cases: Albania Could Lose Potentially 450 million Euro' *Tirana Times* (Tirana, 22 February 2021) <https://tiranatimes.com/?p=149362> accessed 27 June 2024; Damien Charlotin, 'Albania Faces Investment Treaty Arbitration Over Solar Park Project' *IAReporter* (21 December 2020) <https://www.iareporter.com/articles/albania-faces-investment-treaty-arbitration-over-solar-park/> accessed 27 June 2024.

191 Open Data Albania, 'Cases Lost in Arbitration: Issues and Liabilities of the Albanian State' (23 May 2023) <https://ndiqparate.al/?p=19599&lang=en> accessed 27 June 2024.

192 Rudolf Dolzer, 'Investment Contracts' in Ursula Kriebaum, Christoph Schreuer, & Rudolf Dolzer (eds), *Principles of International Investment Law* (3rd ed, OUP 2022) 131.

Focusing on the treaty avenue, investors may bring claims related to contractual breaches by the State under different treaty provisions: (i) so-called umbrella clauses[193] requiring the State to observe commitments towards investors, (ii) FET, for example, for failure to respect expectations that arise from the State's contractual undertakings,[194] or (iii) expropriation, where the contract is repudiated.[195] In this context, it bears noting that tribunals have held that to establish a breach of international law, an investor must show something more than a mere breach of contract. That "something more" could be improper court interference,[196] coercive or politically motivated conduct by State bodies,[197] or other acts of a sovereign character.[198] This is to distinguish mere contractual behaviour from the State using its *puissance publique* to interfere with the property rights of investors.

---

193 *Gardabani Holdings B.V. and Silk Road Holdings B.V. v Georgia*, ICSID Case No ARB/17/29, Award, 27 October 2022, para 701; *Garanti Koza LLP v Turkmenistan*, ICSID Case No ARB/11/20, Award, 19 December 2016, paras 346 and 352–354; *EDF International S.A., SAUR International S.A. and León Participaciones Argentinas S.A. v Argentine Republic*, ICSID Case No ARB/03/23, Award, 11 June 2012, para 940.

194 *Total S.A. v Argentine Republic*, ICSID Case No ARB/04/01, Decision on Liability, 27 December 2010, paras 117 and 183–184; *Greentech Energy Systems A/S, NovEnergia II Energy & Environment (SCA) SICAR, and NovEnergia II Italian Portfolio SA v The Italian Republic*, SCC Case No V 2015/095, Award, 23 December 2018, paras 453–455.

195 Johanne Cox, 'Contractual Expropriation' in Andrea Bjorklund, Catherine Kessedjian, & Francisco Vicuña (eds), *Expropriation in Investment Treaty Arbitration* (OUP 2019) para 8.02; *Ampal-American Israel Corp., EGI-Fund (08–10) Investors LLC, EGI-Series Investments LLC, BSS-EMG Investors LLC and David Fischer v Arab Republic of Egypt*, ICSID Case No ARB/12/11, Decision on liability and heads of loss, 21 February 2017, paras 342 and 346–347; *Swisslion DOO Skopje v The Former Yugoslav Republic of Macedonia*, ICSID Case No ARB/09/16, Award, 6 July 2012, para 314.

196 *Yukos Capital Limited (formerly Yukos Capital S.A R.L.) v Russia*, PCA Case No 2013-31, Final Award, 23 July 2021, para 376; *Infinito Gold Ltd. v Republic of Costa Rica*, ICSID Case No ARB/14/5, Award, 03 June 2021, para 701.

197 *CME Czech Republic B.V. v Czech Republic*, UNCITRAL, Partial Award, 13 September 2001, paras 538 and 601; *Caratube International Oil Company LLP and Devincci Salah Hourani v Republic of Kazakhstan*, ICSID Case No ARB/13/13, Award, 27 September 2017, paras 936 and 939.

198 See *The Lopez-Goyne Family Trust and others v Republic of Nicaragua*, ICSID Case No ARB/17/44, Award, 01 March 2023, para 557 ("[t]he unanimous position in the case-law and doctrine is that the termination of a contract by a State acting as private contracting party, in conformity with the private rules governing it, does not constitute an expropriation. It can only rise to the level of an expropriation if it involves an act of sovereign authority."); *Rasia FZE and Joseph K. Borkowski v Republic of Armenia*, ICSID Case No ARB/18/28, Award, 20 January 2023, para 664. See also Nigel Blackaby, Constantine Partasides, & Alan Redfern, *Redfern and Hunter on International Arbitration* (7th ed, OUP 2022) para 8.92.

Against that background, it should be noted that electricity contracts are, by their nature, long-term agreements and that over their lifespan, there may be various reasons why the State could act in a way that the investor may consider to be in breach of both contract and international law, and therefore seek redress.

For example, in the 2000s, Hungary's accession to the European Union led it to interfere with[199] or outright terminate[200] power purchase agreements concluded with power plants owed by foreign investors. In both publicly reported decisions, Hungary was not held liable under international law. In *Electrabel*, where the contract was terminated, the Tribunal held that the investor could not have legitimately expected to face no economic consequences from Hungary's European Union accession because it knew that Hungary was seeking membership at the time they invested and that membership would necessarily entail market liberalisation that might affect its contractual rights.[201] In *AES II*, where the investors retained their power purchase agreement, the tribunal held that Hungary's measure, which here was a luxury tax reducing profits under the contract, was reasonable and non-discriminatory, as the Tribunal considered it rational for States to regulate excessive profits of corporations.[202] At the same time, Hungary was ordered to pay EUR 107 million in a third arbitration, commenced by EDF International, regarding its power purchase agreements.[203] The *EDFI v Hungary* award is not public.

Even if not directly altering a contract, the State may indirectly interfere with contractual rights through the passage of new legislation. Such legislation may, for example, affect how incentives are calculated under those agreements. This was the case in some of the Italian renewable energy cases where Italy's regulations altered the contractual FiTs, granted to investors through contracts with a State-owned corporation (termed GSE Agreements).[204] The so-called

199 In *AES II*, Hungary issued Price Decrees which capped the investor's earnings on their assets and rendered the price formula in their Power Purchase Agreement inoperable: *AES Summit Generation Limited and AES-Tisza Erömü Kft. v Republic of Hungary (II)*, ICSID Case No ARB/07/22, Award, 23 September 2010, paras 4.21–4.23.

200 In *Electrabel*, Hungary outright terminated the Power Purchase Agreement: *Electrabel S.A. v The Republic of Hungary*, ICSID Case No ARB/07/19, Decision on Jurisdiction, Applicable Law and Liability, 30 November 2012, para 2.13.

201 *Electrabel S.A. v The Republic of Hungary*, ICSID Case No ARB/07/19, Award, 25 November 2015, para 178.

202 *AES Summit Generation Limited and AES-Tisza Erömü Kft. v Republic of Hungary (II)*, ICSID Case No ARB/07/22, Award, 23 September 2010, paras 10.3.34–10.3.36 and 10.3.53.

203 *Électricité de France (EDF) International S.A. v Republic of Hungary*, PCA Case No 2009-13, Decision of the Swiss Federal Tribunal 4A_34/2015, 6 October 2015, paras A-B.

204 *See* for example *Belenergia S.A. v Italian Republic*, ICSID Case No ARB/15/40, Award, 6 August 2019, para 613; *CEF Energia BV v Italian Republic*, SCC Case No 2015/158, Award, 16 January 2019, para 238.

"Spalma-incentivi Decree", issued by Italy in 2014, forced solar investors to accept changes to how tariffs grounded in contracts would be calculated.[205] In *ESPF v Italy*, the Tribunal majority concluded that this decree breached the ECT's umbrella clause.[206] It reasoned that forcing the investors to accept a unilateral change to the terms of their contracts was a violation of those agreements, and, therefore, Italy had failed to observe its contractual obligations entered into with the investors.[207]

Even if a claim is not based on the terms of a contract directly, a contract may nevertheless be the basis for an investor's asserted legitimate expectations. In *Greentech*, the majority found that the Spalma-incentivi Decree had frustrated the investors' legitimate expectations formed from, among other things, their contractual rights.[208] They determined that "[a]t the time of investing, Claimants had been led to believe, reasonably, that the incentive tariffs would remain the same as promised in the *Conto Energia* decrees, GSE letters and GSE Agreements throughout a twenty-year period".[209] Italy had "defeated" those expectations, formed at least in part based on contractual rights, through enacting the Spalma-incentivi Decree "irrespective of any other duties in regard to the umbrella clause".[210] In short, it concluded that the contracts –had created legitimate expectations that were then frustrated by regulatory changes.

The Hungarian and Italian experience is highly relevant for the WB6 as they have now moved to a phase where long-term incentives are largely granted by way of contract. At the same time, there is nothing to indicate proclivity on the part of the WB6 to interfere with contracts more than other States. As discussed above, Albania has implemented a mechanism that allows it to ensure that it can legislate while reducing the risk it interferes with contractual rights. This is its contracts-for-difference regime which allows the State to insulate particular investors from regulations which might otherwise impact the market. Those contracts mitigate some of the risk that an investor would normally bear from regulatory changes. The terms of the investment contract also, naturally, impact the risk allocation between investor and State. In discussing North

205 Law Decree No 91/2014 2014 (Italy) Article 26. The law established different options for investors to choose between with each option impacting the investment's profitability.

206 *ESPF Beteiligungs GmbH, ESPF Nr. 2 Austria Beteiligungs GmbH, and InfraClass Energie 5 GmbH & Co. KG v Italian Republic*, ICSID Case No ARB/16/5, Award, 14 September 2020, para 827.

207 *Ibid*, paras 816 and 823.

208 *Greentech Energy Systems A/S, NovEnergia II Energy & Environment (SCA) SICAR, and NovEnergia II Italian Portfolio SA v The Italian Republic*, SCC Case No V 2015/095, Award, 23 December 2018, paras 453–455.

209 *Ibid*, para 447.

210 *Ibid*, para 453.

Macedonia's renewables promotion regime, IRENA highlights that a State offering effective standardised contracts is a potent avenue for speeding the adoption of green investments.[211]

5 Conclusion

The transition away from fossil fuels to renewable energy can only occur with massive capital expenditures. In the Western Balkans, as elsewhere, such investment is and will perforce be foreign, in large part. Properly constructed legal and business regimes for investment will allow the Western Balkan States to decarbonise their electricity generation, stimulate foreign capital influx, and create jobs. Abrupt amendments to the renewables regulatory framework or arbitrary interventions in projects, however, will likely lead to investor-State arbitration.

The auction-based incentives being offered within the region have thus far proved to be powerful tools in driving renewables investment. These incentive schemes, in the abstract, do not appear to expose the Western Balkan States to the wide-ranging lawsuits that have overwhelmed Spain since 2011.[212] Similarly, the WB6 have yet avoided the Czech scenario of using the tax lever to withdraw incentives through the back door.

Nonetheless, where around 60% of electricity in the WB6 continues to be produced from fossil fuels, the transition to renewable energy production will be long. Governments will change and the legal and business framework, including the renewable energy incentive regimes, will continue to evolve. The analysis above has sought to identify the principal arbitration risks that the WB6 will face as they adapt the regulatory framework to their clean energy goals. That analysis is made in the abstract and in light of experience elsewhere. Each actual State measure and investor claim will need to be examined on its own merits and in light of the circumstances. This is trite, but important to observe. Nevertheless, corruption, cronyism, and political deals– which have historically undermined the rule of law in the region – can be said to be the principal reasons for potential future investor-State disputes in the renewable energy sector in the Western Balkans.

211 International Renewable Energy Agency, 'De-Risking Investments in North Macedonia' (October 2021) p. 7.

212 The first known renewables-related arbitration launched against Spain was commenced in 2011: *AES Solar and others (PV Investors) v The Kingdom of Spain*, PCA Case No 2012-14.

CHAPTER 5

The Implications of the New EU Model Clauses for BITs with Third Countries for Candidate States

Nikos Lavranos and Marialena Komi

1 Introduction[1]

On 21 September 2023, the Directorate-General ("DG") for Trade of the European Commission ("EC") published a "non-paper" entitled "Annotations to the Model Clauses for negotiations and re-negotiations of Member States' Bilateral Investment Agreements with third countries".[2]

The main purpose of this contribution is to provide a detailed analysis of the most important model clauses and their implications for the European Union ("EU") Member States' bilateral investment treaties ("BITs") with third countries. Moreover, we will do so by focusing particularly on the implications for the candidate countries, which currently include: Ukraine, Albania, Bosnia and Herzegovina, Georgia, Moldova, Montenegro, North Macedonia, Serbia, and Turkey, since these countries are (at various stages) in the process of preparing for the accession to the EU.

Since a detailed analysis of all the implications for each individual candidate country would go far beyond this chapter, we will necessarily be forced to generalize to a certain degree and to be selective. Nonetheless, it is hoped that this overall assessment will provide useful and practical guidelines for the policy makers in the candidate countries on how to deal with the (potential) implications of this "non-paper".

This contribution is subdivided as follows: First, we will focus on the Preamble, Right to Regulate and certain definitions (section 2).

Second, we will examine several model clauses dealing with substantive protection standards (section 3). Third, we will address model clauses on

1 All views expressed are those of the authors alone and cannot be attributed to any law firm or organization to which they are affiliated with.

2 *Non-Paper on Annotations to the Model Clauses for negotiation or re-negotiation of Member States' Bilateral Investment Agreements with third countries*, DG for Trade, EC (hereinafter EU Model Clause) 21 September 2023 <https://circabc.europa.eu/ui/group/be8b568f-73f3-409c-b4a4-30acfcec5283/library/f9a070c6-16dd-41e6-8fec-d2ce67473870/details?download=true> accessed 07 July 2024.

 | DOI:10.1163/9789004729889_006

environment, Corporate Social Responsibility ("CSR"), climate change and labour (section 4), followed by an analysis of the ISDS-related provisions (section 5). Finally, under each section we will provide a short analysis on the implications of each respective model provision for the candidate countries. In the last chapter (section 6) we will conclude by offering some general policy recommendations, particularly for the candidate countries.

2 The Political and Legal Background of the "Non-Paper"

The "non-paper" itself does not provide any explicit reasons for compiling and publishing these model clauses for EU Member States' BITs with third states. Indeed, the website of the European Commission simply states that:

> Drawing on the EU's approach to investment protection agreements – and on Member States' best practices – the Commission has developed Model Clauses to guide Member States in their negotiation (or re-negotiation) of bilateral investment agreements.[3]

Despite this rather "innocent" statement, given the latest developments in the EU's investment policy, several reasons can be identified which have likely prompted the EC to publish this "non-paper" now.

First and foremost, in the past decade, the EU has developed its own investment policy by adopting an approach of reforming the existing investor-State-dispute settlement ("ISDS") system. Already, in its very first Communication in 2010,[4] the EC indicated that it intended to deviate from the ISDS system to make it more palatable for the European Parliament and the civil society, which became increasingly hostile against ISDS.

Second, this hostility became particularly obvious in the context of the EU's first investment treaty negotiations with the USA (TTIP[5]) and Canada

3 European Commission, Investment <https://policy.trade.ec.europa.eu/help-exporters-and-importers/accessing-markets/investment_en> accessed 07 July 2024.

4 European Commission, *Communication from the Commission to the Council, the European Parliament, the European Economic and Social Committee and the Committee of the Regions, Towards a Comprehensive European International Investment Policy, Brussels,* COM (2010) 343 final, (7 July 2010) https://eur-lex.europa.eu/LexUriServ/LexUriServ.do?uri=COM:2010:0343:FIN:EN:PDF> accessed 07 July 2024.

5 Transatlantic Trade and Investment Partnership [hereinafter TTIP], EU – U.S (not signed).

(CETA[6]). Regarding the TTIP, the civil society protests were so massive that the negotiations were eventually abandoned, mainly due to the fears that the ISDS system could be used for massive claims by American companies against EU Member States. In light of this strong resistance, which permeated into many important trading Member States such as Germany, France and the Netherlands, the EC decided to call "ISDS dead"[7] and replace it with a new Investment Court System ("ICS") which is inspired by the WTO dispute settlement system.[8] In addition to the ICS, EU's desire to deviate from the ISDS system as we knew it, was clear even during the conclusion of CETA. The latter contains numerous stricter substantive protection provisions, which differ significantly from those generally contained in the "traditional" BITs concluded by the EU Member States.

Third, a number of judgments by the Court of Justice of the EU ("CJEU") have contributed and – to some extent – clarified the extent to which the new EU's investment policy is compatible with EU law. More specifically, we can refer to Opinion 2/15[9] on the EU-Singapore Free Trade and Investment Agreement ("EU-Singapore FTA") in which the CJEU among other things decided that ISDS is not an exclusive competence of the EU but rather a mixed one – shared with the EU Member States.[10] A few years later, in Opinion 1/17[11] the CJEU would greenlight the ICS system contained in CETA, declaring it compatible with EU law, but only under very strict conditions.[12]

Fourth, the EU has succeeded in taking the ISDS reform discussions to the global level, namely, by actively promoting the establishment of the UNCITRAL

---

6 Comprehensive Economic and Trade Agreement [hereinafter CETA] EU – Can., 30 October 2016.

7 BakerMcKenzie, New EU-Japan Trade Deal: EU declares ISDS "dead", 17 July 2017 <https://www.globalarbitrationnews.com/2017/07/17/new-eu-japan-trade-deal-eu-declares-isds-dead/> accessed 07 July 2024. The factsheet of the EC appears to have been permanently removed, so reference is made to other sources which refer to the same factsheet.

8 Vanina Sucharitkul, From Arbitration to the Investment Court System (ICS): Comparing CETA, EVIPA, and TTIP, Handbook of International Investment Law and Policy, pp. 2349–2373 (Julien Chaisse et al. eds., Springer, 2021); Charles N. Brower, *Doomed To Failure: Why The EU Investment Court System Is Destined To Fail Both Foreign Investors And Host States – 3rd Annual EFILA Conference Keynote,* 3 European Investment Law and Arb. Rev., pp. 317–327 (2018).

9 Opinion 2/15 (EU-Singapore FTA) May 16, 2017, ECLI:EU:C:2017:376.

10 Nikos Lavranos, *Mixed Exclusivity: The CJEU's Opinion On The EU-Singapore FTA,* 2 European Investment Law and Arbitration Review, pp.1–34 (2017).

11 Opinion 1/17 (CETA) 30 April 2019, ECLI:EU:C:2019:341.

12 Nikos Lavranos, *CJEU Opinion 1/17: Keeping International Investment Law and EU Law Strictly Apart,* 4 European Investment Law And Arbitration Review pp. 240–259 (2019).

Working Group III on ISDS Reforms.[13] Since its establishment, the EU has been the main driving force in the negotiations, pushing in particular for the creation of a Multilateral Investment Court ("MIC"), which is inspired by the ICS, as well as other instruments such as the new Code of Conduct for Arbitrators.[14]

Finally, one cannot ignore the developments regarding intra-EU BITs and ISDS. To cut a long story short, the CJEU's jurisprudence encompassing *Achmea,*[15] *Komstroy,*[16] *Micula*[17] and *PL Holdings*[18] has resulted in the ban of intra-EU ISDS disputes. This has ultimately brought about the Termination Agreement[19] signed among 23 EU Member States, which terminated most intra-EU BITs.

While these developments seem to only have an intra-EU impact, they have now also spilled over into the Energy Charter Treaty ("ECT"), which is in fact a multilateral investment protection treaty with numerous non-EU Contracting Parties, thus also having an extra-EU dimension.

Indeed, the EU's reform agenda was also incorporated in the draft modernized ECT text,[20] which, however, has been effectively abandoned by the very same EU and its Member States which pushed for it in the first place.[21]

While all the above-mentioned developments were taking place, the approximately 1,200 EU Member States' BITs with third states, most dating from the 1980s and until the early 2000s, remained untouched. Consequently,

---

13 *See* UNCITRAL WG III documents, https://uncitral.un.org/en/working_groups/3/investor-state> accessed 02 July 2024.

14 UNCITRAL, Code of Conduct for arbitrators in international investment dispute resolution with commentary, (2023), <https://uncitral.un.org/sites/uncitral.un.org/files/media-documents/uncitral/en/uncitral_code_of_conduct_for_arbitrators_advance_copy_publ.pdf> accessed 02 July 2024.

See for a detailed overview, Fahira Brodlija, *Sorting The Building Blocks Of Investor-State Dispute Settlement Reform: Recent Developments From The UNCITRAL Working Group III*, 9 European Investment Law and Arbitration Review, pp. 69–94 (2024).

15 *Achmea B.V. v. Slovak Republic*, Case C-284/16, Judgment, CJEU (Mar. 6, 2018).

16 *République de Moldavie v. Komstroy LLC*, Case C-741/19, Judgment of the Court (Grand Chamber), CJEU (02 September 2021).

17 *European Commission v. European Food SA and Others*, Case C-638/19 P, Judgment of the Court (Grand Chamber), CJEU (25 January 2022).

18 *Republiken Polen v. PL Holdings Sàrl*, Case C-109/20, Judgment of the Court (Grand Chamber), CJEU (26 October, 2021).

19 Agreement for the Termination of Bilateral Investment Treaties between the Member States of the European Union, 2020 O.J. (L 169) p. 1 [hereinafter Agreement for Terminating Intra-EU BITs].

20 *Agreement in principle reached on Modernised Energy Charter Treaty*, (COM), (June 27, 2022).

21 Nikos Lavranos et al., *The Meltdown of ECT: How the ECT was ruined by the EU and its Member States*, 21 SchiedsVZ, pp. 38–46 (2023).

an increasing divergence has been emerging between the EU's new "CETA-approach" and the "old-school" Member States' BITs. It seems that in the eyes of the EC, this divergence needs to be addressed now, by aligning those Member States' BITs with the approach as encompassed in CETA.

The first steps towards facilitating this alignment have already been taken by the adoption of new model BIT texts by several EU Member States.[22] These model BIT texts have been composed after consultation with the EC and civil society. Although these model BIT texts have not yet been implemented in new BITs which have been signed and ratified, they signal to prospective contracting parties from third states and to the EC, their intention to adopt the "CETA approach" – albeit to a varying degree.[23]

However, not all EU Member States have updated their model BIT texts so far. This means that a certain level of heterogeneity still exists among the 27 EU Member States. Similarly, not many candidate countries have updated their model BIT texts either. Thus, the level of heterogeneity would increase even further if they were to join the EU with those "old school" BITs remaining unreformed.

Arguably, it is this political and legal landscape that has prompted the EC to publish this "non-paper" to "guide" the EU Member States in their BIT policy by providing model BIT clauses that should be included in their future BITs, as well as in existing BITs that will be renegotiated.

3 The Legal Nature of the "Non-Paper"

Before delving into the analysis, it should be noted that the "non-paper" does not contain an explanatory paragraph regarding its legal nature and purpose. Therefore, it seems appropriate to first clarify the legal nature of this "non-paper" and subsequently consider its intended purpose. This will be important for the purpose of understanding the legal and political framework of EU investment policy vis-à-vis its Member States regarding their BITs with third countries.

22 *See* Model BIT (2019) (Netherlands.); Model BIT (2022) (Italy.); Model BIT (2022) (Belgium.-Luxembourg.), https://investmentpolicy.unctad.org/international-investment-agreements/model-agreements.

23 *See* Nikos Lavranos & Adam Paschalidis, *Comparative Analysis Between The 2018 And 2004 Dutch Model Bilateral Investment Treaty Texts*, 4 European Investment Law and Arbitration Review, pp. 89–123 (2019); Max Kremer et al., *The 2019 BLEU Model BIT: BLEU's Vision Of The Future Of Investment Protection*, 9 European Investment Law and Arbitration Review, pp. 41–68 (2024).

From the outset, it should be emphasized that a "non-paper" is by its very nature a legally non-binding document. Indeed, a "non-paper" is not listed as one of the legally binding acts of the EU as per Article 288 TFEU.[24] So, what is the legal nature of this "non-paper" published by the EC?

As mentioned above, the EC does not say anything more than that the "non-paper" is supposed to "guide" the Member States without any further explanations as to its legal nature. To that end, commentators have attempted to interpret its nature and purpose as follows:

> Non-papers are informal documents usually put forward in closed negotiations with EU institutions. The views in this non-Paper do not necessarily communicate an official position. The Model Clauses may reflect a broader investment protection approach of the Commission and promote best practices for Member States, but they are not an official EU Model BIT. They are suggested for inclusion by Member States in BITs with third countries, to ensure wider compliance with EU policy.[25]

However, this description does not provide any additional explanations, thus highlighting the vague legal nature of this "non-paper".

On one hand, the model clauses incorporated in the "non-paper" are clearly not legally binding on the Member States, but have been developed by the EC to merely "guide" the Member States in their (re)negotiations of their BITs with third countries. On the other, given the fact that the "non-paper" is very detailed and 39 pages long, containing not only the proposed model clauses but also extensive commentaries for each clause, it is obvious that it represents EC's current viewpoint on what the precise contents of the Member States' BITs with third countries should be. Given DG Trade officials' effort to develop this extensive "non-paper", it must be assumed that this is not only to be understood as a "guide" but rather, as a strong invitation towards the Member States to diligently adhere to these model clauses in their BITs with third countries, otherwise legal consequences could follow.

Thus, in our view, this "non-paper" should be considered a soft-law instrument, which *de jure* is not legally binding on the Member States, but carries

24 Article 288 of the Treaty of the Functioning of the European Union [TFEU] lists only Regulations, Directives, Decisions, Recommendations and Opinions as legal acts of the EU.

25 Patricia Nacimiento et al, *European Commission Publishes Non-Paper of Model Clauses for Member States' Bilateral Investment Agreements with Third Countries*, Kluwer Arbitration Blog (19 February 2024) <https://arbitrationblog.kluwerarbitration.com/2024/02/19/european-commission-publishes-non-paper-of-model-clauses-for-member-states-bilateral-investment-agreements-with-third-countries/> (accessed on 6 September 2024).

significant force and effectively imposes a *de facto* obligation on the Member States to implement these model clauses quickly.

This conclusion is further supported by the EC's power to control the contents of the Member States' BITs with third countries as per the so-called "grandfathering" Regulation 1219/2012.[26] This Regulation was the first secondary EU law instrument adopted by the EU legislator after the EU had obtained exclusive competence regarding foreign direct investments ("FDI") as per Article 207 Treaty for the Functioning of the European Union ("TFEU"). The purpose of this Regulation was to regulate the legal status of the ca. 1,200 BITs of the existing Member States' BITs with third countries (extra-EU BITs), which had been in force before the exclusive competence on FDI was granted to the EU by the entering into force of the Lisbon Treaty on 1 December 2009.

To cut a long story short, the Council (i.e., the Member States) demanded from the EC and the European Parliament that these 1,200 extra-EU BITs be grandfathered; that they should stay in force until replaced by EU investment treaties signed with the respective third countries.[27] In that way, a smooth transition from a Member State BIT to an EU BIT could be guaranteed without the risks of creating legal gaps. This is referred to as the "replacement principle". In return, the EC as well as the European Parliament demanded the power to control any future new Member States' BITs with third countries as well as issues relating to the renewal or renegotiation of existing extra-EU BITs. As a result, the EC would be able to harmonize the extra-EU BITs and align them with the EU's model investment treaty over time, which is effectively CETA. Consequently, Member States are required to obtain prior authorization from the EC when negotiating new extra-EU BITs or renewing or renegotiating existing ones.[28] This is referred to as the "authorization principle". Indeed, Article 9(2) of Regulation 1219/2012 explicitly empowers the EC to force a Member State:

> [...] to include or remove from such negotiations and prospective bilateral investment agreement any clauses where necessary to ensure consistency with the Union's investment policy or compatibility with Union law. (emphasis added).

---

26 Regulation 1219/2012, of the European Parliament and of the Council of 12 December 2012 establishing transitional arrangements for bilateral investment agreements between Member States and third countries, 2012 O.J. (L 351) 40.

27 *See for a detailed analysis* Nikos Lavranos, *In Defence of Member States' BITs Gold Standard: The Regulation 1219/2012 Establishing a Transitional Regime for Existing Extra-EU BITs – A Member State's Perspective*, p. 2, Transnational Dispute Management, (2013).

28 *Supra* (n 25), Arts. 8–11.

Accordingly, the "non-paper" on model clauses for Member States' BITs must be understood in this context as an efficient – albeit soft-law – tool, the purpose of which is to signal to all Member States, through one instrument, what the contents of their extra-EU BITs should be in order to be considered to be consistent with the EU's investment policy, thereby remaining safe from interferences by the European Commission or, ultimately, by the CJEU.

4 Overview of the Key Model Provisions and Their Implications for the Candidate Countries

In this section, we will analyse several "foundational" model clauses, in particular the Preamble, the description of the objectives of future Member States' BITs, the "right to regulate" provision as well as the general definitions relating to the scope of application of those BITs regarding the investors and investments that are covered by those model clauses, the key substantive protections, modern provisions related to climate change and the environments, as well as the dispute resolution clause. We will also highlight some of the implications for candidate countries, related to each type of clause, thereby providing more context as to how those model clauses should be understood.

4.1 *Preamble and Objectives*

In line with modern investment treaties, the proposed preambular text explicitly mentions that the investment relations must be aligned with the objective of sustainable development and must be in accordance with internationally recognized environmental, social, and labour standards and international treaties.

As far as the model clause on the objectives of a BIT is concerned, it is notable that the usual language of promoting and protecting investments, which is already contained in the title of several BITs,[29] has been completely dropped. Instead, the relevant provision simply states that:

> The objective of this Agreement is to enhance the investment climate between the Parties, in accordance with the following provisions. (emphasis added).

29 *See* Preamble of the Agreement on encouragement and reciprocal protection of investments, Nicaragua-Netherlands, 28 August 2000.

This seems to suggest a significantly lower level of ambition, thereby subordinating the aim of promoting and protecting investments under the aims contained in the other model clauses. However, more relevant and interesting for this contribution is the following provision:

> [For agreements with third countries that have a status of 'EU (potential) candidate country': BEARING IN MIND that, in light of the judgment of the Court of Justice of the European Union in Achmea (C-284/16), this Agreement should be terminated in the event of the [xx country] accession to the European Union [...]. (emphasis added).

Accordingly, this signals to all the candidate countries that their existing BITs with the current EU Member States must be terminated upon accession to the EU. In other words, as soon as such extra-EU BITs transform into an intra-EU BIT due to the accession to the EU, those BITs must be terminated.

4.1.1 Implications for Candidate Countries

It appears therefore, that candidate countries are advised to consider the consequences of any such termination of their BITs for existing investments made by EU investors as well as future investments. This also raises the issue of any applicable sunset clauses that are contained in these existing extra-EU BITs with candidate countries.[30] A host of difficult legal questions thus arises: Will these sunset clauses also be declared to never have had any legal effect like the Termination Agreement for intra-EU BITs?[31] What would be the impact for pending or any new investment arbitration disputes?

Given that these and many other related issues remain unresolved regarding intra-EU BITs, it would seem highly advisable to include clear transitional provisions in any BITs of the candidate countries, guaranteeing the acquired rights of foreign investors, while simultaneously respecting EU law.

4.2 *Right to Regulate*

This re-orientation and re-balancing of the objectives of a BIT is also clearly visible in the rather detailed model clause on "Investment and Regulatory measures", which effectively contains a broadly formulated right to regulate.[32]

---

30 *See* Agreement on Promotion and Reciprocal Protection, Bosnia and Herzegovina-San Marino [hereinafter Bosn..& Herz.-San Marino BIT] 02 August 2011, Art.14 (4); *See* Agreement on Promotion and Protection of Investments Serb.-Can., Sep. 7, 2014 art. 42 (3).

31 *See* Agreement terminating intra-EU BIT s, *supra* (n 19), Arts. 2–3.

32 Model Clause, *supra* (n 1), at 7.

The model clause explicitly reaffirms the Contracting Parties' right to regulate for a long list of public policy objectives, which includes in addition to the usual reasons, (e.g., protection of health, environment and climate), interesting new ones such as privacy and data protection.

This model clause also intends to clarify some issues that have recently been decided by arbitral tribunals in various ways. For example, it is now clearly stated that there is no protection against regulatory changes by States, even if they negatively affect investments. Similarly, to avoid the flood of renewable energy cases against Spain and other Member States due to the withdrawal of subsidies for renewable energy producers,[33] the model clause explicitly states that the withdrawal of subsidies cannot constitute a breach of this treaty.

Moreover, probably as a reaction to the *Micula*[34] dispute, the model clause explicitly states that nothing in this agreement can prevent a contracting party from discontinuing a subsidy (in the form of state aid) or requesting the reimbursement of such subsidy, if so, obliged by the EC or the CJEU. Clearly, the intention of the EC is to prevent the repetition of those disputes and to avoid the legal problems that have arisen when EU law interferes with BIT obligations of the Member States.[35]

4.2.1 Implications for Candidate Countries

This broad provision stipulating the right to regulate, arguably provides more policy space and legal certainty for the candidate countries in the sense that they could adopt certain measures for the protection of public goods with significantly less exposure to potential ISDS claims from foreign investors. This is particularly true in case subsidies or state aid are reduced or withdrawn, which in the past has caused a high number of ISDS disputes against Spain, Italy, Romania and other EU Member States.

33 *See* Nikos Lavranos, *Report on Compliance with Investment Treaty Arbitration Awards 2023* (2nd ed.), October 2023; *See* Nikos Lavranos & Cornelis Verburg, *Recent Awards in Spanish Renewable Energy Cases and The Potential Consequences of the Judgment for Intra-EU ECT Arbitrations*, 3 European Investment Law and Arbitration Review, pp. 197–222 (2018).

34 *Ioan Micula, Viorel Micula, S.C. European Food S.A, S.C. Starmill S.R.L. and S.C. Multipack S.R.L. v. Romania [I]*, ICSID Case No. ARB/05/20, Final Award (11 December 2013).

35 Nikos Lavranos, *Regime Interaction in Investment Arbitration: EU Law; From Peaceful Co-Existence to Permanent Conflict*, Kluwer Arbitration Blog (13 February 2022) <https://arbitrationblog.kluwerarbitration.com/2022/01/13/regime-interaction-in-investment-arbitration-eu-law-from-peaceful-co-existence-to-permanent-conflict/> (accessed on 6 September 2024).

4.3 *Investment*

The model clause regarding the definition of investments appears to be very much aligned with Article 8.1 of CETA.[36] More important, however, is the explicit use of the *Salini*[37] criteria for characterizing the necessary elements of an investment. Accordingly, assets qualify as an "investment" only if they are of a certain duration, there is commitment of capital or other resources, and there is assumption of risks or the expectation of gain or profit.

While the *Salini* criteria (with variations) are nowadays generally accepted and discretionally applied by most arbitral tribunals – both in ICSID and non-ICSID disputes, the *Salini* criteria are not explicitly contained in all Member States' extra-EU BITs. For example, Dutch BITs typically simply define "investments" as follows:

> (a) the term "investments" means every kind of asset and more particularly, though not exclusively [...].[38]

followed by a non-exhaustive list of examples of the types of investments that fall within the scope of the BIT.

Thus, the explicit inclusion of the *Salini* criteria aligns the BITs with the current state of understanding as illustrated through the consistent jurisprudence of arbitral tribunals,[39] and is arguably, narrower than the broad definition contained in numerous BITs.

In addition, the model clause further restricts the definition of investment by explicitly excluding commercial transactions from the scope of the definition of "investments". More importantly, the model clause also explicitly excludes arbitral awards from the scope of definition of "investments", which effectively prevents commercial parties which finance and/or purchase such awards from relying on the provisions of the BIT.

4.4 *Investor*

The most important "innovation" as regards the definition of "investor" relates to the addition of the requirement of "*substantive business operations in the*

---

36 CETA, *supra* (n. 6).

37 *Salini Costruttori S.P.A. and Italstrade S.P.A. v. Kingdom of Morocco*, ICSID Case No. ARB/00/4, Decision on Jurisdiction, (23 July 2001).

38 *See* Agreement on Promotion and Protection of Investment, Netherlands-Bahrein, 5 February 2007, Art. 1.

39 *See* Darius Chan & Justin Lai, *Two decades after Salini v Morocco: The case for retaining the Salini test with modifications*, 39 Arb. Int. pp. 63–84 (2023).

territory of a Party".[40] This effectively excludes empty so-called "letter box" or "mailbox" companies from the scope of the definition of "investor".

While this is in line with CETA[41] and for example with the recent Dutch Model BIT text of 2019,[42] it is a significant restriction of the definition as contained in many current extra-EU Member States' BITs, which do not include such a requirement. This does not only affect Dutch extra-EU BITs but also for example German extra-EU BITs as the Germany-Trinidad and Tobago BIT illustrates. The latter requires that companies (investors) only be incorporated in Trinidad and Tobago or have their seats in Germany.[43] The same applies for example to the France-Iraq BIT (2010).[44]

4.4.1 Implications for Candidate Countries

In general, these definitional model clauses are not hugely innovative but rather incorporate the current jurisprudence of arbitral tribunals and mirror provisions which are not only found in the EU's investment treaties such as CETA, but also, for example, in the CPTPP[45] concluded by Asian countries. They rather reflect the general trend of clarifying and – in many cases – restricting the broad definitions that have been used in many existing extra-EU BITs of the Member States. As such, they provide a rebalancing to the advantage of the Contracting Parties, while at the same time excluding certain types of investments and investors.

Additionally, the right to regulate, which States already have under the existing extra-EU BITs, is reaffirmed more explicitly and more extensively, thereby providing significantly more policy space for Contracting Parties, while at the same time excluding such measures from the scope of the BIT. This is arguably a positive development for candidate countries, which should be considered as an invitation to align their existing BITs to the extent necessary. For example, the Bosnia-Herzegovina-Slovakia BIT (2008)[46] does not include the *Salini*

40 EU Model Clause, *supra* (n 1), at 4.

41 CETA, *supra* (n 5), Art. 8.1.

42 Netherlands Model BIT, *supra* (n 21), art. 1.

43 *See* Agreement concerning the Encouragement and Reciprocal Protection of Investments, Germany-Trinidad and Tobago, September 8, 2006, art 1 (4).

44 *See* Agreement on Promotion and Protection of Investments, France-Iraq October 31, 2010, art. 1 (2).

45 Comprehensive and Progressive Agreement for Trans-Pacific Partnership, 08 March 2018, 57 I.L.M.

46 Agreement for the Promotion and the Reciprocal Protection of the Investments, Bosnia and Herzegovina-Slovakia, 02 June 2008, Art. 1.

criteria nor the "substantive business activities" requirement. The same applies for example to the Bosnia-Herzegovina-San Marino BIT (2011).[47]

5 Model Clauses on Substantive Protection Standards

In this section, we will discuss the model clauses on the main substantive protection standards, such as fair and equitable treatment ("FET"), expropriation, taxation, transfer of capital as well as the general and security exception clause in more detail.

Despite fact that the model provisions on most favoured nation ("MFN") and national treatment ("NT"), do not contain any significant new elements as compared to those usually found in Member States' BITs, they have not been analysed.

5.1 *Fair and Equitable Treatment (FET)*

The FET provision has become one of the most important substantive investment protection standards on which investors have relied in most, if not all, ISDS cases. Due to its importance, FET has also developed into one of the most controversial provisions in BITs, which is partially because the FET standard has been interpreted in various ways, depending on the specificities of eachcase.

Generally, in EU Member States' BITs, the FET provision reads as follows:

> Each Contracting Party shall ensure fair and equitable treatment of the investments of investors of the other Contracting Party and shall not impair, by unreasonable or discriminatory measures, the operation, management, maintenance, use, enjoyment or disposal thereof by those investors. Each Contracting Party shall accord to such investments full physical security and protection.[48]

The recent Serbia-Turkey BIT (2022) contains even stronger language by including the wording "*at all times*":

> 2. Investments of investors of the State of each Contracting Party shall at *all times* be accorded fair and equitable treatment in accordance with

47 Bosn. & Herz.- San Marino BIT, *supra* (n. 29), Art. 1.

48 Agreement on encouragement and reciprocal protection of investments Netherlands-Armenia 05 June 2010, Art. 3.

> the principles of international law and full protection and security in the territory of the State of the other Contracting Party. Neither Contracting Party shall in any way impair the management, maintenance, use, operation, enjoyment, extension, sale, liquidation or disposal of such investments by unreasonable or discriminatory measures.[49] (emphasis added)

However, the broad FET standard faced resistance in North America soon after the first North American Free Trade Agreement ("NAFTA") awards were rendered in the late 1990s, which interpreted the FET standard broadly. In reaction to these awards, the NAFTA Contracting Parties adopted a Joint Interpretative Note in 2001,[50] in which they limited the level of protection of the FET standard to the minimum standard under customary international law.

The *Waste Management* NAFTA tribunal summarized the NAFTA FET standard as follows:

> Taken together, the S.D. Myers, Mondev, ADF and Loewen cases suggest that the minimum standard of treatment of fair and equitable treatment is infringed by conduct attributable to the State and harmful to the claimant if the conduct is:
> - arbitrary,
> - grossly unfair,
> - unjust or idiosyncratic,
> - is discriminatory and exposes the claimant to sectional or racial prejudice,
> - or involves a lack of due process leading to an outcome which offends judicial propriety – as might be the case with a manifest failure of natural justice in judicial proceedings
> - or a complete lack of transparency and candour in an administrative process.
>
> In applying this standard, it is relevant that the treatment is in breach of representations made by the host State which were reasonably relied on by the claimant.[51]

---

49 Agreement Concerning the Reciprocal Promotion and Protection of Investments, Türkye-Serbia [hereinafter Türk.-Serb. BIT], 07 September 2022, Art. 3.

50 The NAFTA Joint Interpretation (2001) explicitly restricted the level of protection under the FET and FPS to the minimum standard of treatments under customary international law.

51 *Waste Management, Inc. v. United Mexican States*, ICSID Case No. ARB(AF)/00/3, Award, para. 98 (03 April 2004).

Inspired by this NAFTA jurisprudence regarding the FET standard, Canada and the EU went one step further by introducing a closed list of specific FET breaches rather than the broadly formulated language found in EU Member States' BITs.

The model clause on "*Treatment of investors and covered investments*" contains a similar CETA-style closed list of potential FET breaches:

> Treatment of Investors and of Covered Investments
>
> 1. Each Party shall accord in its territory to covered investments and to investors of the other Party with respect to their covered investments fair and equitable treatment and full protection and security in accordance with paragraphs 2 to 5.
> 2. A Party breaches the obligation of fair and equitable treatment referenced in paragraph 1 through measures or series or measures that constitute:
>   a. denial of justice in judicial or administrative proceedings; or
>   b. fundamental breach of due process, including a fundamental breach of transparency in judicial and administrative proceedings; or
>   c. manifest arbitrariness; or
>   d. targeted discrimination on manifestly wrongful grounds, such as gender, race or religious belief; or
>   e. abusive treatment such as harassment, duress or coercion.
> 3. When determining a breach of paragraph 2, a tribunal may take into account whether a Party made a specific representation to an investor to induce a covered investment that created a legitimate expectation, upon which the investor relied in deciding to make or maintain the covered investment, but that the Party subsequently frustrated.
> 4. For greater certainty, "full protection and security" refers to the Party's obligations to ensure the physical security of investors and covered investments.
> 5. For greater certainty, a breach of another provision of this Agreement, or of any other international agreement, does not constitute a breach of this Article.

Accordingly, it is striking to note the high degree of similarity between the FET breaches mentioned by the NAFTA tribunals and the closed list of FET breaches in the model clause.

Consequently, only measures that fall within this closed list can be considered by the arbitral tribunal as possible FET breaches, which is significantly narrower than the broadly worded FET provision in EU Member States' BITs. In addition, the model clause contains further restrictions by prescribing to the arbitral tribunal that legitimate expectations cannot be considered as a standalone violation of the FET standard, but can only be considered as a relevant element when assessing the listed FET breaches.

Finally, the model clause also limits the scope of the full protection and security ("FPS") standard to physical security only, thereby excluding the broader definitions that arbitral tribunals have applied in the past in some cases.[52]

5.2 *Expropriation*

The model clause on expropriation is very similar to the one in CETA. As is commonly the case, this clause differentiates between direct and indirect expropriation. A standard EU Member States' BITs clause on expropriation reads as follows:

> Neither Contracting Party shall take any measures depriving, directly or indirectly, investors of the other Contracting Party of their investments unless the following conditions are complied with:
> a. the measures are taken in the public interest and under due process of law;
> b. the measures are not discriminatory or contrary to any undertaking which the Contracting Party which takes such measures may have given;
> c. the measures are taken against prompt, adequate and effective compensation and in case these measures are carried out in the Republic of Armenia compensation is paid in advance. Such compensation shall represent the genuine value of the investments affected, shall include interest at a normal commercial rate until the date of payment and shall, in order to be effective for the claimants, be paid and made transferable, without delay, to the country designated by the claimants concerned and in the currency of the country of which the claimants are investors or in any freely convertible currency accepted by the claimants.[53]

However, inspired by CETA, the model clause on expropriation refers to an "Annex to the Expropriation" clause dealing with indirect expropriation in particular, which introduces the most important difference compared to Member States' BITs. The relevant paragraph 3 reads as follows:

---

52 *See*, for example, *Biwater v. Tanzania*, ICSID Case No. ARB/05/22), Award, 24 July 2008, para. 7.29; *Siemens v. Argentina* (ICSID Case No. ARB/02/8) Award, 6 February 2007, para. 308.

53 Agreement on encouragement and reciprocal protection of investments, Netherlands-Armenia, 10 June 2005, Art. 6.

> For greater certainty, *except in the rare circumstance* when the impact of a measure or series of measures is so severe in light of its purpose that it appears manifestly excessive, non-discriminatory measures by a Party that are designed and applied to *protect legitimate policy objectives,* such as the protection of public health, social services, public education, safety, environment including climate change, public morals, social or consumer protection, privacy and data protection, or the promotion and protection of cultural diversity *do not constitute indirect expropriations.*[54] (emphasis added)

Accordingly, non-discriminatory measures for the protection of any kind of "*legitimate policy objectives*", such as for example the closure of fossil fuel power plants for the protection of the climate or the withdrawal of the permission for the exploitation of a gold mine for the protection of the environment,[55] could be adopted without running any risk of facing an ISDS claim – "except in rare circumstances".

Furthermore, the model clause also contains additional clarifying language regarding the valuation criteria for determining the damages as well as explicitly stating that the compensation shall include interest at a normal commercial rate until the date of payment.

5.3 *Taxation*

The model clause on taxation deviates significantly from the majority of recent taxation provisions incorporated in investment treaties. While many similarities exist with e.g., CETA and NAFTA, several differences in the model clause underline the EC's choice to deviate from the "norm" when it comes to taxation measures. Primarily, the model clause recognizes the supremacy of existing tax conventions over the provisions of the BIT. If there is any inconsistency between the BIT and a tax convention, the tax convention shall prevail.

Similarly, the "non–paper" (similar to CETA) allows for differentiation in taxation measures based on factors such as residency or investment location, provided that such differentiation does not lead to arbitrary discrimination or trade/investment restrictions. They also both permit the adoption and

54 EU Model Clause, *supra* (n 1), p. 32.

55 Such as for example the decision of the Dutch Government to shut down coal fired power plants, which resulted in the *RWE/UNIPER v. Netherlands* ECT dispute, (ICSID Case No. ARB/21/4), or Romania's decision to withdraw the permission for the exploitation of a gold mine which resulted in the *Gabriel Resources Ltd. v.. Romania* (ICSID Case No. ARB/15/31), Award, 8 March 2024. The *RWE/UNIPER* dispute has been withdrawn, while Romania prevailed over Gabriel Resources.

maintenance of taxation measures aimed at preventing tax avoidance or evasion in accordance with domestic laws or tax conventions. Importantly, and according to recent treaty practice, the model clause stipulates that nothing in the BIT shall affect the rights and obligations of either Party under any tax convention.

The non-paper contains a "general carve-out" according to which under no grounds will investors be eligible to enjoy the protection of the BIT in relation to taxation measures. To provide at least some kind of balance between investors and States, the clause conditions that the general "carve-out" is subject to the requirement that:

> such measures are not applied in a manner which would constitute a means of arbitrary or unjustifiable discrimination between countries where like conditions prevail, or a disguised restriction on trade and investment".

This contrasts with most BITs concluded after 2010,[56] which contain certain claw-back provisions, *i.e.,* exceptions that allow investors to bring a tax-related claims despite the tax carve-out, in particular claims concerning expropriation, FET etc.

Evidently, taxation remains a politically sensitive issue for any State because the authority to tax is one of the fundamental features of sovereignty.[57] Given that the number of tax-related disputes is steadily rising,[58] it seems that the EC has opted for a general taxation carve-out without exceptions, thereby minimizing the risk of tax-related disputes arising out of BITs, while permitting Member States to lawfully perform their regulatory and legislative functions regarding taxation.

5.4 *Transfer of Capital*

An often-overlooked protection standard is the right of investors to transfer their capital without restrictions and delays. For example, Article 5 of the Germany-Jordan BIT (2007) contains a typical transfer of capital provision found in many EU Member States' BITs, which unreservedly guarantees the right to capital transfer:

56 Danielle Morris et al, *Empirical Study: Tax-Related Measures in Investor-State Arbitration* 4 British Institute of International and Comparative Law and WilmerHale (2024).

57 Allison Christians, *Sovereignty, Taxation, and Social Contract*, 18 Minn. J. Int'l. L. 99, p. 104 (2009).

58 *Ibid.*

> *Free Transfer Each Contracting Party* ***shall guarantee to investors*** *of the other Contracting Party the free transfer of payments in connection with an investment, in particular:*
> a. *the principal and additional amounts to maintain or increase the investment;*
> b. *the returns;*
> c. *the repayment of loans;*
> d. *the proceeds from the liquidation or the sale of the whole or any part of the investment;*
> e. *the compensation provided for in Article 4.*[59] (emphasis added)

However, in sharp contrast to this provision, the model clause on capital transfers in the "non-paper" does not guarantee any longer the "right" to capital transfer but only obliges contracting parties to "*permit all transfers* [...] *without restriction or delay*". This is similar to Article 8.13 CETA. This is a significant deviation from the general European BIT practice, as is also illustrated by the language for example in the Bosnia-Herzegovina-San Marino BIT (2011) which provides that:

> each Contracting Party shall ensure the free transfer of payments".60 (emphasis added)

Because in the past, host states have used their powers to restrict the flow of capital in cases of financial crisis, the guarantee of unrestricted capital transfer is of particular importance for foreign investors. Consequently, the fact that this guarantee has now been diluted to a mere obligation "to permit" capital transfers is noteworthy. Indeed, this model clause confirms yet again that the "non-paper" is heavily inspired by CETA.

5.5 *General and Security Exceptions*

From the outset, it should be noted that most EU Member States' BITs do not contain any general or security exceptions clauses.[61] In contrast, the "non-paper" contains two separate exception clauses: (i) a general exception clause and (ii) a security exception clause.

---

59 Agreement concerning the Encouragement and Reciprocal Protection of Investments, Germany-Jordan, 13 November 2007 [hereinafter Ger-Jordan BIT].

60 Bosn. & Herz.-San Marino BIT, *supra* (n. 29), Art. 7.

61 Agreement on encouragement and reciprocal protection of investments, Netherlands-Cambodia, 26 June 2003; Germany-Jordan BIT, *supra* (n. 58).

5.5.1 General Exception Clause

The general exception clause stipulates that Contracting Parties are not prevented from adopting measures that are deemed necessary in pursuing to protect public security, public morals, public order, the environment and to ensure compliance with various laws and regulations – as long as they are not arbitrary or unjustifiably discriminatory. This model clause is almost identical to Article 28.3 of CETA, however, it contains a greater number of exceptions, for example including data protection and protection against fraudulent practices regarding contracts. It is also noteworthy that according to the commentary of the EC in the "non-paper", this general exception provision is modelled after Article XIV GATS. The EC highlights that the general exception clause also extends to the transfer of capital clause discussed in the previous paragraph.

5.5.2 Security Exception

Turning to the model clause regarding Security Exceptions, this clause effectively enables contracting parties to adopt measures which are considered to be necessary for the protection of "essential security interests." This applies in particular to the production or traffic in arms, ammunition, and other military (dual use) goods. In addition, the clause also covers measures taken in times of war or other emergency in international relations, including for the implementation of UN Security Council obligations. The security exception is becoming particularly relevant due to the ongoing wars in Ukraine and Gaza, as well as the increasing use of sanctions.

The inclusion of such a Security exception clause in Member States' BITs would also help to prevent a potential conflict between the right to free capital transfer of investors as discussed above and the obligation of EU Member States to implement UN Security Council sanctions (or EU sanctions adopted for the purpose of implementing UN sanctions). In fact, such a (potential) already arose more than a decade ago regarding several extra-EU BITs of three EU Member States, which did not include a Security exception thereby creating the risk that those EU Member States would be prevented from imposing sanctions freezing financial assets because of the free capital transfer provision contained in the respective BITs. Unsurprisingly, the CJEU found the EU Member States in breach of their EU law obligations and ordered them to take steps in resolving this potential conflict by either re-negotiating or terminating those BITs.[62]

62 *See*, Nikos Lavranos, *Case Note, Case C-205/06, Commission v. Austria; Case C-249/06, Commission v. Sweden; Case C-118/07, Commission v. Finland*, 103 Am. J. Int'l L., pp. 716–722 (2009).

The security exception has also featured in a different context, namely, in the context of economic distress and financial crisis. In the early 2000s when Argentina was at the brink of bankruptcy, it relied on the "essential security clause" of the Argentina-USA BIT to convert US dollar-denominated contracts into worthless Argentinian peso-denominated contracts.[63] However, in the ensuing arbitration proceedings initiated by US investors, the decisions of the arbitral tribunals have been divided. Whereas some arbitral tribunals interpreted the "essential security clause" in the Argentina-US BIT extensively by also covering severe economic problems which could endanger the very existence of the State and thus also its essential security interests, other tribunals interpreted the security exception clause much more narrowly and limited it to military aspects only.[64]

While neither the general exception nor the Security exception provision of the "non-paper" explicitly mentions economic distress as an exception, the "non-paper" deals with this aspect in specific provisions, such as the prudential carve-out for protecting the stability of the financial system, temporary safeguard measures and a separate Annex on public debt. These provisions effectively exclude ISDS claims against measures, which have been adopted for the protection of the financial system broadly understood.

5.6 *Implications for Candidate Countries*

As far as the model clauses of the "non-paper" regarding substantive protection standards is concerned, it can be concluded that their intention is to "cetarize" the EU Member States' BITs with third states as much as possible (i.e. to align the BIT substantive standards with the CETA provisions).

Generally, this means more policy space for host States, while at the same time, protection standards for investors are lowered. On the one hand, this will probably be welcomed by candidate countries as these model clauses clearly lower the risks of facing ISDS claims when adopting certain policy measures. On the other, the lowering of the protection standards could make the candidate countries less attractive for foreign investors and their investments. This could especially be the case if non-candidate countries are competing to attract the same investors by maintaining their old school BITs.

63 *See* Agreement Concerning the Reciprocal Encouragement and Protection of Investment, U.S.-Argentina, 14 November 1991, Art. XI.

64 *See* e.g., William J. Moon, Essential Security Interests in International Investment Agreements (10 April 2012), 15 Journal of International Economic Law 481 (2012), Available at SSRN: <https://ssrn.com/abstract=2039522>.

Moreover, given the unstable situation that has been unfolding since the start of the war in Ukraine, and more recently in Gaza, it seems that the EC has intended to protect Member States from situations that could potentially jeopardize their essential security interests by including explicit general and security exceptions. This gives Member States significantly more policy space for protecting their public policy and essential security interests without running the risk of facing ISDS claims.

6 Model Clauses on CSR, Environment, Change, Labour Climate

Consistent with recent EU free trade and investment agreements such as CETA, this "non-paper" contains several model clauses dealing specifically with CSR, environment, climate change and labour. Indeed, the commentary of the EC regarding the "*CSR and responsible business conduct*" model clause underlines the point that sustainable development is an essential part of the EU's trade and investment agenda, particularly by reinforcing and promoting the existing obligations regarding CSR and the protection of the environment, labour etc.

Given their recent development, it is unsurprising that most, if not all, existing Member States' BITs lack these types of provisions. As such, their inclusion in this "non-paper" is already of great significance and underlines their importance for the Member States' BITs.

6.1 *CSR and Responsible Business Conduct*

The CSR model clause reiterates first of all the due diligence obligations of investors as far as any adverse impacts of their investments are concerned. Second, the Contracting Parties of the BITs are called upon to promote the uptake by investors of relevant CSR practices in order to contribute to sustainable development and responsible investments.

Secondly, and more specifically, the contracting parties are called upon to support the dissemination and use of relevant internationally agreed instruments, such as the UN Global Compact, the UN Guiding Principles on Business and Human Rights, the ILO Tripartite Declaration of Principles concerning multinational enterprises and social policy and the OECD guidelines for multinational enterprises.

Thirdly, the contracting parties agree to exchange information and best practices regarding the above. Despite the increasing importance of CSR, it is notable that the language of this model clause is rather vague, non-committal, and without any negative consequences for failure to implement those obligations.

It does not go beyond what can be found in CETA, which was negotiated 10 years ago.

This can probably be (at least partially) explained by the fact that – in principle – CSR obligations are soft-law obligations, which are legally non-binding on the companies. Nonetheless, as the Dutch Model BIT (2019) illustrates, CSR obligations can be turned into hard-law obligations if investors which have been found to have violated those CSR obligations are "punished" by the arbitral tribunal by a reduction of the amount of compensation they would otherwise receive.[65] In this way, CSR obligations can actually "have teeth" and "bite" investors. Therefore, it seems strange that such a clause was not included as a model clause in the "non-paper".

6.2 *Investment and Environment*

The model clause on investment and environment contains two elements.

Firstly, it explicitly underlines the right of each contracting party to determine their sustainable development policies and priorities, and to establish the levels of domestic environmental protection they deem appropriate. This model clause is essentially part of the general "right to regulate" model clause discussed above.

Secondly, the contracting parties are prohibited to reduce the levels of protection regarding their environmental laws in order to attract investments. This is effectively a so-called "non-regression" clause, which should prevent contracting parties from starting a race to the bottom.

6.3 *Investment and Climate Change*

In contrast to the previous model clause on CSR and environment, this model clause on climate change imposes the explicit obligation on the contracting parties to "effectively implement the United Nations Framework Convention on Climate Change ("UNFCCC") and the Paris Agreement, including the commitments with regard to the Nationally Determined Contributions ("NDCs")".

It also calls upon the contracting parties to promote investments to assist the climate change mitigation and adaptation efforts, such as investments in renewable energy, low-carbon technologies, and energy efficient products and services.

The obligation to implement the Paris Agreement climate reduction targets is identical to the one that has been included in the draft modernized ECT

65 *See* Model BIT (Netherlands), *supra* (n 21) Art. 23.

text,[66] from which – ironically – the very same EU has recently decided to formally withdraw[67] and from which indeed several EU Member States have already done so.[68]

6.4 *Investment and Labour*

Consistent with CETA, the "non-paper" also contains a model clause provision on investment and labour, which effectively imposes a non-regression obligation on the contracting parties and explicitly requires that they implement the relevant ILO Conventions. Moreover, the contracting parties are called upon to promote other relevant ILO Declarations.

6.5 *Implications for Candidate Countries*

In sum, it seems that these model clauses on pressing societal issues are common and do not go beyond what is currently standard practice. In other words, they consolidate the recent trade and investment treaty practice of the EU, including CETA and the draft modernized ECT text, and reflect what has been included in recent model BIT texts of several EU Member States such as, for example, the Netherlands,[69] Belgium, and Luxembourg.[70]

Nonetheless, it is likely that most of the candidate countries would need to update their existing BITs in order to incorporate all those CSR, environment, climate, and labour obligations. For example, the very recent Serbia-Türkiye BIT (2022) does *not* include the obligation to implement the Paris Agreement or the ILO Conventions, while it *does* refer to the obligation to promote the relevant CSR standards.[71] Also, for example, the Denmark-Macedonia (the former Yugoslav Republic) BIT (2015) does not include any of those "modern" model clauses.[72] Therefore, it seems inevitable that the BITs of the candidate countries need to be significantly updated in this regard.

---

66 *See,* the modernized draft of the ECT <https://www.bilaterals.org/IMG/pdf/reformed_ect_text.pdf> accessed 02 July 2024.

67 Council of the EU, Press release, *Energy Charter Treaty: Council gives final green light to EU's withdrawal,* (30 May 2024) https://www.consilium.europa.eu/en/press/press-releases/2024/05/30/energy-charter-treaty-council-gives-final-green-light-to-eu-s-withdrawal/ (last visited June 13, 2024).

68 Poland, France, Germany, Luxembourg, Portugal, Slovenia, Spain, Ireland have formally withdrawn from the ECT. Italy withdrew from the ECT already as of 2016.

69 Nikos Lavranos & Adam Paschalidis, *supra* (n 22), at 89 – 123.

70 Max Kremer et al., *supra* (n 22), at 41–68.

71 Türk.-Serb. BIT, *supra* (n 48), art. 11.

72 Agreement for the Promotion and Reciprocal Protection of Investments, Den.-Maced., May 8, 2015.

7 ISDS–Related Provisions

For many years, the EU has been advocating that the current ISDS system has been suffering from "*a fundamental lack of trust*".[73] The EU had been actively negotiating alternative dispute resolution mechanisms with non–EU countries in the context of free trade agreements, which will allow investors to bring claims before independent tribunals against States for breaches of the agreements.[74]

The turning point, however, occurred when the CJEU ruled in *Achmea* that arbitration clauses in intra–EU BITs were contrary to EU law[75] because it strengthened the EU's argument that the traditional ISDS system allowed non-EU adjudicatory bodies to interpret and apply EU law without the possibility of requesting a preliminary ruling from the CJEU.

The model clauses contained in the "*ISDS – related Provisions*" section of the "non–paper" illustrate just that. The EC, through its model clauses, promotes the establishment of a multilateral dispute settlement mechanism which also includes an appellate mechanism. In addition, it addresses several procedural issues that will be discussed below. Surprisingly, however, the "non–paper" does not make any further references to the traditional ad hoc ISDS system. Rather, it simply suggests that

> [t]he Parties shall pursue with each other and other interested trading partners the establishment of a permanent multilateral investment court which includes an appellate mechanism" (emphasis added).

This wording unavoidably raises the question as to the future and fate of the *ad hoc* ISDS mechanism based on arbitration, which is neither explicitly forbidden nor limited for disputes arising out of BITs with third countries.

From the wording of the provisions in the "non-paper", it appears that the EC chose to maintain the current ISDS system – at least until the establishment of a Multilateral Investment Court (MIC), which, as we discuss below, is currently negotiated in UNCITRAL Working Group III. Thus, the "non-paper"

---

73 *Commission proposes new Investment Court System for TTIP and other EU trade and investment negotiations,* Press Release, (Sep. 15, 2015), https://ec.europa.eu/commission/presscorner/detail/en/IP_15_5651.

74 European Commission, Investment Disputes, https://policy.trade.ec.europa.eu/enforcement-and-protection/dispute-settlement/investment-disputes_en (last visited June 12, 2024).

75 *Achmea B.V. v. Slovak Republic, supra* (n 14).

covers only a specific set of procedural issues without, however, providing any further guidance as to its operation and the rules that will govern it.

7.1 *UNCITRAL Working Group III and Its Effect on the Model Clauses*

The scepticism of many States against the current ISDS system has led UNCITRAL to address these concerns by tasking its Working Group III with proposing reforms to the ISDS system.[76] The EU, having been very vocal about its opposition to the current ISDS system, proposed – among many other elements – the replacement of the existing system with a permanent court system, the MIC. The EU considers the MIC the "*only available option that effectively responds to all the concerns identified in the Working Group*"[77] and "*the only option that captures the intertwined nature of those concerns*".

Among other things, Working Group III has already adopted the Code of Conduct for Arbitrators in ISDS disputes,[78] as well as the Notes on ISDS Mediation and Guidelines for Mediation in ISDS.[79]

7.2 *The Multilateral Investment Court (MIC)*

While the negotiations in Working Group III regarding the MIC are becoming increasingly concrete,[80] the EU has already incorporated the Investment Court System (ICS) in several of its recent bilateral free trade and investments agreements, such as in CETA, the EU–Singapore Investment Protection Agreement[81] as well as the EU-Vietnam Investment Protection Agreement.[82] Interestingly, the EU–Mexico Agreement contains a provision on the Multilateral

76 U.N. Secretariat, Possible Reform of Investor-State Dispute Settlement (ISDS), at 2, U.N. Doc. A/CN.9/WG.III/WP.166/Add.1 (30 July 2019).

77 U.N. Secretariat, Possible Reform of Investor-State Dispute Settlement (ISDS): Submission from the European Union and Its Member States, U.N. Doc. A/CN.9/WG.III/WP.159 (18 January 2019).

78 *See generally*, UNCITRAL Code of Conduct for Arbitrators in International Investment Dispute Resolution (2024).

79 UNCITRAL, Report of Working Group. III (Investor-State Dispute Settlement Reform) on the Work of Its Forty-Sixth Session, Vienna, 9–13 Oct. 2023, U.N. Doc. A/CN.9/1160 (2023).

80 U.N. Secretariat, Possible Reform of Investor-State Dispute Settlement (ISDS): Draft Statute of a Standing mechanism for the resolution of international investment disputes – Note by the Secretariat, U.N. Doc. A/CN.9/WG.III/WP.239 (8 February 2024); U.N. Secretariat, Possible Reform of Investor-State Dispute Settlement (ISDS): Annotations to the Draft Statute of a Standing mechanism for the resolution of international investment disputes – Note by the Secretariat, U.N. Doc. A/CN.9/WG.III/WP.240 (10 February 2024).

81 Investment Protection Agreement, EU-Singapore, 15 October 2018, Art. 3.12.

82 Investment Protection Agreement, EU-Vietnam, 30 June 2019, Art. 3.14.

Dispute Settlement Mechanism, which is fairly similar to the one incorporated in the "non-paper".[83] The EU envisages the ICS as a blueprint for the MIC.[84]

As mentioned above, the model clause in the "non-paper" encourages the parties to the BIT to commit themselves to pursuing the establishment of a permanent MIC, which includes an appellate mechanism. This commitment promotes a collective effort to address concerns surrounding the currently fragmented nature of investment dispute resolution mechanisms. By advocating for a multilateral approach, the EC aims to enhance coherence, consistency, and predictability in the resolution of investment disputes.

The second paragraph of the model clause provides that upon the entry into force of an international agreement between the parties providing for such a MIC, the relevant parts of the agreement in question shall cease to apply. This provision effectively forces the EU Member States to replace the ISDS in their extra-EU BITs with the MIC once it has been established. This, however, raises an unavoidable question: how will this provision be interpreted in light of all existing sunset clauses, and what will be the fate of already initiated and pending cases?

7.3 *Ethics*

The idea to regulate the arbitrators' conduct and ethics has been long awaited. The inclusion of such a provision is consistent with the recent practice following the Working Group's discussions on the need to address concerns about the perceived lack of independence and impartiality among international arbitrators.

The model clause, which is similar to the respective provision in CETA, stipulates the requirement for arbitrators engaged in investment disputes to maintain independence, along with delineating procedures for arbitrator challenges, to be adjudicated by an impartial individual external to the arbitral tribunal. Notably, the model clause also mandates that appointed arbitrators must abstain from serving as legal representatives in any ongoing or prospective investment protection dispute under the BIT or any other agreement or domestic law.

Interestingly, while the draft article solely addresses arbitrators' independence, the accompanying annex introduces a "Code of Conduct for members of tribunals and mediators", which addresses both independence and

83 Investment Protection Agreement, EU-Mexico, 28 April 2020, Art. 14.

84 *See* Friedrich Rosenfeld, *The MIC*, in International Arbitration and EU Law, (Nikos Lavranos & Stefano Castagno eds., 2d ed., Elgar, 2024) Chapter 13.

impartiality. This model clause resembles Annex 29-B to CETA – albeit with some deviations.

The annex encompasses provisions concerning the impartiality and independence of arbitrators, along with imposing obligations of disclosure and confidentiality, extending to arbitrators' assistants. More specifically, Article 3 of the document establishes the disclosure obligations for candidates and members involved in dispute settlement proceedings. It mandates that candidates disclose any potential conflicts of interest, past or present relationships, or matters that could compromise their independence or impartiality prior to their appointment. This disclosure must cover a specified period preceding their consideration for appointment.

Furthermore, appointed members are required to continue disclosing such interests, relationships, or matters throughout their tenure and must promptly inform relevant parties of any breaches of disclosure obligations. Article 4 expands on the duties of members, emphasizing their independence, impartiality, and avoidance of bias. It outlines specific behaviour members must adhere to, including refraining from taking instructions from external entities, avoiding conflicts of interest, and performing their duties diligently and fairly. Article 5 outlines the obligations of former members, prohibiting them from involvement in related investment disputes for a specified period and restricting certain roles they can undertake in such disputes. Lastly, Article 6 addresses confidentiality, prohibiting the disclosure or use of non-public information acquired during proceedings and mandating the confidentiality of deliberations and tribunal decisions until their official publication.

In general, these provisions aim to uphold elevated levels of integrity and diligence, ensuring independence, impartiality, and efficiency in the adjudication of cases. Additionally, the annex delineates specific obligations applicable to former members of arbitral tribunals. It is anticipated that future revisions to the model clauses may incorporate amendments to this code of conduct, potentially referencing the code published by UNCITRAL in February 2024.

7.4 *Transparency*

The "non–paper" explicitly incorporates the UNCITRAL Rules on Transparency in Treaty-based Investor-State Arbitration. This does not come as a surprise, since the Rules constitute by now treaty practice and the EC had adopted them already in 2015 and has been illustrating its intention to promote transparency in ISDS by either including the UNCITRAL Rules verbatim or equivalent wide-ranging rules in several of its finalized treaties. Even prior to that, in 2014, the EC had proposed the application of the UNCITRAL Rules on Transparency to investment treaties that the EU and Member States have in place.

By incorporating these rules, parties to the arbitration are bound to adhere to the transparency standards outlined therein. Notwithstanding that, tribunals retain their discretion, given to them by the Rules to treat confidential or protected information differently. Consequently, confidential business information, information that, if disclosed, would impede law enforcement, or information that is protected against disclosure either by the relevant investment treaty, by the law of the respondent State, or by any law or rules deemed applicable by the tribunal, shall not be made public.

It is noteworthy that the article addresses the exchange of information between the EU and the respective Member State involved in arbitration proceedings. It unequivocally asserts that nothing within the agreement or applicable arbitration rules shall obstruct such exchanges. This provision underscores the importance of fostering communication and cooperation between the EU and its Member States but, more importantly, the obligation that Member States undertake to inform the EU of disputes that have been filed against them or against a third party.

8 Procedural Clauses

The above-mentioned model clauses have been the subject of extensive discussion in the context of Working Group III and have either been adopted or are still being debated. The EC has added several procedural model clauses to the ISDS chapter in the "non–paper" in order to set further promote the reform and harmonization of the ISDS procedural rules.

8.1 *Claims Manifestly without Legal Merit and Claims Unfounded as a Matter of Law*

The "non-paper" contains two provisions, the purpose of which is to disregard claims that either lack legal merit or are unfounded as a matter of law. In the first scenario, the EC included a model clause according to which objections should be filed within 30 days of the establishment of a tribunal or 30 days after becoming aware of the relevant facts. It seems that this provision was inspired by Article 41 of the 2022 ICSID Arbitration Rules. However, in contrast to the model clause, which does not provide any further guidance as to what might be a claim "manifestly without legal merit", Article 41 of the ICSID Rule specifies that "[t]he objection may relate to the substance of the claim, the jurisdiction of the Centre, or the competence of the Tribunal".

As a second "safety net", the EC proposes a mechanism according to which an arbitral tribunal will be able to address and decide as a preliminary question any objection by the Respondent State that, as a matter of law, a claim, or any part thereof, is not a claim for which an award in favour of the claimant may be made, even if the facts alleged were assumed to be true.

These "safety net" provisions aim at preventing the initiation of frivolous claims by allowing the Respondent State to object at an early stage and attempt the dismissal of the investor's case. This serves as a "prevention mechanism" towards investors, since the initiation of claims becomes more difficult and more prone to dismissal.

8.2 *Multiple Proceedings*

The ISDS provisions of the model clauses continue with an article dedicated to multiple proceedings for the purpose of avoiding double recovery, which raise issues of procedural justice.

According to the first paragraph, a tribunal is mandated to dismiss a claim if the claimant has initiated parallel proceedings in any domestic or international court or tribunal regarding the same treatment alleged to breach the respective BIT, unless the claimant withdraws the pending claim, with the exception interim injunctive or declaratory relief from a domestic court or tribunal. Thus, this model clause aims to address this risk by mandating the dismissal of claims filed concurrently in different fora. This risk arises due to the potential application of various legal frameworks when a single investor is impacted by a State's actions, each of which may entail distinct dispute resolution mechanisms. Accordingly, the claimant must furnish evidence demonstrating the withdrawal of any pending proceedings before any relevant court or tribunal, along with a declaration promising not to initiate further proceedings concerning the same treatment under domestic or international law.

The last paragraph of the model clause addresses a recurring issue in ISDS, which is the initiation of parallel proceedings stemming from the same loss or damage based on the complex ownership chain of the investment. This issue arises because investments are often structured through multiple entities. For that purpose, the provision extends the scope of the term "claimant" to include not only the investor, but also any locally established enterprise. Furthermore, it encompasses individuals with an ownership interest in or control over the investor or its locally established enterprise, who claim to have suffered identical loss or damage, thereby preventing multiple claims from different entities in the ownership chain for the same harm.

8.3 *Applicable Law and Rules of Interpretation*

Another interesting addition in the "non-paper" is the model clause on the applicable law and the rules on interpretation. According to that, tribunals are directed to apply the BIT in accordance with the Vienna Convention on the Law of Treaties ("VCLT") and other rules and principles of international law applicable between the parties.

Importantly, the domestic law of the contracting parties, including EU law, does not form part of the applicable law. This provision emphasizes the primacy of international law in interpreting and applying the agreement, ensuring uniformity and predictability in dispute resolution. The same article goes one step further and stipulates that tribunals shall not have jurisdiction to determine the legality of a measure under the domestic law (which includes EU law for EU Member States) of a Party. For greater certainty, in determining the consistency of a measure with this agreement, the tribunal may consider, as appropriate, the domestic law of a party as a matter of fact.

The wording of this clause is informed by the CJEU Opinion 1/17,[85] which found that the ISDS mechanism included in CETA was compatible with EU law, subject to certain conditions. The CJEU emphasized that the ISDS mechanism must not undermine the autonomy of the EU legal order or the jurisdiction of the CJEU to interpret and apply EU law.[86] Accordingly, the authority of investment tribunals should be limited to interpreting the international agreement rather than interpreting or applying EU law. Furthermore, the requirement for tribunals to follow the prevailing interpretation of domestic law by the relevant courts or authorities, as stipulated in the article, reflects a commitment to respecting the autonomy and authority of EU legal institutions – again in line with the principles enunciated in Opinion 1/17.[87]

8.4 *Implications for Candidate Countries*

The procedural model clauses contain a few standard clauses that follow recent investment treaty practices and a few innovative ones. As a general remark, candidate countries need to take into consideration that the standard for dismissal of claims is lower, while at the same time certain provisions leave states in an advantageous position.

However, the EU's reform proposals could appear as unattractive to (potential) foreign investors. Provisions such as the establishment of the MIC, even though innovative and potentially efficient, might intimidate investors since there is no certainty as to their exact implementation. The fact, however, that the "non–paper" refers to the establishment of the MIC without making any reference to ISDS provisions, whilst at the same time addresses issues such

85 Opinion 1/17, *supra* (n. 10), paras. 120 et seq.
86 *Ibid.*
87 *Ibid.*

as the independence and impartiality of arbitrators, might create confusion and uncertainty among investors and their legal advisors.

Bearing that in mind, it is noteworthy that the "non–paper" does not contain any provisions on security for costs or third-party funding. Given the fact that these topics are hotly debated in Working Group III as well as in arbitral decisions, this omission is surprising. In particular, states seem to increasingly ask tribunals to order security for costs against claimants who may appear not to be able to pay any incurred costs of states. Also, there is a clear trend that more transparency is imposed regarding the possible use of third-party funding by claimants in ISDS cases.

As such, this omission – which can be assumed to be deliberate – could potentially create additional obstacles for claimants and reduce the chances of potential claims to move forward. Consequently, it seems advisable if candidate countries go beyond the "non-paper" by explicitly including detailed provisions regarding these issues.

In sum, even though, the protection of States and their right to regulate is paramount, the Western world is currently competing and constantly attempting to attract new investors. To that end, a certain balance needs to be reached, which will on the one hand facilitate investments and safeguard the investors' rights while at the same time reducing the States' exposure to claims.

9 Conclusions / Outlook

The main takeaway from the analysis in this contribution is that the model clauses contained in the "non-paper" are largely reflecting the CETA clauses. As such they reflect the current investment treaty practice, arbitral jurisprudence as well as the results of UNCITRAL Working Group III. Indeed, it seems that they do not contain very innovative clauses. In other words, there are no huge surprises for the candidate countries. Nonetheless, compared to their existing BITs, the consequences for the candidate countries are probably very significant for various reasons.

First and foremost, all BITs between candidate countries and EU Member States will have to be terminated once full accession to the EU has been completed. This will also have implications for pending and new ISDS disputes, as well as for existing investments regarding the possible removal of the respective sunset clauses.

Second, and related to the first point, withdrawal from the ECT will also probably be going to be required from the candidate countries given the formal withdrawal of the EU[88] and several EU Member States and the meltdown of the draft modernized ECT text.

Third, candidate countries will inevitably have to embark on a review process of their existing BITs and start a re-negotiation programme for all BITs whose renewal date is upcoming with the view of implementing the model clauses of the "non-paper".

Fourth, this will arguably also require candidate countries to update their model BIT texts in close cooperation with the EC. In this way, the candidate countries signal to any potential new BIT contracting parties that the new model BIT text will be the starting point for new BIT negotiations.

Fifth, while many model clauses of the "non-paper" will most likely expand the policy space of the candidate countries, some provisions will impose additional obligations, particularly in the area of the protection of the environment and labour. These obligations could become burdensome and have negative implications for foreign investors but also in terms of regulatory implementation.

Finally, despite the clear aim of the "non-paper" to "cetarize" the Member States' BITs, it must be noted that neither CETA, nor the other EU investment agreements are yet in force. Therefore, it remains unclear how these model clauses would be interpreted and applied by arbitral tribunals, and more generally, what their implications will be – for both States and foreign investors. Therefore, it is suggested that each candidate country makes a careful balancing assessment when crafting the protection standards in their future BITs. This could also mean using slightly different language than is suggested in the "non-paper" or in some instances go beyond it.

Given that the accession process to the EU will take another couple of years, the candidate countries should use this time to align their BITs to these model clauses in order to avoid legal problems with the EC and the CJEU.

---

88 IA Reporter, *Analysis: EU publishes text of inter-se Declaration on non-applicability of ECT arbitration clause to intra-EU disputes*, (1 July 2024) <https://www.iareporter.com/articles/analysis-eu-publishes-text-of-inter-se-declaration-on-non-applicability-of-ect-arbitration-clause-to-intra-eu-disputes/>; IA Reporter, *EU notifies withdrawal from the ECT, following a declaration and agreement by the EU and its member states clarifying that ECT investor-state arbitration provisions do not apply in intra-EU context* (*27 June* 2024) <https://www.iareporter.com/articles/eu-member-states-sign-declaration-and-initial-agreement-clarifying-that-ect-investor-state-arbitration-provisions-do-not-apply-in-intra-eu-context/> accessed on 6 September 2024.

CHAPTER 6

The Modernization of International Investment Agreements in the Western Balkans: What Do the New Model BITs Tell Us?

Kabir Duggal, Kevin W. Gray, and Samiha Gopal

Clean your own yard before asking others to clean theirs.
Bosnian quote*

∴

1 Introduction[1]

Countries in the Western Balkans[2] have often been on the receiving end of the stick when it comes to investment treaty claims. They have been labelled the "usual defendants," especially in proceedings under European Bilateral Investment Treaties (BITs).[3] This is perhaps not particularly surprising, given that Balkan states are largely capital importing countries.[4]

The propensity of Western Balkan states to be respondents may also be explained by the fact that many of their older BITs contain unqualified investor

* Unofficial translation of the Bosnian quote: "Prvo očistite svoje dvorište prije nego tražite od drugih da čiste svoje."

1 The authors gratefully acknowledge the comments of Mark Feldman on an earlier draft of this article. All mistakes, naturally, remain their own.

2 For the purposes of this Chapter, we define the "Western Balkans" to include all states that made up Yugoslavia (other than those that have now acceded to the European Union), *viz.* Bosnia and Herzegovina, Kosovo, Montenegro, North Macedonia, and Serbia, as well as Albania.

3 Csongor Istvan Nagy, Introduction: Intra-EU BITs After *Achmea*–A Cross-Cutting Issue, in Csongor Nagy (ed.) Investment Arbitration in Central and Eastern Europe: Law and Practice (1st ed. 2019), at 2.

4 *Cf.* Christian Bellak & Markus Leibrecht Investor-State Disputes in Balkan, post-Soviet Union and Near and Middle East Countries: An Empirical Appraisal, Journal of Balkan and Near Eastern Studies 23(1) J. Near East and Balkan Studies 101–121 (2020) https://www.tandfonline.com/doi/full/10.1080/19448953.2020.1818037.

 | DOI:10.1163/9789004729889_007

protections and lack express provisions to protect a state's regulatory powers.[5] Most original BITs entered into by Western Balkan states followed the traditional European approach – short in length and containing generous and vague substantive provisions – at least as interpreted by tribunals.[6]

These treaties were meant to signal the openness of these newly independent, democratic states for foreign investors otherwise been reluctant to invest in transitional economies, especially as many of these countries were emerging out form a brutal war.

The effects of the generous investment regime established by BITs based on the old models has been felt by several states, and their risks are no longer theoretical. At least fifty treaty claims have been made against the relatively small economies of the Western Balkans since 1995.[7] Out of these, thirty-four were brought in the last 10 years, including fourteen since 2020 alone.[8] For example, the Bosnia and Herzegovina (BIH)-Slovenia BIT has led to a pending claim for over 750 million EUR.[9] In another recent case, an award was issued against BIH for violations related to an investment covered under the Energy Charter.[10] Montenegro faced a claim from an investor claiming that retroactive application of certain laws violated its right to "legal certainty,"[11] a subsidiary prong of the FET standard, while an award was made against Serbia for failing to uniformly enforce its legislation on the handling of hazardous animal by-products.[12]

5 UNCTAD, Phase 2 of IIA Reform: Modernizing the Existing Stock of Old-Generation Treaties, (IIA Issues Note 2, 2017) https://unctad.org/system/files/official-document/diaepcb2017d3_en.pdf (referring to older generation treaties as those entered into before 2010) (noting that "old generation" treaties "bite").

6 UNCTAD, Trends in the investment treaty regime and a reform toolbox for the energy transition (IIA issues note 2, 2023) https://unctad.org/publication/trends-investment-treaty-regime-and-reform-toolbox-energy-transition.

7 UNCTAD Investment Policy Hub, Investment Dispute Settlement Navigator, https://investmentpolicy.unctad.org/investment-dispute-settlement (listing out all publicly known ISDS claims), accessed March 31, 2024.

8 UNCTAD Investment Policy Hub, Investment Dispute Settlement Navigator, https://investmentpolicy.unctad.org/investment-dispute-settlement (listing out all publicly known ISDS claims), accessed March 31, 2024.

9 Elektrogospodarstvo Slovenije–razvoj in inzeniring d.o.o. v. Bosnia and Herzegovina, ICSID Case No. ARB/14/13 (EGS v BiH); Pramod Mittal and others v. Bosnia and Herzegovina (UNCITRAL).

10 Viaduct d.o.o. Portorož and Vladimir Zevnik v. Bosnia and Herzegovina, ICSID Case No. ARB/16/36 (Viaduct).

11 Addiko Bank AG v. Republic of Montenegro, ICSID Case No. ARB/17/35.

12 Zelena N.V. and Energo-Zelena d.o.o Inđija v. Republic of Serbia, ICSID Case No. ARB/14/27.

This chapter considers the evolution of Model BITs across several countries in the Western Balkans region. It divides such BITs into three periods. An early period, where BITs were drafted on the European model, a middle transition period, and the final period, where BITs reflected contemporary state concerns against the expansive interpretation of investment provisions. We provide three representative examples for each of the three periods. The North Macedonia Model BIT,[13] adopted in 2009, the first of the Model BITs examined in this chapter, is one of the last of the first-generation Model BITs (entered into prior to 2010) in the Western Balkans. It exemplifies the generosity of older BITs, even though in it we begin to see the introduction of carve outs and exceptions to investor protection standards. The Serbia Model BIT (2014)[14] symbolizes an intermediate step. Standards of protection are still provided for in broad terms, but there are exceptions and carve-outs, especially in response to positions adopted by investment arbitration tribunals. Finally, the Bosnia and Herzegovina (BIH) Model BIT, adopted in 2023,[15] reflects language used in new BITs that form part of modern investor-state relations. The BIH Model BIT contains sharply defined investor protections that reflect contemporary attitudes towards state obligations. Montenegro adopted a Model BIT in July 2021, but that draft model treaty has not yet been made public.

This chapter will chart the evolution of Model BITs in the Western Balkans, by examining earlier BITs, including the North Macedonia Model BIT of 2009, an old generation BIT in Part II,[16] moving on to the Serbia Model BIT of 2014, an intermediate step in Part III, and finally the BIH Model BIT of 2023 in Part IV. This evolution parallels the change in Balkan state attitudes to foreign direct investment. The older BITs generally track what might be termed the traditional European approach while the newer BITs reflect contemporary state concerns with this investment treaty regime. This chapter then concludes in Part V by exploring the possible consequences of the modernization of Model BITs in the Western Balkans, and what this might mean for the region, and the international investment community at large.

---

13 Model Agreement between the Republic of Macedonia and ____ concerning the Encouragement and Reciprocal Protection of Investments (2009) (North Macedonia Model BIT).

14 Model Agreement between Serbia and ____ on Reciprocal Promotion and Protection of Investments (2014) (Serbia Model BIT).

15 Model Agreement between Bosnia and Herzegovina and ____ on the Promotion and Protection of Investments (2023) (BiH Model BIT).

16 UNCTAD, Phase 2 of IIA Reform: Modernizing the Existing Stock of Old-Generation Treaties, (IIA Issues Note 2, 2017) https://unctad.org/system/files/official-document/diaepcb2017d3_en.pdf (referring to older generation treaties as those entered into before 2010).

2 First Generation BITs – the Example of North Macedonia

The BITs entered into by North Macedonia are an example of the early treaty practice of other countries in the Western Balkans. Treaties from the early period were meant to signal an openness of newly independent, democratic states for foreign investors who may have otherwise been reluctant to enter into these transitional markets.[17] These treaties, sometimes combined with the Energy Charter Treaty, form the basis of all the known ISDS cases filed against countries in the region.[18]

Very little has been written about North Macedonian investment policy, including state strategies for treaty drafting.[19] Most North Macedonian BITs were entered into in the first ten years after its split from Yugoslavia in 1991,[20]– perhaps signifying, like its former Yugoslav neighbors, its willingness to embrace market capitalism. North Macedonia adopted its Model BIT in 2009 at a turbulent time in the country's history. Most subsequent BITs entered into by North Macedonia have adhered to the model in large part, with a few variations.[21]

In 2009, a dispute with foreign investors in newly privatized state power supply company,[22] a newly elected government disputed its predecessor's approval of the sale of shares owned by the state pension fund in a large Serbian company,[23] and a large money-laundering scandal[24] led to North Macedonia's first ever BIT claims.

---

17 Some treaties were inherited from the former Yugoslavia, maintaining the old-generation provisions. This includes the BIT s with Canada and Montenegro.

18 UNCTAD report, *see* n 7. Most ISDS cases filed against Western Balkans states (76%) were initiated since 2013, with all but three of these cases based on treaties concluded before 2010. For BiH, the claims were based on a combination of BIT and ECT standards in *EGS v. BiH, see* n 8 and *Viaduct v. BiH, see* n 9.

19 Ivan Bimbilovski and Elizabeta Spiroska, Macedonia, in Csongor Nagy (ed.) Investment Arbitration in Central and Eastern Europe: Law and Practice (1st ed. 2019), 261 (lamenting the lack of research into ISDS in Macedonia, and the absence of coordinated state policy).

20 UNCTAD Investment Policy Hub, International Investment Agreements Navigator, North Macedonia, https://investmentpolicy.unctad.org/international-investment-agreements/countries/124/north-macedonia.

21 *Cf.* Ivan Bimbilovski and Elizabeta Spiroska, Macedonia, in Csongor Nagy (ed.) Investment Arbitration in Central and Eastern Europe: Law and Practice (1st ed. 2019), 262 (describing the general model of the various treaties entered into by North Macedonia).

22 EVN AG v. The Former Yugoslav Republic of Maced., ICSID, Case No. ARB/09/10.

23 Swisslion DOO Skopje v. The Former Yugoslav Republic of Maced., ICSID Case No. ARB/09/16.

24 Guardian Fiduciary Trust, Ltd, f/k/a Capital Conservator Savings & Loan, Ltd v. The Former Yugoslav Republic of Maced., ICSID Case No. ARB/12/31 (which arose out of events that took place in 2009).

2.1 *"Investor" and "Investment"*

The definition of "investments" in the North Macedonia Model BIT is asset-based, encompassing any kind of asset invested by an investor in the state, including money claims, contractual claims, and "any claims of a financial nature granted by law or agreement", as well as concession agreements in respect of natural resources.[25] The Model BIT also requires the asset to be invested "in accordance with the laws and regulations" of the host state, incorporating the legality requirement[26] into the definition.[27] Similarly, an "investor" under the Model BIT need only be a citizen of one of the Contracting Parties; no provision is made for dual nationals.[28]

Natural persons retain a lower threshold for jurisdiction under the treaty. Juristic persons, however, must both be "established or organized" in the host state and have their "seat and their main activities" in the host state.

2.2 *FET and MFN*

Like many contemporaneous BITs,[29] the North Macedonia Model BIT simply provides that the host state shall "ensure fair and equitable treatment" (FET) of investments and shall not "impair by discriminatory measures" the management of investments.[30] The clause makes no additional references to legitimate expectations or a minimum standard of treatment (MST) or to the full protection and security (FPS) standard.

The exclusion of FPS is odd, as every subsequent BIT entered into by North Macedonia contains reference to FPS[31] without qualification as to its scope.

---

25 North Macedonia Model BIT, Art. 1(1).

26 The requirement that an investment be made in accordance with host state laws is considered an additional requirement on top of the *Salini* factors; it has been applied, for example, in Phoenix Action, Ltd. v The Czech Republic, ICSIC Case No. ARB/06/5, but also rejected in other cases–*see,* Saba Fakes v Republic of Turkey, ICSID Case No. ARB/07/20.

27 North Macedonia Model BIT, Art. 1(1).

28 North Macedonia Model BIT, Art. 1(2)(a).

29 See, e.g., Agreement between the Government of Montenegro and the Government of Qatar for the Reciprocal Promotion and Protection of Investments (Montenegro–Qatar BIT) (2009), Art. 3; Agreement between Bosnia and Herzegovina and the Slovak Republic for the Promotion and Reciprocal Protection of Investments (BiH– Slovakia BIT) (2008), Art. 2; Agreement between the Republic of Serbia and the Portuguese Republic on the Mutual Promotion and Protection of Investments (Serbia–Portugal BIT) (2009), Art. 3.

30 North Macedonia Model BIT, Arts. 3(1), 3(2).

31 See, e.g., Agreement between the Slovak Republic and the Republic of Macedonia for the Promotion and Reciprocal Protection of Investments (North Macedonia–Slovakia BIT) (2009), Art. 2; Agreement between the Government of the Republic of Macedonia and the Government of the Kingdom of Morocco on the Reciprocal Promotion and Protection of Investments (North Macedonia–Morocco BIT) (2010), Art. 2(3); Agreement between

This leaves room for interpretation of the FPS standard to extend to more than just physical security, to include legal and economic security, which can constrain regulatory prerogatives.[32]

The FET protection is combined with most-favored nation (MFN) and national treatment (NT) standards, with the Model BIT providing that "[FET] shall not be less favourable than that granted by each Contracting Party to investments made by its own investors or by investors of a third State."[33]

Such compound clauses had the effect of blurring the lines between different investment protection standards and fortify the expectation of robust and unqualified investment protections, susceptible to broad interpretation. This was a feature common to the treaty practice of the Western Balkans at the time.[34]

2.3 *Expropriation*

The Model BIT covers both direct and indirect expropriation (extending to "any other measure having the same effect [as expropriation]").[35] IT carves out an exception for legal expropriation, which is defined as expropriation having been undertaken in the public interest, on a non-discriminatory basis, following "legal procedure," for effective and adequate compensation, which is termed to be the market value of the asset immediately prior to the expropriation or public knowledge of the expropriation.[36] The Model BIT also allows states to take measures to protect its essential security interests, as well as to deal with balance of payments and external financial issues.[37] Predictably, this

---

the Government of the Republic of Macedonia and the Government of the Republic of Kazakhstan on the Reciprocal Promotion and Protection of Investments (North Macedonia–Kazakhstan BIT) (2012), Art. 2(2).

32 UNCTAD, International Investment Agreements and Their Implication for Tax Measures: What Tax Policymakers Need to Know UNCTAD/DIAE/PCB/INF/2021/3 (2021) at 28, https://unctad.org/system/files/official-document/diaepcbinf2021d3_en.pdf (accessed May 10, 2024).

33 North Macedonia Model BIT, Arts. 3(1), 3(2).

34 See, e.g., Agreement between Montenegro and the Kingdom of Denmark concerning the Promotion and Reciprocal Protection of Investments (Montenegro–Denmark BIT) (2009), Art. 3. ("Each Contracting Party shall in its territory accord to investments made by investors of the other Contracting Party fair and equitable treatment which in no case shall be less favourable than that accorded to its own investors or to investors of any third state, whichever is the more favourable from the point of view of the investor.").

35 North Macedonia Model BIT, Art. 4(1).

36 North Macedonia Model BIT, Art. 4(1).

37 North Macedonia Model BIT, Art. 10.

provision has found expression in North Macedonia's BITs with other Balkan states and developing nations,[38] but not in its treaties with capital exporters.[39]

2.4 *Dispute Settlement*

The Model BIT provides that once a notice of dispute has been received in writing, parties must attempt to settle it by "friendly agreement" for at least six months from the date of the notice.[40] Upon the expiry of the consultation period, the investor is provided with the choice of forum for the dispute– before the courts of the host state, ad hoc arbitration under the UNCITRAL Rules, or institutional arbitration before ICSID.[41] While the Model BIT provides that the investor's election of remedies is definitive,[42] in practice, almost every investor-state dispute involving Macedonia has involved proceedings both before national courts and arbitral tribunals.[43]

3 Intermediate BITs – the Example of Serbia

Serbia, as the primary successor state of Yugoslavia, inherited many BITs from its predecessor.[44] Yugoslavia's BITs passed through three phases as part of the economic transition from socialism to capitalism.[45] Yugoslavia was one of the first communist states to move away from the Soviet orbit. As early as the 1970s, it began a policy shift signaling openness to Western investment. A

38 See, e.g., North Macedonia–Slovakia BIT (2009), Art. 12; Agreement between the Government of the Republic of Macedonia and the Government of Montenegro on Mutual Promotion and Protection of Investments (North Macedonia–Montenegro BIT) (2010), Art. 10; North Macedonia–Kazakhstan BIT (2012), Art. 12.

39 Agreement between the Macedonian Government and the Government of the Kingdom of Denmark for the Promotion and Reciprocal Protection of Investments (North Macedonia–Denmark BIT) (2015).

40 North Macedonia Model BIT, Art. 10(1).

41 North Macedonia Model BIT, Art. 10(2).

42 North Macedonia Model BIT, Art. 10(3).

43 EVN AG v. The Former Yugoslav Republic of Maced., ICSID Case No. ARB/09/10, Swisslion DOO Skopje v. Macedonia, ICSID Case No. ARB09/16, Guardian Fiduciary Trust, Ltd, f/k/a Capital Conservator Savings & Loan, Ltd v. The Former Yugoslav Republic of Maced., ICSID Case No. ARB/12/31. All of these cases were litigated before North Macedonian courts before proceeding to arbitration.

44 It was the successor as a matter of international law to many of the treaties of the former Yugoslavia.

45 Zoltan Vig and Gabor Hajdu, Serbia and Montenegro, in Csongor Nagy (ed.), Investment Arbitration in Central and Eastern Europe: Law and Practice (1st ed. 2019), 414, 415 (describing the three phases of BITs in post-communist Serbia).

second period occurred in the 1990s, during the wars in the former Yugoslavia and the contraction of the economy. Finally, after Slobodan Milosevic lost the elections in fall 2000 and was ultimately extradited to The Hague, the capitalist transition was largely completed, at least as concerned Serbia's entry into the global economic order.

New BITs from that period were drafted to signal maximum openness to foreign capital. Such BITs proved particularly problematic for Serbia. Almost all of the 15 treaty claims brought against Serbia were brough under BITs concluded in the late 1990s and early 2000s.[46]

Serbia adopted its new Model BIT in 2014. The Serbia Model BIT contains certain improvements over the traditional form of investment agreements that was used for Yugoslavian treaties, especially in respect of certain problems that arose for states in prior investment arbitrations. However, only five new BITs were concluded after the adoption of this new model, and as noted above, almost all new treaty disputes continue to be brought under the old generation BITs.[47]

The provisions of the Serbian model BIT represent an intermediate position in Balkan states' investment policy–wary of the wide-ranging claims brought by investors, yet not as strategic as modern state approaches.

3.1 *"Investor" and "Investment"*

Like the North Macedonia Model BIT, the Serbia Model BIT contains an asset-based definition of "investments," but also required that they be made in accordance with the laws and regulations of the host state.[48] In addition to this, there is a specific carve out for contracts for sales of goods and services, and extension of credit.[49] Adopting an element of the *Salini* test, the Model BIT also excludes assets that are not designed to lead to commercial benefits:[50]

The definition of investor has evolved from earlier BITs. Unlike the North Macedonia Model BIT, the Serbia Model BIT makes explicit provisions for natural persons who have dual citizenship in both the home and host states.

---

46 UNCTAD Investment Policy Hub, Investment Dispute Settlement Navigator–Serbia: Cases as Respondent State, https://investmentpolicy.unctad.org/investment-dispute-settlement/country/187/serbia/respondent, accessed March 31, 2024.

47 See, e.g., Coropi Holdings Limited, Kalemegdan Investments Limited and Erinn Bernard Broshko v. Republic of Serb., ICSID Case No. ARB/22/14 (arising out of the Serbia–Cyprus BIT (2005)); APG SGA SA and D.O.O. za promet i usluge Alma Quattro Beograd v. Republic of Serb., ICSID Case No. ARB/21/13 (arising out of the Serbia–Switzerland BIT (2005)).

48 Serbia Model BIT, Art. 1(1).

49 Serbia Model BIT, proviso to Art. 1(1).

50 Serbia Model BIT, Art. 1(1)(g).

TABLE 6.1 The definition of investment in the North Macedonia and Serbia Model BITS

North Macedonia Model BIT, Art. 1(1)	Serbia Model BIT, Art. 1(1)
"The term 'investment' shall mean any kind of asset invested by an investor of one Contracting Party in the territory of the other Contracting Party, in accordance with the laws and regulations of the Contracting Party in whose territory the investment is made and shall include in particular, though not exclusively: a) Movable and immovable property, guarantees and property rights, such as servitude, mortgages and other rights under the law; b) Shares in, stocks, debentures or any other form of participation in companies; c) Claims to money and claims under a contract having financial value and loans directly related to a specific investment; d) Copyrights, trademarks, patents or other intellectual or industrial property rights, know-how and goodwill; e) Any rights of a financial nature granted by law or agreement, such as concessions granted in accordance with applicable regulations, governing the performance."	"The term 'investment' shall mean every kind of assets directly invested by an investor of one Contracting Party in the territory of the other Contracting Party in accordance with the laws and regulations of the latter and in particular, though not exclusively, shall include: a) movable and immovable property and any other rights in rem such as mortgages, liens, pledges, usufructs and other; b) shares in companies, equity stocks as well as other kinds of securities with right of participation in companies; c) claims to money, related with an investment, under loan contract with a duration period of payment more than 5 years, in a form of subordinate claims; d) intellectual property rights (such as copyrights and related rights, patents, industrial designs or models, trademarks) as well as goodwill, technical processes and know-how; e) Public private partnership concluded in accordance with the laws and regulations of the Contracting Party in the territory whereof the investment is being made, including concessions to search for cultivate, extract or exploit natural resources. but "investment" does not mean f) claim to money that arises solely from: (a) commercial contracts, for sale of goods or services by investors in the territory of one Contracting Party to nationals or companies in the territory of the other Contracting Party, or

TABLE 6.1 The definition of investment in the North Macedonia and Serbia Model BITS (*Continued*)

North Macedonia Model BIT, Art. 1(1)	Serbia Model BIT, Art. 1(1)
	(b) the extension of credit in connection with a commercial transaction, referred to in subparagraph (a) of this Article; or g) any other form of investment that is not directed at gaining economic and other commercial benefit. A change in the form in which assets are invested shall not affect their character as investments."

The Model BIT provides that such persons shall be deemed to be exclusively nationals of the State Party to which they have permanent or temporary residence for a period longer than one year.[51] The Model BIT does not clarify which is the relevant period for the purpose of reckoning nationality. For example, is it the most recent year? Or would it be that any residency duration for longer than one year, would qualify? The lack of specificity would result in an indeterminate outcome for an investor who has residence in both home and host states for periods longer than on year.

However, this provision has not been adopted in any subsequent Serbian BITS. Some contain no references to dual citizens.[52] The Serbia–Qatar BIT applies to any individual who is a a "natural" of either State Party.[53] There are exceptions, of course – the Serbia–Canada BIT adopts a more structured effective nationality test, as is set out below.[54] The approach taken in

51 Serbia Model BIT, Art. 1(2)(b).

52 Agreement between the Government of the Republic of Turkey and the Government of the Republic of Serbia concerning the Reciprocal Promotion and Protection of Investments (Serbia–Turkiye BIT) (2018), Art. 1(1)(a); Agreement between the Government of the Republic of Turkey and the Government of the Republic of Serbia on the Reciprocal Promotion and Protection of Investments (Serbia–Turkiye BIT) (2022), Art. 1(1)(a).

53 Agreement between the Government of the Republic of Serbia and the Government of the State Qatar concerning the Reciprocal Promotion and Protection of Investments (Serbia–Qatar BIT) (2016), Art. 1(1)(a).

54 Agreement between Canada and the Government of the Republic of Serbia for the Promotion and Protection of Investments (Serbia–Canada BIT) (2014), §A, Art. 1, "national."

TABLE 6.2 Definition of investor in the Serbian Model BIT and the Serbia–Canada BIT

Serbia Model BIT, Art. 1(2)	Serbia–Canada BIT §A, Art. 1
"2. The term "investor" shall mean: (a) A natural person having the nationality of one Contracting Party and making investments in the territory of the other Contracting Party provided that the person is not a citizen of the other Contracting Party; (b) A natural person who is a dual citizen of the Republic of Serbia and ______ (the proposed counterparty) shall be deemed to be exclusively a national of the Contracting Party in which he have permanent or temporary resident (sic) for a period longer than one year;"	""**investor of a Party**" means a Party, or a national or an enterprise of a Party, that seeks to make, is making or has made an investment (…) "**national**" means: for Canada, a natural person who is a citizen or permanent resident of Canada; and for the Republic of Serbia, a natural person having the nationality of the Republic of Serbia; except that: (a) a natural person who is a dual citizen of Canada and the Republic of Serbia shall be deemed to be exclusively a national of the Party of his or her dominant and effective nationality; and (b) a natural person who is a citizen of one Party and a permanent resident of the other Party shall be deemed to be exclusively a national of the Party of his or her citizenship."

the Serbia–Canada BIT is very different from treaty practice in the Western Balkans at the time, as can be seen below:

Unlike the Serbia Model BIT, the Serbia–Canada BIT makes explicit mention of the "dominant and effective nationality" test that was developed in the context of public international law.[55] The effective nationality test requires

55 Nottebohm (Liech. v Guat.), 1955 I.C.J. 1 (Apr. 6). The test of effective nationality, while first developed in this case, has subsequently been used in private law adjudication by investment tribunals. For example, in *Michael Ballantine v. Dominican Republic*, PCA Case

that the individual claiming nationality demonstrate a genuine connection of existence, interests, and sentiments, together with the existence of reciprocal rights and duties.[56] This is a more demanding requirement than the test set out in the Serbia Model BIT, and the other Serbian BIT's that follow the Model BIT.

With respect to corporations, the Model BIT requires both that the investor corporation be incorporated in the host state, but also that it has substantial business activities in the host state (a combination of the incorporation and place of business test).[57] This provision is bolstered by the fact that the Model BIT also contains a denial of benefits clause. That clause provides that a host state may deny benefits of the BIT to an investor who has no substantial business activities in the home state.[58] Taken together, the Serbian Model BIT contains a strong requirement that investors brining treaty claims actually have their business seat in the home state.

Apart from having substantial business activities in the host state, the Model BIT also requires that the corporation not be directly or indirectly owned by citizens of the host state.[59] his last requirement provided prescient. In 2017, Serbia faced a treaty claim from a Cypriot investment vehicle that was beneficially owned by a Serbian citizen.[60] However, the claim has been brought under the Serbia–Cyprus BIT, which does not contain this proscription,[61] leaving Serbia without the protection of the clause as formulated in the Model BIT.

3.2 *FET and FPS*

The Serbian Model BIT provides explicitly for both FET and FPS. ("investments (…) shall be accorded fair and equitable protection and shall enjoy full

No. 2016-17, the tribunal dismissed a claim against the Dominican Republic under the U.S.–Dominican Republic BIT, by concluding that the claimants' effective nationality was Dominican.

56 Nottebohm (Liech. v Guat.), 1955 I.C.J. 1 (Apr. 6).

57 The *siege social* test, as developed in various cases, including in *Alps Finance and Trade AG v The Slovak Republic,* Preliminary Redacted version of Award (2011), https://www.italaw.com/sites/default/files/case-documents/ita0027.pdf, requires that corporate investors prove that they prove that the state of incorporation is the effective center of administration of business operations, including by showing the locations of board meetings, employees working in the country of operations, the maintenance of a physical location, etc.

58 Serbia Model BIT, Art. 12.

59 Serbia Model BIT, Art. 1(2)(c).

60 Mera Investment Fund Limited v. Republic of Serb., ICSID Case No. ARB/17/2.

61 Agreement between Serbia and Montenegro and the Republic of Cyprus on Reciprocal Promotion and Protection of Investments (Serbia–Cyprus BIT) (2005), Art. 1(3)(b).

protection and security (…)"),[62] even if both of these standards are circumscribed. Art. 2(3) sets out the instances which are deemed to be violations of the FET protection: (a) a denial of justice, (b) fundamental breach of due process, (c) manifest arbitrariness, (d) targeted discrimination, and (e) abusive treatment.

This wording is almost identical to the FET clause in CETA,[63] and has been used in other model BITs that aim to limit the breadth of the FET standard.[64] This formulation is seen to be an evolution on the unqualified "fair and equitable treatment" language in BITs. However, whether these enumerations actually limit BIT claims remains to be seen, since the enumerations themselves contain language that is broad and prone to expansive interpretation. In any case, this provision has not made it into any BIT entered into by Serbia so far.

With respect to FPS, the model BIT clearly provides that the protection does not extend to changes in laws and regulations; however, it does not link the FPS standard to MST or customary international law.[65]

3.3 *MFN and NT*

The model BIT contains standard language incorporating the MFN and NT standards,[66] and also specifically provides that provisions from other international agreements may be imported into and "prevail over" the BIT, if they are more favorable.[67] However, the Model BIT also contains two clauses excluding the importation dispute resolution clauses from other international agreements.[68] As a result, it appears to have been designed to permit only the importation of substantive provisions.

3.4 *Expropriation*

Direct and indirect expropriation are subject to somewhat different standards in the Serbia Model BIT. Treaty protections extend to both direct and indirect

---

62 Serbia Model BIT, Art. 2(2).

63 Comprehensive Economic Trade Agreement between Canada and the European Union (CETA), Art. 8.10(2).

64 See, e.g., Bilateral Investment Treaty between the Government of the Republic of India and ____ (India Model BIT) (2015), Art. 3.

65 Serbia Model BIT, Art. 2(4).

66 Serbia Model BIT, Art. 3(1) ("Each Contracting Party shall in its territory accord investments of the other Contracting Party with equal treatment that it accords to investments of its own investors or to investments of investors of any third state, whichever is the more favourable.").

67 Serbia Model BIT, Art. 15(1).

68 Serbia Model BIT, Arts. 3(2).

expropriation, with a carve out for measures taken in public interest, following due process, on a non-discriminatory basis, and affording compensation at the market value immediately before the expropriation / knowledge of the expropriation became public.[69] In addition, a claim of expropriation is required to be submitted to a judicial authority of the host state, which will decide the investor's rights.[70]

While making this determination, the authority is required to consider (a) the economic impact of the expropriation, (b) the extent to which "reasonable investment-backed expectations" are interfered with, and (c) the character of the expropriatory measures.[71] "Reasonable investment-backed expectations" seems to be a reference to the doctrine of legitimate expectations,[72] which is sometimes used to determine whether there has been a breach of the FET standard. It will likely form part of an expropriation analysis.

Moreover, the intermediate judicial determination is made mandatory before a treaty arbitration for expropriation can be initiated.[73] Besides this, indirect expropriation is also clearly stated to not constitute measures taken with public welfare objectives. It is unclear whether this exception applies independently of the requirement for all legal expropriations to have public policy motives, along with other due process requirements, or whether a public-oriented indirect expropriation need no adhere to due process or offer compensation.

3.5 *ESG-Related Provisions*

In response to environmental concerns and human-rights-related backlash to the ISDS system, many newer treaties have begun to introduce environmental, social, and governance (ESG) provisions.[74] The Serbia Model BIT includes certain corporate social responsibility (CSR) and ESG provisions. Article 10 states that the States Party should "encourage" corporations within their borders to voluntarily adopt standards of corporate social responsibility.[75]

---

69 Serbia Model BIT, Arts. 6(1), 6(2).

70 Serbia Model BIT, Art. 6(3) and Art. 14(5).

71 Serbia Model BIT, Art. 6(4).

72 See, e.g., LG&E Energy Corp. v Arg. Republic, ICSID Case. No. ARB/02/1 (noting that legitimate expectations are created when a state makes specific commitments relating to an investment that an investor relies on).

73 Serbia Model BIT, Art. 14(5).

74 Jesse Coleman, *Modern Provisions in Investment Treaties,* Columbia Centre for Sustainable Investment (2020) https://scholarship.law.columbia.edu/cgi/viewcontent.cgi?article=1202&context=sustainable_investment_staffpubs (accessed March 31st, 2024).

75 Serbia Model BIT, Art. 10.

Similarly, Article 9 bars either State Party from relaxing or offering to derogate from health and environmental regulations in order to attract investment.[76] These provisions are voluntary and do not condition the receipt of treaty benefits upon compliance.[77]

3.6 *ISDS*

The ISDS provision in the Serbia Model BIT is similarly structured to the North Macedonia Model BIT. It requires a six-month negotiation period, following which either party may opt for resolution through (a) domestic courts, (b), ad hoc UNCITRAL arbitration, (c) ICSID arbitration, or (d) ICC institutional arbitration.[78] It is conceivable, therefore, that the state respondent would be able to determine the forum for dispute settlement. As noted in the discussion on the MFN clause, the model also bars the importation of dispute settlement provisions from other treaties,[79] which would probably only be useful to an investor in the event that the state was able to pre-empt the investor by opting for resolution through local courts. The respondent state's ability to elect the remedy is not adopted in any subsequent BIT, however.

4 Modern BITs – the Example of Bosnia and Herzegovina

In the fall of 2023, Bosnia and Herzegovina adopted its most recent Model Bilateral Investment Treaty (BIH Model BIT). The text of the Model BIT reflects BIH's attempt to implement a new reformist agenda, which attempted to eliminate the largest risks to the state contained in investment treaties, focusing in large part on ISDS.

BIH is a signatory to 42 known investment treaties or treaties containing investment protections.[80] Of those, 37 are BITs–these treaties were drafted as typical European-style investment treaties, characterized by their short form

76 Serbia Model BIT, Art. 9.

77 This is similar to that contained in other contemporaneous Model BITs. See, e.g., India Model BIT (2015), Art. 12, which contains non-binding language encouraging parties to "endeavour to voluntarily incorporate internationally recognized standards of corporate social responsibility in their practices and internal policies."

78 Serbia Model BIT, Art. 14.

79 Serbia Model BIT, Art. 15(2).

80 UNCTAD Investment Policy Hub, Country Navigator–Bosnia and Herzegovina <https://investmentpolicy.unctad.org/international-investment-agreements/countries/25/bosnia-and-herzegovina?type=bits> accessed 14 December 2023.

and the standard, generous set of substantive and procedural provisions formulated in vague terms.[81] The modern Model BIT attempts to change this.

4.1 *"Investor" and "Investment"*

Bosnia's older treaties did not include any express language that could prevent covered investors from taking advantage of the treaty protections (e.g. by dual nationals claiming coverage or mailbox companies).[82] The definitions of investment and investor in the new BiH Model BIT impose greater restrictions on qualifying investors and investments. Under, the new BiH Model BIT Art. 1(2):

> The term "investor" means with regard to either Contracting Party: any natural person having the nationality and permanent residence of the Home State under its applicable law. A natural person who is dual national shall be deemed to be exclusively a national of the Contracting Party of his/her dominant and effective nationality; any legal person constituted under the law of the Home State, other than a branch and representative office, and has its seat together with substantial business activities in the territory of the Home State.[83]

---

81 UNCTAD, 'Trends in the investment treaty regime and a reform toolbox for the energy transition' (IIA issues note 2, 2023) <https://unctad.org/publication/trends-investment-treaty-regime-and-reform-toolbox-energy-transition> accessed 14 December 2023. European-style investment treaties ae mostly characterized by their short form and broad provisions, as compared to US-style treaties, such as NAFTA and the USMCA which are more comprehensive as they relate to both trade and investment. However, recent EU treaty practice has evolved in two ways: first, such treaties tend to contain to more detailed provisions, including trade and investment chapters; second, following *Achmea*, focus has been placed on adopting an investment court.

82 Arbitral tribunals and national courts have taken diverging positions on whether dual nationals can file ISDS claims against a state of one of its nationalities. For the most part, tribunals have held that broad BIT provisions neither preclude nor explicitly allow claims by dual nationals, as a result of which they look to the ICSID Convention (1965), The Vienna Convention on the Law of Treaties (1969), or the standard of dominant or effective nationality (for example, Raimundo J Santamarta Devis v Bolivarian Republic of Venezuela, PCA Case No. 2020-56; Serafín García Armas and Karina García Gruber v. Bolivarian Republic of Venezuela, PCA Case No. 2013-3; Burimi SRL and Eagle Games SH.A v. Republic of Alb., ICSID Case No. ARB/11/18; Paris Court of Appeals in Tan Tao Investment & Industry Corp v. Vietnam, (September 2023). The tribunals in *Santamarta* and *Serafin* came to different conclusions, based on the same applicable treaty (the BIT between Spain and Venezuela). The definition adopted in the BiH Model BIT is in line with the provisions of CETA, Art. 8.1.

83 BiH Model BIT, Art. 1(2), Model BIT.

Older BITs apply an "asset-based" definition of investments, creating high exposure risks for ISDS, because this language may cover unexpected asset types, as well as transactions with a dubious relation to the host state's economic development.[84] The newer definition of investment combines the legality requirement (i.e. establishment in accordance with the laws of the host state), with the additional standards known under the *Salini* test:[85] contribution of capital, certain duration, assumption of risks, expectation of profit, as well the contribution to the economic development of the government.[86]

Furthermore, the definition requires that the investor and its investments conduct of substantial business activities in the host state, along with indicators of substantial business activity, which may be helpful in future interpretations and application of the provision.[87] These include the number of qualified employees, registered office or administration in the home state, and annual turnover.[88] The provision explicitly excludes claims to money arising solely out of commercial contracts, as well as their financing and judgments or awards from such transactions, as well as financial instruments traded on non-regulated markets.[89]

This higher standard was designed to provide clarity and attempts to avoid the risk of opportunistic and frivolous claims.[90] Any investor seeking to file a claim against the host state would have the burden of proving their eligibility under these standards, in order to gain access to the available dispute resolution mechanism under the treaty.

---

84 UNCTAD, International Investment Agreements and Their Implication for Tax Measures: What Tax Policymakers Need to Know UNCTAD/DIAE/PCB/INF/2021/3 (2021), https://unctad.org/system/files/official-document/diaepcbinf2021d3_en.pdf (accessed May 10, 2024).

85 Salini Costruttori S.p.A. and Italstrade S.p.A. v. Kingdom of Morocco [I], ICSID Case No. ARB/00/4.

86 BiH Model BIT (2023), Art. 1(1). The *Salini* test is also adopted in recent EU treaty practice as reflected in the CETA (2016), Art. 8.1; EU–Singapore Investment Protection Agreement (2018), Art. 1.2.1 EU–Vietnam Investment Protection Agreement (2019), Art. 1.2(h).

87 BiH Model BIT (2023), Art. 1(1).

88 BiH Model BIT (2023), Art. 1(1). The *Salini* test is also adopted in recent EU treaty practice as reflected in the CETA (2016), Art. 8.1 EU–Singapore Investment Protection Agreement (2018), Art. 1.2.1 EU–Vietnam Investment Protection Agreement (2019), Art. 1.2(h).

89 The BiH BIT lists futures, swaps, forwards, options, and other derivatives in this category. BiH Model BIT (2023), Art. 1(2).

90 Ministry of Foreign Trade and Economic Relations BIH, 'Principles and standards of investment protection in the treaties for the promotion and protection of investments concluded by Bosnia and Herzegovina' (2023).

TABLE 6.3 Features of the definitions of investment and investors in the North Macedonian, Serbian and BiH Model BITs

Category	North Macedonia Model BIT	Serbia Model BIT	BiH Model BIT
Asset-based definition of "investment"	X	X	X
Incorporates all *Salini* requirements into definition of "investor"			X
Excludes sale of goods / services transactions		X	X
Excludes private equity investments and investments in derivative instruments			X
Provision to determine nationality of dual nationals		X	X
Nationality of dual national is determined by test of dominant and effective nationality			X
Requires juristic persons to have "substantial business activities" in the host state	X	X	X
Enumerates requirements to be fulfilled to demonstrate substantial business activities			X

4.2 *FET and FPS*

Consistent with the global trends, FET was the most frequently invoked and most successful claim made against Bosnia (with or without other standards). As earlier treaties contained no carve-outs or exception, they allowed claims for, *inter alia*, denial of justice, interference with investments, violations of legitimate expectations, and lack of transparency.[91]

91 For example, the claimants in the *Aggarwal* case alleged that the government engaged in a series of retaliatory measures following the investor's complaints of misrepresentations in the privatization prospectus for a state-owned insurance company, on which the investors relied in purchasing 50% of the company shares. Such measures included alleged raids of the company premises and the referral of potential users to competitors. In *Viaduct* the investors alleged that the government failed to issue the necessary permits,

Typical FET clauses contained a promise of fair and equitable treatment, often coupled to offers of full protection and security (FPS) and non-discrimination (generally, most favored nation and national treatment clauses). The problem with such clauses is that they tended to blur the lines between different investment protection standards.

Conversely, the FET standard in the new Model BIT is inspired by the CETA model. It contains an exhaustive list of potential violations, including denial of justice, due process and transparency, manifest arbitrariness, targeted discrimination on manifestly wrongful grounds, and abusive treatment.[92] There is one additional provisions included in the BIH Model BIT: the frustration of legitimate expectations, but restricts it to situations where the investor received clear and specific representations or commitments from the government, and where the investor can show that the expectations were central for its decision to invest or maintain its investment.[93]

FPS clauses in Bosnia's old-generation BITs were similarly susceptible to broad interpretations by foreign investors and arbitral tribunals, as they did not limit its scope to physical protection.[94] For example, the investors in the *Pramod Mittal* case alleged a violation of FPS, even though the claims related to shareholder rights and alleged political interference with the investment.[95]

---

or to approve proposed alterations of the construction project under the concession agreement.

92 BiH Model BIT, *Art.* 5(2). In addition to CETA (2016), Art. 8.10.2, the EU also included this closed list in the EU–Singapore Investment Protection Agreement (2018), Art. 2.4.2 and the Investment Protection Agreement between the European Union and its Member States, and the Socialist Republic of Viet Nam (2019) (EU–Vietnam Investment Protection Agreement), Art. 2.5.2.

93 BiH Model BIT (2023), *Art.* 5(2).

94 Agreement between the Belgo-Luxembourg Economic Union and Bosnia and Herzegovina on the Reciprocal Promotion and Protection of Investments (2004) (BiH–BLEU BIT), Art. 3 ("Except for measures required to maintain public order, such investments shall enjoy continuous protection and security, excluding any unjustified or discriminatory measure which could hinder, either in law or in practice, the management, maintenance, use, possession or liquidation thereof."). But see, Agreement on Encouragement and Reciprocal Protection of Investments between Bosnia and Herzegovina and the Kingdom of the Netherlands (1998) (BiH-Netherlands BIT), Art. 3, which guarantees 'full physical security and protection.' , and Agreement between the Republic of San Marino and Bosnia and Herzegovina on the Promotion and Reciprocal Protection of Investments (2011) (BiH-San Marino BIT), Art. 3 (the FPS clause in the BiH-San Marino BIT even provides that each treaty party shall 'extend in its territory full legal protection and security' to the investors of the other treaty party).

95 The claimants initiated *ad hoc* arbitral proceedings under the UNCITRAL Arbitration Rules in April 2023, based on the BiH-India BIT. The BiH government is in the process of retaining external counsel and the outcome is not known on this issue, or the

TABLE 6.4 Features of the FET and FPS provisions in the North Macedonian, Serbian and BiH Model BITS

Category	North Macedonia Model BIT	Serbia Model BIT	BiH Model BIT
Unqualified definition of FET	X		
FET is clubbed with MFN and NT	X		
Follows CETA Model of enumerated instances of FET breaches		X	X
Frustration of legitimate expectations enumerated as a breach of the FET standard			X
Provides for FPS		X	X
Limits FPS to physical protection only		X	X
Provides that breaches of other provisions of BIT are not breaches of FPS			X

The new Model BIT provides instead that the FPS standard refers to the Contracting Party's obligations relating only to physical security of investors and investments."[96] Furthermore, the breach of another provision of the BIT or domestic law of a treaty party do not quality as a breach of FET or FPS, creating a self-contained framework for interpretation.

4.3 *MFN and NT*

Bosnia's earlier BITs did not require that the treatment be limited to "like circumstances" or clarify whether they excluded dispute resolution clauses from the scope of MFN.

---

appointment of the tribunal. Council of Ministers BiH, 'Report from the 19th Regular Session of the Council of Ministers of Bosnia and Herzegovina' (25 July 2023); Council of Ministers BiH, 'Reports from the 28th and 29th Regular Sessions of the Council of Ministers of Bosnia and Herzegovina' (20 November 2023) <https://www.vijeceministara.gov.ba/saopstenja/sjednice/saopstenja_sa_sjednica/default.aspx?id=41864&langTag=bs-BA> accessed 14 December 2023.

96 BiH Model BIT (2023) *Art.* 5(3). This is consistent with the EU treaty practice in the CETA (2016), Art. 8.10.5; the Investment Protection Agreement between the European Union and its Member States, and the Republic of Singapore, (2018) (EU–Singapore Investment Protection Agreement), Art. 2.4.5; and the EU–Vietnam Investment Protection Agreement (2019), Art. 2.5.5.

The new BIH Model BIT contains MFN and NT provisions which attempt to address the deficiencies of the old-generation treaties and fills potential interpretative gaps which have been highlighted in previous ISDS jurisprudence.[97] It attempts to reduce the risk of investors circumventing the higher thresholds for FET, FPS and indirect expropriation claims, or the multi-layered and more demanding criteria for accessing ISDS.

4.4 *Expropriation*

Bosnia's first-generation BITs contained no guidance on the scope of provisions on expropriation or the threshold triggering a right to compensation. As with FET, indirect expropriation provisions did not contain carve outs for legitimate state measures or public interest and contained very few general exception clauses.[98] Moreover, the provisions were generally drafted in general terms, forbidding direct takings of property and measures with equivalent effect, immediately followed by the formula for the compensation of lawful expropriation.[99]

The BIH Model BIT limits the scope of claims for indirect expropriation. As drafted, the provision states that:

> [I]ndirect expropriation occurs if a measure or series of measures of a Contracting Party has an effect equivalent to direct expropriation, in that it substantially deprives the investor of the fundamental attributes of property in its investment, including the right to use, enjoy and dispose of its investment, without a formal transfer of title or outright seizure.[100]

97 BiH Model BIT (2023), Art. 6.

98 The essential security exception is provided in the BITs BiH concluded with Finland, India, and Qatar, while the general exception clause is featured in the BITs with India and Spain. See, Agreement between Bosnia and Herzegovina and the Republic of India for the Promotion and Protection of Investments (2006) (BiH–India BIT), Agreement on the Promotion and Protection of Investments between the Government of the Republic of Finland and Bosnia and Herzegovina (2000) (BiH–Finland BIT), Agreement on the Promotion and Reciprocal Protection of Investments between Bosnia and Herzegovina and Spain (2002) (BiH–Spain BIT), Agreement concerning the Reciprocal Promotion and Protection of Investments between Bosnia and Herzegovina and the Government of the State Qatar (1998) (BiH–Qatar BIT), Art. 7.

99 Agreement between Bosnia and Herzegovina and the Republic of Slovenia for the Reciprocal Promotion and Protection of Investments (2001) (BiH–Slovenia, BIT), Art. 5; BiH–Netherlands BIT, Art. 3; Agreement on the Promotion and Reciprocal Protection of Investments between Bosnia and Herzegovina and the Kingdom of Denmark (2004) (BiH–Denmark BIT), Art. 4; BiH Qatar BIT, Art. 5.

100 BiH Model BIT (2023), Art. 7.

It additionally provides a list of factors that arbitral tribunals should consider in their assessment of allegations of indirect expropriation, including the economic effects of challenged measures, their object, context and intent, as well as any reasonable, investment-backed expectations.[101] Furthermore, there is an exception for any measures taken in good faith and for a public purpose (including health, environment and climate change), provided that the measures are non-discriminatory and not excessive.[102] Finally, it contains an exception to measures that are compliant with the TRIPS Agreement.[103] The provision attempts to bring Bosnia's future treaties into lines with approaches accepted under international law, while also protecting the state's ability to take measures in the public interest which may be tantamount to expropriation, without incurring liability for compensation.

4.5 *ESG-Related Provisions*

As with many modern investment agreements, the treaty contains broader provisions on corporate social responsibility and environmental protection. Investors are required in specific to comply with domestic laws on "human rights, environmental protection and labour laws."[104] Additionally, it includes as interpretative principles several soft law instruments, including the OECD Guidelines for Multinational Enterprises, the United Nations Guiding Principles on Business and Human Rights, and the Recommendation CM/REC(2016) of the Committee of Ministers to Member States on human rights and business.[105]

With respect to climate change, the BIH Model BIT (2023) calls on states parties to comply with the United Nations Framework Convention on Climate

101 BiH Model BIT (2023), Art. 7(7). Such a provision exists in the CETA (2016), Annex 8-A, para 2; the EU–Singapore Investment Protection Agreement (2018), Annex 1, para 2; and the EU–Vietnam Investment Protection Agreement (2019), Annex 4, para 2.

102 BiH Model BIT (2023), Art. 7(8). This is consistent with the EU–Singapore Investment Protection Agreement (2018), Annex 1, para 2; and EU–Vietnam Investment Protection Agreement (2019), Annex 4, para 3.

103 Ibid. Art. 7(9–10). 'TRIPS Agreement' refers to the Agreement on Trade-Related Aspects of Intellectual Property Rights in Annex 1C to the WTO Agreements. This reference is also made in the CETA (2016), Art. 8.12.5-6a; EU–Singapore, Art. 2.6.3, and Annex 3c; EU–Vietnam Investment Protection Agreement, Art. 2.7.4. The EU treaties further clarify that a measure inconsistent with the TRIPS agreement would still not, in and of itself, amount to an expropriation.

104 BiH Model BIT (2023), Art. 16(1).

105 BiH Model BIT (2023), Art. 16(2).

Change (UNFCCC).[106] Arbitral tribunals are required, in ISDS proceedings, to apply the commitments of the parties to preventing climate change.[107]

4.6 *Other Provisions*

All ISDS cases to date against Bosnia have related to investment contracts and concessions. For that reason, umbrella clauses have provided further avenues for foreign investors to transform contract claims into ISDS disputes and to claim treaty protections.[108] For example, the *Viaduct* case related to a concession agreement for the construction, operation and maintenance of two hydro power plants on the Vrbas river, while in *EGS v BiH,*[109] which is still pending, the investor alleged a breach of an agreement for the construction of a power plant unit, which also entitled the investor to a share of the electricity output.[110] The BIH Model BIT does not provide for an umbrella clause, which should limit the investor's pursuit of contractual claims to the forum stipulated in the relevant investment contacts.

Older treaties contained sunset clauses, which extended investment protection standards and dispute resolution clauses to protected investors for substantial periods of time following treaty termination. In the case of BIH BITS, these sunset clauses range from 5 to 20 years.[111] As a result, the new Model BIT

106 BiH Model BIT (2023), Art. 17(1).

107 BiH Model BIT (2023), Art. 17(3).

108 Agreement between the Republic of Austria and Bosnia and Herzegovina for the Promotion and Protection of Investments (2000) (BiH–Austria BIT), Art. 9 'Other Obligations–Each Contracting Party shall observe any obligation it may have entered into with regard to specific investments by investors of the other Contracting Party.' Umbrella clauses are featured in 16 BiH BIT s, including the treaties with the United Kingdom, Qatar, Finland, Switzerland, Iran, Italy, Hungary, Denmark, etc. See, e.g., *EGS v. BiH.*

109 Elektrogospodarstvo Slovenije – razvoj in inzeniring d.o.o. v. Bosnia and Herzegovina, ICSID Case No. ARB/14/13 (*EGS v BiH*).

110 Viaduct d.o.o. Portorož and Vladimir Zevnik v. Bosn. & Herz., ICSID Case No. ARB/16/36.

111 20-year sunset clauses are provided in the BiH BIT s with Finland, France, Kuwait, Germany; 15-year sunset clauses are provided in the BiH BIT s with the United Kingdom, India, Canada, the Netherlands; 10-year sunset clauses are provided in 30 BiH BIT s, including those with Slovenia, Malaysia, San Marino, Switzerland, Portugal; a 5 year sunset clause was provided in the BiH BIT with Italy (running currently until 2025, after the treaty was terminated in 2020). It was the 15-year sunset clause in the BIT between BiH and India that enabled the *Pramod Mittal* investors to file their claim 4 years after its termination. The BiH-India BIT was terminated in the wave of treaty terminations India conducted in the aftermath of the *White Industries Australia Limited v. The Republic of India* case. The treaty was terminated in 2019 but remains in effect for investments made before the termination for another 15 years (until 2034).

contains a much shorter window–five years–for treaty protections.[112] In fact, the 5-year sunset clause in the BIH Model BIT is shorter than the similar clause in the CETA, or in the modernized ECT (both of which maintained the 20-year clause).[113]

4.7 *ISDS*

Older BITs contained reactive ISDS clauses which largely left the initiation and dynamics of the dispute resolution process to foreign investors. Under these treaties, the state gave advance consent to arbitration, and would engage with the investor only after the notice of dispute, when the cooling-off period was triggered and opportunities for dispute prevention or mitigation were all but lost.[114] However, there were no formal requirements, and typically no duty on the part of investors to meaningfully engage with host state institutions prior to engaging in adversarial proceedings, which is exactly the area in which BIH identified areas of concern in previous cases.[115]

The new Model BIT addresses this challenge through a robust ISDS framework. It first excludes all investments acquired illegally or through abusive corporate restructuring.[116] The same provision also applies the *Broche* test to investors who are state-owned enterprises.[117]

Additionally the BIH Model BIT provides concrete instructions for the pre-dispute phase, with a mandatory cooling-off period and consultation phase.[118] The request for consultations must include details identifying the investor, specifying the treaty provisions allegedly breached by a state measure, and the relevant factual and legal background of the claim, as well as the relief

112 BiH Model BIT (2023), Art. 34.

113 CETA, Art. 30.9; Proposal for the Modernized ECT Text (2022) <https://www.bilaterals.org/IMG/pdf/reformed_ect_text.pdf> accessed 14 December 2023.

114 BiH–Austria BIT, Art. 10; BiH–Netherlands BIT, Art. 9; BiH–Qatar BIT, Art. 8; Agreement between Bosnia and Herzegovina and the Swiss Confederation on the Promotion and Reciprocal Protection of Investments (2003) (BiH–Switzerland BIT), Art. 9; BiH–Denmark BIT, Art. 8 'Any dispute concerning an investment between an investor of one Contracting Party and the other Contracting Party shall, if possible, be settled amicably.'

115 For example, Art. 10 of the BiH-Germany BIT simply provides that the parties should attempt amicable settlement for 6 months, and if this attempt is not successful, the investor can initiate ICSID arbitration, unless the parties agree to another forum.

116 BiH Model BIT (2023), Arts 11, 25(1).

117 BiH Model BIT (2023), Art. 25(1)(d).

118 Old-generation ISDS clauses generally establish a timeframe (usually between three to six months) for the disputing parties to attempt amicable settlement, following which the investor can proceed to arbitration. For example, Art. 10 of the BiH-Germany BIT only provides a 6-month cooling off period, following which the investor can file for ICSID arbitration.

sought.[119] Claimants must prove their status as investor, their home state, and their ownership over their investment. The ISDS clause also establishes time limits for specific claims, including the preclusion of claims related to the same measure that have been notified for consultations, but have not been pursued in arbitration after 18 months.[120] Consultations and arbitral proceedings would be suspended in case the parties decide to attempt amicable settlement at any point of the proceedings.[121]

If the parties are unable to resolve the dispute in the cooling-off stage, the investor can submit the claim to the competent national courts or arbitration under the ICSID Convention, *ad hoc* arbitration under the UNCITRAL Rules, or other rules agreed to by the parties.[122] The claims can only relate to the alleged treaty breaches identified in the request for consultations.[123] In keeping with modern treaties, it requires disclosure of third-party funding.[124]

Finally, the ISDS clause limits the applicable law exclusively to the provisions of the treaty and international law, as interpreted under the Vienna Convention on the Law of Treaties.[125] With respect to the EU, although the EU has replaced investment arbitration with an investment court system in recent treaties, BIH has opted to maintain ISDS in an improved form in its Model BIT. However, the Model BIT provides that the ISDS clause would no longer be valid for disputes with EU investors upon its accession to the EU.[126]

5 Conclusion

Treaty practice across the Western Balkans has evolved in line with evaluations seen at the international level. Older BITs–brief and loosely worded–were designed to attract FDI. Over time, expansive interpretations by tribunals prompted state response. Newer agreements incorporate best practices and

119 BiH Model BIT (2023), Art. 19.

120 BiH Model BIT (2023), Art. 19.

121 Ibid.

122 BiH Model BIT (2023), Art. 20(1).

123 Ibid Art. 20(2).

124 BiH Model BIT (2023), Art. 22(3).

125 Ibid. Art. 24(1).

126 The EU has announced multilateral efforts to establish a standing investment court within and beyond its borders, which would replace the bilateral systems established in its recent treaty practice. *See,* e.g., the Joint Interpretive Statement of the EU and Canada issued in the context of the CETA negotiations <http://data.consilium.europa.eu/doc/document/ST-13541-2016-INIT/en/pdf> (accessed 27 April 2024).

more sharply defined provisions, reflecting a global trend towards a more balanced investor-state relationship. In addition, these new models have been formulated to ready states for accession to the EU.

The Western Balkans experience is a microcosm of the ongoing dialogue surrounding ISDS and the importance of clear, calibrated agreements that foster both investor confidence and state sovereignty. This ongoing evolution will be crucial as the Western Balkans navigate their path towards European integration and a more robust investment climate.

CHAPTER 7

Navigating Definitions of "Investor" and "Investment" and Jurisdictional Issues in the Context of ISDS

A Study on Investment Protection Frameworks and Jurisprudence in the Western Balkans

Vlora Maxhuni

1 Introduction

The main goal of international investment treaties negotiated by the Western Balkan ("WB") countries is to enhance economic cooperation between the contracting parties by promoting and protecting investments made by nationals of one contracting party in the territory of the other.[1] The success of this objective, to a certain extent, depends on the definitions of "investment" and "investor" in international investment agreements ("IIAs") and investment protection laws.

The WB investment protection framework generally provides broad definitions with lenient and unclear criteria for "investor" and "investment." This has resulted in legal uncertainties and the protection of unintended categories of "investors" and "investments." The aim of this study is to reveal the categories of "investors" and "investments" covered by the legal framework of WB Economies and expose the risks associated with the definitions of the current investment protection framework in the WB region.

This chapter is divided into two main sections: the definition of "investor" and the definition of "investment." Each section will unfold the various practices of these definitions present in the bilateral investment treaties ("BITs")

1 *See* the preambles of the international investment agreement signed by WB countries, e.g. Agreement on Reciprocal Promotion and Protection of Investments, Alb.-Qatar., Oct. 18, 2011.; *See* the Agreement on Promotion and Reciprocal Protection of Investments, Bosn. & Herz.-San Marino., Aug. 2, 2011.; *See* Agreement on Promotion and Reciprocal Protection of Investments, Azer. – Croat., Oct. 2, 2007.; *See also* Agreement for the Promotion and Protection of Investments, Kos.-Can., Mar. 6, 2018.

 | DOI:10.1163/9789004729889_008

negotiated by the WB Economies[2] and their respective laws on investment protection. This study is based on the analysis of over 150 BITs; however, given that the same definitions have been replicated in numerous BITs, only 57 selected BITs are referred to for illustrative purposes.

Each section will offer a comprehensive analysis of the key jurisdictional issues (ratione personae and ratione materiae) addressed in the ISDS jurisprudence of the Western Balkan countries.[3]

Finally, the chapter will offer insights and recommendations on overcoming issues associated with the current investment protection framework's definitions of "investor" and "investment," aiming to safeguard the best interests of both foreign investors and WB Economies in accordance with best international practices.

2 General Aspects of the Definition of "Investor"

The definition of "investor," referred to as the ratione personae aspect of a claim, sets forth the categories of persons entitled to investment protection under a particular investment treaty or law. The majority of the BITs negotiated by the WB Economies provide broad definitions and low thresholds for natural and legal persons to qualify as investors, fostering opportunities for "nationality shopping." As a consequence, numerous disputes were initiated by nationals of the respondent states, including high-profile individuals in the respective countries, or by companies that did not have sufficient links with their home States or were owned by nationals of the country where investment is made. In some of these disputes, jurisdiction (ratione personae) was successfully established.

The following subsections will address the criteria for natural and legal persons as provided in the current investment protection framework in the WB countries, as well as the jurisdictional issues (ratione personae) examined in ISDS case law involving these countries.

2.1 *Natural Persons*

BITs negotiated by the WB countries provide for a low threshold for natural persons, requiring only that the investor has the nationality of the other

2 Geographically, WB countries include Albania, Bosnia & Herzegovina, Croatia, Kosovo, Montenegro, North Macedonia, and Serbia.

3 Due to the non-availability of materials for the disputes against Bosnia & Herzegovina, its case law is not addressed in this study.

contracting party.[4] Few BITs exhibit greater caution by including additional criteria, such as requesting that the natural person also has "permanent residence,"[5] "domicile,"[6] or "principal place of business"[7] in the home State. Very few treaties explicitly exclude dual nationals from receiving treaty protection.[8]

It is noteworthy to observe the contrasting provisions of the Kosovo-Austria BIT concluded in 2010, and the BIT concluded between the Former Yugoslav Republic ("FYR") and Austria in 1989, which was ratified by Kosovo in 2011.[9] While the BIT of 2010 refers to the "dominant and effective nationality"[10] the succeeded BIT provides a lower threshold by simply requiring that the investor has the nationality of the other contracting party.[11]

Broad definitions have also been employed in national laws on the protection of foreign investments. In Albania[12] and Montenegro,[13] two alternative criteria are required: nationality of a foreign country (without excluding dual nationals) or permanent domicile abroad. According to Serbian investment law, an investor is a domestic or foreign person who has made a direct or indirect investment in Serbia.[14]

Kosovo's Law on Sustainable Investments covers investments of both Kosovars and foreigners.[15] It upholds the principle of "equality before the law," providing that foreign investors have the same rights and obligations as

4 *See* Agreement on the Promotion and Reciprocal Protection of Investments, Croat.-Arg., art 8(2)(a), Dec. 2, 1994.; *See also* Agreement on the Reciprocal Promotion and Protection of Investments, Jul. 14, 1995, North Maced.-Turk., art. I (2)(a); *See also* Agreement on the Reciprocal Promotion and Protection of Investments, Kaz.-North Maced., Art 1. para. 2, Jul. 2, 2012.

5 *See* Agreement on the Reciprocal Promotion and Protection of Investments, Bosn. & Herz.-Alb., Art. 1 (2) (i), June 17, 2008.

6 *See* Agreement on the Promotion and the Reciprocal Protection of Investments, Kos.-Switz., Art. 1(2)(a), Oct. 27, 2011.

7 *See* Agreement on the Reciprocal Promotion and Protection of Investments, Bosn. & Herz. – Slovn., Art. 1 (2), May, 30, 2001.

8 *See* Agreement for the Reciprocal Promotion and Protection of Investments, Croat.-Isr., art. 1(3), Aug. 8, 2000, *See also* Agreement on Reciprocal Promotion and Protection of Investments, Serb.&Mont. – Isr., art. 1(5)(a), Jul. 28, 2004.

9 Ratification of the Agreements Listed on the Exchange of Notes to Undertake Bilateral Agreements Concluded Between the R. of Austria and the Former SFRY, Kos.-Austria, https://gzk.rks-gov.net/ActDocumentDetail.aspx?ActID=8543.

10 Agreement on Promotion and Protection of Investments, Kos.-Austria, art, 1(1) (a), Jan. 22, 2010.

11 *Supra* note 9, art. 1(2)(a).

12 Foreign Investment Law, art.1(a)(b), (1993) (Alb.).

13 Foreign Investment Law, art. 2, (2011) (Montenegro).

14 Law on Investments, art. 3(2), (2015) (Serb.).

15 Law on Sustainable Investments (Kos.).

domestic investors. This includes the right to initiate ISDS proceedings and use the same methods to resolve investment disputes.[16]

BiH's foreign investment law employs a narrower definition, covering only natural persons who are not residents of Bosnia and Herzegovina or have their principal place of business therein; it also covers its nationals as long as they do not reside in BiH and have their principal place of business elsewhere.[17]

2.1.1 Case Law

Two cases were initiated by dual nationals against Kosovo, both filed in the International Chambers of Commerce ("ICC"), namely *Selmani v. Kosovo* and *Devolli v. Kosovo*, under the Kosovo Law on Foreign Investment of 2014 ("2014 LFI").

In *Selmani v. Kosovo*, the Claimant, Mr. Bedri Selmani, a former member of the Parliament of Kosovo and a dual national of Croatia and Kosovo, initiated the proceedings as a Croatian national. The Respondent argued that the Tribunal lacked jurisdiction ratione personae, as the Claimant's "dominant and effective" nationality is Kosovo.[18]

The Tribunal rejected the Respondent's invitation to apply the "dominant and effective nationality" stipulated in Article 17, paragraph 2 (the Applicable Law to Investment Disputes) of the 2014 LFI, which, in its relevant part, provides:

> The court or arbitral tribunal considering an Investment Dispute shall determine the issues in dispute in accordance with the substantive rules or laws agreed upon by the parties in writing. 2. In the absence of such an agreement, the court or arbitral tribunal shall apply the substantive law applicable in the Republic of Kosovo – excluding the private international law rules thereof – and such rules of public international law as may be applicable to the issues in dispute.[19]

The Tribunal considered that since the 2014 LFI is a domestic instrument, its definitions should not be interpreted by reference to customary international law. The Tribunal emphasized that article 17.2 of the 2014 LFI only applies to substantive matters and not to interpreting the definitions section of the

16 *Id.* art. 6.
17 Law on the Policy of Foreign Direct Investment, art. 2 (Bosn. & Herz.).
18 Bedri Selmani v. Republic of Kosovo, Case No. 24443/MHM/HBH, para. 277, (2022) (ICC Int'l Ct. Arb).
19 Law on Foreign Investment, art. 17(2) (2014), (Kos).

legislation, "as those definitions pertain to issues of jurisdiction or specifically to interpreting the Assembly's chosen definition of "foreign person," reflected in the wording of Article 2.1.3.1."[20] Consequently, the Tribunal accepted that the Claimant's Croatian citizenship qualifies him as a foreign person under the 2014 LFI, regardless of his Kosovar nationality. In *Devolli v. Kosovo*, a case brought forward by a prominent Kosovar businessman alleging to qualify as a foreign investor based on his Montenegrin nationality, the Tribunal reached an opposite conclusion to the Tribunal in *Selmani v. Kosovo*. It considered that the Claimant did not qualify as a foreign investor and consequently dismissed the claims.[21]

In *Mihaljevic v. Croatia*, a case initiated at ICSID under the Croatia-Germany BIT by a dual national of Croatia and Germany, the Respondent argued that the Tribunal lacked jurisdiction due to the Claimant's dual nationality, arguing that the negative requirement of Article 25 (2) (a) of the ICSID Convention was not met.[22] The Claimant argued that he had successfully initiated the renunciation of Croatian citizenship prior to filing the Request for Arbitration ("RA"), but due to the delays on the Respondent's side, the renunciation was not completed successfully prior to the filing of the RA.[23]

The Tribunal dismissed the claims for lack of jurisdiction, considering that the Claimant had failed to meet the criteria under the ICSID Convention because the Claimant "had not discharged his burden to show that he had objectively manifested a clear and unequivocal will or intent to obtain an immediate "renunciation."[24]

2.1.2 Key Takeaways and Recommendations

The case law above shows that in the absence of additional qualifying criteria, such as "dominant and effective nationality" or exclusion of host State nationals from treaty protection, the tribunals, especially those operating outside the

---

20 *Supra* note 18, paras. 296–297.

21 Erik Brouwer, *Revealed: ICC tribunal in Blerim Devolli v. Kosovo declines jurisdiction under foreign investment law, seeing insufficient evidence of a foreign contribution of value and finding that the claimant does not qualify as a foreign national*, Investment Arbitration Reporter, May 23, 2023, https://www.iareporter.com/articles/revealed-icc-tribunal-in-blerim-devolli-v-kosovo-declines-jurisdiction-under-foreign-investment-law-seeing-insufficient-evidence-of-a-foreign-contribution-of-value-and-finding-that-the-claimant-doe/.

22 Marko Mihaljevic v. Republic of Croatia, ICSID Case No. ARB/19/35, Award, para. 42 (May 19, 2023).

23 *Id.* paras. 55–61.

24 *Id.* para. 124.

ICSID Convention, will not determine the nationality of the investor based these criteria.

To avoid claims of the host State's nationals and prevent "nationality shopping," it is recommended that additional criteria, such as "permanent residence," "domicile," "principal place of business," or "dominant and effective nationality," be incorporated into the investment protection laws or IIAS. Implementing these supplementary requirements is preferable, rather than completely excluding dual nationals from treaty protection. This approach allows for the inclusion and protection of investments from the diaspora without necessitating the renunciation of their citizenship.

2.2 *Legal Persons*

The largest source of claims in ISDS comes from legal persons (also referred to as legal entities/juridical persons), a pattern mirrored in the context of the WB. To determine the nationality of legal persons, the WB investment protection framework provides the following as alternative or cumulative requirements: (i) the place of the constitution or incorporation in accordance with the legislation of the home State;[25] (ii) the place of the seat;[26] (iii) the main place of business;[27] (iv) the place of real economic activities;[28] and (v) the place of control.[29]

In the next subchapters, the "place of incorporation," "seat," and "foreign control" criteria will be analyzed as the most relevant in the disputes involving the WB countries.

---

25 *See* Agreement on Mutual Promotion and Protection of Investments, Alb.-Bulg., art.1 (3), Apr. 27, 1994.; *See also* For the Promotion and Reciprocal Protection of Investments, Alb. – Isr., Art. 1(3), Jan. 29, 1996.; *See also*, Kuwait-North Maced., art. 1 (2), *supra* note 29.; *See also* Agreement on Agreement on the Reciprocal Promotion and Protection of Investments, Croat.-Serb., art. 1(2), Aug. 8, 1998.

26 *See* Agreement on the Promotion and Reciprocal Protection of Investments, Alb.-Mold., art. 1 (3), Jun. 11, 2004.; *See also* Agreement on the Promotion and Reciprocal Protection of Investments, Serb. – Switz., art. 1(2), Dec. 7, 2005.

27 Mostly the treaties negotiated by Bosnia and Herzegovina, e.g., *see* Agreement for the Promotion and Reciprocal Protection of Investments, Bosn. & Herz. – Lith., art. 1(2), Jun. 7, 2007.; *See also* Agreement for the Promotion and Reciprocal Protection of Investments, Bosn. & Herz. – Slovk., art. 1 (3), Jun. 2, 2008.; *See also* Agreement for the Promotion and Reciprocal Protection of Investments, North Maced. – Viet., art.1(2), Oct. 15, 2014.

28 *See* Agreement on the Promotion and Reciprocal Protection of Investments, Croat.-Switz., art. 1 (1), Oct. 30, 1996.; *See also* Croat.-North Maced., art. 1(4), Jul. 6, 1994.

29 *See* Agreement on Encouragement and Reciprocal Protection of Investments, Bosn. & Herz.-Neth., art. 1 (b), May. 13, 1998.

2.2.1 The Place of Incorporation

The place of incorporation is rarely used as a sole criterion.[30] It is considered a formal criterion contingent upon the company law requirements in the country of incorporation. The requirement for this criterion is the same across all company laws of the WB countries: registration with the company authority is obligatory.[31] A business registration certificate suffices to demonstrate the incorporation of a legal entity in a specific jurisdiction.[32] However, while public documents are often treated as prima facie evidence of the facts they attest to, it is still at the tribunal's discretion to verify the reliability of the information contained therein.[33]

2.2.2 Case Law

The dispute Mera Investment v. Serbia was initiated before the ICSID Centre under the Cyprus–Serbia & Montenegro BIT by Mera Investment Fund Limited ("Mera Investment"), a company established in Cyprus. The Respondent argued that Mera Investment did not meet the criteria for a foreign investor under Article 1 (3) (b) of the BIT.[34] The Respondent's contention was based on Mera Investment's purported lack of the right to use the premises of its registered office in Cyprus, which claimed was necessary for the incorporation test under the BIT.[35]

---

30 *See* Agreement for the Promotion and Protection of Investments, Alb.-U.K., art 1 (d), Mar. 30, 1994.; *See also* North Maced.-Taiwan, art. 1(c), 09/06/1999 Jun. 9, 1999.09/06/1999 Macedonia, The former Yugoslav Republic of–Taiwan Province of China BIT (1999) | International Investment Agreements Navigator | UNCTAD Investment Policy Hub. The ECT also adopts a single incorporation test, *see* International Energy Charter, art. 1(6), 1994.

31 Law on Business Enterprises, art. 3 (Alb).; *See also*, Company Law, (Bosn. & Herz.).; *See also* art. 177(2).; *See also* Kosovo Law on Business Organizations, art. 23, (Kos). *See also* Law on Business Organizations (Montenegro).; *See also*, Law on Companies, art. 3 (Serb.); *See also* Law on Trade Companies, art. 2 (1) (North Maced.).; *See also* Companies Act, (Croat.). The Croatia Companies Act, art. 70, provides that the company is established by contract, but it also regulates the procedure of registration.

32 *See* Mera Investment Fund Limited v. Republic of Serbia, ICSID Case No. ARB/17/2, para. 70, Decision on Jurisdiction, (Nov. 30, 2018).

33 *See* CEAC v. Montenegro, ICSID Case No. ARB/14/8, at 155, Award (Jul. 26, 2016).; *See also* Soufraki v. UAE, ICSID Case No. ARB/02/7, para. 62, Award, (Jul. 7, 2004).

34 Article 1(3) (b) of the Cyprus-Serb. & Montenegro BIT stipulates that an investor shall mean a legal entity incorporated, constituted, or otherwise duly organized according to the laws and regulations of one Contracting Party having its seat in the territory of that same Contracting Party and investing in the territory of the other Contracting Party.

35 *Supra* note 32, Mera Investment Fund Limited v. Republic of Serbia, para. 64.

The Tribunal considered that, according to the BIT, the Claimant did not need to have a "physical presence" in Cyprus nor demonstrate "some right of use over the property" where it claims to be incorporated to satisfy the incorporation test, a condition it considered nonetheless fulfilled.[36] Regarding the authenticity of the registration certificate, the Tribunal accepted the incorporation certificates submitted by the Claimant as proof of its valid incorporation in Cyprus without any flaws that would prevent the Tribunal from recognizing it as duly issued by the competent authorities.[37]

Moreover, the Tribunal did not find it relevant to the incorporation test that the lease agreement was not signed in the presence of the two parties, as required by laws in Cyprus, as the Lease Agreement clearly demonstrates the intention of the parties to enter into a legally binding agreement and in the absence of a contract in the written form, the payments serve as evidence to when the contract was concluded.[38]

Anglo-Adriatic v. Albania was a dispute initiated by a company incorporated in the British Virgin Islands with its legal seat therein. The Respondent argued that the Claimant was not a protected investor as it did not exist at the time the dispute arose. The Tribunal considered that the incorporation test under the Albanian Foreign Investment Law is met, solely relying on the Certificate of Good Standing, which showed that the Claimant was a limited liability company incorporated and operating under the laws of the British Virgin Islands with its legal seat therein and was deemed to exist at all relevant times in the British Virgin Islands.[39]

2.3 *The Seat*

The "seat" criterion is frequently used to ascertain the nationality of foreign investors. This criterion is usually used alternatively with the place of incorporation and sometimes the main place of business activities or cumulatively.

In international law, as it currently stands, there is no single understanding of the term "seat." The "seat" criterion typically refers to the place of effective or central management–where the key decision-making functions are exercised.[40] Some treaties use the term "registered seat" instead, which is typically understood to imply the place of incorporation. However, in certain treaties,

---

36 *Id.* paras. 71, 94, 95.

37 *Id.* para. 70.

38 *Id.* para. 72.

39 Anglo-Adriatic Group Limited v. Republic of Albania, ICSID Case No. ARB/17/6, para. 220, Award, (Feb. 7, 2019).

40 UNCTAD, 'Scope and Definition, A Sequel' UNCTAD Series on Issues in International Investment Agreements II (2011) at 83.

mainly those negotiated by BiH, the term "registered seat" is used interchangeably as "seat" or "central place of management."[41]

In practice, a company's "real seat" is presumably the place where it is formally registered. However, in the absence of sufficient evidence confirming that the seat is indeed in the location of the registered office, the tribunals have delved further into factual evidence to determine the company's actual seat.[42] Therefore, the meaning of the "seat" criterion depends on the specifics of each case.

2.3.1 Case Law

Two notable cases in the region that address the "seat" criterion are *CEAC v. Montenegro* and *Mera Investment v. Serbia*. While both cases were initiated before the ICSID under the Cyprus–Montenegro & Serbia BIT, and in both cases, Claimants asserted their seats in Cyprus, the Tribunals had contrasting views on the meaning of the "seat" criterion under the BIT.

Article 1 (3) (b) of the Cyprus–Montenegro and Serbia BIT reads:

> The term "investor" shall mean […] a legal entity incorporated, constituted, or otherwise duly organized according to the laws and regulations of one Contracting Party having its seat in the territory of that same Contracting Party and investing in the territory of the other Contracting Party.[43]

In *CEAC v. Montenegro*, the Claimant and Respondent invoked different interpretations of the "seat" criterion. While the Claimant referred to the "registered office," which claimed that it should be interpreted according to Cypriot municipal law, the Respondent argued that the term "seat" should be interpreted autonomously under the Treaty, which refers to the place where a legal entity is effectively managed and financially controlled and where it carries out its business activities. The Tribunal, after finding that the Claimant did not have its "registered seat" in Cyprus and that it was not managed and controlled from Cyprus, considered it unnecessary to determine the precise meaning of the term "seat" as employed in Article 1(3)(b) of the BIT.[44]

41 *See* Agreement on Promotion and Protection of Investments, Fin,-Bosn. & Herz., art. (2) (b) (II), Nov. 1, 2000.

42 *See* discussion below on Mera v. Serbia and CEAC v. Montenegro.

43 Agreement on the Promotion and Reciprocal Protection of Investments, Serb. & Montenegro–Cyprus., art. 1(3) (b), Nov. 9, 1995.

44 CEAC Holdings Limited v. Montenegro, ICSID Case No. ARB/14/8, Award, para. 148 (Jul. 26, 2016).

The Tribunal examined the fulfillment of these requirements brought forward by an expert-witness as minimum requirements to establish the "seat" under Cypriot law: (i) the existence of physical premises in Cyprus; (ii) a lease or license to use the premises; (iii) accessibility of the premises for at least two hours per day the keeping of books and registers, and; (iv) the company's name affixed to the outside of the building.[45]

The Tribunal considered that the premises in which the Claimant purports to have its registered office appear unoccupied and inaccessible and showed no sign of any activity. It also noted that the Claimant did not bring any evidence to document that he indeed had an office in Cyprus. Additionally, the Tribunal considered that certificates issued by domestic authorities "constitute only prima facie evidence of the facts they attest to" and that an international tribunal "must make its own determination under international law."[46]

Regarding the Respondent's request to interpret the term "seat" autonomously under the Treaty with reference to the place of effective management and control, the Tribunal noted that the Claimant did not provide any documents in the record attesting that it was managed and controlled from Cyprus at the time the Request for Arbitration was filed, and therefore it did not meet the "seat" requirement brought forward by the Respondent.[47]

On the other hand, in his separate opinion, Prof. William Park observed that the notion of "seat" comes from civil legal tradition, and although Cyprus's company law comes from English tradition, he considered the analogy with the Brussels Regulation, considering that in Cyprus, a "statutory seat" alternatively means a "registered office," "place of incorporation," or "the place under the law of which the company formation took place."[48] Moreover, he considered that an arbitral tribunal could not add such adjectives on its own initiative in the absence of a "real" seat requirement in the BIT.[49] He considered that the "registered office," which only requires an office to be registered, is the requirement under the treaty, and adding any additional requirement "would require arbitrators to assume policy-making mission in excess of their authority."[50]

45 *Id.* para. 171.

46 *Id.* para. 155.

47 *Id.* paras. 207–208.

48 *Id.* para. 14, Separate Opinion of Arbitrator William Park.

49 *Id.* para. 16.

50 *Id.* para. 21.

The Claimant filed an application for annulment ("Application") of the award, which the Committee dismissed entirely.[51] One of the grounds in the Application was that the Tribunal had exercised manifest excess of power by, inter alia, assuming a policy-making role by adopting the minimum requirements presented by the expert, which, according to the Claimant, are not based in either domestic or international law.[52] The Committee noted that the Tribunal only considered them in the context of applying the Claimant's argument that international law requires renvoi to the law of Cyprus and did not find that such requirements constituted part of an autonomous international law definition of "seat."[53]

In MERA *Investment v. Serbia*, the Tribunal agreed with Professor William Park in CEAC *v. Montenegro* that unless stipulated in the treaty, the tribunal cannot add additional requirements on its own initiative. The Tribunal considered that requirements addressed by the Tribunal in the CEAC case go beyond the assessment of the confirmation of a registered office by the relevant authorities and are without a basis in domestic or international law.[54]

The Tribunal considered that the placement of the "seat" criterion in the BIT, alongside the "constituted or otherwise duly organized according to the laws and regulations of one Contracting Party," implies that "seat" is a different and separate criterion from "incorporation."[55] The Tribunal understood the meaning of the term "seat" to refer to an actual location, place, or address. Thus, the equivalent of this condition under Cypriot law is considered to be the "registered office" of an entity.[56] Regarding the probative value of the certificates issued by the relevant authorities, the Tribunal considered them to be conclusive evidence of the registered seat.[57] The Tribunal ultimately decided that the Claimant has its seat in Cyprus.

2.4 *Foreign Control*

Many BITs negotiated by the WB Economies contain "foreign control" clauses. However, the majority of these clauses are drafted vaguely without any specific

51 CEAC Holdings Limited v. Montenegro, ICSID Case No. ARB/14/8, Decision on Annulment, para.142 (May 1, 2011).

52 *Id.* para. 67.

53 *Id.* para.128.

54 *Supra* note 32, paras. 86–94, Mera Investment Fund Limited v. Republic of Serbia.

55 *Id.* para. 91.

56 *Id.* para. 90.

57 *Id.* para. 93.

indicators of what constitutes "foreign control."[58] Only a few BITs include a substantial ownership[59] or the exercise of dominant influence,[60] as indicators to ascertain control. Sometimes, ownership and control are provided alternatively.[61] A good example of a foreign control clause can be found in the North Macedonia–Switzerland BIT,[62] which stipulates that foreign control is established based on the percentage of equity interest owned or the power to name a majority of its directors or otherwise legally direct its actions.

A common issue addressed in disputes involving WB countries is how to determine who controls the company in the absence of one majority shareholder.[63] Other distinctive issues include the levels of share ownership which the tribunal should review to determine "foreign control," specifically whether only the first layer of the controller or the ultimate controller should be reviewed and whether "foreign control" can be applied reversely – to deny jurisdiction;[64] whether the dual nationality of the controller is an issue to establish ratione personae jurisdiction;[65] and the implications of restructuring the company's ownership to gain "foreign control" in establishing jurisdiction.[66] The WB framework does not regulate issues related to restructuring the ownership of the company to gain foreign control prior to initiating ISDS proceedings.

As shown below, tribunals have weighted a combination of factors to determine effective control beyond the mere share ownership, such as the power to block decisions, appoint and dismiss directors, initiate legal proceedings, and independently manage company activities.

---

58 *See* Agreement on encouragement and reciprocal protection of investments, Neth.-Maced., Jul. 7, 1998; *See also supra* note 34, art. 1 (b) (iii).

59 *See* Agreement on the Reciprocal Promotion and Protection of Investments, Alb.-Pol., art. 1(1)(c), Nov. 1, 2006.

60 *See* Agreement on the Promotion and Reciprocal Protection of Investments, Mold. – Montenegro, art. 1(2)(c), June 20, 2014.; *See also* Agreement on the Promotion and Reciprocal Protection of Investments, Crot.-Mold., art. 1(2)(c), Dec. 5, 2011.; *See also*, Croat.-Malta, art. (1)(2)(c), July 11, 2001.; *See also*, Croat.-Austria, art. 1(2)(c), Sept. 26, 1996.

61 *See* Agreement for the Encouragement and Reciprocal Protection of Investments, Bosn. & Herz.-Kuwait, art. 1 (3), Jun. 13, 2001.

62 *See* Agreement on the Promotion and Reciprocal Protection of Investments, Maced. – Switz., art. 2 (2) (c), Sep. 26, 1996.

63 *See section below* Guardian Fiduciary Trust v. Macedonia

64 *See section below* Swisslion v. Macedonia.

65 *See section below* Burimi SRL v. Albania.

66 *See section below* BRIF TRES v. Serbia and MNSS v. Montenegro.

2.4.1 Case Law

In *Guardian Fiduciary Trust v. Macedonia*, the Claimant, a New Zealand-incorporated company, claimed to be under the control of a Dutch entity, Stichting Intertrust, and therefore qualify as a foreign investor under the Netherlands–Macedonia BIT. However, the ownership of the Claimant's immediate holding company, CCT, was divided between two companies: IN Asset Management, a New Zealand company wholly owned by Stichting Intertrust, a Dutch foundation, and CCG, a Marshall Islands company located outside Stichting Intertrust's corporate chain.[67] On the other hand, the Respondent argued that the Claimant is not controlled by Stichting Intetrust but by the CCG.[68]

The Tribunal acknowledged that ownership usually refers to the legal right or the capacity to exercise control. However, it recognized the difficulty of establishing control solely based on ownership when the ownership of the Claimant's immediate holding company is divided between companies of two different countries.[69] To determine the factual control over the company, the Tribunal examined the terms of the agreement between the two owners of the Claimant's immediate holding company (CCT) by focusing on specific provisions, such as the declaration of beneficial ownership, restrictions on share transfer without consent, and the accountability of the legal owner to the beneficial owner. The Tribunal observed that the agreement did not explicitly address certain crucial aspects, particularly the direction and control of CCT's business activities and the exercise of voting rights. In the absence of the provisions within the agreement clearly stipulating control, and due to lack of additional evidence supporting the Claimant's assertions that the controller of the Claimant's immediate beneficial owner is Stichting Intertrust, the Tribunal concluded that the Claimant was not under the direct or indirect control of Stichting Intetrust. Instead, it found that the Claimant is indirectly controlled by CCG and its director, who, inter alia, commenced arbitration on behalf of the Claimant and authorized the Claimant's counsel.[70] Consequently, the Tribunal dismissed the Claimant's claims for lack of ratione personae jurisdiction.

In *Burimi SRL v. Albania*, the dispute involved Burimi SRL, an Italian company owned and controlled by Ilir Burimi, a dual national of Albania and Italy, and Eagle Games, an Albanian company owned by Albanian nationals,

---

67 Guardian Fiduciary Trust, Ltd, f/k/a Capital Conservator Savings & Loan, Ltd v. Macedonia, former Yugoslav Republic of, ICSID Case No. ARB/12/31, Award, at. 2, 3 (Sept. 22, 2015).

68 *Id.* para. 7.

69 *Id.* para. 131.

70 *Id.* para. 137.

including Alma Leka and Ilir Burimi. Albania raised few objections regarding the nationality of the Claimants.

Regarding Burimi SRL, the Respondent argued that since Burimi SRL is under the ownership and control of an Albanian citizen, it does not qualify as a foreign investor. According to the Respondent, Article 8 (2) (c) of Italy-Albania BIT "requires to pierce the corporate veil of the company to identify the nationality of the person or legal entity holding the majority of the capital for purposes of the first clause of Article 25(2)(b) of the ICSID Convention."[71] The Tribunal disagreed with the Respondent, stating the requirement of Article 8 (2) (c) is to "determine whether companies with the nationality of the State party to the dispute (Albania), can be considered under foreign control and therefore should be treated as a "national of another Contracting State" for the purposes of the ICSID Convention."[72] Therefore, the Tribunal concluded that it has jurisdiction ratione personae with respect to the claims of Burimi SRL.[73]

Regarding the nationality of Eagle Games, according to the Claimants, it should be regarded as an Italian investor, although it is incorporated in Albania. The Claimants argued that given that Mr. Ilir Burimi, the General Director and sole shareholder of Burimi SRL, holds 65 percent of the shares in Eagle Games, this puts Eagle Games under the control of Burimi SRL, and, consequently, qualifies it as a foreign investor under Italy-Albania BIT and Albania's Law on foreign investments.[74]

The Tribunal dismissed claims over Eagle Games, considering that grating jurisdiction to legal entities of the host State controlled by its dual nationals goes against the purpose of Article 25(2) (b) of the ICSID Convention.[75]

In *Swisslion v. Macedonia*, the dispute involved Swisslion, a company organized under the laws of the former Yugoslav Republic of Macedonia, owned by DRD Swisslion AG, a company incorporated under the laws of the Swiss

71 *See* Burimi SRL and Eagle Games SH.A v. Republic of Albania, ICSID Case No. ARB/11/18, Award, para. 126, (May 29, 2013).

72 *Id.* para. 132.

73 *Id.* para. 133.

74 *Id.* paras. 97–99.

75 While neither the ICSID Convention nor relevant precedents address the potential for a dual national invoking one of his two nationalities to establish jurisdiction over a claim brought in the name of a juridical person under the second clause of Article 25(2)(b), it strikes the Tribunal as anomalous that the principle against use of dual nationality in 25(2)(a) would not transfer to the potential use of dual nationality in 25(2)(b). Otherwise, any dual national who is a national of the Contracting State to a dispute could circumvent the bar on claims in Article 25(2)(a) by establishing a company in that state and asserting foreign control of that company by virtue of his second (foreign) nationality. *Id.* para. 121.

Confederation, and by Mr. Rodoljub Draskovic, a dual national of Switzerland and Serbia.

To determine jurisdiction ratione personae, the Tribunal only reviewed the first layer of the controller upon which it established that it has jurisdiction while disregarding the nationality of the ultimate owner:

> It is not disputed that more than 50% of its equity interest is beneficially owned by a Swiss company, DRD Swisslion, which has the power to legally direct Swisslion's action. The Claimant meets both conditions alternatively fixed by subparagraphs (i) and (ii) of Article 2 (2) (c) of the BIT and it is a Swiss investor in Macedonia, whatever the nationality of the ultimate owner of DRD Swisslion may be. The Tribunal has jurisdiction ratione personae.[76]

Two notable cases involving the WB address the issue of ownership restructuring to gain "foreign control," namely BRIF TRES v. Serbia and MNSS v. Montenegro.

The dispute, *BRIF TRES v. Serbia*, involved two Claimants, "BRIF TRES" and "BRIF TC,"[77] Serbian-incorporated companies allegedly controlled by Luxembourg nationals. In 2004, they engaged in a public tender by the City of Belgrade for the revitalization of the Danube waterfront property and the construction of a shopping center. However, in 2007, a third party claimed property rights over the property leased to the claimants by the City of Belgrade. Administrative authorities and the court upheld these claims, declaring the lease agreement with the claimants null and void.[78] Over the years, claimants' ownership changed from Luxembourg nationals to Adriatic, a Serbian national, and then,

---

76 Swisslion DOO Skopje v. Macedonia, former Yugoslav Republic of, ICSID Case No. ARB/09/16, para. 132, (Jul. 6, 2012).

77 The preceding company was Montmontaža d.o.o. Beograd, which was incorporated in Serbia on 18 September 2003 as a wholly owned subsidiary of the Croatian company Montmontaža d.o.o. Zagreb, with the purpose of participating in a public tender by the City of Belgrade for the Ada Huja Project. On 12 July 2006, BRIF TRES was incorporated in Serbia as a wholly owned subsidiary of the Luxembourgish company BRIF SICAR. In January 2007, the ownership of Montmontaža, originally controlled by the Croatian parent company Montmontaža d.o.o. Zagreb changed hands to the Serbian company BRIF TRES, which was, in turn, wholly owned by BRIF SICAR, a Luxembourg company. The company designation of Montmontaža changed to BRIF-TC only in March 2009.

78 BRIF-TC d.o.o. Beograd v. Republic of Serbia, ICSID Case No. ARB/20/12, Award, paras. 74–77, (Jan. 30, 2023)

just months before initiating ISDS proceedings, to Beauvallon, a company incorporated in Luxembourg.[79]

The interesting aspect of this case is that the claimants were initially protected under BLEU–Serbia BIT but lost that protection when acquired by Adriatic, regaining it upon acquisition by the Beauvallon. The BLEU-Serbia BIT recognizes nationality based on "foreign control" exercised directly or indirectly.[80]

Respondent argued that the acquisition of BRIF-Tres by the Luxembourg company occurred when the dispute was already foreseeable, thereby alleging that such restructuring constitutes an abuse of process.[81] The Tribunal observed that restructuring of a company to benefit from treaty protection and access international arbitration is typically done by a company lacking "investor" qualification to another company in the same corporate group, organized under the laws of a country that benefits from treaty protection. Regardless of the restructuring's specifics and intentions, the original owner maintains a connection to the investment through corporate ownership affiliations. However, in the present case, the claimants were initially protected investors.[82]

The Tribunal also noted that the acquisition of an investment not protected by a BIT by a company enjoying such protection "does not per se lead to abuse, just because the unprotected investment becomes protected as a result. Otherwise, every case of investment restructuring and acquisition would be found to be abusive, which does not count for the myriad of cases where investment restructuring and acquisition were found to be legitimate."[83]

To determine whether there was an abuse through restructuring or acquisition, the Tribunal addressed these questions: (i) whether the investment claims brought before the tribunal were already crystallized or foreseeable at the time of the restructuring or, in this case, at the time the acquisition took place; and (ii) whether the restructuring or acquisition was made for normal business purposes and had an economic rationale, with the intention of engaging in economic activity in the host State.[84]

Whether the dispute was already foreseeable prior to the restructuring of the ownership was scrutinized based on three questions: (i) to whom the dispute should have been foreseeable, (ii) the degree of the foreseeability

79 *Id.* at 10–23.

80 Agreement on the Reciprocal Promotion and Protection of Investment, art. 1(1), Belg.-Lux.-Serb., Apr. 3, 2004.

81 *Supra* note 78, at 29.

82 *Id.* at 47.

83 *Id.* para. 150.

84 *Id.* para. 151.

required, and (iii) what needs to be foreseeable.[85] The Tribunal considered that the entities restructuring or acquiring investments with the intention of filing claims related to foreseeable disputes rather than genuinely investing in the host State are considered abusers. On the degree of foreseeability, the Tribunal considered that it is met "when the relevant party can see an actual dispute or can foresee a specific future dispute as a very high probability and not merely as a possible controversy."[86] Regarding the third question, the Tribunal found that what needs to be foreseeable is "a dispute originating from deteriorated circumstances affecting an investment in the host State."[87] The Tribunal considered that the dispute was "foreseeable" or "highly probable" if not "crystallized" to the Claimant a minimum of 12 years prior to Beauvallon taking control of BRIF TRES.[88]

Additionally, the Tribunal affirmed that Beauvallon's interest in BLEU-Serbia BIT was not "to assess the protection that future business in Serbia would enjoy. Its interest was evidently directed to the past" as just two weeks after Beauvallon became a registered owner of BRIF TRES, it engaged a law firm "to advise and represent Beauvallon [...] and any relevant affiliates, including Serbian affiliates BRIF-TRES [SIC] and BRIF-TC [...] in connection with a dispute and possible arbitration against the Republic of Serbia concerning the rights of BRIF-TC [...] under a Lease Agreement dated 2 September 2004 for the construction of a shopping centre in Serbia."[89]

The Tribunal thus concluded that the acquisition of BRIF SICAR's dormant investment enshrined in BRIF TRES by Beauvallon, which aimed to acquire a previously crystalised ICSID claim without an independent economic purpose, amounts to an abusive manipulation of the investment treaty system, hence an abuse of process.[90]

In the *MNSS B.V. and Recupero Credito Acciaio v. Montenegro*, a dispute initiated by MNSS, a private company constituted under the laws of the Netherlands, and Recupero Credito Acciaio N.V. ("RCA"), a private company constituted under the laws of Curaçao, concerning the privatization of Zeljezara Niksic

85 *Id.* para. 204.
86 *Id.* para. 207.
87 *Id.* paras. 205–208.
88 *Id.* paras. 209–210.
89 *Id.* para. 219.
90 Beauvallon's acquisition of BRIF SICAR's dormant investment enshrined in BRIF TRES, which aimed to acquire a previously crystalised ICSID claim without an independent economic purpose, amounts to an abusive manipulation of the investment treaty system. The Luxembourgish control of Claimants at the time of the filing of the ICSID claim is the result of such manipulation and thus constitutes an abuse of process. *Id.* para. 222.

("ZN"), the sole electric arc furnace steel in Montenegro at that time. In 2006, MN Specialty Steel Limited ("MN") (UK company) acquired 66.7% of ZN's shares through a privatization agreement with the government of Montenegro. In 2008, MN sold its shares to MNSS. Following the sale, MNSS provided significant loans to ZN between 2008 and 2011, in the amount of 63.75 million euros, for multiple purposes, including working capital and operational needs. However, ZN underwent financial strains, leading to agreements with the Montenegrin government to restructure debts and ensure ongoing operations, which culminated in 2012 when it went bankrupt.[91]

The Responded argued that the Claimants are shell companies without any genuine business activity and are ultimately UK-held, claiming that the Dutch nationality had been fabricated after the dispute emerged because MNSS B.V.'s entry in ZN in February 2008 came at a time when the dispute had already arisen, or was foreseeable. According to the Respondent, "by interposing the Dutch shell company, the effectively British investors attempted to obtain the protection of a BIT for a previously unprotected investment." The Respondent claimed that when MNSS B.V. took over the immediate shareholding of ZN, at the same time "took over" and continued MNSS Limited's dispute, which behavior it considers to be abusive forum shopping.[92]

The Tribunal dismissed the Respondent's objection to the jurisdiction, stating that the elements for an abuse of process were not met as the dispute was not foreseeable at the time of the restructuring:

> to structure an investment with the aim to seek protection of a BIT is not per se in breach of the good faith expected of an investor. Tribunals have found that an investor would not qualify for the protection of the BIT concerned only if the nationality is changed after the dispute has arisen or "when the relevant party can see an actual dispute or can foresee a specific future dispute as a very high probability and not merely as a possible controversy [...] in the instant case, the dispute with MNSS arose after the Assignment Agreement and the Respondent was party to the Assignment Agreement.[93]

91 MNSS B.V. and Recupero Credito Acciaio N.V. v. Montenegro, ICSID Case No. ARB(AF)/12/8, Award, at 15–21, (May 4, 2016).

92 *Id.* at 26–28.

93 *Id.* paras. 182, 183.

2.5 *Key Takeaways and Recommendations*

As observed above, the typical tests for the nationality of legal persons in the WB investment protection framework are the "incorporation test" and the "seat." Both these tests are interpreted under the laws of the state where the legal person claims to be incorporated or have a seat. To avoid "forum shopping" by "mailbox" or "shell" companies, it is important that "place of incorporation" is not used as a single test. This criterion does not require sufficient links with the country of incorporation. On the other hand, the "seat" criterion requires more links with the country where it claims to have its seat. However, it is a vaguer concept and leaves plenty of room for interpretations.

To ensure that the legal person has a sufficient link with the home State, it is important that "the place of incorporation" together with the "seat" is also accompanied by the criterion of "substantive business operations" or "real economic activities."

When providing for the possibility of nationality based on "foreign control," for greater certainty, some indicators for its determination are recommended to be included, such as a certain amount of share ownership along with, e.g. the authority to manage the company, to appoint and dismiss the board of directors, or the dominant influence. Additionally, in order to avoid claims from companies controlled by dual nationals of the country where investment is made, the "foreign control" clause should also indicate that companies owned or controlled by the dual nationals of the country where investment is made do not qualify as an investor unless this person has its dominant and effective nationality or domicile in the other contracting party.

Finally, it is recommended that a "denial of benefits" clause is included in order to deny protection to "mailbox" companies or investments controlled by persons with whom the denying party does not maintain diplomatic relations or is subject to economic sanctions. An example of a denial of benefits clause may taken from the BITs negotiated by WB countries such as Albania-Azerbaijan BIT,[94] Kosovo-Austria BIT,[95] and Serbia-Turkey BIT.[96]

---

94 *See* Agreement for the Promotion and Reciprocal Protection of Investments, Alb.-Azer., Feb. 9, 2012, art 11.

95 *See supra* note 10, Agreement on Promotion and Protection of Investments, Kos-Austria, art. 11.

96 *See* Agreement on the Reciprocal Promotion and Protection of Investments, Serb.-Turk., art 13, Jan. 30, 2018.

3 General Aspects of the Definition of "Investment"

Referred to as the ratione materiae part of the claim, foreign investment constitutes a fundamental element of international investment law and dispute resolution. The BITs negotiated by WB countries and their investment protection laws typically employ the asset-based definition.[97] Only a limited number of BITs, mainly those concluded with NAFTA countries, feature elements of enterprise-based definitions.[98]

The majority of BITs cover a wide variety of assets, invested directly and indirectly.[99] Certain BITs limit the scope of definition by enlisting a number of attributes that investment should have, such as those of the Salini test.[100] Others limit the scope by excluding certain assets from the treaty's protection, such as commercial transactions designated solely for the sale of goods or services[101] or credits or loans provided to the state institutions.[102]

Loans are usually included as standalone investments. However, certain treaties provide that they must be directly related to a specific investment,[103] or to an enterprise.[104]

The risks associated with an open-ended asset-based definition without being limited by any additional requirement is that it is understood to suggest that the term embraces everything of economic value, virtually without limitation.[105] The Western Balkans ISDS jurisprudence shows that tribunals, especially those operating outside the scope of the ICSID Convention, tend to

97 One exception is BiH's Law on Foreign Direct Investment, which adopts an enterprise-based definition. *See supra note* 17, art. 2

98 *Supra* note 1, Agreement for the Promotion and Protection of Investments between Kos.-Can., art.1. *See also* Agreement for the Promotion and Protection of Investments, Can.-Serb., art. 1, Sept. 1, 2014.

99 *See e.g.,* Agreement on the Promotion and Protection of Investments, Bosn. & Herz. – Swed., art. (1)(1), Oct. 31. 2000.; *See also* Agreement on the Reciprocal Promotion and Protection of Investments, Kos.-BLEU, art.1(2), Mar. 9, 2010.

100 *Supra* note 10., Kos-Austria, art. 1(2).; *see also, supra* note 101, Turk.-Serb., art. 1(1).

101 *Supra* note 27 North Maced.-Viet, art. 1 (1).; *See also* Can.-Serb., art. 1, *supra* note 1.; Kos.-Can., *see also*, Turk.-Serb, *supra* note 2; *See supra* note 1, Can.-Serb.; *See also* Agreement on the Reciprocal Promotion and Protection of Investments Serb.-Morocco, art. 1(1), Jun. 6, 2013. w

102 Agreement for the Promotion and Protection of Investments, Austria-Bosn. & Herz., art 1(2), Oct. 2, 2000.

103 Agreement on the Promotion and Protection of Investments, Fin.-Alb., art. 1(c), Jun. 24, 1997).

104 *See supra* note 1, Kos-Can., art 1(d); *See also supra* note 98, Can.-Serb., art. 1 (d).

105 U.N. Conference on Trade and Development, *International Investment Agreements: Key Issues*, UNCTAD/ITE/IIT/2004/10 (Vol. 1) (Sept. 2004).

interpret such terms very broadly to encompass a wide range of assets that do not provide any contribution to the host State.

3.1 *Shareholding*

Most BITs negotiated by WB Economies cover direct and indirect shareholders by employing an open-ended list of protected assets held directly or indirectly, including shares, stocks, and debentures of companies or interests in the property of such companies.[106] As a result shareholders are protected from direct harm caused by the State's actions or omissions, such as the seizure of shares as well as for "reflective loss."[107] Some BITs explicitly foresee compensation for reflective loss,[108] while others impose limitations, such as requiring a minimum shareholding in a company.[109]

3.1.1 Case Law

In the *Addiko v. Montenegro* case, the Claimant, an Austrian bank, issued Swiss Franc-indexed mortgage loans through a locally incorporated entity in Montenegro. The Tribunal found that the Claimant's shares in the Bank, coupled with the follow-on investments in the form of capital contributions and a subordinated loan, correspond to the objective definition of an investment under the ICSID Convention and the BIT.[110]

Additionally, the Tribunal noted that "owning shares in a company cannot be deemed to be beyond the "outer limits" of Article 25(1) of the ICSID Convention, as it is not in any way equivalent to an ordinary commercial transaction, such as a one-off sale agreement [...]."[111] As for meeting the Salini criteria, the Tribunal determined that the purchase of shares in a bank, coupled with subsequent investments in the form of capital contributions and a subordinated

---

106 *See supra* note 25, Kuwait-North Maced, art. 1(1).; *See also* Investment Treaty, U.S.-Alb., art.1(1)(d), Nov. 11, 1995.

107 "Reflective loss" consists of reductions in the value of shares or dividends resulting from actions taken by the host State against the company in which the shareholders hold an interest. *See* OECD, Shareholder Claims for Reflective Loss in Investment State Dispute Settlement: A "Component-by-Component" Approach to Reform Proposals Informal Discussion Paper, December 2021, pp. 7–8.

108 *See e.g.*, Agreement on the Promotion and Reciprocal Protection of Investments, Serb.-U.A.E., art. 6(6), Feb. 17, 2013.; *See also* Agreement on the Promotion and Reciprocal Protection of Investments, art. 6(3) North Maced.-Qatar, Oct. 17, 2011.

109 *See* Agreement on the Reciprocal Promotion and Protection of Investments, Montenegro-Turk., art.1(1), Mar. 13, 2012.

110 Addiko Bank AG v. Montenegro, ICSID Case No. ARB/17/35, Excerpts of the Award, para. 316, (Nov. 24, 2021).

111 *Id.* para. 320.

loan, to satisfy the commitment of capital, duration, and risk as well as the contribution to the economic development of the host State, elements.[112] However, the Tribunal did not definitely assess whether ownership of shares alone meets the criteria under the Salini test.

In *Mera Investment v. Serbia*, the Respondent argued that the Tribunal lacked jurisdiction ratione materiae over any claims that arise from the rights in assets held by the Claimant's subsidiary Mera Invest. According to the Respondent, the Claimant, as a shareholder, did not have standing to directly pursue claims concerning the assets of its subsidiary.[113] The Tribunal observed that the objective and purpose of the treaty outlined in its preamble are "to create favourable conditions for greater economic cooperation between the Contracting Parties" and "to create and maintain favourable conditions for reciprocal investments." The Tribunal considered this formulation to foster broad investment protection. Additionally, the Tribunal noted three elements relevant for determining which assets are covered under the BIT: the broad asset-based definition of investment with a non-exhausted list of covered assets and a clause on the alteration of the form of investment; the silence of the treaty regarding on distinguishing between direct or indirect investment; and Serbia's treaty practice, noting that in other treaties where it wished to exclude indirect investment from the scope of protection, it did so with expressive language.[114] Consequently, the Tribunal found that the assets held by the Claimants constitute protected investments pursuant to the Cyprus-Serbia BIT, in respect to which the Claimant, as its shareholder, may bring claims not only for the impairment of the value of its shares in its subsidiary but also for its reflective loss.[115]

In *Burimi SRL v. Albania*, Burimi SRL claimed to have made an indirect investment by financing Alma Leka's purchase of shares in Eagle Games.[116] Despite the broad language used in the Albania-Italy BIT's definition of investment, the Tribunal found that the financing agreement does not establish Burimi SRL's ownership of the shares.[117] Instead, it considered such an agreement to represent a private loan arrangement between the two parties.[118]

---

112 *Id.* at 89–95.
113 *Supra* note 32, Mera Investment Fund Limited v. Republic of Serbia, para. 113.
114 *Id.* paras. 122–128.
115 *Id.* para. 135.
116 *Supra* note 71, Burimi SRL and Eagle Games SH.A v. Republic of Albania, paras. 134,135.
117 *Id.* paras. 144,146.
118 *Id.*

3.2 *Claims Arising out of Contracts and General Law*

"Claims to money" and "rights conferred pursuant to law," such as licenses and permits, are frequently included as investments under the treaties negotiated by the WB Economies.[119]

While the typical forms of intangibles are usually manifested as contracts and the rights they confer, the WB jurisprudence shows that "rights granted by the general laws" are also considered investments.[120]

3.2.1 Case Law

Mytilineos v Serbia was a case brought before the Permanent Court of Arbitration ("PCA") under the UNCITRAL rules concerning the Claimant's rights and obligations stemming from contracts concluded between the Claimant and RTB-BOR, a state-owned company involved in mineral extraction and metallurgy. According to these contracts, the Claimant provided financing and spare parts to RTB-BOR in exchange for the sale of copper, and the Claimant would have priority in purchasing a stake in RTB-BOR if privatized. However, the cooperation failed, as RTB-BOR struggled to pay its debts. All these contracts between private parties contained choice-of-law clauses providing for English law to govern, and most of them included choice-of-forum clauses in favor of English courts.[121] Respondents argued that there is no jurisdiction as the dispute arose out of commercial activity and, thus, was not covered under the BIT.[122]

To determine whether the Claimant's business operations' and consequently, claims to money stemming out of the agreements between the Claimant and RBT-BOR are investments under the Greece-Serbia BIT, the majority of the Tribunal's arbitrators analyzed three elements: (i) the preamble of the treaty, which emphasized the parties' intention to intensify the economic cooperation to the mutual benefit of both countries on a long-term basis and to create favorable conditions for investments by investors of either Contracting Party in the territory of the other Contracting Party; (ii) the broad asset definition in the treaty which encompasses "every kind of asset invested" including "claims to money or any other claim under contract having an economic

119 *See* Agreement on the Encouragement and Reciprocal Protection of Investments, U.S.-Croat., art. 1(vi), Jul. 13, 1996; *See also* Agreement on the Reciprocal Promotion and Protection of Investments, Alb.-Croat., art.1(1) (e), May 10, 1993.

120 Rudolf Dolzer et al., Principles of International Investment Law, 89, (3rd ed. 2022).; *See also* the discussion on the case Mabco v. Kosovo.

121 Mytilineos Holdings SA v. The State Union of Serbia & Montenegro and Republic of Serbia, UNCITRAL, Partial Award on Jurisdiction, paras. 5–40, (Sept. 8, 2006).

122 *Id.* para. 41.

value"; and (iii) narrow definitions of "investment" in other BITs negotiated by the Respondent which indicated that Greece–FRY BIT covered assets and activities beyond traditional notions of foreign investment.[123]

The Majority noted that the definition of "investment" in the Treaty was "deliberately very broad so as to cover the widest possible economic activities and to encourage economic cooperation between the two countries, as expressly stated in the BIT's Preamble."[124] The Tribunal considered there was no reason to exclude claims arising from purely commercial activities, such as sales contracts, from such a broad definition of investment.[125]

Given that the arbitration was conducted under the UNCITRAL Rules, the majority of the Tribunal's arbitrators noted that to determine jurisdiction, they need to analyze only the attributes of the alleged investment under the requirements of the BIT.[126] However, with neither party contesting the application of criteria under the ICSID Convention but rather arguing whether such criteria were met, upon a comprehensive evaluation of the Claimant's business activities in Serbia, the majority of the Tribunal found that the agreements between the Claimant and RTB-BOR met the investment criteria of the Salini test as well.[127]

In *Mabco v. Kosovo*, the dispute concerned the privatization of Grand Hotel, a socially owned enterprise ("SOE") in Kosovo. The privatization process was carried on by the Privatization Agency of Kosovo ("PAK")[128] through a Special Spin-Off Privatization procedure.[129] UTC, a local company, emerged as the successful bidder; however, lacking sufficient funds to meet its obligations under the tender, UTC sought help from other businessmen, including Mr. Pacolli, the owner of Mabco (the Claimant), and Mr. Ejupi. Among others, they agreed that the Claimant would contribute EUR 4 million for the purchase of the Grand Hotel. According to the Claimant, he transferred the money to UTC in April

123 *Id.* paras. 96–110.

124 *Id.* para. 108.

125 *Id.* para. 109. "Indeed, it has been pointed out that language including "claims to money or any other claim under contract having an economic/a financial value" suggests that "investment" may embrace contractual rights for the performance of services. Read literally there is also no reason why claims arising from pure commercial activities, such as sales contracts, should be excluded from such a broad definition of investment".

126 *Id.* para. 118.

127 *Id.* paras. 111–125.

128 Before Kosovo's declaration of independence, the Kosovo Trust Agency ("KTA") managed and dealt with the privatization of SOEs.

129 The Special Spin-Off Privatization Procedure entailed the creation of a new company (hereinafter "NewCo"), to which an SOE's assets were transferred, followed by a public tender for bids for the purchase of the NewCo's assets.

2006, and the Share Purchase Agreement ("PA") between UTC and PAK was concluded in August 2006. Under the PA, UTC was obliged, inter alia, to invest a minimum capital of EUR 20,200,000.00 and ensure the employment of over 1000 persons in the Grand Hotel.[130] According to the PA, the shares could be withdrawn if the UTC fails to honor its commitments.[131]

According to the Claimant, in January 2007, they signed an "Agreement of Good Understanding" ("AGU") to formalize arrangements with Mr. Ejupi and the owner of the UTC. Under this agreement, UTC would temporarily hold the legal ownership of the shares, while Messrs. Pacolli and Ejupi, the "actual purchasers," would formally become owners after two years. The Claimant would own 40% of the shares.[132]

However, UTC failed to meet the PA requirements, and as a consequence, PAK deliberated the withdrawal of shares.[133] Despite Mabco's requests not to withdraw the shares, PAK officially decided to withdraw the shares in Grand Hotel in May 2012.[134]

Given that the Claimant did not directly participate in the tendering process, he never received the shares, nor was he registered as the owner of the shares. As a consequence, the Tribunal had to determine whether a claim of entitlement to ownership of the shares could constitute an "investment." In light of a broad definition of "investment" in the BIT, the majority of the Tribunal considered that a claim does not need to be rooted in a contract to qualify as an investment:

> [...] As the language of BIT Article 1(1) itself shows, intangibles qualifying as assets take numerous forms. Nor are the intangibles identified in Article 1(1) themselves to be viewed as the only qualifying intangibles. There is no reason why, in logic or practice, intangibles taking other forms cannot be covered investments. The intangibles listed in the BIT do not constitute a "closed set". In sum, the Tribunal is not prepared to exclude the possibility that a claim of entitlement cognizable in investor-State arbitration can arise other than by contract or other than in the form of the specific intangibles enumerated in Article 1(1)".[135]

130 Mabco Constructions v. Republic of Kosovo, ICSID Case No. ARB/17/25, Decision on Jurisdiction, at 29–30, Oct. 20, 2020).

131 *Id.* para. 177.

132 *Id.* para. 179

133 *Id.* at 32–42.

134 *Id.* para. 208.

135 *Id.* para. 306.

Article 1(1) of Kosovo-Switzerland BIT, in its relevant part reads:

> 'investment' means every kind of asset established or acquired [...] that has such characteristics as the commitment of capital or other resources, the expectation of gain or profit, or the assumption of risk, including: [...] (c) claims to money or to any performance having an economic value, [...].[136]

Both the Majority and the Dissenting Arbitrator agreed that "claims to money" must be "established" or "acquired" in order to be considered an investment under the BIT. However, while the Majority considered that Mabco's claim of entitlement was both established and acquired,[137] the dissenting Arbitrator considered that there was only an attempt to acquire an asset and, therefore, there was no investment under the BIT.[138]

Moreover, the Majority found that the requirements of the ICSID Convention were satisfied as well. The financial support provided for the purchase of shares in Grand Hotel constituted a contribution and entailed risk, especially considering the underdeveloped tourism sector in Kosovo at the time. The duration criterion was evaluated under the assumption that if the investment was made it would have endured sufficient duration.[139] Additionally, while not mandatory, considering the importance of the tourism sector in Kosovo and the importance of the Grand Hotel in that regard, the Majority considered that the contribution criterion would have been satisfied.[140]

In contrast, the Dissenting Arbitrator considered that merely making a claim to acquire assets does not constitute an investment until the contractual claim is fulfilled.[141] Additionally, he considered the elements of "certain duration" and "element of risk" not to be met due to the failure to actually acquire an asset in return for the monetary contribution.

---

136 *Supra* note 6, art 1(1), Agreement on the Promotion and the Reciprocal Protection of Investments, Kos.-Switz., Oct. 27, 2011.

137 *Supra* note 130, para. 311, Mabco Constructions v. Republic of Kosovo.

138 *Id.* Dissent on Jurisdiction, para. 20, (Oct. 29, 2020).

139 *Id.* Decision on Jurisdiction, para. 300.

140 *Id.* Decision on Jurisdiction, paras. 300–301.

141 *Id.* Dissent on Jurisdiction para. 29. "Where only a transfer of money is made, leading to a claim to acquire assets, this in itself does not yet constitute an investment. As long as the contractual claim to ownership of assets has not been fulfilled by the other party, the usual commercial, counterparty risk materialized, but not yet an investment risk as a typical characteristic of an investment."

Finally, the Majority considered the prima facie test sufficient to establish ratione materiae jurisdiction.[142] Conversely, the Dissenting Arbitrator considered that while the prima facie test may suffice for assessing potential violation of the applicable BIT or investment law, it is insufficient for establishing whether ratione materiae requirement of an "investment."[143]

3.2.2 Key Takeaways and Recommendations

The case law above illustrates that a broad definition of investment, followed by an open-ended list of assets, creates legal uncertainties and extends protection to unintended categories of investments. These may include claims arising out of commercial contracts, claims to ownership of shares, indirect shareholding, or other assets that do not provide any contribution to the host State's economy. Moreover, it shows that treaties' preambles, which aim at attracting investments by nationals and enterprises of one Contracting Party in the territory of the other, are used in favor of broad interpretations of investment.

To mitigate these risks and ensure a more secure and predictable legal framework where protection is afforded to a targeted group of investments that contribute to the economy and sustainable development of the host State, certain attributes that an "investment" should have can be included, such as the commitment of capital, certain duration, risk, contribution to the host State's economic and sustainable development and employment generation.

Additionally, certain types of assets can be excluded from treaty protection, such as:

i. commercial transactions designed exclusively for the sale of goods or services;
ii. credits to finance commercial transactions (can also be limited for only a certain period, for example, with a duration of less than three years);
iii. credits granted to the State or to a state enterprise;[144]
iv. any order or judgment entered in a judicial or administrative action;
v. costs preceding the establishment of the investment, including costs for licenses, permissions, or permits;
vi. non-business assets;
vii. intellectual property rights which are not protected under the national legislation;
viii. market-share, market access, or similar intangibles;
ix. portfolio investments (can be excluded altogether or have a certain threshold for shareholding).

142 *Id.* Decision on Jurisdiction, para. 337.
143 *Id.* Dissent on Jurisdiction, para. 35.
144 This can also be narrowed down to certain types of financial instruments.

The definition of "investment" can also be narrowed by adopting an enterprise-based definition where protection is provided to the enterprise (including all its assets) controlled by the investor. In this scenario, it is recommended that "control" is defined by either referring to the majority of share-ownership or other forms of control elaborated in section 2.2.3. However, such an approach is very narrow and strips off the protection from all assets not related to the enterprise.

Additionally, the case law above illustrates that the state's treaty practice plays a crucial role in interpreting the broad definition of investments. Therefore, to avoid backlash, any reform targeting definitions should be holistic and target all investment treaties and investment protection laws.

3.3 *The Origin of the Capital*

In addition to the nationality of the investor, the nationality of the investment has also been raised as a jurisdictional issue in the disputes against WB countries. It is widely acknowledged by scholars and tribunals that the origin of the capital invested is irrelevant to the investment's international nature; the only requirement for determining the foreignness of an investment in terms of its origin is the nationality of the investor that owns or controls it.[145] This thesis is also supported by the jurisprudence in the Western Balkans. The requirement of the origin of capital is not found in any of the WB countries' IIAs or investment protection laws.

3.3.1 Case Law

In the dispute *Tradex v. Albania*, the Tribunal considered the origin of capital for the purposes of jurisdiction ratione materiae only relevant when required in the treaty:

> The 1993 Law, in its definition of "Foreign investment" in Art. 1 (3), nowhere requires that the foreign investor has to finance the investment from his own resources [...] quite to the contrary, the law provides for a broad interpretation of "investment". In the present context it may be particularly noted that Art. 1 (3) expressly includes "every kind of investment ... owned directly or indirectly by a foreign investor", "loans, claim to money or claim to performance having economic value" and "any right conferred by law or contract ...".[146]

145 Rudolf Dolzer et al., *Supra* note 126, at 102–104.

146 Tradex Hellas S.A. v. Republic of Albania, ICSID Case No. ARB/94/2, Award, para. 109 (Apr. 29, 1999).

In MERA *Investment v. Serbia*, the Respondent argued that the capital originates from the host State and, therefore, the assets invested are not "investments" under the Cyprus-Serbia BIT. The Tribunal noted that when the treaty is silent regarding the origin of the capital, the Tribunal cannot disregard the intention of the Contracting States by adding such requirements on its own.[147]

In *Rand Investments v. Serbia*, the Tribunal noted that the origin of the investment is irrelevant as long as "the investor is the one ultimately bearing the financial burden of the contribution."[148]

3.3.2 Key Takeaways and Recommendations

Despite being raised as an objection in numerous disputes by WB Economies, their BITs do not provide for any requirement concerning the investment's nationality. To ensure that tribunals consider the investment's origin when deciding on jurisdiction (ratione materiae) and to safeguard against investments originating from the host State, such a criterion should explicitly be included in the treaty. However, such restriction would narrow the range of assets considered "investments" and could often pose challenges in determining the real origin of the investment.

3.4 *Investment Made in Accordance with Legislation of the Host State*

The legality criterion provides an additional safeguard that investments are made in compliance with the host State's legislation. However, treaties do not specify the degree of non-compliance that would violate this criterion. Thus, it is not determined whether only investments made through a serious violation of the host State's law, such as corruption or fraud, or also those not being made in compliance with secondary legislation, violate the legality criterion for the purposes of the jurisdiction (ratione materiae). However, the Western Balkans jurisprudence shows that, for the purpose of jurisdiction, not every minor deviation from the host State's legislation results in violation of this criterion.

3.4.1 Case Law

In *Mamidoil v. Albania*, the dispute involved a Greek investor who invested in the petroleum sector in Albania. The investment consisted of shareholding, a lease contract, and a tank farm.

---

147 *Supra* note 32, Mera Investment Fund Limited v. Republic of Serbia, paras. 168–171.

148 Rand Investments Ltd. and others v. Republic of Serbia, ICSID Case No. ARB/18/8, Redacted Award, para. 237, (Jun. 29, 2023).

The Respondent objected to the Tribunal's jurisdiction, claiming that the investment was made illegally, alleging that (i) the Claimant did not receive nor apply for the necessary permits for the safeguarding of the public, social, environmental, and economic interests; (ii) the Claimant did not conduct due diligence prior to making the investment; (iii) the construction of the tank farm was carried on the basis of only internal approval and lease contract without a written assurance by Government authorities; (iv) the Claimant disregarded the warnings impending change in the Durres port area supported by the international organizations and public interest.[149]

The Tribunal assessed the investment's legality under both the Energy Charter Treat ("ECT")[150] and the Greece-Albania BIT.[151] Although the ECT does not specifically address the investment's legality, the Tribunal considered that it nevertheless does not protect investments made unlawfully.[152]

The Tribunal considered that for an investment to be considered illegal, there must first be "an inner link between the illegal act and the investment itself."[153] Second, it noted that the mere occurrence of minor breaches of the law should not result in denial of jurisdiction.[154]

Additionally, the Tribunal observed that Albania did not exercise its legal authorizations to order the demolition of the tank farm, which the Law on Urban Planning allowed it to do, nor had it imposed any sanctions, which the Law on Control and Regulation of the Construction Works allowed it to impose, but instead, it had "consistently, and in good faith, tried to cooperate with Claimant by repeatedly requesting and inviting it to submit the applications in the proper form and accompanied by the necessary documentation as enumerated in the laws."[155]

The Tribunal considered Albania's proposals to suspend the works in the present and repair them for the future and its readiness to enter into a debate about the legal framework of the investment and not repudiate it as indications of its willingness to overlook the illegality. According to the Tribunal, this suggests that Albania considered such illegality insignificant and something

149 Mamidoil Jetoil Greek Petroleum Products Societe S.A. v. Republic of Albania, ICSID Case No. ARB/11/24, Award, para. 358, (Mar. 30, 2015).

150 International Energy Charter, 1994.

151 Agreement for the Encouragement and Reciprocal Protection of Investments, Alb. – Greece, Aug. 1, 1991

152 *Supra* note 149, Mamidoil Jetoil Greek Petroleum Products Societe S.A. v. Republic of Albania, para. 293.

153 *Id.* para. 481.

154 *Id.* para. 483.

155 *Id.* para. 490.

that could be cured. Consequently, the Tribunal dismissed Albania's objections regarding ratione materiae jurisdiction on the grounds of the illegality of investment.[156]

In *Selmani v. Kosovo*, the Respondent's jurisdictional objections (ratione materiae) were based on the alleged illegality of the investments centered around numerous legislative and institutional changes stretching over the period of 2000–2011. The genesis of the dispute dates from early 2000, when UNMIK[157] had issued to the Claimant a sui generis Permission to Operate Previously State-Owned Fuel Outlets and Establishments (Known as Beopetrol & Jugopetrol) in exchange for payment of rent and taxes.[158] The record shows that Kosova Petrol ("KP")[159] made some rent payments in 2000 and 2001 and stopped in August 2001.[160] According to the Claimant, UNMIK had agreed orally to suspend the rental payments due to some debts owed to KP by other public institutions to which it had supplied petrol during a critical period.[161]

In December 2001, the UNMIK sent Mr. Selmani a Termination Letter stating that the Permission granted to the Claimant was terminated effective 31 December 2001. However, the Letter continued stating that the Claimant is "required to continue to operate these establishments until such time as they are ready to be handed over to the successful tender bidders and recipients of licenses [...]."[162]

In 2005, UNMIK adopted a new Regulation requiring parties to apply for a license to operate petroleum stations. According to this regulation, all licenses

---

156 *Id.* paras. 493–495.

157 United Nations Interim Administration Mission In Kosovo was established with UN Resolution 1244, with the purpose of providing an interim administration for Kosovo, including all legislative and executive powers and administration of the judiciary. Following the declaration of independence by the Kosovo authorities and the entry into force of a new constitution on 15 June 2008, the tasks of the Mission have significantly been modified to focus primarily on the promotion of security, stability, and respect for human rights in Kosovo.

158 *Supra* note 18, Bedri Selmani v. Republic of Kosovo, at 23–25.

159 Mr. Selmani was the manager of Kosova Petrol. Kosova Petrol was alternately described as a "state-owned enterprise" and as "controlled by the former Provisional Government of Kosova." Kosova Petrol was not registered at the business registries. The record shows that with the UNMIK's Permission, Mr. Selmani is recognized as the designated manager of "Kosova Petrol," pending the registration of businesses in Kosovo. According to the Mr. Selmani, Kosova Petrol was not yet registered as a business in Kosovo, because there was no such registration service available at the time.

160 *Supra* note 18, Bedri Selmani v. Republic of Kosovo, paras. 92–95.

161 *Id.*

162 *Id.* para. 105.

issued before its enactment would remain valid for only four months.[163] The record shows no evidence that KP applied for or was issued any licenses between 2005 and late January 2008, according to the new Regulation.[164] According to the Claimant, UNMIK Permission gave him a continuing right to operate even after the enactment of the new Regulation; thus, he did not need to apply for a license. He also noted that the relevant authorities did not raise any objections to KP's continuing operation of the petrol stations from 2005 to early 2008. Moreover, he noted that in 2008, after Kosovo's independence, the Ministry of Trade and Industry ("MTI") had issued several licenses to the Claimant, which, according to him, "confirms that the MTI must have considered the UNMIK Permission still formed a valid and continuing basis for his entitlement to petroleum trading licenses, even under the licensing regime reflected in the 2005 Petroleum Law."[165]

Respondent argued that the Claimant's investment was "tainted with illegality" as after 2001, he did not pay the rent to operate in petroleum stations as required in the permissions issued by UNMIK. Also, according to Kosovo's submission, UNMIK terminated the Claimant's permission in 2001, and even if arguendo it was not terminated in 2001, it was terminated in 2005 with the entry into force of the new regulation, claiming that Mr. Selmani did not obtain the required permits and permissions or pay the necessary taxes after 2005.[166]

To analyze the lawfulness of the investment for the purposes of jurisdiction, the tribunal analyzed the UNMIK Regulation of 2005, the 2014 LFI, the UNMIK's permission issued in 2000, and its Termination Letter of 2001, and the licenses issued by the MTI.

Firstly, the Tribunal noted that the criterion of legality does not require perfect compliance with the host State's laws, and non-compliance with the terms of a lease or contract is a merits issue, but it would not strip the investment of its status as such, for purposes of arbitral jurisdiction. The Tribunal noted that under the Article 2.1.4 of 2014 LFI, the status of being an "investment" is granted "so long as the mechanism authorizing the holding (e.g., the lease, concession, license or contract) remains validly in effect, in the sense that it has not been revoked, terminated, or otherwise invalidated as a matter of law."[167]

However, the Tribunal observed that the Permission did not meet the temporal requirement as the Permission was not valid post-declaration of

163 *Id.* para. 140, at 40.
164 *Id.* para. 143.
165 *Id.* para. 145.
166 *Id.* paras. 144, 306.
167 *Id.* para. 340.

independence of Kosovo, considering legislative and institutional changes in the country. However, given that the Termination Letter required KP to continue operating the petrol stations until they were ready to be handed over to new bidders and recipients of licenses, the Tribunal considered KP to "have "lawfully held" the stations for so long as this ad hoc instruction reasonably could be considered to remain in effect."[168]

The Tribunal considered the absence of affirmative efforts by Kosovo authorities to stop the Claimant's continued operation on the petrol stations insufficient to convert the Claimant's status into that of a lawful holder of rights within the meaning of the 2014 LFI. The Tribunal noted that as of the Republic of Kosovo in February 2008, which is a critical legal marker for purposes of the 2014 LFI's definition of investment, neither the UNMIK Permission nor the Termination Letter's requirement to continue operating, created rights that Mr. Selmani continued to "lawfully hold."[169]

However, the licenses issued by the MTI to Mr. Selmani from 2008 until March 2011 authorized him to import, store, and sell petroleum products, and therefore, the Tribunal considered them to form a valid legal basis for the investment to be deemed lawfully held under 2014 LFI.[170] As a result, the Tribunal considered that the Claimant had made a qualifying investment in Kosovo.

In *Gavrilovic d.o.o. v. Croatia*, the dispute concerned the privatization of 5 companies engaged in meat production by the Claimant (George Gavrilovic) through a purchase agreement in 1991. The Respondent argued that the alleged investment was not made in accordance with the host State's laws. The alleged illegalities involved the manifold irregularities in the bankruptcy procedures of the companies that were sold to the Claimant during the privatization process.[171]

Based on the balance of probabilities, the Tribunal found that the government had orchestrated the bankruptcy as a quid pro quo for the currency smuggling services rendered by Mr. Gavrilović to Croatia. Based on the evidence presented, the tribunal found that the investment was not made according to the Croatia's legislation due to the State's organs actions. Thus, under Article 7 of the ILC Articles, "the conduct of an organ of a State shall be considered an act of the State under international law if the organ exceeds its authority or contravenes instructions."[172]

---

168 *Id.* para. 345.

169 *Id.* paras. 348–349.

170 *Id.* paras. 350–353.

171 Georg Gavrilovic and Gavrilovic d.o.o. v. Republic of Croatia, ICSID Case No. ARB/12/39, Award, at 70–100, (Jan. 30, 2015).

172 *Id.* para. 384.

If the Claimant had orchestrated this situation, the Tribunal reasoned, it would have deemed the investments not made in conformity with Croatian legislation.[173]

Given that the State was involved in actions leading to the illegality of investment, the Tribunal concluded that it could not reject jurisdiction on the grounds of illegality.[174]

Rand v. Serbia is another dispute concerning the termination of the privatization agreement for the acquisition by the Claimant of 70% of shares in BD Agro, a dairy farm in Belgrade. The Respondent argued that the investment was not made in accordance with the laws and regulations of the host State. Such allegations included: (i) the transfer of shares was not performed over the Belgrade Stock Exchange, thus, in violation of Serbian 2002 and 2006 Securities Laws; (ii) alleged non-disclosure of the beneficial ownership to the Privatization Agency; (iii) accusations of siphoning funds from the privatized company; and (iv) and allegations of fraudulent land activities by extracting millions of euros through "land machinations."[175] The Tribunal found these allegations unbased. Additionally, the Tribunal emphasized that compliance with the host State's legislation is not an inherent element of the objective definition under Article 25 (1) of the ICSID Convention, considering that in the absence of such a requirement in the applicable treaty (in the present case Canada-Serbia BIT), the Tribunal is not obliged to apply them.[176]

In the *Anglo-Adriatic v Albania* case, the dispute was related to the privatization vouchers issued by Albania and their collection by the Anglo Adriatika Investment Fund S.H.A. ("AAIF"), a company registered in Albania. The Claimant Anglo-Adriatic Group ("AAG"), a company registered in the British Virgin Islands with the main business purpose of holding shares in the AAIF, argued that it made an investment in Albania by, inter alia, providing loans to AAG.[177]

While the Tribunal was not convinced that the Claimant provided any loan to AAIF, it noted that even if such a loan was made, it would still not qualify as a protected investment under the Albanian Law on the Investment Funds due to the prohibition therein that an investment fund is not entitled to "borrow money or take loans of any kind."[178] According to the Tribunal, such prohibition aimed at reducing insolvency risks, as the Funds authorized to borrow money

173 *Id.* paras. 324–325.
174 *Id.* paras. 396–400.
175 *See* the arguments on the illegality of investments, Rand Investments Ltd. and others v. Republic of Serbia, ICSID Case No. ARB/18/8, Redacted Award, at 93–107, (Jun. 29, 2023).
176 *Id.* para. 229.
177 *Supra* note 39, Anglo-Adriatic Group Limited v. Republic of Albania, at 19–24.
178 *Id.* paras. 281–293.

could eventually become unable to repay the amounts received.[179] Additionally, since investment funds could directly approach Albanian citizens and exchange their privatization vouchers against participation in the fund, such restriction was considered necessary to protect the general public from being deprived of their investments.[180]

According to the Tribunal, "the prohibition on funds to incur indebtedness pursued a compelling public purpose, which any investor was expected to know and observe. In this context, it follows that – should AAG have provided any type of financing to the AAIF – such asset would never qualify as a protected investment under Art. 1 LFI."[181]

3.4.2 Key Takeaways and Recommendations

The analysis above shows that while most of the tribunals have found that an investment made illegally does not qualify as an investment, in Rand v. Serbia, the tribunal emphasized that in the absence of such a criterion in the applicable treaty or law, the tribunal will not take it into account. Therefore, it is important that investment treaties and protection laws explicitly require that investment be acquired and established in conformity with the host State laws and regulations.

4 Conclusion

This analysis showed that the majority of investment treaties and investment protection laws of the WB Economies adopt vague definitions of "investor" and "investment," leading to their controversial interpretations and legal uncertainties. The current investment protection framework extends protection to unintended categories of "investor" and "investments," which contravenes the very purpose of these instruments.

This study unfolded the several qualifying criteria for "investors" and "investment," which have caused major challenges in determining ratione personae and ratione materiae jurisdiction. From high-profile figures to claims arising from commercial transactions, WB Economies have faced ISDS arbitration against their own nationals or companies controlled by them over assets with no contribution whatsoever to their development.

179 *Id.* para. 290.
180 *Id.* para. 291.
181 *Id.* para. 292.

The key lessons learned from the perspective of ratione personae jurisdiction in the WB context are:

1. Regarding natural persons:
   i. The majority of BITs do not exclude their own nationals or require that they have their "effective and dominant nationality," "domicile," or "main place of business" in the other contracting party; the only criteria for them to qualify as foreign investors is to have the nationality of the other contracting party. As a consequence, non-ICSID tribunals can accept dual nationals of the host State as foreign investors (e.g.,Selmani v. Kosovo).
2. Regarding legal persons:
   i. The place of incorporation is the weakest criterion for ascertaining nationality and provides more opportunities for claims from "mailbox" companies.
   ii. There is no single understanding of the "seat" criterion, leading to controversial interpretations, some more restrictive than others.
   iii. The "foreign control" criterion as drafted in current BITs is mainly vague, leaving plenty of discretion for the Tribunals to interpret them.
   iv. In the absence of treaty regulation, "foreign control" clauses do not apply reversely to deny jurisdiction to the companies controlled by the nationals of the host State.
   v. The WB framework does not address or limit a company's restructuring to gain treaty protection prior to ISDS proceedings or after the dispute arises.

The key lessons learned from the ratione materiae perspective in the WB context are:

i. The WB investment protection framework employs a broad asset-based definition with an open-ended list of assets and additional qualifying criteria and exclusions are rarely used.
ii. Tribunals tend to interpret these broad, open-ended asset-based definitions to cover everything of economic value, including commercial transactions.
iii. Without a requirement in the investment protection instrument that the investment is made in accordance with the host State's laws, tribunals are not obligated to take it into account for determining ratione materiae jurisdiction.
iv. In the absence of the criterion regarding the origin of the investment in the BIT, states' attempts to invoke this criterion in ISDS proceedings have been unsuccessful.

v. When interpreting broad definitions of investments, tribunals may view the practice of narrower definitions in other treaties as an indicator that broad asset-based definitions are intentional.

While the recommendations provided in this study will help address these issues, overcoming them would require a holistic reform. This includes reviewing the existing BITs and investment protection laws and strategically addressing the identified issues in line with best international practices. Methods to address these issues could include joint interpretations of BITs, renegotiations of investment treaties, and amendments to existing laws.

CHAPTER 8

Designing a Robust Fair and Equitable Treatment Standard for the Western Balkans

Filip Balcerzak

1 Introduction

The realm of international investment law has grown significantly since the first bilateral investment treaties ("BITs") were concluded almost 70 years ago.[1] The modern legal reality encompasses approximately 3,200 BITs currently in force globally.[2] Based on this network of treaties, a body of over 1,200 treaty-based, investor-state arbitral cases has grown over more than three decades, since the first claims were presented 30 years ago.[3]

This body of case law reveals a significant evolution in the understanding of the standards of protection included in the "*old generation*" BITs. This chapter focuses on one of the standards of protection typically encountered in investment treaties – the Fair and Equitable Treatment ("FET") standard – which is included in approximately 95% of all currently-existing BITs.[4]

The FET standard "*has existed as a sleeping beauty for about fifty years tucked away in a number of documents but was rarely, if ever, kissed awake.*"[5] This situation has changed drastically over the last 20 years. Already in 2006, the FET standard was perceived as "*an attractive catch-all cause of action for investors*".[6] Some commentators described it as "*the grundnorm or basic norm*

---

1 Whilst the roots of investment protection can be tracked further back in history, the current "*phase*" of investment-treaty making began in 1959, when the Germany-Pakistan BIT was concluded. See: Jeswald W. Salacuse, The Law of Investment Treaties (OUP 2021), p. 110.

2 There were 3,265 concluded BITs in 2022, of which 2,584 were in force. See: UNCTAD, World Investment Report 2023. Investing in Sustainable Energy for All (2023), p. 19.

3 Ibid, p. 20. The most recent online data reveals a total of 1,332 known treaty-based ISDS cases as of 31 December 2023 – <https://investmentpolicy.unctad.org/investment-dispute-settlement> accessed 02 July 2024.

4 Patrick Dumberry, "Has the Fair and Equitable Treatment Standard become a Rule of Customary international Law?", Journal of International Dispute Settlement (2017) 8(1), p. 157.

5 Christoph Schreuer, "Fair and Equitable", Transnational Dispute Management (2005) 2(5), p. 1.

6 Ryan Suda, "The Effect of Bilateral Investment Treaties on Human Rights Enforcement and Realization," in: Olivier De Schutter, "Transnational Corporations and Human Rights" (Hart Publishing 2006), p. 101.

 | DOI:10.1163/9789004729889_009

of the investment treaty system".[7] Currently, the FET standard is of the "*highest practical relevance*", and probably the most frequently invoked treaty standard in investor-state arbitrations.[8]

The FET standard's interpretation is considered by many as having evolved in a direction which states never imagined when negotiating the first-generation BITs. The plain meaning of the three typically used words – "*fair and equitable*" – offers little, if any, guidance to anyone seeking to interpret the FET standard literally.[9] This explains why, as early as 2006, it was noted that "*the most controversial words*" of the whole Chapter 11 of the North American Free Trade Agreement ("NAFTA"), regulating investment protection, were those encompassing the FET standard.[10]

Within this context, one can observe that the way in which international investment law ("IIL") has developed resulted in the public perception of this field of law being "*unjust, undemocratic and dysfunctional*".[11] Related investor-state dispute settlement ("ISDS") is perceived by public opinion as enabling arbitral tribunals to "*routinely prioritize foreign investment and corporate interests above environmental and human rights considerations*".[12] The body of ISDS case law and the related evolution of interpreting the FET standard can be understood as one of several factors leading to the existing backlash against IIL.[13] There are visible consequences of this state of affairs. For example, several EU member states, including Poland, Germany and France, withdrew from the Energy Charter Treaty ("ECT"), despite the ongoing process

7 Salacuse, *supra* note 1, p. 291.

8 Rudolf Dolzer, Ursula Kriebaum, Christoph Schreuer, Principles of International Investment Law (OUP 2022), p. 186.

9 GPF v. Poland, SCC Case No. V 2014/168 (29 April 2020), para. 539.

10 Meg N. Kinnear, Andrea K. Bjorklund, John F.G. Hannaford, "Investment Disputes under NAFTA. An Annotated Guide to NAFTA Chapter 11" (Kluwer Law International 2006), pp. 1105–16. Art. 1105(1) of NAFTA reads as follows: "*Each Party shall accord to investments of investors of another Party treatment in accordance with international law, including fair and equitable treatment and full protection and security*". NAFTA has been replaced by the United States-Mexico-Canada Agreement ("USMCA").

11 Report of the Special Rapporteur on the issue of human rights obligations relating to the enjoyment of a safe, clean, healthy and sustainable environment, David R. Boyd, *Paying polluters: the catastrophic consequences of investor-State dispute settlement for climate and environment action and human rights*, A/78/168 (13 July 2023), para. 1.

12 Ibid, para. 7.

13 Little (or no) responsiveness of IIL to human rights and environmental concerns, or towards protecting investments in fossil fuels, can be identified as examples of many other reasons.

of its modernization.[14] Another example can be found in the termination of the intra-EU BITs.[15]

Withdrawals from, and the termination of BITs are, however, an extreme approach. Despite having a tremendous impact on certain regions, and notwithstanding the EU's recent role at the centre of these developments, IIL continues to be a relevant body of public international law in the global context. There are no indications suggesting that, from the global perspective, IIL will cease to exist in any foreseeable future.

Within this context, it comes as no surprise that states learn from the development of the ISDS case law and react to undesired interpretations of the FET standard. Sometimes this takes the form of contracting parties formulating joint interpretations of a particular treaty. More significant in practice, however, is the approach adopted by states at the time of negotiating modern, "*new generation*" BITs, or renegotiating existing ones.

Against this background, this chapter analyses the FET standard in the context of the Western Balkans. First, it provides a brief overview of the region's experience with investor-state arbitrations, including the FET standard. Second, it analyses the current understanding of the content of the FET standard, emerging from the general body of case law. Third, it looks at current attempts to impose certain limits on the content of the FET in recent treaty-making practice. The research question which this chapter seeks to address is whether the Western Balkans states can successfully regain control over the interpretation of the FET standard, thus putting the genie back in the bottle.

2 Western Balkans' Experience with Investor-State Arbitrations

Given the expanding body of cases around the world, it comes as no surprise that the Western Balkans are no exception and that they have been respondents in several investor-state arbitrations. This section provides a short overview of this experience. Whilst this section is limited to treaty-based arbitrations, the

14 The ECT is a multilateral treaty, as opposed to a bilateral treaty, so formally speaking it is not a BIT. However, its investment protection and ISDS provision are comparable to typical BITs, which makes it a suitable example for the present analysis. For the purposes of this chapter, the term BIT is understood as applying to multilateral treaties, such as the ECT, and to free trade agreements which contain investment chapters.

15 Agreement for the Termination of Bilateral Investment Treaties between the Member States of the European Union (OJ L 169, 29 May 2020, pp. 1–41). Other examples include denunciations of the ICSID Convention by Honduras in 2024, and earlier by Bolivia, Venezuela and Ecuador.

Western Balkans states have been parties to arbitrations based on domestic laws and contracts other than those addressed below.

This section is not intended to provide a comprehensive review of all the existing ISDS cases against Western Balkans states. More detailed reviews can be found in the respective country-specific chapters of this book, as well as the chapter authored by Diana Rosert. Rather, this section aims to provide the relevant background, explaining the respective governments' experience with ISDS claims, including the FET standard. This is because such experience shapes the current approaches to IIL, as well as negotiating new and renegotiating existing treaties.

2.1 *Albania*

Albania has been the respondent state in at least 14 known ISDS cases. It prevailed in: (i) *Pantechniki v. Albania*,[16] concerning contracts for construction works on bridges and roads,[17] (ii) *Mamidoil v. Albania*,[18] related to the construction of an oil container port terminal,[19] (iii) *Burimi v. Albania*,[20] concerning legislative reforms and their impact on a gambling company,[21] and (iv) *Albaniabeg Ambient v. Albania*,[22] related to a waste management and a renewable energy production project.[23] Albania lost only one case, *Hydro v. Albania*,[24] concerning investments in a hydroelectric plant, a waste management facility, and a TV station.[25]

16 Pantechniki v. Albania, ICSID Case No. ARB/07/21, Award (30 July 2009).

17 <https://investmentpolicy.unctad.org/investment-dispute-settlement/cases/267/pantechniki-v-albania> accessed 02 July 2024.

18 Mamidoil v. Albania, ICSID Case No. ARB/11/24, Award (30 March 2015).

19 <https://investmentpolicy.unctad.org/investment-dispute-settlement/cases/402/mamidoil-v-albania> accessed 02 July 2024.

20 Burimi v. Albania, ICSID Case No. ARB/11/18, Award (29 May 2013).

21 <https://investmentpolicy.unctad.org/investment-dispute-settlement/cases/409/burimi-v-albania> accessed 02 July 2024.

22 Albaniabeg Ambient v. Albania, ICSID Case No. ARB/14/26, Award (20 March 2020). Whilst the award is not publicly available, the claimants have applied for its annulment, which suggests that the state prevailed. See: Albaniabeg Ambient v. Albania, ICSID Case No. ARB/14/26, Decision on the Applicants' Request for the Continuation of the Provisional Stay of Enforcement of the Award (10 August 2021), para. 3.

23 <https://investmentpolicy.unctad.org/investment-dispute-settlement/cases/577/albaniabeg-ambient-v-albania> accessed 02 July 2024.

24 Hydro v. Albania, ICSID Case No. ARB/15/28, Award (24 April 2019).

25 <https://investmentpolicy.unctad.org/investment-dispute-settlement/cases/637/hydro-and-others-v-albania> accessed 02 July 2024.

It settled two cases: (i) *Leaf Tobacco v. Albania,*[26] concerning tobacco products,[27] and *ČEZ v. Albania,*[28] concerning an investment in a power distribution company.[29] One case, *Arka Energy v. Albania,* concerning an investment in a photovoltaic park,[30] was discontinued for other reasons.[31] Five cases remain pending: (i) *Valeria Italia v. Albania,*[32] relating to an agricultural join-venture,[33] (ii) *Durres v. Albania,*[34] concerning a concession contract for a shipping terminal,[35] (iii) *Ndroqi v. Albania,*[36] concerning investment in programming and broadcasting activities,[37] (iv) *Ivicom v. Albania,*[38] relating to investment in electricity, gas, steam and air conditioning supply,[39] and (v) *EMS Shipping v. Albania,*[40] concerning warehousing and support activities for transportation.[41]

26 Leaf Tobacco v. Albania, ICSID Case No. ARB/95/1, Order of the Secretary-General taking note of the discontinuance dated 30 January 1997, pursuant to Arbitration Rule 44 (30 January 1997).

27 <https://investmentpolicy.unctad.org/investment-dispute-settlement/cases/6/leaf-tobacco-v-albania> accessed 02 July 2024.

28 ČEZ v. Albania, UNCITRAL.

29 <https://investmentpolicy.unctad.org/investment-dispute-settlement/cases/522/-ez-v-albania> accessed 02 July 2024.

30 <https://investmentpolicy.unctad.org/investment-dispute-settlement/cases/1072/arka-energy-v-albania> accessed 02 July 2024.

31 Arka Energy v. Albania, ICSID Case No. ARB/20/54, Order taking note of the discontinuance of the proceeding pursuant to ICSID Administrative and Financial Regulation 14(3)(d) (20 July 2022).

32 Valeria Italia v. Albania, PCA Case No. 2018-49.

33 Damien Charlotin, UNCITRAL tribunal upholds jurisdiction over claims stemming from Albanian agricultural venture, IA Reporter (20 September 2021), <https://www.iareporter.com/articles/uncitral-tribunal-upholds-jurisdiction-over-claims-stemming-from-albanian-agricultural-venture/> accessed 02 July 2024.

34 Durres v. Albania, ICSID Case No. ARB/20/37.

35 <https://investmentpolicy.unctad.org/investment-dispute-settlement/cases/1087/durres-and-others-v-albania> accessed 02 July 2024.

36 Ndroqi v. Albania, UNCITRAL.

37 <https://investmentpolicy.unctad.org/investment-dispute-settlement/cases/1307/ndroqi-v-albania> accessed 02 July 2024.

38 Ivicom v. Albania, SCC Case No. 2021/155.

39 <https://investmentpolicy.unctad.org/investment-dispute-settlement/cases/1228/ivicom-v-albania> accessed 02 July 2024.

40 EMS Shipping v. Albania, ICSID Case No. ARB/23/9.

41 <https://investmentpolicy.unctad.org/investment-dispute-settlement/cases/1285/ems-shipping-v-albania> accessed 02 July 2024.

2.2 *Bosnia and Hercegovina*

Bosnia and Hercegovina has been the respondent state in at least 5 known ISDS cases. It lost one, *Goljevšček v. Bosnia and Herzegovina,*[42] concerning the construction of hydroelectric power plants.[43] It prevailed in *Aggarwal v. Bosnia and Herzegovina,*[44] concerning an investment in an insurance company, and settled another one, *ALAS International v. Bosnia and Herzegovina,*[45] concerning a long-term supply agreement between a cement production company and a state-owned company.[46] Two cases remain pending: (i) *EGS v. Bosnia and Herzegovina,*[47] related to investment in a thermal power plant and a coal mine,[48] and (ii) *Mittal v. Bosnia and Herzegovina,*[49] related to an investment in a metallurgical coke mine.[50]

2.3 *Montenegro*

Montenegro has defended at least 6 known ISDS claims. To date, it has not lost a single one. It prevailed in: (i) *CEAC v. Montenegro,*[51] which concerned an investment in a local company which owned a smelting plant and produced

42 Goljevšček v. Bosnia and Herzegovina, ICSID Case No. ARB/16/36, Award (18 April 2022). Whilst the award is not publicly available, the respondent has filed for its annulment, which suggests that the claimant prevailed in the arbitration. The ICSID Annulment Committee rejected the annulment application, thus making the award final and binding on the parties. See: <https://icsid.worldbank.org/cases/case-database/case-detail?CaseNo=ARB/16/36> accessed 02 July 2024.

43 <https://investmentpolicy.unctad.org/investment-dispute-settlement/cases/752/goljev-ek-and-others-v-bosnia-and-herzegovina> accessed 02 July 2024.

44 Aggarwal v. Bosnia and Herzegovina, UNCITRAL. Award was issued in 2020, but it is not publicly available: <https://investmentpolicy.unctad.org/investment-dispute-settlement/cases/823/aggarwal-and-others-v-bosnia-and-herzegovina> accessed 02 July 2024.

45 ALAS International v. Bosnia and Herzegovina, ICSID Case No. ARB/07/11, Order taking note of the discontinuance issued by the Tribunal pursuant to ICSID Arbitration Rule 43(1) (27 December 2007).

46 <https://investmentpolicy.unctad.org/investment-dispute-settlement/cases/285/alas-international-v-bosnia-and-herzegovina> accessed 02 July 2024.

47 EGS v. Bosnia and Herzegovina, ICSID Case No. ARB/14/13. The case is formally suspended since 30 October 2020.

48 Patricia Živkovic, Yancy Cottrill, Bosnia and Hercegovina, in: Csongor István Nagy, Investment Arbitration in Central and Eastern Europe. Law and Practice (2019), p. 20, Nb 1.16.

49 Mittal v. Bosnia and Herzegovina, UNCITRAL.

50 <https://investmentpolicy.unctad.org/investment-dispute-settlement/cases/1299/mittal-v-bosnia-and-herzegovina> accessed 02 July 2024, Živkovic, Cottrill, *supra* note 48, p. 20, Nb 1.19.

51 CEAC v. Montenegro, ICSID Case No. ARB/14/8, Award (26 July2016).

aluminium,[52] (ii) *Medusa v. Montenegro*,[53] relating to oil and gas exploration rights,[54] (iii) *Deripaska v. Montenegro*,[55] concerning investments in a bauxite mine and in an aluminium production company,[56] and (iv) *Addiko Bank v. Montenegro*,[57] concerning investments in the banking industry.[58] The outcome of *MNSS and RCA v. Montenegro* – which concerned an investment in a local steel production company[59] – can be considered as a stalemate, since the tribunal found a violation of the applicable BIT, but awarded no compensation.[60] One case, *Atlas and Knežević v. Montenegro*, concerning an investment in banks and in a medical centre, remains pending.[61]

2.4 *Kosovo*

Kosovo has faced at least two known ISDS claims: (i) *ACP v. Kosovo*,[62] concerning the privatization of a postal and communications company,[63] and (ii) *Mabco v. Kosovo*,[64] concerning the privatization of a hotel.[65] It won the first case, whilst the second one remains pending.

---

52 <https://investmentpolicy.unctad.org/investment-dispute-settlement/cases/597/ceac-v-montenegro> accessed 02 July 2024.

53 Medusa v. Montenegro, PCA Case No. 2015-39, Award (17 July 2019), which is not publicly available.

54 <https://investmentpolicy.unctad.org/investment-dispute-settlement/cases/908/medusa-v-montenegro> accessed 02 July 2024.

55 Deripaska v. Montenegro, PCA Case No. 2017-07.

56 <https://investmentpolicy.unctad.org/investment-dispute-settlement/cases/765/deripaska-v-montenegro> accessed 02 July 2024.

57 Addiko Bank v. Montenegro, ICSID Case No. ARB/17/35, Award (24 November 2021).

58 <https://investmentpolicy.unctad.org/investment-dispute-settlement/cases/849/addiko-bank-v-montenegro> accessed 02 July 2024.

59 <https://investmentpolicy.unctad.org/investment-dispute-settlement/cases/494/mnss-and-rca-v-montenegro> accessed 02 July 2024.

60 MNSS and RCA v. Montenegro, ICSID Case No. ARB(AF)/12/8, Award (04 May 2016).

61 <https://investmentpolicy.unctad.org/investment-dispute-settlement/cases/1103/atlas-and-kne-evi-v-montenegro> accessed 02 July 2024.

62 ACP v. Kosovo, ICSID Case No. ARB/15/22, Award (03 May 2018).

63 Vladislav Djanic, Analysis: in the latest case to turn on tender process, ICSID tribunal finds that having a winning bid does not constitute an investment, IA Reporter (07 May 2018), <https://www.iareporter.com/articles/analysis-in-latest-case-to-turn-on-tender-process-icsid-tribunal-finds-that-having-a-winning-bid-does-not-constitute-an-investment/> accessed 02 July 2024.

64 Mabco v. Kosovo, ICSID Case No. ARB/17/25.

65 Damien Charlotin, Analysis: tribunal majority in Mabco v. Kosovo finds that claim to ownership of shares qualifies as investment; full tribunal takes no issue with claims ultimately benefitting a Kosovar government member, IA Reporter (24 December 2020), <https://www.iareporter.com/articles/analysis-tribunal-majority-in-mabco-v-kosovo-finds-that-claim-to-ownership-of-shares-qualifies-as-investment-full-tribunal-takes-no

2.5 *North Macedonia*

North Macedonia has faced at least 11 known ISDS claims. It prevailed in one case, *Guardian Fiduciary v. Macedonia,*[66] concerning the closure of bank accounts and the arrest of one of the local company's directors,[67] and lost one case, *Swisslion v. Macedonia,*[68] concerning the acquisition of shares in a food production company from the state.[69] It also settled one case, *EVN v. Macedonia,*[70] concerning the acquisition of Macedonia's national electricity distributor.[71]

Two cases were discontinued for other reasons: (i) *Cunico v. Macedonia,*[72] concerning investments in ferro-nickel mining and production operations,[73] and (ii) *Binani v. North Macedonia (I),*[74] concerning concessions to mine lead and zinc.[75]

Six other cases remain pending: (i) *Tasev v. North Macedonia,*[76] concerning an investment in a lead and zinc mine,[77] (ii) *Skubenko v. North Macedonia,*[78] concerning claims related to the termination of a concession for the exploitation

-issue-with-claims-ultimately-benefitting-a-kosovar-government-mem/> accessed 02 July 2024.

66 Guardian Fiduciary v. Macedonia, ICSID Case No. ARB/12/31, Award (22 September 2015).

67 <https://investmentpolicy.unctad.org/investment-dispute-settlement/cases/486/guardian-fiduciary-v-macedonia> accessed 02 July 2024.

68 Swisslion v. Macedonia, ICSID Case No. ARB/09/16, Award (06 July2012).

69 <https://investmentpolicy.unctad.org/investment-dispute-settlement/cases/360/swisslion-v-macedonia> accessed 02 July 2024.

70 EVN v. Macedonia, ICSID Case No. ARB/09/10, Award embodying the parties' settlement agreement (02 September 2011).

71 <https://investmentpolicy.unctad.org/investment-dispute-settlement/cases/342/evn-v-macedonia> accessed 02 July 2024.

72 Cunico v. Macedonia, ICSID Case No. ARB/17/46, Order taking note of the discontinuance of the proceeding pursuant to ICSID Arbitration Rule 43(1) (31 January 2020).

73 <https://investmentpolicy.unctad.org/investment-dispute-settlement/cases/859/cunico-v-macedonia> accessed 02 July 2024.

74 Binani v. North Macedonia, PCA Case No. 2018-38, Award (17 February 2020). From the judgment of the Swiss court, it seems that the decision of discontinuance was caused by lack of payment of the advance costs – judgment of the Swiss Federal Tribunal of 01 October 2020, case no 4A_156/2020.

75 <https://investmentpolicy.unctad.org/investment-dispute-settlement/cases/946/binani-v-north-macedonia-i-> accessed 02 July 2024.

76 Tasev v. North Macedonia, PCA Case No. 2019-09.

77 <https://investmentpolicy.unctad.org/investment-dispute-settlement/cases/1068/tasev-v-north-macedonia> accessed 02 July 2024, Vladislav Djanic, Uncovered: dispute over lead/zinc mine prompts treaty-based UNCITRAL BIT arbitration, IA Reporter (08 May 2020), <https://www.iareporter.com/articles/uncovered-dispute-over-lead-zinc-mine-prompts-treaty-based-uncitral-arbitration/> accessed 02 July 2024.

78 Skubenko v. North Macedonia, ICSID Case No. ARB/19/9.

of copper, gold and silver,[79] (iii) *Binani v. North Macedonia (II)*,[80] concerning concessions to mine lead and zinc,[81] (iv) *GAMA v. North Macedonia*,[82] relating to a gas-fired power plant,[83] (v) *Ambiente v. North Macedonia*,[84] concerning a waste disposal enterprise,[85] and (vi) *Amadeus v. North Macedonia*,[86] relating to an investment in a real estate project.[87]

2.6 *Serbia*

Serbia has faced at least 16 known ISDS claims. It has prevailed in four: (i) *Mytilineos v. Serbia (I)*,[88] concerning an investment in a mineral extraction and metallurgy business,[89] (ii) *Tvornica* Šećera *v. Serbia*,[90] concerning an investment in sugar production,[91] (iii) *Kornikom v. Serbia*,[92] relating to an underwater

79 <https://investmentpolicy.unctad.org/investment-dispute-settlement/cases/960/skubenko-and-others-v-north-macedonia> accessed 02 July 2024.

80 Binani v. North Macedonia (II), UNCITRAL.

81 <https://investmentpolicy.unctad.org/investment-dispute-settlement/cases/1229/binani-v-north-macedonia-ii-> accessed 02 July 2024.

82 GAMA v. North Macedonia, ICC Case No. 26696/HBH.

83 IAReporter, Balkan state is facing under-the-radar treaty arbitration, with a tribunal already in place (01 November 2022), available at: <https://www.iareporter.com/articles/balkan-state-is-facing-under-the-radar-treaty-arbitration-with-a-tribunal-already-in-place/> accessed 02 July 2024.

84 Ambiente v. North Macedonia, ICSID Case No. ARB/23/31.

85 <https://investmentpolicy.unctad.org/investment-dispute-settlement/cases/1268/ambiente-v-north-macedonia> accessed 02 July 2024.

86 Amadeus v. North Macedonia, ICSID Case No. ARB/23/35.

87 <https://icsid.worldbank.org/cases/case-database/case-detail?CaseNo=ARB/23/35> accessed 02 July 2024.

88 Mytilineos v. the State Union of Serbia & Montenegro and Serbia, UNCITRAL, Award (23 September 2009). The award remains confidential.

89 <https://investmentpolicy.unctad.org/investment-dispute-settlement/cases/200/mytilineos-v-serbia-i-> accessed 02 July 2024.

90 Tvornica Šećera v. Serbia, ICC Case, Award (15 July 2015). The award remains confidential.

91 Jarrod Hepburn, Balkans update: Serbia prevails over Croatian investor in rare ICC-rules treaty claim; unrelated claim under Kosovo investment statute threatened by a Serbian investor, IA Reporter (23 October 2015), <https://www.iareporter.com/articles/balkans-update-serbia-prevails-over-croatian-investor-in-rare-icc-rules-treaty-claim-unrelated-claim-under-kosovo-investment-statute-threatened-by-a-serbian-investor/> accessed 02 July 2024.

92 Kornikom v. Serbia, ICSID Case No. ARB/19/12, Award (20 September 2023).

coal mine,[93] and in (iv) *BRIF v. Serbia*,[94] concerning a real estate project.[95] It has lost six cases: (i) *Mera Investment v. Serbia*,[96] concerning investments in a construction company and banks,[97] (ii) *UAB v. Serbia*,[98] concerning the privatisation of a fertiliser manufacturer,[99] (iii) *Mytilineos v. Serbia (II)*,[100] concerning an investment in a mineral extraction and metallurgy business,[101] (iv) *Zelena v. Serbia*,[102] relating to an investment in an animal-rendering facility and the allegedly unequal enforcement of legislation on the handling of hazardous animal by-products,[103] (v) *Kunsttrans v. Serbia*,[104] relating to an art storage contract with a national museum,[105] and (vi) *Rand Investments v. Serbia*,[106] relating to an investment in a dairy farm.[107]

93 <https://investmentpolicy.unctad.org/investment-dispute-settlement/cases/963/kornikom-v-serbia> accessed 02 July 2024.

94 BRIF v. Serbia, ICSID Case No. ARB/20/12, Award (30 January 2023).

95 <https://investmentpolicy.unctad.org/investment-dispute-settlement/cases/1042/brif-v-serbia> accessed 02 July 2024.

96 Mera Investment v. Serbia, ICSID Case No. ARB/17/2, Award (10 March 2021). Whilst the award remains confidential, on 13 July 2021 ICSID registered an application for annulment of the award filed by Serbia, which suggests that it lost the case. <https://icsid.worldbank.org/cases/case-database/case-detail?CaseNo=ARB/17/2> accessed 02 July 2024.

97 <https://investmentpolicy.unctad.org/investment-dispute-settlement/cases/790/mera-investment-v-serbia> accessed 02 July 2024.

98 UAB v. Serbia, ICSID Case No. ARB/09/21, Award (16 March 2015). The award remains confidential.

99 <https://investmentpolicy.unctad.org/investment-dispute-settlement/cases/365/uab-v-serbia> accessed 02 July 2024.

100 Mytilineos v. Serbia, PCA Case No. 2014-30, Award (22 August 2017). The award remains confidential.

101 <https://investmentpolicy.unctad.org/investment-dispute-settlement/cases/560/mytilineos-v-serbia-ii-> accessed 02 July 2024.

102 Zelena v. Serbia, ICSID Case No. ARB/14/27, Award (09 November 2018). The award remains confidential.

103 <https://investmentpolicy.unctad.org/investment-dispute-settlement/cases/582/zelena-v-serbia> accessed 02 July 2024.

104 Kunsttrans v. Serbia, ICSID Case No. ARB/16/10, Award (19 November 2018). The award remains confidential.

105 <https://investmentpolicy.unctad.org/investment-dispute-settlement/cases/709/kunsttrans-v-serbia> accessed 02 July 2024.

106 Rand Investments v. Serbia, ICSID Case No. ARB/18/8, Award (29 June 2023).

107 <https://investmentpolicy.unctad.org/investment-dispute-settlement/cases/877/rand-investments-and-others-v-serbia> accessed 02 July 2024.

Serbia settled one case, *Loutraki v. Serbia*,[108] concerning a licence to operate casinos.[109] Four cases remain pending: (i) *United Group v. Serbia*,[110] concerning an investment in programming and broadcasting activities,[111] (ii) *APG v. Serbia*,[112] concerning an outdoor advertising concession,[113] (iii) *Coropi v. Serbia*,[114] relating to an investment in a real estate project,[115] and (iv) *Kent Kart v. Serbia*,[116] related to transportation fare collection services.[117] Details of at least one case remain unknown to the public.[118]

2.7 *Conclusions on the Experience of Western Balkans States in Investor-State Disputes*

As can be seen from the above brief description, the Western Balkans states have faced numerous ISDS claims. Commentators analysing these cases have noted that many of the investment disputes are "*of a political nature*".[119] This means that the actions (or omissions, in situations where action was required by law) of politicians, and specific representations made by them, play a relevant role in the region's ISDS reality. Other commentators underline the importance of a safe political and legal environment and note that that the

108 Loutraki v. Serbia, ICSID Case No. ARB/11/4, Order taking note of the discontinuance of the proceeding pursuant to ICSID Arbitration Rule 44 (18 January 2012).

109 <https://investmentpolicy.unctad.org/investment-dispute-settlement/cases/434/loutraki-v-serbia> accessed 02 July 2024.

110 United Group v. Serbia, ICSID Case No. ARB/21/5.

111 <https://investmentpolicy.unctad.org/investment-dispute-settlement/cases/1144/united-group-and-others-v-serbia> accessed 02 July 2024.

112 APG SGA and Alma Quattro v. Serbia, ICSID Case No. ARB/21/13.

113 <https://investmentpolicy.unctad.org/investment-dispute-settlement/cases/1137/apg-sga-and-alma-quattro-v-serbia> accessed 02 July 2024.

114 Coropi v. Serbia, ICSID Case No. ARB/22/14.

115 <https://investmentpolicy.unctad.org/investment-dispute-settlement/cases/1214/coropi-and-others-v-serbia> accessed 02 July 2024.

116 Kent Kart v. Serbia, ICSID Case No. ARB/24/10.

117 Investor in public transportation sector makes good on earlier threat to bring treaty claim against Serbia, IA Reporter (05 April 2024), <https://www.iareporter.com/articles/investor-in-public-transportation-sector-makes-good-on-earlier-threat-to-bring-treaty-claim-against-serbia/> accessed 02 July 2024.

118 Civis-Ing v. Serbia, see: <https://investmentpolicy.unctad.org/investment-dispute-settlement/cases/1029/civis-ing-v-serbia> accessed 02 July 2024.

119 See, for example: Ivan Bimbilovski, Elizabeta Spiroska, Macedonia, in: Csongor István Nagy, Investment Arbitration in Central and Eastern Europe. Law and Practice (2019), p. 281, Nb 9.52: "*The unequivocal conclusion stemming from the previous analysis is that the main reasons that lead to investment disputes in the Republic of Macedonia are of a political nature.*"

Western Balkans states must strive to increase political stability and to provide a perspicuous legal system and an efficient judiciary.[120]

This experience highlights certain sectors where the inflow of foreign investments exposes the Western Balkans states to greater-than-usual potential of facing ISDS claims, namely: (i) the energy sector, understood not only as energy production, but also its distribution,[121] and (ii) natural resources, understood as the exploration, extraction and processing of extracted ore.[122] There is at least one common feature shared by these two sectors, which is of particular relevance for the FET standard – they are highly regulated.

One consequence of the above is that investments in these sectors are more vulnerable to regulatory changes than investments in less regulated economic sectors. In this context, legitimate expectations regarding stability (or stability understood as a separate element) become essential for any FET standard analysis.

Another consequence is that investments in these economic sectors often require concessions or other types of authorizations, and can be subject to certain state subsidies. This opens the door to possible collisions between how the law is applied, and certain assurances made by various state agents, commonly politicians. This is why consistency becomes yet another element of the FET standard and plays a vital role in the analysed context.

3 The FET Standard and Its Substance as Emerging from the Case Law

According to the general rules of treaty interpretation under Art. 31(1) of the Vienna Convention of the Law of Treaties ("VCLT"), treaty text should primarily be analysed in light of its ordinary meaning.[123] With this in mind, one can try to establish the ordinary meaning of *"fair and equitable"* – three words which typically embody the FET standard in BITs. However, as already noted in the introduction, a literal interpretation of these three words offers little, if any, guidance.

120 Zoltán Víg, Gábor Hajdu, Serbia and Montenegro, in: Csongor István Nagy, Investment Arbitration in Central and Eastern Europe. Law and Practice (2019), pp. 436–437, Nb 12.71 and 12.74.

121 See, for example, footnotes 22, 24, 29, 30, 39, 43, 48, 71 and 83 above.

122 See, for example, footnotes 48, 50, 52, 54, 56, 59, 73, 75, 77, 79, 81, 89, 93 and 101 above.

123 *"A treaty shall be interpreted in good faith in accordance with the ordinary meaning to be given to the terms of the treaty in their context and in the light of its object and purpose."*

To borrow McLachlan's words, an analysis of the ordinary meaning of these terms "*may result in little more than an exchange of synonyms.*"[124] This explains why arbitral tribunals consider the plain meaning of the terms "*fair*" and "*equitable*" to be of limited practical relevance.[125] Perhaps because of these features, neither arbitral tribunals nor scholars have been able to agree on one, generally accepted abstract definition of the FET standard.[126]

In broad terms, one can observe that some BITs contain provisions which refer to the FET as a stand-alone standard, whereas others link it with the protection guaranteed by (customary) international law ("CIL") or with general principles of international law.[127] However, whilst this remains subject to debate and with the usual reservation that each case is different, arbitral tribunals tend to consider this differentiation as "*more theoretical than substantial*",[128] or "*more theoretical than real*".[129]

What is, however, rather undisputed is that the FET is an "*absolute*" standard.[130] It is irrelevant to analyse how the respondent state treats third persons (such as its own nationals, or the nationals of third states) in order to assess

124 Campbell McLachlan, Investment Treaties and General International Law, International and Comparative Law Quarterly, (2008) 57, p. 371.

125 See, for example: GPF v. Poland, *supra* note 9, para. 539, Micula v. Romania, ICSID Case No. ARB/05/20, Award (11 December 2013), para. 504.

126 See, for example: Kaj Hobér, The Energy Charter Treaty. A Commentary (OUP 2020), p. 189: "*In fact, it is probably impossible to provide a definition in the abstract which would be relevant for all types of alleged violations of the standard.*"

127 Salacuse, *supra* note 1, p. 293. Although each treaty is differently worded, certain generalizations are useful for the purposes of academic analysis.

128 Murphy v. Ecuador, PCA Case No 2012-16, Partial Final Award (06 May 2016), para. 206.

129 Rumeli v. Kazakhstan, ICSID Case No. ARB/05/16 Award (29 August 2008), para. 611. However, case law under NAFTA, which links the FET standard with CIL, led in several cases to a more "*restrictive*" interpretation when compared to non-NAFTA case law. See, for example: Adelina Prokop, Martyna Darczuk, Chapter Eight of CETA, Article 8.10 [Treatment of investors and of covered investments], in: Moritz Keller (ed.), EU Investment Protection Law: Article-by-Article Commentary (C.H. Beck 2023), pp. 173–212, Nb 11. As a matter of example, the EU was hesitant to link the FET standard with CIL in CETA in a manner comparable to the one applied in NAFTA, "*as it may significantly reduce the level of protection for investment afforded by the FET standard itself*" – see: Council of the EU, 'Meeting Document from the European Commission to the Trade Policy Committee on EU Canada Comprehensive and Economic Trade Agreement – landing zones' (06 November 2012) DS 1744/12, p. 9, available at: <https://thetyee.ca/Documents/2012/11/27/EU_Postion_Nov2012.pdf> accessed 02 July 2024.

130 See, for example: Garanti v. Turkmenistan, ICSID Case No. ARB/11/20, Award (19 December 2016), para. 380.

whether the disputed measures complied with, or violated the FET standard.[131] In that sense, it differs from "*relative*" standards, such as the Most-Favored Nation ("MFN") or the National Treatment ("NT") standards, which require a "*comparator*" to be identified and an analysis to be performed *vis-à-vis* a third person in like circumstances.[132]

In practice, in order to determine whether the FET standard has been violated, arbitral tribunals tend to identify certain non-cumulative "*elements*" of that standard, such as (i) legitimate expectations, (ii) proportionality, (iii) non-arbitrariness and non-discrimination, (iv) good faith, (v) due process, and (vi) transparency.[133] If a tribunal concludes that any of them was infringed, typically this results in a finding that the FET standard was violated.

"*The dominant element*" of the FET standard is the first of the elements listed above, namely the investors' legitimate expectations.[134] The protection of legitimate expectations is often considered as "*the most important function*" of the FET standard.[135] Legitimate expectations are, however, considered as an element of the FET standard and, therefore, as falling within its scope of protection only insofar as investors rely on them when deciding to invest.[136] This means that investors must have subjective expectations, which are at the same time objectively reasonable.[137] It is essential that the expectations exist "*at the time when the investor made the decision to invest*" if they are to be protected.[138]

One hot topic which generates lively discussion is to what extent, if at all, the legitimate expectations forming part of the FET standard include the stability of the host state's legislation.[139] Some argue that stability of the host state's legal

131 UNCTAD, Fair and Equitable Treatment. UNCTAD Series on Issues in International Investment Agreements II (2012), available at: <https://unctad.org/system/files/official-document/unctaddiaeia2011d5_en.pdf> accessed 02 July 2024, p. 6.

132 Hobér, *supra* note 126, p. 188.

133 See, for example: Philip Morris v. Uruguay, ICSID Case No. ARB/10/7, Award (08 July 2016), para. 320, GPF v. Poland, *supra* note 9, para. 543, Rumeli v. Kazakhstan, *supra* note 129, para. 609.

134 Saluka v. Czech Republic, UNCITRAL, Partial Award (17 March 2006), para. 302.

135 Electrabel v. Hungary, ICSID Case No. ARB/07/19, Decision on Jurisdiction, Applicable Law and Liability (30 November 2012), para. 7.75.

136 Enron v. Argentina, ICSID Case No. ARB/01/3, Award (22 May 2007), para. 262.

137 See, for example: Micula v. Romania, *supra* note 125, para. 671. When analysing whether expectations are objectively reasonable, tribunals should "*take into account all circumstances, including not only the facts surrounding the investment, but also the political, socioeconomic, cultural and historical conditions prevailing in the host State*" – see: Duke Energy v. Ecuador, ICSID Case No. ARB/04/19, Award (18 August 2008), para. 340.

138 Bayindir v. Pakistan, ICSID Case No. ARB/03/29, Award (27 August 2009), para. 190.

139 Some consider that legitimate expectations may be based on "*the presumed stability of the overall legal framework*" – see for example: Roland Kläger, Fair and Equitable Treatment

frameworks is so relevant that it should be treated separately from legitimate expectations, as another element of the FET.[140] For example, in *Mamidoil v. Albania* the tribunal stated that "*even when legislative changes seem legitimate, they must not have the character of a continuous oscillation and unpredictability.*"[141] Stability is often closely related to consistency, understood as how legislation is applied by domestic administrative and judicial authorities.[142]

If interpreted too broadly, an expectation of stability may entail a collision course with the state's right to regulate.[143] This is why tribunals in investor-state arbitrations are sometimes forced to decide whether the disputed changes to the host state's regulatory framework were within an "*acceptable margin of change*".[144] It is, however, uncontroversial that stability cannot be understood as a prohibition of states exercising their sovereign powers, and it "*does not mean a freezing of the legal system or making it impossible for the State to reform laws and other regulations* [...]".[145]

On the one hand, the FET standard protects legitimate expectations "*founded on specific assurances or representations*".[146] On the other hand, these representations do not necessarily arise exclusively from explicit promises, and they may be implicit in nature.[147] There are diverging views as to whether

in International Investment Agreements (OUP 2011), p. 164. See also, for example: Suez v. Argentina, ICSID Case No. ARB/03/19, Decision on Liability (30 July 2010), para. 222, LG&E v. Argentina, ICSID Case No. ARB/02/1, Decision on Liability (3 October 2006), para. 311. Others consider this approach to be "*expansive*" – see, for example: Ely Caetano Xavier Junior, Fabio Costa Morosini, El estándar de trato justo y equitativo, in: José Manuel Álvarez Zárate, Maciej Żenkiewicz (eds.), El derecho internacional de las inversiones. Desarrollo actual de normas y principios, Derecho Económico Internacional (2021), p. 449.

140 August Reinisch, Christoph Schreuer, International Protection of Investments. The Substantive Standards (CUP 2020), p. 462. See also, for example: Lemire v. Ukraine, ICSID Case No. ARB/06/18, Decision on Jurisdiction and Liability (14 January 2010), para. 284.

141 Mamidoil v. Albania, *supra* note 18, para. 621.

142 Reinisch, Schreuer, *supra* note 140, p. 468.

143 See, for example: South American Silver v. Bolivia, PCA Case No. 2013-15, Award (22 November 2018), para. 649, Arif v. Moldova, ICSID Case No. ARB/11/23, Award (08 April 2013), para. 537.

144 El Paso v. Argentina, ICSID Case No. ARB/03/15, Award (31 October 2011), para. 402.

145 Levy v. Peru, ICSID Case No. ARB/10/17, Award (26 February 2014), para. 319.

146 Gavrilovic v. Croatia, ICSID Case No. ARB/12/39, Award (25 July 2018), para. 956. The representations must be "*specific and unambiguous*" – Andrew Newcombe, Lluís Paradell, Law and Practice of Investment Treaties: Standards of Treatment (Kluwer Law International 2009), p. 281–282, quoted for example in White Industries v. India, UNCITRAL, Final Award (30 November 2011), para. 10.3.7.

147 See, for example: United Utilities v. Estonia, ICSID Case No. ARB/14/24, Award (21 June 2019), para. 576, Gold Reserve v. Venezuela, ICSID Case No. ARB(AF)/09/1, Award (22 September 2014), para. 571.

legitimate expectations to stability can be based solely on the host state's legislation, in the absence of additional representations given to a particular investor. Although the most recent cases concerning changes to legislation which regulates renewable energy sectors reveal that general legislation can create legitimate expectations that are protected as an element of the FET standard,[148] some tribunals have taken a different approach.[149]

4 Efforts to Re-Shape the FET Standard

Under the "*old-generation*" BITs, the FET standard has been described as "*maddeningly vague, frustratingly general and treacherously elastic*".[150] Many have perceived the development of the investor-state treaty-based arbitration case law and, above all, of the FET standard together with legitimate expectations as its central element, as favouring investors at the expense of states.[151] Critics underline that the manner in which the FET standard has been interpreted is grounded neither in the texts of the applicable BITs nor in the principles of treaty interpretation.[152] Sornarajah noted that *"few instances illustrate the*

148 Filip Balcerzak, Renewable Energy Arbitration – Quo Vadis? Implications of the Spanish Saga for International Investment Law (Brill 2023), pp. 309–318. Similarly, see for example: Rahmi Kopar, Stability and Legitimate Expectations in International Energy Investments (Hart 2021), p. 210.

149 For example, the tribunal in *Horthel v. Poland* stated that: "*general statutory norms thus do not give rise to legitimate expectations unless they contain a specific commitment of stability*", and that "*general rules of law do not generate legitimate expectations because they can be repealed or amended by the state*" – see: Horthel v. Poland, PCA Case No. 2014-31, Final Award (16 February 2017), paras. 240 and 248. A similar approach was taken, for example, by the tribunal in *Philip Morris v. Urugay,* which stated that *"no undertaking or representation may have been grounded on legal rules of general application"* – see: Philip Morris v. Uruguay, *supra* note 133, para. 431.

150 Salacuse, *supra* note 1, p. 294.

151 See, for example: Emmanuel T. Laryea, Legitimate Expectations in Investment Treaty Law: Concept and Scope of Application, in: Julien Chaisse, Leïla Choukroune, Sufian Jusoh (eds.), Handbook of International Investment Law and Policy (Springer 2021), p. 113: *"Application of the legitimate expectation concept overwhelmingly benefits investors. Considering that developing countries are mostly the respondents in investor – State arbitration cases, it stands to reason that they suffer the most from the application of the legitimate expectation principle, at least to the extent that the principle disadvantages host-States."* Similarly, for example, see: Christopher Campbell, House of cards: the relevance of legitimate expectations under fair and equitable treatment provisions in investment treaty law, Journal of International Arbitration (2013) 30(4), pp. 361–380.

152 See, for example, Suez v. Argentina, ICSID Case No. ARB/03/19, Separate Opinion of Arbitrator Pedro Nikken (30 July 2010) para. 3: *"The assertion that fair and equitable treatment*

rapidity of law-making in international law as the emergence into prominence of the fair and equitable standard from out of the shadows of over half a century of disuse, with content attributed to it in six short years."[153]

States could not have ignored this. As noted in the introduction, some states decided to exercise a "*nuclear*" option and abandon the IIL regime. Others have undertaken the effort to re-balance the content of the FET standard, using their powers as public international law actors – by negotiating new treaties, renegotiating existing ones, and providing joint statements on how to interpret treaties in force.

As early as 2012, UNCTAD observed that there is "*an emerging trend in IIA rule making* [...] *to add substantive content to FET clauses. This is also a way of being more precise about the content of the FET obligation and more predictable in its implementation and subsequent interpretation."*[154] Several recent examples can help to shed light on the most current direction of this trend in the context of the FET standard.

4.1 *The CETA Model of the FET Clause*

The Comprehensive Economic and Trade Agreement ("CETA") between the EU and Canada can serve as the first example. Art. 8.10 of CETA regulates the FET standard, alongside the Full Protection and Security ("FPS") standard.

Following a rather typically worded section 1, which embodies the FET and FPS standards,[155] section 2 stipulates that the FET standard will be infringed "*if a measure or series of measures constitutes:* (*a*) *denial of justice in criminal, civil or administrative proceedings;* (*b*) *fundamental breach of due process, including*

---

includes an obligation to satisfy or not to frustrate the legitimate expectations of the investor at the time of his/her investment does not correspond, in any language, to the ordinary meaning to be given to the terms "fair and equitable." Therefore, prima facie, such a conception of fair and equitable treatment is at odds with the rule of interpretation of international customary law expressed in Article 31.1 of the Vienna Convention on the Law of Treaties (VCLT). *In addition, I think that the interpretation that tends to give the standard of fair and equitable treatment the effect of a legal stability provision has no basis in the* BITs *or in the international customary rules applicable to the interpretation of treaties."*

153 Muthucumaraswamy Sornarajah, Resistance and Change in the International Law on Foreign Investment (CUP 2015), p. 246. On p. 247 he added that "[...] *In a leading article on the clause written in 1999, Vasciannie found it difficult to identify the content of the fair and equitable standard of treatment. Yet writing six years later, Schreuer maintained that the standard had been fleshed out with sufficient meaning within that period by arbitral awards."*

154 UNCTAD, *supra* note 131, p. 29.

155 *"Each Party shall accord in its territory to covered investments of the other Party and to investors with respect to their covered investments fair and equitable treatment and full protection and security in accordance with paragraphs 2 through 7."*

a fundamental breach of transparency, in judicial and administrative proceedings; (c) manifest arbitrariness; (d) targeted discrimination on manifestly wrongful grounds, such as gender, race or religious belief; (e) abusive treatment of investors, such as coercion, duress and harassment; or (f) a breach of any further elements of the fair and equitable treatment obligation adopted by the Parties in accordance with paragraph 3 of this Article".

Section 3 establishes that the contracting parties shall "*review the content of the obligation to provide*" the FET standard, and a specialized committee "*may develop recommendations in this regard and submit them to the CETA Joint Committee for decision.*" Next, section 4 adds that, when applying the FET standard, an arbitral tribunal "*may take into account whether a Party made a specific representation to an investor to induce a covered investment, that created a legitimate expectation, and upon which the investor relied in deciding to make or maintain the covered investment, but that the Party subsequently frustrated.*" Sections 6 and 7 "*for a greater certainty*" clarify that, respectively, "*a breach of another provision of this Agreement, or of a separate international agreement does not establish a breach of this Article*" and that "*the fact that a measure breaches domestic law does not, in and of itself, establish a breach of this Article.*"

The wording reproduced above shows that the CETA contracting parties undertook significant effort to limit the content of the FET standard, seeking to curb any undesired interpretations.[156] They have formally underlined that their intention was to "*clearly define investment protection standards*", including the FET standard, and to provide "*clear guidance to dispute resolution Tribunals on how these standards should be applied.*"[157] The European Commission further explained that the FET standard included in CETA is intended as "*neither a*

156 In the negotiations, the EU's initial position was to include an "*unqualified*" ("*standalone*") clause, typical for "*old-generation*" BITs. However, based on its experience as a respondent state, Canada insisted on a more detailed clause. See: Patrick Dumberry, Article 8.10 Treatment of investors and of covered investments, in: Marc Bungenberg, August Reinisch (eds.), CETA Investment Law. Article-by-Article Commentary (Nomos 2022), p. 264, Nb 13. As a result, although the provision's text does not explicitly link the FET standard with CIL, Canada issued a statement on CETA implementation, according to which "*Article 8.10 provides for an absolute minimum standard of treatment, informed by customary international law.*" See: Canada-European Union Comprehensive Economic and Trade Agreement – Canadian Statement on Implementation (2017) <https://www.international.gc.ca/trade-commerce/trade-agreements-accords-commerciaux/agr-acc/ceta-aecg/canadian_statement-enonce_canadien.aspx?lang=eng#a13> accessed 02 July 2024.

157 Joint Interpretative Instrument on the Comprehensive Economic and Trade Agreement (CETA) between Canada and the European Union and its Member States (OJ L 11, 14 January 2017, p. 3–8), point 6(c).

floor or a minimum standard nor an evolving concept. Rather, a clear, closed text defines precisely the standard of treatment without leaving unwelcome discretion to arbitrators".[158]

The CETA regulations described above are an attempt to clarify the boundaries of how to interpret the respective elements of the FET standard which emerge from the current case law. They do not seek to eliminate a majority of the "*elements*" of the FET standard which had been identified in the case law. Rather, they stipulate that a breach of due process must be "*fundamental*", arbitrariness must be "*manifest*", and discrimination must be "*targeted*". Whilst the inclusion of such adjectives in the wording of these provisions certainly elevates the threshold of the respective elements, and impacts the burden of proof during proceedings, they do not seem to constitute a fundamental shift away from how the FET standard has been interpreted in practice.[159] Rather, they seem to adjust the broader interpretation present in the general body of ISDS cases to the narrower interpretation, identifiable in the NAFTA case law.[160]

A different conclusion can be reached with respect to one, albeit crucial, element of the FET standard – legitimate expectations. Whilst CETA reaffirms that legitimate expectations form part of the FET standard, the wording of Art. 8.10(4) introduces two substantial limitations: (i) legitimate expectations do not constitute stand-alone elements of the FET standard but, rather, must be considered when interpreting other elements, and (ii) they must be based on specific representations.[161] Additionally, Art. 8.9(2) of CETA clarifies that legislative changes do not amount to a violation of legitimate expectations.[162] This

158 European Commission, Investment Provisions in the EU-Canada Free Trade Agreement (CETA) (26 September 2014), p. 1, available at: <https://services.djoef.dk/-/media/documents/djoef/j/investment-provisions-in-ceta.ashx> accessed 02 July 2024.

159 Dumberry notes that the content of this provision "*is to a very large extent based on how*" arbitral tribunals have interpreted Art. 1105 of NAFTA – a provision which contains the FET standard in this treaty. See: Dumberry, *supra* note 156, p. 262, Nb 9.

160 Prokop, Darczuk, *supra* note 129, pp. 173–212, Nb 27–29.

161 This should not be ignored in the future, as it is confirmed by the CETA negotiation process. Initially, the EU wanted to include a violation of legitimate expectations as one of the FET standard's elements, as proposed by Canada. See: Bernasconi-Osterwalder, Commentary to the Draft Investment Chapter of the Canada-EU Comprehensive Economic and Trade Agreement (CETA)', IISD Report, May 2013, pp. 17–19, <https://www.iisd.org/system/files/publications/commentary_investment_chapter_CETA.pdf> accessed 02 July 2024.

162 "*For greater certainty, the mere fact that a Party regulates, including through a modification to its laws, in a manner which negatively affects an investment or interferes with an investor's expectations, including its expectations of profits, does not amount to a breach of an obligation under this Section*" [i.e. Section D – Investment protection, which includes Art. 8.10 Treatment of investors and of covered investments, embodying the FET standard]. The

is a significant deviation from the general body of case law under the *"old-generation"* BITS.[163]

Another significant diversion from the current case law is that CETA provides a *"closed list"* of FET standard elements, being *"in fact the first FET clause contained in an IIA that specifically enumerates the different situations resulting in a breach of the obligation"*.[164] This is a major shift from the current understanding of the FET standard, which is categorised by an open list of non-cumulative elements.[165]

It remains to be seen how effective these efforts will be in practice. Whilst CETA provisionally entered into force in 2017, its investment chapter remains inapplicable until all EU member states ratify CETA.[166] This being said, the CETA contracting parties seem to be confident in the outcome of their efforts to eliminate any undesired interpretation, and recently have undertaken efforts to *"help SMEs with dispute resolution under CETA"*.[167]

CETA is not a single, one-time solution, as the EU has followed this path in its subsequent treaty-making practice. Newly negotiated treaties, such as the EU-Singapore Investment Protection Agreement[168] or the EU-Vietnam Investment Protection Agreement,[169] both contain similar solutions. This makes CETA a significant example of the current trends in treaty-making.

---

commentators understand that *"the Parties to CETA appear to have shifted the balancing exercise towards the greater protection of the Parties' right to regulate."* See for example: Monika Diehl, Martyna Darczuk, Chapter Eight of CETA, Article 8.9 [Investment and regulatory measures], in: Moritz Keller (ed.), EU Investment Protection Law: Article-by-Article Commentary (C.H. Beck 2023), pp. 158–172, Nb 36. The contracting parties underlined that they intended to guarantee *"that governments may change their laws, regardless of whether this may negatively affect an investment or investor's expectations of profits"* – EU-Canada Joint Statement, *supra* note 157, point 6(b).

163 For a more detailed analysis of this issue, see for example: Balcerzak, *supra* note 148, pp. 309–318.

164 Dumberry, *supra* note 156, p. 259, Nb 2.

165 See footnote 133 above.

166 <https://www.consilium.europa.eu/en/documents-publications/treaties-agreements/agreement/?id=2016017&DocLanguage=en> accessed 02 July 2024.

167 <https://policy.trade.ec.europa.eu/news/commission-proposes-new-rules-help-smes-dispute-resolution-under-ceta-2024-04-26_en> accessed 02 July 2024. Introduction of the investment court system, replacing the originally planned arbitration, may be a relevant factor increasing this confidence.

168 Arts. 2.2(2) and 2.4.(2)-2.4(4).

169 Art. 2.5.(2) and 2.5.(4). This treaty shows certain intended diversions from the path designated by CETA: (i) it does not contain a provision explicitly excluding the applicability of legitimate expectations to regulatory changes, and (ii) an explicit possibility that *"treatment not listed in paragraph* 2 [list of elements of the FET standard] *may constitute a breach of fair and equitable treatment where the Parties have so agreed in accordance*

Furthermore, an almost identical approach to the FET standard has been embodied in a relevant provision of the EU Model Clauses for BIT 2023, including the "*Treatment of Investors and of Covered Investments*".[170] The official commentary on the provisions mirroring the relevant CETA provisions confirms that the intention behind the adopted wording is to limit the scope of the FET standard as it currently exists in ISDS case law. The commentary explains that the adopted wording provides "*a closed list of improper and reprehensible State conduct that would constitute a violation of*" the FET standard, and limits the standing of legitimate expectations, so that they "*may only be treated as a relevant consideration when assessing an allegation of violation of the FET standard through any of*" the listed elements, "*and not as a standalone element that in itself would give rise to a violation of the FET standard.*"[171]

4.2 *The USMCA Model of the FET Clause*

The United States–Mexico–Canada Agreement ("USMCA") serves as another example of "*new-generation*" treaties which redefine the FET standard. Art. 14.6(1) of USMCA links the FET standard with CIL in the same manner as its predecessor (NAFTA) did.[172]

Section 2 of this provision clarifies that the FET standard, together with FPS, "*do not require treatment in addition to or beyond that which is required by*" CIL "*and do not create additional substantive rights*". It adds that the FET standard "*includes the obligation not to deny justice in criminal, civil, or administrative adjudicatory proceedings in accordance with the principle of due process embodied in the principal legal systems of the world*", and that "*a determination that there has been a breach of another provision of this Agreement, or of a separate international agreement, does not establish that there has been a breach of this Article*".

Whilst the sections reproduced above are in line with the wording used in the 2012 US Model BIT,[173] section 4 goes beyond by clarifying that "*the mere fact that a Party takes or fails to take an action that may be inconsistent with an*

---

with the procedures provided for in Article 4.3" (although the latter diversion seems of little practical importance, since broadening the list of the FET elements requires a treaty amendment, which is possible whenever the contracting parties so desire, even in the absence of such an explicit clause).

170 <https://investmentpolicy.unctad.org/international-investment-agreements/treaty-files/8390/download> accessed 02 July 2024, pp. 9–10.

171 *Ibid.*

172 Wording of the relevant part of Art. 1105 of NAFTA is reproduced in footnote 10 above.

173 <https://investmentpolicy.unctad.org/international-investment-agreements/treaty-files/2870/download> accessed 02 July 2024.

investor's expectations does not constitute a breach of this Article, even if there is loss or damage to the covered investment as a result."

Similarly to CETA, USMCA reacts to the crucial role played by legitimate expectations as a separate element of the FET standard in the ISDS case law. USMCA attempts to limit, or even eliminate legitimate expectations as an element protected by the FET standard, and therefore to recalibrate the direction in which ISDS case law evolved. Whilst this effort is clear, it remains to be seen how tribunals will interpret section 4. Its wording, reproduced above, allows diverging interpretations as to whether it refers to (i) the concept of "*legitimate expectations*" as established in the ISDS case law, or to a different term (mere "*expectations*", as worded in the relevant provision).

It is possible that this will be interpreted as implying a differentiation between "*legitimate*" expectations (which remain protected as part of the FET standard) and "*simple*" expectations (understood as the subjective beliefs of investors, as opposed to objectively reasonable expectations, thus falling outside of the scope of the FET standard). This, in fact, could be considered as confirming the current case law, which requires more than a subjective perception to create legally protected expectations. Additionally, USMCA is silent on the impact of specific representations from the host state to the investor on legally protected expectations, which creates another layer of possibly diverging interpretations.

4.3 *The ECT Model of the FET Clause*

The ECT serves as yet another example of the current trend in treaty-negotiations.[174] This comment is true even if attempts at modernization ultimately fail, as a consequence of the EU and the EU member states withdrawing from, rather than modernizing, the ECT.[175] The decision to withdraw

174 Four out of the six Western Balkans states are contracting parties to the ECT: Albania, Bosnia and Hercegovina, Montenegro, and North Macedonia. This makes this example even more relevant for this chapter.

175 In 2023, the European Commission called for a "*coordinated withdrawal*" by the EU and its member states. This is a surprising shift, given that the European Commission considers the text of the modernized ECT "*to be in line with the mandate*" it received to negotiate the ECT modernization from the Council of the European Union. Due to "*the abstention of a blocking minority of four Member States (Germany, France, Spain and the Netherlands) at the COREPER meeting*" (of 18 November 2022), the "*modernisation package*" was taken off the agenda of the Energy Charter Conference scheduled on 22 November 2022. The EU cannot participate in the voting due to the lack of consensus between its member states, and since its number of votes is equal to the number of its member states (which are the contracting parties to the ECT), without the EU there is no voting quorum in the Energy Charter Conference. This effectively blocks any modernization of the ECT. Additionally,

does not alter the fact that the EU and its member states have participated in the process of negotiating the modernized ECT since its commencement in 2017[176] until its finalization in 2022.[177]

The modernization of the ECT sought to, among other things, redefine the FET standard and expand the space for the state's right to regulate.[178] For example, the European Commission was mandated to negotiate an FET standard which is "*appropriately circumscribed for interpretation purposes*".[179] The official public communication underlined that, among several other important issues, the efforts aimed to "*increase legal certainty*" as regards the definition of the FET standard.[180] The approach adopted in the modernized ECT was to "*provide for a list that designates certain measures or series of measures that constitute a violation of this protection standard. Among such measures or series*

"*the entry into force or provisional application of a modernised Treaty would require the consent of the European Parliament, which has clearly stated that it does not support the reform of the Treaty and calls on the EU and Member States to organise a coordinated withdrawal from the ECT.*" See: Explanatory memorandum of a proposal for a Council Decision on the withdrawal of the Union from the Energy Charter Treaty, COM(2023) 447 final, 2023/0273(NLE) (07 July 2023), pp. 1–2. Back in October 2022, the European Commission recommended to "*adopt*" the modernized ECT – see: Proposal for a Council Decision on the position to be taken on behalf of the European Union in the 33rd meeting of the Energy Charter Conference, COM(2022) 521 final, 2022/0324(NLE) (05 October 2022), Art. 1. Currently, the European Commission recommends "*not to prevent*" modernization of the ECT by the EU and its member states – see: Proposal for a Council Decision on the position to be taken on behalf of the European Union in the Energy Charter Conference, COM(2024) 104 final, 2024/0057(NLE) (01 March 2024), Art. 1. Several EU member states have already either withdrawn or notified their withdrawals from the ECT, namely: Italy, France, Germany, Poland, Slovenia and Portugal. Others (i.e. Spain, the Netherlands and Denmark, as well as a former EU member state, the United Kingdom) have announced their plans to withdraw – see: Toby Fisher, EU Council approves withdrawal from ECT, Global Arbitration Review (08 March 2024).

176 See: Decision of the Energy Charter Conference (28 November 2017), CCDEC 2017 23 STR, available at: <http://dev.energychartertreaty.org/fileadmin/DocumentsMedia/CCDECS/2017/CCDEC201723.pdf> accessed 02 July 2024.

177 The negotiations on the Modernisation of the Energy Charter Treaty finalized on 24 June 2022, when the contracting parties reached an agreement in principle – see: Decision of the Energy Charter Conference (24 June 2024), CCDEC 2022 10 GEN, available at: <https://www.energycharter.org/fileadmin/DocumentsMedia/CCDECS/2022/CCDEC202210.pdf> accessed 02 July 2024.

178 Report by the Chair of the Subgroup on Modernisation, Annex to the Decision of the Energy Charter Conference, CCDEC 2018 21 NOT (27 November 2018), para. 6.

179 Annex to the Decision of the Council of the European Union, 10745/19 ADD 1, p. 4 (02 July 2019).

180 Finalisation of the negotiations on the Modernisation of the Energy Charter Treaty, annex to the decision of the Energy Charter Conference, CCDEC 2022 10 GEN (24 June 2022).

of measures, the new provision specifies the frustration of Investor's legitimate expectations and it describes circumstances that give rise to Investor's legitimate expectations and the conditions under which legitimate expectations may be considered."[181] In this context, the contracting parties "*reiterated and strengthened*" their right to regulate.[182] The above reveals the intention underpinning the wording of the modernized ECT, and how the ECT's contracting parties understand the new wording of its Art. 10.[183]

The approach taken in the modernized ECT shares many features that are present in CETA. Above all, it lists situations which will result in a violation of the FET standard. Whilst the list is not identical, it can be noted that: (i) the wording of two modernized ECT sections match the wording of two sections of the CETA list,[184] (ii) the wording of two sections of the modernized ECT

---

181 Decision of the Energy Charter Conference (24 June 2024), CCDEC 2022 10 GEN, available at: <https://www.energycharter.org/fileadmin/DocumentsMedia/CCDECS/2022/CCDEC202210.pdf> accessed 02 July 2024., p. 4.

182 "*Additional wording in the preamble and throughout the Treaty are introduced to reiterate and strengthen the right of Contracting Parties to regulate within their territories. For legal certainty, a new stand-alone article on the right to regulate is introduced in Part III of the Treaty to reaffirm the Contracting Parties' right to regulate vis-a-vis Investments and Investors in the interest of legitimate public policy objectives. Such objectives may include the protection of the environment, including climate change mitigation and adaptation, protection of public health, safety or public morals. A new structure is introduced in provisions on the exceptions from the Treaty to complement the existing general exceptions building on the provisions of GATT and GATS and clarify a possibility of taking measures for the maintenance of international peace and security*" – ibid, p. 5.

183 "*(1) Each Contracting Party shall accord to Investments of Investors of other Contracting Parties, and to such Investors with respect to their Investments, Fair and Equitable Treatment and Full Protection and Security in its Area.*
(2) A Contracting Party breaches the obligation to accord Fair and Equitable Treatment set out in paragraph (1) through a measure or series of measures that constitute
i. *arbitrariness, such as blatant unreasonableness;*
ii. *targeted discrimination on wrongful grounds, such as, gender, race or religious belief;*
iii. *fundamental breach of due process, including a fundamental breach of transparency in judicial and administrative proceedings;*
iv. *denial of justice in criminal, civil or administrative adjudicatory proceedings;*
v. *abusive treatment such as harassment, duress or coercion; or*
vi. *frustration of an Investor's legitimate expectations where these were central to its Investment, and arose from a clear and specific representation or commitment by that Contracting Party upon which the Investor reasonably relied in deciding to make or maintain the Investment.*
For greater certainty, a breach of another provision of this Treaty, or of any other international agreement, does not establish a breach of this paragraph."

184 The wording of sections a) and b) of the CETA list is identical to the wording of, respectively, sections iv) and iii) of the modernized ECT list.

sections is similar to the wording of two sections of the CETA list,[185] (iii) and the wording of one section of the modernized ECT differs from the respective section of CETA.[186]

Contrary to CETA and the more nuanced approach of UMCSA, the FET standard in the modernized ECT continues to protect legitimate expectations as a separate element of that standard. Building on the extensive case-law under the "*old*" ECT, it clarifies that legitimate expectations must: (i) be "*central*" to the investment, (ii) arise from a "*clear and specific representation or commitment*", and (iii) have been relied upon in deciding whether to make or maintain the investment.

Moreover, the modernized ECT further clarifies that "*for greater certainty, an Investor's legitimate expectations do not include general expectations, such as an expectation (in the absence of clear and specific representations or commitments to that effect) that a Contracting Party's legal or regulatory framework will not change*"[187] and that the "*determination of whether there is a clear and specific representation or commitment requires a case-by-case, fact-based inquiry that considers, among other factors, laws and regulations and the Contracting Party's relevant publicly known policies and their objectives.*"[188] These clarifications of the protection of the legitimate expectations should be read in conjunction with the new wording underlining the right to regulate. First, this is reaffirmed in the preamble.[189] Second, a new provision is to be added in Part III of the ECT, regulating investment promotion and protection.[190]

The above confirms that the ECT's contracting parties are sensitive to the case law in which arbitral tribunals have analysed the creation of legitimate

185 The wording of section d) of the CETA list is almost identical to the wording of section ii) of the modernized ECT list, except that the latter does not use the adjective "*manifestly*" before "*wrongful grounds*". Section e) of the CETA lists contains the same examples of abusive treatment as are listed in section v) of the modernized ECT list, albeit in a different order. It also clarifies the concept of abusive treatment "*of investors*" which is missing in the modernized ECT.

186 Section i) of the modernized ECT refers to "*arbitrariness, such as blatant unreasonableness*", whereas section c) of CETA refers to "*manifest arbitrariness*".

187 Footnote 2 on p. 33 of the Agreement in Principle on the Modernization of the Energy Charter Treaty ("Agreement in Principle").

188 Footnote 3 on p. 33 of the Agreement in Principle.

189 "*Acknowledging the inherent rights of the Contracting Parties to regulate investments within their territories in order to meet legitimate and public policy objectives*" – Agreement in Principle, p. 4.

190 "*The Contracting Parties reaffirm the right to regulate within their territories to achieve legitimate policy objectives, such as the protection of the environment, including climate change mitigation and adaptation, protection of public health, safety or public morals*" – Agreement in Principle, p. 31.

expectations based on legislation (in the absence of specific representations), and the violation of such expectations by changes to the regulatory framework which affect a group of investors (as opposed to measures affecting an individual investor). The often-commented-upon Spanish saga cases, as well as other cases initiated against EU member states in connection with the renewable energy sector, concern this kind of disputes, where claimants allege that a violation of the FET standard has occurred due to changes to the regulatory framework.

However, it is unclear whether the modernized ECT would lead to different outcomes when compared to the case-law based on the "*old*" ECT. This can be assessed by analysing the examples of cases initiated against Spain. First, the facts which led to the Spanish saga cases included an important factor, namely that Spain made certain assurances in addition to its general legislation, such as a press release reaffirming certain guarantees, "*road-shows*" conducted by state agencies around the world and promoting the regulatory framework in place, as well as a report reaffirming its understanding of the legal regime at the relevant time.[191] These could be classified as "*clear and specific representations or commitments"* even within the meaning of the first clarification of the modernized ECT.

Moreover, the relevant legislation's purpose was to incentivize private investments in the clean energy sector, so that Spain could meet its international obligations regarding its level of renewable energy supply.[192] This would be a relevant factor in the fact-finding exercise within the meaning of the second clarification of the modernized ECT. Indeed, when facing ISDS claims concerning its regulatory changes, Spain argued during various arbitral proceedings that its legislation "*does contain a general commitment to investors investing in renewables in Spain*", even though Spain disagreed with the claimants as to its scope.[193]

191 Balcerzak, *supra* note 148, pp. 36–37.

192 By way of example, the *Antin* tribunal arrived at this conclusion by relying on arguments presented by Spain in its submissions, filed during the proceedings – Antin v. Spain, ICSID Case No. ARB/13/31, Award (15 June 2018), paras. 82 and 84. See also, for example: Foresight v. Spain, SCC Case No. V 2015/150, Final Award (14 November 2018), para. 53, The PV Investors v. Spain, PCA Case No. 2012-14, Final Award (28 February 2020), para. 591, Masdar v. Spain, ICSID Case No. ARB/14/1, Award (16 May 2018), paras. 103–104, Stadtwerke v. Spain, ICSID Case No. ARB/15/1, Award (02 December 2019), paras. 51–52.

193 The dissenter in the *Cavalum* case reproduced part of Spain's post-hearing brief – Cavalum v. Spain, ICSID Case No. ARB/15/34, Dissenting Opinion of David R. Haigh Q.C. (31 August 2020), para. 53:

"Spanish legislation does contain a general commitment to investors investing in renewables in Spain, but it is not the commitment that Claimant claims. The Commitment that

4.4 *Joint Statements*

Negotiating new treaties and modernizing existing ones is not the only tool available to states wishing to react to undesired interpretations of the FET standard. Joint statements on correct treaty interpretations offer another possibility. The most recognised example of this is a statement issued by the Free Trade Commission entitled "*Notes of Interpretation of Certain Chapter 11 Provisions*". This was issued by the NAFTA contracting states in 2001, as a reaction to three awards previously rendered under that treaty:[194] *Metalclad v. Mexico*,[195] *S.D. Myers v. Canada*,[196] and *Pope & Talbot v. Canada*.[197]

The NAFTA contracting states intended to restrict the meaning of the FET standard to CIL. As noted earlier in this chapter, the effectiveness of this attempt remains debatable, and the NAFTA contracting parties "*have not fully regained "control" over the interpretation of Article 1105*".[198]

4.5 *The Western Balkans Modern Treaty-Making Practice*

The Western Balkans states have decided to follow the same path in treaty-making in the realm of IIL.[199] These efforts have resulted in at least two new model BIT s, recently adopted by Western Balkans states: (i) by Bosnia and Hercegovina in 2023 and (ii) by Montenegro in 2021.[200] Publicly available

Spanish legislation contained at the time of Claimant's investment and that is maintained in the Spanish legislation currently in force, after the disputed measures, is that investors obtain a reasonable return to their investment in accordance with the cost of money in the capital markets."

194 Dumberry, *supra* note 156, p. 260, Nb 4.

195 Metalclad v. Mexico, ICSID Case No. ARB(AF)/97/1, Award (30 August 2000).

196 S.D. Myers v. Canada, UNCITRAL, Partial Award (13 November 2000).

197 Pope & Talbot v. Canada, UNCITRAL, Award on the Merits of Phase 2 (10 April 2001).

198 Patrick Dumberry, Moving the Goal Post! How Some NAFTA Tribunals Have Challenged the FTC Note of Interpretation on the Fair and Equitable Treatment Standard Under NAFTA Article 1105, World Arbitration & Mediation Review (2014) 8:2, p. 292. See also footnote 129 above.

199 One recent example is that experts from the Western Balkans participated in early 2024 in a "Training on the Negotiation Skills for International Investment Agreements" – see: <https://www.linkedin.com/posts/samira-sulejmanovicba_westernbalkan-regional-cooperation-bits-activity-7188094127501164544-eQ3D> accessed 02 July 2024. Another example of re-shaping the experience with IIL is the initiative of Bosnia and Hercegovina to establish a mechanism for "Prevention and Early Detection of International Investment Disputes." See: D Tavilović, BiH pokušava odgovoriti investitore od arbitraže (Capital.ba, 24 April 2024) <https://www.capital.ba/bih-pokusava-odgovoriti-investitore-od-arbitraze/> accessed 02 July 2024.

200 <https://investmentpolicy.unctad.org/international-investment-agreements/model-agreements> accessed 02 July 2024.

information shows that these processes started several years ago, and that the region was not delayed in its activities regarding IIL when compared to the globally visible shifts.[201]

Whilst, unfortunately, none of these model BITs have been made publicly available, the "*Regionally Accepted Standards for Negotiating IIAs*" ("Standards") adopted by the Western Balkans states in 2020 have been made available to the public.[202] They shed light on the approach of the region's states towards negotiating new BITs and renegotiating existing ones. Looking at the example of the FET standard, this approach seems to be fully aligned with the approach adopted by the EU, as described earlier in this chapter.[203] In new BITs, the

201 As noted in footnote 154, such trends were already visible in 2012, whereas Bosnia and Hercegovina started along this path back in 2014 – Samira Sulejmanovic, Reform of IIAs regime in Bosnia and Herzegovina or BIH version of The Fellowship of the Ring (10 January 2024), <https://www.linkedin.com/pulse/reform-iias-regime-bosnia-herzegovina-bih-version-samira-sulejmanovic-l728f> accessed 02 July 2024.

202 <https://www.rcc.int/docs/562/wb6-regionally-accepted-standards-for-negotiating-iias> accessed 02 July 2024. As regards the FET standard, the document states as follows: "*Inclusion of a fair and equitable treatment clause with the following elements:*

- *Protecting investors against serious instances of arbitrary, discriminatory or abusive conduct by host economies;*
- *Clarifying the scope of the term "fair and equitable treatment" by enumerating actions in a closed list that constitute FET violations such as, for example, denial of justice in criminal, civil and administrative proceedings; a fundamental breach of due process; manifestly arbitrary conduct; harassment, coercion, abuse of power or similar bad faith conduct; and targeted discrimination on manifestly wrongful grounds, such as gender, race or religious belief;*
- *Clarifying the scope by describing actions that are outside the scope of the FET clause, for example, by a statement that the mere disappointment of investors' legitimate expectations does not in itself amount to a breach of fair and equitable treatment.*
- *Clarifying that a breach of another provision of the respective agreement or another international agreement is not considered a breach of the FET clause.*"

203 As one of the officials involved in drafting the Standards noted, they "*were prepared with assistance of*" the European Commission, to "*make sure the investment policy reflected in IIAs is in line with the one of the Commission*" – <https://www.linkedin.com/posts/samira-sulejmanovicba_regional-iias-standards-in-wb6-activity-7026566701815054336-_PPK> accessed 02 July 2024. In a note prepared by a state official of Bosnia and Hercegovina who was involved in preparing the Standards, it has been confirmed that the Standards were prepared in a "*complex process*" in cooperation with, among others, the European Commission. The authors "*undertook to make a full mapping and comprehensive review of IIAs currently in force as well as to benchmark them with new generation IIAs and EU standards to identify gaps and develop recommendations to enhance alignment with reform-oriented standards in new generation IIAs / EU standards and drafting a new model of BiH BITs.*" See: Alma Daut, Regionally Accepted Standards of the Western Balkan's for Negotiating IIAs, <https://www.linkedin.com/posts/samira-sulejmanovicba_regional-iias-standards-in-wb6-activity-7026566701815054336-_PPK> accessed 02 July 2024, p. 1.

FET standard should be defined by a closed list of elements (explicitly excluding the protection of legitimate expectations), with adjectives added to elevate the threshold required for finding violations of those respective elements (as in recent treaties concluded by the EU, a breach of due process must be "*fundamental*", arbitrariness must be "*manifest*", and discrimination must be "*targeted*"). In addition, the Standards re-affirm the right to regulate.

There is only one BIT which has been recently negotiated by a state from the region – the Serbia-Turkey BIT – which is available in the public domain.[204] It reflects the approach towards the FET standard that is proposed in the Standards for treaty negotiation. Art. 3(3) of that BIT contains a closed list of the FET standard's elements, containing the same adjectives as those adopted in the Standards.

5 Conclusions

The Western Balkans states are far from abandoning IIL. On the contrary, publicly available information shows that they are striving to re-shape the content of existing and future investment treaties.

Some commentators note that the role of IIL will grow alongside the process of joining the EU.[205] Five of the Western Balkans states are recognized candidates for membership in the EU: Albania, Bosnia and Hercegovina, Montenegro, North Macedonia and Serbia. The sixth one, Kosovo, has filed an application for membership, and is considered as a potential candidate. A crucial element of the efforts underway to accede to the EU is the process of harmonizing the respective states' domestic laws with EU law. Therefore, it comes as no surprise that the same efforts can be seen, or at least can be expected, when one looks at the Western Balkans' approach towards IIL, which is aligned with the approach of the EU and its member states.[206]

204 This was signed in 2022 but, at the time of writing, is not yet in force. In 2023, Serbia concluded another BIT, with South Korea, which is not in public domain, <https://investmentpolicy.unctad.org/international-investment-agreements/treaties/bilateral-investment-treaties/5080/korea-republic-of---serbia-bit-2023-> accessed 02 July 2024. In 2021, North Macedonia signed a BIT with the United Arab Emirates, which entered into force in 2023. Unfortunately, the text is not publicly available in English. <https://investmentpolicy.unctad.org/international-investment-agreements/treaties/bilateral-investment-treaties/4969/north-macedonia---united-arab-emirates-bit-2021-> accessed 02 July 2024.

205 Živkovic, Cottrill, *supra* note 48, p. 23, Nb 1.23.

206 In the context of accession to the EU, one can expect the existence of certain transition clauses regarding BITs which would become intra-EU after the Western Balkans states'

Building on their experience with treaty-based investor-state claims and on the recent examples of treaty-making visible globally, the Western Balkans states have begun efforts to regain control over the interpretation of the FET standard, and to mitigate their exposure for claims based on newly negotiated BITs. They have the tools to put the genie back into the bottle, at least when it comes to securing enough space for their right to regulate and, potentially, limit or eliminate legitimate expectations regarding regulatory stability.

It will be a harder task to ensure consistency regarding potential claims related to specific assurances frivolously given by politicians. Even new-generation BITs will, most likely, offer some kind of protection to legitimate expectations based on such specific assurances. In this context, it is crucial to continue the process of modernizing domestic legislation, to ensure that it offers internal mechanisms of checks-and-balances to correct any frivolously made statements in a timely manner. If such domestic mechanisms are in place and are effective, any expectations which go beyond them can be expected to fall within the category of subjective beliefs, as opposed to objectively reasonable expectations, and therefore to fall outside the scope of protection of the FET standard.

---

accession to the EU. This is in line with the section of the Standards entitled "*Compliance with EU law*", which requires that any new and renegotiated BITs should include a "*horizontal REIO clause, i.e. provisions ensuring that, upon becoming an EU Member State, the party to the BIT has an obligation to ensure that its BITs are interpreted and applied in a manner that is consistent with the obligations resulting from its membership in the European Union, as well as to take the necessary steps to ensure fulfilment of such obligations.*"

CHAPTER 9

Unlocking the Benefits of Investor-State Dispute Prevention Mechanisms

Existing and Potential Solutions for the Western Balkans

Fahira Brodlija

1 Introduction

In recent years, policy makers, scholars and practitioners have dedicated intensive attention to the process of investor-State dispute settlement (ISDS), especially investment arbitration as the default ISDS procedure.[1] However, a sole focus on the adversarial stage of ISDS leaves behind the rich landscape of dispute prevention opportunities and mechanisms available in the pre-dispute phase.[2] While it is undeniable that the existing framework for ISDS should be addressed to respond to the concerns of the relevant stakeholders, there is nothing preventing States from also considering and enabling mechanisms that could help identify and prevent investment claims at their root.[3]

In this sense, investment claims can be approached as an indication of underlying gaps in communication and coordination between foreign investors and competent government institutions. These gaps block communications and prevent timely responses to investor grievances, although they may be readily available within the competent government agencies.[4] In other

1 Since 2018, the UNCITRAL Working Group III (ISDS Reform) has been the forum for States, international organizations and other stakeholders discussing the reform of the ISDS system from the procedural perspective. The reform discussions also include systemic issues, such as the possibility of establishing a standing multilateral investment court and/or appellate mechanism. The developments and working documents are all available on the UNCITRAL WGIII website here: <https://uncitral.un.org/en/working_groups/3/investor-state> accessed 29 April 2024.

2 UNCITRAL Secretariat, 'Possible reform of investor-State dispute settlement (ISDS) Dispute prevention and mitigation – Means of alternative dispute resolution' (UNCITRAL, 15 January 2020) 10 <https://documents-dds-ny.un.org/doc/UNDOC/LTD/V20/002/56/PDF/V2000256.pdf?OpenElement> accessed 29 April 2024.

3 According to the UNCTAD Investment Policy Hub, there are 1257 known ISDS cases registered as of 19 April 2023 <https://investmentpolicy.unctad.org/> accessed 29 April 2024.

4 John Bonnitcha and Zoe Williams, 'Investment Dispute Prevention and Management Agencies: Toward a more informed policy discussion', (International Institute for Sustainable

 | DOI:10.1163/9789004729889_010

words, the different ends of the dispute resolution spectrum co-exist in information silos, missing valuable opportunities for coordinated responses to investor grievances, and ultimately for the prevention of potential investment disputes.

By mobilizing internal coordination and communication mechanisms, States could have the best of both worlds: they would retain existing and attract new investments by creating an agile, responsive and transparent investment protection framework, while mitigating the risk of legal exposure and short-term and long-term losses.[5] Regardless of the many potential benefits of dispute prevention mechanisms, they are either absent or underutilized in most jurisdictions. In investment treaty practice, they are virtually non-existent in both old-generation and new-generation treaties.

This chapter explores the potential of dispute prevention mechanisms to become a powerful instrument for investment protection policies in the Western Balkans, regardless of the outcome of the ongoing ISDS reform process. Following a (1) general overview of the concept and features of investment dispute prevention mechanisms, (2) the chapter analyzes the specific issues and concerns identified and shared by the Western Balkans governments, (3) as well as the treaty-based and institutional reforms undertaken in the region to address these issues. (4) The analysis will be rounded out with proposals developed in other regions, within the UNCITRAL Working Group III (ISDS Reform) (WGIII), as well as other international organizations and institutions). Finally, (5) the chapter will conclude with reflections on some common features of dispute prevention mechanisms around the world, which may be beneficial for the Western Balkans, as potential staples of investment protection for both gradual and systemic reform.

Development (IISD) Report, January 2022). It is reported that investors publicly complained that they initiated arbitral proceedings against the host state because they could not establish a proper communication with the competent institutions, and that arbitration was "simply the only option left to limit the severe financial damage." Jack Ballantyne, 'Albania faces claim over gas turbine power plant' (Global Arbitration Review, 05 May 2022) <https://globalarbitrationreview.com/article/albania-faces-claim-over-gas-turbine-power-plant> accessed 29 April 2024.

5 *See*, Priyanka Kher and Dongwook Khun, 'Policy Options to Mitigate Political Risk and Attract FDI' (The World Bank Group, 2020) p. 16 <https://openknowledge.worldbank.org/bitstream/handle/10986/34380/Policy-Options-to-Mitigate-Political-Risk-and-Attract-FDI.pdf?sequence=1> accessed 29 April 2024.

2 The Sea Change in the ISDS System and the Island of Dispute Prevention

International investment arbitration has long been the default dispute resolution mechanism for investment disputes.[6] Enshrined in a network of thousands of (bilateral and multilateral) investment treaties,[7] foreign investment laws and investment contracts since the 1960s, investment arbitration has flourished since the 1980s – demonstrating the "bite" of ISDS clauses to treaty parties.[8] A relatively young mechanism in a nascent field of international investment law, investor-State dispute settlement (ISDS) is experiencing growing pains after an explosion of cases starting from the early 2000s to date.[9]

The ongoing reform process spearheaded by the UNCITRAL Working Group III (ISDS Reform) is aimed at addressing the main concerns identified in the existing ISDS system, i.e., the perceived lack of consistency and coherence in the arbitral awards, bias and lack of accountability of arbitrators in ISDS, duration of the proceedings and, perhaps most importantly, the sometimes high damages awards in favor of foreign investors and high costs of arbitral proceedings and legal representation.[10] During the entire lifetime and operations of a long-term investment, issues and complications may arise at various stages of the conflict continuum, which need to be adequately addressed.[11]

Dispute prevention mechanisms have not been deliberated in detail at the WGIII. However, recently, the UNCITRAL Commission has adopted instruments

6 Joachim Pohl, Kekeletso Mashigo and Alexis Nohen, 'Dispute Settlement Provisions in International Investment Agreements: A Large Sample Survey' (OECD Working Papers on International Investment, 2012/02, OECD Publishing, 2012) p. 15 <https://papers.ssrn.com/sol3/papers.cfm?abstract_id=2187254> accessed 29 April 2024.

7 UNCTAD (n 3).

8 UNCTAD, 'Treaty-Based Investor–State Dispute Settlement Cases and Climate Action' (IIA Issues Note, Issue 4, September 2022) p. 2 <https://unctad.org/system/files/official-document/diaepcbinf2022d7_en.pdf> accessed 29 April 2024.

9 UNCTAD (n 3).

10 UNCITRAL Secretariat, 'Possible reform of investor-State dispute settlement (ISDS)' (UNCITRAL, 30 July 2019) <https://documents-dds-ny.un.org/doc/UNDOC/LTD/V19/082/01/PDF/V1908201.pdf?OpenElement> accessed 29 April 2024.

11 The World Bank has illustrated the various stages of the investor-State relations as a continuum with multiple points on which issues and disputes may arise, which require different types of reactions and dispute resolution mechanisms. Kher and Khun (n 5) p. 16. Similarly, ICSID has referred to an Investment Dispute Chronology to highlight the different stages on a timeline during which direct negotiations and mediation are available, through the lifecycle of the investment. ICSID, 'Background Paper on Investment Mediation' (ICSID, July 2021) p. 4 < https://icsid.worldbank.org/sites/default/files/publications/Background_Paper_on_Investment_Mediation_Oct.2021.pdf> accessed 29 April 2024.

for mediation as an alternative dispute settlement mechanism: UNCITRAL Model Provisions on Mediation, the UNCITRAL Guidelines on Mediation for International Investment Disputes.[12] Such mechanisms are usually activated during the so-called "cooling-off stage", which, depending on the respective investment treaty, lasts from three to six months, once the notice of dispute has already been submitted to the host State and the clock ticks before the initiation of the arbitral proceedings.[13] While there are no emerging multilateral solutions, countries around the world have developed a variety of mechanisms aimed at facilitating foreign investments and preventing possible disputes. The WGIII has published a compilation of best practices demonstrating the mechanisms established in countries around the world, as well as draft Guidelines for Dispute Prevention and Mitigation (which will be further discussed below). However, the Guidelines remain a neutral proposal, left to the discretion of each adopting State.

The period before investor grievances has not yet escalated into a full-blown dispute provides the highest chances of coming to an efficient, direct, and painless solution, if the foreign investor is facing an administrative or

12 The WGIII has developed two concrete instruments dedicated to the facilitation and promotion of mediation as a dispute resolution mechanism in ISDS, available to State as guidance and models for policy and procedural reforms. UNCITRAL Secretariat, 'Possible reform of investor-State dispute settlement (ISDS): Draft provisions on mediation' (UNCITRAL, 25 April 2023) <https://uncitral.un.org/sites/uncitral.un.org/files/media-documents/uncitral/en/draft_provisions_advance_copy.pdf> accessed 29 April 2024; UNCITRAL Secretariat, 'Possible reform of investor-State dispute settlement (ISDS): Draft UNCITRAL guidelines on investment mediation' (UNCITRAL, 21 April 2023) <https://uncitral.un.org/sites/uncitral.un.org/files/media-documents/uncitral/en/draft_guidlines_advance_copy.pdf> accessed 29 April 2024; United Nations press release, 'UN Commission on International Trade Law finalizes four legal texts during the first week of its 56th Session in Vienna' (13 July 2023) https://unis.unvienna.org/unis/en/pressrels/2023/unisl344.html> accessed 29 April 2024.

13 The cooling-off period is determined in most international investment agreements as the first step in the dispute resolution process, before initiating arbitration, requiring the parties to engage in a good faith effort to resolve the dispute amicably (through negotiations, mediation or conciliation) for a specific period of time (three to six months in most treaties). None of these provisions in old-generation treaties provide any guidance on the pre-dispute phase or the proper communication channels for possible early resolution of disputes. They also generally do not indicate that non-adversarial processes, such as mediation, are available even after the initiation of arbitral proceedings. *See,* for example, North Macedonia – Lithuania BIT, Art 8, which only establishes the duty of the parties to attempt amicable settlement for six months, following which the investor can initiate arbitration.

operational issue affecting their investment.[14] With a prompt and coordinated response from the competent institution or agency, these issues could be addressed immediately, or referred to the appropriate high political level for further attempts of amicable settlement or dispute resolution. Nevertheless, it is precisely in this phase when the best opportunities for dispute prevention and avoidance are missed.[15]

Direct lines of communication and interest-based resolutions of issues are also preferred by foreign investors who have already stressed that arbitration and litigation are the last resort solutions which they would rather avoid.[16] In fact, some investors stated that they use the initiation of arbitral proceedings as leverage to progress in direct negotiations or settlement.[17] The following sections will provide a terminological framework of the analysis, followed by a comparative showcase of dispute prevention models proposed by international organizations or adopted by some States.

3 Defining the Vocabulary of Dispute Prevention and Management

Before engaging in a deeper analysis of existing and potential forms of dispute prevention mechanisms in ISDS, it is important to clarify the terminology used in this chapter. In theory and practice, dispute prevention, dispute management, and dispute resolution, are used somewhat loosely and interchangeably as umbrella terms, although in their essence, they refer to very distinct processes.[18] Others refer to early grievance mechanisms, claim management tools, or early alert systems to describe tools and mechanisms that are applied in the pre-dispute phase, before an investor claim is officially notified.[19] It is

14 The World Bank Group and the Energy Charter Secretariat, 'Enabling Foreign Direct Investment in the Renewable Energy Sector: Reducing Regulatory Risks and Preventing Investor-State Conflicts' (World Bank Group, April 2023) 56.

15 Ziad Obeid, Moiz Mirza Baig, Mollie Lewis and Maria Paschou, 'Initial Stages of a Dispute: The State's Perspective' (Global Arbitration Review, 14 January 2022) <https://globalarbitrationreview.com/guide/the-guide-investment-treaty-protection-and-enforcement/first-edition/article/initial-stages-of-dispute-the-states-perspective> accessed 29 April 2024.

16 Queen Mary University of London (QUML) and Corporate Counsel International Arbitration Group (CCIG), 'Survey: Investors' Perceptions of ISDS' (QUML, May 2020) p. 8 <https://arbitration.qmul.ac.uk/media/arbitration/docs/QM-CCIAG-Survey-ISDS-2020.pdf> accessed 29 April 2024.

17 *Ibid.*

18 UNCITRAL (n 2).

19 UNCITRAL Secretariat, 'Possible reform of investor-State dispute settlement (ISDS): Mediation and other forms of alternative dispute settlement' p. 10 <https://uncitral.un.org

not surprising that there is no firmly established definition of dispute prevention mechanisms, since they have emerged in practice from different legal and institutional frameworks in diverse legal cultures, and have not been studied systematically in the past.[20]

For the purpose of clarity, in this chapter, dispute prevention mechanisms refer to the agencies, institutions, or coordination bodies whose mandate falls anywhere between the investment aftercare phase, to the very brink of the "cooling-off" period. The activities and processes that take place beyond this point will be referred to as "dispute management" and "dispute resolution" in this chapter. Although in some instances dispute prevention bodies may play a role in the latter phases, they will be analyzed mostly from the perspective of their preventive roles.

The key distinction between the dispute prevention and dispute resolution bodies, as analyzed in this chapter, is in the object of their intervention. Thus, dispute prevention mechanisms address *investor issues or grievances* that have not been formulated and notified as an investor claim. The notification of a *dispute* and intent to initiate arbitration or litigation initiates the *cooling-off period*. During this limited amount of time (usually 3–6 months), the competent institutions should engage with the foreign investor in an attempt to amicably settle the underlying dispute. If the adversarial proceedings are initiated (typically investment arbitration), a *legal dispute* has emerged. At this stage, the parties enter into the dispute resolution phase which can still be settled but can no longer be prevented.

Dispute prevention mechanisms can be established as an independent agency, ombudsperson for investment protection, a department within a government ministry, or a coordination body comprising several competent institutions and agencies.[21] In some cases, the dispute prevention function can be entrusted to a single focal point institution, while other institutions or coordination bodies can be included at the dispute management and resolution stage.[22]

As a general matter, dispute prevention mechanisms can be mandated with a variety of functions, including: investment aftercare, assistance, responses to direct investor inquiries, serving as a designated focal point for investor

---

/sites/uncitral.un.org/files/media-documents/uncitral/en/draft_guidelines_on_media tion.pdf> accessed 29 April 2024.

20 An overview of the variety of approaches taken in different jurisdictions is available in the UNCITRAL Compilation of Best Practices on Investment Dispute Prevention and Mitigation <https://uncitral.un.org/sites/uncitral.un.org/files/media-documents/uncitral/wg_iii _compilation_on_dispute_prevention_and_summary.pdf> accessed 29 April 2024.

21 *Ibid.*

22 *Ibid.*

grievances,[23] establishing a clear communication and coordination channel for investors and the competent institutions, including by ensuring the proper flow of information across the government and elevating sensitive issues to state-level institutions,[24] proposing solutions for investor grievances,[25] centralizing information about investment agreements, maintaining records of investor grievances and State responses, identifying risks and trends in the operations of investors, including the most sensitive sectors,[26] conducting capacity development and awareness raising campaigns,[27] proposing administrative and legislative improvements based on direct experiences,[28] etc.

---

23 *See,* for example, the Energy Charter Secretariat Model Instrument https://www.energychartertreaty.org/model-instrument/; The Investment Assistance Committee (IAC) of Myanmar; Office of Administration of International Commercial Agreements and Treaties (DICOEX) of the Dominican Republic, etc.

24 For example, in the Czech Republic, the International Arbitration and Investment Protection Unit at the Ministry of Finance of the Czech Republic <https://www.mfcr.cz/cs/o-ministerstvu/zakladni-informace/organizacni-struktura/sekce09/odbor-71-legislativa-a-sporne-agendy/oddeleni-7103-mezinarodni-arbitraze-a-oc> accessed 29 April 2024; Creation of an Inter-ministerial Committee for Defence of the State in International Investment Disputes and Regulation of Coordination for Resolution of such Disputes. Decree 125 (27 December 2016) <https://www.leychile.cl/N?i=1098279&f=2016-12-27&p=> accessed 29 April 2024; in Chile, Directorate of Foreign Investment and Services established within Ministry of Commerce. High-Level Government Instance for the prevention and management of international investment disputes; See Decree No. 1939 (2013) <https://www.suin-juriscol.gov.co/viewDocument.asp?id=1373623> accessed 29 April 2024; in Peru, the Coordination and Response System for International Investment Disputes (SICRECI in Spanish) Law No. 28933, Peru (December 2006) <https://docs.peru.justia.com/federales/leyes/28933-dec-15-2006.pdf> accessed 29 April 2024.

25 For example, The World Bank's Systemic Investor Response Mechanism SIRM; in Colombia, the High-level government body (HLGB) of Colombia; Inter-Institutional Commission for the settlement of international trade and investment disputes (CIDS) of Costa Rica; the SICRECI in Peru, etc.

26 For example, the mechanisms established in the Czech Republic, Peru, the Dominican Republic, Colombia, Chile, etc. (n 24).

27 For example, the mechanisms established in Peru, Colombia, etc. (n 25). UNCITRAL Working Group III is currently deliberating the establishment of an Advisory Centre for States, which would provide capacity development and technical assistance, and could serve as the repository for international investment treaties and other resources relevant for dispute prevention and settlement. UNCITRAL Secretariat, 'Possible reform of investor-State dispute settlement (ISDS) Advisory Centre' (03 January 2021) <https://documents-dds-ny.un.org/doc/UNDOC/LTD/V21/090/91/PDF/V2109091.pdf?OpenElement> accessed 29 April 2024.

28 For example, Office of the Foreign Investment Ombudsman (OFIO) of South Korea; Direct Investments Ombudsman (DIO) of Brazil.

4 The Challenges and Roadblocks to Dispute Prevention in ISDS

For the most part, States have clearly acknowledged the benefits of and need for establishing a robust system for dispute prevention and management, as a safeguard from lengthy arbitral proceedings.[29] In fact, the WGIII delegations have emphasized dispute prevention as a key element of ISDS reform.[30] However, there are some unique internal and external challenges that obstruct State efforts to meaningfully engage in dispute prevention or alternative dispute resolution mechanisms with foreign investors.

The main challenges faced by the States relate to limited institutional and personnel capacities, as most of them do not have a dedicated agency or institution for dispute prevention. Although it falls within the broader mandate of most foreign investment protection agencies (at least as it relates to communication and coordination with foreign investors), there is an acute lack of human capacities, expertise in, or even awareness of the international investment protection framework, including international investment treaties.[31] The existing institutions and coordination bodies are authorized to act once a grievance has matured into a claim, and a dispute has been notified.[32] As noted above, even with best efforts at this stage, the institutions are already facing a legal claim which can be mitigated or settled, but not prevented.

In terms of internal early grievance notification efforts within the government, there are many tales of letters and inquiries of foreign investors being sent from ministry to ministry, or from department to department, none of which consider the issue to be within their competence. Even if the notification arrives at the right address, if the government officials consider that there was no treaty breach under the alleged facts, they do not address the issue or engage directly with the foreign investor. In either of these scenarios,

29 Submission from the Government of Morocco, para 14; Submission from the Government of Thailand, paras 24–25; Submission from the Governments of Chile, Israel and Japan, p. 7; Submission from the Government of Brazil; Submission from the Government of Sthe Republic of Korea, paras 40–41 and paras 47–48; Submission from the Government of China, p. 5.

30 UNCITRAL Secretariat (n 19) p. 15.

31 German Organization for International Cooperation (GIZ), 'The Regional Mapping Report of ISDS Structures for the Western Balkans' (GIZ, 2020) <https://www.giz.de/en/downloads_els/ORF%20Legal%20Reform%20-%20Regional%20Mapping%20Report%20on%20Investor%20State%20Dispute%20Settlement.pdf> accessed 29 April 2024.

32 Council of Ministers Bosnia and Herzegovina, Decision on the Establishment of the Permanent Negotiating Body for the Amicable Settlement of Investment Disputes, Bosnia and Herzegovina (24 November 2017) (Official Gazette BiH, no 17/18) <http://www.sluzbenilist.ba/page/akt/1boIlQelogztz5k76kjn45hA=> accessed 29 April 2024.

the clock will run down on the cooling-off period and the foreign investors will refer the dispute to an arbitral tribunal.[33] There is a prevalent lack of a clear and transparent roadmap for the flow of information from the foreign investor to the competent institutions, and at the intra-governmental level, which ultimately hinders the likelihood of a timely response to investor grievances.[34]

Among the political risks that concern foreign investors, the lack of predictability, transparency and communication with the competent institutions take the highest ranks.[35] In several surveys, foreign investors have placed political risks, in their various forms, higher on their list of concerns than the breach of contract, expropriation, civil unrest, war and terrorism.[36] These issues are the most important considerations foreign investors take into account when deciding to establish, expand, reduce or withdraw their investments. Foreign investors are particularly concerned with adverse regulatory changes which are not transparently announced and a lack of responsiveness from the competent institutions to address the emerging issues at an early stage.[37]

Although the effectiveness of the investment protection framework is mostly measured by the outcomes of investment arbitrations, most foreign investors consider any adversarial proceedings to be a matter of last resort. This is exactly the issue cited by a foreign investor who initiated investment arbitration against a Western Balkans State, only because the competent institutions were not engaging in any sort of communication with them on the issues related to their covered investment.[38] While formal investment claims are a bellwether for problems foreign investors experience in the host State,

33 In most investment protection treaties, the cooling-off period lasts between 3 to 6 months, and there are no specific parametres or requirements that the parties have to fultill to discharge of the duty to attempt amicable settlement during this time. Ganesh Aravind, 'Cooling Off Period (Investment Arbitration)' (Max Planck Institute Luxembourg for International, European and Regulatory Procedural Law, MPILux Working Paper 7, 2020) 2 <https://www.mpi.lu/fileadmin/mpi/medien/research/MPEiPro/WPS7_2017_Ganesh_Cooling_Off_Period__Investment_Arbitration_.pdf> accessed 29 April 2024.

34 Nikos Lavranos, 'Assessment of the Legal Framework for Dispute Prevention in the Western Balkans' (GIZ, 2022).

35 Kher and Khun (n 5).

36 *Ibid.*

37 *Ibid.* Aside from being a deterrent factor for foreign investors considering entry into a host State, the lack of transparency and predictability of the legal system in the host State are also a common basis for investor claims under the Fair and Equitable Treatment standard, viewed as a breach of their legitimate expectations.

38 Ballantyne (n 4).

the vast majority of aggrieved foreign investors withdraw their investments or cancel planned expansions, without notifying any claims.[39]

The aversion of foreign investors from pursuing adversarial proceedings against host states is also notable from the reported outcomes of the known ISDS cases. Namely, according to data published by UNCTAD, 19.2% of the ISDS disputes are settled,[40] while ICSID reported an even higher settlement rate of 36–38%.[41] While there is little to no information about the modalities of reaching the amicable resolution of the disputes, these statistics indicate the willingness of both investors and states to avoid lengthy disputes, to the extent possible.

A study has shown that only around 25% of foreign investors choose to litigate or arbitrate their grievances and investment related claims, while others either relinquish their rights or withdraw or reduce their investments.[42] Therefore, these silent losses are less scandalous than large damages awards issued against host States in investment arbitration, but they could be more economically devastating because they cannot be detected or measured without the proper communication and engagement with foreign investors.

Finally, a common challenge in the realm of investment protection and dispute prevention is the absence of a calibrated and effective tool to track the frequency and nature of investor grievances, as well as the nature and success of State responses to investor grievances, claims, and disputes. Such a tool could track to multiple factors, including the economic gains, transfer of know-how, employment, and other value (gained or lost), as well as the monetary amounts in damages or arbitral costs (lost or saved) through the operation of dispute prevention measures.[43] Systematic data collection and impact assess-

39 The World Bank Group (n 14).

40 UNCTAD Investment Policy Hub, Investment Dispute Settlement Navigator <https://investmentpolicy.unctad.org/investment-dispute-settlement> accessed 29 April 2024.

41 ICSID, 'The ICSID Caseload Statistics, Issue 2023-02 (2023) p. 13 <https://icsid.worldbank.org/sites/default/files/publications/2023.ENG_The_ICSID_Caseload_Statistics_Issue.2_ENG.pdf> accessed 29 April 2024.

42 *Ibid.* citing the World Bank Group, 'Global Investment Competitiveness Report 2019/2020: Rebuilding Investor Confidence in Times of Uncertainty' (2020) <https://openknowledge.worldbank.org/entities/publication/ac1e9078-9cdf-5dcb-84be-16f5e30a6e6a> accessed 29 April 2024.

43 Law No. 28933, Peru (December 2006) Art 5, <https://docs.peru.justia.com/federales/leyes/28933-dec-15-2006.pdf.> accessed 29 April 2024; The World Bank Group, 'Retention and Expansion of Foreign Direct Investment, Political Risk and Policy Findings – Summary of Research Findings and Policy Implications' (2019) p. 7 <https://documents1.worldbank.org/curated/en/528401576141837231/pdf/Political-Risk-and-Policy-Responses-Summary-of-Research-Findings-and-Policy-Implications.pdf> accessed 29 April 2024.
Ibid.

ments are a crucial part of effective dispute prevention because they allow the State to identify recurring risks, assess the quality of the existing mechanisms and enable agile policy and procedural adjustments.

5 Existing Models of Dispute Prevention Mechanisms

Over the past two decades, several dispute prevention and management models (DPMMs) have been discussed as international best practices (including the proposed models by World Bank, Energy Charter Secretariat) or country-specific models (such as those established in Brazil, Peru and South Korea). Most recently, the UNCITRAL Secretariat has published Guidelines for the prevention and mitigation of investment disputes.[44] It should be noted at the outset that none of the international proposals outlined below are endorsed as a best practice, but merely provide useful and viable models which each State can adapt to its own framework and needs. The national models are examples of such adaptations, each providing valuable elements that may inspire the Western Balkans countries, and otherwise demonstrate how dispute prevention mechanisms operate in practice.

6 The World Bank's Systemic Investor Response Mechanism (SIRM)

The World Bank Group has developed the Systemic Investor Response Mechanism (SIRM) as a tool to "identify, track and resolve, in a timely manner, investor–state grievances that put investment projects at risk of withdrawals and cancellations."[45] The SIRM was piloted in 2019 in several countries, to help them design a mechanism that would enable a timely identification of early investor grievances, a coordinated response by the competent institutions, and ultimately the prevent or settle the dispute before it escalates to arbitration.[46]

Regardless of the policy orientation and strategic purpose of the SIRM as a model, some common elements have emerged in all the mechanisms developed in the pilot countries:[47] The lead agency would operate in the pre-dispute phase, collecting and transmitting information about investor grievances and

44 UNCITRAL Secretariat, 'Possible reform of investor-State dispute settlement (ISDS) – Draft legislative guide on investment dispute prevention and mitigation' (UNCITRAL, 19 January 2023) <https://uncitral.un.org/sites/uncitral.un.org/files/media-documents/uncitral/en/wp_228_advance_copy.pdf> accessed 29 April 2024.

45 The World Bank Group (n 43).

46 Bonnitcha and Williams (n 4) p. 3.

47 The World Bank Group (n 43) p. 7.

potential disputes to the competent institutions before the foreign investor files a formal claim. If the preliminary direct exchange with the competent institutions at the technical level does not yield results, the lead agency could raise the matter to the political level, where necessary.[48] This can be a single competent institution or agency, as well as a coordination body composed of representatives of several competent institutions, including those directly involved in the dispute.

The specific design and dynamics of this mechanism should be defined country-by-country, depending on the structure of their government and economy, as well as the specific priorities and risks that are associated with their investment protection framework.

7 The International Energy Charter Secretariat's Model Instrument on the Management of Investment Disputes

The Model Instrument on the Management of Investment Disputes (the Model Instrument) was developed by the International Energy Charter Secretariat as a policy framework for the effective prevention, management, and resolution of investment disputes, as a matter of public interest.[49] With a focus on coordination, the Model Instrument explains in detail its key components, including the centralization of information, the consistency of dispute settlement provisions, an early alert mechanism, and coordinated management at all stages of an investment dispute.[50] The early alert system would require any institution in the government that becomes aware of the existence or likelihood of an investment dispute to notify the identified responsible body immediately, along with the available information and documentation.[51]

The Model Instrument explicitly defines the relevant public entities that could be implicated in an investment dispute and the "responsible body" that will be directly engaging with the foreign investor in the relevant dispute (competent ministry, inter-ministerial coordination body or another appropriate designated agency).[52] The responsible body would thus be explicitly identified in the instrument establishing the dispute prevention mechanism, making

48 *Ibid.*

49 Energy Charter Secretariat, 'Explanatory note, Model Instrument on the Management of Investment Disputes', p. 20 <https://www.energychartertreaty.org/fileadmin/DocumentsMedia/Library/CCDEC201826_-_INV_Adoption_by_correspondence_-_Model_Instrument_on_Management_of_Investment_Disputes.pdf> accessed 29 April 2024.

50 *Ibid.* Arts 5–8 and Chapter II.

51 *Ibid.* Art 8.

52 *Ibid.*

it easier for the investor to properly communicate their grievances or claims to the right "address". This could effectively bridge the transparency gaps and remove a significant obstacle to the effective prevention of investment disputes.[53]

The responsible body is expressly authorized and encouraged to engage in amicable settlement proceedings (negotiations, conciliation, mediation, good offices, etc.), with authority to settle the dispute on behalf of the State.[54] This is a significant factor for the consistency, efficiency, and effectiveness of amicable settlement proceedings.

The World Bank and ECT Secretariat models envisage the parallel operation of a focal point (or lead agency) for dispute prevention and communication related to investor grievances, and a coordinating body that acts on potential disputes, notified by the focal point. If both components are well connected and coordinated, there is a higher likelihood of early detection and prevention of possible investment disputes. On the so-called "investor-State conflict continuum," such models could span from the moment a grievance arises in the investment aftercare phase, until the notice of a legal dispute is submitted.[55] The coordinated decision-making in the pre-dispute and amicable settlement period also helps distribute the responsibility among the competent institutions related to any potential settlement, which should ease the concerns of political or public backlash at home.

8 The Draft UNCITRAL Guidelines for the Prevention and Mitigation of Investor-State Disputes

The Draft UNCITRAL Guidelines for Dispute Prevention and Mitigation (Draft Guidelines), developed by the WGIII, are a tool to assist States developing the

53 *Ibid.* Art 3.6.

54 *Ibid.* Art 2.2.

55 Council of Ministers Bosnia and Herzegovina (n 35). The Council of Ministers of Bosnia and Herzegovina established a 'Permanent Negotiating Body for Investment Disputes' comprising the key ministries involved in foreign trade and investment, the State Attorney's Office and ad hoc members relevant for each particular case. By its mandate, the Permanent Negotiating Body acts upon a notice of dispute from a foreign investor, in order to attempt amicable settlement during the cooling off period. If the dispute escalates to international arbitration, the SAO takes over the case as the legal representative of the State. There is no established early grievance mechanism in Bosnia and Herzegovina to date, but the first proposal was submitted to the Council of Ministers, following an online public consultation.

legal framework for a dispute prevention mechanism for ISDS.[56] They also define the key terms, making a clear distinction between grievances, disputes, and legal disputes, indicating the different processes to address them: dispute prevention for grievances, amicable settlement for disputes, and resolution for formulated legal disputes.[57]

The Draft Guidelines propose the establishment or designation of a lead agency that would take the central coordination role, similar to the SIRM and Model Instrument, with an indicative list of their possible mandates and functions, including the possibility to demand compliance of other government agencies with proposed dispute prevention measures.[58]

Communication and coordination are at the heart of the dispute prevention and mitigation mechanism proposed by the Draft Guidelines,[59] where the lead agency would be the first contact point for foreign investors, the repository of information, and the conduit for communication within the government. The Guideline also proposes the establishment of an inter-ministerial coordination body that would be activated at the earliest stages to address grievances or attempt to amicably resolve any possible dispute.[60]

The Draft Guidelines also promote the harmonization among the instruments of consent (defined as international investment agreements, investment contracts, and national legislation governing foreign investment protection),[61] through the continuous exchange of information and experiences among the competent institutions.[62] With such a systemic harmonization of investment standards across various legal instruments applicable in the State, there will be fewer risks of the government setting unrealistic expectations in investment contracts or negotiating investment treaties that will expose certain institutions to frequent disputes.[63]

---

56 UNCITRAL Draft Legislative Guide (n 12). Although the WGIII has not deliberated any concrete proposals since it was discussed at the 35th session, UNCITRAL published a compilation of existing dispute prevention and management mechanisms established around the world, including some that are considered best practices. UNCITRAL Secretariat (n 20).

57 UNCITRAL Draft Legislative Guide (n 44), Recommendation 2.

58 *Ibid.* Recommendation 5, 6.

59 *Ibid.* Recommendation 3.

60 *Ibid.* Recommendation 4.

61 UNCITRAL Draft Legislative Guide (n 44), Recommendation 8.

62 *Ibid.* This can include Model investment treaties and model clauses for international investment contracts.

63 Examples of this approach can be found in the Dominican Republic, Decree No. 303-2015, Art. 4 (available in Spanish) <https://studylib.es/doc/5157825/decreto-sistema-de-prevenci%C3%B3n-de-controversias-no.-303-15> accessed 29 April 2024; Also see in Peru, Law No. 28933 (December 2006) Art. 13 <https://docs.peru.justia.com/federales/leyes/28933

The Draft Guidelines also recommend the exclusion of legal liability for State representatives engaging in negotiation, conciliation, and mediation, with the aim of preventing investment disputes.[64] This is an important factor to ensure effective engagement in amicable settlement, alleviating the concerns of government officials ofr possible allegations of corruption or abuse of power in the aftermath of their engagement in successful settlements with foreign investors.[65]

Such a provision in the legislation underlying the dispute prevention mechanism would be a great step towards destigmatizing early engagement between foreign investors and the competent government bodies, to avoid adversarial proceedings.[66]

9 Examples of National Dispute Prevention Mechanisms

9.1 *Office of the Foreign Investment Ombudsman* (OFIO) *of South Korea*

The South Korean OFIO67 is widely recognized as one of the best practices at the international level, and it has directly inspired legislation and institutional frameworks for investment facilitation and dispute prevention in other jurisdictions.[68] It is an independent body responsible only to the Prime Minister,

---

-dec-15-2006.pdf. The South African Development Community (SADC) Model BIT (2012) was drafted as a guideline for the negotiation of future investment treaties, but also as an educational tool for Government officials.

64 UNCITRAL Draft Legislative Guide (n 44), Recommendation 14.

65 *Ibid.* With the exception of willful misconduct or negligence. Previous studies found that the fear of allegations of corruption and fear of criticism were among the main obstacles for State engagement in amicable settlement of ISDS disputes. *See* for example, Seraphina Chew, Lucy Reed, J Christopher Thomas, 'Report: Survey on Obstacles to Settlement of Investor-State Disputes', (National University of Singapore, Research Paper No. 18/01) pp. 12–13 <https://deliverypdf.ssrn.com/delivery.php?ID=406105097031080068031088090075099030017003038044067033122100111020920171240870300070070190551190060030211081130040921160970010300870110400860661261031211220901181070180220320741191201120241200700891221150681120071220690930050301251070951131130850870 76&EXT=pdf&INDEX=TRUE> accessed 29 April 2024.

66 *Ibid.*

67 More information is available on the official OFIO website <https://ombudsman.kotra.or.kr/ob-en/bbs/i-2638/list.do> accessed 29 April 2024.

68 For example, the Myanmar delegation visited Korea during the development of their Investment Law. OFIO representatives also frequently presented about their work at various international conferences and other fora, such as APEC, OECD and UNCTAD events. A Choong Yong (July 2010) 'Ombudsman services for foreign investors as a dispute prevention and FDI promotion measures' (APEC document 2010/IEG/WKSP1/012) APEC Workshop on Dispute Prevention and Preparedness <http://mddb. apec.org/documents/2010/ieg/wksp1/10_ieg_wksp1_012.pdf> accessed 29 April 2024.

established within the Korean Trade and Investment Promotion Agency.[69] The Ombudsman has a broad mandate, including the ability to require the collaboration of government agencies on particular matters, to resolve foreign investor complaints and issue recommendations to improve the investment protection system and climate.[70]

Where the competent agency does not adopt the recommendation within 30 days, the OFIO may request the submission of the issue to the Foreign Investment Committee.[71] In addition to activities related to ensuring compliance with international standards, and addressing operational issues faced by foreign investors, the Ombudsman works on improving living conditions of the foreign investors and their workers.[72] Beyond its primary role, the OFIO can also make legislative recommendations based on their direct experiences with foreign investors.[73]

The OFIO can also assign staff members ("home doctors") to particular regions or foreign investors to facilitate the resolution of grievances.[74] Home doctors are experts in different fields, and they are available to provide information remotely and to conduct site visits. Foreign investors can file their grievances through an online platform accessible on the OFIO website.

The OFIO website also hosts a user-friendly and up-to-date database of legislative and other governmental acts of interest for foreign investors.[75] The OFIO system provides foreign investors a one-stop platform to obtain the necessary information and get in touch with the competent institutions with direct inquiries or grievances, thus serving the combined function of an investment aftercare and grievance mechanism.

69 Foreign Investment Promotion Act South Korea, Art 15-2 para 10.

70 The Enforcement Decree of the Foreign Investment Promotion Act South Korea, Art 21-3, paras 2–5.

71 The Foreign Investment Promotion Act South Korea, Art 15-2, para 6.

72 Ibid para 3.3.

73 IISD (n 4) p.28.

74 *Ibid.* paras 5–6.

75 The database of the laws and regulations in force in Korea is available here <https://ombudsman.kotra.or.kr/ob-en/cntnts/i-2642/web.do> accessed 29 April 2024.

10 Direct Investments Ombudsman (DIO) of Brazil

The DIO is largely inspired by the Korean OFIO and is tailored to the unique investment protection regime in Brazil. Namely, Brazil has abandoned the typical network of bilateral investment treaties (BITs) and replaced it with a special treaty regime established through its Cooperation and Facilitation Investment Agreement (CFIA) program.[76] These treaties focus on investment facilitation and dispute prevention, only allowing investment disputes to be resolved through State-to-State proceedings.[77] Each individual CFIA establishes a joint committee of the treaty parties and an ombudsperson to facilitate the dialogue between foreign investors and the host State, and provide the necessary support.[78] Since 2019, the DIO is available to all foreign investors in Brazil and not only those registered in countries which have concluded a CFIA with Brazil.[79]

The DIO is established as part of the Brazilian Chamber for Foreign Trade (CAMEX), to fulfill the obligations undertaken by the State under its CFIAs,[80] as the single contact point for foreign investors, to communicate specific inquiries and investor grievances to the competent institutions through its network of institutional focal points.[81] Through this coordination and exchange, the DIO collects and compiles the relevant information from the designated staff members of the focal point institutions, which it submits as a response to the investor in question.[82]

Unresolved issues from the preliminary procedure can be referred to a grievance settlement body that the DIO establishes, comprising a representative of the DIO and the agency involved in the grievance.[83] The DIO prepares

76 Government of Brazil, Resolution No. 43, de 4 de maio de 2020: Aprova o regimento interno do Ombudsman de Investimentos Diretos, no âmbito da Câmara de Comércio Exterior.

77 World Bank Group, 'Improving Business Environment for Prosperity, Retaining foreign investment in Brazil' (March 2020) <http://pubdocs.worldbank.org/en/258701593542404722/ibepcountry-successStories-brazil-foreigninvestment.pdf> accessed 29 April 2024.

78 IISD (n 4) p. 17.

79 Brazilian Decree No 9.770/2019.

80 Submission of the government of Brazil to the UNCITRAL WGIII (11 June 2019) p. 4 <https://documents-dds-ny.un.org/doc/UNDOC/LTD/V19/045/74/PDF/V1904574.pdf?OpenElement> accessed 29 April 2024.

81 Direct Investments Ombudsman – DIO Brazil <https://oid.economia.gov.br/en/menus/8> accessed 29 April 2024.

82 DIO Frequently Asked Questions <https://oid.economia.gov.br/en/menus/1> accessed 29 April 2024.

83 *Ibid.*

recommendations to the competent institution, but it cannot compel any specific actions by any agency.

Like the Korean DFIO, the DIO does not engage in any claim evaluation, amicable settlement, conciliation, or dispute resolution processes, which are the mandate of the Joint Committee of the treaty parties – through an assessment of the alleged measures that breach the CFIA, and ad hoc State-to-State arbitration, if an amicable solution is not possible.[84]

Both of these mechanisms are characterized by some key features that are crucial for their effective operations: (1) they are tailored to the particular jurisdiction in which they are established; (2) they enable a hands-on approach providing foreign investors constant support and clear channels of communication in case of potential issues and grievances; (3) the staff and government officials involved in the process are highly specialized and well informed about the policy and practice of investment protection; (4) the investment aftercare and dispute prevention components are clearly separated from the resolution of legal disputes; (5) both mechanisms focus on proactive investment facilitation rather than reactive investment protection; (6) the experiences of such institutions can be leveraged to propose legislative amendments and policy improvements.

11 The Coordination and Response System for International Investment Disputes (SICRECI) in Peru

The Coordination and Response System for International Investment Disputes (SICRECI) in Peru is a tailor made coordinating intra-governmental body providing a comprehensive framework for dispute prevention and settlement.[85] The SICRECI is composed of the competent ministries and agencies involved

84 Government of Brazil (n 80) p. 4.

85 The SICRECI (Sistema de Coordinación y Respuesta del Estado en Controversias Internacionales de Inversión in original Spanish) was established in 2006 by Law No. 28933. Peru developed this model based on its previous experiences of the State in ISDS, including the lack of coordination between the competent institutions, particularly for the exchange of information, uncertainties regarding the delegation of responsibilities, the appointment of external counsel and the payment of the costs of the proceedings. El Ministerio de Economía y Finanzas Peru <https://www.mef.gob.pe/es/?option=com_content&language=es-ES&Itemid=101010&lang=es-ES&view=article&id=5245> accessed 29 April 2024.

in investment protection and promotion, and those relevant for a specific dispute.[86]

Any agency which becomes aware of an investor grievance must notify the SICRECI within 5 days, and foreign investors can register direct complaints to the Ministry of Economy and Finance through an online platform.[87] Once a formal notice of dispute is filed, the Special Committee has the authority to negotiate a settlement with the foreign investor in the cooling-off period, and it otherwise coordinates the State defense in arbitration proceedings.[88]

The SICRECI also supports the capacity development of all relevant institutions and agencies through training programs and dispute prevention manuals.[89] The SICRECI also maintains a database of all agreements providing for ISDS, making them accessible to all institutions.[90] All government agencies that conclude an agreement providing for international arbitration are required to report it within 30 days.[91] This ensures that all competent institutions are aware of the international obligations undertaken by the State, which allows the proper risk assessment.

86 IISD (n 4) p. 30. The body consists of the Ministry of Economy and Finances, as coordinator and a Special Commission (SC) comprising the Ministry of Foreign Affairs, ProInversión, and the Ministry of Justice, chaired by the Ministry of Economy and Finances, as well as other agencies relevant for a specific dispute. If the dispute arises out a free trade agreement, the Ministry of Foreign Trade and Tourism is also involved.

87 A similar early grievance mechanism exists in the Dominican Republic, whose Office of Administration of International Commercial Agreements and Treaties (DICOEX) works through an online form through which investors can notify potential disputes. Any entity that is notified of or obtains knowledge about a dispute must inform the DICOEX within 3 days, which is registered in the DIOCEX database. After this registration, DICOEX officials conduct a legal evaluation of the case, and interview the investor and the relevant government entities to determine if the allegations of a treaty breach are viable, as well as the possible costs of the dispute. UNCITRAL, Commercial Profile Dominican Republic (Report from the 2nd Inter-Sessional Meeting on ISDS Reform <commercial_profile_dominican_republic.pdf (un.org)> accessed 29 April 2024; State Secretariat for Industry and Commerce of the Dominican Republic, 'Trade Capacity Building National Action Plan: Addressing Globalization Challenges' (2007) p. 38 <https://ustr.gov/archive/assets/Trade_Agreements/Regional/CAFTA/asset_upload_file240_13690.pdf> accessed 29 April 2024.

88 *Ibid.*

89 Ministry of Economy and Finance Peru (2019) MEF capacitó a funcionarios públicos en solución de controversias internacionales <https://www.mef.gob.pe/?lang=en> accessed 29 April 2024.

90 Ministry of Economy and Finance Peru, Sistema de Coordinación y Respuesta del Estado en Controversias Internacionales de Inversión – SICRECI <https://www.mef.gob.pe/es/?option=com_content&language=es-ES&Itemid=101974&lang=es-ES&view=article&id=3252> 29 April 2024.

91 *Ibid.*

12 EU Perspective on Dispute Prevention and Alternative Dispute Resolution (UNCITRAL Working Group III and Recent Treaty Practice)

In the broader context of ISDS reform, the EU and its member states have not advocated for, or proposed, a concrete dispute prevention mechanism.[92] However, the EU has consistently emphasized the value of dispute prevention as a component of ISDS reform and its support for the promotion and effective use of mediation and other amicable settlement mechanisms for investment disputes.[93] Thus, it actively contributed to the deliberations on the UNCITRAL Model Provisions on Mediation and the UNCITRAL Guidelines on Mediation for International Investment Disputes.[94]

This is consistent with the more recent EU treaties, as reflected in the investment chapters of the treaties concluded with Canada, Singapore, Vietnam, and Angola.[95] The investment chapters of all of these treaties provide for mediation, which is available at any time to the disputing parties (before or after the

92 The UNCITRAL Secretariat noted the general view of the WGIII delegations that the Draft Legislative Guide on Dispute Prevention Mechanisms in Investor-State Dispute Resolution should be revised into a neutral guide, to avoid any legislative directives for sovereign states. The EU did not take any specific position on this issue otherwise. (n 16) <https://documents-dds-ny.un.org/doc/UNDOC/GEN/V23/024/83/PDF/V2302483.pdf?OpenElement accessed 29 April 2024.

93 Comments of the EU and its Member States on the UNCITRAL Secretariat Note, Possible reform of investor-State dispute settlement (ISDS) – Mediation and other forms of alternative dispute resolution (ADR) (2021) <https://uncitral.un.org/sites/uncitral.un.org/files/media-documents/uncitral/en/21.12.17_draft_clauses_on_mediation_eu_and_ms_comments.pdf> accessed 29 April 2024.

94 United Nations press release, 'UN Commission on International Trade Law finalizes four legal texts during the first week of its 56th Session in Vienna' (13 July 2023) <https://unis.unvienna.org/unis/en/pressrels/2023/unisl344.html> accessed 29 April 2024. At the 56th session the delegations discussed the draft guidelines on investment mediation, where they noted that mediation could be used as a component of the state strategy to prevent and mitigate investment disputes. Dispute prevention was also noted as a key element of ISDS reform. UNCITRAL Secretariat, (n 16) pp. 14–15.

95 EU-Canada Comprehensive Economic and Trade Agreement (CETA) (2017); EU-Singapore Investment Protection Agreement (2019); EU-Vietnam Investment Protection Agreement (2019); EU-Angola Sustainable Investment Facilitation Agreement (2023). These treaties have been concluded by the EU and their counterparts, the relevant investment protection chapters have not entered into force, pending their ratification by each EU member state. Their provisions are used for information only. UNCTAD Investment Policy Hub (as of 29 April 2024) <https://investmentpolicy.unctad.org/international-investment-agreements>.

submission of a claim).[96] The mediators would be appointed from the roster of adjudicators established for each treaty,[97] and subject to the same code of conduct.[98] It should be noted that these provisions have not yet entered into force, pending their ratification by all EU member States, so their real impact is yet to be tested.

Further, the text of the Sustainable Investment Facilitation Agreement between the EU and Angola (SIFA) provides some insights into the possible contours of a future EU model for investment dispute prevention.[99]

This treaty is the first of its kind proposed by the EU, geared towards investment facilitation and management, and establishing a more collaborative framework between the treaty parties towards common sustainability goals.[100] In this sense, the treaty encourages the creation of intra-governmental coordination mechanisms for the institutions of the treaty parties, in charge of policies and procedures affecting the investment protection framework.[101] This includes the designation of lead agencies for investment facilitation and coordination, aimed at ensuring a stable and coherent legal framework for investment across different levels of government.[102] In addition, SIFA provides that each treaty party shall seek to establish problem-solving mechanisms for existing and potential investors, who may need assistance related to the application of the relevant domestic regulation.[103] The provision explicitly notes the

96 For example, CETA, Article 8.20.1; EU-Singapore Investment Protection Agreement, Annex 6, art 2; EU-Viet Nam Investment Protection Agreement, Annex 10, art 2;

97 See for example, CETA Rules on Mediation, Article 3.1; EU-Singapore Investment Protection Agreement, Annex 6 art3.1., etc.

98 For example, CETA, Annex 29-B; EU-Singapore Investment Protection Agreement, Annex 11; EU-Viet Nam Investment Protection Agreement, Annex 8.

99 The EU-Angola Sustainable Investment Facilitation Agreement (SIFA) is available publicly for information purposes, but it is pending approval for signature by the EU Council, after which it can enter into force once approved by the EU Parliament. European Commission, 'EU-Angola Sustainable Investment Facilitation Agreement' moves towards approval (16 June 2023) <https://policy.trade.ec.europa.eu/news/eu-angola-sustainable-investment-facilitation-agreement-moves-towards-approval-2023-06-16_en> accessed 29 April 2024.

100 *Ibid.*

101 European Commission, 'EU and Angola conclude first-ever Sustainable Investment Facilitation Agreement' (18 November 2022) <https://ec.europa.eu/commission/presscorner/detail/en/IP_22_6136≥29 April 2024; SIFA text, Art. 24.

102 SIFA text, Art. 22.

103 Ibid Art. 23. The dispute resolution clause for the treaty parties also refers to the avoidance of disputes, through consultations, mediation and arbitration. The dispute resolution mechanisms do not provide for detailed rules, leaving them to the discretion of the

importance of making such mechanisms available and accessible to small and medium-sized enterprises, in line with the broader objectives of the treaty.[104]

Although this provision does not provide any further detail on the structure, functions or scope of such mechanisms, it expressly includes a dispute prevention function into the investment protection framework established by the treaty.

The EU policy position on ISDS mediation, expressed in its treaty practice and contributions at the UNCITRAL WGIII, reflects the following common features:

- General support for mediation and other forms of alternative dispute resolution as cost-effective, flexible and efficient way to resolve investment disputes - The EU and its member states consider mediation as a viable and preferable alternative to litigation of investment disputes.[105] It is recognised as such in the previously mentioned EU treaties, and it is already contemplated as a likely feature in the framework of the multilateral investment court.[106]
- Availability of mediation at any time to the disputing parties – The EU has clearly expressed its preference for the availability of mediation to the disputing parties prior to and during the dispute. This is relevant from the perspective of the present analysis as it opens the door to mediation as a dispute prevention tool, and not only a one for the peaceful resolution of disputes which have already emerged.[107]
- Express mediation provisions in the treaty and mandatory commencement of mediation – The EU and its member states consider it preferable to have the agreement to mediate provided in the treaty text itself, rather than leaving it as an option for subsequent agreement by the disputing parties.[108] In this sense, the EU supports the mandatory commencement of mediation as a preliminary step in the dispute resolution process, in order to ensure its

---

parties or the arbitrators if the parties choose to pursue arbitration. SIFA text, Chapter VI Dispute Avoidance and Settlement.

104 SIFA text, Art. 23.2.

105 Comments of the EU and its Member States to the UNCITRAL Draft Provisions on Mediation (2021) p. 4 <https://uncitral.un.org/sites/uncitral.un.org/files/media-documents/uncitral/en/21.12.17_draft_clauses_on_mediation_eu_and_ms_comments.pdf> accessed 29 April 2024.

106 *Ibid.* 9.

107 For example, the CETA Mediation Rules refer to „disputes and problems" which can be referred to mediation, indicating that the parties can mediate issues which have not yet escalated to a dispute. CETA Mediation Rules, Art 3(4).

108 EU Submission to the UNCITRAL WGIII (n 105) pp. 11–12.

effective and meaningful use.[109] The EU's concluded treaties have been somewhat less assertive, leaving it to the requested party to "give sympathetic consideration to the request and accept or reject it in writing within 10 days of its receipt."[110]

- Big picture: the multilateral investment court as the framework for ISDS mediation – Consistent with its proposal for systemic ISDS reform, EU packaged its proposals on investment mediation in the context of the multilateral investment court, outlining the potential benefits of integrating this mechanism into the administrative and operational structure of the court.[111]

Despite the uneven and multi-track ISDS reform efforts unfolding at the international, regional, and national levels, it appears that investment mediation is a stabilizing factor which will be a viable reform option in any context, including in the EU. Although there is still room for more clarity on the rules and dynamics of investment mediation within the EU framework, it will likely find its place as a tool for dispute prevention and amicable settlement in the future.

13 The Dispute Prevention and Management Mechanisms in Bosnia and Herzegovina

In the Western Balkans region, Bosnia and Herzegovina (BiH) intuitively made an early start in considering and building institutional coordination mechanisms for the prevention and mitigation of investment disputes. Although a formal early detection and dispute prevention mechanism is not formalized to date, The Ministry of Foreign Trade and Economic Relations (MoFTER BiH) has been closely coordinating with the Foreign Investment Protection agency (FIPA BiH) to exchange timely information about detected investor complaints..

The "Permanent Negotiating Body for Investment Disputes" (BiH coordination body), established in 2017, comprises representatives of the key competent ministries and the State Attorney's Office as standing members, as well as ad hoc members for each specific case.[112] Its purpose is to consider in mutual

109 EU Submission (n 105) p. 13.

110 CETA Mediation Rules, Art. 3(3).

111 *Ibid.* p. 9.

112 Decision of the Council of Ministers of BiH on the Establishment of the Negotiating Body for the Amicable Settlement of International Investment Disputes (Official Gazette of BiH, no 17/18) issued on the 121st session of the Council of Ministers dated 24 November 2017 <http://www.sluzbenilist.ba/page/akt/1boIlQelogztz5k76kjn45hA=> accessed 29 April 2024; Decision of the Council of Ministers of BiH on the Appointment of the Members of the Permanent Negotiating Team for the Amicable Settlement of International

coordination, and propose an amicable settlement of notified investor claims, during the cooling-off period, i.e. once a notice of dispute is already submitted. If a settlement cannot be reached at this stage, the State Attorney's office will take over the case in investment arbitration, along with external counsel and with continued support of the BiH Coordination Body.[113]

Under its current mandate, the BiH Coordination Body does not have any early grievance mechanism, but MoFTER BiH BiH has conducted public consultations for its proposal for a mechanism for the early identification and prevention of investment disputes. This would close an important institutional gap, and systematically connect the activities already conducted by the FIPA BiH to the existing coordination mechanism.[114]

The new BiH Model BIT (developed in 2023) provides a robust and layered dispute resolution clause, starting from the earliest consultation phase to formal dispute resolution.[115] This is already a step towards the systemic integration of the dispute prevention, mitigation, and resolution frameworks established in other instruments of consent (investment contracts and the national law for investment protection).[116]

BiH has also taken steps for the systemic integration of its dispute resolution clauses. The BiH Model BIT addresses this challenge through a robust and layered ISDS framework, starting with an exclusion of investors who acquire the investment illegally, through an abuse of corporate restructuring solely to file the investment claim, or whose claims are manifestly without legal merit.[117]

Investment Disputes (Official Gazette BiH, no 58/18); Samira Sulejmanovic, 'Investor-State Dispute Prevention and Resolution Mechanism in Bosnia and Herzegovina', in Ben Beaumont, Fahira Brodlija, et al. (eds), The Future of Investor-State Dispute Settlement: Reforming Law, Practice and Perspectives for a Fast Changing World, (Kluwer Law International 2024) 167 – 184 at 126–127.

113 Decision of the Council of Ministers of BiH on the Establishment of the Negotiating Body for the Amicable Settlement of International Investment Disputes, art 6.

114 *Ibid.* In 2018, FIPA BiH reported that the joint efforts with the collaborative network helped remove 150 obstacles identified by investors. „A large number of these issues are solved by the active commitment and participation of institutions. For 12 companies, it is currently working to resolve open issues. 204 reform measures were passed out of which 20 were fully implemented, 25 partially, 45 are in procedure, and activities were not yet started for 10 obstacles."

115 The author analyzed a copy of the BiH Model BIT, which is not publicly available at the time of writing.

116 The Law on the Foreign Investment Protection Policy in Bosnia and Herzegovina (Official Gazette of BiH no. 4/1998, 17/1998, 13/2003, 48/2010 and 22/2015).

117 BiH Model BIT (2023), Art 25.

Unlike the old generation BITs, the BiH Model BIT provides concrete instructions for the pre-dispute phase, with a mandatory cooling-off period and consultation phase.[118] The request for consultations must include details identifying the investor, specifying the alleged treaty breaches, and the relevant factual and legal background of the claim, as well as the relief sought.[119] The claimant must also prove their status as investor of their home state, and their ownership over their investment, placing the burden of proof on the investor to prove their standing under the dispute resolution clause.[120]

The parties are encouraged to seek to resolve any dispute through amicable settlement (negotiations, conciliation, or mediation) without prejudice to any other rights under the treaty. Amicable settlement is available at any time before or after the initiation of arbitration.[121] Unlike the CETA model,[122] the BiH Model BIT does not provide detailed procedural rules for mediation, but it leaves the agreement on these aspects to the discretion of the parties.[123] Here, the BiH Model BIT provides additional space for the State to participate in the selection of the applicable rules, thus balancing its rights with the investor in the design of the process.

Importantly, the BiH Model BIT expressly refers the investors to the direct notification channels and to the competent authorities which should intervene in the early stages of a dispute,[124] thus putting into motion the available institutional mechanisms in BiH (the early grievance mechanism and coordination body) to possibly prevent the escalation of disputes to international arbitration.

Currently, the BiH Model BIT references: (1) the network of foreign investment protection agencies (FIPAs) as first contact points and the early grievance mechanism, which would transmit the information to the competent institutions and seek an early resolution of the issue; and (2) the BiH Negotiation Body as the next instance for the amicable settlement of investment disputes,

118 ICSID analysis of treaty dispute resolution clauses. Old-generation ISDS clauses generally establish a timeframe (mostly between three to six months) for an attempt of amicable settlement, upon which the investor can proceed to arbitration. For example, Art 10 of the BiH-Germany BIT only provides a 6-month cooling off period, and after its lapse the investor can file for ICSID arbitration.

119 BiH Model BIT (2023), Art 20.

120 *Ibid.* Art 11.

121 *Ibid.* Art 19.

122 CETA (2016), Annex 29-C.

123 BiH Model BIT (2023), Art 29; CETA Art 8.20.

124 BiH Model BIT (2023), Art 20(2).

if the issue could not be resolved locally[125] MoFTER BiH would bridge the two phases and provide the necessary information and guidance on the application and interpretation of the applicable treaty.[126]

The UNCITRAL WGIII only recently issued its Draft Guidelines for the Prevention and Mitigation of International Investment Disputes,[127] which propose the establishment of lead agencies and coordination bodies for dispute prevention, and focus on transparency and enhanced communication flows, similar to the framework established in BiH.[128] Therefore, BiH was ahead of the curve in the international reform process, designing a mechanism which is just now recognized as a best practice at the international level.

With the two-phased dispute prevention and mitigation system in place, and combined with the modernized investment treaties, BiH should be in a better position to avoid lengthy and expensive disputes, while projecting a robust and attractive framework for foreign investors. In addition, and in the context of the broader ISDS and treaty reform initiatives, these modern institutional mechanisms are viable in the existing ISDS framework, but also within the possible standing investment court promoted by the EU, which BiH will have to accept upon EU accession.[129]

If the parties are unable to resolve the dispute in the cooling-off stage, the investor can submit the claim to the competent national courts or arbitration

125 Art 5. Decision of the Council of Ministers of BiH on the Establishment of the Negotiating Body for the Amicable Settlement of International Investment Disputes (Official Gazette of BiH, no 17/18) issued on the 121st session of the Council of Ministers dated 24 November 2017 <http://www.sluzbenilist.ba/page/akt/1boIlQelogztz5k76kjn45hA=> accessed 29 April 2024; Decision of the Council of Ministers of BiH on the Appointment of the Members of the Permanent Negotiating Team for the Amicable Settlement of International Investment Disputes (Official Gazette BiH, no 58/18).

126 Information of the Ministry of Foreign Trade and Economic Relations BiH, p. 30.

127 Agenda of the 47th Session of the UNCITRAL WGIII <https://undocs.org/en/A/CN.9/WG.III/WP.234> accessed 29 April 2024; UNCITRAL Secretariat, 'Draft Guidelines for the Prevention and Mitigation of International Investment Disputes' (November 2023) <https://uncitral.un.org/sites/uncitral.un.org/files/media-documents/uncitral/en/2322784e_-_advance_copy_0.pdf> accessed 29 April 2024.

128 'Draft Guidelines for Prevention and Mitigation', *see* n 91.

129 The dispute prevention and mitigation mechanism proposed by BiH was highlighted as a best practice at the UNCITRAL Forum on Dispute Prevention in Investor-State Dispute Settlement (7 July 2023), on the occasion of the 56th Session of the UNCITRAL Commission in Vienna <https://uncitral.un.org/en/forumondisputeprevention> accessed 29 April 2024. The EU has openly supported dispute prevention and amicable settlement as important components of the reform of ISDS. The submissions by the EU and its member states on the topic are available here: <https://uncitral.un.org/en/investmentmediationanddisputeprevention> accessed 29 April 2024.

under the ICSID Convention, *ad hoc* arbitration under the UNCITRAL Rules, or other rules agreed to by the parties.[130] The claims can only relate to the alleged treaty breaches identified in the request for consultations.[131] To enhance procedural efficiency, the ISDS clause also expressly authorizes the arbitral tribunal to order security for costs and consolidation, and requires the disclosure of the names and addresses of third party funders.[132]

Although the EU has replaced investment arbitration with an investment court system in recent treaties and is advocating for the establishment of a multilateral investment court, BiH has opted to maintain ISDS in an improved form in its Model BIT. The ISDS clause would no longer be valid for disputes with EU investors upon its accession to the EU,[133] and BiH would have to transition to the multilateral investment court, if one is established by the time it becomes an EU member state.[134] Since its establishment is not expected in the near future, BiH moved forward with concrete improvements of the existing ISDS mechanisms, while acknowledging that EU rules will prevail once BiH becomes an EU member state.[135]

14 Common Set of Elements for Effective Dispute Prevention Mechanisms

The previous sections illustrated only a fragment of the tapestry of existing dispute prevention models and established mechanisms that could inspire policymakers considering their own solutions. The analysis also highlighted that there is no universal approach. Some states relied on existing agencies and

130 BiH Model BIT (2023), Art 21(1).

131 Ibid Art 21(2).

132 Ibid Art 22 and 23.

133 The EU has is pursuing multilateral efforts to establish a standing investment court within the EU and internationally. *See* for example, the Joint Interpretive Statement of the EU and Canada issued in the context of the CETA negotiations <http://data.consilium.europa.eu/doc/document/ST-13541-2016-INIT/en/pdf> accessed 29 April 2024.

134 Agreement on the Termination of Intra-EU BITs (2020), Art. 1.

135 Ibid Arts 32, 34. The ICS provisions in the recent treaties the EU concluded with Canada, Singapore and Vietnam have still not entered into force, pending the ratification of the investment chapters of these treaties by each EU Member State. The MIC proposal will be discussed further at the UNCITRAL WGIII, but there is no consensus or open support at the international level. UNCITRAL Secretariat, 'Summary of the inter-sessional meeting on investor-State dispute settlement (ISDS) reform submitted by the Government of Singapore' (September 2023) <https://undocs.org/en/A/CN.9/WG.III/WP.233> accessed 29 April 2024.

institutions to perform particular functions for investment aftercare, information exchange, and resolution of investor grievances to the degree possible. Others have established focal points with (or without) a coordinating body to identify and react to issues related to the operations of foreign investors. Ultimately, all of these mechanisms aim to prevent grievances from escalating into investment disputes, risking long arbitral proceedings and large damages awards.

It is difficult to measure the effectiveness of these mechanisms, for two main reasons. Firstly, there is a lack of systematic statistical data on the number of interventions, the value of investments at stake and the value of investments retained or damage claims averted through successful interventions.[136] Relatedly, assessing the benefits would require proof of a negative, i.e. how many investors were considering the withdrawal their investment or initiating arbitral proceedings, but ultimately changed course due to a timely response by the investment ombudsman or early grievance mechanism of the host State? Nevertheless, the fact that States are dedicating significant efforts and resources to the establishment and operations of dispute prevention mechanisms is a good indicator of their perceived value.

14.1 *No One Size-Fits All Approach*

As a starting point, states should pursue tailor-made solutions, fitted to their economic priorities, governmental structure of each state, aligned with the broader foreign investment priorities and policies. International exchange and consultations are a valuable resource in the deliberations and development of a dispute prevention mechanism, but the ultimate decision should remain close to home with a view towards sustainable and effective operations. Furthermore, the foundations of a suitable dispute prevention mechanism may already be built in the existing governmental structure and could be repurposed by developing the capacities and expanding the authority of the agencies and inter-ministerial coordination bodies operating in the State. Thus, there is no need to reinvent the wheel or adopt brand new proposals simply because they are considered best practices elsewhere. Ideally, dispute prevention mechanisms will be designed as flexible and responsive bodies whose competence and duties can be upgraded and refined over time to meet the strategic goals and policy priorities of the State.

136 IISD (n 4) p. 30.

14.2 *Clear Communication*

The next key feature of functional dispute prevention mechanisms is clear, open and ongoing communication. There should be well-established channels for information exchange and the notification of smaller and larger issues alike, ensuring that all competent institutions are regularly informed about potential risks, regardless of whether they are called to action in a particular case.

The communication channels should operate vertically and horizontally within the government, also in relation to the compliance with international treaty obligations and the possible consequences of State measures. The intra-governmental communication should flow directly from the information channels available to foreign investors, such as the network of focal points or other investment grievance mechanisms directly communicating with foreign investors. Ideally, the various avenues of communication will be merged in an online platform that could centralize and store the relevant information, thus enabling subsequent analysis and identification of recurring issues, pitfalls and solutions.

14.3 *Online Platforms*

Robust and systematic communication through online platforms has the added value of reducing the response time to investor grievances teetering on the brink of investment disputes and coordinating the State defense in case an investor files a notice of dispute. Where possible, states should seek to develop accessible and user-friendly online platforms that can serve as databases for the key legislative acts and international instruments, relevant industry updates, ready-to-use administrative forms and templates, and most importantly, a platform for the submission of inquiries and grievances by foreign investors. Such a one-stop shop would place all stakeholders on an equal information footing and ensure the timely flow of notifications to the competent institutions.

14.4 *Transparency*

Key success factors for dispute prevention through effective communication is transparency and accessibility. Foreign investors should be informed immediately upon establishment about their respective contact points, available grievance mechanisms and competent authorities for the resolution of potential issues. Government institutions, from the local to the central levels, should also be aware of and have access to the established communication mechanisms, relying on a set of guidelines and standardized protocols for the proper management of investor grievances and potential disputes.

14.5 *More Detailed Provisions in Investment Treaties*

As noted above, dispute prevention mechanisms are not a common feature of international investment treaties or ISDS clauses. If the focal points and competent authorities for dispute prevention and resolution were explicitly identified in the investment treaties, investment contracts or foreign investment laws of the host state, it would increase the level of legal certainty for all stakeholders and reassure the foreign investors that their grievances would be heard and addressed in a timely manner. Therefore, states should consider including guidance on their respective dispute prevention mechanisms in their model investment treaties and contracts, with direct references to the focal points (if designated).

Ideally, the dispute prevention mechanism would also be placed on a legislative footing, either in a law establishing the dispute prevention mechanism, or in the law governing foreign investments. Such provisions would reduce the risk of miscommunication or lost opportunities for dispute prevention, which characterize the current frameworks with the added value of signaling to the foreign investors that the host State is prepared to effectively respond to their needs and concerns.

14.6 *Capacity Building*

The comprehensive capacity development and training of all competent institutions involved in the conflict resolution spectrum in the host State apparatus will be vital for the functioning of any dispute prevention mechanism. All stakeholders should be educated on the applicable international investment treaties and the investment protection guarantees undertaken by the State, as well as the most frequent grounds for investment claims. The capacity development program should also include protocols of the dispute prevention and dispute resolution phase, and various soft skills necessary for effective communication with foreign investors. Such training could become a feature of periodical and mandatory professional development of public officials throughout the government body, strengthening the institutional knowledge at all levels. If a state disposes of an online platform supporting the dispute prevention mechanism, the materials of the training program could be made available to all users of the platform.

The consistency and quality of the trainings and capacity building for Western Balkans governments can be sustained through membership in the Advisory Centre for States whose draft Statue was adopted in principle at the 57th session of the UNCITRAL Commission. The Centre, once established, would provide technical assistance, training, and legal advisory services to member states, prioritizing developing and least developed States.[137] Among the various potential benefits of the services to be provided by the Centre, the WGIII delegations and the UNCITRAL Secretariat emphasized the possibility of fostering and promoting dispute prevention and amicable settlement methods.[138]

The Western Balkans governments have been actively following the deliberations on the Advisory Centre and its features, and expressed their views in a joint submission to the WGIII, along with the international partners which currently provide technical assistance in the region.[139] Since the region has recognized the potential benefits and interest in the idea of an institution such as the Advisory Centre, the governments, along with their international partners, could consider establishing a regional Centre in case of the delay or abandonment of the international version.[140]

14.7 *Clear Distribution of Roles and Responsibilities*

Considering the sensitive nature of handling investment disputes beyond operational issues faced by foreign investors often resulting in investor grievances, it is important to clearly distinguish the roles of the dispute prevention mechanisms operating outside of the cooling-off period and the dispute management and resolution mechanisms that are activated following a notice of dispute. If certain institutions or coordination bodies should act across several phases, their role and authority should be clearly set forth in the legislation or other instrument establishing the dispute prevention and management mechanisms. A particularly important component is the determination of the institution with settlement authority, and its ability to request collaboration, propose and accept settlement agreements, and allocate costs among

137 Draft statute of an advisory centre on international investment dispute resolution, A/CN.9/WG.III/WP.242 (April 2024) Art. 6.

138 *Ibid.*

139 Submission to the UNCITRAL Working Group III (ISDS Reform) by the Deutsche Gesellschaft fur Internationale Zusammenarbeit (GIZ) GmbH and the Regional Cooperation Council (RCC) Comments on the Proposal for the Establishment of the Advisory Centre on International Investment Law.

140 The option of establishing regional offices of the Advisory Centre was already discussed at the 47th session of UNCITRAL WGIII, where the governments of France, Ghana, the Netherlands, Paraguay and Thailand offered to host such offices. *See,* UNCITRAL Secretariat, Report of Working Group III (Investor-State Dispute Settlement Reform) on the work of its forty -seventh session (Vienna, 22–26 January 2024) <https://documents.un.org/doc/undoc/gen/v24/008/72/pdf/v2400872.pdf?token=nxx5mH62fVT2SVmRkO&fe=true> accessed 02 July 2024.

government institutions. All the institutions in the dispute prevention and management chain should operate under a clear structure of oversight and reporting to the highest levels of government.

14.8 *Lead Agency*

A coordination body comprising several competent institutions from the central government and the agencies directly involved in the dispute should take the lead in the dispute management and resolution phase. This will distribute the responsibility in the cooling-off period, relieving the pressure that comes with negotiating settlements with foreign investors, and the surrounding scrutiny of the public. Should the investor opt to proceed with investment arbitration, the State will be in a better position to raise a cohesive defense with the extensive preliminary work of the competent institutions during the cooling-off period.

Finally, and parallel to all the activities of the government in establishing a robust regulatory and institutional response system for potential and actual investment disputes, there should be a continuous public awareness-raising campaign providing information about the existing mechanisms, and their purpose and benefits for the population and economy. Over time, this should normalize the discourse surrounding investor-State relations and diffuse the intensive backlash against the existing international investment protection framework.

15 Conclusion

States around the world are on an intensive path to reform and strengthen the investment protection frameworks, with a particular emphasis on dispute resolution through investment arbitration. While these processes are important, they also narrow the area of intervention to the far end of the investor-State dispute resolution spectrum, overlooking the dispute prevention and amicable settlement opportunities that arise much earlier.

Importantly, dispute prevention mechanisms allow the governments to take greater control over the process and outcomes of investor grievances, while conducting in parallel the necessary reforms of investment treaties and dispute resolution mechanisms. In addition, they improve the attractiveness of the state for prospective foreign investors and help retain existing investments.

Several model frameworks for dispute prevention mechanisms have emerged over the years, the best practices from individual States are tailored to the specific national legal framework, as well as their institutional structure and capacities. Although the design of a layered dispute prevention mechanism may sound challenging, as the example of the BiH model showed, it may only require a clear vision and the systemic connection and coordination of existing mechanisms, coupled with the proper authority in investment disputes.

If established and used transparently and effectively, the dispute prevention mechanism can help to retain and attract foreign investments, relieving their concerns about political risks and instability. On the other hand, it can also streamline the inter-governmental coordination throughout the life cycle of foreign investments, allowing timely interventions to prevent or at least mitigate investment claims, before they escalate to arbitral proceedings. For States starting from "scratch", the regional and international models provide a variety of options for focal points and coordination bodies that can be adopted and adapted to the national context.

This chapter has highlighted that the Western Balkans governments are already in a good position to take full advantage of the presented best practices, while remaining compliant to the EU legal framework as they progress towards EU membership. While the effectiveness of dispute prevention mechanisms in the Western Balkans can only be measured in the future, there is a promising outlook for dispute prevention as a valuable tool in the investment protection framework, which is worth further efforts.

CHAPTER 10

Investment Mediation: a Means for Resolving Investor-State Disputes in the Western Balkans?

Frauke Nitschke

1 Introduction

Cross-border investment is vital to achieving the United Nations Sustainable Development Goals (SDGs), set forth in the 2030 Agenda for Sustainable Development, adopted by all United Nations Member States in 2015. International investment flows that impact the SDGs have significantly increased in 2022, in particular in the infrastructure, energy, and health and education sectors.[1] One aspect of cross-border investment, foreign direct investment (FDI), is key to connecting domestic economies to flows of capital, technology, knowhow, and global value chains.[2] A comprehensive approach to investment policy and promotion can therefore optimize the benefits of FDI. To retain FDI, encourage re-investment, and support investment expansion and spillovers for the local economy, any investment disputes that may arise between States or State entities and investors must be addressed effectively.[3] Processes employed to resolve such investor-State disputes include direct negotiations, mediation, conciliation or arbitration between the investor and the State or State entity involved.

The vast majority of investor-State disputes are administered by the International Centre for Settlement of Investment Disputes (ICSID), established by the Convention on the Settlement of Investment Disputes between States and Nationals of Other States,[4] which entered into force in 1967. The founding State

1 United Nations Conference on Trade and Investment, World Investment Report 2023, p. 8. (https://unctad.org/publication/world-investment-report-2023).

2 World Bank Group, World Bank Brief, June 8, 2021 (https://www.worldbank.org/en/topic/investment-climate/brief/investment-policy-and-promotion).

3 World Bank Group, Investment Policy and Promotion Diagnostics and Tools: Maximizing the Potential Benefits of Foreign Direct Investment for Competitiveness and Development (2017), p. 5. (https://elibrary.worldbank.org/doi/epdf/10.1596/28281).

4 Convention on the Settlement of Investment Disputes between States and Nationals of Other States (opened for signature 18 March 1965, entered into force 14 October 1966) (ICSID Convention).

 | DOI:10.1163/9789004729889_011

parties created ICSID to provide a neutral, delocalized framework to settle disputes between investors and States or State entities by way of arbitration and conciliation. In 1978, the ICSID Administrative Council expanded the process offerings to include fact-finding procedures, and also expanded the mandate of ICSID to also provide arbitration and conciliation procedures for disputes where only one disputing party, but not both, have a nexus to an ICSID Member State.[5] Following amendments to the ICSID arbitration and conciliation frameworks in 1984, 2003 and 2006,[6] the ICSID Administrative Council, following a 6-year consultation process,[7] amended the existing rules and regulations in 2022, and at the same time adopted an expansion of the Centre's dispute

5 1978 Rules Governing the Additional Facility for the Administration of Proceedings by the Secretariat of the International Centre for Settlement of Investment Disputes (Additional Facility Rules). These types of proceedings include (i) conciliation and arbitration proceedings for the settlement of investment disputes where either the State party to the dispute or the home State of the foreign national is a contracting State of the Convention; (ii) conciliation and arbitration proceedings for the settlement of investment disputes between parties at least one of which is a contracting State or a national of a contracting State for the settlement of disputes that do not arise directly out of an investment; and (iii) fact-finding proceedings. The Additional Facility Rules were last updated and amended in 2022. The 2022 amendments broadened the scope of application of the Additional Facility to authorize the ICSID Secretariat to administer arbitration and conciliation proceedings for the settlement of legal disputes arising out of an investment between a State or a Regional Economic Integration Organization on the one hand, and a national of another State on the other hand, where (i) none of the parties to the dispute is a Contracting State or a national of a Contracting State, (ii) either the State party to the dispute or the State whose national is a party to the dispute, but not both, is a Contracting State or (iii) an REIO is a party to the dispute. The 2022 amendments also updated the former Additional Facility Fact-Finding Rules and moved these to a stand-alone framework.

6 ICSID, *Brief history of amendments to the ICSID Rules and Regulations* (https://icsid.worldbank.org/news-and-events/speeches-articles/brief-history-amendment-icsid-rules-and-regulations).

7 ICSID, *Proposals for Amendment of the ICSID Rules – Working Paper # 1* (August 3, 2018) https://icsid.worldbank.org/sites/default/files/publications/WP1_Amendments_Vol_3_WP-updated-9.17.18.pdf 9 ("WP 1"); ICSID, *Rule Amendment Project – Member State & Public Comments on Working Paper # 1 of August 3, 2018*, https://icsid.worldbank.org/sites/default/files/amendments/Compendium_Comments_Rule_Amendment_3.15.19.pdf ("Comments on WP 1"); ICSID, *Proposal for Amendments to the ICSID Rules –Working Paper # 2*, vol 2 (March 15, 2019), https://icsid.worldbank.org/sites/default/files/amendments/Vol_1.pdf ("WP 2"); ICSID, *Proposal for Amendments to the ICSID Rules – Working Paper # 3*, vol 1 (August 16, 2019), https://icsid.worldbank.org/sites/default/files/amendments/WP_3_VOLUME_1_ENGLISH.pdf ("WP 3"); ICSID, *Proposals for Amendment to the ICSID Rules – Working Paper # 4*, vol 1 (February 28, 2020), https://icsid.worldbank.org/sites/default/files/amendments/WP_4_Vol_1_En.pdf ("WP 4"); ICSID, *Proposals for Amendments to the ICSID Rules – Working Paper # 5*, vol 1 (June 15, 2021) https://icsid.worldbank.org/sites/default/files/documents/WP%205-Volume1-ENG-FINAL.pdf) ("WP 5"); ICSID, *Proposals for Amendments to the ICSID*

resolution service offerings by adopting a set of mediation rules tailored to investor-State dispute settlement. The ICSID Mediation Rules complement the Centre's rules for arbitration, conciliation, and fact-finding, and may be used either independently of, or in conjunction with, arbitration proceedings.

The States in the Western Balkans region, namely Albania, Bosnia & Herzegovina, Kosovo, Montenegro, North Macedonia, and Serbia, have in recent years put particular emphasis on investment policy development and effective management of investor-State disputes. This article will examine (1) the landscape of investment disputes at ICSID involving the Western Balkan region to date and (2) reviewing empirical data on outcomes in concluded investment arbitrations. The following section (3) will commence with an analysis of the empirical data involving amicable settlement in the Western Balkans and (4) provide an overview of investor-State mediation at the ICSID. The article concludes by (5) offering an outlook on the use of investment mediation in the Western Balkans in the future.

2 Empirical Data on ICSID Cases Involving States from the Western Balkans Region

By the end of December 2023, ICSID had registered 967 requests under its ICSID frameworks for dispute resolution proceedings outlined above. One of the cornerstones for ICSID dispute settlement is the parties' written consent.

As illustrated in the chart below, most ICSID cases are instituted on the basis of the State's advance consent to ICSID dispute settlement contained in bilateral investment treaties (BITs) and multilateral investment agreements. Parties have also relied on contractual ICSID clauses and provisions in domestic investment laws providing for ICSID dispute settlement in the event a dispute between an investor and a State or State entity arises.

ICSID Cases involve disputes relating to a variety of economic sectors. About one quarter of ICSID cases relate to the oil, gas, and mining sector (23%), followed by the construction (18%), transportation (18%) and electric power and other energy sectors (12%). The remainder of ICSID cases relate to a variety of industrial activities.

Of the 967 cases registered at ICSID at the end of 2023, 39 have involved State parties from the Western Balkans, comprising about 4% of all ICSID cases. Within the region, the largest portion of cases involves Albania (12 cases),

---

Rules – Working Paper # 5, vol 1 (November 12, 2021) https://icsid.worldbank.org/sites/default/files/documents/ICSID_WP_Six.pdf) ("WP 6").

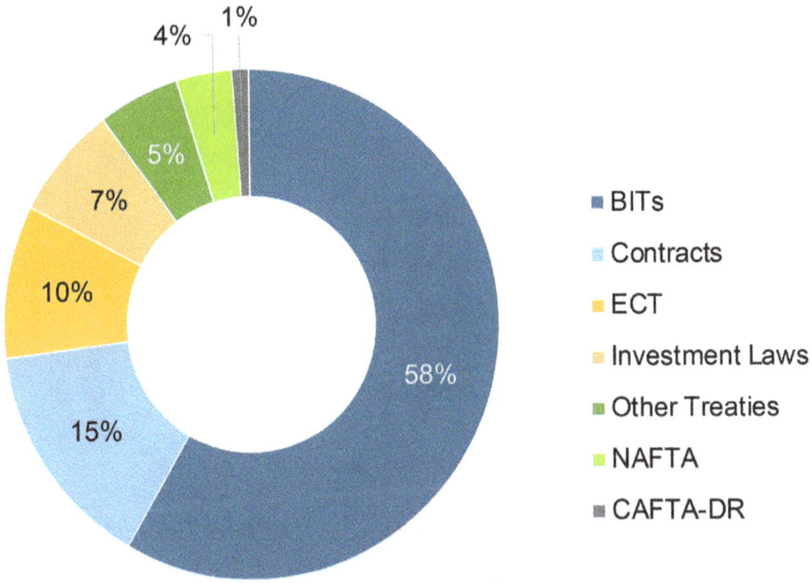

FIGURE 10.1 All ICSID cases – basis of consent

SOURCE: ICSID, THE ICSID CASELOAD-STATISTICS (ISSUE 2024-1), P. 7 (HTTPS://ICSID.WORLDBANK.ORG/SITES/DEFAULT/FILES/PUBLICATIONS/ENG_THE_ICSID_CASELOAD_STATISTICS_ISSUE%202024.PDF)

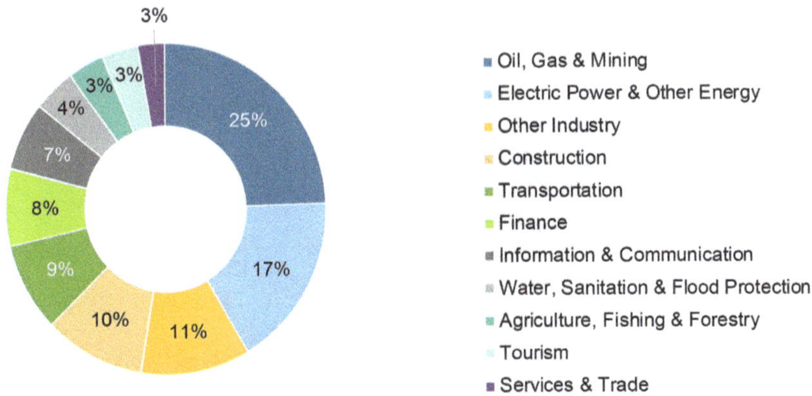

FIGURE 10.2 All ICSID cases – economic sectors

SOURCE: ICSID CASELOAD-STATISTICS (ISSUE 2024-1), *SUPRA* N 8, P. 10

followed by Serbia (11 cases), North Macedonia (7 cases), and Bosnia and Herzegovina, Kosovo and Montenegro (three cases each).

In the following section, the overall landscape of ICSID investment disputes involving a State or State entity from the Western Balkans will be reviewed.

FIGURE 10.3 ICSID cases involving a State party from the Western Balkans

2.1 *Albania*

Of the 12 ICSID cases involving Albania, eleven were ICSID Convention arbitrations and one a conciliation proceeding. In four of the 12 cases involving Albania, ICSID jurisdiction was asserted on two alternative bases, a bilateral investment treaty and the investment law. In six further cases, parties relied on the ICSID dispute settlement provision contained in bilateral investment treaties. The ICSID dispute settlement provision set out in the Energy Charter Treaty was relied on in one case, and in one further case, parties invoked the ICSID dispute settlement clause contained in an investment contract.

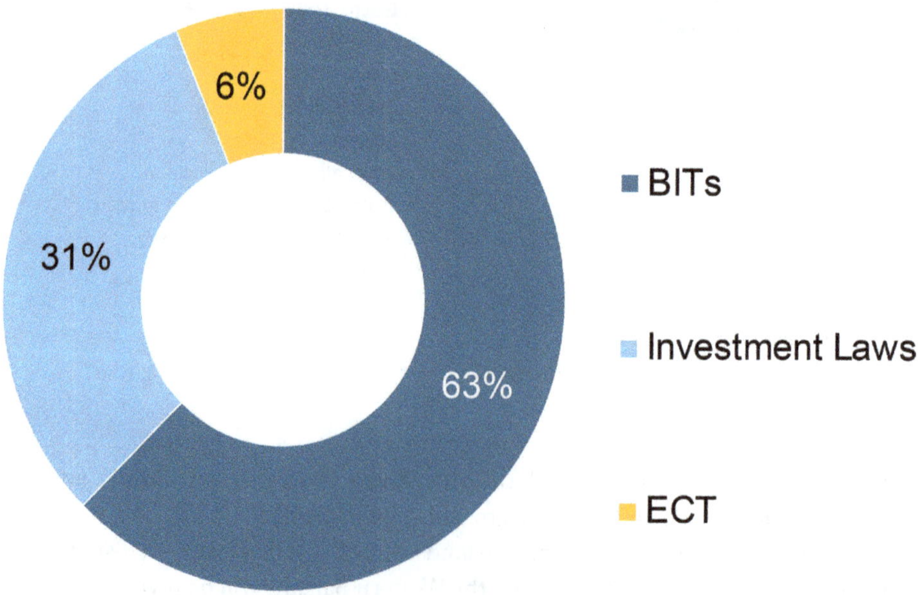

FIGURE 10.4 ICSID cases involving Albania – basis of consent to jurisdiction

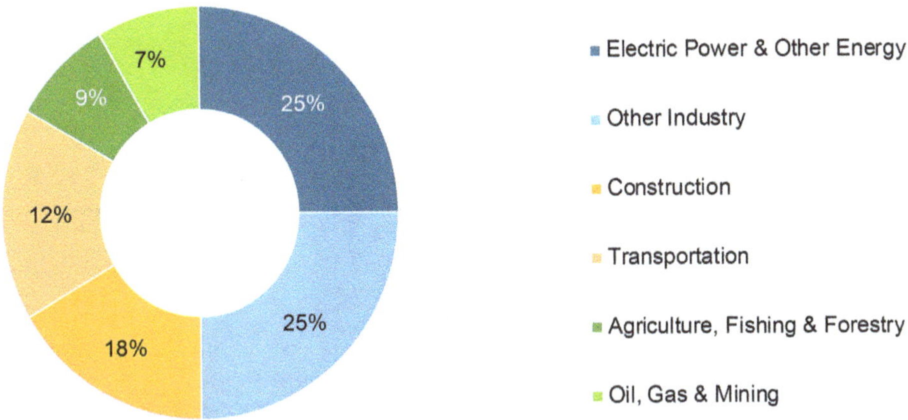

FIGURE 10.5 ICSID cases involving Albania – economic sectors involved

Three of the cases involving Albania related to the electric power and other energy sector, followed by the transportation and construction sectors (two cases each). One case involved agriculture, fishing and forestry and one case related to the oil, gas, and mining industry sector. The remaining three cases involved a variety of industry sectors, including tobacco manufacturing and warehousing, gaming, and privatization vouchers.

2.2 *Bosnia and Herzegovina*

The three ICSID cases involving Bosnia and Herzegovina were ICSID arbitration cases. Two cases were instituted on the basis of two alternative bas es for ICSID dispute settlement, a bilateral investment treaty and the Energy Charter Treaty, and one further case was instituted on the basis of a bilateral investment treaty only. Two of the cases involving Bosnia and Herzegovina related to the electric power and other energy sector, and one case involved the construction sector.

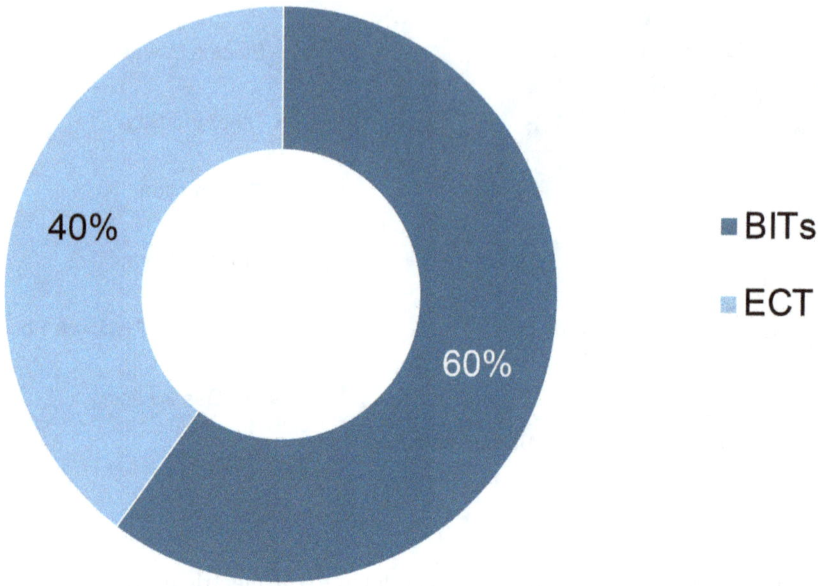

FIGURE 10.6 ICSID cases involving Bosnia and Herzegovina – basis of consent to jurisdiction

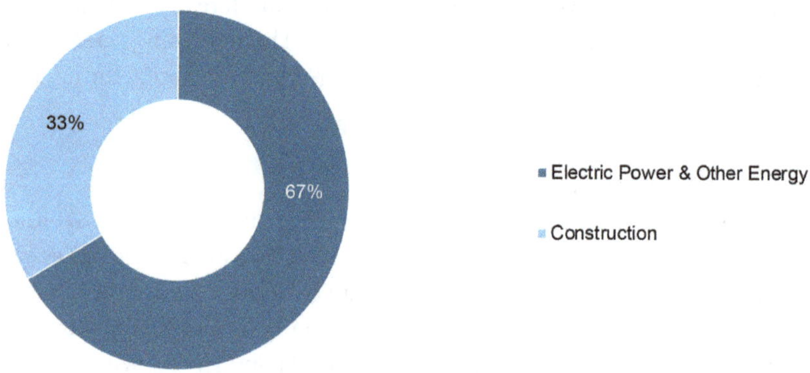

FIGURE 10.7 ICSID cases involving Bosnia and Herzegovina – economic sectors involved

2.3 *Kosovo*

The three cases instituted involving Kosovo were all ICSID Convention arbitrations. In two cases, parties invoked two alternative bases for ICSID jurisdiction, the ICSID dispute settlement provision in a bilateral investment treaty and in the investment law. In one further case, parties relied on the ICSID arbitration clause contained in a contract.

In terms of economic sectors, the three cases involving Kosovo related to the electric power and other industry sector, information and communication sector and the tourism sector in equal parts (one case each).

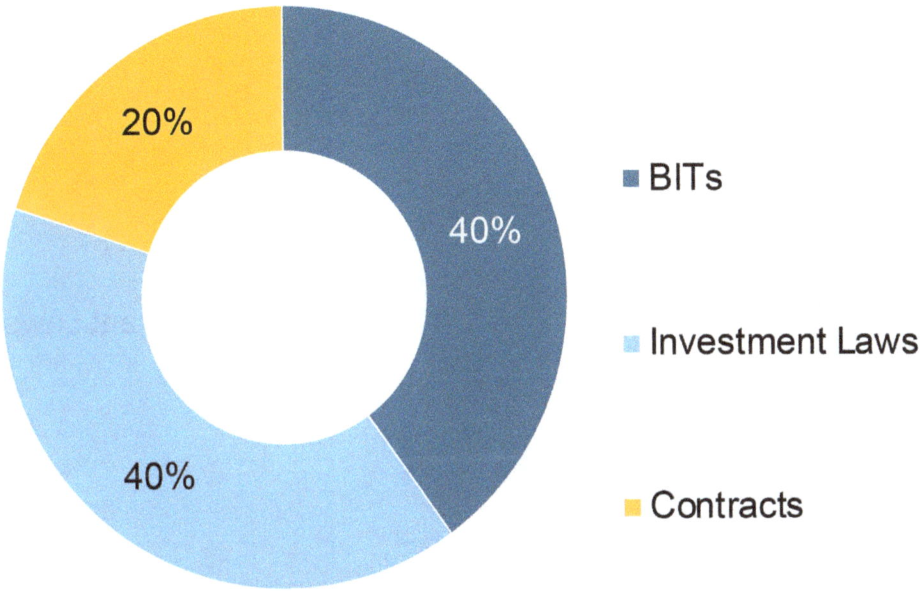

FIGURE 10.8 ICSID cases involving Kosovo – basis of consent to jurisdiction

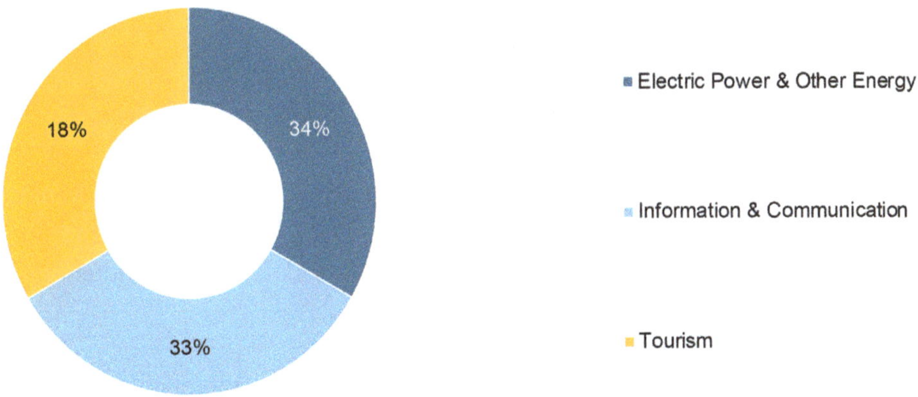

FIGURE 10.9 ICSID cases involving Kosovo – economic sectors involved

2.4 *Montenegro*

All three cases involving Montenegro were arbitrations conducted under the ICSID Convention. All three cases relied on an ICSID dispute settlement provision contained in a bilateral investment treaty. In one of these cases, the Claimant relied upon the ICSID dispute settlement provision in the investment law as an alternative basis to establish ICSID jurisdiction. Regarding the economic sectors, one case involved the finance sector, one case the oil,

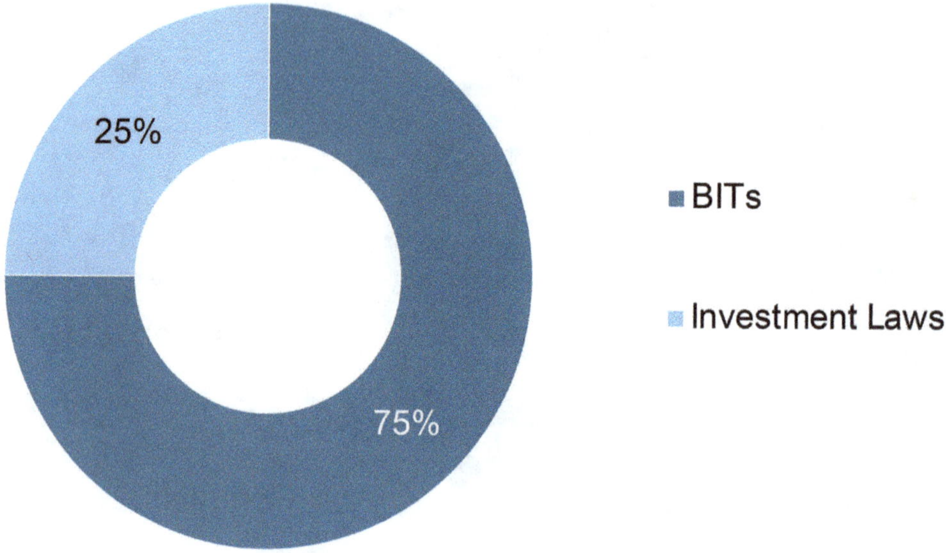

FIGURE 10.10 ICSID cases involving Montenegro – basis of consent to jurisdiction

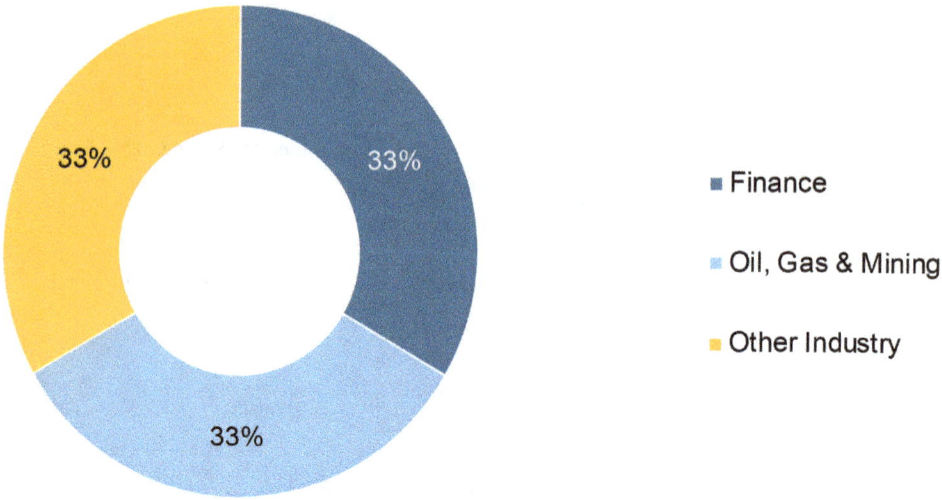

FIGURE 10.11 ICSID cases involving Montenegro – economic sectors involved

gas, and mining sector and one case related to the other industry sector and involved steel production.

2.5 *North Macedonia*

All three cases involving North Macedonia are ICSID Convention arbitrations. All seven cases were instituted on the basis of a bilateral investment treaty. In one of these cases, the ICSID dispute settlement clause in the Energy Charter Treaty was also relied upon.

The cases involving North Macedonia related to a variety of economic sectors. Two cases related to the construction industry, one to the electric power and other energy sector, one case involved the oil, gas, and mining sector, and one further case related to the finance sector. Two cases involved other industries and related to food products and the metal industry.

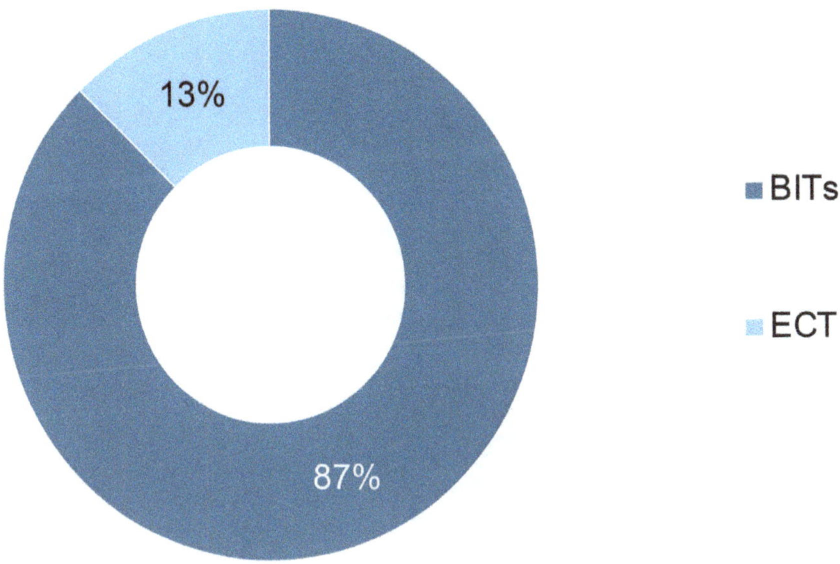

FIGURE 10.12 ICSID cases involving North Macedonia – basis of consent to jurisdiction

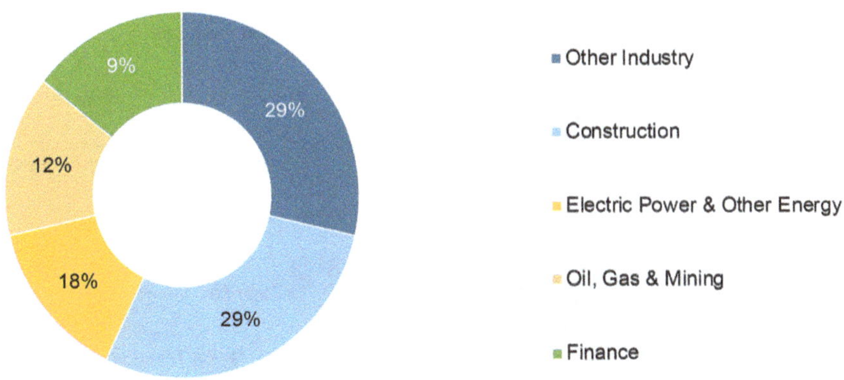

FIGURE 10.13 ICSID cases involving North Macedonia – economic sectors involved

2.6 *Serbia*

All 11 cases involving Serbia were arbitrations conducted under the ICSID Convention. All eleven cases were instituted on the basis of ICSID dispute settlement provisions in bilateral investment treaties.

The cases involving Serbia relate to a variety of economic sectors. Two cases involve the information & communication sector. One case each related to the

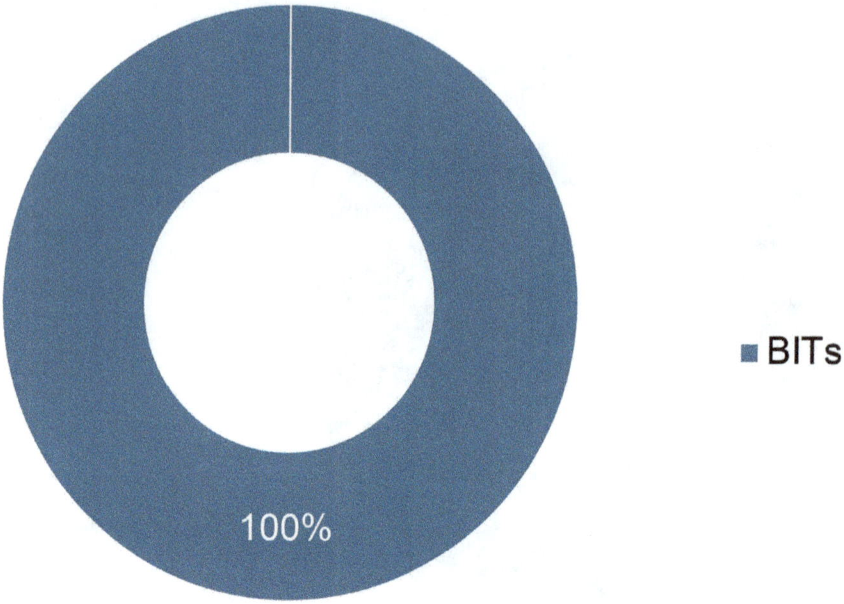

FIGURE 10.14 ICSID cases involving Serbia – basis of consent to jurisdiction

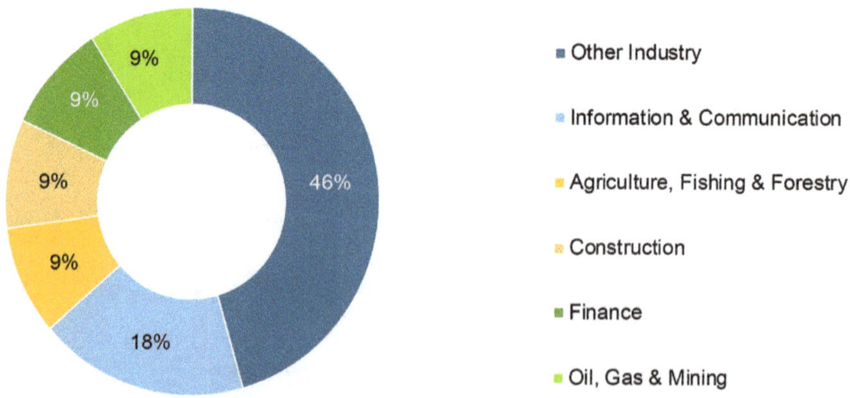

FIGURE 10.15 ICSID cases involving Serbia – economic sectors involved

construction sector, the finance sector and the oil, gas and mining sector. Five further cases are related to a broad range of industry activity, including gaming and entertainment facilities, waste management services, real estate, and the chemical industry.

3 Empirical Data on Outcomes of ICSID Arbitrations Involving States from the Western Balkans

Generally, investment arbitrations at ICSID may be terminated with an award issued by a tribunal or be settled or otherwise discontinued. Tribunal decisions may take the form of an award declining jurisdiction,[8] an award upholding claims in part or in full,[9] or an award deciding that the claims are manifestly without legal merit.[10]

Parties may further request a tribunal to embody the parties' settlement agreement into an award,[11] or cases may be discontinued upon request of both parties[12] by way of request from one party to which the other party does not object,[13] or if the parties have failed to take step in a proceeding for more than six months,[14] or failed to pay the requested advances.[15]

Looking at outcomes in ICSID cases, and specifically at ICSID arbitrations, historically, about 36% of these arbitrations settle or are otherwise discontinued without a ruling by the Tribunal. This proportion of dispute settlement outcomes is an indication that parties continue to be interested in amicable dispute resolution even after the institution of an arbitration process.

Looking only at ICSID arbitrations involving the Western Balkans, the question arises whether this trend in the overall ICSID caseload is also reflected in the Western Balkans or whether more, or fewer, arbitrations settle amicably than the overall ICSID data indicates. If the available data for tribunal awards involving each of the Western Balkan States cannot be reported in the aggregate, the data is provided as it is available in the public domain. Information on discontinuances is reported based on the data available on ICSID's website.

---

8 2022 ICSID Arbitration Rule 44(3)(c).
9 2022 ICSID Arbitration Rule 59(1)(i).
10 2022 ICSID Arbitration Rule 41(3).
11 2022 ICSID Arbitration Rule 55(2)(b).
12 2022 ICSID Arbitration Rule 55(2)(a).
13 2022 ICSID Arbitration Rule 56.
14 2022 ICSID Arbitration Rule 57.
15 2022 ICSID Administrative and Financial Regulation 16.

FIGURE 10.16 Outcomes in ICSID arbitrations
SOURCE: THE ICSID CASELOAD – STATISTICS (ISSUE 2024-1), *SUPRA* N 8, P. 12

3.1 *Albania*

Of the nine ICSID arbitrations involving Albania that have concluded, two cases were settled or otherwise discontinued, and in seven cases, a tribunal rendered an award. Of the seven cases decided by tribunals, four dismissed all claims, two awards declined jurisdiction, and one award upheld the claims in part or in full. One case was discontinued at the request of a party to which the other party did not object, and one case was discontinued for lack of payment of the required advances.

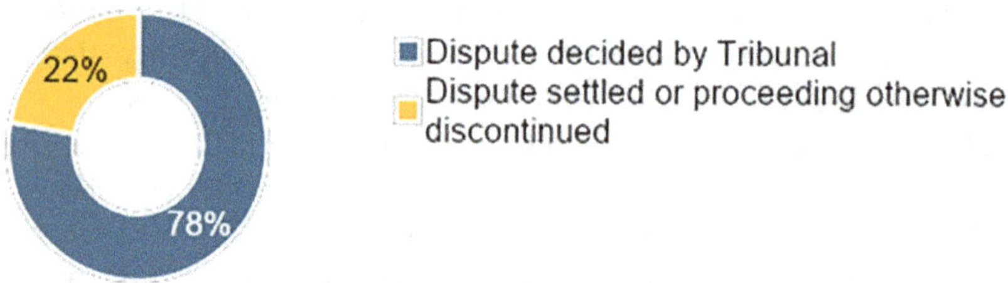

FIGURE 10.17 ICSID arbitrations involving Albania – outcomes

3.2 Bosnia and Herzegovina

Of the two ICSID arbitrations concluded involving Bosnia and Herzegovina, one resulted in an award upholding the claims in full or in part,[16] and one was discontinued at the request of both parties.

16 Viaduct d.o.o. Portorož, Vladimir Zevnik and Boris Goljevšček v. Bosnia and Herzegovina, ICSID Case No. ARB/16/36, *reported in* Global Arbitration Review (March 3, 2024) (https://globalarbitrationreview.com/article/bosnia-fails-annul-hydroelectric-plant-award#:~:text=An%20ICSID%20annulment%20committee%20has%20upheld%20an,Slovenian%20investors%20in%20two%20hydroelectric%20power%20plants).

FIGURE 10.18 ICSID arbitrations involving Bosnia and Herzegovina – outcomes

3.3 *Kosovo*

To date, two ICSID arbitration proceedings involving Kosovo concluded, one with a ruling by a tribunal declining jurisdiction,[17] the other discontinued at the request of both parties.

FIGURE 10.19 ICSID arbitrations involving Kosovo – outcomes

3.4 *Montenegro*

Of the three ICSID arbitrations involving Montenegro that have concluded to date, all three resulted in a ruling by the tribunal. Two awards dismissed all claims and one award declined jurisdiction.

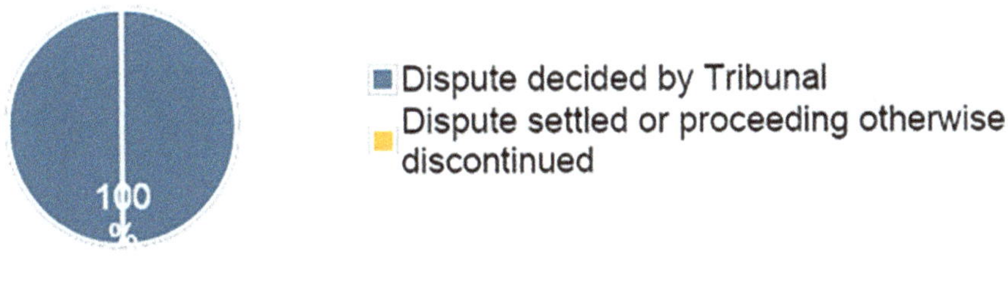

FIGURE 10.20 ICSID arbitrations involving Montenegro – outcomes

17 ACP Axos Capital GmbH v. Republic of Kosovo, ICSID Case No. ARB/15/22, Award (May 3, 2018) (https://www.italaw.com/cases/3907).

3.5 *North Macedonia*

To date, four arbitrations involving North Macedonia have concluded. Two of these resulted in a ruling by the tribunal, one upholding claims in full or in part,[18] for the other, the rulings contained in the award are not publicly available. Two further proceedings terminated without a ruling, one was discontinued at the request of both parties, the other terminated with the parties' settlement agreement being embodied in an award.[19]

FIGURE 10.21 ICSID arbitrations involving North Macedonia – outcomes

3.6 *Serbia*

Of the eight concluded arbitrations involving Serbia, seven resulted in a ruling by the tribunal. One tribunal declined jurisdiction, one dismissed all claims, and five awards upheld the claims in part or in full. One further arbitration was discontinued at the request of both parties.

FIGURE 10.22 ICSID arbitrations involving Serbia – outcomes

18 Swisslion DOO Skopje v. The Former Yugoslav Republic of Macedonia, ICSID Case No. ARB/09/16, Award (July 6, 2012) (https://www.italaw.com/cases/1516).

19 EVN AG v. The former Yugoslav Republic of Macedonia, ICSID Case No. ARB/09/10, Award (September 2, 2011) (https://www.italaw.com/cases/427).

4 ICSID Mediation as an Additional Tool to Resolve Investment Disputes in the Western Balkans

4.1 *Introduction*

As the empirical data of ICSID's overall arbitration shows,[20] a considerable number of investment disputes are resolved without a tribunal ruling, even after arbitration proceedings have been instituted.

From the empirical data relating to outcomes in disputes involving the Western Balkans, it is notable that all States from the Western Balkan region except for Montenegro have either agreed, or not objected to, one or more arbitrations to being discontinued or settled without a ruling of a tribunal. In fact, as noted above, looking at the outcomes involving three of these six States, i.e., Bosnia and Herzegovina, Kosovo, and North Macedonia, 50% of investment arbitrations have resulted in a discontinuance or settlement. For Albania and Serbia, the proportion of disputes is lower, with 22% for Albania and 13% for Serbia.

While concluded arbitrations involving Montenegro all resulted in a tribunal ruling, it should be recalled that two of these terminated with a dismissal of all claims and one further award declined jurisdiction. This data could indicate that Montenegro manages investment disputes effectively prior to the commencement of arbitral proceedings and resolves disputes amicably where in the interest of the State. In relation to the three disputes that came before ICSID and were decided by a tribunal, the government may have prepared a comprehensive assessment of these three disputes, reviewing the government conduct at the heart of the disputes, weighing the interests of the State and the prospects of a potential ruling in favor of the State on the basis of the available information. Such review may have led to the determination that arbitrating these three disputes was in fact in the interest of the State.

This empirical data illustrates that States in the Western Balkans are familiar with resolution of investment disputes other than by ruling by a tribunal. Notably, while the settlement rate for Albania is about half of that of Bosnia and Herzegovina, Kosovo, and Montenegro, Albania is the only Western Balkan country that is a party to an ICSID conciliation proceeding conducted under the ICSID Convention.[21]

ICSID's mediation services could be a possible avenue for States and investors in the region alike to consider. Making a conscious determination regarding what would be an adequate investment dispute resolution process, whether arbitration, conciliation, mediation, or negotiation, is beneficial for any party

20 *See* above, Figure 16.

21 Xenofon Karagiannis v. Republic of Albania, ICSID Case No. CONC/16/1.

faced with a dispute – regardless of whether it is the investor or a State or State entity. Even if a State is faced with a request for arbitration, or the State and the investor are already engaged in an arbitration, that does not necessarily exclude the possibility of engaging in parallel in an amicable settlement process. As the data above indicates, parallel amicable settlement discussions are not unusual. The question that arises, therefore, (and is addressed in the next section), is how the suitability of a dispute for mediation – as a form of facilitated mediation – can be ascertained.

4.2 *ICSID Mediation – Background*

The ICSID Mediation Rules were drafted in response to inquiries by ICSID Member States requesting that ICSID as the trusted international forum offer investor-State mediation services. Certain developments leading up to the adoption of the ICSID Mediation Rules are also worth recalling.

On a policy level, mediation is offered as a mechanism to settle disputes between foreign investors and host States in numerous new-generation bilateral and multilateral investment agreements,[22] some of which provide for mediation during the "cooling-off" period while others envision mediation as a stand-alone process that parties may pursue either separately or in parallel to an ongoing arbitration.[23] The ICSID Mediation Rules were intended *inter alia* to support the implementation of the State's policy choices to offer mediation alongside conciliation.

The ICSID Mediation Rules further coincided with the work of the international community that culminated in the Singapore Convention on Mediation which opened for signature in the fall of 2019.[24] During the drafting stages, the

---

22 ICSID, Overview of Investment Treaty Clauses on Mediation (July 2021) (https://icsid.worldbank.org/sites/default/files/publications/Overview_Mediation_in_Treaties.pdf).

23 *See, e.g.*, EU-Canada Comprehensive Economic and Trade Agreement (signed October 30, 2016, provisionally entered into force September 21, 2017) Annex 29-C on Mediation (https://investmentpolicy.unctad.org/international-investment-agreements/treaties/treaties-with-investment-provisions/3546/canada—eu-ceta-2016-); EU-Vietnam Investment Protection Agreement (signed June 30, 2019, not yet in force), Ch 3, Art. 3.4 (https://investmentpolicy.unctad.org/international-investmentagreements/treaties/treaties-with-investment-provisions/3616/eu—viet-nam-investment-protectionagreement-2019); EU-Singapore Investment Protection Agreement (signed October 15, 2018, not yet in force), Annex 6 (https://investmentpolicy.unctad.org/international-investment-agreements/treaties/treaties-with-investment-provisions/3545/eu—singapore-investment-protection-agreement-2018-).

24 United Nations Convention on International Settlement Agreements Resulting from Mediation (adopted on December 20, 2018 and opened for signature on August 7, 2019) ("Singapore Convention on Mediation").

ICSID Secretariat closely cooperated with the UNCITRAL Secretariat to align the ICSID Mediation Rules with the formal requirements set out in the Singapore Convention Article 4(1).

4.3 *Differences between ICSID Mediation and ICSID Conciliation*

As noted above, the ICSID framework has provided, since 1967, for amicable dispute settlement by way of conciliation. ICSID mediation differs from the ICSID conciliation process in a number of ways. Key differences include:

- *Scope of Application*: in ICSID mediation, unlike in ICSID conciliation, there is no foreign nationality requirement and therefore investment mediations at ICSID may be conducted between States and investors of the State party to the mediation. Further, there is no requirement for either party to be linked to an ICSID Convention Member State; hence, ICSID mediation is available where neither home State of the investor nor the host State is an ICSID Contracting State.[25]
- *Commencement of Proceeding*: In ICSID conciliation, a request for conciliation must indicate the parties' written consent to ICSID conciliation. In mediation, a request for mediation may contain such written consent to ICSID mediation. However, there is a further avenue to commence a mediation at ICSID in the event there is no pre-existing consent to ICSID mediation: a Request for mediation may also be submitted that contains simply an offer to the other party to mediate the issues in dispute.[26] ICSID will then transmit the offer to mediate to the other party, inviting that party to state whether it accepts or rejects the offer. If the offer is rejected or no response is received within 60 days, no further action will be taken by the ICSID Secretariat. If the offer is accepted, the review of the Request for mediation will continue with the registration of the Request as the next step.[27]
- *Unilateral withdrawal at any time*: Unlike ICSID arbitration and conciliation, where unilateral withdrawal of consent is not possible, the ICSID Mediation Rules explicitly provide for an option to withdraw from the mediation at any time; hence, mediation requires "ongoing consent" to mediate.[28]
- *Number of Mediators & Method of Appointment*: In ICSID mediation, there is either one mediator or two co-mediators who is/are appointed by the parties jointly. If the parties do not agree on the number of mediators, the default is one mediator appointed by party agreement. In ICSID conciliation, the

25 ICSID Mediation Rule 2(1).
26 ICSID Mediation Rule 6.
27 ICSID Mediation Rule 7.
28 ICSID Mediation Rule 22(1)(c).

framework provides for an uneven number of conciliators, with the default being a three-member commission under the ICSID Convention.

- *Role of the Mediator*: The mediator's role is limited to assisting the parties in reaching a mutually acceptable resolution of all or part of the issues in dispute,[29] and there is no determination of "jurisdiction" by the mediator, nor does the mediator have the ability to issue *status quo* recommendations. In ICSID conciliation, a "jurisdictional" determination is made by the conciliation commission, whose role further also encompasses the clarification of the issues in dispute and the ability to issue recommendations for the parties to maintain the *status quo*.
- *Information Disclosure by ICSID*: Information relating to a conciliation or a mediation and all documents generated in or obtained during the process are confidential, unless (i) the parties agree otherwise, (ii) the information or document is independently available, (iii) disclosure is required by law. No information concerning the mediation will be published by ICSID absent party agreement.[30] This differs from ICSID conciliation, where the Administrative and Financial Regulations require ICSID to publish the names of the parties and basic case details on its website.

The ICSID Mediation Rules are also a reflection of a trend observed over the years that investors and States are looking for amicable resolution of the conflicts arising between them even after an arbitration has been commenced. This is evident from the empirical data on settlement and discontinuance in investment arbitration at ICSID described above.[31]

4.4 *How to Determine the Suitability of Investment Mediation?*

A comprehensive assessment of the dispute and the parties or entities involved is recommended as a helpful starting point to determine the suitable dispute resolution process in the particular circumstances. Such assessment benefits from analyzing the stakeholders involved – on the one hand those stakeholders and entities involved in the circumstances leading to the dispute, and on the other hand those stakeholders that may be relevant and may need to be involved in finding a negotiated resolution. In investment disputes in particular, the entities at the heart of the dispute and those required for its resolution are not necessarily the same.

---

29 ICSID Mediation Rule 17.

30 ICSID Mediation Administrative and Financial Regulation 3 and ICSID Mediation Rule 10(2)).

31 *See above*, Section 3.

Based on a comprehensive assessment of the dispute, further aspects to consider when assessing the suitability of mediation for the resolution of an investment dispute are:

- *Willingness to engage in negotiations.* First, since mediation is in principle a facilitated negotiation between the disputing parties, a party's willingness to engage in negotiations with the other party is fundamental. Absent such willingness to negotiate, mediation is not a suitable process.
- *Desire to maintain the relationship.* Another aspect that disputing parties may give thought to is whether they desire to maintain their relationship or wish for an amicable termination of such relationship. Given the non-adversarial nature of mediation, it has been considered a suitable process in such instances.
- *Desired structure/design/form of the dispute resolution process.* When determining the suitability of mediation as a form of facilitated negotiation, parties are encouraged to reflect which procedural features and characteristics they consider of vital. For example, in cases in which interim relief is of utmost importance to the parties, arbitration or litigation may be more suitable, as the mediator does not possess a function of ordering such interim relief. On the other hand, if the disputing parties wish to involve third parties in the dispute resolution process in a flexible manner, mediation may offer that opportunity more so than arbitration.
- *Desire to shape the resolution/maintain control of the outcome.* Disputing parties should also reflect on whether they wish to maintain the ability to shape the eventual resolution (possibly including aspects other than pecuniary relief available under most legal instruments), or whether they prefer for a third party neutral to determine the outcome and issue a final and binding ruling. If the latter is desired, it is important to understand that the mediator is not vested with the function of imposing a resolution on the disputing parties.[32]
- *Financial resources to cover the costs of the dispute resolution process.* As a practical matter, parties may also consider the financial resources available and the relative costs of pursuing the various dispute resolution processes. Based on the information available on investment mediations, process costs relating to investment mediation range between 25,000 and 200,000 USD.
- *Desired time frame to resolve the dispute.* Another consideration relates to a party's desired speed of resolution of a particular dispute. In certain circumstances, a rapid resolution may be essential to a disputing party or

32 ICSID Mediation Rule 17(1).

an investment activity as a whole. Based on the data available, investment mediations take on average between six and nine months, counted from the appointment of the mediator.

It is important for parties to keep in mind that the assessment of what would be a suitable dispute resolution process may change over time. As evidenced by the empirical data on ICSID arbitrations above, even if an arbitration process were commenced by one disputing party with the goal of obtaining a final resolution from a tribunal, that does not preclude the parties from engaging in negotiations and resolving the dispute amicably. Likewise, parties may, and have, engaged in ICSID mediation as a form of facilitated negotiations, while a parallel arbitration was ongoing. In practice, the arbitration is likely going to be suspended by party agreement while the mediation is ongoing.

4.5 *When to Mediate?*

Contrary to a longstanding perception, mediation is conceptually not only available following a notice of dispute and prior to the commencement of arbitration. Mediation, as a form of facilitated negotiation, is available during the entirety of an investment dispute continuum, i.e., mediation could be used to resolve disagreements, problems, or grievances during investment operations. Mediation could also be resorted to prior to commencement of arbitration following a notice of dispute (during the so-called cooling-off period), and mediation is also available alongside arbitration. In practice, mediation has also occurred after an arbitration is concluded.[33] Investors and States could even consider mediation to facilitate negotiations at the outset of an investment during the initial negotiations. It should be noted that unresolved investment disputes may lead to the withdrawal of the actual investment, or cancellation of investment plans given the difficulties in resolving disputed issues that have arisen during the investment relationship. The graphic below illustrates the lifecycle of an investment dispute, mapped against available dispute resolution processes.

33 ICSID, Background Paper on Investment Mediation (July 2021), p.7 (https://icsid.worldbank.org/sites/default/files/publications/Background_Paper_on_Investment_Mediation_Oct.2021.pdf).

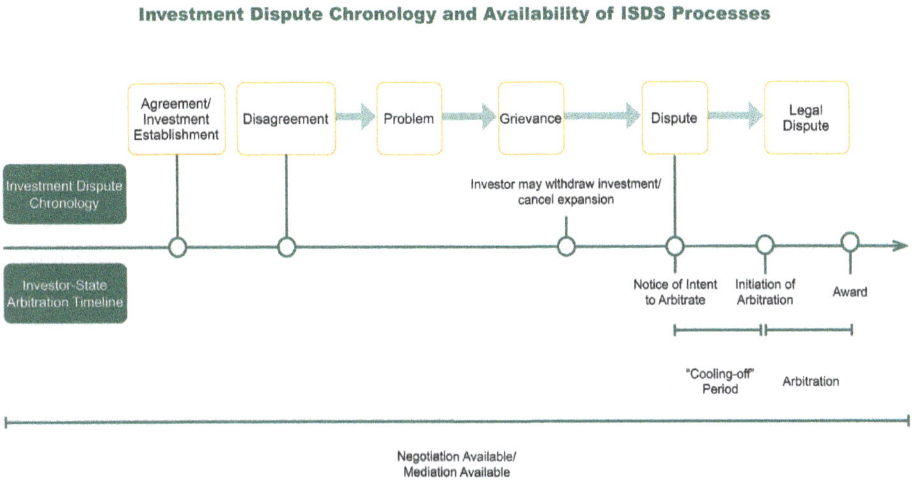

FIGURE 10.23 Investment dispute continuum and available investment dispute settlement processes

4.6 *The Mediation Process*

While many dispute resolution practitioners are familiar with investment arbitration and direct negotiations, mediation theory or mediation skills training are not featured prominently in formal legal education or practical training around the globe. While mediation practice and style differ depending on geographic region or cultural approaches, process principles of mediation appear universal. Mediation is generally considered an informal, flexible process providing for collaborative problem-solving, consideration of legal and non-legal interests and direct party participation.[34] Narrowing to investment mediation, investment mediation is typically understood as a mediation involving a State, State entity or Regional Economic Integration Organization and relates to an investment.[35]

Although mediation is flexible and informal, that does not mean that the process lacks structure. Many different process models exist to set out the phases of a mediation. Generally speaking, a mediation consists of a process-organization phase (at ICSID this concludes with the adoption of the Mediation Protocol), followed by a phase focusing on the parties' gaining

34 World Bank Group, Mediation Essentials (2017), p. 40 (http://documents1.worldbank.org/curated/en/153761503566770915/pdf/119068-WP-MediationEssentials-PUBLIC.pdf).

35 *See also* ICSID Mediation Rule 2(1).

clarity about the disputed issues and their views on these, a phase to generate potential solutions, a negotiation phase, and a closing phase.[36]

4.6.1 Process-Organization Phase

Following the mediator's appointment, the structure and organization of the mediation is discussed at the outset between the mediator and the parties. In ICSID mediation, the parties' initial written statements are to describe the issues in dispute and a party's views on these issues as well as on matters of mediation procedure.[37] Subsequently, the mediator may meet with the parties jointly or separately to prepare the guiding framework of the mediation, the "Mediation Protocol" on the basis of which the mediation will be conducted.[38] The Mediation Protocol addresses *inter alia* the language of the mediation, the method of communication, place of meetings, treatment of information relating to, and documents generated in or obtained during, the mediation,[39] the division of advances payable to cover the costs of the mediation, the participation of other persons in the mediation, and any agreement between the parties not to initiate or pursue other proceedings in respect of the issues being mediated.[40]

The ICSID Mediation Protocol also usually reflects the tools a mediator may use when conducting the mediation and engaging in the various process phases described below. ICSID Mediation Rule 17 identifies that the mediator's duties are to "assist the parties in reaching a mutually acceptable resolution of all or part of the issues in dispute" and at the same time makes clear that "[t]he mediator has no authority to impose a resolution of the dispute on the parties."[41] Both the parties and the mediator have the duty to conduct the mediation in good faith and in an expeditiously and in a cost-effective manner.[42]

The mediator further has a duty to treat the parties equally and provide each party with a reasonable opportunity to participate in the mediation.[43] The mediator may meet and communicate with the parties jointly or separately,

36 Mediation Essentials, *supra* n 37, p. 40; American Society of International Law, 2024 Annual Meeting (April 5, 2024), Putting Mediation to the Test (https://soundcloud.com/americansocietyofinternationallaw/putting-mediation-to-the-test?in=americansocietyofinternationallaw/sets/2024-asil-annual-meeting).

37 ICSID Mediation Rule 19(1).

38 ICSID Mediation Rules 20 and 21(1).

39 ICSID Mediation Rule 10 sets forth the basic principles of treatment of information with non-mediation participants, whereas ICSID Mediation Rule 17(4) regulates the sharing of information received by the mediator from one party may not be disclosed to the other party without authorization from the disclosing party.

40 ICSID Mediation Rule 20(3).

41 ICSID Mediation Rule 17(1).

42 ICSID Mediation Rules 17(2) and 18.

43 ICSID Mediation Rule 17(3).

in person or in writing, and by any appropriate technological means.[44] ICSID Mediation Rule 17(4) specifies that information received by the mediator from one party is not to be disclosed to the other party without authorization from the disclosing party. The mediator may further request additional information or written statements from the parties,[45] and may obtain expert advice with the agreement of the parties. Only with the agreement of all parties may the mediator make recommendations for the resolution of any disputed issues.[46]

4.6.2 Gaining Clarity

Once the Mediation Protocol is adopted, the mediator and the parties continue the dialogue with the aim of gaining clarity about the disputed issues, each party's views on the issues and the reasons underlying a party's views. This typically involves a legal analysis and a review of non-legal aspects such as other priorities important to a party. Such priorities in the context of investor-State mediation may relate to economic, financial, political, environmental or governance priorities. At this stage, the mediator usually also engages each party in considering what the other party may be thinking about the disputed issues, and what the underlying reasons for that party are to hold these views. In essence, this phase aims at generating a comprehensive understanding of the disputed issues and each party's perceptions and priorities in relation to these issues, considering past history, and a party's priorities for the future – be it a continuation of a relationship or an amicable termination thereof.

4.6.3 Developing Solutions

Based on the clarity obtained, the mediator will then work with each party to develop potential solutions that reflect both, a party's views on the legal considerations and its other priorities, and the risks and benefits attributable to each of those. The mediator assists parties in gaining deeper clarity about the issues and the party's priorities and parameters and rationale for potential settlement options. Particularly in the State context, States require clear and objectively justifiable rationales for the settlement of disputes involving sovereign entities.

4.6.4 Negotiating

Having developed prospective solutions reflecting a party's clarity about the disputed issues and its priorities (legal or otherwise) going forward, as well as the considered risks and benefits of any such possible solution, proposals are made and received. On the basis of these proposals, negotiations between the

44 ICSID Mediation Rule 17(4).
45 ICSID Mediation Rule 21(2)
46 ICSID Mediation Rule 21(4).

parties begin to evolve. It is not infrequent for several rounds of proposals to be exchanged, often facilitated by the mediator conveying a proposal.

In addition, it should be noted that the negotiation process may not necessarily be linear – when considering proposals, a party may revert to earlier steps, realizing the need to gain more clarity about its priorities when faced with a concrete settlement proposal from the other party, which reflects that party's priorities.

Negotiating an amicable solution does not require either disputing party to compromise or 'give up' any of its priorities. The goal of the mediation process is collaborative problem solving. Solutions are developed that reflect each party's priorities, the weight given to those priorities and the associated risks. It may indeed be that a non-negotiated solution better aligns with a party's priorities than a negotiated one that does not sufficiently reflect a party's priorities. Through that lens, it becomes clear that mediation is a process that revolves around decision-making by a party in its own best interests.

One aspect that has been cited as an obstacle to settlement in investment disputes during direct negotiations is the desire on the part of the State to avoid the (political) responsibility for a negotiated solution.[47] Mediation in fact offers process support to address this aspect: The mediator engages with the parties throughout the mediation, including at the original process organization phase, to identify key players for a negotiated solution.[48] This includes addressing the question which key players and which process may be applicable, or advisable, to adopt a resolution. In a number of settlements in the investment dispute context, the political responsibility was allocated to a broader political base involving numerous officials and/or entities, such as a council of ministers[49] or parliament.[50] Some countries build in a review by the attorney general's office, other options involve the government financial accountability office, comptroller general or audit department to review any negotiated solution prior to its finalization.[51]

---

47 National University of Singapore, Centre for International Law, Survey on Obstacles to Settlement of Investor-State Disputes (2018) (https://cil.nus.edu.sg/publication/survey-on-obstacles-to-settlement-of-investor-state-disputes/).

48 This is also reflected in ICSID Mediation Rule 20(4) and memorialized in the Mediation Protocol.

49 Vicat S.A. v. Arab Republic of Egypt, ICSID Case No. ARB/21/35, reported in Global Arbitration Review (March 23, 2022) (https://globalarbitrationreview.com/egypt-settles-french-cement-claim-icsid).

50 AngloGold Ashanti (Ghana) Limited v. Republic of Ghana, ICSID Case No/ ARB/16/15, reported in Global Arbitration Review (23 July 2018) (https://globalarbitrationreview.com/article/ghana-gold-mine-dispute-settles).

51 Ximena Bustamante, Mediation in the Public Sector, p.2.

4.6.5 Closing

The closing phase may take different shapes in mediation. A mediation may or may not lead to a settlement agreement. Agreeing to mediation only entails that the parties participate in a process that offers them an opportunity to reflect on the dispute and the parties' priorities and explore whether negotiated solutions are possible. There is no requirement to find such an amicable settlement.

In the closing phase, if the parties reach an agreement, the parties will then work out the detailed terms, the practical implementation and desired or applicable enforcement frameworks. For example, in the ICSID context, if a mediation is conducted alongside an ongoing arbitration parties have the option to revert to the Tribunal requesting to embody their settlement agreement in an award,[52] which then benefits from the simplified enforcement mechanism contained in the ICSID Convention. A settlement may also take the form of a renegotiated concession, or another contract between the investor and the host State. In some instances, the implementation of the settlement agreement required the adoption of a law.[53]

In the event the parties do not reach a settlement within an agreed timeframe, or following extensive negotiations they determine that no negotiated solution may be reached through the mediation, they may agree to terminate the mediation and the mediator will take note of such agreement in the termination notice to be issued in ICSID mediations.[54] In practice, parties have reported that even if a mediation did not lead to a settlement agreement, the process and reflection by the parties as regards their priorities and associated risks has proven helpful for a comprehensive understanding of the dispute and possible outcomes.

As the statistics quoted above on settlements in ICSID arbitration indicate, while the parties may not be able to resolve a dispute at a certain point in time, (and for example pursue investor-State arbitration), a settlement may be possible at a later stage, in particular if the circumstances change – such as certain developments in the arbitration and/or regarding the situation surrounding the dispute and/or its resolution.

---

52 *See e.g., supra* n 21, Swisslion DOO Skopje v. The Former Yugoslav Republic of Macedonia, ICSID Case No. ARB/09/16, Award (July 6, 2012).

53 *See e.g.,* the settlement agreement reached in Vattenfall AB and others v. Federal Republic of Germany, ICSID Case No. ARB/12/12, implemented by an amendment to the German Atomic Law (https://www.mannheimerswartling.se/en/assignment/vattenfall-secures-eur-1-6-billion-settlement/).

54 ICSID Mediation Rule 22.

5 Outlook

Since the ICSID Mediation Rules took effect in July of 2022, less than two years ago, ICSID received numerous mediation requests. The policy trend, as reflected in the bilateral investment agreements and free trade agreements providing for mediation and in the discussions at ICSID's consultations and UNCITRAL's Working Group III, indicate that States and investors consider mediation as a viable alternative to other investment dispute settlement processes.

In addition, mediation with its lower process costs may be attractive for disputing parties, as may be the opportunity to retain control over the outcome and ability to shape future investment relationships based on the disputing parties' priorities – economic, political, environmental, financial or otherwise.

The World Bank estimates that only about 6% of investment disputes are resolved by way of arbitration, while the other 94% of disputes remain unresolved, possibly leading to cancellation of investment expansions or withdrawal of investments altogether. Therefore, mediation with its informal nature may be of particular interest for that portion of disputes where parties decide not to pursue a resolution by way of arbitration.

Structural challenges remain to pursuing mediation as an investor-State dispute resolution process, which may be described as institutional readiness, especially on the part of the State, but also on the part of the investor. This aspect is at times discussed under the umbrella of the establishment of a government lead entity in charge of dealing with investment dispute management – it may be a separate entity, an inter-ministerial commission or another standing body composed of relevant government officials.[55] A number of structural questions must be considered in this context, such as: Who is in charge of managing investment grievances/disputes? Who/which entity conducts a comprehensive dispute and stakeholder assessment which can then shed light on the most suitable dispute resolution procedure? Who determines the appropriate dispute resolution process? How are entities/ministries involved in the dispute's resolution being coordinated (to gain information and develop a negotiation strategy)? Who coordinates public statements, reviews compliance with public disclosure obligations? What is the basis of the authority to enter into mediation/negotiate? Who has the budgetary authority to mobilize funding for the mediation process? Is there a settlement sign-off process in place or an entity already identified vested with such authority?

---

55 Carballo Leyda, Alejandro and Nitschke, Frauke, Investment Dispute Management: The importance of the domestic dimension, Columbia FDI Perspectives, No. 345 (November 28, 2022) (https://ccsi.columbia.edu/sites/default/files/content/docs/fdi%20perspectives/No%20345%20-%20Leyda%20and%20Nitschke%20%20-%20FINAL.pdf).

Besides the structural questions associated with a lead entity in charge of or coordinating investment dispute management and dispute resolution processes, anchoring mediation not only in international treaties but also in the domestic legal framework is vital. Such domestic framework increases stakeholders' confidence and provides a clear legal basis for government officials to engage in mediation and negotiate solutions on the basis of a state's policy priorities. Effective participation in mediation also presupposes capacity building among government officials in relation to mediation generally and investment mediation in particular.

The Western Balkans region as a whole has embarked on a remarkable journey – each of the six countries is engaging in determining customized solutions for investment dispute management, including investment mediation. Such efforts have focused *inter alia* on

i. *legislative reform* (including introducing provisions regulating settlement of investor-State disputes through mediation in draft legislation, reforming domestic mediation laws to explicitly encompass investor-State mediation, drafting model *ad hoc* mediation consent clauses);
ii. *institutional reform* by *inter alia* introducing procedures to engage in investor-State mediations at the international level; establishing an agency or inter-institutional body coordinating engagements between the investor and the State entities involved in the amicable settlement process; creating a multi-stakeholder/ coordinating body to oversee the implementation of government contracts/ investment treaties and serve as a point of contact for the amicable resolution of investment grievances/conflicts/disputes;
iii. *treaty reform* by, *inter alia*, initiating updates to model treaties, re-negotiating investment treaties and more generally reviewing a State's internal mechanism and procedures for early and amicable resolution of investment disputes;
iv. *capacity development* – States in the Western Balkans have also engaged and invested in capacity development by participating in trainings by ICSID or the World Bank on practical aspects of investment mediation and negotiation, collaborated with universities and raising awareness more generally about the availability and practice of investment mediation among government entities by organizing conferences and creating a regional exchange on investment mediation.

Through these efforts, the States of the Western Balkans have done remarkable work and are laying a solid foundation for amicable investor-State dispute settlement. This indeed provides promising waters for investment mediation to set sail into an amicable dispute settlement future.

PART 2

Regional Perspectives on International Investment Law and Investor-State Disputes

Chapter 11

Investment Protection and Investor-State Dispute Resolution in Albania

Flutura Kola Tafaj and Silvana Cinari

1 Introduction

Albania showed its commitment to creating a favorable climate for foreign investments since the early stages of the new political and economic regime established in the '90s by enacting the Washington Convention on Settlement of Investment Disputes between States and Nationals of Other States (ICSID) and signing several bilateral investment treaties (BIT) since 1991 and enacting a law on foreign investment in 1993. To promote the economic development of the country coming from an isolated economy, Albania aimed to become an attractive market for foreign investments by granting protection to foreign investors and providing them with neutral and reliable legal remedies for the protection of their legal and economic rights.

The enactment of the law on foreign investment and entry into force of the ICSID Convention and BITs were also accompanied by the establishment of an institutional framework for the protection of foreign investors, which would facilitate the implementation of foreign investment projects. A solid legal and institutional framework for the protection of foreign investors certainly plays a role in the increase of the foreign direct investment (FDI) inflow into the country.

This chapter aims to analyze the trends and key sectors of foreign direct investments in Albania and the legal and institutional framework for foreign investment protection, placing particular emphasis on the ongoing reforms of domestic and international legal instruments and on the investor-state dispute settlement (ISDS) cases in which Albania has been involved.

1 Foreign Direct Investment Trends and Key Sectors

Until 1990, Albania was a highly centralized economy. Afterwards, the Albanian economy moved towards a free-market economy. Since then, the economic policies of Albania have been oriented towards openness to foreign

 | DOI:10.1163/9789004729889_012

investors, considering that foreign direct investments (FDI) are generally seen as the main promoter of economic growth. Statistics show that throughout these years, FDI flows have continuously supported the Albanian economy.[1] Referring to the data from the Bank of Albania,[2] the FDI flow for the year 2022 was €1372 million. This marks a record figure in the flow of FDI in the country, compared to lower numbers of previous years.[3]

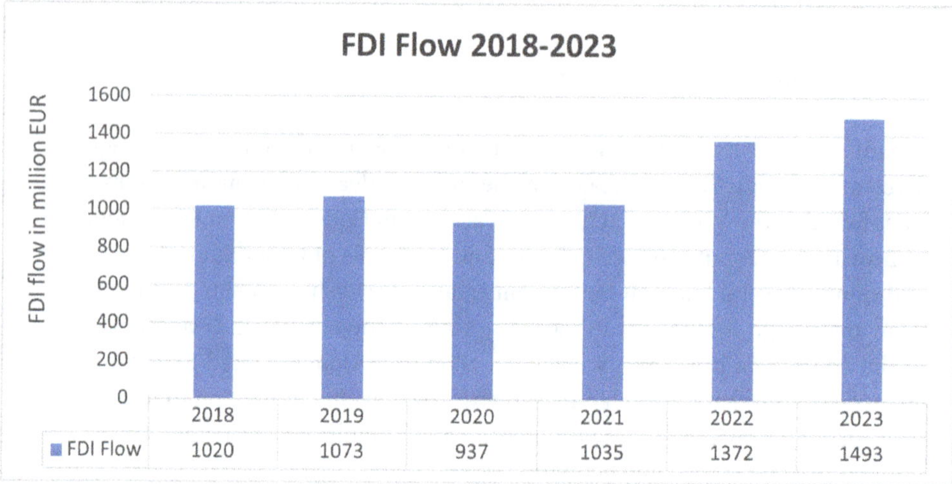

FIGURE 11.1 FDI flow 2018–2023
SOURCE: AUTHORS BASED ON THE BANK OF ALBANIA DATA, URL: HTTPS://WWW.BANKOFALBANIA.ORG/STATISTIKAT/STATISTIKAT_E_SEKTORIT_TE_JASHTEM/INVESTIMET_E_HUAJA_DIREKTE/SERI_KOHORE-INVESTIMET_E_HUAJA.HTML

For 2023, the FDI in the country has been dominated by the Netherlands, which has contributed with a flow of € 302 million, comprising about 20% of the total flow, followed by Italy with € 203 million (13.6% of the total flow), Türkiye with € 179 million (12% of the total flow), Austria with € 119 million (8% of the total flow), Kosovo with € 73 million (5% of the total flow), France

1 The FDI inflow has constituted 8.1% of the GDP in 2014, 8% in 2015, 8.7% in 2016, 8.6% in 2017, 8% in 2018, 7.6% in 2019, 6.7% in 2020, 7.5% in 2021 and 7.7% in 2022. Data obtained from <https://pubdocs.worldbank.org/en/764381588143421027/RER17-Albania-Country-Note-ALB.pdf

2 Data obtained from <https://www.bankofalbania.org/Statistikat/Statistikat_e_Sektorit_te_Jashtem/Investimet_e_huaja_direkte/Seri_Kohore-Investimet_e_Huaja.html> accessed 02 July 2024.

3 For the year 2021, the FDI flow was €1035 million, 937 million for 2020, 1073 million for 2019, 1020 million for 2018, etc. Data obtained from <https://www.bankofalbania.org/Statistikat/Statistikat_e_Sektorit_te_Jashtem/Investimet_e_huaja_direkte/Seri_Kohore-Investimet_e_Huaja.html> accessed 02 July 2024.

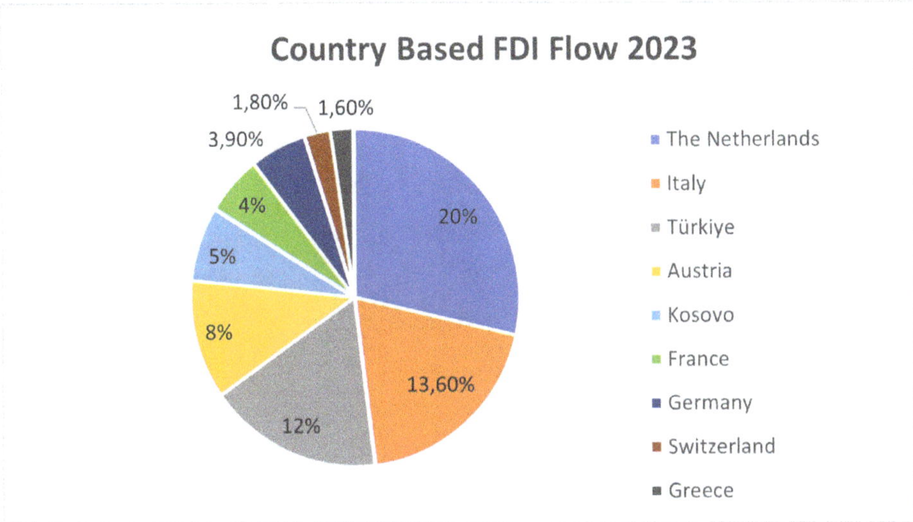

FIGURE 11.2 Country based FDI flow 2023
SOURCE: AUTHORS BASED ON THE BANK OF ALBANIA DATA, URL: HTTPS://WWW.BANKOFALBANIA.ORG/STATISTIKAT/STATISTIKAT_E_SEKTORIT_TE_JASHTEM/INVESTIMET_E_HUAJA_DIREKTE/SERI_KOHORE-INVESTIMET_E_HUAJA.HTML

with € 60 million (4% of the total flow), Germany with 59 million (3.9% of the total flow), Switzerland with 27 million (1.8% of the total flow) and Greece with 24 million (1.6% of the total flow).[4]

During 2023, the main source of FDI inflows in flow terms was the real estate activities sector which represented about 21.8% of the total flow, followed by other economic sectors such as the extractive industry sector with 18.1%, financial and insurance activities with 16%, electricity, and water supply with 10.6%, wholesale and retail trade, vehicle and motorcycle repair with 8.37%, and the processing industry with 8.31% of the total flow.[5]

Even the FDI stock reached a record figure in 2023, with a value of €13309 million, 16.8% of which was contributed by the Netherlands, followed by Switzerland with 15.7%, Canada with 12.6%, Italy with 11.1%, Turkey with 7.71%., etc.[6]

For 2023, the main source of FDI inflows in stock terms was electricity, gas, and air conditioning supply representing 25% of the total stock, followed by other sectors such as the extractive industry sector with 16.4%, financial and

4 *Ibid.*

5 https://www.bankofalbania.org/Statistikat/Statistikat_e_Sektorit_te_Jashtem/Investimet_e_huaja_direkte/Seri_Kohore-Investimet_e_Huaja.html

6 *Ibid.*

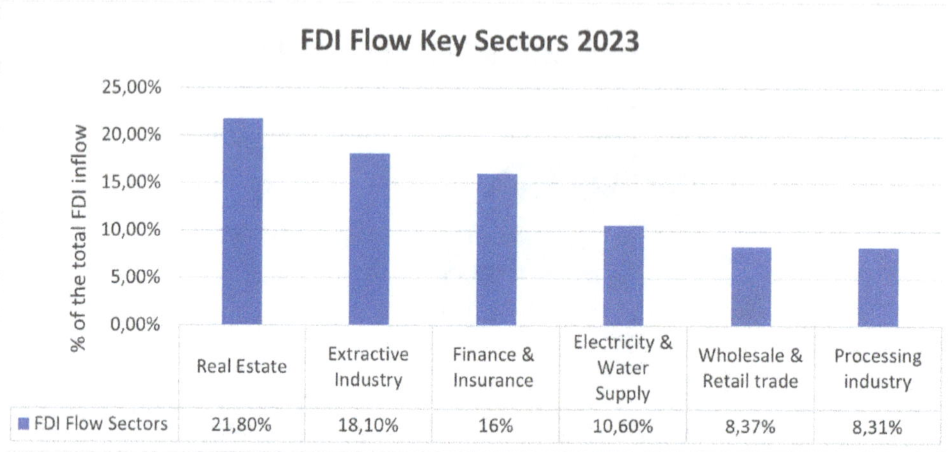

FIGURE 11.3 FDI flow key sectors 2023
SOURCE: AUTHORS BASED ON THE BANK OF ALBANIA DATA, URL: HTTPS://WWW.BANKOFALBANIA.ORG/STATISTIKAT/STATISTIKAT_E_SEKTORIT_TE_JASHTEM/INVESTIMET_E_HUAJA_DIREKTE/SERI_KOHORE-INVESTIMET_E_UAJA.HTML

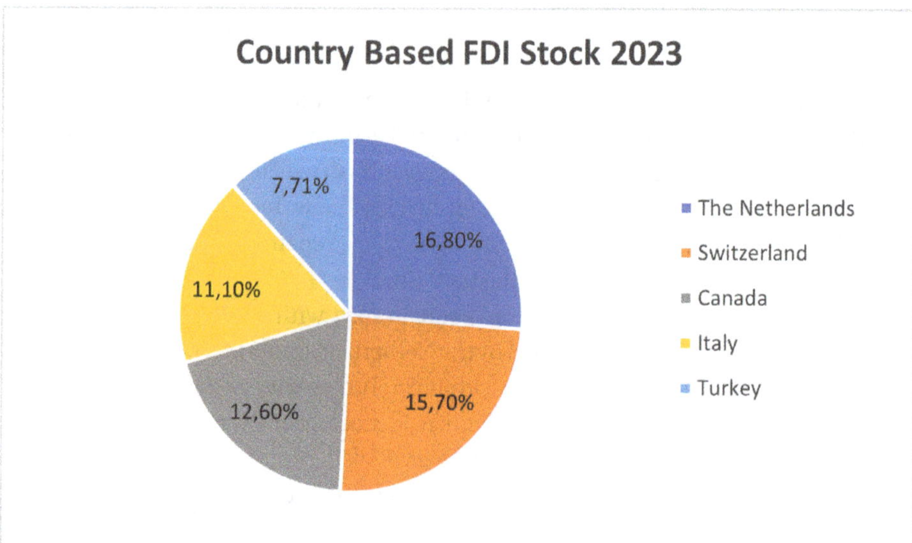

FIGURE 11.4 Country based FDI stock 2023
SOURCE: AUTHORS BASED ON THE BANK OF ALBANIA DATA, URL: HTTPS://WWW.BANKOFALBANIA.ORG/STATISTIKAT/STATISTIKAT_E_SEKTORIT_TE_JASHTEM/INVESTIMET_E_HUAJA_DIREKTE/SERI_KOHORE-INVESTIMET_E_HUAJA.HTML

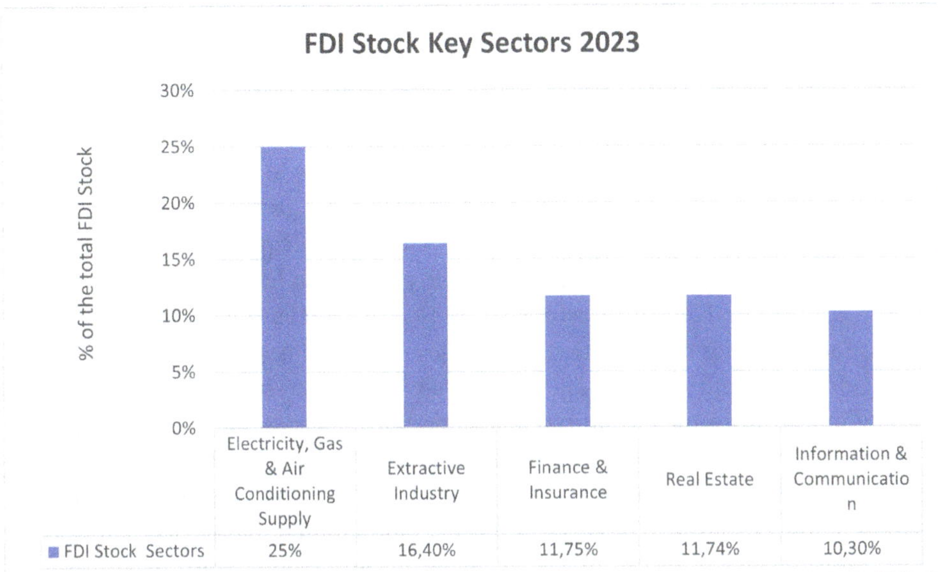

FIGURE 11.5 FDI stock key sectors 2023
SOURCE: AUTHORS BASED ON THE BANK OF ALBANIA DATA, URL: HTTPS://WWW.BANKOFALBANIA.ORG/STATISTIKAT/STATISTIKAT_E_SEKTORIT_TE_JASHTEM/INVESTIMET_E_HUAJA_DIREKTE/SERI_KOHORE-INVESTIMET_E_HUAJA.HTML

insurance activities with 11.75%, real estate activities with 11.74% and information and communication with 10.3% of the total stock.[7]

2 Legal Framework for Foreign Investment Protection

2.1 *Domestic Legal Framework*

The existence of legislation that grants investors appropriate legal guarantees for the protection of their investments is an important instrument that influences the absorption of foreign investments. Albania has long adopted a liberal legislation regarding protection of foreign investments. The most important laws in this area are Law no. 7764, dated 02.11.1993 "On Foreign Investment", as amended, and Law no. 55/2015 "On Strategic Investments", as amended.

The Foreign Investment Law provides for protection of foreign investors in Albania. A *foreign investor* is defined as a natural person who is a citizen of a foreign country, an Albanian citizen without a permanent residence in Albania, a legal person, which is established according to the law of a foreign

7 https://www.bankofalbania.org/Statistikat/Statistikat_e_Sektorit_te_Jashtem/Investimet_e_huaja_direkte/Seri_Kohore-Investimet_e_Huaja.html

country, or a "community company", in the sense of Article 49 of the Stabilization-Association Agreement, which directly or indirectly tries to make or is making an investment in the territory of the Republic of Albania in accordance with its laws, or has made an investment in accordance with laws during the period from 31.7.1990 onwards (Art. 1). According to the same law, *foreign investment* means any type of investment owned directly or indirectly by a foreign investor, consisting of property, money, participation in company, IP rights, and other rights recognized by law, contract, or license (Art. 1).

Under the Foreign Investment Law (Art. 2), foreign investments are not subject to prior authorization. They enjoy equal and impartial treatment, full protection, and security, and are allowed and treated no less favorably than domestic investments under similar conditions, except for land ownership. In any case, they have treatment no less favorable than that provided by the generally accepted norms of international law. In addition, foreign investments are protected against direct or indirect expropriation or nationalization. Such procedures are allowed only if they are in the public interest, without discrimination, with immediate, appropriate, and effective compensation and in accordance with legal procedures (Art. 4). Foreign investors also have the right to repatriate all capital and contributions in kind (Art. 7).

The 2010 amendments to the Foreign Investment Law provided for special legal protection granted to foreign investors investing in public or tourist infrastructure, energy or agriculture that were involved in litigation with private third parties (Arts. 8/a – 8/dh). The Albanian state could substitute the investor in a civil legal dispute with third private parties or even assume the obligations of a foreign investor to the benefit of third private parties, under certain conditions stipulated in the law. In 2018, special legal protection was also extended to investors having the "strategic investor" status in accordance with the Strategic Investments Law. This special legal protection was in force until 31 December 2019.

The Foreign Investment Law also provides for the national security exception (Art. 10) and for domestic or ICSID arbitration, in addition to national courts of Albania, as a mechanism of settling disputes failing amicable settlement. Consent to ICSID jurisdiction, however, is limited to disputes relating to expropriation, compensation for expropriation or discrimination, and transfer of capital (Art. 8).

Law No. 55/2015 "On strategic investments" aims to encourage and attract investments, domestic and foreign, in strategic sectors of the economy, such as energy and mining, transport, electronic communications infrastructure and urban waste, agriculture, and tourism, through the establishment of special supportive administrative procedures that favor, facilitate, or accelerate the services provided to investors.[8] Pursuant to this law, the administrative procedures which concern the preparation, development, and implementation of a strategic investment project, as well as the issuance of licenses/permits/authorizations and opinions, are prioritized, and follow an accelerated procedure before all public institutions and state authorities, directly or indirectly involved in these procedures. Strategic investors can benefit from one of the following two statuses: (i) status "Strategic Investment/Investor, assisted procedure", (ii) status "Strategic Investment/Investor, special procedure". Under this Law, the Albanian Investment Development Agency (AIDA) serves as the Secretariat of the Strategic Investment Committee (SIC) which approves the status for each strategic investor and at the same time serves as a unique window for foreign investors in relation to the Albanian institutions.

2.2 *International Investment Agreements Framework*

As early as its first years of the new political system, Albania ratified the 1965 Washington Convention on Settlement of Investment Disputes between States and Nationals of Other States (ICSID) and signed several bilateral and multilateral investment treaties. Albania is a contracting party to a total of 45 bilateral treaties for the promotion and mutual protection of investments, (otherwise known as BITS) and to seven treaties with investment provisions (TIPS). In addition, Albania is party to 21 investment related instruments (IRI).[9]

The TIPS ratified by Albania are provided in the table below.[10] With the exception of the Free Trade Agreement between Albania and Serbia and

---

8 Articles 1 and 8 of the Law No. 55/2015 "On strategic investments", as amended.

9 TRIPS, TRIMS, Islamic Corporation for the Insurance of Investment Credit, MIGA Convention, New York Convention, ICSID Convention Fifth Protocol to GATS, Fourth Protocol to GATS, GATS, Draft Supplementary Treaty to the Energy Charter Treaty, UN Code of Conduct on Transnational Corporations, Doha Declaration, World Bank Investment Guidelines, ILO Tripartite Declaration on Multinational Enterprises, ILO Tripartite Declaration on Multinational Enterprises, ILO Tripartite Declaration on Multinational Enterprises, Singapore Ministerial Declaration, UN Guiding Principles on Business and Human Rights, Permanent Sovereignty UN Resolution, New International Economic Order UN Resolution, Charter of Economic Rights and Duties of States, available at: <https://investmentpolicy.unctad.org/international-investment-agreements/countries/2/albania?type=tips> accessed 02 July 2024.

10 The list of bilateral investment treaties concluded by Albania is available at: <https://investmentpolicy.unctad.org/international-investment-agreements/countries/2/albania?type=bits> accessed 02 July 2024.

Montenegro, which was replaced by the CEFTA Agreement in 2008, all the other TIPs are in effect. Also, other than the Agreement amongst the Member States of the Organization of the Islamic Conference (OIC), which was signed in 1981 and the Energy Charter Treaty (ECT), signed in 1994, the other TIPs belong to the 2000s. Out of the TIPs, only the ECT and OIC Agreement provide for investors' right to directly resort to dispute settlement mechanisms against contracting states, including arbitration. The other TIPs only allow for state-to-state disputes to be submitted to Joint Committees.

Albania is a contracting party to a total of 45 BITs. Forty of the BITs have been signed and have entered into force, while the remaining five have only

TABLE 11.1 Overview of treaties with investment provisions concluded by Albania

No.	Short title	Status	Date of signature	Date of entry into force
1	Free Trade Agreement between the Republic of Albania and EFTA states	In force	17/12/2009	01/10/2010
2	Free Trade Agreement between Turkey and Albania	In force	22/12/2006	01/05/2008
3	Central European Free Trade Agreement and the Agreement on Amendment of and Accession to the Central European Free Trade Agreement (CEFTA)	In force	19/12/2006	22/11/2007
4	Stabilization and Association Agreement between the European Communities and their Member States, of the one part, and the Republic of Albania, of the other part	In force	12/06/2006	01/04/2009
5	Free Trade Agreement between Albania and Serbia and Montenegro	Terminated/ Replaced by CEFTA	13/11/2003	01/08/2004
6	The Energy Charter Treaty (ECT)	In force	17/12/1994	16/04/1998
7	Agreement on Promotion, Protection and Guarantee of Investments amongst the Member States of the Organization of the Islamic Conference (OIC)	In force	05/06/1981	01/02/1988

TABLE 11.2 Overview of bilateral investment treaties (BITs) concluded by Albania

No.	Short title	Status	Date of signature	Date of entry into force	Amendment protocols
1	Albania–United Arab Emirates BIT (2015)	In force	15/10/2015	17/02/2017	No
2	Albania–San Marino BIT (2012)	Signed	18/05/2012		No
3	Albania–Azerbaijan BIT (2012)	In force	09/02/2012	13/07/2012	No
4	Albania–Qatar BIT (2011)	Signed	18/10/2011		No
5	Albania–Malta BIT (2011)	In force	27/01/2011	31/12/2011	No
6	Albania–Cyprus BIT (2010)	In force	05/08/2010	07/11/2011	No
7	Albania–Bosnia and Herzegovina BIT (2008)	In force	17/06/2008	06/04/2009	No
8	Albania–Kuwait BIT (2007)	In force	12/12/2007	14/05/2013	No
9	Albania–Lithuania BIT (2007)	In force	28/03/2007	07/12/2007	No
10	Albania–Poland BIT (2006)	Signed	01/11/2006		No
11	Albania–Moldova, Republic of BIT (2004)	In force	11/06/2004	23/12/2004	No
12	Albania–Korea, Republic of BIT (2003)	In force	15/12/2003	18/05/2006	No
13	Albania–Spain BIT (2003)	In force	05/06/2003	14/01/2004	No
14	Albania–Serbia BIT (2002)	In force	26/11/2002	14/05/2004	No
15	Albania–Iran, Islamic Republic of BIT (2002)	Signed	18/11/2002		No
16	Albania–Ukraine BIT (2002)	In force	25/10/2002	30/04/2004	No
17	Albania–BLEU (Belgium-Luxembourg Economic Union) BIT (1999)	In force	01/02/1999	18/10/2002	No
18	Albania–Portugal BIT (1998)	In force	11/09/1998	10/06/2007	No
19	Albania–Macedonia, The former Yugoslav Republic of BIT (1997)	In force	04/12/1997	03/04/1998	No
20	Albania–Slovenia BIT (1997)	In force	23/10/1997	22/03/2000	No
21	Albania–Finland BIT (1997)	In force	24/06/1997	20/02/1999	No
22	Albania–Israel BIT (1996)	In force	29/01/1996	18/02/1997	No
23	Albania–Hungary BIT (1996)	In force	24/01/1996	01/04/1998	No

TABLE 11.2 Overview of bilateral investment treaties (BITs) concluded by Albania (*cont.*)

No.	Short title	Status	Date of signature	Date of entry into force	Amendment protocols
24	Albania–Denmark BIT (1995)	In force	05/09/1995	18/01/1996	No
25	Albania–France BIT (1995)	In force	13/06/1995	14/06/1996	No
26	Albania–Russian Federation BIT (1995)	In force	11/04/1995	29/05/1996	No
27	Albania–Sweden BIT (1995)	In force	31/03/1995	01/04/1996	No
28	Albania–United States of America BIT (1995)	In force	11/01/1995	04/01/1998	No
29	Albania–Czech Republic BIT (1994)	In force	27/06/1994	07/07/1995	– sign date: 08/10/2010, entry into force date: 08/10/2010
30	Albania–Romania BIT (1995)	In force	11/05/1994	02/09/1995	– sign date: 15/07/2005, entry into force date: 15/07/2005
31	Albania–Bulgaria BIT (1994)	In force	27/04/1994	28/01/1996	No
32	Albania–Netherlands BIT (1994)	In force	15/04/1994	01/09/1995	No
33	Albania–United Kingdom BIT (1994)	In force	30/03/1994	30/08/1995	No
34	Albania–Malaysia BIT (1994)	In force	24/01/1994	11/04/1994	No
35	Albania–Tunisia BIT (1993)	Signed	30/10/1993		No
36	Albania–Egypt BIT (1993)	In force	22/05/1993	06/04/1994	No
37	Albania–Croatia BIT (1993)	In force	10/05/1993	16/04/1994	– sign date: 10/02/2009, entry into force date: 10/02/2009
38	Albania–Austria BIT (1993)	In force	18/03/1993	01/08/1995	No
39	Albania–Poland BIT (1993)	In force	05/03/1993	09/08/1993	No
40	Albania–China BIT (1993)	In force	13/02/1993	01/09/1995	No
41	Albania–Switzerland BIT (1992)	In force	22/09/1992	30/04/1993	No
42	Albania–Turkey BIT (1992)	In force	01/06/1992	26/12/1996	No

TABLE 11.2 Overview of bilateral investment treaties (BITs) concluded by Albania (*cont.*)

No.	Short title	Status	Date of signature	Date of entry into force	Amendment protocols
43	Albania–Germany BIT (1991)	In force	31/10/1991	18/08/1995	No
44	Albania–Italy BIT (1991)	In force	12/09/1991	29/01/1996	No
45	Albania–Greece BIT (1991)	In force	01/08/1991	04/01/1995	No

been signed. The BITs to which the Republic of Albania is a party are shown in the table below:[11]

Out of the 45 BITs signed by Albania (29 in total) were concluded in the 1990s, while 16 were concluded in the 2000s, with the latest in 2015 (the Albania-UAE BIT). Thus, generally, the BITs concluded by Albania are old treaties which share some common features, such as: granting protection after the establishment of investment, providing for unqualified fair and equitable treatment (FET), national treatment (NT), and most favored nation (MFN) clauses, and no clarification for indirect expropriation, not including exception clauses, etc. Some of the BITs also contain the controversial so-called umbrella clauses.[12]

All of the BITs also contain the typical dispute resolution clauses for state-to-state disputes and ISDS. All of them also require an attempt to resolve disputes amicably and provide for cooling-off periods before initiating court or arbitration proceedings, which vary from treaty to treaty between three[13] to six[14] months. While under most of the BITs the investors have the right to submit their dispute before national courts, ICSID, UNCITRAL Rules, or rules of other arbitral institutions, only a few of them include fork in the road provisions.[15]

11 UNCTAD, Investment policy Hub–Country Navigator, Albania <https://investmentpolicy.unctad.org/international-investment-agreements/countries/2/albania?type=bits> accessed 02 July 2024.

12 See for instance: Albania Malta BIT (2011), Albania–Switzerland BIT 1992, Albania–Austria BIT (1993), Albania–United Kingdom BIT (1994), Albania–Netherlands BIT (1994), Albania–Denmark BIT (1995).

13 See for instance: Albania Finland BIT (1997), Albania USA BIT (1995).

14 See for instance: Albania San Marino BIT (2012), Albania Azerbaijan BIT (2012), Albania Spain BIT (2003), Albania Italy BIT (1991).

15 See for instance: Albania Azerbaijan BIT (2012), Albania Qatar BIT (2011).

There are only a few BITs that provide for alternative mechanisms to arbitration, such as conciliation.[16]

2.3 *Institutional Framework for Promotion and After-Care of Investors*

Under the Albanian domestic legislation several institutions responsible for the promotion and assistance of foreign investments are established. The main institutions are Albanian Investment Development Agency (AIDA), the Albanian Investment Council (IC), the Strategic Investment Committee (SIC), the Ministry of State for the Protection of Entrepreneurship (MSPE), and the State Advocate Office (SAO).

AIDA is the official investment promotion, Small and Medium Enterprise (SME) development and export promotion agency in Albania that facilitates and supports direct investments in Albania. They do this through the identification and promotion of investment opportunities and offering services and support to existing or potential investors.[17] AIDA ensures access to updated information, provides efficient means of communication with the administrative bodies, and serves as a "One-Stop-Shop," supporting investors throughout each step of their investment process.[18] AIDA mediates in the relations between investors and central or local state bodies. At their request, the Agency may represent investors and their interests against state bodies and institutions, except for in courts of all levels.[19]

IC is a specialized, intermediary advisory body within the Council of Ministers that facilitates the dialogue between the representatives of the business community, the donors and the government, to develop a favorable, non-discriminatory and transparent business/investment environment.[20] IC's main responsibilities are: (i) the facilitation of a constructive dialogue and exchange

16 See for instance: Albania–Moldova BIT (2004), Albania–France BIT (1995) Albania–Sweden BIT (1995) Albania–Romania BIT (1995) Albania–United Kingdom BIT (1994) Albania–Greece BIT (1991).

17 AIDA is established with the law No. 10 303, dated 15 July 2010 "On the establishment and the manner of organization and operation of the Albanian Investment Development Agency (AIDA)."

18 The details about the structure, functions, and activities of AIA are available on its official website <http://aida.gov.al/en/about-aida/> accessed 02 July 2024.

19 Article 6(e) the law No. 10 303, dated 15 July2010 "On the establishment and the manner of organization and operation of the Albanian Investment Development Agency (AIDA)"

20 The Investment Council is established with the Decision of the Council of Ministers No. 294, dated 8 April 2015 "On the Establishment of the Investment Council" based on the Agreement concluded between the Government of the Republic of Albania and the European Bank for Reconstruction and Development on Cooperation in Support of the Investment Climate and Good Governance, signed on 24 February 2014.

of views between the Council of Ministers, the Ministries and the other executive Agencies under their subordination on the one hand and the private sector on the other hand, in terms of improving and encouraging a sound investment climate and execution of an effective measures plan against corruption in accordance with the principles of the Albanian National Anti-Corruption Strategy; (ii) Preparation of legal and economic analysis, and specific recommendations with a focus in the improvement of the existing legislative framework and development of policies for the promotion of investments.

SIC[21] is a collegial administrative body within the Council of Ministers, which is headed by the Prime Minister and composed by the Deputy Prime Minister, Ministers of Finance, Tourism, Infrastructure, Energy and Industry, Urban Development Issues, Agriculture, Environment, and the minister in charge of a specific area as the case might be, including the State General Advocate. SIC aims for the most efficient implementation of the law and is responsible for monitoring the functioning of the one stop shop system for services to the strategic investor, and the performance of the impact of strategic investments and their performance. SIC also approves projects with the status of "project with strategic potential" and the action plan for measures, procedures, and deadlines relating to services and facilities of procedures for the design and implementation of a strategic investment project, setting out specific commitments, tasks, and deadlines for central institutions and local government units for all stages of project implementation.

MSPE's mission is to assist and protect private enterprises which operate in Albania, as well as to promote inter-institutional cooperation to improve public services to the enterprises.[22] MSPE is responsible for: (i) investigating and handing administrative complaints of private enterprises, including those of strategic and/or foreign investors against public institutions, (ii) promoting transparency and inter-institutional cooperation for the improvement of public services, (iii) assisting enterprises in protecting their legal rights related to their entrepreneurial activities towards public institutions, (iv) mediating the enterprises' communication with public institutions for the implementation of contracts and developing mechanisms for preliminary settlement of disputes between them, (v) encouraging the development of partnership and communication between public institutions and enterprises as well as their representative organizations.[23]

---

21 SIC is established under the Law no. 55/2015 "On the Strategic Investments in the Republic of Albania".

22 Decision of the Council of Ministers No. 511, dated 03 September 2017.

23 *Ibid.*

MSPE is considered an Investor Grievance Management (IGM) mechanism.[24] The main practical role of the MSPE is addressing investor complaints to the appropriate administrative body and following the case until the investor receives a response from the institution. According to the Internal Regulation of MSPE,[25] the complaints/requests of domestic or foreign entrepreneurs should be registered in the register of the Archive Office. The latter should immediately forward the complaint/request to the Secretary of the Minister who also registers and sends them to the Director of the Cabinet. After reviewing the nature of the complaints/requests, the Director of the Cabinet appoints the Advisors responsible for handling the practice and assigns specific tasks. Advisors review and address complaints/administrative claims of private enterprises, including those of foreign investors, against public institutions. At the end of the analysis, they draft their opinion and send it for approval to the Director of the Cabinet, who, if there are no observations on the manner of treatment, forwards it to the Minister of SPE for final approval. After getting the approval by the Minister, the letter-response will be recorded by the Secretary of the Minister, who submits it to the Archive Office.

Documents (complaints/request) or administrative acts are circulated and reviewed within the deadlines set in the delegation of tasks. These deadlines can be normal, priority, or urgent. In cases when the review of the case is not completed within the set deadline, the responsible structures must inform in writing of the reasons of the delay in handling the case, as well as proposing another possible deadline for the completion of the task. The Minister of SPE and the Director of the Cabinet report and publish the status of complaints handled and monitor the inter-institutional process to the Prime Minister at the beginning of each month. In the framework of transparency, the Minister of SPE publishes the report of complaints handled every month on the website www. sipërmarrja.gov.al

SAO26 is a public legal entity subordinate to the Prime Minister, which provides legal assistance to state institutions, public entities, and companies established or operating under the Law on Entrepreneurs and Companies, where the State has the right to appoint most of the members of the governing bodies of the company or owns more than half of the shares or quotas. SAO

24 Albania Investment Council, "Summary Paper, Legal Framework on Investments, Current Debates and Challenges", June 2018, p. 10 <https://www.investment.com.al/wp-content/uploads/2018/06/AL_Prezantimi-18-06-2018.pdf

25 <https://sipermarrja.gov.al/wp-content/uploads/2018/12/RREGULLORE-E-BRENDSHME-.pdf> accessed 02 July 2024.

26 Law No. 10 018, dated 13 November 2008, "On State Advocacy Office", as amended in 2018 by the Law No. 86/2018.

is headed by the State Advocate-General. SAO is the representative body for the protection of the interests of the Albanian State before foreign courts and tribunals and international organizations of a judicial or supervisory nature, regardless of the subject matter of disputes. The latest amendments of the Law on State Advocacy Office in 2018 have foreseen that SAO provides mandatory preliminary counseling to the public administrative bodies when there are complaints by foreign investors of violations by the Republic of Albania of the law, treaties, or international agreements for the protection of foreign investments.[27] SAO also has the authority to mediate a settlement for a dispute in which the legal persons represented by it are involved.[28] Prior to signing, the draft settlement agreement is submitted to the Ministry which is responsible for the issues addressed by the agreement, and the Ministry responsible for finance, in case the agreement is accompanied by financial effects on the state budget. The responsible ministries must express their opinion within 30 days of the submission of the draft agreement.

2.4 *Ongoing Reforms of Domestic and International Legal Instruments*

In the past decade, the Albanian government has clearly expressed its commitment to creating a favorable climate for domestic and foreign investments through the implementation of a reform program which will enable the attraction of new investments, increase exports, and employment and thus, lead to the promotion of a sustainable economic development of the country. To that end, the government has prepared an Investment Policy Guide[29] which sets out the principles and some priorities for reforms to be implemented by the Albanian government. According to this guide, the government aims to: "a) guarantee an efficient, effective and transparent system for attracting and making investments; b) improve and modernize the legal framework for investments in accordance with international best practices; c) promote the development and implementation of international standards and best practices in relation to investments."

The guide also identifies the principles of good investment policies that should be guaranteed by the domestic investment legislation, such as ensuring non-discrimination between domestic and foreign investors and the effective protection of ownership, following good regulatory practices by ensuring the

27 Article 15(4)(ç) Law No. 10 018, dated 13.11.2008, "On State Advocacy Office", as amended in 2018 by the Law No. 86/2018.

28 Article 17 Law No. 10 018, dated 13.11.2008, "On State Advocacy Office", as amended in 2018 by the Law No. 86/2018.

29 Approved with the Decision of the Council of Ministers No. 579, dated 03.08.2016.

transparency of the decision-making and legislative process, implementing effective mechanisms for the management of investor complaints, guaranteeing environmental and social standards, facilitating the entry and temporary stay of personnel etc.[30]

To achieve the above goals, the guide has foreseen the implementation of the following reforms: (1) drafting a unified law on investments, which shall replace the law on foreign investments and the law on strategic investments; (2) improving the confidence of investors by creating mechanisms for preserving, maintaining investments and handling their complaints (grievance mechanisms) and (3) improving the institutional framework.

The implementation of the reforms has already started, although it is not progressing according to the action plan foreseen in the Investment Policy Guide. The work on drafting a new law on investments has started as of 2017. A law on investments has been drafted and publicly consulted, but it has not been approved yet. The aim of this new law is "a) to establish a new, unified and competitive legal scheme to attract new local and foreign investments; b) to include in the legislation the best international investments standards; c) to establish an efficient mechanism for the quick and fair settlement of investment disputes."[31]

The Explanatory Report of the Draft-law indicates that some of the novelties that this new draft-law brings are found: "(i) in the definitions, which are in line with the bilateral investment agreements between Albania and other countries; (ii) in the investors' rights and obligations, which are in line with the international standards; (iii) in the competition principles that the investment incentives must meet to not distort competition and the free market; (iv) in establishing a dispute resolution mechanism."[32] In our opinion however, the draft-law does not fully reflect the best international standards for the protection of investments/investors. To mention but a few criticisms, the NT and MFN clause[33] does not set any criteria for determining the "like circumstances", nor restrict their scope. The FPS clause does not refer to customary international law, but to the minimal standard of treatment under international law and does not clarify whether it is limited only to physical protection (although it states that FPS does not create additional substantive rights.)[34] Similarly, the FET clause incorporates investors' legitimate expectations without specifying

30 UNCITAD, Investment Policy Guide, approved with the Decision of the Council of Ministers no. 579, dated 03 August 2016.

31 Explanatory Report of the Draft-law no.__/2020 "On Investments", p. 6.

32 *Ibid.*. p. 12.

33 Article 8 of the Draft-law no.__/2020 "On investments"

34 Article 7(1)(4) of the Draft-law no.__/2020 "On Investments".

the conditions and circumstances which would give rise to them.[35] While there is a public policy exception in pursuit of objectives related to public health and security, environment, consumer and competition, its scope is limit only to the expropriation clause.[36]

A particularly interesting feature of the draft law is its Art. 24(2) concerning ISDS, which, unlike the current law,[37] does not provide for the consent of the Albanian state to ICSID jurisdiction. Rather, it provides for the submission of disputes to the competent courts in accordance with domestic law, and/or the treaty in which Albania is a contracting party and/or the contract in force between the investor and the state. In addition, the draft law provides for a grievance mechanism, although it does not determine which will be the responsible institution playing such a role and leaving this decision to the Council of Ministers.[38] According to Art. 23 of the draft law, complaints relating to an investment against a public institution shall be reviewed within a reasonable time in a procedure which allows the responsible institution to summon the officials involved in the proceedings subject to complaint, examine evidence, require the public institutions to deliver a detailed, written report on the matter within seven days, find mechanisms to resolve the dispute, and issue a written report with the findings. It then must notify the complaining investor, the heads of public institutions involved, and the ministers. A complaint before the grievance mechanism does not affect the investor's right to submit the dispute to the competent court.

The undertaking of this reform in the Albanian domestic legislation on investments also comes in the framework of an initiative taken at a regional level, such as the Reform for the Regional Economic Area (REA), which also includes a Regional Investment Reform Agenda (RIRA).[39] RIRA aims for

---

35 Article 7(2) of the Draft-law no.__/2020 "On Investments".

36 Article 13(3) of the Draft-law no.__/2020 "On Investments".

37 Art. 8(2) of the Law No. 7764, dated 2.11.1993 "On foreign investments", amended. "If a dispute regarding a foreign investment arises between a foreign investor and the state administration of the Republic of Albania, which has not been resolved amicably, then the foreign investor may refer the dispute to a competent court or arbitration of the Republic of Albania, in accordance with its laws. In case the dispute arises out of or relates to expropriation, compensation for expropriation or discrimination, as well as transfers according to Article 7 of this law, then the foreign investor can also refer the dispute to the International Center for Settlement of Investment Disputes (the Center) set up by the Convention on the Settlement of Investment Disputes between States and Nationals of Other States adopted in Washington, on March 18, 1965.

38 Article 23(6) of the of the Draft-law no.__/2020 "On Investments".

39 The Regional Investment Reform Agenda (RIRA) was formalized during a meeting organized within the framework of the regional initiative of 6 Western Balkan countries, in Tivat, Montenegro, in May 2018.

"greater harmonization of investment policies in the Western Balkans (WB) with European Union standards and international best practices", within the framework of the South East Europe (SEE) 2020 Strategy, the Central European Free Trade Agreement (CEFTA) and the admission processes to the EU.[40] As shown in the RIRA policies framework and reform actions, reforms in the policy area concerning investment protection and retention foresee upgrading domestic legislation and WB IIAs, particularly BITs in line with standards provided in new generation IIAs and EU standards. It is also foreseen to extend the role of the SEE Investment Committee–CEFTA Joint Working Group as a mechanism that would assist in the modernization/revision of IIAs of the WB.

3 Investor-State Dispute Settlement Cases and Outcomes

3.1 *ICSID Cases*

The Republic of Albania has been a party in 12 ICSID cases, nine of which are concluded, and three others still in process.[41] In all of these cases, the Republic of Albania has been in the position of the Respondent and most of the issues have been with Italian and Greek investors. Recently, there has been a change in the nationalities of the claimant investors, which now include those from Germany, the Netherlands, and the UK.

The subject-matter of the disputes relates to different areas, such as privatization vouchers issued by Republic of Albania,[42] waste management and renewable energy production projects,[43] the construction and operation of an oil container terminal,[44] renewable energy generation enterprises;[45]

40 Regional Investment Reform Agenda for the Western Balkans Six, 11 May 2018, p. 5 <https://www.rcc.int/download/docs/RIRA%20final%2011%20May%202018.pdf/e03b87efe764ca1a03de62b15ac0babf.pdf> accessed 02 July 2024.

41 For more detailed information see the table below. Updated information about the status of the respective cases can be found on the ICSID website <https://icsid.worldbank.org/cases/case-database> accessed 02 July 2024.

42 *Anglo-Adriatic Group Limited v. Republic of Albania* (ICSID Case No. ARB/17/6).

43 *Albaniabeg Ambient Sh.p.k, M. Angelo Novelli and Costruzioni S.r.l. v. Republic of Albania* (ICSID Case No. ARB/14/26).

44 *Mamidoil Jetoil Greek Petroleum Products Societe S.A. v. Republic of Albania*, ICSID Case No. ARB/11/24.

45 *Hydro S.r.l. (Italian), Costruzioni S.r.l. (Italian) and others v. Republic of Albania* (ICSID Case No. ARB/15/28).

TABLE 11.3 Overview of ICSID investment arbitrations against Albania

No.	Case no.	Claimant(s)	Respondent(s)	Status	Economic sector	Instrument invoked
1	ICSID ARB/23/9	EMS Shipping & Trading GmbH	Republic of Albania	Pending	Transportation	BIT Germany–Albania 1991
2	ICSID ARB/20/54	Arka Energy B.V.	Republic of Albania	Concluded–discontinuance of proceedings	Electric Power & Other Energy	BIT Netherlands–Albania 1994
3	ICSID ARB/20/37	Durres Kurum Shipping SH. P.K. and others	Republic of Albania	Pending	Transportation	BIT Albania–United Kingdom of Great Britain and Northern Ireland 1994, BIT United States of America–Albania 1995
4	ICSID ARB/17/6	Anglo-Adriatic Group Limited	Republic of Albania	Concluded	Other industry–privatization vouchers	Albanian Law 7764 "On Foreign Investment" as amended by Law 10316
5	ICSID CONC/16/1	Xenofon Karagiannis	Republic of Albania	Pending	Construction	BIT Greece–Albania 1991–Investment Law–Albania (1993)
6	ICSID ARB/15/28	Hydro S.r.l. and others	Republic of Albania	Concluded	Electric Power & Other Energy	BIT Albania–Italy 1991
7	ICSID ARB/14/26	Albaniabeg Ambient Sh.p.k, M. Angelo Novelli and Costruzioni S.r.l.	Republic of Albania	Concluded	Electric Power & Other Energy	ECT

TABLE 11.3 Overview of ICSID investment arbitrations against Albania (*cont.*)

No.	Case no.	Claimant(s)	Respondent(s)	Status	Economic sector	Instrument invoked
8	ICSID ARB/11/24	Mamidoil Jetoil Greek Petroleum Products Societe Anonyme S.A.	Republic of Albania	Concluded	Oil, Gas & Mining	BIT Greece–Albania 1991
9	ICSID ARB/11/18	Burimi SRL and Eagle Games SH.A	Republic of Albania	Concluded	Gaming industry	BIT Albania–Italy 1991–Investment Law–Albania (1993)
10	ICSID ARB/07/21	Pantechniki S.A. Contractors & Engineers	Republic of Albania	Concluded	Construction	BIT Greece–Albania 1991–Investment Law–Albania (1993)
11	ICSID ARB/95/1	Leaf Tobacco A. Michaelides S.A. and Greek-Albanian Leaf Tobacco & Co. S.A.	Republic of Albania	Concluded–discontinued following a settlement agreement	Tobacco manufacturing and warehousing	BIT Greece–Albania 1991
12	ICSID ARB/94/2	Tradex Hellas S.A.	Republic of Albania	Concluded	Agriculture, Fishing & Forestry	BIT Greece–Albania 1991–Investment Law–Albania (1993)

construction (Cement terminal construction project),[46] the gaming industry,[47] etc.

The ICSID jurisdiction in these cases is established based on the Law No. 7764 "On foreign investment" of November 2, 1993, and/or the Energy Charter Treaty and/or the respective Bilateral Investment Treaties.

In most of the concluded cases, the ICSID tribunals have either declined jurisdiction,[48] rejected the claims on the merits,[49] or discontinued for non-payment of the required advance on costs,[50] or settlement.[51] Only in one case of the concluded cases, investors' claims against Albania were accepted.[52] In this case, the dispute between the Italian investors and the Albanian state arose out of obstacles faced by Hydro s.r.l. and Costruzioni s.r.l, with shareholders Francesco Becchetti and others, while investing in the hydropower plant of Kalivac, the Agonset television and the waste management plant. In 2019, the ICSID tribunal rendered a EUR 110 million award in damages against Albania for the unlawful expropriation of Agon TV in violation of the Albania Italy BIT.[53] The award was upheld by an ad hoc committee in 2021 and Albania's request for revision of the award was dismissed as manifestly without legal merit on 29 March 2023.[54] The dismissal of the revision request led Albanian

46 *Pantechniki S.A. Contractors & Engineers v. The Republic of Albania* (ICSID Case No. ARB/07/21).

47 *Burimi Srl And Eagle Games Sh.A v. Republic of Albania* (ICSID Case No. ARB/11/18).

48 *Anglo-Adriatic Group Limited v. Republic of Albania* (ICSID Case No. ARB/17/6); *Burimi SRL and Eagle Games SH.A v. Republic of Albania* (ICSID Case No. ARB/11/18).

49 *Tradex Hellas S.A. v. Republic of Albania* (ICSID Case No. ARB/94/2); *Pantechniki S.A. Contractors & Engineers v. Republic of Albania* (ICSID Case No. ARB/07/21); *Mamidoil Jetoil Greek Petroleum Products Societe Anonyme S.A. v. Republic of Albania* (ICSID Case No. ARB/11/24);); Durres Kurum Shipping SH. P.K. and others v. Republic of Albania (ICSID Case No. ARB/20/37). In the case *Albaniabeg Ambient Sh.p.k, M. Angelo Novelli and Costruzioni S.r.l. v. Republic of Albania* (ICSID Case No. ARB/14/26) the investors claims of were denied by the arbitral tribunal, but the award was later annulled. See: https://ndiqparate.al/wp-content/uploads/2023/05/Humbje-ne-Arbitrazh-Ceshtje-dhe-Detyrime-te-Shtetit-Shqiptare-Gjendje-Maj-2022.xls

50 *Arka Energy B.V. v. Republic of Albania* (ICSID Case No. ARB/20/54).

51 *Leaf Tobacco A. Michaelides S.A. and Greek-Albanian Leaf Tobacco & Co. S.A. v. Republic of Albania* (ICSID Case No. ARB/95/1); EMS Shipping & Trading GmbH v. Republic of Albania (ICSID Case No. ARB/23/9).

52 *Hydro S.r.l. and others v. Republic of Albania* (ICSID Case No. ARB/15/28).

53 Brussels court maintains Albanian asset freeze (Global Arbitration Review, 23 May 2023) https://globalarbitrationreview.com/article/brussels-court-maintains-albanian-asset-freeze> accessed 02 July 2024.

54 Albania fails to reopen ICSID award after criminal convictions (Global Arbitration Review, 4 April 2023) <https://globalarbitrationreview.com/article/albania-fails-reopen-icsid-award-after-criminal-convictions#:~:text=An%20ICSID%20tribunal%20

Prime Minister to declare that Albania might withdraw from the ICSID Convention.[55] There is no public information available as to whether this is merely a political statement or a thoroughly analysed decision, and whether specific steps are being taken in this regard.[56]

3.2 *Non-ICSID Cases*

Information about non-ICSID cases is scarce. However, from the publicly available data, it results that Albania has been party to several investment treaty arbitrations, either ad hoc or under rules of arbitration of different institutions.

The table opposite presents the number, status, economic sector, and the instrument invoked in the non-ICSID cases against Albania.[57]

Except the *ČEZ case*, which was settled after ad-hoc arbitration proceedings under the UNCITRAL rules of Arbitration were initiated, the three other cases that are pending before arbitral tribunals are established either under the rules of arbitration of the Stockholm Chamber of Commerce Arbitration (SCC), or UNCITRAL.

Investors' treaty claims are based on the ECT and the BITs Albania has concluded with Italy and Bulgaria. The subject matter of the disputes falls in the areas of electricity, gas, steam and air conditioning supply, farming, and telecommunication. Hence, in the *Valeria Italia Srl* case, the investor alleges violation of FET and protection against expropriation clauses of the Albania

has%20refused,by%20the%20Balkan%20state's%20courts> accessed 02 July 2024. See also: *Hydro s.r.l. and Others v. Republic of Albania* (ICSID case no. arb/15/28- revision) https://files.lbr.cloud/public/2023-04/2023.03.29%20-%20ICSID%20ARB-15-28-Revision%20-%20Decision.pdf?VersionId=ds3Sgw3m_k_nf97EorOb_xtKuyJ7llOF> accessed 02 July 2024.

55 Gjergj Erebara, Albanian PM Threatens to Quit International Arbitration Body, Tirana (BIRN, 7 April 2023) <https://balkaninsight.com/2023/04/07/albanian-pm-threatens-to-quit-international-arbitration-body/> accessed 02 July 2024; Toby Fisher, Albania faces new treaty claim over seizure of television station (Global Arbitration Review, 18 April 2023) <https://globalarbitrationreview.com/article/albania-faces-new-treaty-claim-over-seizure-of-television-station> accessed 02 July 2024.

56 Toby Fisher, Albania threatens ICSID withdrawal as German investor brings new claim (Global Arbitration Review, 13 April 2023) <https://globalarbitrationreview.com/article/albania-threatens-icsid-withdrawal-german-investor-brings-new-claim> accessed 02 July 2024.

57 Source for cases listed with no. 1-3 is UNCTAD, Investment Policy Hub – Investment Dispute Settlement, Albania <https://investmentpolicy.unctad.org/investment-dispute-settlement/country/2/Albania> accessed 02 July 2024; Source for case no. 4 is Jus Mundi <https://jusmundi.com/en/document/decision/en-mimoza-ndroqi-v-albania-composition-of-the-tribunal-pending-sunday-1st-january-2023> accessed 02 July 2024; *See supra* (n 55).

TABLE 11.4 Overview of non-ICSID investment arbitrations against Albania

No.	Case no.	Claimant(s)	Respondent(s)	Status	Economic sector	Instrument invoked
1	SCC Case No. 2021/155	Ivicom Holding GmbH	Republic of Albania	Pending	Electricity, gas, steam and air conditioning supply	ECT
2	PCA Case No. 2018-49	Valeria Italia Srl	Republic of Albania	Pending	Crop and animal production, hunting and related service activities	Albania–Italy BIT (1991)
3	UNCITRAL	ČEZ	Republic of Albania	Settled	Electricity, gas, steam and air conditioning supply	ECT
4	PCA Case No. AA900 UNCITRAL	Mimoza Ndroqi	Republic of Albania	Pending	Telecommunication	Albania–Bulgaria BIT 1994

Italy BIT as result of Albania's failure to reactivate an agricultural joint venture between the investor and an Albanian state-owned farm.[58]

The *Ivicom case* concerns a dispute with an Austrian company investing in Albania in a power plant, where Albanian authorities refused the granting of an environmental permit.[59] The *ČEZ case* concerned claims arising out of the revocation of the license of CEZ Shpërndrje, a power distribution company in which the claimant had invested, after a tariff-related dispute.[60] The latest investment treaty arbitration filed against Albania is that of a Bulgarian investor following the seizure of the Ora News television channel and claims arising

58 Jack Ballantyne, Albanian farming claim moves to merits phase (Global Arbitration Review, 21 September 2021) <https://globalarbitrationreview.com/article/albanian-farming-claim-moves-merits-phase> accessed 02 July 2024.

59 Jack Ballantyne, Albania faces claim over gas turbine power plant (Global Arbitration Review, 05 May 2022) https://globalarbitrationreview.com/article/albania-faces-claim-over-gas-turbine-power-plant

60 *ČEZ v. Albania* (UNCITRAL) <https://investmentpolicy.unctad.org/investment-dispute-settlement/cases/522/-ez-v-albania> accessed 02 July 2024.

out of a concession for the construction of a yacht harbor, and other projects concerning mining and hydropower.[61]

4 Conclusions

For more than 30 years Albania has been an open market to foreign investors. Official data show that FDI flows have constantly supported the Albanian economy, reaching a record figure in 2023, where the Netherlands led the FDI flow, and the main source was the real estate activities sector. To create a favorable climate for foreign investments Albania became a party to the ICSID Convention and to several IIAs and enacted a law on foreign investment in the '90s. Nowadays, being aware that most of the BITs concluded by Albania are old treaties, and that domestic legislation also needs to be aligned with standards provided in new generation IIAs, the Albanian government has expressed its commitment to implementing a reform program. The reform is taken both at a domestic and regional level. It aims at the promotion of sustainable economic development of the country and implementation of international standards and best practices concerning investments.

The implementation of the reforms started more than seven years ago, but it is not progressing according to the foreseen action plan and the new draft law on investments does not entirely reflect the best international standards for the protection of investments/investors concerning the NT, MFN, FPS, FET clauses and the public policy exception. It is also interesting to note that the new draft law does not provide any longer for the consent of the Albanian state to ICSID jurisdiction. This might be a response to the recent criticism that has been expressed by the Albanian government towards ICSID arbitration because of the ICSID award in the Hydro S.r.l. and others v. Republic of Albania case, which ordered Albania to pay 110 € million in damages for the unlawful expropriation of Agon Channel TV in violation of the Albania-Italy BIT. This has been the only ICSID case Albania has lost out of the nine concluded ICSID cases in which it is involved. Regardless of the concerns about the time of implementing the reform concerning investments and its substance, the mere undertaking to reform the investment legal framework is a very positive step and should be appreciated. The results remain to be seen, hopefully soon.

61 Ylli Ndroqi padit Shqipërinë në arbitrazh për 130 mln euro (16 PRILL 2023) <https://www.oligarkia.al/ylli-ndroqi-padit-shqiperine-ne-arbitrazh-per-130-mln-euro/> accessed 02 July 2024; Toby Fisher, Albania faces new treaty claim over seizure of television station (Global Arbitration Review, 18 April 2023, <https://globalarbitrationreview.com/article/albania-faces-new-treaty-claim-over-seizure-of-television-station> accessed 02 July 2024.

CHAPTER 12

Investment Protection and Investor-State Dispute Resolution in Bosnia and Herzegovina

Armela Ramić and Ajla Serdarević

1 Introduction

Bosnia and Herzegovina (**"BiH"**) is a state that belongs to the region known as the Western Balkans (**"WB"**). BiH consists of two separate entities, i.e. the Federation of BiH (**"FBiH"**) and the Republika Srpska (**"RS"**), as well as one special autonomous district under the direct sovereignty of the state, i.e. the Brčko District BiH (**"BD BiH"**), where different legal regimes are applicable. Certain issues are regulated by state laws and treaties executed by the BiH as a state, while certain issues fall within the scope of the entities' jurisdiction. The region has a rich history and is developing economically, fuelled by its investment environment. One of the key catalysts behind the development are foreign direct investments (**"FDI"**).

Due to the aftermath of wars and crises, BiH faced legal and economic complexities interfering with its goal of improving the economy and staying committed to goals such as accession to the EU. Political and economic circumstances, along with BiH's aspiration of EU accession have influenced the push for reforms towards a more stable market and attracting sustainable investments. This is particularly relevant for BiH, which is rich in natural resources and opportunities for investments in numerous sectors abound (e.g. infrastructure and energy).

The focus of this chapter is to present an analysis of the legal and institutional framework of BiH for investment protection, the FDI trends and how FDI affects the market and key sectors of BiH, as well as ongoing reforms and future goals of the state. This topic is analysed through the existing regulatory framework and work of relevant institutions which are important for the achievement of such goals.

2 Foreign Direct Investment Trends

FDI are pivotal for achieving economic growth bringing benefits both to the investors and states. To attract FDI, a state must have an environment which

 | DOI:10.1163/9789004729889_013

presents opportunities and provides low risks for investors. BIH, as well as the rest of the region, aims to have an attractive environment for investors by making necessary policy changes. However, change takes time, and for outcomes to show progress, BiH must continue increasing the flow of FDI. States that have attracted the most inflow of direct FDI in the Western Balkans are Serbia, then Albania, Montenegro, BiH, Kosovo, and North Macedonia, which ranked as the lowest.[1] BiH ranks as the fourth state in the region - which shows that the current economic and political fragmentation of the state has slowed down FDI inflow. The state must focus on key reforms to increase FDI and keep up with other Western Balkan states, and broader within the Central and Eastern Europe region.

BiH started intensifying its focus on attracting FDI in the 2000s, which resulted in a record amount of FDI in 2007. This recorded amount of 1.3 billion EUR in 2007[2] was attributed to the privatization of large state-owned enterprises. The global COVID-19 pandemic affected the economies all around the world, including FDI flows in BiH. However, the level of FDI rebounded quickly by reinvestment with the focus on further development of investment policies.

The development prospects, according to the World Investment Report 2023, are the measures including investment facilitation initiatives and the introduction of incentives to promote renewable energy and other climate-related investments.[3] There are numerous analyses of FDI procyclical behaviour in emerging market economies but only in times when states have stable markets. Isakovic and Ilgun (2015) analysed the remittances as one of the major external fundings for BiH and FDI inflows. In the period from 2007 to 2010, due to the global financial crisis, the FDI inflows into BiH were affected. From 2010, FDI inflows started growing more steadily again. In their work, Isakovic and Ilgun presented that FDI inflows were countercyclical compared to the cyclical components of gross domestic product of BiH.

The co-movement was asynchronous, i.e. FDI led the BiH output cycle by one year, and as such, could be used as an instrument for mitigating the consequences of economic downturn or recession in the country.[4] As such, policymakers in BiH can use FDI if there are signs of economic downturn or recession. To use FDI also as an economic instrument to minimize future

1 Lubeniqi, G., Foreign Direct Investments in Western Balkans: Are the Western Balkans countries different? (June 2023).

2 FIPA BiH Report FDI Position and Performance (September 2023).

3 UNCTAD, World Investment Report 2023. p.18, <https://unctad.org/publication/world-investment-report-2023> accessed 1 July 2024.

4 Isakovic, N., & Ilgün, E. (2014). Cyclical Properties of Workers' Remittances: Evidence from Bosnia and Herzegovina. International Journal of Economics and Financial Issues, Vol.5 No.1.

economic downturns, BiH has to have a clear strategy on increasing FDI inflow as well as monitoring the key sectors for FDI. FDI are considered the best source of capital and have an advantage over other sources of capital, such as debt, portfolio investment and foreign aid.[5] Their biggest advantage is that they are long-term investments. The two forms of foreign direct investment are greenfield investments and investments through mergers and acquisitions ("**M&A**").

According to the data provided by the Foreign Investment Promotion Agency of Bosnia and Herzegovina ("**FIPA**"), in 2008, greenfield investments contributed highly to the FDI inflow that year amounting to 684 million EUR.[6] Additionally, the Financial Times issued a Greenfield FDI Intelligence report in which greenfield investments were compared to the size of a specific states' economy. The report showed how Southeast Europe, including BiH, are an area where greenfield FDI investments are increasing, due to BiH having an excellent geographic position for foreign investments.[7] It must be emphasized that the FDI Intelligence report uses data on "announced" projects supposed to generate FDI, however, most of the announced projects might not be realised, especially in business environments such as that in BIH.[8]

Out of the Western Balkan countries Serbia had the highest index for 2019, Montenegro was second and BiH also had a high index showing the states' success in achieving FDI growth. However, in comparison to Serbia or Montenegro, BiH does not hold as strong of a position and presence on the radar for investors. Issues such as corruption, political instability, and complex legislation all affect the FDI possibilities in BiH. Nonetheless, BiH is on a positive trend of FDI according to the FIPA report, showing an 27.5% increase of FDI in 2022 is a positive indicator. The Central Bank ("**CBBH**") of BiH reported that FDI in BiH for 2022 amount to 736.4 million EUR (or 1,440.3 million BAM). This positive indicator and increase of FDI, according to the CBBH, are due to high

5 I Susic, M Stojanovic-Trivanovic, and M Susic "Foreign Direct Investments and Their Impact on the Economic Development of Bosnia and Herzegovina." IOP Conference Series. Materials Science and Engineering (May 2020) <https://doi.org/10.1088/1757-899x/200/1/012019> access 1 July 2024.

6 FDI Position and Performance. (n.d.). http://www.fipa.gov.ba/informacije/statistike/investicije/FDI%20Position%20and%20Performance_October%202023_E.pdf.

7 Prof.dr. Emir Sudžuka Prof. dr. Azra Branković, Legal and Economic Environment for Foreign Investments in Bosnia and Herzegovina: Advantages and Obstacles, Epiphany: Journal of Transdisciplinary Studies, Vol. 9, No. 2, (2016) Faculty of Arts and Social Sciences. <https://doi.org/10.21533/epiphany.v9i2.240.> access 1 July 2024.

8 Bakota , I. Bosnia-Herzegovina economy briefing: Foreign investment in BIH, facts and perceptions Ivica Bakota, Bosnia-Herzegovina Economy Briefing: Foreign Investment in BIH, Facts and Perceptions, *China-CEE Institute*, Sept 2019, Vol.21, No.2.

rates of reinvested earnings of existing non-financial and financial companies with foreign investments, while investments in the form of equity capital and other capital (intercompany lending) amounted to a total of BAM 500 million.[9]

BIH aims to create a climate that attracts investments and complies with the safeguarding of trade zones. The primary step is focused on removing the obstacles for joining the EU and aligning the legal frameworks with the EU *acquis* on the internal market. This is especially important for the state to benefit from the Economic and Investment Plan and the New Growth Plan for the Western Balkans. As stated by EU High Representative for Foreign Affairs and Security Policy/Vice-President of the European Commission, Josep Borrel "*with the Economic and Investment Plan, we are backing our Enlargement Package assessment with action, providing deep and strong support for economic recovery and reform of for a modern, greener and more prosperous Western Balkans delivering better to their citizens on the road to the EU.*"[10]

Adopted with the Economic and Investment Plan for the WB is the Green Agenda for the WB. The Green Agenda sets forth the pillars to achieve climate neutrality and environmental sustainability by 2050 aligned with the goals of the European Green Deal. The region, including BiH, has to undergo regulatory changes and substantial investments to improve sustainability, innovation and green growth.

BiH, with its natural resources, had the potential to move away from use of coal and gas. The Head of the Delegation of the EU to BiH and the EU Special Representative in BiH, Ambassador Johann Sattler stated that "*the reasons to do so are plenty and should convince any skeptics: energy transition will provide affordable and secure energy, help fight climate change, ensure clear air, and boost BiH's economic competitiveness in a rapidly changing world.*" The energy transition to renewable energy sources can be achieved with the use of energy generated from sources such as sun, wind, and water. Furthermore, the state has an opportunity to examine the lessons learned from other states in the region as well as other European states in the energy transition journey.

For BiH it is imperative to foster sustainable and inclusive growth through structural changes and alignment with goals such as accession to the EU. The green transition and sustainable connectivity are key to economic integration

---

9 FIPA FDI Position and Performance, <http://www.fipa.gov.ba/informacije/statistike/investicije/FDI%20Position%20and%20Performance_September%202023_E.pdf> accessed 1 July 2024.

10 European Commission - European Commission. "Press Corner," 2024. <https://ec.europa.eu/commission/presscorner/detail/en/ip_20_1811> accessed 1 July 2024.

within the region and with the EU.[11] Through the effective implementation of the Economic and Investment Plan and the Green Agenda for the Western Balkans, BiH can achieve the goals of joining the EU and improving the investment climate in the state. For foreign investors, it sends a message that BIH is committed to accelerating the development in accordance with current trends and creating an environment that brings benefits to all stakeholders.

Additional improvement has been made with BiH signing the Central European Free Trade Agreement ("**CEFTA**"). CEFTA Parties have committed to EU compliance to decrease the cost of trade and production. Through free trade zones, market access barriers are eliminated. Unlike bilateral agreements (which apply a bilateral cumulation of the goods of origin), CEFTA enables a diagonal cumulation.[12] States can conclude free trade agreements with the CEFTA Common Committee, with certain rules upheld, that the goods will have a status of domestic goods of origin, irrespective of the origin of the materials. BiH exports $1.45 billion to CEFTA countries (17 percent of total exports), and imports from CEFTA countries $1.67 billion (13 percent of total imports), which is approximately 14.3 percent of BiH total trade.[13]

The process of joining the World Trade Organization ("**WTO**") is another goal for BiH. On 2 March 2023, Deputy Director-General Zhang Xiangchen met with Mr. Josip Brkić, Deputy Minister of Foreign Affairs of BiH to discuss the state-of-play in Bosnia's accession process. The meeting of the Working Party indicated that BiH is close to gaining its membership in the WTO. Previously, BiH aspired to become a WTO member in 2013, but due to issues regarding domestic regulation and issues encountered in the phase of multilateral accession negotiations, membership was not acquired. Recently, BiH is advancing both multilateral and bilateral negotiations and improving legislation in order to pave the way to WTO membership.

Taking into consideration above-mentioned aspects of FDI, the trends of FDI indicate that it is a form of international movement of capital which could move production, increase employment, and raise the living standard in Central and Eastern Europe. For the economic development of BiH, EU accession and membership in the WTO are the primary goals that could bring positive

11 European Commission. "Press Corner," (2024) <https://ec.europa.eu/commission/presscorner/detail/en/QANDA_23_5613.> accessed 1 July 2024.

12 Kovač, Helena. INFLUENCE of the CEFTA 2006 AGREEMENT on BIH ECONOMY, *Zbornik Radova Ekonomskog Fakulteta U Istočnom Sarajevu*, Vol.1, No. 13 (May 3, 2017): 41–41. <https://doi.org/10.7251/zrefis1613041k.> accessed 1 July 2024.

13 Bosnia and Herzegovina - Market Overview, *International Trade Administration* | Trade.gov. <https://www.trade.gov/country-commercial-guides/bosnia-and-herzegovina-market-overview.> accessed 1 July 2024.

changes, similar to those BiH achieved with its membership in CEFTA. BiH can attract more foreign investment by leveraging these trade agreements and creating an investor-friendly environment that also promotes market integration, transfer of technology and knowledge, spurs economic growth, and creates additional job opportunities.

3 Key Sectors for Foreign Direct Investment

Due to the state's potential, BiH has several promising areas for investment. The main historic sectors for FDI in BiH are manufacturing, banking, trade, and telecommunications.[14] Investments are most often made in manufacturing, financial, and insurance activities. Foreign investors have been drawn to the manufacturing and banking sectors in BiH due to the states' strong industrial tradition.

The banking sector plays a crucial role in aligning with significant frameworks like the EU directives which also bring financial stability in BiH. Only one bank is majority state-owned, while foreign banks own more than 80% of the banking sector.[15] The financial system of BiH is progressing, and even with crisis periods such as COVID-19 and other geopolitical issues affecting the global economy, this sector in BiH remains stable.

Regarding the BiH credit rating, in February 2024 Standard & Poor's has confirmed the sovereign credit rating of BiH is "B+ outlook stable" and in July 2022, Moody's Investors Service affirmed the sovereign credit rating of BiH at "B3 with stable outlook".[16] This is important for the FDI flow, considering that credit rating and FDI have a positive relationship resulting in the increase of FDI in the state.

Further improvements can be made to additionally prompt FDI flow, such as introducing an e-signature law which other states of the region have established. The law on electronic signature is not aligned with the EU's eIDAS Directive, so it's necessary to amend or enact a new law on electronic identification and services for providing electronic transactions. Despite repeated

14 United States Department of State, Bosnia and Herzegovina - United States Department of State (2023) <https://www.state.gov/reports/2023-investment-climate-statements/bosnia-and-herzegovina/#:~:text=The%20main%20historic%20sectors%20for,banking%2C%20trade%2C%20and%20telecommunications.> accessed 1 July 2024.

15 Fipa.gov.ba. (2020). Banking and Financial Services. <http://fipa.gov.ba/atraktivni_sektori/bankarski_sektor/default.aspx?id=46&langTag=en-US> accessed 1 July 2024.

16 Central Bank BiH, BH Credit Rating (2022) <https://www.cbbh.ba/Content/Read/549?lang=en.> accessed 1 July 2024.

requests, there is still no state-wide harmonisation of the e-signature and the related coordination, cooperation, and data exchange between different administrations is still needed.[17] Advancements in the digitalisation transition and a harmonized state-wide system for e-signature will prompt all sectors vital for FDI to follow suit. Companies around the world have turned towards digital transformation, which affects the business environment and economy in all states including BiH.

Based on CBBH data, by activities, most investments were realised in the area of electricity, gas, steam, and air conditioning supply in the amount of 102 million EUR, followed by the area of financial service activities with 75 million EUR and manufacture of basic metals 63 million EUR.[18] It should be noted that in previous years, the FDI inflow was mainly reinvestment on the existing investments, whilst greenfield investments have been low and mainly linked to the tourism sector. Historically, BiH had a comparative advantage in electricity production because the state is rich with natural hydropower resources and coal reserves. Despite this advantage, the world is changing. Considering that the EU is now more focused on carbon border tax and phasing out financing for new fossil fuel projects, BiH must follow the strategy map and shift away from the use of coal. The EU's Carbon Border Adjustment Mechanism ("**CBAM**") is the EU's tool to put a fair price on the carbon emitted during the production of carbon intensive goods that are entering the EU, and to encourage cleaner industrial production in non-EU countries.[19] Since the EU is pushing towards the decarbonisation of the EU industry aligned with WTO rules, the implementation of CBAM affects the import of goods, and FDI flows. In addition, CBAM compliance is part of the EU Green Deal framework and mandates adjustments from states including BiH. According to the study by Stockholm Environment Institute by analysing financial flows from 2008–2020 in five WB states: BiH, Kosovo, Montenegro, North Macedonia and Serbia, BiH received

17 Communication from the Commission to the European Parliament, the Council, the European Economic and Social Committee and the Committee of the Regions (2023) Communication on EU Enlargement policy <https://neighbourhood-enlargement.ec.europa.eu/system/files/2023-11/SWD_2023_691%20Bosnia%20and%20Herzegovina%20report.pdf.> accessed 1 July 2024.

18 FDI Position and Performance (September 2023) <http://www.fipa.gov.ba/informacije/statistike/investicije/FDI%20Position%20and%20Performance_September%202023_E.pdf>

19 Taxation and Customs Union, Carbon Border Adjustment Mechanism (2023) <https://taxation-customs.ec.europa.eu/carbon-border-adjustment-mechanism_en#:~:text=The%20EU's%20Carbon%20Border%20Adjustment,production%20in%20non%2DEU%20countries.> accessed 1 July 2024.

the highest proportion of finance for non-renewable sources.[20] According to the study, the trend was present even after the adoption of the Paris Agreement, indicating that BiH has not advanced into a decarbonized state that attracts finance for renewable energy. Power generation projects in renewable energy sources are an opportunity for BiH to attract FDI in this sector.

4 Legal Framework for Foreign Investment Protection

The legislation regarding FDI due to the states' specific political makeup is regulated on multiple levels. Firstly, under the BiH constitution, which is the Annex IV of the Dayton Peace Agreement, stipulates that BiH has jurisdiction regarding foreign policy and foreign trade policy. Therefore, BiH kept the previously established agreements on FDI from the earlier makeup of the state after the dissolution of Socialist Federal Republic of Yugoslavia. Much of the responsibilities are placed on the entities of BiH, which includes the foreign trade policy, and consequently, FDI. At the state level, FDI is regulated under the Law on the Policy of Foreign Direct Investments of BiH ("Official Gazette of BiH", nos. 4/1998, 17/1998, 13/2003, 48/2010 and 22/2015). The most significant reforms of the law followed the agreement on Stabilization and Association of BiH with the EU in 2015 with the aim to harmonize the existing legislation with the EU.

BiH became an EU candidate state in 2022 in a move that was widely acknowledged as a political decision rather than a reflection of significant progress on necessary reforms.[21] In a recent report, the European Commission pointed out that this issue extends to positive developments at the state level being in stark contrast to negative developments at the level of the Republika Srpska entity, impacting the country as a whole.[22] Some improvements that

20 Anneli Sundin, Where is development finance going in Bosnia and Herzegovina? *Stockholm Environment Institute* (2024) <https://www.sei.org/features/where-is-development-finance-going-in-bosnia-and-herzegovina/ > accessed 1 July 2024.

21 United States Department of State. (2023). Bosnia and Herzegovina - United States Department of State. <https://www.state.gov/reports/2023-investment-climate-statements/bosnia-and-herzegovina/> accessed 1 July 2024.

22 Communication from the Commission to the European Parliament, the Council, the European Economic and Social Committee and the Committee of the Regions 2023 Communication on EU Enlargement policy. (n.d.). <https://neighbourhood-enlargement.ec.europa.eu/system/files/2023-11/SWD_2023_691%20Bosnia%20and%20Herzegovina%20report.pdf.> accessed 1 July 2024.

affected the FDI climate in RS included the establishment of district commercial courts and one-stop-shops for business registration.

The legal framework for FDI presents a combination of public and private law elements, as well as national and international law overlap. The state-level law on FDI regulates the most significant rights and obligations foreign investors must abide by. The most significant aspect is that foreign investors have national treatment, therefore, the same rights and obligations as domestic investors have in BiH. Only sectors such as manufacturing and sale of weaponry, munition, explosives for military use, and public broadcasting require prior confirmation and approval. The two entities, FBiH and RS, also have regulations relating to FDI. In FBiH the FDI rules are set in the Foreign Investments Act (Official Gazette of FBiH, nos. 61/2001, 50/2003 and 77/2015) and in RS in the RS Foreign Investments Act (Official Gazette of RS, no. 21/2018).

The applicable legislation prohibits any kind of discrimination, such as on the basis of citizenship, origin of investment, or residence. National treatment of investors also sets the same obligations for foreign investors as domestic investors, including the obligation to abide by the public order, the needs of the public health sector of the host state, and the protection of the environment. Additional benefit in BiH is that the tax rates stimulate FDI since they are balanced and non-discriminatory. Previous issues that were seen as obstacles for investors have improved, such as time for registration, reduction of costs in the process of registration, as well as proactive support for green growth investments. Entities of BiH also enact secondary legislation in accordance with the constitution and laws which makes the possibility of investment more attractive to the investors, due to possible benefits such as non-discrimination of investors, no competition between entities, and cooperation between entities for FDI.

BiH in comparison to other states in the region is among one of the more favourable tax environments, which can be seen as an additional benefit for the investors. All foreigners residing in the FBiH and RS pay tax on income generated in the calendar year in the territory of BiH and all foreigners who do not reside in BiH, but who generate income in the FBiH are considered tax payers.[23] In the BD, foreigners are treated as taxpayers if they stay in the territory of the BD for a continuous period of at least 183 days.[24] The income (direct) tax (10%) and value added tax (17%) indicate how the current rates could be favourable for investors.

23 FIPA BiH, Porezi <http://www.fipa.gov.ba/informacije/poslovanje/porezi/default.aspx?id=76&langTag=bs-BA> accessed 1 July 2024.

24 *Ibid.*

To facilitate and improve the inflow of FDI, there are several key institutions. One of the key institutions is the Ministry of Foreign Trade and Economic Relations ("**MoFTER**") which is responsible for foreign trade policy. Specifically, the sector of Foreign Trade Policy through the work of the Department for Foreign Investment Policy and Improving the Investment Climate, implements foreign investment policy through the removal of regulatory and administrative barriers to business in BiH, and undertakes activities to improve the investment climate with the aim of creating a more favourable business environment for foreign investors in coordination with other institutions, agencies, as well as civil society organizations and the private sector.[25] The ministry plays a crucial role in facilitating the FDI inflow to BiH by following the recent trends, especially activities connected to the EU accession.

The agency for the promotion of foreign investment, FIPA, is responsible for promotion of FDI in accordance with the law and decisions of the Council of Ministers of BiH. The agency creates an image of BiH as a modern state - a serious, competitive, and safe partner for capital investment.[26] Through FIPA investors are informed about the legislation in BiH, the potential an investment can have in different regions of BiH, as well as sectors, advantages, and characteristics related to the projects. Moreover, FIPA actively participates in seminars, conferences, and the like, where the goal is to promote BiH to draw in FDI. Investment conditions are also improved through FIPA's involvement in proposing legislation and legal measures as well as participating in negotiations of interstate, bilateral and multilateral investment agreements. Other agencies in different states also cooperate with FIPA to contribute to the shared goal of boosting the image of BiH based on the states' potential.

These activities that FIPA carries out are also aligned with the work program that is approved by the Council of Ministers in BiH. In the work program, FIPA presents the strategic goals and priorities within each of the goals. For 2024, the suggested program sets out the goals of macroeconomic stability, primarily through the improvement of support for current and potential investors. According to the program, Central and Eastern Europe, including Bosnia and Herzegovina, are in a good position to take full advantage of "near-shoring" as well as the opportunity to attract a certain number of companies that have production in Ukraine, where the largest investors are the Netherlands, the

25 *Vanjskotrgovinska politika i strana ulaganja.* (2018) <http://www.mvteo.gov.ba/content/read/vanjskotrgovinska-politika-i-stranja-ulaganja> accessed 1 July 2024.

26 Zakon o FIPA-i. (2024) <http://fipa.gov.ba/o_fipa/zakon/default.aspx?id=285&langTag=bs-BA> accessed 1 July 2024.

United Kingdom, Switzerland, and Germany.[27] This information is supported by the estimates from CBBH mentioned above as a positive indicator for the increase of FDI in BiH.

However, FIPA also indicated that the challenges ahead are connected to larger global challenges and economic uncertainties. Recent geopolitical and macroeconomic uncertainties have been damaging for investments - including the region of Europe, andsubsequently the WB region. Additionally, the energy crisis showed how important it is to have domestic demand fulfilled and to benefit from exports.

It is also important for BiH to achieve the phasing out of fossil fuels – a demanding process, combined with incentivizing investments in renewable energy. Considering how rich BiH is in terms of natural resources and the potential for investments in the attractive renewable energy sector, policymakers have to recognize such potential and align the goals to attract FDI accordingly. Regarding the relevant sectors, FIPA indicates that if it improves its business environment, BiH would be attractive for new investments, especially in the metal processing sector, automotive parts industry, food production, the information and communication technology (ICT) sector, and Business Process Outsourcing (BPO). The most promising areas for new investments in 2024 are the renewable energy sector, the tourism sector, logistics centres, and other manufacturing activities.[28] FIPA plans to mainly focus their activities on the EU market to present the investment potential in BiH and to attend events and activities through which the main goal of the agency can be carried out.

One of the major activities FIPA has carried out since 2007 is post-investment support to investors (“**Aftercare program**”). The Aftercare program was enhanced in 2013 and is carried out in cooperation with the Cooperative Network, representing the first comprehensive program aimed at motivating existing investors in BiH to reinvest, along with improving connections with the local economy and all levels of government in BiH.[29] In the analysis of the 2022 Aftercare program, FIPA states that it actively participated in 898 assistance actions to foreign investors since 2013, and proposed 232 reform measures to improve business conditions.[30] The Aftercare program as such is efficient and cost effective, which enhances that attributes to the investment climate in BiH. The success of the Aftercare program shows how an ongoing

27 Analysis of the Aftercare Program for the Year 2022 with Recommendations for Improving the Business Environment, December 2023

28 *Ibid.*

29 *Ibid.*

30 *Ibid.*

support for investors beyond the initial investment phase also benefits BiH's reputation. This program also serves as a best practice model for investment retention which investors could find advantageous in the long term. Through the work of FIPA there is active cooperation between the public and private sectors.

The activities FIPA carries out and the measures for the improvement of the investment climate in BiH benefits the economic development of BiH. Overall, the business environment has improved in BiH, especially with the states goal of harmonizing with EU legislation and standards. The work of key stakeholders to use this opportunity to increase the FDI levels depends on the legislation, administration and financial environment. It is difficult for investors, especially foreign ones, to navigate through the BiH regulatory network, which applies to all aspects of corporate operations, including business registration, licensing, and permitting, inspections and direct taxation.[31] According to the World Bank's Doing Business ranking, BiH has a score of 90, which indicates that BiH has to improve its business environment to attract investments. Some of the positive reforms which have already taken place in BiH include the reduction of the paid-in minimum capital requirement for limited liability companies and increasing the efficiency of the notary system, replacing the required utilization permit with a simple notification of commencement of activities and by streamlining the process for obtaining a tax identification number.[32] However, compared to the scores of neighbouring states, BiH has to take other necessary steps to bring about changes. The two biggest motivating factors for FDI are resources and markets. These motives can benefit BiH to attract FDI which is also an opportunity for the investors themselves.

5 International Investment Treaty Framework

BiH is a smaller state that must aim for balance in attracting investors while also avoiding investment disputes that result in investment arbitration. Across all its sectors, BiH is undergoing needed development stages. Additionally, BiH faces challenges in achieving the balance due to its political and administrative

31 Prof.dr. Emir Sudžuka Prof.dr. Azra Branković, Legal and Economic Environment for Foreign Investments in Bosnia and Herzegovina: Advantages and Obstacles, Epiphany: Journal of Transdisciplinary Studies, Vol. 9, No. 2, (2016) Faculty of Arts and Social Sciences. <https://doi.org/10.21533/epiphany.v9i2.240.> accessed 1 July 2024.

32 Starting a Business Reforms – Doing Business – World Bank Group (2019) <https://subnational.doingbusiness.org/en/data/exploretopics/starting-a-business/reforms> accessed 1 July 2024.

tensions. This has a negative impact on state development in general, and it can discourage investors from seeking opportunity in BiH. In the post-conflict period, BiH has focused on having a legal framework to ensure both the power of the state to regulate, but also investors to benefit from their investments. Classified as economies in transition, the WB states have gradually tried to implement major economic reforms aimed at the liberalization of their economic, trade and financial systems and the gradual improvement of their business environment.[33] Since the decision makers aimed to create investor friendly environment the most effective step to achieve it was through concluding bilateral investment treaties ("BIT") with other states.

Today, these treaties are considered old-generation BITs that offered the investor-state and state to state mechanism for dispute settlement. The original Model BIT of BiH, which served as the baseline for the negotiation of all the concluded BITs, largely followed the European 'post-establishment' BIT model and contained standard clauses, such as the most-favoured-nation (MFN) treatment, national treatment (NT), fair and equitable treatment (FET), free transfers, and fair compensation in the case of expropriation.[34] The new model BIT that BiH has decided to adopt has not yet been applied because no new BITs have been concluded. Nonetheless, it is a modern and improved model which should strengthen the state's right to regulate, clearly define substantive protections for investors, and provide a broader spectrum of dispute resolution mechanisms, including investment mediation.

BiH is a party to 37 BITs, 20 of which are with EU Member States. BiH *also* has BITs with four states that are aspiring for EU membership, all of which are old-generation BITs.[35] One of the positive changes is the work of MoFTER on a two-phase dispute prevention and mitigation mechanism. This would enhance communication between the host state and investors, serving the goal of preventing possible disputes, but also improve coordination between

---

33 Michail Dekastros and Marios Tokas, 'Chapter 10: Promoting and Protecting Green Investment in Western Balkans BITs: Existing Limitations and Future Opportunities', in Ben Beaumont, Fahira Brodlija, et al. (eds), The Future of Investor-State Dispute Settlement: Reforming Law, Practice and Perspectives for a Fast-Changing World, (Kluwer Law International, 2024) pp. 220.

34 Samira Sulejmanovic, 'Chapter 8: Investor-State Dispute Prevention and Resolution Mechanism in Bosnia and Herzegovina', in Ben Beaumont, Fahira Brodlija, et al. (eds), The Future of Investor-State Dispute Settlement: Reforming Law, Practice and Perspectives for a Fast-Changing World, (Kluwer Law International, 2024) p.175.

35 Fahira Brodlija, 'Chapter 3: The Path of (Re)volution of the International InvestorState Dispute Settlement Regime: A Case Study of Bosnia and Herzegovina', in Alan M. Anderson and Ben Beaumont (eds), The Investor-State Dispute Settlement System: Reform, Replace or Status Quo? (Kluwer Law International, 2020) p.67.

the competent government institutions. The investor community is in favour of gradual ISDS reform, and they will not support reform options which endanger their interests.[36] BiH can align its own aspirations for ISDS reform with the expressed support for reform by the investors themselves.

This achieves the needed balance between the advantages of ISDS and room for improvements that future investors and states can utilize as mechanisms for protection. Even though issues such as transparency have been improved, there still remain concerns about transparency, especially within the context of public interest. Other issues, such has double hatting and "nationality planning" have been raised regarding ISDS reform. An important point to bear in mind is that ISDS is a system of application of the law, therefore improvements to the ISDS system should go hand in hand with progressive development of substantive international investment law itself.[37] BiH BITs provide for ICSID arbitration as an option. Some of these treaties also include the possibility of conciliation or proceedings under the Additional Facility Rules of ICSID.

Besides ICSID arbitration, a frequently used arbitral institution is the ICC in Paris contained in five BiH BITs, two of which are intra-EU BITs: Agreement Between the BelgoLuxembourg Economic Union and Bosnia and Herzegovina on the Reciprocal Promotion and Protection of Investments (2010); Agreement Between the United Kingdom of Great Britain and Northern Ireland and Bosnia and Herzegovina on the Promotion and Protection of Investments(2003); Agreement Between the Ukraine and Bosnia and Herzegovina on the Promotion and Reciprocal Protection of Investments (2004); Agreement Between the Republic of Austria and Bosnia and Herzegovina on the Promotion and Protection of Investments (2002); Agreement Between the Republic of Turkey and the Council of Ministers of Bosnia and Herzegovina Concerning the Reciprocal Promotion and Protection of Investments (2009). The most common form of ad hoc arbitration provided in BiH BITs is arbitration under the UNCITRAL Rules, which are modified directly in the BIT in certain cases, including the modification of the default appointing authority.[38]

Along with the BITs, the investment treaty framework for BiH is regulated by multilateral free trade agreements that do not have the same protection

36 Submission by the Corporate Counsel International Arbitration Group (CCIAG) to UNCITRAL Working Group III – ISDS Reform.

37 UNCTAD, Reform of investor-state dispute settlement: In search of a roadmap (2013) <https://unctad.org/system/files/official-document/webdiaepcb2013d4_en.pdf.> accessed 1 July 2024.

38 Agreement Between Bosnia and Herzegovina and the Government of the Italian Republic on the Promotion and Protection of Investments (2005) and Agreement on the Promotion and Protection of Investments Between Sweden and Bosnia and Herzegovina (2002).

TABLE 12.1 Bosnia and Herzegovina Bilateral Investment Treaties (BITs)

Treaty with	Date of signature	Entry into force	Full text document
Albania	17.jun.08	6.apr.09	Treaty English
Austria	2.okt.00	20.okt.02	Treaty English
Belarus	29.nov.04	22.jan.06	
Belgium	3.mar.04	16.sep.10	Treaty English
Canada	21.dec.79	28.dec.80	
China	26.jun.02	1.jan.05	Treaty English
Croatia	23.jul.02	3.jan.05	
Czech Republic	17.apr.02	30.maj.04	Treaty English
Denmark	24.mar.04	13.jun.08	Treaty English
Egypt	11.mar.98	29.okt.01	Treaty English
Finland	1.nov.00	8.dec.01	Treaty English
France	12.dec.03	7.dec.07	Treaty French
Germany	18.okt.01	11.nov.07	Treaty English
Greece	13.dec.00	15.jun.07	Treaty English
Hungary	26.sep.02	31.aug.05	Treaty English
India	12.sep.06	13.feb.08	Treaty English
Iran	27.jul.96	2.jun.09	Treaty English
Italy	19.maj.00	10.feb.05	Treaty English
Jordan	2.jul.06	25.nov.11	
Kuwait	13.jun.01	23.dec.02	Treaty English
Lithuania	7.jun.07	16.mar.09	Treaty English
Luxembourg	3.mar.04	16.sep.10	Treaty English
Malaysia	16.dec.94	27.maj.95	Treaty English
Moldova	9.apr.03	9.jun.08	Treaty English
Montenegro	18.dec.01		
Netherlands	13.maj.98	1.jan.02	Treaty English
North Macedonia	16.feb.01	26.apr.04	Treaty English
Pakistan	4.sep.01	14.maj.10	Treaty English
Portugal	13.mar.02	3.feb.09	Treaty English
Qatar	1.jun.98	5.feb.09	Treaty English
Romania	20.feb.01	3.dec.01	Treaty English
San Marino	2.aug.11	24.maj.12	Treaty English
Serbia	18.dec.01	25.aug.04	Treaty English
Slovakia	2.jun.08	19.nov.09	Treaty English
Slovenia	30.maj.01	1.jul.02	Treaty English
Spain	25.apr.02	21.maj.03	Treaty Spanish

TABLE 12.1 Bosnia and Herzegovina Bilateral Investment Treaties (BITS) (*cont.*)

Treaty with	Date of signature	Entry into force	Full text document
Sweden	31.okt.00	1.jan.02	Treaty English
Switzerland	5.sep.03	21.maj.05	Treaty French
Turkey	21.jan.98	10.feb.09	Treaty English
Ukraine	13.mar.02	22.jan.04	Treaty English
United Kingdom	2.okt.02	25.jul.03	Treaty English

clauses as the BITS. However, a significant protection was achieved through the Energy Charter Treaty ("ECT") that BiH is signatory to. The ECT underwent the process of modernization but received backlash from the EU and its member states, leading to their steps to officially withdraw from the treaty. The European Commission considers the ECT to be no longer compatible with the EU's climate goals under the European Green Deal and the Paris Agreement, predominantly due to concerns over continued fossil fuel investments.[39] Since BiH is committed to the Green Agenda for the WB states and its accession to the EU, it is significant to assess its membership to the ECT. Through the measures of the EU through the Green Deal, the WB region is on the path of decarbonisation and achieving climate neutrality. An example of such measures is the carbon border tax, whose implementation is planned for the near future. According to the Business Plan for the period from 2023 to 2025, state-owned power utility Elektroprivreda BiH is certain that the CO2 emission tax would come into force in the next three to eight years for coal power plants in BiH.[40]

The region has this obligation because the WB states are signatories to the Sofia Declaration on the Green Agenda. The list of actions undertaken by the signatory states, including climate neutrality and decarbonization, are based on the following pillars of the Agenda: : (1) climate action, including decarbonisation, energy and mobility, (2) circular economy, addressing in particular waste, recycling, sustainable production and efficient use of resources,

39 Strasbourg plenary session, MEPs to vote on EU withdrawal from the Energy Charter Treaty (European Parliament News) <https://www.europarl.europa.eu/news/en/agenda/briefing/2024-04-22/30/meps-to-vote-on-eu-withdrawal-from-the-energy-charter-treaty.> accessed 1 July 2024.

40 Vladimir Spasić (2023). EPBiH foresees CO2 taxation to be introduced in BiH in three to eight years. [online] Balkan Green Energy News <https://balkangreenenergynews.com/epbih-foresees-co2-taxation-to-be-introduced-in-bih-in-three-to-eight-years/> accessed 1 July 2024.

(3) biodiversity, aiming to protect and restore the natural wealth of the region, (4) fighting pollution of air, water and soil and (5) sustainable food systems and rural areas.[41] Environmental concerns and focus on sustainable finance which also impact attracting green investments, encourages new model BITs to contribute to such goals. As a shift from favouring FDI and investors enjoying the protection of BITs, nowadays the focus is on the balance of the states right to regulate in the public interest, but also giving the investors protection.

None of BiH BITs include provisions on 'exception for subsidies', 'substantive environmental obligations', 'corporate social responsibility', 'obligations of environmental impact assessment', and 'differentiating green and non-green investments'.[42] The only exception among the BITs is the one with Finland, where the preamble includes a reference to issues related to sustainable development: "*Agreeing that these objectives can be achieved without relaxing health, safety, and environmental measures of general application.*" Previously the BIT with India also contained a reference to public health, but the treaty is currently in its sunset phase following its termination. Since all BITs BiH has concluded contain the legality of investment obligation, it can be interpreted as the investors' obligation to also adhere to the environmental law and policies the state has implemented.

BiH can also benefit from following the recent trends, such as the environmental social governance principles ("**ESG**"). Some of the examples of model treaties and BITs with provisions indicating the ESG standards and obligations include South African Development Community Model Bilateral Investment Treaty Template, from 2012, the Dutch Model Investment Agreement from 2019, and Morocco–Nigeria BIT from 2016. The Morocco- Nigeria BIT contains some innovative provisions that attempt to strike a balance between the power of the host State to regulate its economy and the need to protect the rights of foreign investors in the host state.[43] Looking at pre-2018 approaches to environmental and health language inclusion as well as state commitments to sustainable development, the standards have been raised even higher in international investment agreements ("**IIAs**").

BiH must ensure that the state and its industrial sectors, such as the energy sector, are free from corruption, are efficient, and are committed to ESG

41 Green Agenda for the Western Balkans <https://neighbourhood-enlargement.ec.europa.eu/system/files/2020-10/green_agenda_for_the_western_balkans_en.pdf.> accessed 1 July 2024.

42 *See supra* (n. 33) pp.226.

43 Stanley Nweke-Eze, BIT between Morocco and Nigeria – A Bold Step in the Right Direction? (Kluwer Arbitration Blog, 22 June 2017) <https://arbitrationblog.kluwerarbitration.com/2017/06/22/bitmorocco-nigeria-bold-step-right-direction/> accessed 1 July 2024.

standards. Even though the public sees ESG as a far distant future for BiH, in reality, ESG is already present. Regulation in BiH incorporates ESG, for example, in tender procedures, cooperating with international companies, and in achieving its EU membership. The ESG commitment evolved from the previous corporate social responsibilities that IIAs referred to.

Finally, some BITs explicitly acknowledge the right of the host state to impose measures in favour of legitimate policy objectives, such as the protection of the environment. Some BITs also recognize that not every change in regulation can be considered to frustrate the legitimate expectations of an investor.[44] This is a significant step in assessing in which manner the legitimate expectation claim is raised and whether the regulation change has affected it. Due to its natural resources, BiH has great potential for green investments. To achieve this potential, existing BITs must reflect the states commitment to phase out coal-fired plants and transition to cleaner, renewable options. The balance for BiH is to pursue a carbon-neutral future while simultaneously steering clear of investment disputes with investors.

The question of intra-EU BITs was resolved, sealing the fate of the BITs BiH has with EU member states since it aims to become a member of the EU. The inter-EU BITs will be considered null and void, which is at this stage, is important for the pending cases. BiH will have to terminate its intra-EU BITs, which will eliminate the majority of the BITs concluded by BiH. Following their termination, EU law's investment protection regime will apply between BiH and foreign investors.

The Agreement for the Termination of Bilateral Investment Treaties Between the Member States of the European Union, will also terminate the sunset clauses—where investors have the right to bring claims against the host state for a specified period after the termination of the BIT.[45] Due to the global goal of ISDS reforms, non-EU BITs can benefit BiH by achieving more enhanced mechanisms of protection. MoFTER BIH, being the competent institution for negotiation and conclusion of BITs, uses every opportunity to raise awareness of other institutions, particularly those at lower levels of administration in BIH, on the state obligations under international investment agreements and specifically about the ISDS mechanism that is available to investors.[46] This indicates that BiH institutions are working together on achieving transparent and effective mechanisms to prevent disputes and achieve mutual benefits for the state and investors.

44 *See supra* (n. 33) pp. 229.

45 Articles 2–4 of the Agreement for the termination of bilateral investment treaties between the Member States of the European Union.

46 *See supra* (n. 34) pp.180.

6 ISDS Cases and Outcomes

The purpose of IIAs and the Investor-State Dispute Settlement ("**ISDS**") systems was based on ensuring stability of investments in developing states. The practice of entering IIAs which include provisions for ISDS significantly increased in the 1990s. First, the opinion that investments can negatively impact the internal market and economy of host states has changed, and globalization has only advanced the presence of FDI and subsequently IIAs. The biggest shift happened due to the frequent clash of protections investors have in IIAs and sustainable development and human rights. Another indication of this issue, is that according to UN Special Rapporteur on Human Rights and the Environment, ISDS hinders climate action and human rights protection, resulting in a "regulatory chill."[47]

Considering that the critiques of ISDS are linked to the rising standards of climate protection and corporate responsibility such as ESG standards, it is important to have IIAs and states domestic regulation addressing the level of protection in this respect, and the standards by which foreign investors must abide. An example is the BIT signed, but not in force, between Nigeria and Morrocco[48] – establishing the way in which foreign investors are to adhere to certain standards and contribute to sustainable development. In case of a dispute, the BIT contains an ISDS clause that provides for arbitration as a dispute mechanism.

This serves as an example of establishing a balance between the protections investors have, but also the protection for policy autonomy of the host state. Respect for States' regulatory space is gaining momentum in the ongoing ISDS reform process.[49] This is an important step, because environmental and health as well as other human rights have not always been explicitly regulated in IIAs – a trend that has been changing rapidly in recent years. The 2011 OECD survey Environmental Concerns in International Investment Agreements

47 Nazar, F., ISDS and ESG: Friends or Foes? (Kluwer Arbitration Blog, February 25, 2024) <https://arbitrationblog.kluwerarbitration.com/2024/02/25/isds-and-esg-friends-or-foes/> accessed 1 July 2024.

48 Morocco – Nigeria BIT (2016), UNCTAD, International Investment Agreements Navigator,| UNCTAD Investment Policy Hub <https://investmentpolicy.unctad.org/international-investment-agreements/treaties/tips/3711/morocco---nigeria-bit-2016-> accessed 1 July 2024.

49 Crina Baltag, Riddhi Joshi, Kabir Duggal, Recent Trends in Investment Arbitration on the Right to Regulate,Environment, Health and Corporate Social Responsibility: Too Much or Too Little?, ICSID Review, Vol.00, No.00 (2023).

studied 1,623 IIAs pertaining to 49 States.[50] The survey was conducted to analyse the extent, type, and frequency of environmental language used in IIAs. The findings from this survey show relevant insights in the pre-2018 era and how far has environmental language has come compared to survey findings. The findings also show that even pre-2018, states had different approaches when it came to the inclusion of environment language in IIAs, including in regard to health. Looking at pre-2018 approaches to environmental and health language inclusion as well as states commitments to sustainable development, the standards have been raised even higher in IIAs.

New types of IIAs, the termination of BITs, and ongoing multilateral discussions on the reform of ISDS mechanisms are all necessary for further development. The World investment report indicated that IIAs reforms have led to the conclusion of several international investment governance instruments with proactive investment facilitation features, and an increased focus on sustainable investment.[51] For states such as BiH, this is an opportunity to terminate IIAs and model new IIAs in a manner to achieve a balance between investor protection and sustainable development. It is up to states themselves to establish regulations that consequently affect the investors legitimate expectations. Investors also see ISDS as an assurance in case of a dispute - there is an ability to bring claims against their host state. As such, ISDS is facing criticism and undergoing reforms, but there is no alternative that could offer what investors or host states can achieve through the ISDS.

With a broad mandate to undertake the multilateral efforts of ISDS reform, the United Nations Commission on International Trade Law (UNCITRAL) Working Group III became the forum for the deliberation of the perceived issues and generation of reform solutions in an open forum lead by states.[52] The Working Group embarked on a structured approach to address the complexities surrounding the ISDS and to reform the framework to enhance the efficacy as well as fairness of this dispute mechanism. Achieving the right balance between the states right to regulate and protect investors is imperative for fostering a fair, equitable, and sustainable investment environment. States can pursue public policy objectives and regulatory measures in the interest of their citizens' welfare, without undermining the confidence and security

---

50 Kathryn Gordon and Joachim Pohl, 'Environmental Concerns in International Investment Agreements: A Survey' (2011) OECD Working Papers on International Investment 2011/01.

51 World Investment Report (2023).

52 Fahira Brodlija, 'Chapter 4: Weeding Out the Issues of ISDS Reform: The Progress and Milestones of the UNCITRAL Working Group III Five Years Later', in Ben Beaumont, Fahira Brodlija , et al. (eds), The Future of Investor-State Dispute Settlement: Reforming Law, Practice and Perspectives for a Fast-Changing World, (Kluwer Law International, 2024).

necessary for attracting and retaining foreign investment. This balance is not just beneficial, but *necessary* for promoting long-term investment that aligns with broader societal goals, including environmental sustainability, social equity, and economic development.

The WB region can create a market for renewable investment opportunities, particularly in the generation and export of green hydropower to Europe. In addition, to prevent and manage likely disputes in this field, it is important to develop the capacities of public and private actors, educate them on the risks and opportunities of the energy transition, and invest time into drafting robust contracts and dispute resolution clauses. The energy transition process will inevitably bring instability to the regulatory framework in the energy sector, which can result in investment arbitrations brought by fossil fuel investors (during the phase out) and renewable investors alike. Spain alone has faced at least 50 investment claims due to the changes in its renewable energy framework and is facing billions of dollars in damages. BiH and other WB states cannot afford such a scenario.

The traditional ISDS mechanism relies on investment arbitration between the investor and the host State, in which the International Centre for Settlement of Investment Disputes (ICSID) plays a major role.[53] The ICSID framework serves to resolve ISDS disputes by providing for conciliation and arbitration. Investors enjoy the protection of a neutral forum that ICSID offers when a claim is brough against a host state. This Attorney General's Office represents BiH and its institutions in international litigation and arbitration.[54]

The largest number of arbitration cases against WB states were filed against Croatia, Albania, and Serbia, whilst BiH has a lower number of (known) cases. BiH has faced five investment treaty cases. The first arbitration case against Bosnia and Herzegovina was initiated in 2007 by the Austrian investor ALAS International. The applicable IIA in this dispute was the Austria-BiH BIT. Claims arose out the alleged Government's failure to prevent a local State-owned company from breaching a long-term supply agreement with ALAS's local subsidiary.[55] The dispute was eventually resolved through a settlement agreement and the proceeding before ICSID was discontinued on 27 December 2007, the details of which remain confidential.

53 Kong Qingjiang and Kaiyuan Chen, 'ISDS Reform in the Context of China's IIAs', in Meg Kinnear and Campbell McLachlan (eds), ICSID Review – Foreign Investment Law Journal, (© The Author(s); Oxford University Press 2021, Volume 36 Issue 3

54 Zakon o pravobranilaštvu Bosne i Hercegovine - Paragraf Lex BA. Article 13, Duties of the Attorney General's Office. https://www.paragraf.ba/propisi/bih/zakon-o-pravobranilastvu-bosne-i-hercegovine.html

55 ALAS International v. Bosnia and Herzegovina, (ICSID Case No. ARB/07/11)

The following case registered under ICSID where BiH was the respondent was in 2014. The case was brought by Slovenian investor 'Elektrogospodarstvo Slovenije – razvoj in inženiring' ("EGS"). Claims arose from payments owed to the claimant for its financial contribution towards the construction of a thermal power plant in BiH. Additionally, compensation was sought for undelivered electricity from the same thermal plant, which is currently fully owned by the government of RS. The basis for the claims is invoked under the ECT and IIA protection. The details of the case have not been made public, but according to the data given in the report of the Attorney General's Office, the EGS v. BiH dispute amounting to 1,359,645,000.00 KM (approximately 693millionEUR) is in the phase of deliberation on the merits of the dispute and it is stated that this arbitration process is highly significant, both due to the exceptionally high value of the dispute and the legal precedent that the arbitration tribunal will establish regarding the issues raised throughout the proceedings.[56] On March 29, 2024 the proceeding was suspended pursuant to the parties' agreement.[57] RiTE Ugljevik has to pay compensation of 67 million euros plus interest of 58.2 million euros to the Electricity of Slovenia, it was agreed to pay compensation in instalments and to deliver a third of the electricity produced in Ugljevik.[58]

Another Slovenian investor in 2016 Viaduct d.o.o. Portorož, Vladimir Zevnik and Boris Goljevšček invoked arbitration under ICSID against BiH based on ECT and BiH-Slovenia BIT protection. Claims arose from purported acts and omissions of the government of RS, which allegedly hindered the claimants' two hydroelectric power plant projects on the Vrbas River. In 2004, the claimants' subsidiary HES Vrbas signed concession contracts to construct and operate the power plants. However, the facilities were never constructed, purportedly due to RS failure to issue necessary permits or approve an updated conceptual project design, as well as RS allegedly granted concession rights to the state-owned company ZP Hidroelektrane to construct a competing power plant on the river without a public tender.[59] The dispute (amounting to approximately 50 million EUR) was decided in favour of the investor in 2022. The amount awarded by the tribunal amounted to 45 million EUR. The

---

56 Report on the Work of the Attorney Generals Office of BiH in the Year 2022 – Arbitration Proceedings p.29

57 Elektrogospodarstvo Slovenije – razvoj in inzeniring d.o.o. v. Bosnia and Herzegovina (ICSID Case No. ARB/14/13).

58 Bojana Ninkovic (2024). Sve naše izgubljene arbitraže: Hoće li iko odgovarati za stotine miliona KM izgubljenih u sporovima? Capital.ba – Informacija je capital. <https://www.capital.ba/sve-nase-izgubljene-arbitraze-hoce-li-iko-odgovarati-za-stotine-miliona-km-izgubljenih-u-sporovima/> accessed 1 July 2024.

59 Goljevšček and others v. Bosnia and Herzegovina (ICSID Case No. ARB/16/36).

government of BiH sought to annul the award in ICSID annulment proceedings, which was rejected on 1 May 2024, making the award final and binding on BiH.[60] The annulment request was declined on May 1st 2024 and the award is final and binding against BiH.

In 2017, Neete Gupta, Neeven Aggarwal and Usha Industries invoked ad hoc arbitration where BiH was the respondent under UNCITRAL arbitration rules. The dispute arose out of the alleged freeze of the claimants' shareholding in the insurance company Krajina and other actions allegedly taken by Bosnian regulatory agencies to prevent the claimants from exercising their majority ownership rights in Krajina, after the claimants had accused the Bosnian authorities of fraudulent misrepresentations in the offering prospectus on which they had relied when purchasing the shares.[61] The investors allege violations of several provisions, including fair and equitable treatment/minimum standard of treatment, denial of justice, national treatment, most favoured nation treatment, and indirect expropriation. The decision of the tribunal under the number PCA Case 2018-03 from 24th November 2020 was in favour of the State. The State was awarded an amount of one million US dollars.

The pending case against BiH is the Mittal v. BiH from 2023. The applicable IIA is the BiH-India BIT from 2006. Even though the BIT with India has been terminated, the case has been filed in accordance with the sunset clause, allowing action within 15 years from the date of termination of the treaty. Indian investor Pramod Mittal initiated arbitration due to a dispute in the company GIKIL of which Mittal is the majority owner. The obligations that BiH allegedly violated under the mentioned Agreement are illegal expropriation, denial of fair and equitable treatment, denial of national treatment and most-favoured-nation treatment, denial of full protection and security to the investors and their investments, as well as failure to comply with obligations related to the plaintiff's investments in accordance with the Association Agreement and the statute of GIKIL.

7 Ongoing Reforms

The WB region is filled with great potential for economic growth. The direction of this growth is the key for the future of the region and individual states such as BiH. In this sense, FDI can be the key to unlock such possibilities. This will require building trust with investors whilst also preserving states power to

60 *Ibid.*

61 Aggarwal and others v. Bosnia and Herzegovina (PCA Case No. 2018-03).

TABLE 12.2 Bosnia and Herzegovina known treaty-based ISDS cases

No.	Year of initiation	Short case name	Summary	Outcome of original proceedings	Respondent state	Home state of investor
1	2023	Mittal v. Bosnia and Herzegovina	Investment: Investment in Global Ispat Koksna Industrija d.o.o. Lukavac ("GIKIL"), a producer of metallurgical coke.	Pending	Bosnia and Herzegovina	India
2	2017	Aggarwal and others v. Bosnia and Herzegovina	Investment: Majority shareholding in Krajina osiguranje a.d. Banja Luka ("Krajina"), a local partly State-owned insurance company. Summary: Claims arising out of the alleged freeze of the claimants' shareholding in the insurance company Krajina and other actions allegedly taken by Bosnian regulatory agencies to prevent the claimants from exercising their majority ownership rights in Krajina, after the claimants had accused the Bosnian authorities of fraudulent misrepresentations in the offering prospectus on which they had relied when purchasing the shares.	Decided in favour of State	Bosnia and Herzegovina	India United States of America

3	2016	Goljevšček and others v. Bosnia and Herzegovina	Investment: Interests in local subsidiary HES Vrbas, a company in the hydroelectric power industry. Summary: Claims arising out of alleged acts and omissions of the Government of Republika Srpska, a region within Bosnia and Herzegovina, which allegedly frustrated the claimants' two hydroelectric power plant projects on the Vrbas river. In 2004, the claimants' subsidiary HES Vrbas signed concession contracts to build and operate the power plants, but the facilities were never built, allegedly due to Republika Srpska's failure to issue the necessary permits or approve an updated conceptual project design, and its granting of concession rights to State-owned company ZP Hidroelektrane to build a competing power plant on the river without a public tender.	Decided in favour of investor	Bosnia and Herzegovina	Slovenia
5	2007	ALAS International v. Bosnia and Herzegovina	Investment: Majority shareholding in a newly-privatized Bosnian cement manufacturing company. Summary: Claims arising out the alleged Government's failure to prevent a local State-owned company from breaching a long-term supply agreement with ALAS' local subsidiary.	Settled	Bosnia and Herzegovina	Austria

regulate the necessary reforms. Considering that ISDS, as any other area of law, is continuously developing, the WB region should use the opportunity to have a positive narrative of investment law and ISDS. The reform of BITs is another important step for BiH, which it has started by developing its modern Model BIT. This reform would benefit the goal of BiH to support green investments and strengthen its candidate status for EU membership. This reform will entail the balancing of investment protections and the public interests that the state regulates. For a state like BiH, such a balance is essential for the avoidance of ISDS claims against the state.

BiH must stimulate the environment for FDI, especially in light of the recent trends of green investing and sustainability. Over the years, BiH has improved in this goal, but further steps have to be taken to achieve desired outcomes that benefit all stakeholders. In recent years, the Council of Ministers of Bosnia and Herzegovina has been working on reforms to make positive structural changes. Reforms not only benefit BiH, but also investors, because an investment in a state that has as many resources as BiH and a reformed administrative make-up is expected to draw in investments.

8 Special Features

BiH is the only state in the WB region that has a special feature in a sense of a Permanent Negotiating Body in BiH for the Peaceful Settlement of International Investment Disputes ("**the Negotiating Body**") which represents BiH and protects its interests. The Negotiating Body, since its establishment in 2017, is responsible for facilitating the process of the peaceful settlement of international investment disputes in the best interest of BiH. These disputes are arbitrations initiated against BiH. The Negotiating Body analyses the request of a foreign investor, collects information, and provides the Office of the Attorney General of BiH with recommendations and guidelines with the aim of improving the negotiation process and achieving success in the process of peaceful resolution of disputes.[62]

According to Article 1 of the Decision on the formation of the negotiating body, the Permanent Team includes:

a. the Attorney General's Office of Bosnia and Herzegovina, the chairman;
b. Ministry of Finance and Treasury of Bosnia and Herzegovina, member;
c. Ministry of Foreign Trade and Economic Relations of Bosnia and Herzegovina, member; and

62 *See supra* (n. 34) p. 177.

d. Ministry of Justice of Bosnia and Herzegovina, member.

Ad hoc members that can be appointed include:

a. a legal entity that, according to the foreign investor's claims, caused the dispute by its actions or omissions, subject to peaceful resolution;
b. the relevant ministry/institution of the state, entity, canton or Brčko District of Bosnia and Herzegovina, directly responsible for the area from the request of the foreign investor, depending on the subject of the dispute; and
c. the competent attorney general's office of the entity or canton or Brčko District of Bosnia and Herzegovina, depending on the subject of the dispute.

External experts with relevant background in international arbitration can also be included on the team, which can support the work of the Negotiating Body.[63] In case the work of the Negotiating Body is not successful and the foreign investor initiates the arbitration procedure, the Office of the Attorney General of BiH continues the procedure and undertakes all actions necessary to protect the interests of Bosnia and Herzegovina, taking into account the deadlines established by the rules of the international arbitration forum to which the dispute was submitted.[64] It is the Office of the Attorney General BIH, with the consent of the Council of Ministers of BIH, that decides on the appointment of the arbitrator on behalf of BIH, the engagement of experts, and external domestic or international legal counsel for the preparation of defence and the representation of BIH, as well as all other matters essential for the effective and successful conduct of the arbitral proceedings.[65]

The work of the Negotiating Body is an efficient way to strive for an amicable solution. It also sheds a light on ISDS as a way of protecting the interests of the state while providing investors an opportunity to consider not bringing claims against the state. Moreover, the activities of MoFTER, FIPA, and the Negotiating Body are linked. Currently, BiH is establishing a mechanism for the prevention and early detection of international investment disputes. With this mechanism, BiH aims to prevent arbitration and court disputes. The decision for this mechanism was proposed by MoFTER and will be an activity that it would carry out in coordination with FIPA and the Negotiating Body. The draft decision proposes the following procedure:

1. The Ministry (MoFTER) performs the necessary consultations and analyses all available facts, and within 30 working days from the date of receipt

63 Odluka o formiranju Pregovaračkog tijela Bosne i Hercegovine za mirno rješavanje međunarodnih investicijskih sporova, Službeni glasnik BiH, broj 17/18.

64 *Ibid.*

65 *See supra* (n 34) p.178.

of the notification from FIPA, makes a recommendation to the state body or public company for the solution of the foreign investor's problem.[66]

2. If the problem is still not resolved, the Ministry informs the Negotiating Body and submits all the relevant information for early warning of a possible court or arbitration dispute, for the amicable settlement stage.[67]

The single mechanism for prevention of the dispute would benefit both the state and the investor. For the investor, it would give clear timeframes, and in case no amicable solution is reached, the option to bring claims against the state remain. However, this can be prevented with a clear and streamlined line of communication with the responsible institution on behalf of the state, that could seek to minimize the risk of a dispute. BiH is taking the step of improving efficiency, with a transparent and timely reaction to possible issues with investments. This model of Negotiating Body in BiH also serves as an example for the rest of the WB region that could consider establishing a similar structure.

9 Conclusion

The WB region, including BiH, is made up of states which have great potential for drawing in FDI and consequently improving the economic development of the region. This chapter has outlined the legal and institutional framework for FDI, investment protection, and dispute resolution in BiH. BiH is on the path of increasing its FDI flow, achieving sustainable development, and becoming a member of the EU.

Recent positive trends, such as the increase in FDI, reflect growing investor interest driven by reinvested earnings and new investment policies. BiH is committed to aligning with EU standards, promoting green growth, and improving its regulatory frameworks. The ISDS reforms go alongside the improvements BiH can achieve, as reflected in the significant work of the key institutions (such as MoFTER and FIPA) in promoting FDI. The goal is to balance investor protection with the state's regulatory rights. By leveraging its natural resources and improving its business environment, BiH can attract more FDI and increase economic growth, which will advance its EU integration prospects.

---

66 Nacrt odluke o uspostavljanju mehanizma za prevenciju i panu detekciju međunarodnih investicionih sporova: Cilj je sprečavanje arbitraže i sudskih sporova <https://www.paragraf.ba/dnevne-vijesti/24042024/24042024-vijest4.html> accessed 1 July 2024.

67 *Ibid.*

CHAPTER 13

Investment Protection and Investor-State Dispute Resolution in Croatia

Irena Alajbeg

1 Introduction

The past three decades of Croatia's transition to market economy and integration to the European Union (EU) have been marked with continued reforms and upgrades to its legal system, including its legal framework for the protection of foreign investment. Accession to the EU has significantly shaped Croatian investment treaty policy, especially considering that investment protection agreements with EU Member States (intra-EU BITs) have been terminated, and most of Croatia's Foreign direct investment (FDI) stock comes from EU states. Even though the investment treaty regime in EU has been fully reformed and modernised, none of the concluded treaties are yet in force. Croatia still has a stock of old-style BITs in force, out of which only a limited number are likely to be renegotiated. Croatia has been exposed to ISDS claims, mostly based on Intra-EU BITs. Although Croatia was mostly successful in defending these cases, high arbitration costs and reputational risks made Croatia organize an early dispute prevention mechanism to reduce the number of cases that reach arbitration.

2 Foreign Direct Investment Trends in Croatia

Over the last 30 years of independence, Croatia has gone through the arduous process of its economic transition and integration to the global economy, starting with accession to the World Trade Organisation in 2000, to the European Union in 2013, and finally to joining the Eurozone and Schengen area in 2023.

Throughout this period, Croatia substantially improved its living standard, experienced substantial economic growth, and reached the status of a high-income economy in 2017. In this process, FDI has been an important source of external financing, fostering, and contributing to overall growth.

The highest inflow of FDI was during the early 2000s, with a wave of the privatisation of state-owned companies. FDI stock grew steadily until the global

 | DOI:10.1163/9789004729889_014

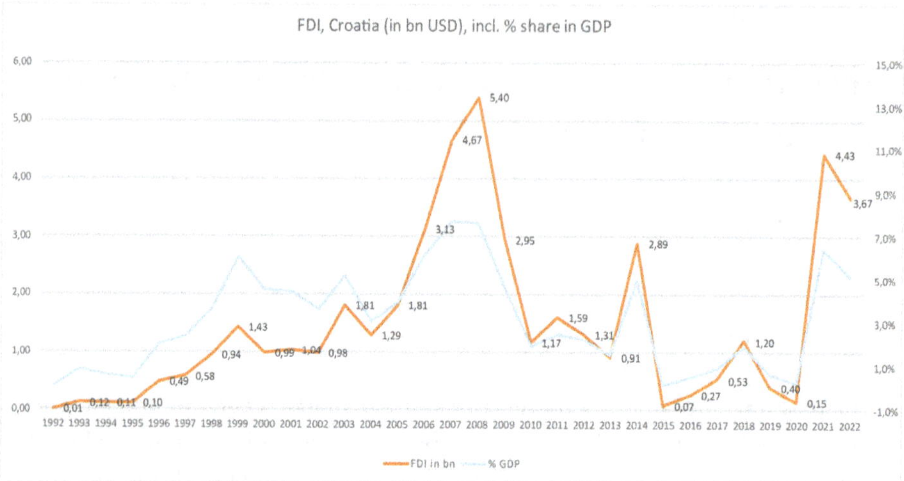

FIGURE 13.1 FDI levels in Croatia (in USD) including the share in the GDP
SOURCE: UNCTAD, WORLD INVESTMENT REPORT 2022 DATABASE

financial crises in 2008, when Croatia (in line with global developments), experienced divestment. FDI stocks started to recover after 2015 and reached the pre-2008 crisis levels only around 2020.[1]

Croatia's stock of FDI relative to GDP has been growing comparably to other economies in CEE region, from 13% of the GDP in 2000, to 40% in 2008 and 59% in 2021. However, according to OECD analysis, Croatia is far below the average of other economies in absolute terms. By 2021, Croatia's FDI stock corresponded to only 0.1% of the OECD total and about 40% of the average FDI stock in other CEE countries.[2]

Some authors note that (despite its geographical attractiveness and active investment promotion policies) Croatia lost some of its competitive advantage to attract FDI with the enlargement of the EU in 2004, when comparable CEE economies (such as Czechia, Hungary, Slovenia and Slovakia) joined the EU, and some Western European production moved to those new EU Member States.[3]

1 OECD, FDI Qualities Review of Croatia: Advancing the Strategic Framework for Investment Promotion and Facilitation, OECD Publishing, Paris (2023) <https://doi.org/10.1787/79b2345b-en> accessed 29 June 2024.

2 *Ibid.*

3 Matej Bule and Andrijana Ćudina, "Foreign Direct Equity Investments and Foreign Ownership Premium: the Case of Croatia" <https://www.hnb.hr/repec/hnb/wpaper/pdf/w-058.pdf> accessed 29 June 2024.

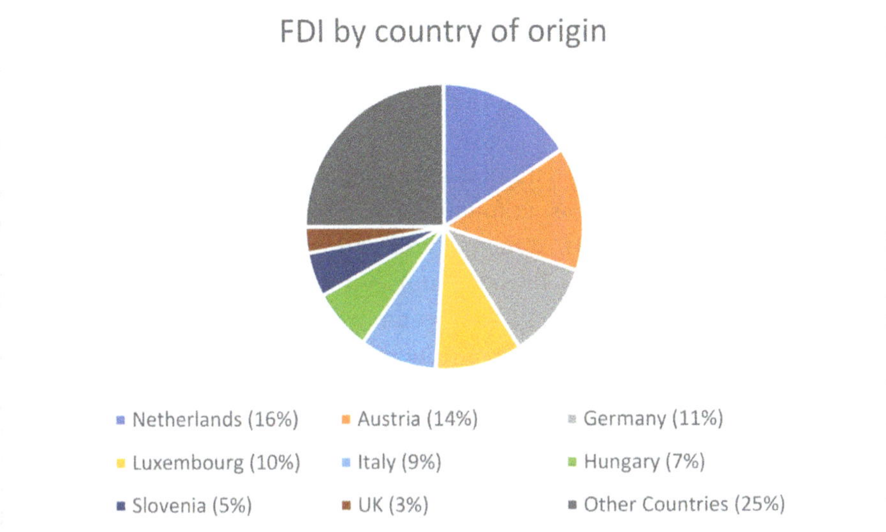

FIGURE 13.2 FDI in Croatia by country of origin
SOURCE: MINISTRY OF ECONOMY AND SUSTAINABLE DEVELOPMENT, HTTPS://INVESTCROATIA.GOV.HR/EN/ABOUT-CROATIA/

In total numbers, between 1993 and 2022, Croatia has received foreign direct investments in the amount of EUR 42.55 billion, by investors mostly from EU countries (along with the UK).[4]

Although for many years statistics show that the biggest inflow of investment came from the Netherlands, the major value of FDI from the Netherlands is largely influenced by a 2014 roundtripping transaction by Croatia's largest conglomerate Agrokor, which took over Slovenia's biggest retail company through a company in the Netherlands.[5] Similarly, there are other investments that are registered as Dutch investments, but were actually made through Dutch established companies (as will be mentioned later with reference to ISDS cases). The second largest origin country for FDI in Croatia is Austria, with EUR 4.0 billion of FDI primarily in the banking sector, followed by Germany, Luxembourg, and Italy.

---

4 Information obtained from the Croatian Investment Promotion Website, Invest Croatia, <https://investcroatia.gov.hr/en/about-croatia/> accessed 29 June 2024.

5 Josip Tica, Tomislav Globan, , Marin Levaj, FDI in Croatia. In Joel I. Deichmann (ed), Foreign Direct Investment in the Successor States of Yugoslavia. Economic Geography. Springer, Cham (2021) <https://doi.org/10.1007/978-3-030-55739-3_3> accessed 29 June 2024.

3 Key Sectors for Foreign Direct Investments

Croatian FDI, both brownfield and greenfield, throughout the entire transition period has been largely connected to the services sector and non-production industries.[6]

The largest share of Croatian total FDI, 25%, is concentrated in financial services, insurance, and pension funding. Predominantly, these investments in the financial sector relate to the privatization and recapitalization of foreign-owned domestic banks. In the manufacturing sector, which represents 17% of total FDI, most of the FDI is concentrated in refined petroleum products, the pharmaceutical industry, and the production of other non-metallic mineral products.

Other than financial and industrial sectors, a significant share of FDI is also in trade, real-estate and construction, tourism, and other services, all related to the robust growth of tourism sector in Croatia.

However, after 2017, Croatia attracted a substantial share of greenfield FDI in infrastructure activities related to ICT and internet infrastructure (communications), as well as electricity generation from renewables.

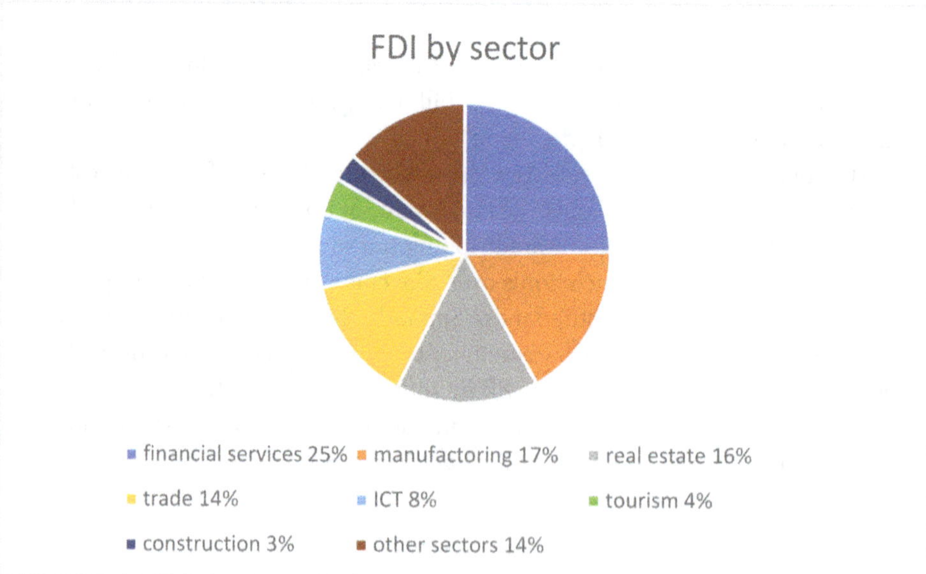

FIGURE 13.3 FDI in Croatia by sector
SOURCE: MINISTRY OF ECONOMY AND SUSTAINABLE DEVELOPMENT, HTTPS://INVESTCROATIA.GOV.HR/EN/ABOUT-CROATIA/

6 *Ibid.*

4 The Legal Framework for Foreign Investment Protection

Croatia's legal framework for foreign investment, both in terms of market openness and investment protection, has been constantly reviewed and upgraded as a result of the integration processes to the EU, Eurozone, and Schengen area. Currently, it is again a subject of review and adaptation to the OECD standards during accession to the OECD.[7]

As a result of these constant efforts, the Croatian legal framework for investment is generally described and evaluated as a modern policy regime; open, non-discriminatory for foreign investment and with high standards of protection guarantees for investors.

Croatia does not have a specific law or act regulating particular foreign investment and investors, but a general legal framework applies to all investors equally.

The Constitution itself guarantees several rights to (foreign) investors, starting from equal legal status to all entrepreneurs. It also stipulates that all rights acquired by investing capital will not be limited by law or other legal act, and that foreign investors are guaranteed free transfer and repatriation of profits and invested capital.[8]

4.1 *Market Openness and Admission of Investment*

The establishment and operation of companies in Croatia is regulated by the Companies Act, which provides for equal treatment between domestic and foreign-owned enterprises established in Croatia. A foreign investor may establish a company, participate in establishing a company, or acquire any rights or commitments same as any domestic investor. For a non-WTO member country, there is a reciprocity requirement for establishing a branch in the territory of Croatia, but this requirement does not apply in the case of the incorporation of a company in Croatia.

Croatia does not have an investment screening mechanism for inbound FDI, and there are only a few limited regulatory restrictions for the participation of foreign investors in economic activities. These measures are mainly limited to conditions on the entry of foreign investors (e.g., local incorporation

7 On 25 January 2022, the OECD Council opened accession discussions with Croatia and a Roadmap for Accession has been adopted on 10 June 2022, stating *inter alia* that „ (...) the OECD will work closely with Croatia to support the adoption of long-lasting reforms to align with OECD standards, best policies and best practices."

8 The Constitution of the Republic of Croatia (consolidated text) <https://www.sabor.hr/en/constitution-republic-croatia-consolidated-text> accessed 29 June 2024.

requirement or reciprocity, as mentioned above) in a few specific sectors, as well as limitations in some services in line with GATS commitments (e.g. in legal services, freshwater fisheries and air transport). Most of these do not apply to investors incorporated in the European Union or the European Economic Area (EU/EEA).

Even in cases of some limitations, such as the ability to acquire real estate or agricultural land in Croatia, there are no impediments to these acquisitions if carried out through an enterprise incorporated in Croatia.

The OECD Investment Policy Review of Croatia, conducted in 2019 as a prerequisite for Croatia to accede to the OECD Declaration on Multinational Enterprises, attested the openness of the Croatian investment regime under the OECD FDI Regulatory Restrictiveness Index, as shown in the figure below.

According to the Index, the extent of discrimination against foreign investors in Croatia's regulations is below the OECD and non-OECD average, it is lower than most of the 73 countries benchmarked under the Index.

On a sectoral basis, Croatia is also less restrictive than the OECD average. Regulatory restrictions on FDI are present business services, essentially reflecting some discriminatory measures in legal services sectors. In financial services, some restrictions exist in insurance, banking, and other financial services. Nonetheless, Croatia is now undergoing another review with a view to accede to the OECD Codes of Liberalisation of Capital Movements and of Current Invisible Operations, so some of these restrictions may be further reduced through this process.

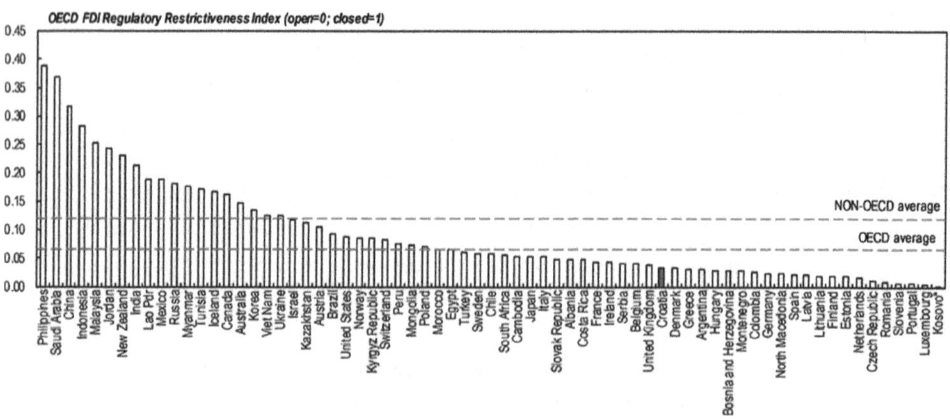

FIGURE 13.4 OECD FDI regulatory restrictiveness index 2017
SOURCE: OECD INVESTMENT POLICY REVIEW FOR CROATIA, OECD RESTRICTIVENESS INDEX 2017

4.2 *Property Rights and Guaranties against Expropriation*

The right to private ownership in Croatia is also established in the Constitution and further confirmed by the Law on Property and Other Property Rights,[9] stipulating (again) that foreign entities incorporated under Croatian law are viewed as Croatian legal persons and thus may acquire property without restrictions.

Ownership rights may be exceptionally restricted by law for the purposes of protecting the interests and security of the Republic of Croatia, nature and the human environment, and human health (Article 50 of the Constitution), but this rule applies equally to domestic and foreign investments. The same Article of the Constitution guarantees compensation equal to the market value of the investment, in cash, or by assignment to another appropriate property (whose value reflects the market value of the property subject to expropriation in the same municipality or town, which provides the owner of the expropriated property with the same living conditions as the expropriated real estate).

The expropriation rules are further regulated by the Act on the Expropriation and Determination of Compensation.[10] The Law along with relevant by-laws determines the conditions for an expropriation and provides guidelines for the calculation of the amount of compensation. Expropriation rules as established by the law are fully based on four guiding principles: expropriation is permitted in the (1) public interest, (2) without discrimination, (3) against the payment of prompt, adequate, and effective compensation and under (4) due process of law. The process is public and transparent, and investors have the right to remedy, i.e. to raise expropriation claims with respect to both the decision to expropriate and conditions of expropriation.

4.3 *Judicial System and Alternative Dispute Resolution*

Croatia has well established judicial system, based on the principle of independence of the judiciary, which is guaranteed by the Constitution. The Judicial system consists of courts of general and specialized jurisdictions. Regular courts are municipal courts, county courts, and the Supreme Court of the Republic of Croatia as Croatia's highest court. Specialised courts are administrative courts, misdemeanour courts, and commercial courts.

Commercial courts have jurisdiction in disputes between companies, intellectual property disputes, bankruptcy proceedings, and unfair market competition. They also conduct proceedings for the recognition and enforcement of

9 Zakon o vlasništvu i drugim stvarnim pravima, Narodne novine 91/96, 68/98, 137/99, 22/00, 73/00, 129/00, 114/01, 79/06, 141/06, 146/08, 38/09, 153/09, 143/12, 152/14, 81/15, 94/17.

10 Zakon o izvlaštenju i određivanju naknade, Narodne novine 74/14, 69/17, 98/19.

foreign judicial decisions and arbitral awards in commercial cases. The High Commercial Court has appellate review of lower commercial court decisions.

The Administrative Court has jurisdiction over the decisions of administrative bodies of all levels of government. The Supreme Court is the highest court in the country and, as such, enjoys jurisdiction over civil and criminal cases. It hears appeals from the County Courts, High Commercial Court, and Administrative Court.

In regional and international comparisons, the judicial system in Croatia typically ranks above average.[11] Despite that, investors and the public continue to report lack of confidence in Croatian courts. Investors often report problems with unusually protracted court procedures, lack of clarity in legal proceedings, contract enforcement, and judicial efficiency. The European Commission Country Report for Croatia from 2020 also addresses the length of court proceedings as a burden for business. The OECD reports also recognize some weaknesses in the judicial system, like insufficient professionalization (especially at the local level), insufficient e-procedures, and a backlog of cases.

The Government has invested significant efforts to conduct reforms to address these grievances. The Judicial Reform Strategy and its Action Plan for the period 2013–2018 addressed five areas of action: Independence, impartiality, and professionalism of the judiciary; efficiency; Croatian judiciary as part of the European judiciary; human resources management; and using the potential of modern technologies.

European Union membership has been an important catalyst for change particularly, during the accession negotiations, but also afterwards. In addition, Croatia has received significant donor assistance from various international organisations in implementing judicial reform, e.g. ongoing Justice for Business Project financed by World Bank loan, aimed to support ICT infrastructure upgrades, court process improvements, and other reforms to judicial services to improve the business climate.[12]

As a result of these reforms, the performance of the justice system has improved in recent years and Croatia now has rates of case efficiency for civil, commercial, administrative, and other cases comparable with other EU member states. Important progress has also been made in reducing the number of

11 OECD, OECD Investment Policy Reviews: Croatia 2019, OECD Investment Policy Reviews, OECD Publishing, Paris (2019) <https://doi.org/10.1787/2bf079ba-en> accessed 29 June 2024.

12 Ministry of Justice, Public Administration and Digital Tranformation Croatia, Announcement of the Justice for Business Project (J4B) <https://mpudt.gov.hr/highlights/projects/world-bank-loan-agreements/justice-for-business-project-just-b/25439> accessed on 19 June 2024.

pending cases. According to the World Bank analysis, the number of pending cases has fallen by half over the past decade.[13]

Croatian authorities have also invested significant effort in promoting out-of-court settlements. An alternative dispute resolution system has been seen as an additional and efficient tool to cope with an over-burdened judiciary, particularly with regards to small-value commercial cases.

Croatia's legal framework for arbitration and mediation is defined by the Arbitration Act of 2001 and the Act on the Peaceful Resolution of Disputes, entered into force in 2023, replacing the then-existing Mediation Act.[14] In addition, other acts promoting and regulating access to arbitration and mediation include the Civil Obligations Act, the Trades and Crafts Act, and most recently, the Act on Alternative Consumer Dispute Resolution.[15]

The Arbitration Act is based on the UNCITRAL Model Law. It applies to commercial and non-commercial disputes, including disputes with an international element (those where at least one of the parties is a foreign person or legal entity) if the seat of Arbitration is in Croatia.[16] Arbitration rulings have the force of a final judgment but can be appealed.[17] The major arbitration institution in Croatia is the Permanent Arbitration Court at the Croatian Chamber of Economy first established in 1853 and re-established in 1965. The Permanent Arbitration Court has developed its own arbitration rules, called Zagreb Rules, which are based on UNCITRAL Arbitration Rules.

The Act on the Peaceful Resolution of Disputes provides that mediation can be conducted in all regular and specialised first and second instance courts (municipal, county, commercial courts and the High Commercial Court) in all stages of the proceedings, including during the appeal proceedings.[18] Mediation can also be carried out outside of courts by various mediation centres established at professional associations (such as the Centre for Mediation at the Croatian Chamber of Economy, or the Centre for Mediation at the Croatian Association for Mediation).

The promotion of use of mediation and the efforts to improve the overall framework for mediation has been rising significantly in the past decade, with many successful projects aimed at reinforcing the system of court-annexed

13 OECD (2019), OECD Investment Policy Reviews: Croatia 2019, OECD Investment Policy Reviews, OECD Publishing, Paris (2019) <https://doi.org/10.1787/2bf079ba-en> accessed 29 June 2024.

14 Zakon o mirnom rješavanju sporova, Narodne novine 67/23

15 Zakon o alternativnom rješavanju potrošačkih sporova, Narodne novine 121/16, 32/19

16 Zakon o arbitraži, Narodne novine 88/01

17 Ibid.

18 Ibid.

mediation which resulted with the rise of cases submitted to mediation as well as rise of successfully concluded mediations. According to the data of the Ministry of Justice, around 177 cases in Croatia are resolved in court-annexed mediation procedure per year.[19]

5 International Investment Treaty Framework

Since gaining its independence in 1991, Croatia began to actively conclude bilateral investment treaties (BITs), along with double taxation treaties and economic cooperation agreements, mainly as a part of its economic diplomacy efforts.

Similarly, to other transition economies and newly established states, the motivation to conclude these agreements was twofold: to support the recognition of a newly established statehood and build bilateral economic ties on one hand, but also to position itself as an attractive destination for investment on the other hand.

During the period from 1993 to 2008, Croatia negotiated and concluded 58 BITs.[20] The first BIT was signed in 1993 with Albania, more than half of the Croatian BITs were signed between 1996 (when 11 treaties were signed in one year alone) and 2000. The latest BIT was concluded with Lithuania in 2008. In addition to BITs, Croatia has been a party to the Energy Charter Treaty since 1994.

As far as geographical distribution is concerned, 23 of the Croatian BITs, or 41%, had been concluded with EU member states, 27% with Asian countries, and 17% with other economies in transition. The remaining 15% were concluded with countries from the Americas and Africa.[21]

Geographical distribution of these BITs, or the choice of treaty partners, does not necessarily reflect a certain strategy or policy. It seems that it was mostly dependent on the course of establishing diplomatic relations with certain countries. Croatia has thus concluded treaties with a wide range of high-income economies as well as developing countries, whereas with some

19 <https://mpudt.gov.hr/UserDocsImages//dokumenti/ISTAKNUTO/Medijacija//INFOGRAFIKA%20-%20Mirenje%20statistika.png> accessed 29 June 2024.

20 Ministry of Foreign and European Affairs, https://mvep.gov.hr/o-hrvatskom-izvozu/trgovinska-politika-europske-unije/ugovori-o-poticanju-i-zastiti-ulaganja-i-zajednicka-politika-ulaganja-eu/244676

21 Full list of Croatian BITs is available at the web-page of the Ministry of Foreign and European Affairs: <https://mvep.gov.hr/UserDocsImages/gospodarska_diplomacija/Tablica-%20Ugovori%20o%20poticanju%20i%20uzajamnoj%20zastiti%20ulaganja%20-%20kolovoz%202022(1).docx> accessed 29 June 2024.

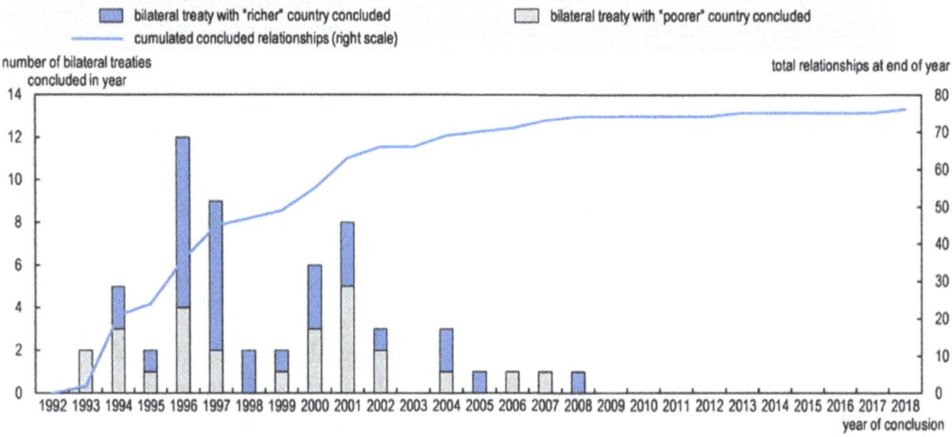

FIGURE 13.5 Treaty relationships with other countries: Croatia (2019)
SOURCE: OECD INVESTMENT POLICY REVIEW 2019

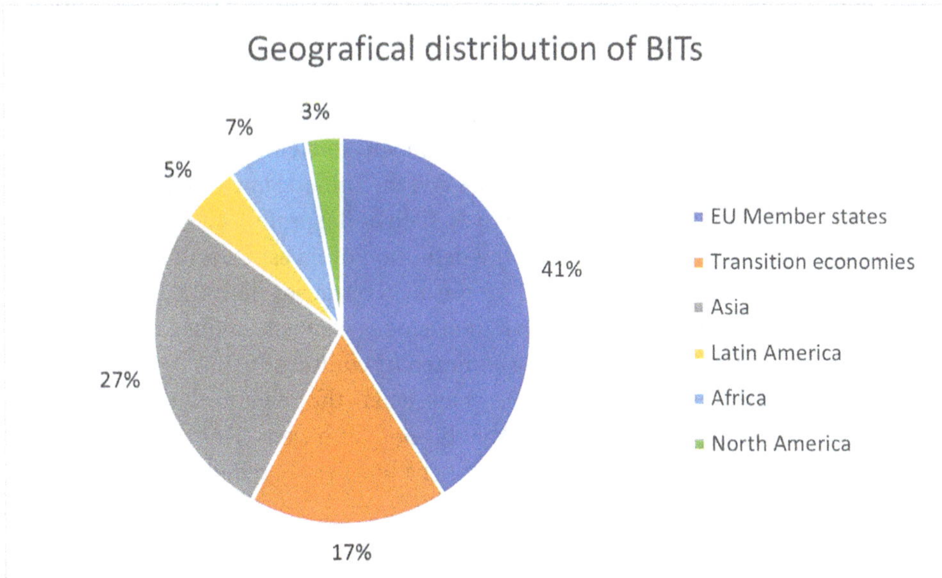

FIGURE 13.6 Geographical distribution of BITs concluded by Croatia
SOURCE: UNCTAD, MINISTRY OF FOREIGN AND EUROPEAN AFFAIRS

of these countries there has been no obvious economic interest (no inbound or outbound investment), and some of these treaties never entered into force.[22]

22 Treaties with Indonesia, Cuba, Mongolia, Morroco, Oman, Russia and Zimbawe were not ratified either by Croatia or the other Contracting Party.

Nevertheless, since the source of most of inward FDI was from the European countries with which Croatia concluded its first treaties, the stock of FDI covered by concluded treaties was very high, up to 95%. According to the OECD Investment Policy Review from 2019, the BITs with the Netherlands, Austria, and Hungary combined brought almost half of Croatia's inward FDI stock under treaty cover, and the BITs concluded with the Netherlands, Bosnia and Herzegovina, and Slovenia cover around two thirds of Croatia's outward FDI stock.[23] On substance, Croatian investment treaties are old style investment treaties, with typical features of "first generation" treaties, like most others concluded in the 1990's.

Croatian treaties typically include a broad, asset-based definition of investment, mostly an unqualified fair and equitable treatment clause (only exceptionally linked to minimum standard of treatment in international law), a very broad most favoured nation clause and a typical expropriation clause, with no qualifiers for indirect expropriation. Except for amendments that were made to comply with the EU law (as explained later in text), Croatian BITs do not contain specific exceptions clauses to safeguard the right to regulate in public interest or for prudential or security reasons.

Only few Croatian BITs, namely the more recent one with Azerbaijan and the treaties with partners with highly developed treaty polices such as Canada and United States, contain some more sophisticated features. For example, the preambles of the BITs with Azerbaijan and the United States include language concerning key public policy objectives, such as the protection of health, labor standards, and the environment; the definition of investment in the BIT with Canada excludes assets not used for business purposes from the scope of the treaty;[24] and the BIT with Azerbaijan excludes claims to money or claims to performance arising solely from a commercial contract.[25]

All of that suggests that in the years when the dynamics of conclusion of treaties was most intense, Croatia did not yet have a clear and consistent approach regarding the substance of BITs but mostly relied on model BITs proposed by treaty partners.

23 OECD Investment Policy Reviews: Croatia 2019, OECD Investment Policy Reviews, OECD Publishing, Paris (2019) <https://doi.org/10.1787/2bf079ba-en> accessed 29 June 2024.

24 Croatia–Canada BIT <https://investmentpolicy.unctad.org/international-investment-agreements/treaties/bilateral-investment-treaties/780/canada---croatia-bit-1997-> accessed 29 June 2024.

25 Croatia–Azerbaijan BIT <https://investmentpolicy.unctad.org/international-investment-agreements/treaties/bilateral-investment-treaties/292/azerbaijan---croatia-bit-2007-> accessed 29 June 2024.

Since 2008 Croatia has not concluded any new BITs. There are two separate set of events that led to this "negotiation chill." First, as a part of the process of accession to the EU, Croatia was required to review all its international agreements and align them with the *aquis communitaire*. As a result, Croatia engaged in amending the existing treaties to ensure compatibility with the Treaties on which the EU was founded, i.e., with the findings of the European Court of Justice (ECJ) in its decisions against Sweden, Finland, and Austria (see further text). Also, first concerns were communicated by the European Commission on the compatibility of Intra EU BITs with the EU law, leading to the first calls to terminate intra-EU BITs, which made their future uncertain.[26]

The second reason for a more cautious approach to treaty negotiation relates to the beginning of investment arbitrations against Croatia, as well as a rise of investment treaty cases globally. Croatia received its first investment treaty claim in 2004,[27] and second in 2007[28] and it was the beginning of the awareness of treaty commitments and their implications. Even though both cases were concluded in favour of the state, the costs of the arbitrations were high enough to raise concerns and trigger discussions on the need for reform.

5.1 *Impact of the Accession to the European Union*

Accession to the European Union in July of 2013 has significantly shaped Croatia's investment treaty policy, both in terms of BITs with third countries and with regard to intra-EU BITs.

As mentioned previously, Croatia has already started to renegotiate its old BITs before its accession to the EU, as one of the preconditions for its accession was to align its international treaties with the *aquis communitaire*. The amendments requested of Croatia were based on the decisions that the ECJ brought in the cases Commission v Sweden (Case no C 249/06), Commission v Austria (Case no C 205/06) and Commission v Finland (Case no C 118/07) concerning the compatibility of these countries pre-accession BITs with the EC Treaty. In these decisions, the ECJ held that the provisions on the transfer of capital which allow investors to move capital freely into and out of the territory of the other signatory, were incompatible with certain provisions in the

26 European Commission Press Release, Commission asks Member States to terminate their intra-EU bilateral investment treaties <https://ec.europa.eu/commission/presscorner/api/files/document/print/en/ip_15_5198/IP_15_5198_EN.pdf> accessed 29 June 2024.

27 Ulemek v. Croatia, UNCITRAL <https://www.italaw.com/cases/1130> accessed 29 June 2024.

28 Adria Beteiligungs GmbH v. The Republic of Croatia, UNCITRAL <https://www.italaw.com/cases/47> accessed 29 June 2024.

EC Treaty that empower the Council to restrict such payments to or from third countries.

In line with these guidelines, Croatia has renegotiated 11 of its BITs with third countries – mainly with countries that have already been engaged in some kind of accession relation with the EU – i.e. Western Balkans economies, Turkey, and CIS economies. The amendments were limited to provisions on the transfer of funds and essential security interest clause, as well as certain modifications of the regional economic integration organization (REIO) exception.

When Croatia entered the EU, investment treaty policy had already been part of common commercial policy and the exclusive competence of the EU, as defined by Article 207 of the TFEU. Also, Regulation (EU) No 1219/2012 of the European Parliament and of the Council of 12 December 2012, establishing a transitional arrangement for bilateral investment agreements between the member states and third countries had already been in place, allowing Croatia to maintain its old treaties until they are replaced by the treaties on the EU level. At the same time, in accordance with the Regulation, to negotiate or renegotiate agreements, Croatia as a Member State must seek authorisation from the Commission to ensure that those agreements would not conflict with the EU competences and are consistent with the EU's investment policy.

To obtain the authorization to negotiate and conclude treaties, among other conditions, Regulation (EU) No 1219/2012 requires the Member State "to include or remove from such negotiations and prospective bilateral investment agreement any clauses where necessary to ensure consistency with the Union's investment policy". In the case of Croatia, that meant to create a new Model BIT fully aligned with the EU approach, which was no longer limited only to provisions on transfer of funds and security exceptions.

At that point in time, the EU investment treaty reform process had already started with TTIP public consultations and resulted in a new model investment treaty in 2015[29] that had been used by the EU to negotiate either chapters on investment protection in FTAs or stand-alone investment treaties.

As opposed to existing Croatian treaties, the EU model agreement introduced well-defined provisions on fair and equitable treatment, indirect expropriation, strong reference to right of the state to regulate in public interest, security exceptions, prudential carve-out etc. The EU model also contains fully

29 European Commission Press Release, EU finalises proposal for investment protection and Court System for TTIP (12 November 2012) <https://ec.europa.eu/commission/presscorner/api/files/document/print/en/ip_15_6059/IP_15_6059_EN.pdf> accessed 29 June 2024.

reformed system of investment dispute resolution, i.e. the Investment Court System (ICS).

Croatia has continuously supported these reforms, advocating for a better balance between the right of the state to regulate its public policies and protection of investors rights. As previously mentioned, by that time, Croatia had already been hit with several ISDS. Thusly, Croatia is fully aware of the weaknesses of broad and undefined standards of protection in its BITs. Being in favour of replacing its old BITs with "new generation" agreements, Croatia was among the first Member States that ratified CETA[30] and investment protection agreements with Vietnam[31] and Singapore.[32] However, none of these agreements are yet in force and it remains to be seen how the future of investment protection in EU will develop.

Apart from concluding these new agreements on the EU level, Croatia has not engaged in any new negotiations of BITs on its own behalf. It has communicated publicly on many occasions[33] its intention to renegotiate its old BITs first, based on the new and reformed approach, but has not yet opened any of these negotiations.

It seems that with the elimination of intra-EU BITs and with ongoing or concluded negotiations on the EU level with main partners, the remaining treaties cover a relatively small stock of FDI. The sense of urgency to modernize the stock of remaining treaties is gone.

In Croatia, BITs with 28 countries are still in force: Albania, Argentina, Azerbaijan, Belarus, Bosnia and Herzegovina, Cambodia, Canada, Chile, China, Egypt, Iran, Israel, Jordan, Kuwait, Libya, Malaysia, Moldova, Montenegro, North Macedonia, San Marino, Serbia, South Korea, Switzerland, Thailand, Turkey, Ukraine, The United Kingdom, and The United States.

With some of these countries, the EU has already negotiated or is currently negotiating investment protection agreements. Some of them are in the process of accession to the EU and their agreements with Croatia will be

---

30 Zakon o potvrđivanju Sveobuhvatnog gospodarskog i trgovinskog sporazuma (CETA) između Kanade, s jedne strane, i Europske unije i njezinih država članica, s druge strane, Narodne novine 9/2017.

31 Zakon o potvrđivanju Sporazuma o zaštiti ulaganja između Europske unije i njezinih država članica, s jedne strane, i Socijalističke Republike Vijetnama, s druge strane, Narodne novine 7/21.

32 Zakon o potvrđivanju Sporazuma o zaštiti ulaganja između Europske unije i njezinih država članica, s jedne strane, i Republike Singapura, s druge strane, Narodne novine 7/21.

33 OECD (2019), OECD Investment Policy Reviews: Croatia 2019, OECD Investment Policy Reviews, OECD Publishing, Paris (2019) <https://doi.org/10.1787/2bf079ba-en> accessed 29 June 2024.

terminated upon accession. This leaves Croatia with a limited stock of treaties to be modernized in the near future.

5.1.1 Intra-EU BITs

As with BITs with third countries, and even more so, the destiny of Croatia's intra-EU BITs has been determined by its accession to the EU.

Croatia had announced its intention to terminate intra-EU BITs already in the process of its accession to the EU. At that point, the discussions on compatibility of intra-EU BITs with the EU law had been ongoing, the issue had not yet been brought before Court of Justice of European Union (CJEU), and there was no consent by other Member States to terminate those agreements – so Croatia waited for a common solution on the EU level.[34]

The issue was finally resolved in March 2018 by the decision of CJEU in case C-284/16, Achmea v. Slovak Republic (the Achmea decision), where the CJEU held that "Articles 267 and 344 [... of the Treaty on the Functioning of the European Union] must be interpreted as precluding a provision in an international agreement concluded between Member States [...]" allowing intra-EU investment arbitration.

The Decision was followed by signing the Declaration of the Representatives of the Governments of the Member States on the legal consequences of the Judgment of the Court of Justice in Achmea and on Investment Protection in the European Union, by which Member States committed to terminate all their intra-EU BITs.[35]

Finally, on 5 May 2020, 23 Member States, including Croatia, signed the agreement for the termination of intra-EU bilateral investment treaties. The Termination Treaty entered into force for Croatia on 25 October 2020, and at this point, all intra-EU BITs are terminated. With Member States that didn't sign the Termination Treaty, namely Austria, Sweden, and Finland, BITs were terminated bilaterally, by mutual consent.

Without getting into detailed legal arguments on the relationship between EU law and international law that has been extensively discussed in both

34 Although public reports and documents from the accession period do not have explicit details on Croatia's attempts to terminate BITs with some Member States, this information was communicated in the process of interpellation at Croatian Parliament in 2016 <https://sabor.hr/sites/default/files/uploads/sabor/2022-05-04/142801/m_INTERPELACIJA_ARBITRAZA.pdf> accessed 29 June 2024.

35 Declaration of EU Member States on the legal consequences of the *Achmea* judgment of the CJEU (15 January 2019) <https://finance.ec.europa.eu/publications/declaration-member-states-15-january-2019-legal-consequences-achmea-judgment-and-investment_en> accessed 29 June 2024.

academic papers and in jurisprudence, it might be interesting to note that one of the Croatian BITs, the BIT with Austria, has a unique provision which stipulates that EU law prevails over treaty provisions. Article 11(2) of the said treaty reads:

> „The Contracting Parties are not bound by the present Agreement insofar as it is incompatible with the legal acquis of the European Union (EU) in force at any given time."

Nevertheless, based on this provision Croatia has been unable to challenge the jurisdiction of tribunals in any of seven cases brought under that particular treaty (see next subchapter). From publicly available decisions on jurisdiction in cases under the Croatia-Austria BIT, where this provision has been raised and discussed, it seems that neither Party has been able to track, in *travaux préparatoires* of this treaty, the rationale behind including this provision.[36] Croatia does not have such a provision in any other of its BITs, and Austria has otherwise only included in its BIT with Bolivia[37] (negotiated in the same year as the Croatian BIT.)

6 ISDS Cases and Outcomes

By 2024, 19 investment treaty claims had been brought against Croatia. The vast majority of these cases were brought by EU investors, under intra-EU BITs, two cases under the BIT with Canada, and one under the BIT with Israel. Two cases were based on the Energy Charter Treaty, also brought by EU investors.[38]

The Croatian government has been mostly successful in defending these claims. Only two of all cases were concluded in favour of the investor and in both, the investor had been awarded less than 2% of its requested damages.[39]

36 Detailed analyisis of this provision in the Decision on Croatia's Jurisdictional Objection Related to the Alleged Incompatibility of the BIT with the EU Acquis in ICSID Case No. ARB/17/37 <https://www.italaw.com/sites/default/files/case-documents/italaw11546.pdf> accessed 29 June 2024.

37 Austria-Bolivia BIT (1997) <https://investmentpolicy.unctad.org/international-investment-agreements/treaties/bilateral-investment-treaties/229/austria---bolivia-plurinational-state-of-bit-1997-> accessed 29 June 2024.

38 UNCTAD, Investment Policy Hub, Croatia <https://investmentpolicy.unctad.org/investment-dispute-settlement/country/51/croatia> accessed 29 June 2024.

39 Data from annual reports by State Attorney's Office <https://dorh.hr/hr/izvjesca-o-radu> accessed 29 June 2024.

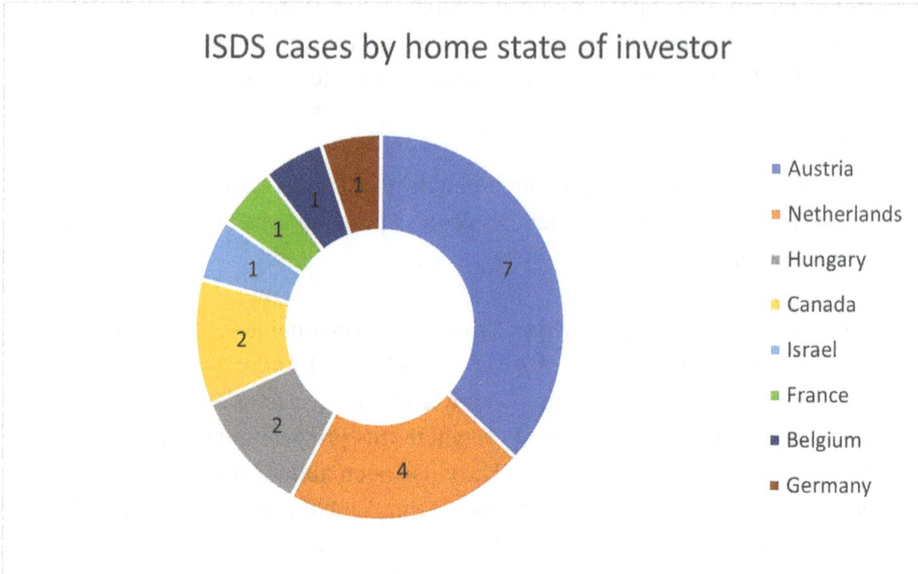

FIGURE 13.7 ISDS cases filed against Croatia by home state of the investor
SOURCE: UNCTAD, CROATIA STATE ATTORNEY'S OFFICE

Croatia also has a high rate of settlements of disputes, five cases were settled during the arbitration. There are also several cases that were settled prior to arbitration, after the notice of dispute had been received. At the time of writing this chapter, only four arbitration cases are still pending.

Investment arbitration cases against Croatia arose in various sectors and from various measures, but can be roughly grouped into four categories: a) claims brought by foreign banks (seven cases) all associated with the same measure, (the legislation that converted Swiss francs denominated loans into Kuna denominated loans in late 2015); b) claims arising from various issues related to privatisation from the late 90s; c) claims arising from spatial planning and local measures; and d) claims arising out of the Government's takeover and restructuring of the largest national food and retail conglomerate.

Cases brought by banks concerning conversion of CHF loans are interesting and significant not only because of their high financial value (which was approximated to 1.2 bil € altogether), but also because they opened yet another debate on the relationship between EU law and international investment law (i.e. between consumer protection rights under EU law and investment protection under BITs), because they triggered public debate on investment protection in Croatia and interpellation in Croatian Parliament with a call to terminate intra-EU BITs, as well as due to the Government having successfully reached settlement with five of seven banks – and finally discontinued at ICSID.

Another landmark case was the case is the case initiated by Raiffeisenbank Austria, in 2020 (again under Croatia–Austria BIT)[40] concerning the adaptation of Law on the Procedure of Extraordinary Administration in Companies of Systemic Importance for the Republic of Croatia from 2017 (as mentioned, one of the two cases provoked by the restructuring of Agrokor group by the mentioned Law; the other case is initiated by Agrokor group owners and mentioned later in text). The case was initiated under UNCITRAL Arbitration Rules, and the parties agreed on Frankfurt as the seat of arbitration. Croatia used an option found in the German Civil Procedure Code to contest the admissibility of the claim before the High Regional Court in Frankfurt (OLG-Oberlandesgericht).

In 2021, the OLG decided in favour of Croatia, finding that the arbitration proceedings were inadmissible due to the invalidity of the arbitration clause, following the CJEU decision in the Achmea case. That decision was confirmed by the German Federal Court of Justice (Bundesgerichtshof-BGH) later in 2021.[41] Following that decision, the parties jointly requested the Tribunal to suspend the proceedings, and on 14 June 2022 the arbitration proceedings were concluded in accordance with UNCITRAL Arbitration Rule 34(2). Croatia was also awarded the costs of these proceedings.[42] This is the first case that Croatia successfully defended based on non-admissibility of intra-EU arbitration due to the invalidity of intra-EU arbitration clauses. It also served as an inspiration for some other Members States of the EU to use a similar approach in their defence.[43]

In all other intra-EU cases that started after the accession of Croatia to the EU, whether before and after the Achmea decision, Croatia tried to challenge the jurisdiction of tribunals by using the intra-EU argument, without success.

Out of the remaining cases, the largest two cases are *MOL Hungarian Oil and Gas Company Plc v. Republic of Croatia* (ICSID Case No. ARB/13/32) under ECT and Adria Group B.V. and *Adria Group Holding B.V. v. Republic of Croatia* (ICSID Case No. ARB/20/6) under the BIT with the Netherlands. These cases are not

40 Savezni vrhovni sud Njemačke potvrdio je odluku visokog regionalnog suda u Frankfurtu <https://dorh.hr/hr/priopcenja/savezni-vrhovni-sud-njemacke-potvrdio-je-odluku-visokog-regionalnog-suda-u-frankfurtu> accessed 29 June 2024.

41 *Ibid.*

42 Annual report for 2022 by State Attorney Office, page 217, accessible at <https://dorh.hr/hr/izvjesca-o-radu/izvjesce-o-radu-drzavnih-odvjetnistava-u-2022-godini> accessed 29 June 2024.

43 The Netherlands later used the same approach in two ICSID cases that German energy companies RWE and Uniper brought under the ECT.

only relevant in terms of the level of damages, but in terms of impact of these two companies on the Croatian economy and the public interest they raised due to the involvement of the highest governmental officials – including criminal proceedings against the prime minister at the time (in MOL case).

In the case that Hungarian MOL initiated against Croatia in 2013, the Tribunal rendered its award in 2022, after almost nine years of proceedings – making it one of the lengthiest in arbitration practice in general. The case was decided in favour of the investor, and MOL was awarded damages in the amount of $184 million USD, out of the $1.1 billion USD the investor claimed.

The case was complex in legal, factual, and procedural terms. It was based on several decisions and measures by various Croatian institutions and officials from 2003 to 2014, starting with the privatization of the national oil company (INA) in 2003, then the conclusion of the amendment to the gas business agreement which was connected with the alleged corruption. This was followed by criminal cases against both the prime minister and the board director of the company, and finally the decisions of the Government relating to the liberalisation of the gas market.

The other case, initiated by Adria Group under the Dutch BIT, is the case of a Croatian company, Agrokor, and its Croatian owner where the investment is structured through a company established in the Netherlands, and thus falls under the protection of the Croatia–Netherlands BIT. The case is still pending, and it remains to be seen whether Croatia could be successful in raising the jurisdictional objection based on the effective nationality of the investor.

On that note, the Croatia–Netherlands BIT was also used in *Elitech B.V. and Razvoj Golf d.o.o. v. Republic of Croatia* (ICSID Case No. ARB/17/32), a case concerning the development of a golf project in city of Dubrovnik, which could not be realized within ten years due to numerous actions of environmental NGOs, activists, and influential politicians who have allegedly influenced courts to block the project. The investor behind the project is Israeli businessman Aaron Frankel, but the investment has been structured through a Dutch-established company. However, once the terminations of intra-EU BITs started, the Israeli investor initiated a case on the same factual and legal grounds under the BIT between Croatia and Israel (*Ahron G. Frenkel v. Republic of Croatia* (ICSID Case No. ARB/20/49). Elitech's case concluded in 2023 in favour of the State, and the other case is still pending.

Although Croatia defended those cases mostly successfully, whether on jurisdiction or merits, the costs of these arbitrations are high and negatively impact the reputation of the country as an attractive investment destination. Therefore, Croatia has made efforts in the past decade to create an internal system for the amicable resolution of investment disputes.

6.1 *Institutional Set-up for Defence against Treaty-based Claims*

Once an investment arbitration claim against Croatia is filed, irrespective of the rules and forum for such an arbitration, the country is represented by the Attorney General's Office, which procures services from private law firms.

However, to manage emerging investor-state disputes against Croatia, with the rise of investment arbitration cases in 2012 and 2013, the Government has established an early-warning system in relation to disputes with foreign investors.

By way of Government Decree,[44] the Government has as established an Interdepartmental Committee to act on claims of foreign investors related to disputes arising from international agreements of the Republic of Croatia in the field of investment promotion and protection. The members of the Committee are State Secretaries from four ministries, Foreign and European Affairs, Finance, Economy and Sustainable Development and Justice and Administration, one Deputy State Attorney and a representative of the Office of the Prime Minister. Other competent authorities participate in the work of this Committee if necessary, depending on the field from which the specific dispute arose.

The role of the Committee is to analyze investor requests, collect the necessary information from the competent authorities, and assess the potential liability of the state, as well as potential damages. Upon these assessments, the Committee proposes the resolution to the Government. In each individual case for an amicable resolution of the dispute, the decision to settle is formally made by the Government.

The biggest case Croatia has settled through this approach is a case with the U.S. investor Colgate/McCallum Ltd, settled in 2022, arising from the conduct of the Croatian Privatization Fund in the late 1990s. Through a settlement agreement, Croatia agreed to reimburse the investor 297 million HRK (around 40 mil EUR) and the investor waived the right to initiate any court and arbitration proceedings against the Republic of Croatia and additionally committed to invest at least HRK 100 million back in Croatia over the next five years. The settlement agreement prevented an ICSID arbitration and a lawsuit by the U.S. International Development Finance Corporation, over an investor's investment guarantee.[45]

---

44 Government Decree establishing the Interdepartmental Committee <https://vlada.gov.hr/UserDocsImages/2016/Sjednice/2020/Studeni/24%20sjednica%20VRH/24%20-%2019.docx> accessed 29 June 2024.

45 Ministry of Foreign and European Affairs Croatia, press release <https://mvep.gov.hr/press/priopcenje-mvep-a-245657/245657> accessed 29 June 2024.

There are many benefits to the approach of amicable dispute settlement, even when the settlement of a dispute cannot be reached. By engaging in dialogue with investors, the Government sends a signal of political commitment and responsibility, the officials involved in process get more insight and awareness of treaty commitments for future policy considerations, and both government institutions and the State Attorney get the opportunity to prepare for the future arbitration case.

7 Ongoing Reforms

As a member of the EU, Croatia has been engaged in all developments related to investment treaty reform at the EU level. As described in this chapter, Croatia welcomed and adopted the new approach to investment treaties, as negotiated in EU agreements with Canada, Vietnam, and Singapore. Croatia also participates in the work of UNCITRAL Working Group III on the reform of investor-state dispute settlement as well as in the work of the OECD on the Future of Investment Treaties.

Since investment treaty policy is a part of EU trade policy and falls within the exclusive competence of the EU, Croatia is not in a position to pursue any further reforms on its own behalf, other than those at the EU level. As the investment treaty regime at the EU level is already significantly reformed and modernized, it remains to be tested in the renegotiations of old-style BITs concluded by Croatia. Croatia has not announced any plans for future negotiations of new BITs.

CHAPTER 14

Investment Protection and Investor-State Dispute Resolution in Kosovo

Lyra Çela

1 Introduction

A free-market economy is one of the fundamental values and principles upon which the constitutional order of the Republic of Kosovo is based, according to Article 7 [Values] of its Constitution.[1] Article 10 [Economy] of the Constitution further stipulates that '*A market economy with free competition is the basis of the economic order of the Republic of Kosovo.*'[2] Kosovo has experienced steady economic progress over the past decade, with a nearly 50% increase in per-capita income and a 35% reduction in poverty. Its economy is characterized by a constant expansion in consumption and investment, a strong impetus from diaspora inflows, public investment in infrastructure, and financial deepening.[3] A limited Foreign Direct Investment (FDI) trend has continued during recent years, with a stagnating low level since 2015 and up to 2022.[4] Diaspora remittances continue to be the country's main economic driver. In 2022, remittances accounted for 19.7% of the country's GDP.[5] In 2023, remittances saw an increase of 9.9% in comparison to the previous year and accounted for 13.9% of Kosovo's GDP.[6]

Kosovo's young population, with a median age of 35, low labour costs, low tax rates, proximity to the affluent European Union (EU) market, natural resources,

1 *See* Constitution of the Republic of Kosovo (2008), Art. 7(2): '*The constitutional order of the Republic of Kosovo is based on the principles of freedom, peace, democracy, equality, respect for human rights and freedoms and the rule of law, non-discrimination, the right to property, the protection of environment, social justice, pluralism, separation of state powers, and a market economy.*'

2 *Ibid.* Art. 10.

3 International Development Association International Finance Corporation Multilateral Investment Guarantee Agency Country Partnership Framework for Republic of Kosovo for the Period FY23-FY27, The World Bank Group (10 April 2023), at 3.

4 Annual Report 2022, Central Bank of the Republic of Kosovo (June 2023), at 20; Boosting Foreign Direct Investment, The World Bank Group (November 2021), at 7.

5 Annual Report 2022 (n 4), at 20.

6 Annual Report 2023, Central Bank of the Republic of Kosovo (June 2024), at 36.

 | DOI:10.1163/9789004729889_015

and high-level internet access, among others, represent major strengths to attracting FDI.[7] Continuous efforts to improve the efficiency and efficacy of the legal, regulatory, and administrative frameworks through the years have resulted in the betterment of the business climate in Kosovo, as evidenced by Kosovo's relative standing in the World Bank (WB) Doing Business Survey.[8] In 2020, Kosovo ranked 57th out of 190 countries in the World Index of Ease of Doing Business.[9] However, while Kosovo has ranked 12th out of 190 surveyed in terms of starting a business, the trend of limited FDI levels can be attributed to numerous economical and structural challenges, ranging from limited regional and global economic integration, inadequate access to finance, significant infrastructure heaps, inadequate competition, including due to a large informal sector, difficulties of establishing property rights, to corruption, tenuous rule of law, including a lack of contract enforcement and challenges to investor protections.[10] The ongoing dispute with Serbia and limited international recognition also represent obstacles to doing business for foreign investors.[11]

FDI inflows show a positive trend. The net flow of FDI in 2023 reached EUR 884.3, million.[12] In 2022, FDI the net flow of NDI was estimated at EUR 778.2 million, representing a significant increase of 85% compared to the net amount in 2021, driven primarily by diaspora-dominated real estate investment, but also with notable increases in mining and quarrying, financial and insurance activities, and manufacturing.[13] There is a minimal presence of FDI in sectors that tend to significantly impact innovation, productivity gains, and job creation, such as export-oriented or higher-value-added manufacturing and services sectors.[14] Due to its limited impact on productivity-enhancing spillovers, constrained by the characteristics of the sectors FDI has continuously been concentrated in, FDI in Kosovo has not been a significant driver of structural transformation.[15]

---

7 Boosting Foreign Direct Investment (n 4), at 7.

8 *Ibid.* at 14.

9 Doing Business 2020: Economy Profile Kosovo, The World Bank Group (2021), at 4.

10 2023 Investment Climate Statements: Kosovo, US Department of State (29 October 2023), https://www.state.gov/reports/2023-investment-climate-statements/kosovo/; Competitiveness in South East Europe 2021: A Policy Outlook, OECD (5 July 2021), at 1048; Boosting Foreign Direct Investment, The World Bank Group (November 2021), at 7.

11 2023 Investment Climate Statements: Kosovo (n 9); Boosting Foreign Direct Investment (n 4), at 7.

12 Annual Report 2023 (n 6), at 36.

13 Annual Report 2022 (n 4), at 20; Country Partnership Framework for Republic of Kosovo (n 3), at 4.

14 Boosting Foreign Direct Investment (n 4), at 7.

15 Competitiveness in South East Europe 2021 (n 10), at 1046.

2 FDI Trends and Key Features

FDI has represented a pillar of many transition economies' structural transformation and modernization efforts. FDI has the potential, therefore, to benefit Kosovo's economy by enabling the creation of more and better jobs and spurring greater and more resilient economic growth.[16]

Up to the year 2020, the FDI trend has been at a stagnating low level. An increased FDI trend started in 2020, with FDI equalling EUR 341.7 million and an increase of 34.2% compared to the previous year.[17] In 2021, FDI totalled EUR 415.3 million, amounting to an increase of 20.1% compared to the previous year.[18] In 2022, FDI has had an annual increase of 85%, totalling EUR 778.2 million. According to recently published data by the Central Bank of Kosovo (CBK), the positive trend continued in 2023, with FDI totalling EUR 884.3 million.[19] Sectors such as real estate, mining, and construction saw the most increase in FDI.[20]

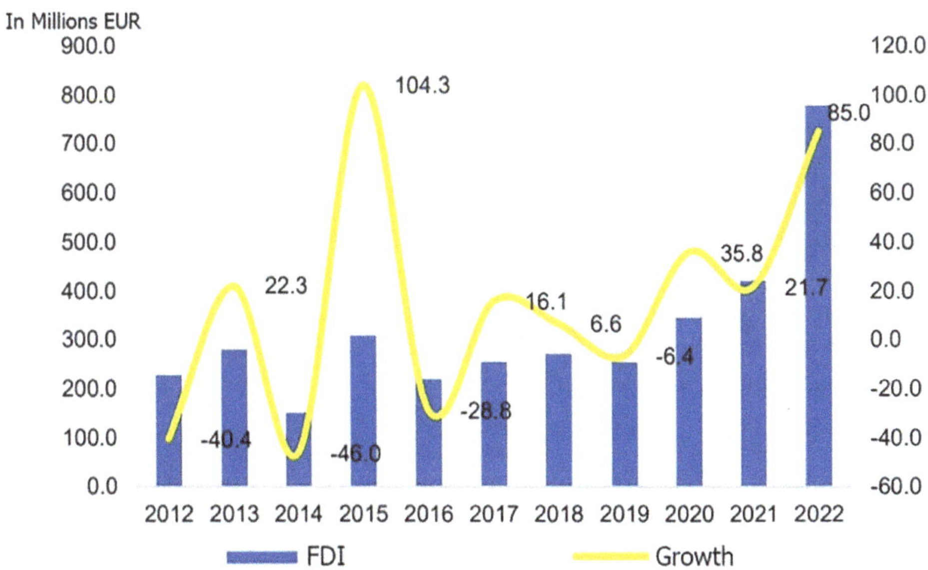

FIGURE 14.1 FDI inflow in Kosovo 2012–2022
SOURCE: CENTRAL BANK OF KOSOVO (CBK)

16 Boosting Foreign Direct Investment (n 4), at 7.
17 Annual Report 2022 (n 4), at 39.
18 *Ibid.* at 38.
19 Annual Report 2023 (n 6), at 35.
20 Annual Report 2022 (n 4), at 37.

2.1 *Key Sectors*

FDI in the real estate sector accounted for 60.6% of the net FDI inflow in Kosovo in 2023.[21] It totalled EUR 523.7 million, accounting for 67.3% of the overall FDI in Kosovo for the year 2022. This increase in 2022 compared to the trend between 2007–2019, a period during which real estate accounted for around 43% of FDI annually, has been attributed mainly to the 35% estimated increase in prices for acquiring real estate.[22] Other important service sectors receiving FDI included financial services, construction and transportation, storage, and communications.[23]

Although 53% of the land in Kosovo is considered arable and the agriculture sector has the potential to spur economic growth, FDI inflows in this sector during 2021 and 2022 account for approximately 9.2% of total FDI inflows.[24] Despite the overall energy trends in Europe and beyond and the fact that Kosovo ranks fifth worldwide in terms of lignite reserves and is rich in other minerals including aluminium, lead, zinc, copper, Kosovo has experienced negative inflows into mining and quarrying activities.[25] The lack of FDI in this sector is mainly attributed to factors such as political instability, disputes over territories with large mineral reserves, lack of investment in equipment, facilities, and development of new mines.[26]

2.2 *FDI Origin*

A key feature of FDI in Kosovo is the pattern related to the origin of the investments. It is common for FDI flowing into developing and fragile economies to originate from countries with a strong diaspora presence. FDI in Kosovo originates predominantly from source markets with a strong diaspora presence, such as Germany, Switzerland, the UK, Turkey, Austria, and the US, along with other countries in the region.[27]

21 Annual Report 2023 (n 6), at 36.
22 Annual Report 2022 (n 4), at 37.
23 Boosting Foreign Direct Investment (n 4), at 13.
24 *Ibid.*
25 Foreign Direct Investment in Kosovo – The Investment Climate, Potential and Barriers, Institute for Free Market Economy (IFME) (December 2019), at 37.
26 *Ibid.*
27 Annual Report 2022 (n 4), at 177; Boosting Foreign Direct Investment (n 4), at 15.

TABLE 14.1 Incoming FDI in 2022 by originating country / in Million EUR

Country	Incoming direct investments		
	Total incoming direct investments	**Equity**	**Other capital transactions**
Austria	329.3	303.4	25.9
Belgium	70.8	62.8	8
Bulgaria	38.7	8.3	30.4
Cyprus	15.6	4.4	1.5
France	56.1	52.2	3.9
Germany	897.6	824.8	72.8
Greece	68	55	14
Croatia	12.5	13.5	-1
Italy	74.4	61.7	12.4
Netherlands	88.5	46.7	41.8
Romania	0.3	1.9	1.6
Slovenia	238.9	182.8	56.1
Sweden	99.5	99.1	0.5

SOURCE: CBK ANNUAL REPORT 2022

3 Legal Framework

According to the Organisation for Economic Co-operation and Development (OECD), the legal framework for investment activities and conducting business in Kosovo is clear and comprehensive.[28] Kosovo had the best score out of other Western Balkans countries in the 2019 OECD FDI Regulatory Restrictiveness Index, which assessed and benchmarked market access and exceptions to national treatment.[29] This score indicates limited restrictions to foreign investments and that foreign firms are not discriminated against and enjoy the same privileges as local businesses.[30]

28 Competitiveness in Southeast Europe 2021 (n 10), at 1059.

29 *Ibid.*

30 *Ibid.*

However, a recent investor survey conducted by the World Bank (WB) finds that while Kosovo provides sufficient investor protection as pertains to its laws, the challenge is enforcement.[31] Strong investor protection guarantees are fundamental to enhancing investor confidence and attracting FDI, particularly in contexts with high perceived political risk, such as Kosovo.[32] The legal framework in Kosovo is comprised of both a set of (3.1) internal laws, as well as a number of international (3.2) bilateral and (3.3) multilateral treaties.

3.1 *Internal Laws*

As of 6 September 2024, investment activities in Kosovo are governed by the Law on Sustainable Investment (3.1.1). Until very recently, two main internal laws governed investment activities in Kosovo, the Law on Foreign Investment, passed by the Assembly of the Republic of Kosovo in 2014 (3.1.2), and Law on Strategic Investments, passed by the Assembly in 2017 (3.1.3), as well as a set of other laws and sub-legal acts.

With the recent entry into force of the new law, the former have been abrogated. Although the two primary laws above were relatively recent, the internal legal framework in Kosovo is not necessarily as novel. United Nations Mission in Kosovo (UNMIK) Regulations, acts that had the effect of laws at the time, established the initial rules pertaining to foreign investment as early as 2001. This contribution analyses in detail the recently abrogated Law on Foreign Investment and Law on Strategic Investment, as they have governed Kosovo's investment landscape for a substantial period. Moreover, all investment arbitration cases discussed herein have proceeded when the latter were still in force.

3.1.1 Law on Sustainable Investment

The Law on Sustainable Investment (LSI) aims to establish a comprehensive legal framework for promoting and protecting investment and enhancing economic development by addressing the shortcomings of the legal framework currently in force. In its nine chapters, LSI lays out the governing principles of sustainable investment and the rights and obligations of investors, establishes a novel institutional structure and specialized bodies to promote, encourage, and protect sustainable investment, sets the rules on strategic investment, the procedure for awarding the status of a strategic investment project and its screening, and establishes the rules and procedures concerning dispute resolution.

31 Competitiveness in South East Europe 2021 (n 10), at 33.

32 Competitiveness in South East Europe 2021 (n 10), at 1059.

This Law has entered into force in early September 2024, following approval by the Parliament in October 2023 and review by the Constitutional Court upon an application filed by deputies of the Parliament in November 2023. In its Judgement in case KO243/23 of 2 August 2024, the Constitutional Court found that the provisions alleged by the applicants as unconstitutional, did not violate Kosovo's Constitution, ultimately paving the way for LSI's entry into force.[33]

This Law's purpose is to promote, encourage, and protect the sustainable investments and exports in the Republic of Kosovo, in line with the United Nations', OECD, and European principles, standards, and best practices. In Article 14, LSI lists the following of Kosovo's 'national objectives' it intends to fulfil through the promotion and protection of investment: increasing of manufacturing and export; promotion of the circular economy; increasing of competitiveness of domestic industry; development of innovation and technology; enhancement of the industrial ecosystem; training and employment of workforce; empowerment of youth, women, non-majority communities and marginalized groups; sustainability of the movement of people; engagement of the diaspora; regional development; and environmental sustainability.[34] Against this backdrop, LSI introduces the manufacturing and processing industry, agriculture, information and communication technology, education and training, research and information, health, tourism, sewage and waste administration, transport, energy, and mines as investment priority sectors in Kosovo.[35] Strategic investments according to LSI, may be made by both Kosovar and foreign persons.[36]

Intending to increase Kosovo's attractiveness towards foreign and other investors, LSI begins by stipulating the highest standards and guarantees of the investor's rights and investment protection. In its initial provisions, LSI sets forward the investor and investment's equality before the law, protection and security, respect of rights from public institutions, and protection from expropriation.[37] Further, this Law provides several facilitation services investors may benefit from, including exemption from export duties, subsidies for the salaries of the Kosovar employees, support for research and development, and support for access to finance.[38] LSI foresees the leasing of public property

33 Judgement in case KO245/23, with applicants Ferat Shala and nine deputies of the Assembly of the Republic of Kosovo.

34 Law no. 08/L-209 on Sustainable Investment (22 August 2024), Art. 14.

35 *Ibid.* Art. 15.

36 *Ibid.* Art. 29(1).

37 *Ibid.* Arts. 6, 7, 8, 10.

38 *Ibid.* Art. 16(1).

for strategic investment purposes, for a duration of up to 99 years, upon the approval of Kosovo's Assembly, municipal assembly, or in accordance with the Law on publicly-owned enterprises, depending on the type of property.[39] The law includes detailed provisions on non-discrimination, fair and equitable treatment, and protection from expropriation.[40]

In Chapter IV, LSI establishes a novel institutional structure, setting out the institutional framework and the respective responsibilities and mandates of the so-called 'competent bodies for investment'.[41] LSI foresees the establishment of the Agency of Investments and Exports (AIE), specifically tasked to provide certain enumerated investment promotion, investment facilitation, and investor care services.[42] AIE coordinates the other ministerial bodies involved in the processes of evaluation and additional verification of investments.[43] Another novel body, established as an executive agency of the Ministry for Industry, Entrepreneurship, and Trade, is the Agency for Innovation and Support of the Enterprises in the Republic of Kosovo (AISEK), primarily competent for innovation and development of entrepreneurship, development of production capacities destined for export, promotion of tourism, and administration of industrial and technological parks.[44]

The creation of an inter-ministerial Investment Council, with powers to evaluate, select, implement, supervise, and decide on strategic investment projects, is also foreseen, with the Prime Minister as Chair, and members representing the following ministerial departments: industry, entrepreneurship, and trade, finance, environment and special planning, agriculture, local governance, and other members as determined by a Government decision.[45] Among the primary competencies and responsibilities of the Council are the issuance of decisions on strategic investment, conclusion of strategic investment agreements, and oversight of strategic investment implementations.[46]

Chapter V of LSI details the general conditions, application, and awarding procedure of a strategic investment. A strategic investment project must help in fulfilling the 'national objectives' as stipulated by this Law and belong to the priority sectors in the same sets.[47] Different from the former Law on Strategic

39 *Ibid.* Art. 28.
40 *Ibid.* Arts. 6, 7, 10.
41 *Ibid.* Arts 17–23.
42 *Ibid.* Art. 19.
43 *Ibid.* Art. 19(5).
44 *Ibid.* Art. 20.
45 *Ibid.* Art. 21(2).
46 *Ibid.* Art. 21 (4).
47 *Ibid.* Art. 24(2).

Investment that had set a threshold value of EUR 30 million, a strategic investment project under LSI, must reach the value of at least EUR 10 million.[48] An investment project may be prepared, proposed, or implemented by persons of both Kosovar citizens and foreigners.[49] Proposals are submitted and initially reviewed by AIE, which verifies the data and documents and undertakes a technical, financial, and legal evaluation of the proposal.[50] The Council then decides based on AIR's recommendation within strict deadlines and may also require screening before moving forward with a final decision.[51] Finally, following negotiations with the announced strategic investor, the Council enters into an agreement with the investor.[52] Such an agreement should have a duration of at least five years.[53] The Council is competent to annul or abrogate the decision for strategic investment under the circumstances foreseen in Article 39 of LSI.

LSI contains more detailed provisions for disagreements and disputes in a special chapter on the matter. In the event of a disagreement, LSI foresees that the parties shall first enter consultations, facilitated by AIE.[54] The investor may refer a complaint to a Complaints Panel, another specialized structure established by LSI.[55] However, the exhaustion of this remedy is not conditional for pursuing a matter through litigation or arbitration.[56] Article 47 of the said act stipulates the legal remedies available in courts.[57]

Ultimately, Article 47 of LSI introduces a highly anticipated change to the existing legal framework as per the 2014 LFI. This provision sets that the Republic of Kosovo and the investor may agree to resolve the investment dispute through mediation or arbitration only if the terms and conditions have been agreed in advance. It states that the arbitration shall take place in the Republic of Kosovo or an EU member state that is party to the New York Convention.[58] Consequently, with the entry into force of LSI, the controversial Article 16 of the 2014 LFI further elaborated below, will cease to serve as a basis for Kosovo's advance consent to arbitration. Moreover, for the first time, Kosovo introduces mediation as a means of resolving investor-state disputes.

48 *Ibid.* Art. 24(3).
49 *Ibid.* Arts. 29 (1), 29(2).
50 *Ibid.* Arts. 31, 32.
51 *Ibid.* Arts. 33, 36.
52 *Ibid.* Art. 38.
53 *Ibid.* Art. 38(4).
54 *Ibid.* Art. 44.
55 *Ibid.* Art. 45.
56 *Ibid.* Art. 46(4).
57 *Ibid.* Art. 46.
58 *Ibid.* Art. 48.

3.1.2 Law on Foreign Investment (2014 LFI)

Since its entry into force in 2014 and up until its abrogation in 2024, the 2014 LFI provided a set of fundamental rights and guarantees to ensure investor protection and fair treatment. It contained provisions with respect to the standards for investor and investment protection, obligations of Kosovo towards the investor, dispute settlement, including the mechanism, applicable law, and recognition and enforcement of arbitral awards. A key feature of this law was that through its effect, the Kosovo Investment and Enterprise Support Agency (KIESA) was established as a specialized body mandated to protect and promote investment.[59] With the entry into force of the Law on Sustainable Investment, KIESA ceases to exist and is replaced by two novel specialized bodies, namely the Agency of Investments and Exports and the Agency for Innovation and Support of the Enterprises. The 2014 LFI was the principal law protecting, promoting, and encouraging foreign investment and the basis for rights and guarantees to foreign investors willing to invest in Kosovo.[60]

This law set Kosovo's commitment as a host country to treat foreign investors and their investments in Kosovo fairly and equitably and to provide them with full and constant protection and security.[61] Its Articles 7 and 8 provided for protection against expropriation without fair compensation. Article 7 guaranteed explicitly that direct or indirect expropriation measures were to be taken in a non-discriminatory manner, for a public purpose, under due process of law, and against '*immediate, adequate and effective compensation*'.[62] Article 8 indicated the modalities for compensation, which shall be made in a timely manner and based on fair market prices.[63]

Article 2 of the 2014 LFI delimitated the law's material, personal, and temporal scopes. A foreign person for the purposes of this law was defined as (i) any natural person who is a citizen of a foreign country; (ii) any natural person who is a citizen of the Republic of Kosovo, but has residence abroad; or (iii) a legal person established according to the law of a foreign country.[64] Pursuant to Article 2(1)(1.4), an investment was defined as '*any asset owned or otherwise lawfully held by a Foreign Person in the Republic of Kosovo for the purpose of conducting lawful commercial activities*'.[65] According to the Tribunal's interpretation in *Bedri Selmani v. Republic of Kosovo*, discussed in more detail below,

---

59 Law No. 04/L-220 on Foreign Investment (9 January 2014), Art. 23.
60 *Ibid.* Art. 1.
61 *Ibid.* Arts. 3(1), 3(2).
62 *Ibid.* Art. 7.
63 *Ibid.* Art. 8.
64 *Ibid.* Art. 2(1)(1.3).
65 *Ibid.* Art. 2(1)(1.4).

the reference to 'Republic of Kosovo' sets the temporal scope of the 2014 LFI as well, rendering the law applicable to investments made after the Republic of Kosovo came into being, on 17 February 2008.[66]

Article 16 of the 2014 LFI contained provisions related to the mechanism for the resolution of investment disputes. It gave priority to the parties' choice, namely any applicable requirements or procedures that have been agreed upon in writing between the foreign investor and the Republic of Kosovo. In the absence of an agreement between the parties, the foreign investor may have resorted to litigation before a court in Kosovo, or to local or international arbitration.[67]

A special feature of the 2014 LFI was Article 16(3), according to which the unilateral consent of Kosovo to the submission of an investment dispute to arbitration is given by effect of law.[68] Therefore, an arbitral tribunal could establish jurisdiction based on the provisions of the 2014 LFI only, regardless of whether a bilateral investment treaty (BIT) is in force between the investor's state and Kosovo. This method of consenting in advance, through the effect of a law has been highlighted as a concern by the United Nations Conference on Trade and Development (UNCTAD) through its Investment Policy Review for Southeast Europe, conducted in 2017. According to UNCTAD, reserving consent to international arbitration on a case-by-case basis assessment allows the host country flexibility with respect to the choice of forum and provides them better control over their exposure to investor claims.[69]

Article 18 stipulated that any arbitral award in connection with an investment dispute falling within the scope of the law at hand shall be deemed final and binding between the parties and shall be enforceable within the Republic of Kosovo as if the highest court of competent jurisdiction of Kosovo rendered it.[70]

3.1.3 Law on Strategic Investment (2017 LSI)

This Law represented a step forward to further improving the existing legal framework, among others, since it differentiated strategic investors from small investors. LSI too has been abrogated as of 6 September 2024 with the entry into force of the new Law on Sustainable Investment. A key highlight of this

66 ICC International Court of Arbitration, Case No. 24443/MHM/HBH, Mr. Bedri Selmani (Croatia) v. Republic of Kosovo (1 August 2022), par. 337, at 96.

67 2014 LFI (n 59), Art. 16(1).

68 *Ibid.* Art. 16(3).

69 Investment Policy Review: South-Eart Europe, UNCTD (2017), at 15.

70 2014 LFI (n 59), Art. 18.

law was its Article 2(1), which enlisted the priority sectors for investment in Kosovo as follows: energy with infrastructure and mining, transport and telecommunication, tourism, processing industry, agriculture, and food industry, health, industrial and technological parks, and wastewater and waste management, thereby introducing a policy-orientation layer. Projects for each respective sector must meet a specific minimum threshold initial investment value, varying from EUR 10 million to 30 million.[71]

In addition to being projects from priority sectors as above, projects must also '*contribute to the economic growth, employment, and implementation of new technologies, increase of competitive economic capabilities of Kosovo, increase of export and reduction of trade deficit and the ones having a general impact in the growth of welfare and living conditions of the citizens of the Republic of Kosovo*'.[72]

Foreign investors, domestic investors, public investment authorities, and any public investment authority in cooperation with any foreign or domestic investor can be granted the status of a strategic investor.[73] The LSI did not contain any dispute resolution provisions. According to the said Law, however, the mechanisms for dispute resolution between the Government of the Republic of Kosovo and the strategic investor must be included in the agreement for the realisation of a strategic project.[74]

LSI was very specific in terms of standards for transparency and the obligation of KIESA to make the registry of lists of projects granted the status of strategic projects at least twice a year.[75] The registry available online and last updated in December 2022, listed only four projects for which the Government has granted the status of strategic project. Two of them, however, are pending approval by Parliament.[76]

3.2 *Treaty Framework*

The treaty framework pertaining to international investment in Kosovo is comprised of a set of international multilateral treaties (3.2.1), regional multilateral treaties (3.2.2), as well as bilateral treaties (3.2.3).

71 *Ibid.* Art. 2(2).
72 *Ibid.* Art. 2(1).
73 *Ibid.* Art. 4(1).
74 *Ibid.* Art. 17.
75 *Ibid.* Art. 22(2).
76 Registry of Projects having obtained the status of strategic investors (29 October 2023) https://kiesa.rks-gov.net/desk/inc/media/51A06562-D287-454B-A8FD-8C89B01FAF41.pdf

3.2.1 Multilateral Treaties: the ICSID Convention and New York Convention

Kosovo became a party to the International Centre for Settlement of Investment Disputes (ICSID) Convention in 2009. Currently, three of seven cases brought by investors against Kosovo as host country were filed under the ICSID framework and decided by an ICSID Tribunal.

Foreign arbitral awards and judgments are enforceable in Kosovo. Regarding the arbitral awards' enforcement framework, Kosovo is not formally a member of the New York Convention on the Recognition and Enforcement of Arbitral Awards (NYC). However, the NYC is rendered applicable by reference pursuant to the applicable Law Contested Procedure.[77]

3.2.2 Regional Multilateral Treaties: Central European Free Trade Agreement (CEFTA)

CEFTA is a regional multilateral trade agreement aiming at developing and integrating the Western Balkans regional market through establishing a free-trade zone as a pre-EU-integration phase. The agreement seeks to eliminate trade barriers and foster trade between the member economies.[78] The members of CEFTA include Albania, Bosnia and Herzegovina, Bulgaria, Croatia, North Macedonia, Moldova, Montenegro, Romania, Serbia, and Kosovo. It must be noted, however, that UNMIK is a member of CEFTA on behalf of Kosovo.

3.2.3 Bilateral Treaties: the Stabilization and Association Agreement (SAA) and Bilateral Investment Treaties (BITS)

The SAA signed between Kosovo and the EU in 2015, represents a framework for Kosovo to gradually align its policies and regulations with the EU and, over time, promote economic and political integration with the EU. While the reaches of the SAA are cross-sectorial, one of the aims of the agreement, as stated in its preamble, is '*to create a new climate for economic relations between the Parties and, above all, for the development of trade and investment, factors crucial to economic restructuring and modernisation*'.[79] This commitment is

77 *See* Law No. 04/L-118 on Amending and Supplementing the Law No. 03/L-006 on Contested Procedure, amending Article 511, Art. 26: '*The recognition and enforcement of foreign arbitral awards shall be implemented in consistence with the New York Convention on the Recognition and Enforcement of Foreign Arbitral Awards*'.

78 Kosovo's Contested Representation in CEFTA – A Political and Legal Overview, Balkans Policy Research Group (22 November 2021), at 7.

79 Stabilisation and Association Agreement between the European Union and the European Atomic Energy Community, of the one part, and Kosovo, on the other part, Official Journal of the European Union (16 March 2016), Preamble.

further materialized in Article 98, titled 'Investment promotion and protection', wherein the contracting parties, the EU and Kosovo, undertake to cooperate in the field of investment promotion and protection to bring about a favourable climate for investment.[80]

BITs constitute an additional layer of protection for foreign investors.[81] According to the list publicly available in the Official Gazette, Kosovo has entered the BITs as follows:

1. Agreement between the Government of the Republic of Kosovo and the Government of the Republic of Austria;[82]
2. Agreement between the Government of the Republic of Kosovo and the Belgium–Luxembourg Economic Union;[83]
3. Agreement between the Government of the Republic of Kosovo and Swiss Confederation;[84]
4. Agreement between the Government of the Republic of Kosovo and the Republic of Turkey;[85]
5. Agreement between the Government of the Republic of Kosovo and the Government of Macedonia;[86]
6. Agreement between the Government of the Republic of Kosovo and United Arab Emirates;[87]
7. Agreement between the Government of the Republic of Kosovo and the Council of Ministers of the Republic of Albania;[88]

80 *Ibid.* Art. 98.

81 Competitiveness in South East Europe 2021 (n 10), at 1060.

82 Agreement between the Government of the Republic of Kosovo and the Government of the Republic of Austria on the reciprocal promotion and protection of investments (25 February 2010).

83 Agreement between the Government of the Republic of Kosovo and the Belgium-Luxembourg Economic Union on the reciprocal promotion and protection of investments (3 June 2010).

84 Agreement between the Government of the Republic of Kosovo and Swiss Confederation on the reciprocal promotion and protection of investments (17 November 2011).

85 Agreement between the Government of the Republic of Kosovo and the Republic of Turkey on the reciprocal promotion and protection of investments (1 October 2012).

86 Agreement between the Government of the Republic of Kosovo and the Government of Macedonia on mutual promotion and protection of investments (9 March 2015).

87 Agreement between the Government of the Republic of Kosovo and United Arab Emirates on the reciprocal promotion and protection of investments (4 November 2016).

88 Agreement between the Government of the Republic of Kosovo and the Council of Ministers of the Republic of Albania on the reciprocal promotion and protection of investments (27 June 2016).

8. Agreement between the Government of the Republic of Kosovo and the Government of Canada;[89]
9. Agreement between the Government of the Republic of Kosovo and the Government of Hungary for the promotion and reciprocal protection of investments.[90]

In addition to the list above, of BITs entered by the Republic of Kosovo as an independent country, it is interesting to note that arbitral tribunals have found Kosovo bound by BITs concluded by the former Socialist Federal Republic of Yugoslavia (SFRY) by succession. In the matter of *ACP Axos Capital GmbH v. Republic of Kosovo*, further discussed below, a claim was brought and decided by an ICSID Tribunal under a BIT between the Federal Republic of Germany and SFRY from 1990.[91] Therefore, it cannot be ruled out that the BITs list presented here is not definitive and that the number of all potentially binding BITs to Kosovo which may be invoked in investor-state disputes may be rather open.

4 Investor-State Disputes

The first claims against Kosovo as a host country were brought by ACP Axos Capital GmbH in 2015, before an ICSID Tribunal. The number of cases has since been increasing, and as shown in the table below, seven investor-state dispute cases have been brought against Kosovo, six of which have been concluded. It must be noted that, in the absence of official sources, this information is inferred from various online sources, and the number of pending cases may vary.

The pattern of the cases is tightly linked with the historical, political, and economic context of Kosovo: a new country and market, formerly belonging to a socialist system, that for the first time was being introduced to the economy of free trade; newly established state institutions, with little to no experience with foreign investments – let alone alternative dispute resolution mechanisms; ambiguity and questions of public international law in the context of

89 Agreement between the Government of the Republic of Kosovo and the Government of Canada on the reciprocal promotion and protection of investments (10 May 2018).

90 Agreement between the Government of the Republic of Kosovo and the Government of Hungary for the promotion and reciprocal protection of investments on the reciprocal promotion and protection of investments (16 March 2021).

91 International Centre for Settlement of Investment Disputes ICSID Case No. ARB/15/22, ACP Axos Capital GmbH v. Republic of Kosovo (3 May 2018), par. 2, at 2.

TABLE 14.2 Status table of ISDS cases against the Republic of Kosovo

	Year of introduction	Parties	Tribunal/ Institution	Legal basis	Case status
1	2015	ACP Axos Capital GmbH (Germany) v. Republic of Kosovo	ICSID	Germany-SFRY BIT	Decided in favour of the state
2	2017	Mabco Construction SA (Switzerland) v. Republic of Kosovo	ICSID	Kosovo-Switzerland BIT	Final award pending; In 2020 an Award on Jurisdiction was issued
3	2019	Bedri Selmani (Croatia) v. Republic of Kosovo	ICC	2014 LFI	Decided in favour of the state
4	2020	Fox Marble Holdings Plc (UK) v. Republic of Kosovo	Ad-hoc Arbitration	2015 LFI	Pending
5	2020	Blerim Devolli (Montenegro) v. Republic of Kosovo	ICC	2016 LFI	Decided in favour of the state
6	2020	Iute Credit (Estonia) v. Republic of Kosovo	ICC	2017 LFI	Decided in favour of the state
7	2020	Contour Global (US) v. Republic of Kosovo	ICSID	2018 LFI	Discontinued ambiguity as to official status

SOURCE: REGIONAL MAPPING REPORT ON INVESTOR STATE DISPUTE SETTLEMENT: STATUS QUO AND PROSPECTIVE REFORMS OF THE ISDS STRUCTURES IN THE WESTERN BALKANS – KOSOVO REPORT, KUJTESA NEZAJ (FEBRUARY 2021)

attribution of liability to Kosovo for acts or omissions of UNMIK; intricate scenarios involving questionable privatization processes of formerly socially owned property, at times allegedly tainted by corruption.

A brief analysis of three concluded cases, the awards in relation to which are accessible publicly, will be presented. The full text of the awards of the other cases as listed is not available publicly.

4.1 *ACP Axos Capital GmbH v. Republic of Kosovo*

The Claimant in this case, ACP Axos Capital GmbH, brought claims against the Republic of Kosovo in relation to the acquisition of shares of the Post and

Telecom of Kosovo (PTK), the postal and telecommunications authority in Kosovo. The case was submitted before the ICSID on 22 April 2015 based on the BIT between the Federal Republic of Germany and the Socialist Republic of Yugoslavia concerning the Reciprocal Protection and Encouragement of Investments, which entered into force on 25 October 1990, and the ICSID Convention.[92]

4.1.1 Facts of the Case

Following Kosovo's independence in 2008, the Government decided to offer for tender and sale 75% of PTK.[93] The process was carefully crafted in several phases and included several filters, and the award of the contract was ultimately subject to Parliamentary consent. Only once the Parliament had approved the privatization with a simple majority vote, could Kosovo enter into a Sale and Purchase Agreement with the successful bidder.

Kosovo formally announced a public invitation for participation in the public tender process, with a pre-qualification stage as the first step in the tendering process. Among those potential investors was a consortium comprising of Columbia Capital V LLC, acting as lead member, and Axos.[94] In September 2012, the successful bidders from the first phase were provided with Instructions for the Tender Participants in the second phase. This document contained a very general legal disclaimer shielding Kosovo from any sort of liability in the unlikely event the privatization process would get cancelled. It followed:

> 'The Contracting Authority further reserves the right to cancel the Tender or declare it void or otherwise without effect either in relation to the entire Tender or in relation to an individual Bidder, for any reason whatsoever, until the signing of the Transaction Documents, and that such action does not entitle the Bidder/Selected Bidder to any claim whatsoever against the Government Privatization Committee, the Government of Kosovo, or any of their respective agents, representatives, advisors or consultants'.[95]

A few months later, in December 2012, Columbia, which up to that point had been the lead member of the Consortium, including Axos, withdrew from the Consortium. Another company, Najafi Companies, joined instead. The relevant

92 *Ibid.* par. 1, at 1.
93 *Ibid.* par. 50, 51, 52, at 13.
94 *Ibid.* par. 56, at 14.
95 *Ibid.* par. 62, at 17.

authorities in Kosovo were duly informed of these changes in the Consortium structure and approved them.[96]

In April 2013, the tendering process entered its final phase, and the Government Privatization Committee (GPC) issued a summary report, declaring the Axos and Najafi Consortium as the winning bidder in the privatization tender.[97] The letter, however, denoted that the contract award was provisional and conditional on potential requests for review by unsuccessful tenderers.[98] In the following weeks, a formal contract award notice followed.[99] However, on 24 April 2013, the very day that the formal contract notice was issued, Najafi terminated its cooperation agreement with Axos and requested that Axos notify the authorities of Kosovo of the same.[100] However, Axos did not immediately act upon this request.[101]

In parallel, developments in the internal scene were as dynamic as those concerning the Consortium. In May 2013, the Government submitted the privatization process to scrutiny by the Parliament.[102] The Parliamentary Economic Committee held a public hearing the following month, endorsed the privatization process, and referred the Privatization Report to a plenary session of the Parliament for approval on 30 July 2013.[103] In September 2013, the Privatization Report was brought before the plenary session in three consecutive sessions. However, the Parliament did not have the necessary quorum in either of those sessions to vote on it.[104] Voting failed a fourth time on 26 December 2013 due to lack of quorum.[105]

In December 2013, the GPC held one last meeting to discuss on the unlikely prospect of the Report receiving Parliamentary approval and concluded that there was no basis for further postponement of the transaction, thereby implicitly deciding to cancel the privatization process.[106] This decision was conveyed to Axos the following day, 31 December 2013, during a conference call, and subsequently publicly announced on the Ministry of Economic Development

96 *Ibid.* par. 74, at 20.
97 *Ibid.* par. 88 at 24.
98 *Ibid.* par. 91, at 25.
99 *Ibid.* par. 93, at 26.
100 *Ibid.* par. 94, at 26.
101 *Ibid.* par. 95, at 27.
102 *Ibid.* par. 117, at 33.
103 *Ibid.* par. 120, at 34.
104 *Ibid.* par. 121, at 35.
105 *Ibid.* par. 126, at 36.
106 *Ibid.* par. 127, at 36.

website.[107] A formal letter was sent to Axos on 6 January 2014.[108] On 30 January 2014, Axos notified Kosovo of its intention to file for arbitration.[109]

4.1.2 Claims and Counterclaims of the Parties

Axos as Claimant, sought that the Tribunal (i) declare that it had jurisdiction over the dispute; and as regards the merits of the case, contended that Respondent had breached its obligations under the BIT by (ii) expropriating Claimant's investment; (iii) failing to accord to it fair and equitable treatment; (iv) taking arbitrary measures that have prejudicated Claimant's use of its investment; (v) failing to observe obligations entered into with regard to Claimant's investments; and in effect, Claimant requested that the Tribunal order (vi) Respondent to make full reparation for Claimant's loss arising out of Respondent's treaty violation in the amount of EUR 380.3 million as well as interest thereon; and (vii) bear the costs of the present arbitration proceedings, including those incurred by Claimant.[110]

Kosovo as Respondent sought for its part a Final Award: (i) declaring that the Tribunal did not have jurisdiction; (ii) alternatively, dismissing Axos' claims; (iii) awarding Kosovo such other relief as the Tribunal considers appropriate; and (iv) ordering Axos to pay the costs of this arbitration, including the costs of the Arbitral Tribunal and the legal and other costs incurred by Kosovo on a full indemnity basis, plus interest in an amount to be determined by the Tribunal.[111] Kosovo primarily raised several jurisdictional and admissibility objections. Interestingly, Kosovo did not object the application of the BIT, concluded between Germany and former Yugoslavia.

In response, Axos presented two jurisdictional theories to justify the existence of a protected investment under the Treaty. Claimant contended that the Tribunal had jurisdiction, by claiming that a contract had been concluded between the parties based on Kosovo's Law on Obligations, arising from the exchanges between the parties on 3 April 2013 and 18 April 2013.[112] In the alternative, Claimant asserted that the jurisdiction of the Tribunal stemmed from the Claimant's rightful 'claim to money', arising from the monies spent for the preparation of the tender and know-how it said it had transferred to Kosovo.[113] Interestingly, with respect to the former, Respondent in its submission, did not

107 *Ibid.* par. 129, at 37.
108 *Ibid.* par. 130, at 37.
109 *Ibid.* par. 131, at 38.
110 *Ibid.* par. 46, at 11, 12.
111 *Ibid.* par. 48, at 12.
112 *Ibid.* par. 135, 136, at 39.
113 *Ibid.* par. 137, at 40.

contest the Tribunal's jurisdiction to examine the existence of a valid contract under Kosovo law, but claimed that to establish whether the parties entered into a valid contract, the Tribunal must turn to the relevant administrative public laws, including the Law on Public Procurement, rather than the Law on Obligations.[114]

4.1.3 The Tribunal's Findings

The Tribunal concluded that no valid contract for the purchase of the shares of PTK between Claimant and Respondent ever came into being.[115] Moreover, the Tribunal noted that the bidder at the time of exchanging the letters was not the Claimant, but rather a Consortium comprised of Axos jointly with Najafi. The Tribunal recognized that there could not have been a valid contract prior to the signing of the Sale and Purchase Agreement, as Kosovo had effectively reserved the right to '*cancel the Tender*', as instructed in the tender documents.[116]

The Tribunal further found that the applicable law to the question of contract formation was the administrative law in Kosovo. Therefore, the ICSID Tribunal concluded that it did not have jurisdiction to resolve the present dispute, as it lacked jurisdiction ratione materiae.[117] Finally, the Tribunal dismissed all the other claims raised by Claimant.

Kosovo was entitled to reimbursement from Axos for its reasonably incurred costs, including the costs of arbitration and Kosovo's legal fees and expenses.[118] The award amount totalled USD 1,713,349.40 and EUR 132,446.20.[119]

4.2 *Mabco Construction SA v. Republic of Kosovo*

Mabco Construction SA v. Republic of Kosovo was introduced to ICSID on 15 May 2017. A final award has not been issued yet. However, in late 2020 the Tribunal issued a Decision on Jurisdiction, which is publicly available online. It is unclear from the sources available why the Tribunal bifurcated the proceedings.

The case concerns a very complex set of facts relating to the privatization process of the Grand Hotel, a hotel in the centre of Kosovo's capital, formerly a socially owned enterprise. The claimant brought the proceedings under both the BIT between Switzerland and Kosovo and the 2014 LFI. The Claimant

114 *Ibid.* par. 145, 146, at 42.
115 *Ibid.* par. 152, at 44.
116 Ibid.
117 Ibid.
118 *Ibid.* par. 268, at 72.
119 *Ibid.* par. 274, at 73.

asserts that the Respondent violated its obligations primarily by unlawfully expropriating Claimant's property, denial of fair and equitable treatment, and denial of justice.[120]

4.2.1 Facts of the Case

Until the end of the war in Kosovo in June 1999, Grand Hotel was a socially owned enterprise (SOE). In 2002, UNMIK entrusted the management of the Grand Hotel and other SOEs to a public entity established for that purpose, named the Kosovo Trust Agency (KTA).[121] Shortly after Kosovo's declaration of independence on 17 February 2008, the KTA was transformed into the Privatization Agency of Kosovo (PAK).

Just like KTA, PAK was charged with administering the SOEs and disposing of their assets by creating new companies, known as 'NewCos' and offering them for sale/privatization in a tender process.[122] KTA, and after that PAK, conducted the privatization of Kosovo's SOEs through a Special Spin-Off Privatization Procedure that entailed the creation of a NewCo, to which an SOE's assets were transferred.[123]

Following the conclusion of a very complex tendering process, UTC, a local company owned by Mr. Berisha, was selected as the successful bidder. However, according to the records, Mr. Berisha did not have the necessary financial means to fulfil his obligations under the tender and sought help from other businessmen, the owner of Claimant, Mr. Pacolli, and the owner of NTSH, Mr. Ejupi. According to Mr. Pacolli's testimony during the hearings of this arbitration, the three men had a meeting in Vienna, at which Mr. Berisha told him that he had already paid EUR 500,000 as a deposit for being admitted to the tender process but could not afford to pay the balance of the total price of about EUR 8 million. At that meeting, Messrs. Berisha, Ejupi, and Pacolli decided by oral agreement, allegedly as representatives of their respective companies, to purchase together the Grand Hotel shares, with Claimant and NTSH contributing EUR 4 million and EUR 1 million, respectively.[124]

Claimant maintains that in January 2007, in order to formalize the prior arrangements among UTC, NTSH, and Claimant, Messrs. Pacolli, Ejupi, and Berisha signed an 'Agreement of Good Understanding' (AGU). Under the AGU,

120 International Centre for Settlement of Investment Disputes, ICSID Case No. ARB/17/25 – Decision on Jurisdiction, Mabco Constructions Sa v. Republic of Kosovo (30 October 2020), par. 138, at 21.

121 *Ibid.* par. 142, at 21.

122 *Ibid.* par. 143, 144, at 22.

123 *Ibid.* par. 160, at 24.

124 *Ibid.* par. 166, at 26.

UTC would become the formal owner of the shares of Grand Hotel for two years. Thus, according to paragraph 2 of the AGU, UTC was initially the 'legal purchaser', while Messrs. Ejupi and Pacolli were the 'actual purchasers. With the passing of two years, Claimant, NTSH, and UTC were to officially become joint owners of the shares, with the shares distributed among the three owners as follows: UTC 40%, NTSH 20%, and Claimant 40%.[125]

To that effect, Claimant made a EUR 4 million wire transfer to NTSH. Claimant's first attempt to pay the sum failed, and NTSH was required to return the funds to Mabco. The letter from CBK to Mabco reporting that its initial transfer of funds was unsuccessful was copied to KTA. From what is inferred from the record, KTA did not express any concerns about the fact that the funds were being paid by a party other than the winning bidder.[126] Thus, according to Claimant, KTA knew about and approved of the agreement and the source of the funds. However, according to the PAK leadership, PAK was never made aware of the AGU or any other agreement between the three businessmen.[127]

4.2.2 Claims and Counterclaims

Claimant alleged that it had made a qualifying investment within the meaning of the BIT, the 2014 LFI, and the ICSID Convention.[128] Claimant maintained that it satisfied the jurisdictional requirements since (i) the dispute is a legal one arising directly out of an investment; (ii) the dispute is between a Contracting State and a national of the other Contracting State; and (iii) the parties consented to the settlement of the dispute through ICSID arbitration given that, according to Claimant, Respondent consented to arbitration under both the BIT and the 2014 LFI.[129] In addition, Claimant asserts that its purchase of shares meets all the criteria for an investment under the ICSID Convention established by arbitral jurisprudence: a substantial capital contribution, entailing a certain risk, promising a regular profit and return, and having a certain duration.[130]

Respondent contested the Tribunal's jurisdiction under Article 25(1) of the ICSID Convention on numerous grounds, notably, that it did not consent to arbitration under either the BIT nor the 2014 LFI.[131] Respondent claims that (i) the Tribunal lacks jurisdiction ratione materiae, since Claimant owns no

125 *Ibid.* par. 179, at 30.
126 *Ibid.* par. 330, at 84.
127 *Ibid.* par. 181, at 31.
128 *Ibid.* par. 230, at 48.
129 *Ibid.* par. 244, at 52.
130 *Ibid.* par. 245, at 52.
131 *Ibid.* par. 248, at 53.

qualifying asset in order for either the BTI or the 2014 LFI to apply since it never acquired ownership of, or a right or interest in, the asset at issue in this case.[132] According to Respondent, (ii) the Tribunal lacks jurisdiction ratione personae as well since Claimant is neither an investor nor a foreign investor. If any investment was made, it would have been made by Mr. Pacolli, a national of Kosovo, in his personal capacity. In addition, according to Respondent, neither can Claimant itself be considered a foreign national, in this case, a national of Switzerland, due to the absence of any real economic activity in Switzerland.[133]

4.2.3 The Tribunal's Findings

The main question before the Tribunal concerning its material jurisdiction was whether the particular intangible that Claimant asserts, namely, a claim of entitlement to ownership of shares, may constitute a protected investment under the BIT and the 2014 LFI.[134] The Tribunal found that, depending on the circumstances, a claim of entitlement to an asset is itself capable of constituting an investment under the BIT, provided that it was 'established or acquired'. In the Tribunal's view, Claimant's entitlement claim was established and acquired.[135]

In the Tribunal's view, Claimant's claim of entitlement in the case falls within Article 2(1) of the 2005 LFI. Like the BIT, the 2005 LFI specifically recognizes intangibles as assets amenable to treatment as investments.[136] The Tribunal accordingly considers a claim of entitlement to ownership of shares to be cognizable as a qualifying investment, although that entitlement must eventually be established as a merits matter.[137] Finally, the Tribunal found that, solely to establish jurisdiction on a prima facie basis, and without prejudice to any decision on the merits, Claimant's claim of entitlement may be regarded as an investment.[138]

Concerning the Tribunal's ratione personae jurisdiction, the Tribunal found that the record shows more indication that Mr. Pacolli was representing Claimant and that he had not been acting in an individual capacity. The Tribunal noted that the EUR 4 million transfer was made from Claimant's bank account, was reflected on its balance sheets, and was confirmed by its external auditor. In addition, the decision to invest in Kosovo was brought before and voted

132 *Ibid.* par. 249, at 53.
133 *Ibid.* par. 250, at 54.
134 *Ibid.* par. 307, at 76.
135 *Ibid.* par. 311, at 78.
136 *Ibid.* par. 316, at 79.
137 *Ibid.* par. 318, at 80.
138 *Ibid.* par. 337, at 87.

upon by Claimant's shareholders. The Tribunal thus concluded that the investment was Claimant's.[139]

Interestingly, Respondent also raised denial of justice claims. It contended that Mr. Pacolli, at that time Deputy Prime Minister and Minister of Foreign Affairs of Kosovo, as a member of the Government, would have access to documents and other information, including confidential information, that a party does not ordinarily enjoy vis-à-vis its opponent in an adversarial proceeding. As a Government member, he would also participate in decisions the Respondent will take in this proceeding, including even the decision to advance payment to ICSID of the costs of the arbitration that Mr. Pacolli has himself brought.[140] The Tribunal, however, did not give merit to this claim, recalling that it has already established that the putative investor is Mabco and not Mr. Pacolli. That Mr. Pacolli owns, and controls Claimant is of no consequence, at least as long as the Claimant is not a 'shell company' or otherwise purely fictional.[141] The Tribunal pointed out that although this scenario is highly unusual it sees no basis for treating a national of a host state any differently since he or she is a member of that State's government. As a businessman legitimately operating through a foreign company, he was entitled to the same protections as are available to any other businessman.[142]

4.3 *Bedri Selmani v. Republic of Kosovo*

The dispute, *Bedri Selmani v Republic of Kosovo*, concerned the alleged expropriation of Kosovo's largest network of petrol stations with claims quantified more than EUR 45 million, excluding interest. The case was brought before the ICC Court of Arbitration in April 2019, based on the 2014 LFI, invoking Article 16 of the said law that declares in advance Kosovo's consent to arbitrate on matters falling within the scope of the 2014 LFI. The case rested largely on the proposition that an UNMIK Permission, an ad hoc document issued by the interim UN administrative authority during an initially chaotic transitional period, remained in force more than a decade after its issuance, and continued to bind the independent State that later emerged in the same territory, appearing as Respondent in this dispute.[143]

139 *Ibid.* par. 344, at 90.
140 *Ibid.* par. 487, at 140.
141 *Ibid.* par. 490, at 141.
142 *Ibid.* par. 491, at 142.
143 *Ibid.* par. 629, at 174.

4.3.1 Facts of the Case

Following the calamitous war in Kosovo in 1999, in June of the same year, the UN Security Council passed Resolution 1244, establishing UNMIK, as an interim administration in Kosovo to provide '*transitional administration while establishing and overseeing the development of provisional democratic self-governing institutions to ensure conditions for a peaceful and normal life for all inhabitants in Kosovo*'.[144] UNMIK enjoyed broad executive, legislative, and judiciary powers in every field. Among others, pursuant to Regulation No. 2000/54, UNMIK would administer all '*movable or immovable property*' in the territory of Kosovo, '*where UNMIK has reasonable and objective grounds to conclude that such property*' either (i) belonged to the Federal Republic of Yugoslavia or the Republic of Serbia or any of their organs, or (ii) was 'socially owned property'.[145] Such properties were the properties of Jugopetrol and Beopetrol, that in the 80s had been registered in the commercial courts of former Yugoslavia as SOEs.[146]

Mr. Selmani was a Kosovar businessman who had lived in Croatia for several year and had acquired Croatian citizenship.[147] In early 2000, UNMIK issued a sui generis document titled 'Permission to Operate Previously State (Public)-Owned Fuel Outlets and Establishments (Known as Beopetrol & Jugopetrol) Pending the Registration of Businesses in Kosovo', which granted Kosovo Petrol, owned by Mr. Selamni, the permission to operate the 61 fuel and fuel establishments, once belonging to Beopetrol and Yugopetrol. The Permission contained no express provision about its term of validity. However, it did state that:

> the permission extended in this letter is issued as a measure to ensure that the supply of Petroleum Products … is ensured during this vital winter period, a reference that Kosovo says implies an intended short-term duration.

The Permission also denoted that in due course it would give way to a more regularized licensing process, signalling the document's exceptional nature.[148] In addition, pursuant to this Permission, Kosovo Petrol was authorized to perform all the petroleum trading functions associated with their operation, namely importation, transport, distribution, and sale, as referenced in the

144 United Nations Security Council Res. 12/44 (10 June 1999), Annex 2, par. 5.
145 UNMIK Regulation No. 2000/54 (27 September 2000), Sec. 6.
146 Mabco Constructions Sa v. Republic of Kosovo (n 121), par. 72, at 21.
147 *Ibid.* par. 74, at 21.
148 *Ibid.* par. 89, at 24.

expressly cross-referenced UNMIK Regulation No. 1999/9.[149] UNMIK retained its right of revocation at any time in the event Kosovo Petrol failed to meet its obligations, including the obligation to make monthly rental payments, or if it acted improperly or unlawfully.[150]

The record shows that Kosova Petrol made rental payments in 2000 and 2001. It is undisputed between the parties that Kosova Petrol ceased to make any rent payments from August 2001 onwards.[151]

The main disagreement between the parties was whether, and if so, when did UNMIK terminate the Permission. According to Respondent's line of argument, the termination took place and effect in late 2001. In contrast, Claimant argues that he never received any termination letter and that for many years thereafter, various authorities continued to act on the understanding that the Permission remained in effect.[152] Neither scenario could be supported with documented facts. While there is evidence of a 2001 memorandum by an UNMIK executive that UNMIK was in the process of terminating the Permission due to Claimant's failure and/or refusal to pay taxes that is said to have been attached to the termination letter, which was to be forwarded to Claimant, an archived copy of such letter could never be retrieved from UNMIK's archives.[153] The record, however, shows that there was legal clearance of the final text of the termination letter, dated 14 December 2001.[154] Claimant, on the contrary, claims that he was not in knowledge of any contemplation on the side of UNMIK to terminate the Permission.

Fast forward to 2006; the KTA was established, and certain competencies relating to the administration of SOEs and related assets were transferred to it as a trustee for their owners.[155] According to the record, it appears that KTA was under the assumption that the Permission had not been terminated, given that Kosova Petrol had normally continued its operation and UNMIK had not provided any definitive confirmation of termination in response to an informal inquiry by the KTA.[156] In the meantime, Kosova Petrol continued to de facto possess and operate the petrol stations, not paying anyone any rent.[157]

149 *Ibid.* par. 90, at 25.
150 *Ibid.* par. 89, at 24.
151 *Ibid.* par. 93, at 26.
152 *Ibid.* par. 102, at 28.
153 *Ibid.* par. 102, at 28, 29.
154 *Ibid.* par. 114, at 32.
155 *Ibid.* par. 121, at 35.
156 *Ibid.* par. 132, at 37.
157 *Ibid.* par. 133, at 38.

Only in June 2006 did KTA formally inquire to UNMIK concerning the status of the Permission.[158]

Another set of issues concerned the operation of the petrol stations. Following a 2005 Law on Petroleum passed by the Parliament of Kosovo, any engagement in transporting, storing, or selling petroleum products for commercial purposes 'without a currently valid License' issued by a newly founded entity was forbidden. All licenses issued prior to this law's entry into force would continue to remain valid for four months.[159] This effectively meant that Claimant's license to operate as per the Permission should have expired in 2005.

The Claimant argued that it did not need to apply for the license's renewal, as it had a continuing right to operate under the Permission even after the 2005 Petroleum Law. Mr. Selmani also pointed out that the relevant authorities had offered no objection in the 2005 to early 2008 period to Kosova Petrol's continuing operation of the 34 petrol stations that it had run since the Permission. In 2008, after Kosovo's independence, the relevant ministry issued several licenses to Claimant. Claimant thus argued that the issuance of licenses after 2008 confirmed that the authorities had considered the Permission to form a valid and continuing basis for his entitlement to petroleum trading licenses, even under the licensing regime reflected in the 2005 Petroleum Law.[160]

4.3.2 Claims and Counterclaims

The Claimant alleges that Kosovo, in its capacity as host state, has committed numerous breaches of the substantive obligations set forth in one or more of the 2001 UNMIK Investment Regulation, the 2006 LFI, and the 2014 LFI, listing the claims as follows: (i) breach of fair and equitable treatment; (ii) breach of obligations not to impair investments by unreasonable or discriminatory means; (iii) breach of full protection and security obligations; (iv) breach of protections against expropriation; (v) breach of obligations to respect the rights of foreign investors and to comply with obligations towards such investors, with specific reference to obligations undertaken in the Permission.[161]

In addition to denying these claims on their merits, Respondent raised eight objections against the Tribunal's jurisdiction – namely that the Tribunal lacks jurisdiction (i) ratione personae, because Mr. Selmani is not a qualified 'foreign person' under the 2014 LFI; (ii) ratione materiae, because Mr. Selmani had no lawful property rights qualifying as investments that are entitled to protection

158 *Ibid.* par. 134, at 38.
159 *Ibid.* par. 140, at 40.
160 *Ibid.* par. 145, at 42.
161 *Ibid.* par. 265, at 76.

under the 2006 LFI or the 2014 LFI; in addition, (iii) no alleged conduct, obligations or liability of UNMIK or PAK could be attributable to Kosovo; (iv) there is no 'retroactive' jurisdiction over alleged breaches of instruments predating the 2014 LFI; (v) the majority of Claimant's claims are time-barred; (vi) the claims are barred by the 'fork-in-the-road' provision of the 2014 LFI; (vii) claims about PAK conduct are not arbitrable; and (viii) there are 'no substantive obligations' that could give rise to claims with respect to alleged expropriation by UNMIK, or fair and equitable treatment claims under the 2014 LFI.[162]

4.3.3 The Tribunal's Findings

Respondent's allegations that the Tribunal lacks jurisdiction ratione personae were based on the fact that Mr. Selmani was a resident of Kosovo 'at all material times in dispute' and is, therefore, excluded from the protection of the 2014 LFI, and that he had registered his business using his Kosovo identification and not his Croatian passport.[163] It noted that Claimant counter-argued that his Kosovo citizenship, alongside his Croatian one, does not deprive him of protection under the 2014 LFI, as the law neither denies protection to dual nationals nor requires Kosovar citizens to be domiciled outside of Kosovo.[164]

In addition, Mr. Selmani submits he is also a protected foreign person under the 2001 UNMIK Investment Regulation and the 2006 LFI.[165] On deciding on this issue, the Tribunal first clarified that it would assess the question based on the 2014 LFI since it is this law from which the Tribunal's jurisdiction stems.[166] It concluded that, based on the drafting history of the legal text at hand, Claimant's status as a citizen of Croatia qualifies him as a 'foreign person' under the 2014 LFI, although he also held Kosovar nationality after 2008. The Respondent's objection ratione personae was, therefore, denied.[167]

The Tribunal further reemphasized that it would assess all matters arising from the dispute at hand through the lens of the 2014 LFI only. The Tribunal noted that in interpreting the definition of investment under the 2014 Tribunal, it introduced a temporal layer to the definition as well. According to the requirements set by Article 2(1)(4) of 2014 LFI, assets under its scope must be '*lawfully held … in the Republic of Kosovo*'. The Tribunal calls for attention to the fact that the 'Republic of Kosovo' came into existence with the Declaration of

162 *Ibid.* par. 266, at 76, 77.
163 *Ibid.* par. 273, at 80.
164 *Ibid.* par. 279, at 81.
165 *Ibid.* par. 281, at 82.
166 *Ibid.* par. 285, at 83.
167 *Ibid.* par. 297, at 86.

Independence in February 2008, therefore, the said law applies to investments that, even if originally 'made' in the territory of Kosovo prior to the birth of the Republic, continued after Kosovo's independence to be 'lawfully held' under its laws. This interpretation implicitly excludes from coverage pre-independence investments that were no longer recognized as valid after independence.[168]

The Tribunal noted that the requirement that assets be 'lawfully held' refers to the validity of the 'holding', whether by lease, concession, license, contract, or other mechanisms.[169] To that end, non-compliance with the terms of a lease, concession, license, or contract – such as a failure to pay required rent – might be relevant to merits issues in any eventual dispute over State treatment of the investment, but it would not strip the investment of its status as such, for purposes of the Tribunal's jurisdiction.[170] Although the existence of a termination letter was disputed between the parties, the Tribunal recalled that according to Respondent the letter acknowledged that Kosovo Petrol would continue operating the petrol stations 'until such time as they are ready to be handed over to the successful tender bidders and recipients of licenses'.

Therefore, according to the Tribunal, Kosova Petrol may still have 'lawfully held' the stations for so long as this ad hoc instruction reasonably could be considered to remain in effect.[171] However, after the Declaration of Independence in February 2008, Claimant ceased to 'lawfully hold' any rights in a license to operate the petrol stations for petroleum trading.[172] The Tribunal also recalled that Claimant was issued various petroleum trading licenses from the relevant authorities in Kosovo from 2008 on. So long as Kosova Petrol continued to hold valid licenses of this sort, it did to that extent, have a qualifying investment in Kosovo under the 2014 LFI, which would be sufficient for the purposes of establishing ratione materiae jurisdiction.[173] The Tribunal thus concluded that Claimant had a qualifying investment under the 2014 LFI between 2008 and 2013.[174]

However, the Tribunal noted that most of Claimant's contentions related to rights derived from the continued validity of the Permission. The Tribunal found that the Permission was not a qualifying investment under Article 2(1)(4) of the 2014 LFI, because the temporal requirements of that Article were not

168 *Ibid.* par. 337, at 96.

169 *Ibid.* par. 340, at 97.

170 Ibid.

171 *Ibid.* par. 345, at 98.

172 *Ibid.* par. 348, at 99.

173 *Ibid.* par. 351, at 100.

174 *Ibid.* par. 353, at 101.

met. The Permission, therefore, cannot be the basis for any legal claims under the 2014 LFI.[175]

Interesting questions of public international law were also raised during this arbitration, related to the possibility of, and if so, the degree to which acts and omissions of UNMIK could be attributable to Kosovo. The Tribunal noted that following its independence, the Republic of Kosovo would be bound by obligations undertaken by UNMIK or liabilities incurred by UNMIK, only to the extent it expressly agreed to be so bound.[176] Accordingly, based on the Ahtisaari Plan, Kosovo's Declaration of Independence, and its Constitution, Kosovo explicitly agreed to assume obligations certain obligations from the period of UNMIK administration. Nonetheless, the Permission did not qualify as any of these. The Tribunal thus concluded that UNMIK's conduct prior to Kosovo's independence was not attributable to the Republic of Kosovo following its independence, nor did Kosovo agree to assume any liabilities that UNMIK might have had for any pre-independence breach. Therefore, the Tribunal granted Kosovo's jurisdictional objection to any claims predicated on such attribution.[177]

An interesting allegation of Respondent was that the Tribunal lacked jurisdiction due to a 'fork in the road provision' in the 2014 LFI, preventing matters from being referred to arbitration in the event the parties have already elected courts as the fora of choice. However, it interpreted Article 16(2) of the 2014 LFI to mean that it does not preclude the parties from ever pursuing another – regardless of the outcome of the first remedy, or even if the initial proceedings remain pending without resolution. A more explicit text would be required to that effect.[178]

Ultimately, the Tribunal dismissed all of Claimant's claims on their merits – that Kosovo has breached its obligations under the 2014 LFI. It ordered Claimant to pay 75% of Kosovo's costs, without pre-Award interest; and accordingly, awarded Kosovo a total of USD 1,477,165.38 and EUR 71,653.305 from Claimant, comprised of USD 1,302,165.38 and EUR 71,653.305 for Kosovo's costs and fees (excluding arbitration costs) and USD 175,000 for Kosovo's share of the costs of arbitration fixed by the Tribunal.[179]

175 *Ibid.* par. 359, at 102.
176 *Ibid.* par. 390, at 111.
177 *Ibid.* par. 397, at 114.
178 *Ibid.* par. 460, at 130.
179 *Ibid.* par. 644, at 180.

5 Ongoing Reforms

The most substantial recent development in Kosovo concerning investment protection and investor-state dispute resolution is the entry into force of the new Law on Sustainable Investment. This law aims to promote, encourage, and protect sustainable investment and exports in the Republic of Kosovo, through laying out rules and provisions that guarantee a higher level of protection for the investor and investment, supported by newly established specialized bodies.

As discussed above, relevant to this study are especially LSI's dispute settlement provisions, which have finally abrogated the previous contentious provisions on arbitration. Moreover, LSI aligns Kosovo with the newly developing trend worldwide of providing mediation as a means of resolving investor-state disputes. Recent developments in Kosovo have the potential to create synergies for positively affecting the investment landscape. Briefly discussed below, are recent developments concerning the strategic framework (5.1); and the establishment of a specialized Commercial Court (5.2).

5.1 *Strategic Framework Developments*

Several data analyses related to FDI, conducted through the years by organizations such as the WB and OECD, have attributed Kosovo's unsatisfactory performance in attracting FDI to a lack of a comprehensive strategy framework for attracting, promoting, and facilitating FDI, as well as to a lack of solid inter-agency or inter-ministerial coordination mechanisms.[180] In recent years, however, Kosovo seems to have acted upon these findings. In May 2022, the Government passed the National Development Strategy 2023 (NDS 2030), a holistic cross-sectorial and cross-ministerial strategic development document, aiming at providing a vision for the country's sustainable development and serving as a 'horizontal agenda'.[181]

Relevant to this study, the third pillar of NDS 2030, on security and the rule of law, recognizes the increase of access to alternative dispute resolution mechanisms as an indicator of the strategic objective of providing genuine access to justice.[182] Specific strategic aims related to the rule of law sector have been articulated in the Rule of Law Strategy 2021–2026. While this strategy does not

180 Competitiveness in Southeast Europe 2021 (n 10), at 1044, 1045.

181 National Strategy and Action Plan for Development 2030 (March 2023), at 5.

182 *Ibid.* at 43.

specifically refer to ISDS, it calls for measures to promote the use of alternative dispute resolution mechanisms to decrease the backlog of court cases.[183]

5.2 *The Establishment of a Specialized Commercial Court*

In 2022, the Parliament adopted the Law on the Commercial Court, which established a special court for handling business disputes fairly, efficiently, and predictably. The Commercial Court has jurisdiction over economic disputes between legal and natural persons, including reorganization, bankruptcy, and liquidation of economic persons; disputes regarding impingement of competition, and protection of property rights and intellectual property rights across the entire territory of Kosovo.[184] More specifically, according to Article 10(3) of the Law on the Commercial Court, a special division for disputes related to foreign investors, with jurisdiction for the whole territory of Kosovo, is established within the Court's Department for Economic Matters.[185] The Commercial Court now has exclusive jurisdiction concerning the recognition and enforcement of domestic and international arbitral awards.[186]

The Commercial Court has recently completed its first year of operation. Although it started with a massive inherited backlog of cases, its case-resolution rate for the first year was 113%.[187] The creation of this specialized court is aimed at enabling a more foreseeable, sustainable, and business-friendly environment, through providing effective and timely dispute resolution.

---

183 Strategy on Rule of Law 2021–2026 (July 2021), at 27.

184 Law No. 08/L-015 on Commercial Court, Art. 2.

185 *Ibid.* Art. 10(3).

186 Ibid Art. 13(1)(1.3).

187 Kosovo Judicial Council, Një vit me Gjykatën Komerciale (29 October 2023): https://komerciale.gjyqesori-rks.org/2023/08/23/nje-vit-me-gjykaten-komerciale/

CHAPTER 15

Investment Protection and Investor-State Dispute Resolution in Montenegro

Aneta Spaić and Milana Ranković

1 Introduction

The legal framework for international arbitration is tremendously relevant as it underpins the effectiveness and reliability of arbitration as the most common method of resolving international disputes. As such, it enhances global trade and foreign investments. Montenegro's strategic position as an appealing destination for foreign investments has influenced legislators to provide an adequate legal framework and conditions for the development of an attractive business environment in Montenegro.[1]

The European integration process has established standards that Montenegro must meet in order to gain accession to the European Union. The formal start of European integration process, assuming harmonization of the Montenegrin and EU laws, started with the Stabilization and Association Agreement signed in 2007 between the European Communities and their Member States and Montenegro. This agreement envisaged the legal and political development of Montenegrin systems, in accordance with the principles of the rule of law, human and civic freedoms, economic freedoms and institutions and mechanisms of the free market securing equality for all citizens of Montenegro.[2]

Within the area of Rule of Law, enhancing the efficacy of the judiciary, is one of the most important strategic goals and arbitration, as a method of Alternative Dispute Resolution (ADR), emerges as a potent mechanism in the pursuit of this objective.

In fact, the rising costs of litigation and time delays continue to plague litigants, gave more importance to various means of settling disputes outside of the courtroom such as early neutral evaluation, negotiation, conciliation, mediation and arbitration. It is nowadays widely assumed that it is in the best

1 Proposal of the Arbitration Act of Montenegro 2015 <www.skupstina.me> accessed 10 April 2024.

2 Aneta Spaić, *Commercial and Economic Law* (Kluwer Law International 2018), 15.

 | DOI:10.1163/9789004729889_016

interest of commercial entities to have their disputes resolved by means of alternative dispute resolution. In the national arena the Law on alternative dispute resolutions has been adopted in 2020,[3] whereas the Law on Arbitration[4] has been incorporated in the Montenegrin legislation as a separate piece of Montenegrin legislation in 2015.

Sources of law on International Arbitration in Montenegro include Arbitration Act of Montenegro, multilateral and bilateral treaties. The most important Conventions to which Montenegro is a party, and that are analyzed in this Chapter are: New York Convention, European Convention on International Commercial Arbitration 1961 and Washington Convention on the Settlement of Investment Disputes Between States and Nationals of Other States of 1965 (ICSID Convention).

Before the adoption of the Arbitration Act in Montenegro arbitration procedure was regulated by the Civil Procedure Code (IV)[5] and Private International Law Act (which provided provisions on recognition and enforcement), which represented a fusion of the solutions inherited from the Yugoslav system with solutions UNCITRAL Model Law.[6] Having in mind tendency of the contemporary countries worldwide to regulate arbitration in separate piece of legislation, Montenegro in 2015 has adopted Arbitration Act, which regulates international and domestic arbitration, the recognition and enforcement of arbitral awards, and jurisdiction and procedure of courts in relation to arbitration.[7]

Its provisions mostly rely on the on the UNCITRAL Model Law, which sets standards for International Arbitration worldwide and serves as the basis for harmonization of Arbitration Law.[8] Namely, legislation based or influenced by

3 „Official Gazzette of Montenegro“ No. 77/2020.

4 „Official Gazzette of Montenegro“ No . 47/2015.

5 “Official Gazzete of Montenegro“ No. 22/04 and 76/06.

6 Maja Kostić-Mandić, *Međunarodno privatno pravo* (Pravni fakultet Univerzitet Crne Gore 2017) 210.

7 Art. 1, Arbitration Act, “Official Gazette of Montenegro“, No. 47/2015.

8 At the moment of writing this Chapter the procedure for the amendments of the Montenegrin Arbitration Act have been initiated by Ministry of Justice of Montenegro. Namely, the fact that Arbitration Act entered into force more than eight years ago and was not amended, the importance of procedures that are resolved through arbitration, as well as social environment in which the law is applied, imposed the need for amendments to the Arbitration Act, especially in the part that refers to the more detailed provisions on the arbitration proceedings, as well as recognition of all jurisdictions and procedural possibilities. However, suggested amendments will not significantly change existing Act. Government of Montenegro, Information on the need to amend the Arbitration Act, December 2023, available at: <https://www.gov.me/dokumenta/84f26d37-c22e-4fee-8e1d-a4061a3d73da> accessed 10 April 2024.

the Model Law has been adopted in 91 States, in a total of 124 jurisdictions.[9] Modal Law provides legal certainty to parties that their dispute will be resolved by rules that are accepted in many countries and overall, it contributes to the popularity of arbitration as a method of dispute resolution. This fact provided a certain degree of credibility to Montenegro as well, as a territory where legal disputes are being resolved in accordance with highest international standards, therefore strengthening rule of law and attractiveness of Montenegro for foreign investments.

2 Arbitrability

Arbitration can be agreed only if dispute in question is arbitrable. Traditionally, arbitrability is one of the conditions for the validity of arbitration agreement, which imposes general restrictions on the admissibility of arbitration in concrete case. The boundaries have to be taken into consideration not only by the arbitral tribunal, but also by the national courts, who may decide on this issue when deciding upon the annulment of the arbitral award[10] or in procedure of recognition of foreign arbitral awards.

Montenegrin Arbitration Act, however, does not provide clear guidelines on arbitrability and what disputes may be resolved by arbitration. Instead, it provides that arbitration cannot be conducted when another law stipulates that certain disputes cannot be settled by arbitration.[11] If on the other hand, dispute in question is not arbitrable, it will serve as a ground for the annulment of domestic arbitral award (Art. 48, para.2, subpara.1) or it may serve as a ground for refusal of recognition of foreign arbitral award (Art. 52, para.2, subpara.1).

Therefore, one may say that in Montenegrin law, parties are free to agree to resolve via arbitration any property dispute regarding rights over which the parties have full disposal, except for disputes for which the Law provided exclusive jurisdiction of the court – *objective arbitrability*[12] or *arbitrability ratione materiae.*[13] The exclusive jurisdiction of Montenegrin courts exists when it is

9 UNCITRAL Model Law on International Commercial Arbitration (1985), with amendments as adopted in 2006. Status is available at <https://uncitral.un.org/en/texts/arbitration/modellaw/commercial_arbitration/status> accessed 10 April 2024.

10 Art. 47, Arbitration Act.

11 Art. 3, para. 2, Arbitration Act.

12 Jean-Francois Poudret and Sebastien Besson, *Comparative Law of International Arbitration* (Sweet & Maxwell 2007) 281.

13 Gašo Knežević and Vladimir Pavić, *Arbitraža i ADR* (Pravni fakultet Univerziteta u Beogradu, Centar za izdavaštvo i informisanje 2013) 52.

expressly prescribed by law,[14] such as proceedings in which the subject matter is a property right over immovable property or the lease of immovable property located in Montenegro.[15] Further, any natural or legal person may agree to arbitration, including for disputes with the State, its organs, institutions and enterprises in which it has a shareholding – *arbitrability ratione personae.*

In that regard, Art. 2 of Arbitration Act provides that arbitration shall mean conduct of arbitral proceedings before an arbitral tribunal for the resolution of a dispute in which the parties are natural persons with a domicile or habitual residence in Montenegro, and/or legal persons. A legal person means a public authority, state administration body, other legal person exercising public powers, local self-government body, company, public enterprise, public institution, non-governmental organization, investment fund or other fund, as well as other association or organization which within its operations continuously or occasionally gains or obtains assets and manages them. Basically, arbitration can be contracted by anyone who, in accordance with the provisions of the law governing civil proceedings, has the ability to be a party to the proceedings.

With this in mind, the question of whether a dispute can be arbitrable can be raised at different stages of the arbitration procedure:1) at the beginning of the proceedings, before the arbitral tribunal, which shall decide whether it has jurisdiction in the case; 2) may be referred to a state court, which will be required to determine whether the subject matter is in dispute arbitrable; 3) in the context of proceedings before a national court concerning the annulment of decisions; 4) before the court deciding on the recognition and enforcement of the decision.[16]

Some examples of the disputes that are regarded as non-arbitrable in Comparative Law are: competition law, law on intellectual property and bankruptcy law disputes.[17] Also, usually certain family law matters, and inheritance matters are reserved for the national courts. It is important to highlight that domestic law does not make agreement void if the dispute in question is not arbitrable. Therefore, arbitration agreement does not have legal effects only when it comes to the arbitration in question.[18]

---

14 Art. 107, Private International Law Act, "Official Gazette of Montenegro" No. 1/2014, 6/2014 – corr., 11/2014 – corr, 14/2014 and 47/2015 – another law).

15 Art. 119, para. 1, Private International Law Act.

16 Art. 5, para. 2, subpara. (a), New York Convention on the Recognition and Enforcement of Foreign Arbitral Awards of 1958.

17 Maja Stanivuković, *Međunarodna arbitraža sa odabranim prilozima* (JP Službeni Glasnik 2013) 106.

18 *Ibid.*

Finally, we suggest that in proposed amendments of Arbitration Act, it provides clear guidelines when arbitration agreement can be concluded and conditions for arbitrability of the dispute, in order to avoid future disputes over this issue.[19] This will enhance legal certainty, and provide precise answers when it comes to the arbitration.

3 The Arbitration Agreement

Arbitration is a creature of party autonomy.[20] Arbitration exists because of the mutual consent of the parties to settle their dispute in front of the arbitral tribunal,[21] and it also imposes on them negative obligation-not to initiate proceedings in any other forum.[22]Parties should express this intent clearly and unambiguously, the agreement should also be evidenced in writing and signed to ensure its validity according to the applicable law.[23]

Article 9 of the Montenegrin Arbitration Act defines arbitration agreement in terms similar as Modal law,[24] as the agreement to submit to arbitration all or certain disputes which have arisen or which may arise between them in respect of a defined legal relationship, whether contractual or not.

An arbitration agreement may be concluded in the form of a separate agreement or in the form of an arbitration clause as an integral part of a contract

19 This solution is widely accepted in comparative Law of the counties in region. For instance, Article 5 of the Serbian Arbitration Act (Official Journal of the Republic of Serbia, No. 46/2006) defines arbitrability and provides: „Parties may agree to an arbitration for the resolution of a pecuniary dispute concerning rights they can freely dispose of, except for disputes that are reserved to the exclusive jurisdiction of courts. Each natural or legal person, including the State, its instrumentalities, institutions and companies in which a State has a property interest, may agree to an arbitration. Anyone having the capacity to be a party in the civil procedure pursuant to the provisions of the statute regulating civil procedure may agree to an arbitration.“

20 Robert Merkin and Louis Flannery, *Arbitration Act 1996* (Informa Law from Routledge 2014) 101.

21 Margaret L. Moses, *The principles and practice of International Commercial Arbitration* (Cambridge University Press 2012) 19.

22 Philippe Fouchard and Berthold Goldman, *Fouchard, Gaillard, Goldman on International Commercial Arbitration* (Emmanuel Gaillard and John Savage ed, Kluwer Law International 1999) 382.

23 Julian Lew, Loukas Mistelis and Stefan Kroll, *Comparative International Commercial Arbitration* (Kluwer Law International 2003) 8-1.

24 David St John Sutton, Judith Gill and Matthew Gearing, *Russell on Arbitration* (24th edn Sweet & Maxwell 2015) 7-008.

between the parties on a legal transaction between them.[25] In Montenegrin Arbitration Law, the conditions for validity of the arbitration agreement are: written form (that arbitration agreement is concluded in writing), arbitrability[26] and legal capacity of parties.[27]

Art.9 para. 4, similarly like Art. 7 of Model Law, specifies that arbitration agreement is concluded in writing if: 1) it is contained in documents signed by the parties or has been concluded in an exchange of messages by means of communication which provide a written record of the agreement of the parties, whether or not those messages have been signed by the parties; 2) after an orally concluded arbitration agreement one party sends to the other party a notice in writing referring to a previously concluded oral agreement and the other party fails to object to the contents of the received notice in a timely manner, which is considered to constitute acceptance of the offer according to the usages of the trade; 3) the parties in a written contract make a reference to another document containing an arbitration agreement (general terms of business, general terms for conclusion of legal transaction, text of another agreement etc.) provided that the purpose of such reference is to make the arbitration agreement an integral part of the main contract; 4) a bill of lading contains an express reference to an arbitration clause in a charter party; 5) the claimant initiates arbitral proceedings in writing, and the respondent expressly accepts arbitration and agrees to it in writing or in the statement made on the record at the hearing or takes part in arbitral proceedings and does not deny the existence of the arbitration agreement or fails to object to the jurisdiction of the arbitral tribunal before raising issues related to the substance of the dispute.[28]

Parties are advised to commit their due attention to the drafting of the arbitration agreement. Unclear or faulty arbitration agreements may result in prolonged legal disputes over jurisdiction, both initially and when attempting to enforce the arbitration award.

Similarly, as in the other Model Law countries, there are four key elements that arbitration agreement shall contain: clear obligation on the parties, choice of the arbitration as a method of dispute resolution, scope of the issues to be decided in arbitration and it should be clear that decision made by the arbitral

25 Art. 9, Arbitration Act.

26 Art. 48 and 52, Arbitration Act.

27 Maja Kostić-Mandić, *Međunarodno privatno pravo* (Pravni fakultet Univerzitet Crne Gore 2017) 215.

28 Art. 9, Arbitration Act; Maja Kostić-Mandić, *IEL Private International Law of Montenegro* (Kluwer Law International 2023) 694.

tribunal shall be final and binding.[29] If parties have opted for the institutional arbitration, in that case identification of arbitral institution is also essential. Besides these essential elements, arbitration clause can contain additional elements such as: choice of the seat of the arbitration, number of the arbitrators, language, choice of the applicable law and others.

4 Jurisdiction Issues and State Courts

Jurisdiction of arbitral tribunal is derived from the parties' agreement, and it is limited to the matters which they have agreed to submit to arbitration.[30] If the arbitral tribunal exceeds its jurisdiction and decides on matters beyond the scope of the arbitration agreement, then enforcement of that decision can be questioned at a later stage.[31]

Competence-competence principle is enshrined in Art.19 of Montenegrin Arbitration Act,[32] which provides that arbitrator is authorized to consider and decide disputes over its own jurisdiction, which shall be determined by the agreement between the parties.[33] The arbitral tribunal takes into account its competence, as well as the complaint about the existence or validity of the arbitration agreement.[34]

Jurisdiction is notably affected by the fact that arbitration is a product of contract.[35] Therefore, *competence-competence* principle is further related to the principle of the autonomy of the arbitration clause. As relates to the arbitrator's jurisdiction, it is frequently considered together with the overarching authority of arbitrators to make decisions regarding their jurisdiction.[36] The doctrine of separability is embedded in the Art. 19, para.3, and provides that arbitration clause in main contract is separate agreement and shall be treated independently of the other terms of the contract, when ruling on an objection

29 Maja Stanivuković, *Međunarodna arbitraža sa odabranim prilozima* (JP Službeni Glasnik 2013) 106.

30 Nigel Blackaby, Constantine Partasides et al., *Redfern and Hunter on International Arbitration* (6th edn, Kluwer Law International 2017) 1–58.

31 Gašo Knežević and Vladimir Pavić, *Arbitraža i ADR* (Pravni fakultet Univerziteta u Beogradu, Centar za izdavaštvo i informisanje 2013) 58.

32 Gary Born, *International Commercial Arbitration* (Kluwer Law International 2009) 853.

33 Art.19, para. 1, Arbitration Act.

34 Art.19, para. 2, Arbitration Act.

35 Robert Merkin and Louis Flannery, *Arbitration Act 1996* (Informa Law from Routledge 2014) 101.

36 Julian Lew, Loukas Mistelis and Stefan Kroll, *Comparative International Commercial Arbitration* (Kluwer Law International 2003) 6–16.

with respect to the existence or validity of the arbitration agreement. A decision by the arbitral tribunal that the contract containing an arbitration clause is null and void, shall not entail the invalidity of that clause.

The core principle of this doctrine asserts that the validity of an arbitration clause is independent of the validity of the main contract, and similarly, the validity of the main contract is independent of the arbitration clause.[37] Arbitration clause is autonomous contract and has independent legal destiny. Separability safeguards the integrity of the arbitration agreement and serves a crucial function in guaranteeing that the parties' intent to resolve disputes through arbitration remains resilient. Moreover, it safeguards the jurisdiction of the arbitration tribunal. While the doctrine of competence-competence grants authority to the tribunal to determine its jurisdiction independently, the principle of separability ensures its capability to rule on the substantive issues as well.[38]

Plea as to the lack of jurisdiction and exceeding the scope of authority shall be raised by the respondent not later than the submission of the statement of defense in which the respondent raised issues related to the substance of the dispute. A plea that the arbitral tribunal is exceeding the scope of its authority shall be raised by the party as soon as the matter alleged to be beyond the scope of its authority is raised during the arbitral proceedings. A party is not precluded from raising a plea that the tribunal lacks jurisdiction by the fact that he has appointed, or participated in the appointment of, an arbitrator. If delay is justified, arbitral tribunal can decide to accept later plea. The arbitral tribunal may rule on a plea either as a preliminary question or in an award on the merits. If the arbitral tribunal rules on a plea as a preliminary question, any party may request, within thirty days from the date of service of that ruling, the Commercial Court to decide the matter. The court decision shall be subject to no appeal. While the court proceedings for pleas referred are pending, the arbitral tribunal may continue the proceedings and make decision resolving the dispute.[39]

The arbitration agreement is same as the agreement on exclusive jurisdiction of the Courts,[40] and it means that the parties are not allowed to submit their dispute to any other forum.[41] Relatedly, Article 10 of the Arbitration Act,

37 *Ibid.*, 6–9.

38 *Ibid.*, 6–10.

39 Art. 20, Arbitration Act.

40 Gary Born, *International Commercial Arbitration* (Kluwer Law International 2009) 1024.

41 Nigel Blackaby, Constantine Partasides et al., *Redfern and Hunter on International Arbitration* (6th edn, Kluwer Law International 2017) 2-01.

provides that if the parties have agreed to arbitration for the resolution of a certain dispute, the court to which a claim in the same dispute between the same parties has been filed, upon the party's objection submitted no later than in response to a claim, will declare itself incompetent, cancel the actions taken in the procedure and dismiss the claim, unless it finds that the arbitration agreement is not valid, has ceased to be valid or unenforceable.

In Montenegro, the Commercial Court in Podgorica has the jurisdiction to decide on certain matters as to arbitration assistance and has an important role to play through various stages of the arbitral process. In the absence of such intervention and assistance, the fair resolution of disputes before an impartial tribunal may not be achieved.

There is a tendency to limit the possibilities of court intervention in the course of an arbitration.[42] Therefore, the Art. 5 of the Arbitration Act provides that the court shall not intervene except where so provided in this Law. Commercial Court of Montenegro undertakes activities with regards to arbitration assistance: for decision on the appointment of arbitrators, objection as to the lack of jurisdiction of the arbitral tribunal, service of the award, determination of the application for setting aside an arbitral award and the application for recognition of a foreign arbitral award or interim measure. Court can also order an interim measure of protection before or during arbitral proceedings, upon request of a party.[43] When ordering an interim measure in arbitration proceedings, the court shall act in accordance with the rules of procedure of enforcement and security, irrespective of whether the seat of an arbitral tribunal is in the territory of Montenegro, while taking into consideration the specific features of international arbitration.[44]

Also, Art. 39 provides that the arbitral tribunal or a party with the approval of the arbitral tribunal may request from Commercial Court in Montenegro, legal assistance in taking evidence that the arbitral tribunal itself could not take. The court will take evidence within its competence and according to the law governing taking evidence before that court, and also arbitrators can participate in this procedure. Legal assistance in taking evidence and service of a foreign arbitral award shall be provided by a court having subject matter jurisdiction for provision of legal assistance requested, while the court in the territory of which a certain action is to be undertaken shall have territorial jurisdiction.[45]

42 *Ibid.*, 7–63.
43 Art. 11, Arbitration Act.
44 Art. 29, Arbitration Act.
45 Art. 6, Arbitration Act.

5 Constitution of the Arbitral Tribunal, Arbitrator Ethics and Accountability

Arbitration procedure is conducted in front of the arbitral tribunal consisting of one or more arbitrators. Role and position of the arbitrators in Montenegro is provided by the Arbitration Act, which stipulate that the arbitrator can be any natural person with legal capacity, regardless of nationality.[46] Law does not impose limitations regarding capacity of an arbitrator and provides parties with freedom in determining arbitrators as well as the procedure for their nomination.[47]

Rules regarding the composition of arbitral tribunal are provided by Art. 12–18, and are based on the principle of party autonomy. Article 12 of the Law on Arbitration allows parties to determine number of arbitrators and if arbitration agreement provides for more than one arbitrator, there must be an odd number of arbitrators. If the parties did not determine the number of arbitrators, the arbitral tribunal shall consist of three arbitrators.[48] It is considered that three arbitrators will provide the necessary majority, objectivity and professionalism in decision-making, but will not cause significant increase in cost and have other negative consequences on the effectiveness of the arbitration.

The effectiveness of arbitration proceedings significantly relies on the skills and expertise of the selected arbitrators.[49] However, it is essential that arbitrators are impartial and independent in relation to the parties and the subject of the dispute,[50] and to conscientiously and efficiently perform duty of an arbitrator.

Parties are free to agree on procedure for appointment of the arbitrators and if parties fail to reach such agreement, arbitrators will be appointed in accordance with procedure provided by Arbitration Act.[51] In situations when case is to be resolved by sole arbitrator, the arbitrator shall be appointed by mutual agreement of the parties within thirty days, from the date when one party invites the other party to jointly appoint the arbitrator.[52] If a sole arbitrator is not appointed by mutual agreement of the parties, the appointment

46 Art.13, Arbitration Act.

47 Julian Lew, Loukas Mistelis and Stefan Kroll, *Comparative International Commercial Arbitration* (Kluwer Law International 2003) 10-4.

48 Art. 12, para.3, Arbitration Act.

49 Nigel Blackaby, Constantine Partasides et al., *Redfern and Hunter on International Arbitration* (6th edn, Kluwer Law International 2017) 1–71.

50 Art. 15, para 1, Arbitration Act.

51 Art. 13, para 2, Arbitration Act.

52 Art.13, para 3, Arbitration Act.

shall be made by a legal or a natural person designated by the parties under the agreement and if they have not designated appointing authority or if the appointing authority fails to appoint a sole arbitrator, decision on appointment shall be made by Commercial Court of Montenegro. If parties agreed on the institutional arbitration, and if the arbitration rules adopted by an arbitral institution provide for a mechanism for choosing or designating an appointing authority, the appointing authority shall be designated in accordance with those rules.[53]

On the other hand, if a dispute is resolved by three arbitrators, each party shall appoint one arbitrator within thirty days from the date of an invitation to do so from the other party. If the requested party fails to appoint an arbitrator within the set time limit, the arbitrator shall be appointed by the appointing authority, and if the appointing authority has not been designated or if it fails to appoint the arbitrator, decision on appointment shall be made by the Commercial Court of Montenegro.[54] In case a panel of arbitrators is composed of more than three arbitrators, arbitrators shall be appointed in same way, and each party shall appoint an equal number of arbitrators.

The presiding arbitrator of an arbitral tribunal shall be chosen by the appointed arbitrators within thirty days from the date of their appointment. If the arbitrators fail to choose the presiding arbitrator within the set time limit, presiding arbitrator shall be appointed by the appointing authority, and if the appointing authority has not been designated or if it fails to appoint the presiding arbitrator, decision on appointment shall be made by the Commercial Court of Montenegro.[55]

Arbitrators have a duty to give the statement on acceptance of their appointment in writing and to undertake actions in the arbitral proceedings in a timely manner and ensure that any delay in the proceedings is avoided.[56]

Integrity of arbitration proceedings depends on the ethics of the arbitrators, so that independence and impartiality of arbitrators is first and most important duty.[57] Therefore, article 15 of the Arbitration Act imposes an obligation on arbitrators to disclose any circumstances which shall give a rise to justifiable doubts as to his independence or impartiality, from the time of his appointment and throughout the arbitral proceedings. Further, arbitrator can

53 Art.13, para.5, Arbitration Act.

54 Art.13, para.6, Arbitration Act.

55 Art.13, para.7, Arbitration Act.

56 Art.14, Arbitration Act.

57 Julian Lew, Loukas Mistelis and Stefan Kroll, *Comparative International Commercial Arbitration* (Kluwer Law International 2003) 11-1.

be challenged only in case that there are circumstances which give a rise to his independence or impartiality or if he does not possess the required qualifications agreed by parties. These are the only grounds for challenge of the arbitrators. A party may challenge an arbitrator appointed by him, or in whose appointment he has participated, only if the ground for challenge occurred or if the party becomes aware of it after the arbitrator has been appointed.[58]

Procedure for challenging an arbitrator is provided in the article 16 of the Arbitration Act, which provides that parties are free to agree on the procedure for appointing the arbitrators, and if they fail to do so, a party can in fifteen days from the date of becoming aware of the appointment of an arbitrator or of becoming aware of any grounds for challenge, submit a written request for the challenge of an arbitrator to the arbitral tribunal. Unless the challenged arbitrator withdraws from his office or the other party agrees to the request for challenge, the arbitral tribunal, including the challenged arbitrator, shall decide on the challenge without delay. If the parties do not agree on challenging an arbitrator or if the arbitral tribunal rejects the request for challenging an arbitrator, the challenging party may submit such request to the Commercial Court of Montenegro, within thirty days from the date of receipt of the decision rejecting the challenge. This decision is subject to no appeal. The arbitral tribunal can proceed with arbitration and make an arbitral award even if the procedure upon the request for challenging an arbitrator is pending.

The Arbitration Act also provides rules on the termination of the arbitrator's mandate. Therefore, if an arbitrator is no longer able to perform his duty due to legal or factual reasons, his duty as an arbitrator shall cease if he withdraws from that duty or the parties agree on the termination of his duty. Also, if the parties have not agreed otherwise in the arbitration agreement, during the arbitration proceedings they may agree on the termination of the duties of an arbitrator who fails or delays the fulfillment of his duties.

If the parties do not agree on the termination of the duties of the arbitrator, the party who considers that the arbitrator is no longer able to perform his duties or does not take timely actions in the arbitration procedure, may submit a request to the appointing authority or the court referred to in Article 6 paragraph 1 of this law to pass the decision on the termination of the duties of the arbitrator. If the arbitrator withdraws from his duties or the parties have agreed on the termination of the arbitrator's duties, it is not considered that the arbitrator has thereby acknowledged, that is, that the parties have established the validity of the reason for the termination of the arbitrator's duties.[59]

58 Art.15, Arbitration Act.

59 Art. 17, Arbitration Act.

6 Third Parties, Joinder and Consolidation

The Arbitration Act does not contain any provision about third parties, joinder and consolidation, which can cause problems in situations when the seat of arbitration is in Montenegro and when Montenegrin Arbitration Act applies. The questions of consolidation and joinder are often regarded as issues that are likely to cause problems in arbitration practice.[60] Namely, the parties involved in arbitration might consider involving or adding a third party, such as an insurer or in another relevant person, who has a connection to the dispute. Or there are two arbitrations of similar questions of law and fact, between same parties, when an issue arises if those two arbitrations can be consolidated and decided in one proceeding by same arbitral tribunal.

However, the Arbitration Court of the Chamber of Commerce in Montenegro tried to compensate this deficiency in legislation, by adopting new and contemporary Arbitration Rules before the Arbitration Court at the Montenegrin Chamber of Commerce in 2023,[61] which are completely harmonized with the UNCITRAL Arbitration Rules 2021.[62]

These Rules apply if the parties have agreed upon their application or if the parties have agreed that the dispute will be resolved by an arbitral tribunal formed in accordance with these Rules or that they will submit the dispute for resolution to the Arbitration Court, they are considered to have agreed to the application of these Rules, if the arbitration procedure was initiated after their entry into force.[63] Also, the parties may agree that the "Arbitration Rules of the United Nations Commission on International Trade Law (UNCITRAL) before the Arbitration Court of the Chamber of Commerce of Montenegro" will be applied to the conduct of the dispute before the Arbitration Court.

Rules about consolidation are provided in Art. 11 of the Arbitration Rules, which provides that at the proposal of a party, the Presidency can consolidate two or more procedures that follow these rules: if all parties agree to the consolidation or if all claims from the proceedings are within the scope of the

---

60 Nigel Blackaby, Constantine Partasides et al., Redfern and Hunter on International Arbitration (6th edn, Kluwer Law International 2017) 1.111.

61 Arbitration Rules in front of Arbitration Court of the Montenegrin Chamber of Commerce, „Official Gazzete of Montenegro"no. 112/23. Available at: <https://komora.me/pkcg/arbitrazni-sud>, accessed 19. april 2024.

62 UNCITRAL Arbitration Rules 2021. Available at: < https://uncitral.un.org/sites/uncitral.un.org/files/media-documents/uncitral/en/21-07996_expedited-arbitration-e-ebook.pdf>, accessed 19. april 2024.

63 Art. 2 of Arbitration Rules of the Arbitration Court at the Chamber of Commerce of Montenegro 2023.

same arbitration agreement or if all claims from the proceedings are not covered by the same arbitration agreement, but the parties to the proceedings are the same and the claims arise from the same legal relationship, or if the Presidency assesses that the arbitration agreements are mutually harmonized. When deciding on consolidation proceedings, the Presidency considers all the circumstances it deems relevant, including whether arbitrators have already been appointed in at least two proceedings and whether the same or different arbitrators were appointed. Before making a decision, the Presidency will consult with the parties and the already appointed arbitrators. When arbitrations are consolidated, they will be consolidated into the arbitration that was initiated first unless the parties agree otherwise.

Art.12 of Arbitration Rules contains rules about joining third parties. At the request of any party, the arbitral tribunal may allow one or more third parties to join the proceedings as a party, provided that those parties are bound by the same arbitration agreement. After all parties, including the person or persons whose joinder is being decided, have been given the opportunity to express themselves, the arbitral tribunal may refuse to join if it would disproportionately harm the interests of any of the parties.

7 Evidence

Establishing facts is fundamental in arbitration. Parties construct and present facts in support of their arguments. It is crucial to establish the facts and clarify disputed issues, which will facilitate the tribunal in rendering a decision. Therefore, taking and presentation of evidence is crucial in any arbitration.[64]

Montenegrin Arbitration Act follows rules of the Model law also when it comes to taking the of evidence. Namely, principle of procedural flexibility is adopted in taking the evidence, the admissibility of evidentiary means and their probative value. Having in mind that rules contained in Arbitration Act provide summary provisions regarding conduction of the evidence, experienced arbitrators may suggest to the parties to agree on the procedure to be adopted regarding the taking the evidence or on the application of IBA Rules on the Taking of Evidence in International Commercial Arbitration, them being widely accepted international standards in taking the evidence.[65]

64 Julian Lew, Loukas Mistelis and Stefan Kroll, *Comparative International Commercial Arbitration* (Kluwer Law International 2003) 22-4.

65 Gary Born, *International Commercial Arbitration* (Kluwer Law International 2009) 170.

Burden of proof of any particular factual allegation lies upon a party which makes the allegation,[66] and each party has to prove the facts upon which relies. As a rule, arbitrators do not take the initiative from the parties regarding the determination of the factual situation.[67] However, arbitrators may request clarifications or documents they deem essential for making decision. Particularly, the claimant shall state in the statement of claim the facts supporting his claim, the points at issue and the relief or remedy sought, and the respondent shall state in his statement of defense his defense in respect of the claimant's allegations, proposals and claims. In addition, the parties may submit with their statements documents they consider being relevant or may add a reference to the documents or other evidence they intend to submit.[68]

Arbitral tribunal shall decide whether it will decide on basis of the documents only or whether it will hold oral hearings. Oral hearings should be conducted only if party requests so,[69] unless parties agreed that no oral hearings shall be held. The parties shall be given sufficient advance notice of any oral hearing and of any meeting of the arbitral tribunal for the purposes of inspection of goods, other property or documents. All statements, documents or other information supplied to the arbitral tribunal by one party shall be communicated to the other party.[70] Any evidentiary expert report or evidentiary document on which the arbitral tribunal may rely in making its decision shall be communicated to the parties.

Principle of confidentiality of arbitration is explicitly provided in Art. 36, para.3 of Arbitration Act. When seat of arbitration is Montenegro, or when Montenegrin Arbitration Act applies arbitration procedure shall not open to public, unless otherwise agreed by the parties.[71]

Also, arbitral tribunal may appoint one or more experts to report to it on specific issues to be determined by the arbitral tribunal or require a party to give the expert any relevant information or to produce, or to provide access to, any relevant documents, goods or other property for his inspection.[72] Unless otherwise agreed by the parties, if a party so requests or if the arbitral tribunal considers it necessary, the expert shall, after delivery of his written or oral

66 Nigel Blackaby, Constantine Partasides et al., *Redfern and Hunter on International Arbitration* (6th edn, Kluwer Law International 2017) 6–84.

67 Maja Stanivuković, *Međunarodna arbitraža sa odabranim prilozima* (JP Službeni Glasnik 2013) 231.

68 Art. 35, Arbitration Act.

69 Art. 36 para. 2, Arbitration Act.

70 Art. 36, para 3, Arbitration Act.

71 Art. 36, para 6, Arbitration Act.

72 Art. 38, Arbitration Act.

report, participate in an oral hearing where the parties have the opportunity to put questions to him and to present other expert witnesses in order to testify on the points at issue. Grounds for challenging an expert are the same as grounds for challenging an arbitrator, and that is in case that there are circumstances which give a rise to his independence or impartiality or if he does not possess the required qualifications agreed by parties.

8 Interim Measures and Preliminary Orders

There are different approaches regarding the issues of interim measures in comparative law. Some countries provide that only court can order interim measures, which is argued by the fact that arbitral tribunal in order to decide on interim measure may jeopardize its independence, because it will have to decide whether party requesting interim measure may succeed on the merits, and that recourse to courts in some situations may be necessary and will save time.

However, Montenegrin Arbitration Act has adopted different approach, having in mind that it was necessary to safeguard confidentiality of arbitral procedure, which is one of the main principles. Therefore, arbitral tribunal may, at the request of a party order an interim measure and order to: 1) maintain or restore the status quo pending determination of the dispute; 2) take action that would prevent, or refrain from taking action that is likely to cause, current or future harm or prejudice to the arbitral process itself; 3) preserve assets out of which the obligations imposed in the arbitral award may subsequently be enforced; or 4) preserve evidence that may be relevant to the resolution of the dispute.[73]

Arbitral tribunal can grant an interim measure if harm not adequately reparable is likely to result and such harm substantially outweighs the harm to result to the party against whom the interim measure is ordered, and if there is a possibility that the party requesting an interim measure will succeed on the merits of the claim, where such possibility shall not affect the discretion of the arbitral tribunal in making any subsequent determination.[74] The party requesting an interim measure bears a burden of proof to satisfy the arbitral tribunal that conditions for granting it have been fulfilled. In addition, tribunal

73 Art. 21, Arbitration Act.

74 Art. 22, para. 2, Arbitration Act.

can impose an obligation on the party requesting an interim measure to provide appropriate security.[75]

The arbitral tribunal may modify, suspend or decide to terminate an interim measure, upon request of any party or on its own initiative, which can be done only in exceptional circumstances and upon prior notice to the parties.[76]

The arbitral tribunal may at any point during the proceedings, award the costs and damages if later is determined that, in the circumstances, the measure should not have been granted. The party requesting an interim measure is liable for any costs and damages caused by the measure to the other party.

An interim measure ordered by an arbitral tribunal, irrespective of the country in which it was ordered, shall be recognized and enforced by the decision of the court, except if there are grounds for refusing recognition. However, if the arbitral tribunal decides to modify, suspend or terminate the interim measure, then such a decision should not be enforced. The party who is seeking or has obtained recognition or enforcement of an interim measure shall promptly inform the court of any modification, suspension or termination of that interim measure. The court before which recognition or enforcement of an interim measure is sought may, if it considers it necessary, order the requesting party to provide appropriate security if the arbitral tribunal has not already made a determination with respect to security or where necessary to protect the rights of third parties.[77]

Recognition and enforcement of an interim measure may be refused if the court finds that: 1) such refusal is justified because some of the grounds for refusing the recognition and enforcement of the foreign arbitral award exists;[78] 2) party did not provide security which was requested by order of the tribunal; 3) the interim measure has terminated or has been suspended by the arbitral tribunal or by the court of the State in which the arbitration takes place, where the court is so empowered, or of the State under the law of which that interim measure was ordered; 4) the interim measure is incompatible with the powers conferred upon the court in accordance with the legislation of Montenegro, unless the court decides, for the purposes of enforcing the interim measure, to modify that interim measure, in accordance with the legislation, without modifying its substance; The court where recognition and enforcement of an

75 Art. 24, Arbitration Act.

76 Art. 23, Arbitration Act.

77 Art. 27, Arbitration Act.

78 Grounds for refusing the recognition and enforcement of the foreign arbitral award, which can be basis for refusal of recognition of interim measure are provided in Art.52, para 1, point 1 to 4 of the Arbitration Act.

interim measure is sought shall not, in making that determination, undertake a review of the substance of the interim measure.[79]

When ordering an interim measure in the arbitration procedure, the court acts in accordance with the rules of the enforcement and security procedure,[80] regardless of whether the seat of the arbitration tribunal is on the territory of Montenegro, while taking into account the special characteristics of international arbitration.[81]

9 The Arbitral Award

The arbitral tribunal decides the dispute and renders the arbitral award applying the rules chosen by the parties as applicable to the subject of the dispute.[82] To prevent *renvoi* or other Private International Law issues that may arise, Art. 40, para.2, provides that any reference to the law or legal system of a particular country will be interpreted as a direct reference to the substantive law of that country and not to its rules on determining the applicable law, unless the parties have agreed otherwise.[83] Also, the tribunal can decide the dispute on the principle of equity (*ex aequo et bono*), if the parties have expressly agreed on it.

Montenegrin Arbitration Act provides parties with wide autonomy and flexibility to agree on legal rules to be applied in procedure, and if the parties have not determined the applicable law, the arbitral tribunal applies conflict of law rules that are applicable.[84]

Parties can agree on the on the method of voting and making the decisions.[85] In the absence of the party's agreement, the arbitration panel decides by majority of votes of all arbitrators.[86] If an arbitral award cannot be made on this way, the panel of arbitrators continues deliberations on each opinion presented and if after repeated deliberations the arbitral award still cannot be made then it shall be made by the presiding arbitrator. Questions of procedure

79 Art. 28, Arbitration Act.

80 Law on Enforcement and Securing of Claims "Official Gazette of Montenegro, 36/2011".

81 Art. 29, Arbitration Act.

82 Maja Kostić-Mandić, *Međunarodno privatno pravo* (Pravni fakultet Univerzitet Crne Gore 2017) 219.

83 Art. 40, para. 1 and 2, Arbitration Act.

84 Art. 40, para 3, Arbitration Act.

85 Maja Stanivuković, *Međunarodna arbitraža sa odabranim prilozima* (JP Službeni Glasnik 2013) 257.

86 Art. 40, Arbitration Act.

may be decided by a presiding arbitrator alone, if it is authorized by the parties, or all members of the panel of arbitrators. The panel of arbitrators may entrust one of its members to undertake certain evidence-taking activities.[87]

Arbitral proceeding is terminated: by rendering the final arbitral award; when the claimant withdraws claim, unless the respondent objects thereto and the arbitral tribunal recognizes a legitimate interest of the respondent in obtaining a final arbitral award; the parties agree on the termination of the proceedings; the arbitral tribunal finds that the continuation of the arbitral proceedings has become unnecessary or impossible; or the arbitral proceedings have been terminated in accordance with Arbitration Act or in case that parties settle the dispute.[88]

Therefore, arbitral award is the decision of the arbitral tribunal which resolves the issues in dispute between the parties submitted to the tribunal, and is just one of the ways for the termination of the arbitration.[89] The arbitral award shall resolve all requests of the parties, and could also be made in the form of a partial or interim award. The arbitral award shall be made in writing and shall be signed by the members of the panel of arbitrators or the sole arbitrator. The arbitral award shall state the reasons upon which it is based, unless the parties have agreed that no reasons are to be given or the award is an award on agreed terms.[90] An award made by tribunal is final and binding between the parties and on any person claiming through or under them. Therefore, the arbitral award creates a res judicata, which will prevent either party from re-opening the substantive dispute.[91] This does not affect the right of a person to challenge he award by any available arbitral process of appeal or review or in accordance with the provisions of this part.

Arbitration can also be terminated with the settlement of the parties. Decision based on the settlement of the parties can be recorded in the form of an arbitral award, which shall state that it is an arbitral award based on settlement of the parties and it has same legal effect as an arbitral award in resolving the dispute. However, the tribunal will not make such award, if it finds that the content of the settlement is contrary to the public policy of Montenegro.[92]

The party may submit the request for corrections of arbitral award, for specific interpretation of such award or for additional award as to claims presented

87 Art. 41, Arbitration Act.

88 Art. 44, Arbitration Act.

89 Julian Lew, Loukas Mistelis and Stefan Kroll, *Comparative International Commercial Arbitration* (Kluwer Law International 2003) 24-1.

90 Art. 43, Arbitration Act.

91 Art. 49, Arbitration Act.

92 Art. 42, Arbitration Act.

in the arbitral proceedings but not decided in the arbitral award, within thirty days from the date of receipt of the award at the latest.[93]

The parties are subject to an obligation to perform and comply with the terms of the award, and if they do not comply the arbitral award, it can be enforced in a same manner as a judgement of a court. To put it in other words, an arbitral award made by an arbitral tribunal in the territory of Montenegro, has the force and effect of an enforceable document and it can be enforced in accordance with the Law on enforcement and security.[94]

10 Costs, Fees and Interest

An arbitrator has the right to reimbursement of expenses and a fee for work performed unless he or she has waived those rights expressly in writing.[95] The parties shall be jointly and severally liable for the payment of such expenses and fee.[96] If the arbitrator has determined the amount of his expenses and fee, his decision shall not be binding upon the parties if they do not accept it, and in that case decision on arbitrator's expenses and fee shall be made, on a proposal from the arbitrator or a party, by the arbitral institution or the appointing authority and such decision shall be an enforceable instrument.[97]

Also, the party requesting an interim measure shall be liable for any costs and damages caused by the measure to the other party if the arbitral tribunal later determines that, in the circumstances, the measure should not have been granted, these costs can be awarded at any point during the proceeding.[98]

11 Challenge of Arbitral Awards

Arbitral award is final and binding on parties and it represents enforceable document.[99] The only legal remedy is application for annulment to the

93 Art. 45, Arbitration Act.

94 Art. 46, Arbitration Act.

95 Art. 14, para 3, Arbitration Act. See also: Gašo Knežević and Vladimir Pavić, *Arbitraža i ADR* (Pravni fakultet Univerziteta u Beogradu, Centar za izdavaštvo i informisanje 2013) 77.

96 Nigel Blackaby, Constantine Partasides et al., *Redfern and Hunter on International Arbitration* (6th edn, Kluwer Law International 2017) 9–88.

97 Art. 14, Arbitration Act.

98 Art. 26, Arbitration Act.

99 Nigel Blackaby, Constantine Partasides et al., *Redfern and Hunter on International Arbitration* (6th edn, Kluwer Law International 2017) 9–173.

Commercial Court of Montenegro, which shall be made within three months from the date on which the award had been served to the party.[100] One should also bear in mind that under Arbitration Act of Montenegro, parties cannot waive their right to make a claim for annulment of arbitral award.[101] This is a mandatory rule,[102] which cannot be contracted out and it always applies when *lex arbitri* is Montenegrin Arbitration Act.[103]

An arbitral award may be annulled, if the party making the application proves that: 1) the arbitration agreement was not concluded or is not valid under the law designated by agreement of the parties or under the law of Montenegro, unless otherwise agreed by the parties; 2) the party to the proceedings did not have the capacity to conclude the arbitration agreement and to be a party to the dispute or a party was not duly represented; 3) the party making the claim for annulment was not given proper notice of the initiation of the arbitral proceedings or was otherwise unlawfully unable to present its case before the arbitral tribunal; 4) the award deals with a dispute that falls outside the scope of the arbitration agreement or contains decisions on matters beyond the scope of the arbitration agreement, provided that only the part of the award on matters not submitted to arbitration may be set aside if that part of the award can be separated from the decision on matters submitted to arbitration; 5) the composition of the arbitral tribunal or the arbitral procedure was not in accordance with Arbitration Act of Montenegro, or a permissible agreement of the parties, and that fact could have affected the content of the arbitral award; or 6) the award does not contain the statement of reasons or has not been signed.[104]

The court shall annul an arbitral award if it finds that: 1) the subject-matter of the dispute is not arbitrable, 2) the award is in conflict with the public policy of Montenegro.[105]

---

100 Art. 47, Arbitration Act. See also: Maja Stanivuković, *Međunarodna arbitraža sa odabranim prilozima* (JP Službeni Glasnik 2013) 262, Gašo Knežević and Vladimir Pavić, *Arbitraža i ADR* (Pravni fakultet Univerziteta u Beogradu, Centar za izdavaštvo i informisanje 2013) 163.

101 Maja Kostić-Mandić, *Međunarodno privatno pravo* (Pravni fakultet Univerzitet Crne Gore 2017) 225.

102 Art. 48, para 3, Arbitration Act.

103 Maja Stanivuković, *Međunarodna arbitraža sa odabranim prilozima* (JP Službeni Glasnik 2013) 63.

104 Art. 48, para 1, Arbitration Act.

105 Art. 48, para 2, Arbitration Act.

12 Recognition and Enforcement of Foreign Arbitral Awards

Legal framework for recognition and enforcement of foreign arbitral awards in Montenegro is provided by the Arbitration Act 2015 and the New York Convention,[106] latter being the source of outmost importance,[107] being in force in 172 countries signatories.[108]

To ensure that a foreign arbitral award has legal effect in Montenegro, it must be recognized by the court in Montenegro.[109] Arbitration Act, in Art. 50, defines foreign arbitral award as the award made by an arbitral tribunal whose seat is outside of Montenegro and shall be considered to be the award of the State in which it was made. During the recognition and enforcement procedure, the domestic court checks if conditions for recognition and enforcement stipulated by national legislation are fulfilled.[110] The recognition and enforcement of foreign arbitral award in Montenegro are decided by the Commercial Court in a non-litigious procedure.

Party initiating recognition and enforcement of foreign arbitral award in Montenegro, shall submit to court request accompanied by: 1) the original arbitral award or a certified copy; 2) the original arbitration agreement or document on the acceptance of arbitration or a certified copy; 3) certified translation of a foreign arbitral award and arbitration agreement into the Montenegrin language or into the language officially used before the competent court.

When deciding upon request for recognition or enforcement of a foreign arbitral award, the court shall confine itself to determining whether the requirements laid down in Arbitration Act have been met, and if it considers it necessary, it may seek an explanation from the arbitral tribunal that rendered the award, from the parties, and from a court or a notary or other person with which the award was deposited. Therefore, court has a duty to recognize every foreign arbitral award, unless it finds, upon the objection by the opposing party that: 1) there is the ground for refusing recognition and enforcement; 2) the

106 New York Convention on the Recognition and Enforcement of Foreign Arbitral Awards of 1958.

107 Mihailo Dika, Gašo Knežević i Srđan Stojanović, *Komentar Zakona o međunarodnom privatnom i procesnom pravu* (Homos Beograd 1991) 319.

108 Status of New York Convention is available at: <https://uncitral.un.org/en/texts/arbitration/conventions/foreign_arbitral_awards/status2> accessed 10 April 2024.

109 Nigel Blackaby, Constantine Partasides et al., *Redfern and Hunter on International Arbitration* (6th edn, Kluwer Law International 2017) 11.17.

110 Maja Kostić-Mandić, *IEL Private International Law of Montenegro* (Kluwer Law International 2023) 708.

award has not yet become binding on the parties; or 3) it has been set aside or suspended by a court of the country in which, or under the law of which, that award was made.

Art.52 of Arbitration Act provides reasons for refusing the recognition upon request of a party:

1. arbitration agreement is not valid under the law to which the parties have subjected it or under the law of the country where the award was made;
2. party was not given proper notice of the appointment of an arbitrator or of the arbitral proceedings or was otherwise unable to present its case;
3. the award deals with a dispute not contemplated by the arbitration agreement or it contains decisions on matters beyond the scope of that agreement, provided that the recognition and enforcement of that award may be partially refused if it is found that the part of the award which contains decisions on matters beyond the scope of the arbitration agreement can be separated from the remaining part of the award;
4. the arbitral tribunal or the arbitral procedure was not in accordance with the arbitration agreement or, failing such agreement, was not in accordance with the law of the country where the arbitration took place; or
5. the award has not yet become binding on the parties or has been set aside or suspended by a court of the country in which, or under the law of which, that award was made.

Furthermore, law provides two additional reasons when court shall ex officio refuse recognition and enforcement of an arbitral award: the subject-matter of the dispute is not arbitrable or the effects of the arbitral award would be contrary to the public policy of Montenegro.[111]

Commercial Court may, if necessary, decide to adjourn its decision on recognition and enforcement of a foreign arbitral award if the proceedings for annulment or suspension of award commenced in the country in which, or under the law of which, that award was made, until the termination of such proceedings.[112] The Legal remedy against decision made in the proceedings for recognition, shall be submitted to the Appellate Court of Montenegro within fifteen days from the date of service of the decision.[113]

---

111 Maja Kostić-Mandić, *IEL Private International Law of Montenegro* (Kluwer Law International 2023) 711.

112 Gašo Knežević and Vladimir Pavić, *Arbitraža i ADR* (Pravni fakultet Univerziteta u Beogradu, Centar za izdavaštvo i informisanje 2013) 172.

113 Art. 54, Arbitration Act.

13 Investment Arbitration Framework in Montenegro

In the field of investment arbitration, most important multilateral treaty is the Washington Convention on the Settlement of Investment Disputes Between States and Nationals of Other States of 1965 (ICSID Convention).[114] Montenegro has signed ICSID Convention on 19 July 2012.[115] ICSID convention has established International Centre for Settlement of Investment Disputes, with the purpose to encourage cross-border investment in developing states by providing an effective means of enforcing contractual rights, and to provide facilities for conciliation and arbitration of investment disputes between Contracting States and nationals of other Contracting States.[116]

As previously stated, when it comes to initiating arbitration proceedings, there is no national institution responsible for representing the State before international tribunals. Considering all aspects of investment arbitration, its complexity in particular, the approach of the Government is to require that those representing the state in such proceedings must have an appropriate experience and reputation. The Government of Montenegro usually gives consent to the competent ministries (the Ministry of Finance or the Ministry of Economy) to contract external legal counsel. Even though such law firms are hired, the Government appoints working groups consisting of the representatives of ministries and other interested parties, with a task to follow the arbitral proceedings, provide logistics to the legal counsel and inform the Government about the proceedings.

It should be noted that the structure of the working groups is adapted to the subject matter of the dispute (meaning that the members of the working group come from the competent governmental bodies), at the same time taking into account the personal expertise of the members, his/her specialization or experience relevant to the particular case, etc.

According to the information published by ICSID, Montenegro is a party in 9 ICISD proceedings.[117] The success rate of Montenegro in these disputes

114 The ICSID Convention is a treaty ratified by 158 Contracting States

115 Available at: <https://icsid.worldbank.org/about/member-states/database-of-member-states> Accessed 10 April 2024.

116 Maja Stanivuković, *Međunarodna arbitraža sa odabranim prilozima* (JP Službeni Glasnik 2013) 62.

117 Subject matter of the disputes (arbitration proceedings and proceedings before national courts) Montenegro has been the respondent party in eight ISDS arbitration processes so far: MNSS B .V. and Recupero Creditito Accaio NV v Montenegro, CEAC Holdings Limited v Montenegro, Medusa v Montenegro, Oleg Vladimirovich Deripaska v Montenegro , Investment and Development Fund of Montenegro v Montenegro, SIA Multikapitals,

leads to the conclusion that the approach of the state (appointment of external legal counsel, with coordinative working groups providing logistics and monitoring the process) is efficient. From its establishment to date, there were no investment disputes settled before the Arbitration Court of the Chamber of Economy of Montenegro. Speaking about the investment-related proceedings before national courts, in which the State is represented by the Protector of Property and Legal Interests of Montenegro, the respective annual reports of the Protector and the Ministry of Finance do not contain specific information on such cases.

In addition, it is important to note that Montenegro has entered into 26 bilateral investment treaties, focused on the mutual promotion and protection of investments.[118] Out of 26 signed BITs, 24 are in force, one is terminated and one is signed but not ratified.[119] They all include the cooling off clause, requiring the parties to try to settle the dispute through mediation, conciliation/negotiations.[120] Neither piece of the national legislation regarding ISDS

Addiko Bank AG v Montenegro, CEAC Holdings Limited v Montenegro. Three ISDS proceedings were initiated before the International Centre for Settlement of Investment Disputes (ICSID), four under the Arbitration Rules of the United Nations Commission on International Trade Law (UNCITRAL) and one before the foreign District Court. Five disputes were initiated under BITs while three were based on the commercial contracts between investors and the State. Seven disputes were decided in favour of the State, with one still pending.

118 The list of the countries as well as the texts of the treaties are available at: https://investmentpolicy.unctad.org/international-investment-agreements/countries/140/montenegro. BITs in force signed with: Austria, Slovakia, Serbia, Czech Republic, Finland, Denmark, State of Qatar, Republic of North Macedonia, Malta, France, Greece, the Netherlands, Israel, Cyprus, Romania, Germany, Lithuania, Poland, Spain, Swiss Confederation, Azerbaijan, Moldova, United Arab Emirates, Belgium and Luxembourg Economic Union, Turkey, USA. 12 BITs were signed after declaring independence: with Serbia, Czech Republic, Finland, Denmark, State of Qatar, Republic of North Macedonia, Malta, Azerbaijan, Moldova, United Arab Emirates, Belgium-Luxembourg Economic Union and Turkey.

119 Aneta Spaić, Achmea Ripple Effect and Its Reverberations in the Investment Worlds, in University of Montenegro Law Journal, Collection of papers – Part II (Jean Monnet Module in Law of the EU Internal Market: Integrating the Western Balkans into the European Union's Internal Market – Challenges and Prospects), p.74, https://www.ucg.ac.me/objava/blog/1263/objava/157065-novi-broj-zbornika-pravnog-fakulteta-ucg-na-engleskom-jeziku, accessed 16 April 2024. See also: https://investmentpolicy.unctad.org/international-investment-agreements/countries/140/montenegro, accessed 23 January, 2023.

120 There is a six-months cooling-off period time envisaged in BITs with the vast majority of the countries: Moldova, Germany, Turkey, Azerbaijan, Macedonia, Belgium-Luxembourg, Serbia, Qatar, Denmark, Swiss, Cypress, Lithuania, Israel, Spain, Greece, Poland, Slovakia, and Romania. Some of the analysed BITs with Malta, Austria, and Finland have envisaged

reflects on the amicable resolution mechanisms. However, these agreements encourage parties to attempt resolution through negotiation, seeking third-party expertise, diplomatic conciliation, or any other good-faith method.[121]

Furthermore, the Law on Foreign Investments,[122] in Article 30 provides that any dispute arising from foreign investment shall be resolved by the competent court in Montenegro, unless the decision on establishment i.e., investment agreement stipulates that such disputes should be resolved before domestic or foreign arbitration. Further, the Law on Public–Private Partnership[123] allows foreign investors to compete on fair ground against domestic enterprises for concession contracts for public works or public services, or to conclude public–private partnership contracts for public works or public services. Article 80 of this law provides that any dispute arising from a Public–Private Partnership Agreement shall be resolved by the competent court in Montenegro, unless regulated otherwise by that very agreement. Moreover, any disputes arising out of, or in connection to, a Public–Private Partnership Agreement may also be settled before domestic or foreign arbitration, if agreed.

Disputes that are arbitrable under the ICSID Convention are provided in Article 25(1), stating that the jurisdiction of the Centre shall extend to any legal dispute arising directly out of an investment, between a Contracting State (or any constituent subdivision or agency of a Contracting State designated to the Centre by that State) and a national of another Contracting State, which the parties to the dispute consent in writing to submit to the Centre. When the parties have given their consent, no party may withdraw it unilaterally.

In the UNCTAD Investment Policy Hub registry, there are six cases brought against Montenegro – four cases decided in favor of the state, one decided in favor of neither party and one still pending.[124]

So far, Montenegro has been successful in cases brought against it under the ICSID Convention. For example, in 2012 in case *MNSS BV and Recupero Credito*

---

the shorter cooling-off time of three months. However, only one BIT with a nine-month cooling-off period is signed with the United Arab Emirates. The "reasonable lapse of time" in which contracting parties may reach amicable settlement is included in the BIT with the Netherlands, whereas a clause without a time limit is provided in the BIT with the Czech Republic. Proposal on the key elements of ISDS clauses of future BITs in the Western Balkans, GIZ Project "Harmonisation of the Legal Framework for Investment Protection" Report for Montenegro drafted by Aneta Spaić.

121 Aneta Spaić "Proposal on the key elements of ISDS clause of the future BITs" (2020), GIZ ORF LR – "Harmonization of Legal Framework for Investment Protection", C/ORFLR/2020/002.

122 "Official Gazette of Montenegro", No. 18/11 and 45/14.

123 "Official Gazette of Montenegro", No .73/19.

124 Aneta Spaić, *supra* n. 121. See more at: <https://investmentpolicy.unctad.org/investment-dispute-settlement/country/140/montenegro>, accessed January 29, 2023.

Acciaio NV v. Montenegro, the tribunal decided on claims arising out of alleged Government interference with the operation and management of a steel production facility in which the claimants had invested, leading to its bankruptcy. The arbitral tribunal declined its jurisdiction over the contract and the investment law claims and denied all claims except for the breach of the full protection and security standard, while ruling that the investors had suffered no loss because of a violation of this treaty standard.[125]

Further, in *CEAC Holdings Limited v Montenegro*[126] claims arising out of the alleged unlawful interference by the Government in the insolvency process of an aluminium production company in which the claimant Central European Aluminium Company ("CEAC") owned by Oleg Deripaska, a Russian billionaire, had invested. The Arbitral Tribunal declined its jurisdiction, on the ground that Claimant had failed to establish a seat or registered office in Cyprus and thus could not qualify as a foreign investor and bring a claim under Article 1(3)(b) of the Montenegro-Cyprus Bilateral Investment Treaty of 2005. In the case, Montenegro successfully argued that the claimant had no office in Cyprus, that the address provided was in fact an abandoned residence and the tribunal accepted the position that a certificate of tax residency was insufficient to establish a seat for the purposes of this claim. Then, in 2016, Oleg Deripaska initiated proceedings against Montenegro, alleging unlawful expropriation of the claimant's investments in an aluminum production company and a bauxite mine. This case was also decided in favor of Montenegro.

Montenegro was also successful in *Medusa v. Montenegro*[127] investment case about oil and gas exploration rights under a joint venture contract with local petroleum company AD Jugopetrol Kotor. In 2021, Arbitral Tribunal dismissed all claims brought against the Government of Montenegro by Addiko Bank AG, case was about Law on conversion into Euros of mortgages held in Swiss Francs.[128]

14 Institutional Framework and Capacities for International Arbitration in Montenegro

The International Commercial Court of Arbitration, affiliated with the Montenegrin Chamber of Commerce and located in Podgorica, is the only arbitration institution in Montenegro, which was established in 2003. This Arbitration Court decides, conciliates and mediates when its jurisdiction is provided by

125 ICSID Case No. ARB/12/8.
126 ICSID Case No. ARB/14/8.
127 PCA Case No. 15/39.
128 ICSID Case No. ARB/17/35.

the agreement of the parties for commercial disputes between domestic and/or foreign economic entities. The institution adopted an updated version of its arbitration rules in 2023 to align with the UNCITRAL Rules. This type of institutional arbitration has been gaining popularity in recent years in Montenegro.[129]

The parties wishing to resolve the dispute before the Arbitration Court at the Chamber of Commerce of Montenegro are obliged to include in their contract the recommended arbitration clause or to conclude a special contract. By doing so, the parties agree to resolve the dispute in the proceedings before the Arbitration Court and thus provide a quick, efficient and professional resolution of the dispute.[130]

Proceedings before the Arbitration Court at the Chamber of Commerce of Montenegro are conducted in a way that ensures fair and efficient resolution of disputes and avoids unnecessary delays and costs. Arbitration rules before the Arbitration Court at the Chamber of Commerce of Montenegro[131] regulate the conduct of arbitral proceedings before the Arbitration Court at the Chamber of Economy of Montenegro (the ACCEMN) and the organization of the ACCEMN. The Arbitration Court at the Chamber of Commerce of Montenegro has a recommended list of arbitrators. Also, this institution has adopted the Code of Ethics for Arbitrators, which determines the ethical principles and rules of conduct with which the arbitrators must comply in the proceedings.

However, there is space for improvement when it comes to the number of cases referred to arbitration and the number of resolved cases through the arbitration procedure before the Arbitration Court of the Chamber of Commerce of Montenegro. It is reported that at the annual level, the number of cases resolved by the Arbitration Court is insignificant (mostly one case per year), which influenced the Government to initiate procedures for the amendments of the Arbitration Act in 2023.[132] The proposed changes would provide a more detailed legal framework, and encourage parties to incorporate arbitration clauses in their business agreements and to ultimately resolve their disputes in a more efficient manner.

---

129 Maja Kostić-Mandić, *IEL Private International Law of Montenegro* (Kluwer Law International 2023) 692.

130 Available at: <https://www.privrednakomora.me/arbitrazni-sud> accessed 10 April 2024.

131 Adopted at the session of the Assembly of the Chamber of Commerce of Montenegro.

132 Government of Montenegro, Information about the need to amend the Arbitration Act, December 2023, available at: <https://www.gov.me/dokumenta/84f26d37-c22e-4fee-8e1d-a4061a3d73da> accessed 10 April 2024.

CHAPTER 16

Investment Protection and Investor-State Dispute Resolution in North Macedonia

Toni Deskoski and Vangel Dokovski

1 General Overview

Located in the central Balkans, North Macedonia shares borders with Albania to the west, Bulgaria to the east, Greece to the south, and Serbia and Kosovo to the north. It is a landlocked country. Operating as an open economy, North Macedonia actively seeks foreign direct investment (FDI). The country has implemented legislation to provide foreign investors with equal opportunities compared to domestic counterparts and offers various incentives to attract such investments. To facilitate this, North Macedonia has established an agency dedicated to attracting and assisting foreign investors. Additionally, the Office of the Deputy Prime Minister for Economic Affairs serves as the primary point of contact for foreign investors and plays an active role in resolving investor-state disputes.

The Republic of North Macedonia, a candidate country for EU membership and a NATO member since March 2020, is working to establish a legal framework for the protection of foreign investments in accordance with EU law. As part of this effort, the government is in the final stages of adopting a new Draft Model Bilateral Investment Treaty (BIT), which is based on the EU Model clauses.

North Macedonia offers an attractive investment climate with a legal framework that largely complies with international standards. Foreign companies, especially those operating within the Technological Industrial Development Zones (TIDZ), often report positive investment experiences and maintain good relations with government officials.

2 Foreign Investment Trends in North Macedonia

In the absence of adequate domestic savings, foreign investments play a vital role in the development of North Macedonia's economy. According to UNCTAD's World Investment Report 2023, net FDI flows to North Macedonia

 | DOI:10.1163/9789004729889_017

increased to USD 794 million in 2022, a year-on-year rise of 42.6%. By the end of the same period, the total stock of FDI was estimated at USD 7.47 billion, accounting for approximately 54.7% of the country's GDP.[1]

According to data from the Central Bank of North Macedonia, the most of the FDI influx into the country in terms of stocks comes from Austria, with a total of EUR 1,053 million, followed by Greece, with EUR 729 million. The top five also includes the United Kingdom (EUR 634 million), Germany (EUR 572 million), and the Netherlands (EUR 544 million). Regarding investment activities, manufacturing attracts the highest share of FDI, accounting for EUR 2,453 million or 35% of total direct investments, while financial and insurance activities receive EUR 1,520 million or 21.7%. In 2023, the country welcomed total net inflows from direct investments totaling EUR 616.7 million. This sum comprised net inflows from equity amounting to EUR 274.8 million, reinvestment of earnings of EUR 172.9 million, and intercompany lending of EUR 169.1 million, according to the Central Bank.[2]

2.1 *Key Sectors for Foreign Investments*

In North Macedonia, five key sectors can be identified as attractive sectors for foreign investments.

2.1.1 Machine and Automotive Components

North Macedonia has a longstanding tradition in the automotive sector, dating back to the Yugoslav period when local factories began supplying automotive components to the Serbian producer Zastava. Over time, the manufacturing sector evolved, leading to the emergence of several specialized producers of automotive components across the country. The products manufactured in these factories meet the highest standards, complying with automotive standards TS 16949 and ISO 9001. This ensures that the automotive components produced in North Macedonia are of top quality and suitable for export. Currently, North Macedonia's automotive component sector is experiencing

1 *See* Lloyds Bank, North Macedonia: Invest in North Macedonia, https://www.lloydsbanktrade.com/en/market-potential/north-macedonia/investment (data as of May 2024)last Top of Form

2 *See* National Bank of the Republic of North Macedonia, Independent Auditor's Report and Financial Statements prepared in accordance with International Financial Reporting Standards for the year ended 31 December 2022, https://www.lloydsbanktrade.com/en/market-potential/north-macedonia/investment (data as of May 2024).

significant growth, driven by strategic government policies, its advantageous geographical location, and a competitive market environment.[3]

2.1.2 Information and Communication Technology

The Information and Communication Technology (ICT) industry stands out as the fastest-growing sector within the Macedonian economy, assuming a pivotal role as a major source of employment and export revenue. Hardware constitutes the predominant segment (55%) of the ICT market in North Macedonia, followed by ICT services (30%) and software (15%). The ICT sector in North Macedonia has demonstrated a consistent annual growth rate ranging between 2.5% and 8% over recent years.

This growth trajectory is attributable to substantial investments by both the government and telecommunications companies in IT infrastructure, continued financial sector expenditure, a reduction in the price of IT equipment, and a decrease in VAT for such equipment.[4]

2.1.3 Agribusiness and Food Processing

The agribusiness industry in North Macedonia has emerged as one of the fastest-growing sectors, experiencing a remarkable increase of over 10% in recent years. Adding value to high-quality agricultural products, which are in demand in major European markets, has become a cornerstone of Macedonian business practices. The agribusiness sector in North Macedonia benefits from several competitive advantages.

These include a unique combination of Continental and Sub-Mediterranean climates, environmentally friendly production practices, and sound food processing technologies. Additionally, the availability of qualified labor throughout rural areas, good access to regional markets, and a reputation for quality food products contribute to the sector's strength. North Macedonia's favorable natural conditions, combined with its rich agricultural tradition and newly developed skills, create a wide range of opportunities in agriculture. From high mountain pastures exceeding 2000 meters in altitude to the fertile water valleys with a Mediterranean climate, the country offers diverse and promising prospects for agricultural development.[5]

---

3 *See* Machine and Automotive Component, Invest North Macedonia, https://investnorthmacedonia.gov.mk/invest-machine-and-automovite-components (data as of May 2024) [hereinafter INM].

4 *See* Information and Communication Technology, INM, https://investnorthmacedonia.gov.mk/invest-ict/ (data as of May 2024).

5 *See* Agrobusiness and Food Processing, INM, https://investnorthmacedonia.gov.mk/invest-agrobusiness-and-food-processing/ (data as of May 2024).

2.1.4 Textile and Clothing

The textile industry represents one of the most developed and diversified sectors of the economy in terms of industrial production, employment, and export earnings, ranking as the second-largest industrial sector in the country after metallurgy. Contributing 17% to the industry's GDP and 14% to total country exports, the textile and clothing sector plays a significant role in North Macedonia's economy.

Characterized by a customer-focused approach, the availability of experienced labor, and flexibility to quickly respond to customer requirements, the textile and clothing industry in North Macedonia offers substantial opportunities for growth. The country is not only attractive for new foreign direct investment but also for outsourcing, strategic alliances, and joint ventures with numerous well-established local companies.[6]

2.1.5 Energy

The energy sector has been one of the biggest beneficiaries of foreign investments in North Macedonia. With a focus on renewable energy, foreign investors have been attracted to the country's abundant natural resources and favorable regulatory environment. This sector emerges as one of the most promising industries for investment in the Macedonian economy. Recent developments in the country's energy market include the expansion of its internal gas distribution network, ongoing liberalization of the electricity market, and increased regional cooperation for electricity and gas interconnections.

In June 2018, North Macedonia adopted a new Energy Law aimed at harmonizing its energy legislation with the EU Energy Community's Third Energy Package. As a full member of the Union for the Coordination of Production and Transmission of Electricity European Interconnection (UCPTE), the country ensures compatibility with European electric power systems. During the 2000s, Macedonia's state-owned power company underwent unbundling and partial privatization. Since 2006, Austrian utility company EVN has been responsible for electricity distribution in the country, while the state-owned MEPSO operates as the electricity transmission system operator. Furthermore, ESM – Power Generation Plants, a Macedonian state-owned electricity producer, plays a significant role in the sector.[7]

6 *See* Textile and Clothing, INM, https://investnorthmacedonia.gov.mk/invest-textile-and-clothing/ (data as of May 2024 For more visit: https://investnorthmacedonia.gov.mk/invest-textile-and-clothing/ (accessed on 21.03.2024).

7 *See* Energy, INM, https://investnorthmacedonia.gov.mk/invest-energy/ (data as of May 2024).

3 Dealing with Foreign Investments

Foreign investors in North Macedonia can rely on three main agencies and bodies to facilitate their investment: a) Invest North Macedonia, b) North Macedonia Free Zones Authority and c) Foreign Investors Council.

3.1 *Invest North Macedonia*

Established in 2005, Invest North Macedonia is the official government investment and export promotion agency tasked with attracting foreign investments and supporting the export promotion of the Republic of North Macedonia.[8] Its primary mission is to encourage and facilitate new foreign direct investments in the country, foster business cooperation with local suppliers, and promote the export potential of local companies to foreign markets.

Through its Aftercare program, Invest North Macedonia provides assistance to foreign investors by mediating with local authorities and the government. The agency offers various forms of support to investors' business activities, including: a) Support for expansion, reinvestment, and the development of research capacities, b) Assistance in finding suitable industrial zones and business properties, c) Identifying suppliers in the relevant region, d) Providing support in the area of human resources, e) Promoting cooperation between investors and secondary schools, vocational colleges, and universities, f) Facilitating negotiations with local authorities, state administration bodies, and public institutions, g) Guiding foreign national applicants through the process of obtaining or extending temporary residence and work permits, h) Submitting investors' proposals to amend legislation to the Government of North Macedonia, and i) Organizing specialized workshops, working breakfasts with top officials, round tables, and social events.

3.2 *North Macedonia Free Zones Authority*

The North Macedonia Free Zones Authority serves as the governmental body responsible for developing free economic zones across the country.[9] Additionally, it assists foreign investors interested in operating within these zones by managing all administrative affairs and helping investors identify suitable investment locations and facilities. The authority operates under a single entry point and promotes its aftercare system, which is designed to provide personalized support and facilitate active two-way communication,

8 *See* INM, https://investnorthmacedonia.gov.mk (data as of May 2024).

9 *See* North Macedonia Free Zones Authority, https://fez.gov.mk/en/home-english/ (last visited May 20, 2024).

ensuring full professional assistance for each investor. To streamline the process, each company is assigned a dedicated single contact person for direct communication. Investors can submit their requests to the Free Zone Authority online by completing a dedicated form.[10] The authority offers three pillars of services:

1. Pillar I – Support in providing information and processing requests related to the services of the Directorate;
2. Pillar II – Support in providing information and processing requests related to the services of other public institutions; and
3. Pillar III – Support, analysis, and recommendations to meet market-related needs.

3.3 *Foreign Investors Council*

The Foreign Investors Council (FIC) was established on 27 February 2006 following a Decision on the Establishment of a Foreign Investors Council adopted by the President of the Economic Chamber of Macedonia. Functioning as a representative body of the business community, the FIC is dedicated to enhancing the attractiveness of the Macedonian economy for investments by advocating for simplified regulations and increased predictability. The FIC also places a strong emphasis on promoting solid business ethics and high corporate governance standards. Currently, the FIC comprises over 130 companies with foreign capital operating in the country.

The primary aims of the Foreign Investors Council are: a) Improving the investment and business development climate in North Macedonia by proposing concrete reforms; b) Stimulating foreign direct investments; c) Facilitating communication between the FIC and Macedonian authorities; d) Assisting in resolving any differences that may arise in relations with foreign investors; e) Establishing connections with other foreign investor organizations across the Southeast European (SEE) region to share best practices; f) Exploring specific strategies to facilitate regional operations; g) Facilitating the exchange of information between FIC members and the government.

The key roles of the Foreign Investors Council include a) Contributing to the enhancement of the Macedonian legal framework concerning commercial and tax matters; b) Promoting sound business ethics; c) Cultivating a positive image of foreign investments and business in North Macedonia.

10 The request form for foreign investor requests is available here: https://fez.gov.mk/#customer.

4 Domestic Legal Framework for Foreign Investments – Law on Strategic Investments

North Macedonia's legal and regulatory framework is generally favorable to foreign investors and provides numerous incentives to attract them. The country recently adopted a new law to create more advantageous conditions for strategic investments.

According to Article 59 of the Constitution of the Republic of North Macedonia, foreign investors are guaranteed the right to freely export invested capital and profits. Furthermore, any rights acquired based on invested capital cannot be diminished by law or any other regulation.

The Law on Strategic Investments, published on 20 January 2020 in the Official Gazette of the Republic of North Macedonia, came into effect to introduce the category of "strategic investment", providing special treatment to eligible projects. This Law is harmonized with Regulation (EU) no. 347/2013 of the European Parliament, CELEX number 320013R0347 and the Council of 17 April 2013 concerning the trans-European energy infrastructure and repealing Decision no. 1364/2006/EC, as well as the amendment of Regulation (EU) no. 713/2009, Regulation (EU) no. 714/2009 and Regulation (EU) no. 715 / 2009.[11]

The Law on Strategic Investments regulates the criteria, conditions and procedure for application, determination of status, selection, preparation and implementation of investment projects of the highest strategic priority for the country. As per Article 3 of the Law on Strategic Investments, the Law is based on the principles of free movement of goods, services and capital, free competition and equal treatment, non-discrimination and transparency.[12]

To qualify for this status, investment projects must meet certain criteria, including Minimum investment of EUR 100 million in the territory of at least two or more municipalities; Minimum investment of EUR 50 million in municipalities with city status, municipalities in the City of Skopje, or the City of Skopje; Minimum investment of EUR 30 million in municipalities with village status. Additionally, the investment must be in one of the following sectors: energy, transportation, telecommunications, tourism, manufacturing, agriculture and food, forestry and water economy, health, industrial and technological parks, wastewater and waste management, sports, science and education

11 Law on Strategic Investments in the Republic of North Macedonia (Закон за стратешки инвестиции во Република Северна Македонија), published on January 20, 2020 available at https://dejure.mk/zakon/zakon-za – strateshki-investicii-vo-republika-severna -makedonija.

12 *See* ibid Art 3.

and Construction of large multifunctional construction complexes of buildings that have in their composition more than one of the areas listed above. However, the status may also be granted in any other sector if the investment exceeds EUR 150 million.

The implementation of strategic investment projects shall be in the public interest. The strategic investment project should cumulatively meet the following conditions: – the proposed investments must comply with the environmental standards set out in the laws of the Republic of North Macedonia, the proposed investments must not be contrary to the Constitution of the Republic of North Macedonia, the laws and obligations arising from international agreements ratified in accordance with the Constitution, the public strategic projects must be in accordance with the strategic priorities of the Government of the Republic of North Macedonia.

Under the Law on Strategic Investments, the strategic investor is a domestic legal entity or a subsidiary of a foreign legal entity registered for performing activity on the territory of the Republic of North Macedonia in accordance with the law.[13] A strategic investment project can be a private, public-private strategic investment project or a fully public project that meets the criteria prescribed by this Law.[14] While private strategic investment project is a project financed by domestic or foreign legal entities,[15] a public-private strategic investment project is a project implemented according to the model of public-private partnership in accordance with the regulations for public-private partnership.

On the other hand,[16] a public strategic investment project is a project whose bearer is a state administration body, public enterprises established by the state or the municipalities, as well as trade companies that are in full or dominant ownership of the state and the municipalities, the municipalities in the City of Skopje and the City of Skopje and other legal entities established by the Republic of North Macedonia or the municipalities.[17] Finally, large multifunctional construction complexes are buildings on one or more construction plots, single or connected.[18] All of these entities and projects are eligible for protection under the North Macedonian Law on Strategic Investments, and its favorable regime.

13 *See Ibid.* Art 7 (2).
14 *See Ibid.* Art 7 (3).
15 *See Ibid.* Art 7 (4).
16 *See Ibid.* Art 7 (5).
17 *See Ibid.* Art 7 (6).
18 *See Ibid.* Art 7 (7).

5 International Investment Treaty Framework – Bilateral Investment Treaties

In 2009, the Republic of Macedonia (now the Republic of North Macedonia) published its Model Bilateral Investment Treaty (BIT), based on the traditional approach for investment protection. With 13 articles, this Model BIT represents the framework for negotiations of BITs with other countries. After the introduction of the Model BIT, several BITs were concluded, namely those with Slovakia, Morocco, Montenegro, Lithuania, Qatar, Kazakhstan, Azerbaijan, Vietnam, Denmark and the United Arab Emirates. Most of the BITs concluded by the Republic of North Macedonia were concluded before the 2009 Model BIT (32 BITs in total). The first BIT was concluded back in 2004, and the most recent one with the United Arab Emirates in 2021.

TABLE 16.1 List of bilateral investment treaties concluded by North Macedonia

Parties	Status
North Macedonia–United Arab Emirates BIT (2021)	In force
Denmark–Macedonia, The former Yugoslav Republic BIT (2015)	In force
Kosovo–Macedonia BIT (2015)	In force
Macedonia–Viet Nam BIT (2014)	In force
Azerbaijan–Macedonia, The former Yugoslav Republic of BIT (2013)	In force
Kazakhstan–Macedonia, The former Yugoslav Republic of BIT (2012)	In force
Macedonia, The former Yugoslav Republic of–Qatar BIT (2011)	Signed
Lithuania–Macedonia, The former Yugoslav Republic of BIT (2011)	In force
Macedonia, The former Yugoslav Republic of–Montenegro BIT (2010)	In force
Macedonia, The former Yugoslav Republic of–Morocco BIT (2010)	In force
Macedonia, The former Yugoslav Republic of–Slovakia BIT (2009)	In force
Kuwait–Macedonia, The former Yugoslav Republic of BIT (2008)	In force
India–North Macedonia (2008)	Terminated
Macedonia, The former Yugoslav Republic of–Spain BIT (2005)	In force
Czech Republic–Macedonia, The former Yugoslav Republic of BIT (2001)	In force
Belarus–Macedonia, The former Yugoslav Republic of BIT (2001)	In force
Hungary–Macedonia, The former Yugoslav Republic of BIT (2001)	In force
Austria–Macedonia, The former Yugoslav Republic of BIT (2001)	In force
Bosnia and Herzegovina–Macedonia, The former Yugoslav Republic of BIT (2001)	In force
Finland–Macedonia, The former Yugoslav Republic of BIT (2001)	In force

TABLE 16.1 List of Bilateral Investment Treaties concluded by North Macedonia (*cont.*)

Parties	Status
Iran, Islamic Republic of–Macedonia, The former Yugoslav Republic of BIT (2000)	In force
Macedonia, The former Yugoslav Republic of–Romania BIT (2000)	In force
Egypt–Macedonia, The former Yugoslav Republic of BIT (1999)	Signed
Macedonia, The former Yugoslav Republic of–Taiwan Province of China BIT (1999)	In force
Bulgaria–Macedonia, The former Yugoslav Republic of BIT (1999)	In force
BLEU (Belgium-Luxembourg Economic Union)–Macedonia, The former Yugoslav Republic of BIT (1999)	In force
Macedonia, The former Yugoslav Republic of–Netherlands BIT (1998)	In force
Macedonia, The former Yugoslav Republic of–Sweden BIT (1998)	In force
North Macedonia–Ukraine BIT (1998)	In force
France–Macedonia, The former Yugoslav Republic of BIT (1998)	In force
Albania–Macedonia, The former Yugoslav Republic of BIT (1997)	In force
Macedonia, The former Yugoslav Republic of–Malaysia BIT (1997)	In force
Macedonia, The former Yugoslav Republic of–Russian Federation BIT (1997)	In force
Korea, Dem. People's Rep. of–Macedonia, The former Yugoslav Republic of BIT (1997)	In force
China–Macedonia, The former Yugoslav Republic of BIT (1997)	In force
Italy–Macedonia, The former Yugoslav Republic of BIT (1997)	Terminated
Macedonia, The former Yugoslav Republic of–Poland BIT (1996)	In force
Macedonia, The former Yugoslav Republic of–Switzerland BIT (1996)	In force
Germany–Macedonia, The former Yugoslav Republic of BIT (1996)	In force
Macedonia, The former Yugoslav Republic of–Serbia BIT (1996)	In force
Macedonia, The former Yugoslav Republic of–Slovenia BIT (1996)	In force
Macedonia, The former Yugoslav Republic of–Turkey BIT (1995)	In force
Croatia–Macedonia, The former Yugoslav Republic of BIT (1994)	In force

6 International Investment Treaty Framework – Treaties with Investment Provisions and Investment Related Instruments

Treaties with investment provisions (TIPS) are economic agreements that include investment-related provisions, distinct from Bilateral Investment Treaties (BITS). These provisions are found in various agreements such as:

TABLE 16.2 List of treaties with investment provisions concluded by North Macedonia

Title of agreement	Status
Partnership, Trade and Cooperation Agreement between the Republic of North Macedonia and the United Kingdom of Great Britain and Northern Ireland	Signed
Central European Free Trade Agreement and the Agreement on Amendment of and Accession to the Central European Free Trade Agreement	In force
Stabilization and Association Agreement between the European Community, of the One Part, and the Former Yugoslav Republic of Macedonia, of the Other Part	In force
Free Trade Agreement between the EFTA States and the Republic of Macedonia	In force
Free Trade Agreement between Turkey and the Former Yugoslav Republic of Macedonia	In force
The Energy Charter Treaty	In force

- Investment chapters within Economic Partnership Agreements (EPAs)
- Free Trade Agreements (FTA) and
- Regional economic integration agreements.

These provisions aim to facilitate and regulate investment activities between the signatory parties, covering areas such as investment protection, dispute resolution, and the promotion of investment. The Republic of North Macedonia is a party to six (6) such treaties.

As for the Investment Related Instruments, Republic of North Macedonia is a party and signatory to the: Agreement on Trade-Related Aspects of Intellectual Property Rights (hereinafter TRIPS), Agreement on Trade-Related Investment Measures hereinafter TRIMs, Convention Establishing the Multilateral Investment Guarantee Agency (hereinafter MIGA Convention), United Nations Convention on the Recognition and Enforcement of Foreign Arbitral Awards (hereinafter New York Convention), Convention on the settlement of investment disputes between States and nationals of other States (hereinafter ICSID Convention), General Agreement on Trade in Services of the World Trade Organization (hereinafter GATS), Fifth Protocol to GATS, Fourth Protocol to GATS Draft Supplementary Treaty to the Energy Charter Treaty, UN Code of Conduct on Transnational Corporations, the Doha Declaration, World Bank Investment Guidelines, International Labour Organization (ILO) Tripartite Declaration on Multinational Enterprises, the Singapore Ministerial Declaration, UN Guiding Principles on Business and Human Rights, the Permanent Sovereignty UN Resolution, New International Economic Order UN Resolution, and the Charter of Economic Rights and Duties of States.

7 Recent Trends in Reforming the Model Bilateral Investment Treaty

The new Draft Model BIT of the Republic of North Macedonia was drafted in the midst of the global economic crisis and vivid discussions on the reform of the International Settlement of Investment Disputes (ISDS). Therefore, this new Draft Model BIT follows the most recent trends for reform. Also, it may be considered a "new generation BIT" for some of its features and embodied principles, such as the principle of equal opportunities and participation of women and men in the economy, principles of corporate social responsibility (notably the OECD Guidelines for multinational enterprises), best practices of responsible business conduct and a modern dispute resolution clause.

The new Draft Model BIT of the Republic of North Macedonia has been positively evaluated by the European Commission and it is in the final stage of adoption by the Government of North Macedonia. This new Draft Model BIT is fully aligned with the annotated EU Model Clauses for the negotiation or re-negotiation of Member States' Bilateral Investment Agreements with third countries from 2023.

The Draft-Model BIT is composed of a preamble and 5 (five) parts. The first part is named: *Definitions and Scope of Application*. The Draft Model BIT largely retains the definition of "investment" from the 2009 Model, which is broadened to include a definition that begins with a general description, followed by a non-exhaustive list of examples. However, it includes some significant modifications.

The Model BIT, in Article 1, adopts an asset-based definition of investment. For an investment to be covered by the Model BIT, it must be of a certain duration, involve the commitment of capital or other resources, and entail the assumption of risk (following the Salini test). The inclusion of the necessary characteristics of assets that constitute investments aligns with recent treaties, such as the Italian and Dutch Model BITs, which have also incorporated similar characteristics. The first part of the Model BIT stipulates that it applies to measures adopted or maintained by a Contracting Party in its territory concerning: a) Investors from the other contracting party, and b) Protected investments.[19]

The second part is titled: *Promotion and Protection of Investment*. In this part, the following questions are regulated: promotion of investment, transparency, treatment of investors and covered investments, national treatment and most favored nation (MFN) treatment, expropriation and compensation, compensation for losses, transfers, temporary security measures and subrogation. The main novelty in this part is the clear obligation of the Contracting Parties to recognize that it is inappropriate to weaken or reduce the level

19 Draft North Macedonia Model Bilateral Investment Treaty, Art 2 (1).

of protection provided by domestic health, safety, labour or environmental laws, international agreements or standards with the sole intention of encouraging investment. Accordingly, a Contracting Party shall not waive or otherwise waive, or offer to waive or otherwise waive, such laws, regulations or standards to encourage investment by an investor of the other Contracting Party.

The principle of transparency requires each party to publish, or otherwise make publicly available, its laws and regulations of general application, as well as international agreements which may affect investors of the other Party and their covered investments in its territory, including any measures aimed at protecting the environment and labour conditions or that may be affecting the protection of the environment or labour conditions, thereby ensuring awareness and providing reasonable opportunities for interested persons and stakeholders to submit views. As for the national treatment and the MFN clause, the proposed articles are based on the Italian, Dutch and Belgian Model BIT,.

Investments and Sustainable Development is the title of the third part of the new Draft-Model BIT. It represents a complete set of new rules, which are, for the first time, introduced in the Model BIT of the Republic of North Macedonia. The previous 2009 Model BIT did not deal with the questions of investments and sustainable development.

This part includes provisions for the protection of human rights, public health, safety, the environment, public morals, financial stability, social or consumer protection, or the promotion and protection of cultural diversity. Within this part, there is a clear commitment of the Contracting Parties to sustainable development and to promoting the development of international economic cooperation. In that sense, each Contracting Party should encourage enterprises operating within its territory or subject to its jurisdiction to voluntarily incorporate internationally recognized standards of corporate social responsibility in their practices and internal policies, such as statements of principle that have been endorsed or are supported by the Parties.

These principles address issues such as labour, the environment, human rights, community relations and anti-corruption. Also, there is a commitment for the Contracting Parties, to dialogue and cooperate as appropriate on investment-related labour, environmental and climate change issues of mutual interest arising under part three in a manner complementary to the efforts under existing bilateral and multilateral mechanisms.

The fourth part deals with the dispute settlement mechanism, while the last part of the Draft-Model BIT deals with the question of entry into force and termination, consistent with standard practice of the vast majority of other BIT s. The last part of the new Draft-Model BIT contains the final provisions, regulating amendments, entry into force and termination of the agreement, after the accession of the Republic of North Macedonia to the European Union.

7.1 *Definitions of "Investment" and "Investor" Under the New Draft-Model* BIT

Under Article 1 (1) of the new Draft-Model BIT,[20] investment means every kind of asset that has the characteristics of an investment, which includes a certain duration, the commitment of capital or other resources, the expectation of gain or profit, and the assumption of risk. Investments under the treaty may thus include:

a. movable and immovable property as well as any other property rights in rem in respect of every kind of asset, such as mortgages, liens and pledges;
b. rights derived from shares, bonds and other kinds of interests in companies and joint ventures;
c. claims to money, to other assets or to any contractual performance having an economic value;
d. intellectual property rights, including copyrights, trade marks, patents, industrial designs, technical processes, know-how, trade secrets, trade names and goodwill associated with an investment;
e. public private partnership concluded in accordance with the laws and regulations of the Contracting Party in the territory whereof the investment is being made, including concessions to search or cultivate, extract or exploit natural resources.
f claims to money or to any performance under a contract having a financial value associated with an investment.

Further on, the term "investor"[21] means:

a. any natural person having the nationality of that Contracting Party under its applicable law;
b. a natural person who has dual nationality of the Republic of North Macedonia and the other country, shall be deemed to be exclusively a national of the Contracting Party of his or her dominant and effective nationality;
c. The term "legal person" refers with regard to either Contracting Party to any legal person including, enterprises, companies, corporations, business associations and/or organizations established or organized in accordance with the respective state legislation of either Contracting Party having their seat and their main activities in the territory of that Contracting Party;

20 *Ibid.* Art 1 (1)
21 Draft North Macedonia Model Bilateral Investment Treaty, Art 1 (3).

d. an enterprise incorporated or constituted under the law of one Contracting Party, but effectively controlled, directly or indirectly, by nationals or enterprises of the other Contracting Party, shall be treated as an enterprise of the latter Contracting Party;
e. an enterprise incorporated or constituted under the law of one Contracting Party, but owned or effectively controlled, directly or indirectly, by nationals or enterprises of the other Contracting Party, shall be treated as an enterprise of the latter Contracting Party.

7.2 *Promotion of Investments and Transparency under the New Draft-Model BIT*

The new Draft-Model BIT provides that each Contracting Party shall, in its territory, promote as far as possible investments by investors of the other Contracting Party and admit such investments in accordance with its laws and regulations.[22] Further, the Contracting Parties recognise that it is inappropriate to weaken or reduce the level of protection provided by domestic health, safety, labour or environmental laws, regulations or standards with the sole intention of encouraging investment. Accordingly, a Contracting Party shall not waive or otherwise derogate from, or offer to waive or otherwise derogate from, such laws, regulations or standards in order to encourage investment of an investor from the other Contracting Party.[23]

During the transportation of goods and persons related to a specific investment, one contracting party shall not exclude or impede the transport companies of the other contracting party and, if necessary, shall grant permits for the execution of the transportation.[24] Finally, each Contracting Party shall create favorable conditions for the granting of visas and work permits required in its territory in order to enable the nationals of the other Contracting Party to perform their activities connected to the investment.[25]

Transparency in international investment arbitration refers to the extent to which the public can access arbitral proceedings and information related to those proceedings. This includes providing access to hearings, documents, awards, decisions, and the inner workings of arbitral institutions, thereby enhancing the openness and accountability of the arbitration process. This is why the new Draft-Model BIT introduces transparency as one of its cornerstone articles.

---

22 *Ibid.* Art 4 (1).
23 *Ibid.* Art 4 (2).
24 *Ibid.* Art 4 (3).
25 *Ibid.* Art 4 (4).

In principle, each Contracting Party shall ensure that its laws, regulations, judicial decisions, procedures and administrative rulings of general application with respect to any matter covered by this Agreement are promptly published or made available in such a manner as to enable interested persons and the other Contracting Party and its investors to become acquainted with them. Whenever possible, such instruments will be made available through the internet in English. Further, there is no requirement for the Party to publish or allow access to any confidential or proprietary information, including information concerning particular investors or their covered investments, the disclosure of which would impede law enforcement or be contrary to domestic laws protecting confidentiality, or would prejudice legitimate commercial interests of investors and their covered investments.[26]

7.3 *Investments and Sustainable Development – New Trends in the Evolving Economy*

Sustainable Development Investing (hereinafter SDI) refers to deploying capital in ways that make a positive contribution to sustainable development, using the Sustainable Development Goals (hereinafter SDGs) as a basis for measurement. By aligning investment strategies with the SDGs, SDI aims to address global challenges while generating financial returns. The new Draft-Model BIT, for the first time, introduces a special chapter devoted to investments and sustainable development.

7.3.1 Corporate Social Responsibility

Under the new Draft-Model BIT, the Parties acknowledge the importance of investors implementing due diligence to identify and address adverse impacts, such as those affecting the environment and labour conditions, within their operations, supply chains, and other business relationships. The Parties commit to promoting the adoption of corporate social responsibility (CSR) or responsible business practices by enterprises and investors to contribute to sustainable development and responsible investment. Furthermore, the Parties agree to support the dissemination and utilization of relevant internationally agreed instruments, such as the UN Global Compact, the UN Guiding Principles on Business and Human Rights, the ILO Tripartite Declaration of Principles concerning Multinational Enterprises and Social Policy, and the OECD Guidelines for Multinational Enterprises, along with related due diligence guidance.

---

26 *Ibid.* Art 5.

Additionally, the Parties agree to exchange information and best practices on issues covered by this article, including possible ways to facilitate the adoption of corporate social responsibility and responsible practices by enterprises and investors.[27]

7.3.2 Health, Safety and Environmental Measures

Based on Article 14 of the new Draft-Model BIT, the Contracting Parties shall not to encourage investment by relaxing domestic health, safety or environmental measures. Accordingly, a Contracting Party should not waive or otherwise derogate from or offer to waive or otherwise derogate from those measures to encourage the establishment, acquisition, expansion or retention of an investment of an investor in its territory.[28]

7.3.3 Labour Standards

When it comes to the labour, the new Draft-Model BIT provides that the Contracting Parties, in accordance with their obligations under relevant ILO instruments, recognize that the violation of fundamental principles and rights at work cannot be used as an encouragement for the establishment, acquisition, expansion and retention in their territories, of an investment.[29] Each Contracting Party reaffirms its commitment to respect, promote and implement in its law and practices in its whole territory core labour standards as embodied in the fundamental ILO Conventions that it has ratified. The Parties shall make continued and sustained efforts to ratify the fundamental ILO Conventions if they have not yet done so.[30]

7.3.4 Dialogue and Cooperation on Investment-Related Sustainable Development Issues

The new Draft-Model BIT provides that the Parties agree to dialogue and cooperate as appropriate on investment-related labour, environmental and climate change issues of mutual interest in a manner complementary to the efforts under existing bilateral and multilateral mechanisms.[31]

---

27 *Ibid.* Art 13.
28 *Ibid.* Art 14.
29 *Ibid.* Art 15 (1).
30 *Ibid.* Art 15 (2).
31 *Ibid.* Art 16.

8 Mediation and Conciliation – Policy Trends

The Model BIT 2009 provides for a classic dispute-resolution clause that preceded the current stages of reform at the international level. The components of such clauses include:

1. Disputes between one of the Contracting Parties and an investor of the other Contracting Party shall be notified in writing, including detailed information, by the investor to the Contracting Party in whose territory the investment is made. Any dispute between a Contracting Party and an investor of the other Contracting Party should be settled by friendly agreement.
2. If the dispute cannot be settled amicably within six months from the date of the written notification, by which the other Contracting Party was informed about the subject of the dispute, the investor concerned may suggest, at his own choice, for the dispute to be submitted to:
   - the competent court of the Contracting Party in whose territory the investment is made;
   - "ad hoc" arbitration conducted under the Arbitration Rules of the United Nations Commission for International Trade Law (UNCITRAL);
   - the International Center for Settling Investment Disputes (ICSID), in accordance with the Convention on the Settlement of Investment Disputes between States and Nationals of Other States, open for signature since 18.03.1965 in Washington DC, if both Contracting Parties signed this Convention.
3. Once the dispute has been submitted to the competent court of the Contracting Party or to international arbitration, the choice of one or the other procedure shall be definitive (so-called fork in the road clause).
4. The arbitration decision shall be based on:
   - the provisions of the Agreement;
   - the national law of the Contracting Party in whose territory the investment is made, including the rules related to conflicts of law;
   - the rules and the universally accepted principles of international law.
5. The arbitration decisions shall be final and binding on the parties to the dispute. Each Contracting Party shall undertake to execute the decisions in accordance with its national law.[32]

32 Model Bilateral Investment Treaty, Art 7 (2009).

Based on the analysis of concluded BITs of North Macedonia, it appears that there is a lack of treaty regulation regarding mediation as one of the alternative methods for resolving disputes. While all BITs contain a clause that refers to the International Centre for Settlement of Investment Disputes (hereinafter ICSID), no further provisions regarding mediation can be found in the majority of these agreements. However, in six BITs (concluded between North Macedonia and India, Malaysia, Morocco, Netherlands, Sweden, and Switzerland), there is a clear reference to mediation/conciliation. Only the BIT with India provides for international conciliation under the Conciliation Rules of the United Nations Commission on International Trade Law (UNCITRAL), and only if both parties agree.

However, the situation under the new Draft-Model BIT has changed, which now includes a modern and detailed provision.

Under Article 23 of the new Draft-Model BIT:

1. Any disputing party may initiate, at any moment, a mediation or a conciliation process in accordance with ICC Rules on Mediation, the ICSID Rules on Mediation or the ICSID Rules on conciliation or such other rules as the disputing parties may agree.
2. Recourse to mediation or conciliation pursuant to this Article is voluntary and without prejudice to the legal position of either disputing party.
3. Once the disputing parties agree to have recourse to mediation, the time limits set out for the amicable settlement of dispute in Article 20 shall be suspended between the date on which it was agreed to have recourse to mediation or conciliation and the date on which either party to the dispute decides to terminate the mediation or the conciliation, by way of a letter to the mediator or the conciliator and the other disputing party.
4. If an international arbitration has already been initiated pursuant to Article 24, once a mediation or a conciliation request is sent to one of the disputing parties, the disputing parties may agree to request jointly the arbitral tribunal or the court to suspend the proceeding in course for an agreed time period.
5. Upon request of both disputing parties, the arbitral tribunal shall stay its proceedings until the date on which either party to the dispute decides to terminate the mediation or the conciliation, by way of letter to the mediator or the conciliator, the other disputing party and the arbitral tribunal.
6. The mediation or the conciliation shall take place in the territory of the Contracting Party where the investment is established, or upon the disputing parties' agreement in any other location or by video-conferencing or any other means.

7. The mediator or the conciliator shall be a national of neither Contracting Party.
8. The mediator or the conciliator shall be impartial and independent of the disputing parties.
9. The mediator or the conciliator shall have particular expertise or experience in the following fields:
   a. mediation or conciliation as dispute settlement means; or the resolution of disputes arising under International Investment or International Trade Agreements; and
   b. Public International Law; or International Investment or International Trade Law or experience in the industry or economic field of the investment.
10. If the disputing parties do not agree on the remuneration of the mediators or the conciliators, the prevailing ICSID rate for mediators or conciliators shall apply.
11. The mediation or the conciliation shall be terminated by:
   a. adoption of a mutual agreement of the disputing parties, on the date of that agreement;
   b. by a written declaration of the mediator, after consultation with the disputing parties, that further efforts at mediation would be to no avail, on the date of that declaration;
   c. by a written declaration of the investor or the Contracting Party, on the date of that declaration.
12. Any conciliation agreement reached between the disputing parties during the mediation shall comply with the domestic law of the Contracting Party, including its budgetary laws and rules.
13. In case the mediation or the conciliation is terminated without the adoption by the disputing parties of a mutual agreement, any stayed arbitration proceeding shall resume. In such case, the disputing parties shall not rely on or introduce as evidence in arbitration, nor shall the arbitral tribunal take into consideration:
   a. positions taken by the disputing parties in the course of the mediation procedure;
   b. the fact that one of the disputing parties to mediation has indicated its willingness to accept a solution to the alleged breach subject to mediation; or
   c. advice given or proposals made by the mediator.[33]

33 Draft North Macedonia Model Bilateral Investment Treaty, Art 23.

9 Investor-State Disputes Involving North Macedonia

Any investment has the potential to result in a dispute. If such a dispute cannot be resolved amicably, the next step is usually court or arbitration, if so provided under the applicable instrument of consent. In cases where a bilateral or multilateral agreement offers a choice, investors typically opt for institutional or ad hoc arbitration to resolve the dispute. While the settlement of the dispute before the domestic court of the respondent state is an option, it often creates unease among investors and is, therefore, rarely pursued.

As of May 31, 2024, North Macedonia was involved in several disputes with foreign investors, most of which were governed by bilateral investment agreements containing provisions for arbitration settlement. As of that date, there have been 11 publicly available arbitration disputes against the Republic of North Macedonia arising from concluded bilateral investment agreements.

9.1 *Swisslion DOO Skopje v. Macedonia, Former Yugoslav Republic of (ICSID Case No. ARB/09/16)*[34]

Swisslion v. Macedonia is an arbitration dispute arising from the bilateral agreement for the promotion and mutual protection of investments between Macedonia and Switzerland from 1997. Article 10 of the agreement regulates the resolution of potential disputes. Paragraph 2(a) offers the option to resolve the dispute before an ICSID tribunal, while paragraph 2(b) provides for an ad hoc tribunal. In 2009, Swisslion, a Swiss investor in North Macedonia, initiated a dispute against North Macedonia before the ICSID arbitral tribunal.

Swisslion claimed that North Macedonia illegally expropriated part of the shares in Agroplod, which violated Article 5, paragraph 1 of the agreement. Additionally, Swisslion argued that North Macedonia failed to comply with its obligations, thereby breaching Article 12 of the investment contract. Swisslion further alleged that "Macedonia unreasonably interfered with Swisslion's enjoyment" of the investment, contravening Article 4, paragraph 1 of the applicable BIT. The ICSID tribunal ruled in favor of the claimant, finding a violation of Article 4, paragraph 2. As a result, North Macedonia was ordered to pay the investor €350,000, along with semi-annual compound interest calculated at the LIBOR rate from March 30, 2007. North Macedonia was also required to pay €350,000 to the claimant as part of the legal costs. The award is publicly available.

---

34 Swisslion DOO Skopje v. Macedonia, former Yugoslav Republic of, ICSID Case No. ARB/09/16, (Jul. 6, 2012).

9.2 *EVN AG v. Macedonia, Former Yugoslav Republic of (ICSID Case No. ARB/09/10)*[35]

The arbitration dispute arose from the bilateral agreement for the protection and promotion of investments between Austria and Macedonia from 2002. Article 12 of the agreement regulates the resolution of potential disputes. In 2009, EVN initiated a dispute against Macedonia before the ICSID arbitration tribunal, based on this article. The dispute concerns unpaid electricity bills from citizens and companies for the period from 1995 to 2004, totaling a sum of €100 million in claims, plus interest. In 2011, the parties reached a settlement, which was embodied by the ICSID arbitral tribunal in the form of an award. However, this settlement is not available to the public.

9.3 *Guardian Fiduciary Trust, Ltd, f/k/a Capital Conservator Savings & Loan, Ltd v. Macedonia, Former Yugoslav Republic of (ICSID Case No. ARB/12/31)*[36]

The arbitration dispute arose from the bilateral agreement for the protection and promotion of investments between Macedonia and the Netherlands from 1998. Pursuant to the provisions of the agreement, the dispute was brought before the ICSID arbitral tribunal under the 2006 ICSID Arbitration Rules. The dispute revolved around a money laundering investigation. Macedonian authorities arrested one of the Claimant's directors on charges of money laundering and issued a statement disclosing both the Claimant's name and the director's name.

According to the Claimant, the Respondent knew or should have known that the money laundering allegations were false. The Claimant alleged that the actions taken by the respondent, particularly the alleged false statements, forced the Claimant to change its location and name, causing substantial harm to its business. The Claimant claimed that the respondent's behavior constituted a breach of contract and demanded compensation for the losses suffered.

Initially, the claim was quantified at $600 million but was later reduced to approximately $20 million. The dispute was further complicated by ambiguities regarding the ownership of the developer and the nationality of the owner. Consequently, the tribunal dismissed the claims due to a lack of *ratione personae* (personal) jurisdiction. The Claimant was ordered to pay North

35 EVN AG v. Macedonia, former Yugoslav Republic of, ICSID Case No. ARB/09/10, (Sep. 2, 2011).

36 Guardian Fiduciary Trust, Ltd, f/k/a Capital Conservator Savings & Loan, Ltd v. Macedonia, former Yugoslav Republic of, ICSID Case No. ARB/12/31, (Sept. 22, 2015).

Macedonia an amount of US$1,072,708 and £32,000 in legal costs. All other claims of either party were dismissed.

9.4 *Blazo Tasev v. Republic of North Macedonia (PCA Case No. 2019-09)*[37]

The ongoing arbitration arose from the agreement for the protection and promotion of foreign investments between Macedonia and Slovenia, dating back to 1996. The dispute will be adjudicated before the Permanent Court of Arbitration under the UNCITRAL Arbitration Rules of 1976. The dispute, which concerns the mining sector, has limited public information available, with all other details remaining undisclosed.

9.5 *Cunico Resources N.V. v. Macedonia, Former Yugoslav Republic of (ICSID Case No. ARB/17/46)*[38]

An arbitration dispute arose from the bilateral agreement for the protection and promotion of investments between Macedonia and the Netherlands, dating back to 1998. Pursuant to Article 9 of the treaty, the arbitration proceedings are brought before the ICSID Arbitral Tribunal, under the 2006 ICSID Arbitration Rules. The Claimant's claims stem from the alleged interference of the Republic of North Macedonia Government in the planned sale of FENI Industries by the Claimant, which allegedly led to the initiation of bankruptcy proceedings against FENI. The proceedings before the tribunal have been discontinued in accordance with Article 43, paragraph 1 of the rules, as the parties have managed to agree on a settlement of the dispute or have otherwise terminated the proceedings.

9.6 *Gokul Das Binani and Madhu Binani v. Republic of North Macedonia (I) (PCA Case No. 2018-38)*[39]

The claim arose from the bilateral agreement for the protection and promotion of investments between Macedonia and India, dated March 17, 2008. The dispute was brought before the Permanent Court of Arbitration, pursuant to the UNCITRAL Arbitration Rules of 1976. The dispute revolves around a concession for lead and zinc in Dobrevo and Toranica, which the plaintiff claims was arbitrarily expropriated and redistributed. However, the arbitration procedure

37 Blazo Tasev v. Republic of North Maced., PCA Case No. 2019-09 (2020).

38 Cunico Resources N.V. v. Macedonia, former Yugoslav Republic of, ICSID Case No. ARB/17/46, (Dec. 21, 2017).

39 Gokul Das Binani and Madhu Binani v. Macedonia, former Yugoslav Republic of, PCA Case No. 2018-38 (i), (Aug. 7, 2017).

was compicated by the Claimant's inability to cover the costs of the tribunal, leading to its termination.

9.7 *Valentyn Drozdenko, Artem Kadomskyi, Igor Kompanets and others v. Republic of North Macedonia (ICSID Case No. ARB/19/9)*[40]

This dispute arose from the bilateral agreement for the protection and promotion of investments between Macedonia and Ukraine, dated April 28, 1998. Under Article 7 of the agreement, which regulates the resolution of potential investor-state disputes, the investor brought an arbitration dispute against the Republic of North Macedonia before the International Centre for Settlement of Investment Disputes (ICSID), under the 2006 Arbitration Rules. The dispute concerns three mining concessions for the Kazandol, Petroshnica, and Plavush deposits. The claims amount to 380 million EUR and stem from the termination of the concession for the exploitation of copper, gold, and silver in the Kazandol deposit, allegedly due to environmental concerns. As of now, the dispute is ongoing.

9.8 *Gokul Das Binani and Madhu Binani v. Republic of North Macedonia (II)*[41]

This dispute is a continuation of Binani v. North Macedonia (I). The proceedings were initiated before an ad hoc arbitral tribunal under the UNCITRAL Arbitration Rules of 2013. As of the date of writing, the arbitration procedure is still ongoing.

9.9 *GAMA Güç Sistemleri Mühendislik ve Taahhüt A.Ş. v. Republic of North Macedonia*[42]

This arbitration dispute arose from the bilateral agreement for the protection and promotion of investments between Macedonia and Turkey, dated January 30, 1997. Article 7 of this agreement outlines the procedures for resolving potential disputes between investors and the state. The dispute was brought before the International Chamber of Commerce (ICC), under the ICC rules. At present, the proceedings are ongoing, and information regarding the dispute is limited.

40 Valentyn Drozdenko, Artem Kadomskyi, Igor Kompanets and others v. Republic of North Maced., ICSID Case No. ARB/19/9 (2019).

41 Gokul Das Binani and Madhu Binani v. Macedonia, former Yugoslav Republic of, PCA Case No. 2018-38 (ii) (2020).

42 AMA Güç Sistemleri Mühendislik ve Taahhüt A.Ş. v. Republic of North Macedonia, ICC Case No. 26696/HBH, (Nov. 23, 2021).

9.10 *FCL Ambiente S.r.l. v. Republic of North Macedonia (ICSID Case No. ARB/23/31)*[43]

In 2023, an Italian company initiated an ICSID claim against North Macedonia regarding a concession to manage one of Europe's largest landfill sites. Meanwhile, a Canadian mining company has renewed its threat to bring a claim against the state, although details regarding this potential claim are also limited.

9.11 *Amadeus Group and Amadeus Development DOOEL v. Republic of North Macedonia (ICSID Case No. ARB/23/35)*[44]

An Albanian group has filed a $110 million ICSID claim against North Macedonia regarding a halted project to construct a hotel and commercial center in the capital city of Skopje. The Arbitral Tribunal was constituted on February 29, 2024 and no further information is available.

10 Policy Recommendations

The Republic of North Macedonia has adopted an open-door policy for foreign investors, recognizing the need to provide essential international legal protection. As a result, North Macedonia has concluded 42 Bilateral Investment Treaties to date, as well as multilateral treaties such as the Energy Charter Treaty. The arbitration clauses in these treaties typically cover all types of disputes that may arise between foreign investors and the Republic of North Macedonia as the host country. Foreign investors are offered a variety of dispute settlement options, including Macedonian courts and several arbitral tribunals. These options include the possibility for investors to submit disputes to ICSID or to initiate ad hoc arbitration under UNCITRAL Arbitration Rules. Some treaties also allow cases to be submitted to prominent international arbitral institutions such as the International Chamber of Commerce or the Arbitration Institute of the Stockholm Chamber of Commerce (SCC). The choice of law clause consistently stipulates the application of relevant rules and principles of international law.

The new Draft Model Bilateral Investment Treaty is based on contemporary model agreements. Its aim is to provide North Macedonia with a stronger

43 FCL Ambiente S.r.l. v. Republic of North Macedonia, ICSID Case No. ARB/23/31, (Jul. 31, 2023).

44 Amadeus Group and Amadeus Development DOOEL v. Republic of North Maced., ICSID Case No. ARB/23/35, (Oct. 21, 2023).

negotiating position when forming agreements to protect and promote foreign investments, while also aligning its investment policy with that of the European Union.

Observing the investments made in North Macedonia, it is evident that a significant portion comes from the traditional sector, which relies on fossil fuels. This raises the question of how a potential transition by North Macedonia to renewable energy will impact the expectations of investors. Are we potentially moving towards a situation where an increasing number of disputes will arise from this shift? An analysis of previous disputes brought against North Macedonia reveals that the state successfully wins most cases in its favor. Utilizing clear language in drafting agreements for the protection and promotion of investments will enhance legal certainty for foreign investors while clearly defining the boundaries of sustainable development.

CHAPTER 17

Investment Protection and Investor-State Dispute Resolution in Serbia

Dragana Nikolić

1 Introduction[1]

The Republic of Serbia is situated in the west-central part of the Balkans and serves as a junction between Eastern and Western Europe. It is a landlocked country bordering with Hungary, Romania, Bulgaria, Macedonia, Albania, Montenegro, Bosnia and Herzegovina, and Croatia. It covers an area of 88,499 km2 and has a population of 6,647,003 inhabitants.[2] The official currency is the Serbian dinar (RSD).[3]

Serbia was part of the former Yugoslavia for much of the 20th century, becoming independent in 2006 after Montenegro withdrew from their joint state union. Today, Serbia is a parliamentary democracy. Its capital, Belgrade, is home to over 1,600,000 citizens and is one of the largest cities and key financial centers in Southeastern Europe.

2 FDI Trends

The transition in Serbia, including privatization, started in the early 1990s, but it encountered substantial setbacks due to wars, economic sanctions, hyperinflation, and political instability. A more assertive push toward privatization was initiated after the so-called 'Bulldozer Revolution' in October 2000. A significant portion of foreign direct investments (FDI) stemmed directly from

1 The author wishes to express her sincere gratitude to Miss Oleksandra Azizova, whose assistance was essential in the writing of this chapter. The opinions expressed in this publication are those of the author alone and do not purport to reflect the opinions or views of any law firm, organization or institution with which the author is affiliated.

2 Excluding the population of the Autonomous Province of Kosovo and Metohija.

3 Government of the Republic of Serbia, *Basic Info – Get to Know Serbia* <www.srbija.gov.rs/tekst/en/130127/basic-info.php> accessed 11 May 2024. The Autonomous Province of Kosovo and Metohija is treated as an integral part of the Serbia's territory, pursuant to the Constitution of Serbia.

 | DOI:10.1163/9789004729889_018

these privatization activities.[4] However, the privatization efforts in Serbia have only been partially successful.[5] As will be discussed later, a considerable number of international investment arbitrations involving Serbia are related to unsuccessful privatizations.

In recent years, Serbia has experienced significant growth in FDI, largely attributed to improved economic policies, legal reforms, and various incentives such as financial, tax and other subsidies that have effectively drawn-in foreign investors. These initiatives have positioned Serbia as a prime destination for investment, making it the world leader in job creation through FDI relative to population.[6]

Serbia, while not a member of the European Union (EU), is a candidate country that commenced EU accession negotiations in 2014. As a candidate, Serbia enjoys the benefits of the Central European Free Trade Agreement (CEFTA), which establishes a free trade area among its member countries, including Serbia's several neighborhood countries. Serbia also benefits from the 'Economic and Investment Plan for the Western Balkans 2021–2027'. Under this plan, the EU has committed to invest and support investments in sustainable transport, clean energy, environmental and climate initiatives, the digital future, the competitiveness of the business sector, and the development of human capital.[7]

Along with its close economic ties with EU countries, Serbia has expanded its trade networks by signing additional free trade agreements with China, Turkey, the Eurasian Economic Union (EAEU) led by Russia, and the European Free Trade Association (EFTA), among others. This diverse trade engagement is evident in Serbia's FDI performance, where the largest investors – both in terms of the number and value of projects, are predominantly from EU countries. Germany leads with 17% of projects and 13.5% of total investment value, followed by Italy at 11.1% and 11.7%, respectively. Austria, contributing 6.2% of projects and 7.3% of investment value, and France, with 4.9% and 8.5%, are also significant economic partners for Serbia. Additionally, the USA is also a major contributor, being the third largest source of foreign investments with 7.7% and 10.9%.[8]

4 Slaviša Kovačević, Mladen Rebić and Drago Kurišić, 'The Impact of the Inflow of Foreign Direct Investments on the Economic Development of Serbia' (2021) 2 Economics 123, 130, 134.

5 Ivan Vujačić and Jelica Petrović Vujačić, 'Privatization in Serbia – Results and Institutional Failures' (2011) 191 EA pp. 89, 92.

6 IBM Institute for Business Value, *Research Insights – Global Location Trends* (IBM 2019) p. 6.

7 *See* European Union, *Economic and Investment Plan for the Western Balkans 2021–2027* <www.wbif.eu/eip> accessed 11 May 2024.

8 Development Agency of Serbia, *RAS Database December 2023* <https://ras.gov.rs/en/invest-in-serbia/why-serbia/join-the-pool-of-the-successful> accessed 11 May 2024.

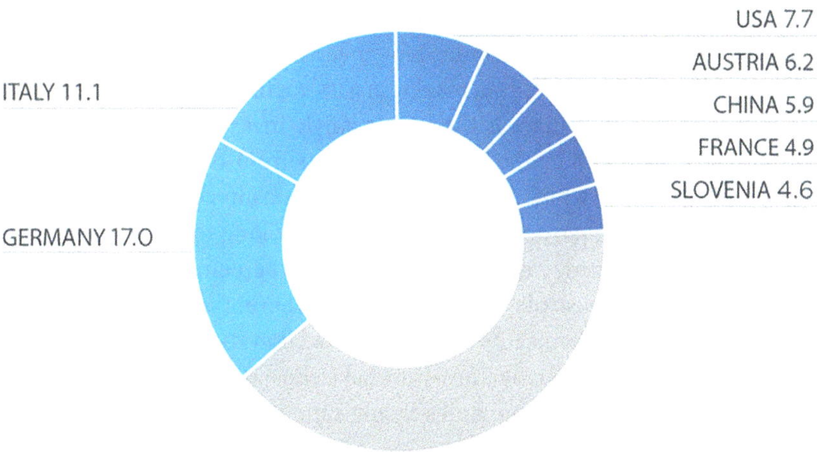

FIGURE 17.1A Largest foreign investors in Serbia by number of projects
AUTHOR: DEVELOPMENT AGENCY OF SERBIA, RAS DATABASE DECEMBER 2023
SOURCE: <HTTPS://RAS.GOV.RS/EN/INVEST-IN-SERBIA/WHY-SERBIA/JOIN-THE-POOL-OF-THE-SUCCESSFUL> ACCESSED 11 MAY 2024

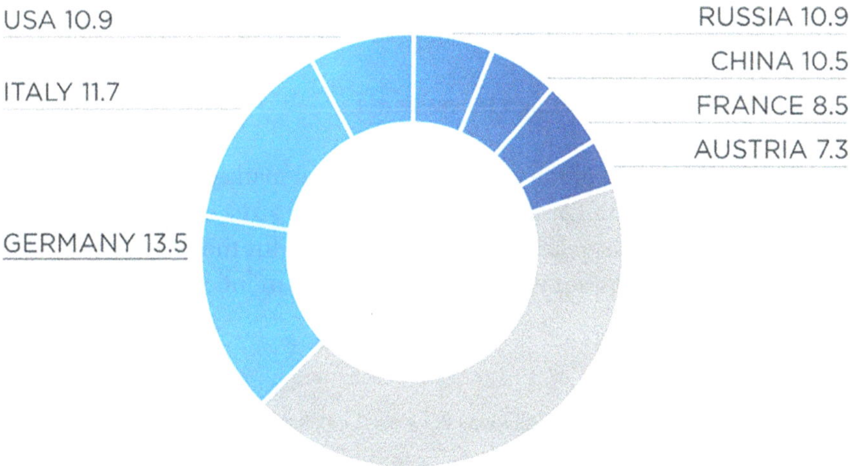

FIGURE 17.1B largest foreign investors in Serbia by value of projects (%)
AUTHOR: DEVELOPMENT AGENCY OF SERBIA, RAS DATABASE DECEMBER 2023
SOURCE: <HTTPS://RAS.GOV.RS/EN/INVEST-IN-SERBIA/WHY-SERBIA/JOIN-THE-POOL-OF-THE-SUCCESSFUL> ACCESSED 11 MAY 2024

In recent years, the involvement of Chinese investors has significantly increased (5.9% of projects and 10.5% of investment value).[9] The value of net investment inflows from China rose from EUR 2.4 million in 2010 to EUR 1.4 billion in 2022. In fact, China was the largest single investor in Serbia in 2022, investing nearly as much as the total investments from the EU combined.[10] The growth in FDI from China is expected to continue after the new free trade agreement takes effect, particularly among those looking to leverage the low customs rates for exporting raw materials under this agreement.

Russian investments also play a significant role in Serbia's economy, accounting for 10.9% by value of projects.[11] It is anticipated that these investments will continue to grow as many Russian investors have chosen to transfer their funds or entire investments from companies facing sanctions to newly established Serbian legal entities.

Turkish investments in Serbia, particularly in infrastructure and the financial sector, have also increased in recent years, as have investments from the United Arab Emirates, including those in real estate, agriculture, and transportation. Key examples of significant foreign direct investments include the Belgrade's airport (France), copper mines and steel mill (China), lithium mine (Australia/UK), automotive plants (Italy, Germany, UK), tire factories (Japan, China) and oil and gas companies (Russia).[12]

3 Key Sectors for Foreign Investments

Serbia opened to FDIs in the early 2000s, a period marked by the sale of key domestic banks to foreign entities. The influx of FDIs increased until the global economic crisis, reaching its peak in 2006 with the privatization of a phone operator.[13] From 2010 onwards, the trend of FDI inflows turned positive

9 *Ibid.*

10 Marina Vulović, 'Economic Relations Between the Western Balkans and Non-EU Countries' [2023] 36 SWP Comment p.3.

11 Development Agency of Serbia, *RAS Database December 2023* <https://ras.gov.rs/en/invest-in-serbia/why-serbia/join-the-pool-of-the-successful> accessed 11 May 2024.

12 For more, *See* László Vasa and Aleksandra Angeloska, 'Foreign Direct Investment in the Republic of Serbia: Correlation Between Foreign Direct Investments and the Selected Economic Variables' (2020) 13(1) JIS pp. 170, 173–174.

13 Ivan Stošić, Draško Nikolić and Mihajlo Đukić, 'Attractiveness of Serbia for Foreign Direct Investments: Tendencies, Obstacles and Perspectives' in Mirjana Radović Marković, Srđan Redžepagić, João Andrade and Paulino Teixeira (eds), *Serbia and the European Union: Economic Lessons from the New Member States* (vol 1, IES 2011) p. 52; Branislav Dudić, Zdenka

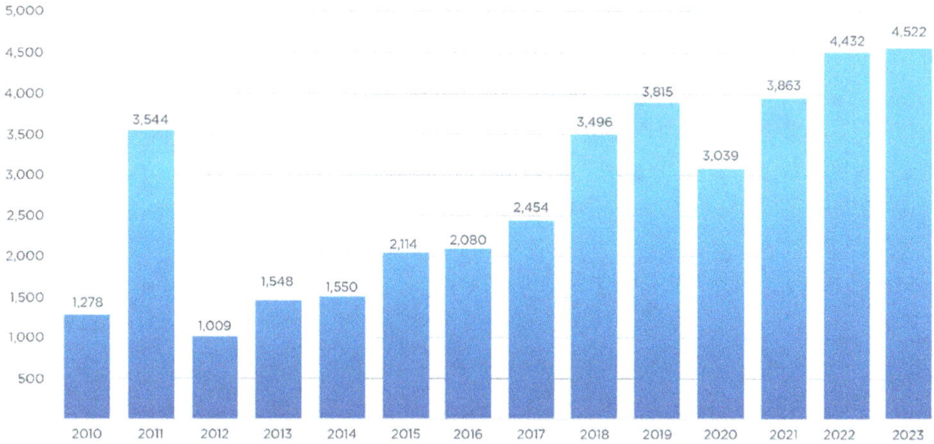

FIGURE 17.2 FDI Inflow (mil EUR)
AUTHOR: NATIONAL BANK OF SERBIA
SOURCE: <HTTPS://RAS.GOV.RS/EN/INVEST-IN-SERBIA/WHY-SERBIA/JOIN-THE-POOL-OF-THE-SUCCESSFUL> ACCESSED 11 MAY 2024

again.[14] The latest reports show that FDI inflows in Serbia are steadily increasing, reaching a record high in 2023 with FDIs valued at EUR 4.5 billion. This represents an increase of almost 15% compared to the pre-COVID year of 2019:

While investments in the financial and telecommunications sectors are now declining, sectors such as electronics, construction, machinery and equipment, and wood and furniture continue to attract investment over the years. Traditionally, the most desirable sectors for investment in Serbia have included automotive, agriculture, food and beverages, and textile and clothing:

More recently, the mining, energy, and information and communication technology sectors are expected to drive significant growth in the coming years.

3.1 *Automotive Sector*

The automotive industry is Serbia's most attractive sector for investment, accounting for approximately 17% of total projects.[15] The impetus for investing in this sector has been driven by historical collaborations with Fiat Chrysler Automobiles, which have spurred interest from other global players. These companies produce wire harnesses, seat covers, tires, wipers, hoses, and

---

Dudić, Ján Smoleň and Vladimir Mirković, 'Support for Foreign Direct Investment Inflows in Serbia' (2018) 169 EA-XXI (1–2) pp. 4, 9–10.

14 Kovačević, Rebić and Kurišić *supra* (n 3) pp. 129–130. *See* also [Fig. 2_Serbia].

15 *See* [Fig. 3_Serbia] above.

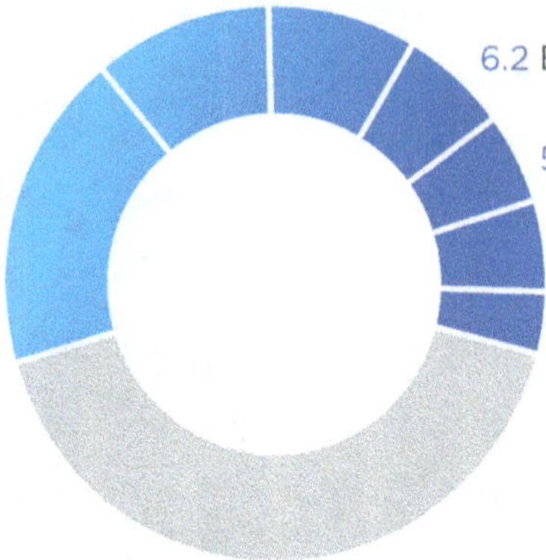

FIGURE 17.3 Most attractive investment sectors by number of projects (%)
AUTHOR: DEVELOPMENT AGENCY OF SERBIA, RAS DATABASE DECEMBER 2023
SOURCE: <HTTPS://RAS.GOV.RS/EN/INVEST-IN-SERBIA/WHY-SERBIA/JOIN-THE-POOL-OF-THE-SUCCESSFUL> ACCESSED 11 MAY 2024

various metal components in plants throughout Serbia. Together, they have contributed to a turnover of more than EUR 5 billion and provided employment to almost 100,000 individuals.[16] As a result, Serbia is now supplying most European car manufacturers. There are also plans to launch the production of electric vehicles in Kragujevac, the heart of the Serbian automotive industry.

3.2 *Agriculture, Food and Beverages*

The northern part of Serbia, known as Vojvodina, boasts some of the cleanest soil in Europe, continually attracting foreign investors specializing in agriculture and the production of food and beverages. Many investors have acquired former Yugoslav giants in this sector, including sugar factories, breweries, chocolate factories, meat plants, dairies, and producers of mineral water and soft drinks. Investing in fruit production has also been profitable. Serbia is also recognized for its potential to export healthy organic food, as the trade and cultivation of genetically modified organisms (GMOs) and products containing GMOs for commercial use are prohibited.[17]

16 Development Agency of Serbia, *Automotive Industry* <https://ras.gov.rs/en/sector/automotive> accessed 11 May 2024.

17 Development Agency of Serbia, *Agri-Food Industry* <https://ras.gov.rs/en/sector/agri-food-industry> accessed 11 May 2024. *See* also the Law on Genetically Modified Organisms (*Official Gazette of RS*, No. 41/2009).

3.3 *Textile and Clothing*

Textile and apparel production in Serbia has a long-standing tradition and has been one of the main export industries for decades. Although its peak years ended with the disbandment of Yugoslavia in the early 1990s, the number of enterprises – primarily small and medium-sized – has recently increased. These businesses mainly provide Cut and Make Trim (CMT) services, importing materials and adding only labor before re-exporting the products. Over the last decade, there has been a shift towards a more design-oriented industry.[18]

3.4 *Mining*

Serbia is rich in high-demand commodities such as gold, copper, zinc, silver, lithium, boron, cobalt, and nickel. Following the adoption of the amendments modernizing the Law on Mining in 2021, Serbia has emerged as a promising hub for mining and exploitation, attracting foreign investors from around the world, including Chinese, Australian and UK companies.[19] However, some of these mining projects have raised significant concerns among the local population due to their environmental impact, leading to mass protests, civil disobedience, and political pressure. Despite this, the sector is expected to grow in the upcoming years, strongly supported by FDIs.[20]

3.5 *Energy*

Serbia has historically generated most of its electricity from coal and hydropower, with only a small percentage coming from renewable sources. This has led the Serbian government to announce an ambitious plan to transition to green energy solutions in the coming years. To facilitate this, in 2021, Serbia adopted the new Law on Use of Renewable Energy Sources, the Law on Energy Efficiency and Rational Use of Energy, and amendments to the Law on Energy.[21] These laws, aligned with EU standards, open opportunities for foreign investors to develop solar power plants, wind farms, biogas, biomass, and

18 Serbia Investment and Export Promotion Agency, *Serbia – Textile Industry* <https://ras.gov.rs/uploads/2016/02/textile-final-small.pdf> accessed 11 May 2024.

19 Law on Mining and Geological Research (*Official Gazette of RS*, Nos. 101/2015, 95/2018 – other law, 40/2021).

20 Government of the Republic of Serbia, 'Zijin Mining to Invest Another $3.8b in Serbia' (9 September 2023) <www.srbija.gov.rs/vest/en/212067/zijin-mining-to-invest-another-38b-in-serbia.php> last accessed 11 May 2024.

21 Law on Use of Renewable Energy Sources (*Official Gazette of RS*, Nos. 40/2021 and 35/2023); Law on Energy Efficiency and Rational Use of Energy (*Official Gazette of RS*, No. 40/2021), and amendments to the Law on Energy (*Official Gazette of RS*, Nos. 145/2014, 95/2018 – other law, 40/2021, 35/2023 – other law and 62/2023).

geothermal plants in Serbia. Additionally, this shift should help reduce Serbia's dependence on Russia, which holds a majority shareholding in Serbia's main oil and gas company.

3.6 *Information and Communication Technology*

The information and communication technology (ICT) sector in Serbia is also well-developed, primarily due to the skilled young workforce and a strong educational system.[22] The Government's support, manifested in a supportive legislative framework, tax incentives, and investments in tech parks, has further contributed to this success. Expertise in this sector is focused on custom, high-end IT development services, including software development, hardware, and solutions. The gaming industry is among the fastest growing in the world. Additionally, the development of blockchain industries is expected to accelerate with the implementation of the new Law on Digital Assets in Serbia.[23]

4 Legal Framework for Foreign Investment Protection

Serbia attracts foreign direct investors not only because of its strategic position as the largest economy in the Western Balkans, but also because it offers a favorable legal framework for investors. The general legal framework for investments in Serbia is outlined in the Law on Investments.[24] Its aim is to enhance the investment environment and encourage direct investments, thereby strengthening economic and commercial development and employment growth.[25] It is accepted in the literature that this law is based on the principles of liberalization, full protection, and promotion of foreign investments.[26]

This law applies to both direct and indirect investments and covers both domestic and foreign investors who have made investments in Serbia in accordance with the law.[27] The Law on Investments also differentiates between

22 Development Agency of Serbia, *ICT* < https://ras.gov.rs/en/sector/ict > accessed 11 May 2024.

23 Law on Digital Assets (*Official Gazette of RS*, No. 153/2020).

24 Law on Investments (*Official Gazette of RS*, Nos. 89/2015 and 95/2018). *See* also Drago Divljak, 'New Legal Framework for Foreign Investments in Serbia – Key Characteristics and Possible Effects' (2016) 2 ZRPFNS p. 423; Vladimir Pavić, 'A Decisive Half-Step Forward – Review of the Law on Investment' (2016) 1 APFBG p. 67.

25 Law on Investments, Article 2.

26 Divljak (n 23) pp. 426–427.

27 Law on Investments, Article 3.

investments of special importance and those of local importance.[28] Significantly, a branch of a foreign company functions simultaneously as both a foreign investor and a foreign investment.

Under Article 4 of the Law on Investments, investors are guaranteed the freedom to invest and protection for their investments, in accordance with the applicable laws. Furthermore, Article 5 of this law ensures that investors have full legal security and protection regarding rights acquired through investment. Additionally, Article 8 grants investors the freedom of foreign payments, while Article 9 secures the right to transfer profits and assets abroad, provided all taxes and other public duties are paid.

Furthermore, foreign investors enjoy equal status and have the same rights and obligations as domestic investors regarding their investments, unless specified otherwise by law. Moreover, foreign investors may acquire ownership rights and other real rights over movable and immovable property located within Serbia's territory, in accordance with the Constitution and applicable laws.[29]

Finally, it is prohibited for investments to be expropriated, either directly or indirectly, through measures that have a goal that is equal to expropriation. The sole exception is if an investor's property and other rights over immovable property are seized or restricted in the public interest.[30]

This can only occur if such action is allowed by the law governing expropriation, carried out in a non-discriminatory manner, following the procedures prescribed by that law, and accompanied by the prompt payment of adequate compensation as defined under Article 6 of the Law on Investments. Notably, adequate compensation encompasses not only payment for the expropriated immovable property but also compensation for any decrease in business value caused by such seizure, in accordance with the law.

In case of expropriation, the investor has the right to seek legal remedies, to have the seizure procedure urgently resolved, and to have the value of the seized property assessed by a court or other competent authority, in accordance with the law.

For their commercial disputes, foreign investors have access to alternative dispute resolution mechanisms, including arbitration and mediation. These are available through the Permanent Arbitration at the Chamber of Commerce and Industry of Serbia and the Belgrade Arbitration Center. Both

---

28 Law on Investments, Article 11.

29 Law on Investments, Article 7.

30 Law on Investments, Article 6.

arbitration institutions have jurisdiction to settle any dispute eligible for arbitration, whether international or domestic.[31]

Under Article 13 of the Law on Investments, investors are eligible for various incentives, including state aid, tax incentives and reliefs, customs exemptions, tariff preferences, and coverage of compulsory social insurance. In addition to the protections provided by the umbrella law on investments, qualified foreign investors may benefit from government cash incentives, which include investments in tangible and intangible assets, the payment of salaries for newly hired workforce, and other eligible costs.[32] It is reported that a major stake of these incentives has been granted to investors investing in projects of low and medium low technological complexity.[33]

The Serbian tax system is also appealing to potential foreign direct investors, offering tax incentives, deductions and credits for transferring construction land, payroll, startups, innovative and research and development (R&D) activities, as well as corporate income tax relief.[34] Additionally, the government has established economic free zones that permit the free, unrestricted, and duty free export and import of goods and services to and from these zones.[35]

Further assistance and support for potential foreign investors are provided by the Serbian government's Development Agency (RAS). Although it was initially envisioned as a one-stop shop for interested domestic and foreign investors, RAS now primarily focuses on promoting investment conditions in Serbia and managing the distribution of government incentives offered to foreign

---

31 *See* Law on Arbitration (*Official Gazette of* RS, No. 469/2006); Rules of the Permanent Arbitration at the Chamber of Commerce and Industry of Serbia (2016); Rules of the Belgrade Arbitration Center (2013).

32 *See* Decree on Determining Criteria for Granting Incentives for Attracting Direct Investments (*Official Gazette of* RS, Nos. 1/2019, 39/2023 and 43/2023). The Government passed separate decrees for certain sectors: Decree on Determining Criteria for Granting Incentives for Attracting Direct Investments in Hotel Accommodation Services Sector (*Official Gazette of* RS, Nos. 33/2019, 42/2019, 18/2022 and 103/2023); Decree on Determining Criteria for Granting Incentives for Attracting Direct Investments in Groceries Production Sector *Official Gazette of* RS, Nos. 1/2019, 23/2023 and 39/2023).

33 Milica Vukajlović, Tamara Milenković Kerković and Dragana Radenković Jocić, 'The Influence of Foreign Direct Investment Treatment in Domestic Legislation on the Economic Development of the Republic of Serbia' (2020) 58 ET pp. 501, 511.

34 Development Agency of Serbia, *Why Invest in Serbia* <https://ras.gov.rs/uploads/2024/05/why-invest-2024.pdf> accessed 11 May 2024, p. 14.

35 Chamber of Commerce and Industry of Serbia, *Benefits for Investors in the Republic of Serbia* <https://api.pks.rs/storage/assets/Benefits%20for%20investments%202024%20DMM.pdf> accessed 11 May 2024.

investors.[36] In addition, the National Register of Investment Locations enables investors to access all necessary information on potential locations for their planned investments.[37] The Law on Investments includes provisions for the establishment and operation of the Council for Economic Development, but this body was never established, and the Development Agency of Serbia.[38]

On the other hand, foreign investors may be subject to certain additional conditions. For example, all foreign investors and their cross-currency financial activities, including internal transfers involving Serbian subsidiaries, are subject to strict scrutiny.[39] Additionally, purchasing real estate also entails specific requirements that vary depending on the buyer and property types.[40] The exception is the ownership of agricultural land, which is only possible for EU citizens under the conditions aligned with the Stabilization and Association Agreement.[41]

Moreover, other limitations apply to specific investment sectors. For example, acquiring qualified shareholdings in banks, insurance companies, and leasing firms requires specific regulatory approval. Furthermore, licensing requirements are applicable to all investors in certain sectors, regardless of their nationality, including military, finance, energy, mining, tobacco, and pharmaceuticals.

5 International Investment Treaty Framework

Serbia is a signatory to all major multilateral conventions on the protection of foreign investments and has concluded more than fifty bilateral investment treaties to promote and protect these investments.

---

36 Marko Jovanović, 'Serbia Report' in GIZ, *Regional Mapping Report on Investor State Dispute Settlement – Status Quo and Prospective Reforms of the ISDS Structures in the Western Balkans* (GIZ 2021) 121.

37 Republic Geodetic Authority, *National Register of Investment Locations* <www.rgz.gov.rs/register-of-investment-locations#:~:text=The%20National%20Register%20of%20Investment,for%20investment%20in%20one%20place.> accessed 11 May 2024.

38 Law on Investments, Section 5.

39 Law on Foreign Currency Transactions (*Official Gazette of RS*, Nos. 62/2006, 31/2011, 119/2012, 139/2014 and 30/2018).

40 Law on Foundations of Property Law Relations (*19zette of SFRY*, Nos. 6/1980 and 36/1990, *Official Gazette of SRY*, No. 29/1996, *Official Gazette of RS*, No. 115/2005 – other law) Articles 82–85b.

41 Law on Agricultural Land (*Official Gazette of RS*, Nos. 62/2006, 65/2008 – other law, 41/2009, 112/2015, 80/2017 and 95/2018 – other law), Article 1.

5.1 *Multilateral Conventions*

The Convention on the Settlement of Investment Disputes Between States and Nationals of Other States (ICSID Convention) entered into force for Serbia on 8 June 2007.[42] It is worth noting that Serbia deposited a new ratification although the former Yugoslavia had acceded to the ICISD Convention back in 1967.[43]

Serbia has also been a signatory to the United Nations Convention on the Recognition and Enforcement of Foreign Arbitral Awards (New York Convention) since 27 April 1992. Nine years later, Serbia acknowledged the implementation of reservations concerning reciprocity, commercial differences, and the application of the New York Convention only to awards made after its entry into effect. These reservations were initially deposited by the former Yugoslavia in 1982.[44]

Serbia is currently an observer of the Energy Charter Treaty, having signed the European Energy Charter in 1991.[45]

5.2 *Bilateral Investment Treaties*

According to publicly available information, Serbia is a signatory to 46 bilateral investment treaties (BITS) that are currently in force. Additionally, there are several BITS that Serbia has signed but have not yet entered into force.[46] Moreover, five known BITS were terminated before 2024, four of which have been replaced by newer treaties.[47]

---

42 ICSID, *Member States – Serbia* <https://icsid.worldbank.org/about/member-states/database-of-member-states/member-state-details?state=ST119> accessed 11 May 2024.

43 SICE, *ICSID List of Contracting States and Other Signatories to the Convention (as of October 28, 1997)* <https://sice.oas.org/dispute/comarb/icsid/w_csig.asp and https://icsid.worldbank.org/about/member-states/database-of-member-states> accessed 11 May 2024.

44 UNCITRAL, *Status: Convention on the Recognition and Enforcement of Foreign Arbitral Awards (New York, 1958)* <https://uncitral.un.org/en/texts/arbitration/conventions/foreign_arbitral_awards/status2> accessed 11 May 2024. On recognition and enforcement of foreign arbitral awards in Serbia, *see* Maja Stanivuković, 'National Report for Serbia (2020 through 2023)' in Lise Bosman (ed), *ICCA International Handbook on Commercial Arbitration*, Supplement No. 25 (Kluwer 2023) pp. 53–59.

45 Energy Charter, *Members and Observers to the Energy Charter Conference* <www.energycharter.org/who-we-are/members-observers/> accessed 11 May 2024

46 According to publicly available information, these are the BITS with Indonesia (2011), Morocco (2013), Turkey (2018), Turkey (2022), and the Republic of Korea (2023). In the absence of official information, it is unclear whether the BITS with Zimbabwe (1996), Italy (2000), Nigeria (2002), and Finland (2005) had been signed and enforced.

47 According to publicly available information, these are BITS with India (2003); with Egypt (1977) replaced in 2005 by another BIT; with Poland (1979) replaced in 1996; with

Serbia's oldest BIT still in force is the treaty from 1974 signed between the former Yugoslavia and France. After Yugoslavia dissolved, the validity of this BIT was reaffirmed in 2003 by another treaty concerning the succession of bilateral treaties previously signed by Yugoslavia, which Serbia then automatically inherited.[48] Additionally, Serbia assumed Yugoslavia's position in BITs originally signed with Egypt (1977), Sweden (1978), The Netherlands (1979), Austria (1989), and Germany (1989). The BITs with Egypt, The Netherlands, Poland, and Austria have since been replaced by newer treaties.[49]

The first wave of BITs, signed by Serbia (along with Montenegro), began in 1990s, during which 14 new BITs were signed. Notably, 10 of these, including treaties with China and Russia, were signed in 1995 and 1996. It is assumed that this surge in BITs was likely driven by the desire to quickly capitalize on the lifting of sanctions and by the understanding that signing investment treaties could be portrayed positively to the public.[50]

Interest in bilateral investment treaties intensified in the 2000s following Serbia's adoption of 'a liberal stance on foreign investment'.[51] This approach is evident in both the list of signatories and the content of the treaties, which arguably exhibit a lack of coherent strategy.[52] Serbia signed treaties with neighboring countries (eg Bosnia and Herzegovina, Hungary, Albania) and EU countries (eg Spain, United Kingdom, Finland). It has also entered into treaties with countries from which investments were unlikely (eg Ghana, Nigeria, Iran), as well as countries that facilitate the establishment of special purpose vehicles (eg Cyprus and the Belgium–Luxembourg Economic Union (BLEU)).

After the dissolution of the State Union of Serbia and Montenegro in 2006, Serbia automatically succeeded all bilateral treaties signed between 1991 and

---

The Netherlands (1979) replaced in 2002; and with Austria (1989) replaced in 2001 by another BIT.

48 Law on the Ratification of the Agreement Between the Council of Ministers of Serbia and Montenegro and the Government of the French Republic on the Succession of Bilateral Agreements Concluded Between the Socialist Federal Republic of Yugoslavia and France (*Official Gazette of SMN – International Agreements*, No. 6/2003). *See* also fn 52 below.

49 *See supra* (n 45). *See* also Christian Tams, 'State Succession to Investment Treaties: Mapping the Issues' in Meg Kinnear and Campbell McLachlan (eds), *ICSID Review – Foreign Investment Law Journal* (OUP 2016) pp. 329–331.

50 Vladimir Pavić, 'The Future of Investment Protection in Serbia after *Achmea*' (2018) 7(1) Harmonius pp. 170, 176

51 Radovan Kastratović and Predrag Bjelić, 'The Effectiveness of Bilateral Investment Treaties in Attracting Foreign Direct Investment: The Case of Serbia' (2023) 68(237) EA pp. 37, 42

52 Pavić, 'The Future of Investment Protection in Serbia after *Achmea*' (n 49) p. 176

2006.[53] Since then, Serbia has signed 15 more treaties, only three of which were with EU member countries, the last of these being signed in 2010.[54] The last five BITs were signed with the Republic of Korea (2023), Turkey (2022 and 2018), Qatar (2016), and Canada (2014). Negotiations on new treaties have been announced for Angola, Bahrain, Uzbekistan, India, and the Kyrgyz Republic.[55]

There are currently 21 BITs in force that were signed with EU members, including one signed with the BLEU. These include BITs with countries that are major investors in Serbia, such as France, Germany, and Austria.[56]

It should be noted that the BIT with France, dating back to 1974, is an atypical old-generation BIT containing several ambiguous provisions, the applicability of which remains untested in practice. For example, this BIT does not contain definitions of 'investor' and 'investment', nor does it contain a typical dispute resolution clause.[57] In contrast, the BITs with Austria and Germany provide investors with a contemporary set of protection standards and include provisions for arbitration in case of any disputes with the Serbian government.[58]

Two additional BITs were signed with Italy and Finland, but it appears that these never came into effect. Consequently, Italian investors, who are the second largest investors in Serbia, do not enjoy additional protection for their investments beyond that provided by Serbian law.

Serbia has not signed BITs with three EU countries: Estonia, Latvia, and Ireland. Given the EU's restrictive approach to signing new intra-EU BITs, it is unlikely that these treaties will be signed in the near future. In fact, according to the European Commission's report on Serbia for 2023, Serbia should develop a strategy for 'amending or terminating existing treaties that fall short of EU standards and expose the country to risks due to the broad and open language used'.[59]

---

53 Decision on the Obligations of State Authorities of the Republic of Serbia in Exercising the Competencies of the Republic of Serbia as a Successor of the State Union of Serbia and Montenegro (*Official Gazette of RS*, No. 48/2006)

54 Serbia signed BITs with Denmark (2009), Portugal (2009), and Malta (2010).

55 European Commission, *Serbia 2023 Report* p. 147

56 *See* Section 2 above.

57 Agreement Between the Government of the French Republic and the Government of the Socialist Federal Republic of Yugoslavia Concerning the Protection of Investments dated 28 March 1974.

58 Agreement Between the Government of the Republic of Austria and the Federal Government of the Federal Republic of Yugoslavia for the Reciprocal Promotion and Protection of Investments dated 12 October 2001; Treaty Between Federal Republic of Germany and Yugoslavia Concerning the Reciprocal Protection and Encouragement of Investments (with Protocol) dated 10 July 1989.

59 European Commission, *Serbia 2023 Report* p. 147.

As mentioned above, Chinese and Russian investors are protected under BITs signed with Serbia. While the BIT with Russia provides broad investment protection and access to *ad hoc* UNCITRAL arbitration, the BIT with China restricts access to international arbitration solely to disputes 'involving the amount of compensation for expropriation'.[60]

Serbia has also signed applicable BITs with other significant non-European economies, including Qatar (2016), Canada (2014), United Arab Emirates (2013), Switzerland (2005), Israel (2004), United Kingdom (2002), and Turkey (2001).

Significantly, Serbia does not have BIT with the USA, despite having established close economic ties.[61] Other countries from which Serbia receives substantial FDI, but has not signed any treaties, include Japan, India, and Norway.

According to some analyzes, Serbian BITs are generally perceived as moderate to high-quality treaties. Their provisions on temporal scope, arbitration, national treatment standard, and transfer of funds provisions are evaluated as high-quality. In contrast, areas such as the investment definition, umbrella clauses, indirect expropriations, and limitations to the most-favored-nation treatment could have been defined more precisely.[62]

The vast majority of concluded BITs fall into the first and second generations, typically offering broad investment protections. These include basic standards such as fair and equitable treatment, prohibition of discrimination, protection against expropriation without compensation, national and the most-favored-nation treatment. Almost all of them facilitate access to international arbitration for dispute resolution.[63] Most BITs allow for *ad hoc* arbitration under the UNCITRAL Rules or for ICSID arbitration. Additionally, some treaties also grant jurisdiction to the ICC.[64]

One prominent exception is the BIT with Canada from 2014, which was drafted based on the Canadian Model BIT. This treaty places special emphasis on promoting sustainable development, transparency, protection of health,

60 Agreement Between the Government of the Russian Federation and the Federal Government of the Federal Republic of Yugoslavia on Promotion and Mutual Protection of Investments dated 11 October 1995; Agreement between the Government of the People's Republic of China and the Government of the Federal Republic of Yugoslavia Concerning the Reciprocal Encouragement and Protection of Investments dated 18 December 1995, Article 9.

61 *See* Section 2 above.

62 Kastratović and Bjelić (n 50) p. 44.

63 Petar Đundić, 'Potential Reform of Serbian Network of Bilateral Investment Treaties: An Opportunity for a New Beginning' (2022) 1 ZRPFNS pp.145, 149.

64 Stanivuković, 'National Report for Serbia (2020 through 2023)' (n 43) p. 67.

safety and environment, and corporate social responsibility.[65] Similarly, the BIT signed with Turkey in 2018, which has not yet been enforced, also contains provisions characteristic of the newer generations of BITs.[66]

Finally, it is worth mentioning that the Serbian government has so far adopted two model treaties. The first, adopted in 2007, limits the scope of investors eligible for protection ensured under the BIT.[67] Another model BIT was adopted in 2012. Its main features include a restrictive definition of the fair and equitable treatment standard; protection of health, safety, and environmental measures; encouragement of corporate social responsibility; and the country's freedom to regulate certain areas of public importance.[68] There is no publicly available information that an internal version of this model BIT was ever used in negotiations before its official publication.[69]

6 ISDS Cases and Outcomes

As explained above, Serbia primarily imports capital. Therefore, it is not surprising that information about arbitrations involving Serbian claimants is scarce. According to available literature, there is only one such case, initiated under the Macedonia-Serbia BIT.[70]

Conversely, Serbia is one of the most active SEE countries as a respondent in investment arbitrations. The first known case dates to 2005, and since then, there have been 16 known investment arbitrations:

To date, foreign investors have initiated 12 proceedings against Serbia before ICSID, with seven already concluded. Five ICSID proceedings are pending, one of which is at the annulment stage.[71] Of the remaining four cases, three were governed under UNCITRAL rules, and one was an ICC case.

65 Agreement Between Canada and the Republic of Serbia for the Promotion and Protection of Investments dated 1 September 2014, Articles 12, 15, and 16.

66 Agreement Between the Government of the Republic of Serbia and the Government of the Republic of Turkey on Mutual Promotion and Protection of Investments dated 30 January 2018.

67 Agreement Between the Republic of Serbia and the [...] on the Reciprocal Promotion and Protection of Investments (2007), Article 1.

68 Agreement Between the Republic of Serbia and the [...] on Reciprocal Promotion and Protection of Investments (2012).

69 Pavić, 'The Future of Investment Protection in Serbia after *Achmea*' (n 49) p. 176.

70 Maja Stanivuković, 'Dispute Resolution Clauses in Serbia's Bilateral Investment Treaties' [2017] 1 PŽ pp. 78, 87.

71 ICSID, *Cases Database* < https://icsid.worldbank.org/cases/case-database> accessed 11 May 2024.

TABLE 17.1 List of international investment arbitrations involving Serbia

Claimant(s)	Year	Case no.	Applicable BIT	Subject matter	Status
			ICDIS Cases		
UAB 'ARVI' ir ko and UAB 'SANITEX'	2009	ARB/09/21	Lithuania–Serbia 2005	Fertilizer plant	Concluded
Club Hotel Loutraki S.A. and Casinos Austria International Holding GMBH	2011	ARB/11/4	Greece–Serbia 1997 Austria–Serbia 2001	Operation of gaming and entertainment facilities	Concluded
Zelena N.V. and Energo-Zelena d.o.o Inđija	2014	ARB/14/27	Belgium-Luxembourg–Serbia 2004	Waste management services	Concluded
Kunsttrans Holding GmbH and Kunsttrans d.o.o. Beograd	2016	ARB/16/10	Austria–Serbia 2001	Art storage facility	Concluded
Mera Investment Fund Limited	2017	ARB/17/2	Cyprus–Serbia 2005	Financial services	Concluded
Rand Investments Ltd. and others	2018	ARB/18/8	Canada–Serbia 2014 Cyprus–Serbia 2005	Agricultural enterprise	Pending (annulment)
Kornikom EOOD	2019	ARB/19/12	Bulgaria–Serbia 1996	Termination of privatization agreement	Concluded
BRIF TRES d.o.o. Beograd and BRIF-TC d.o.o. Beograd	2020	ARB/20/12	Belgium-Luxembourg–Serbia 2004	Construction project	Concluded
United Group B.V. and others	2021	ARB/21/5	Netherlands–Serbia 2002	Telecommunica-tions enterprise	Pending
APG SGA SA and D.O.O. za promet i usluge Alma Quattro Beograd	2021	ARB/21/13	Switzerland–Serbia 2005	Advertising enterprise	Pending

TABLE 17.1 List of international investment arbitrations involving Serbia (*cont.*)

Claimant(s)	Year	Case no.	Applicable BIT	Subject matter	Status
Coropi Holdings Limited, Kalemegdan Investments Limited and Erinn Bernard Broshko	2022	ARB/22/14	Canada–Serbia 2014 Cyprus–Serbia 2005	Real estate project	Pending
Kent Kart Anadolu Elektronik Sanayi ve Ticaret Anonim Şirketi and others	2024	ARB/24/10	Turkey–Serbia 2001	Transportation fare collection services	Pending
Other Cases					
Mytilineos Holdings SA (I)	2005	/	Greece–Serbia 1997	Mining	Concluded
Civis-Ing Kft	2007	/	Hungary–Serbia 2001	Agricultural enterprise	Concluded
Mytilineos Holdings SA (II)	2013	PCA Case 2014-30	Greece–Serbia 1997	Mining	Concluded
Tvornica Šećera Osijek d.o.o.	2013	ICC Case 19881/MHM	Croatia–Serbia 1998	Manufacture of food products	Concluded

SOURCE: ICSID CASE DATABASE AND UNCTAD INVESTMENT POLICY HUB

According to available information, tribunals in five of these cases found breaches of the applicable BITs.[72] Similarly, decisions in five other known cases favored Serbia, with two claims being dismissed during the jurisdiction phase.[73] One case was settled,[74] while the outcome of another remains undisclosed.[75]

72 See below *UAB 'ARVI' ir ko and UAB 'SANITEX' v Serbia, Zelena N.V. and Energo-Zelena d.o.o Inđija v Serbia, Kunsttrans Holding GmbH and Kunsttrans d.o.o. Beograd v Serbia, Rand Investments Ltd. et al. v Serbia, Mytilineos Holdings v Serbia (II)*.

73 See below *Kornikom EOOD v Serbia, BRIF TRES d.o.o. Beograd and BRIF-TC d.o.o. Beograd v Serbia, Mytilineos Holdings SA v The State Union of Serbia and Montenegro and Republic of Serbia (I), Civis-Ing Kft v Serbia, Tvornica Šećera Osijek d.o.o. v Serbia*.

74 *Club Hotel Loutraki S.A. and Casinos Austria International Holding GMBH v Serbia.*

75 *Mera Investment Fund Limited v Serbia.*

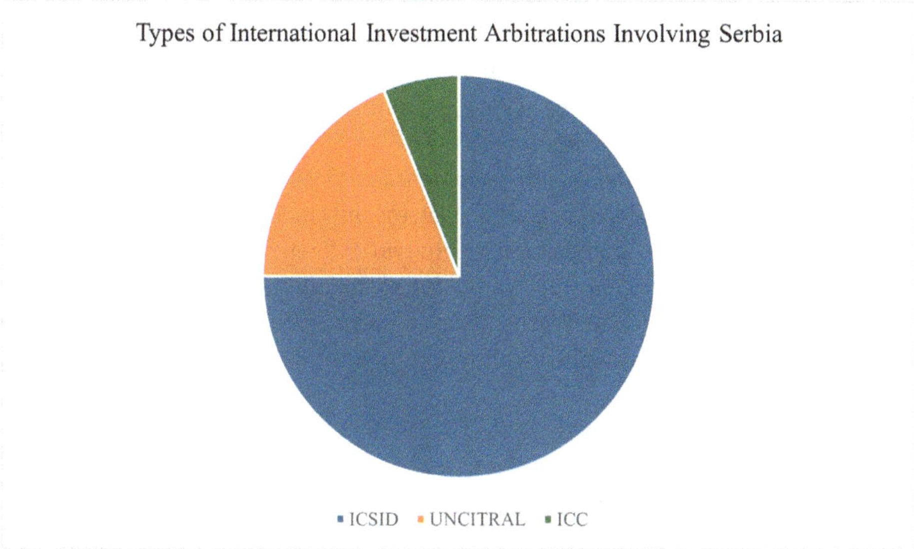

FIGURE 17.4 Types of International Investment Arbitrations involving Serbia

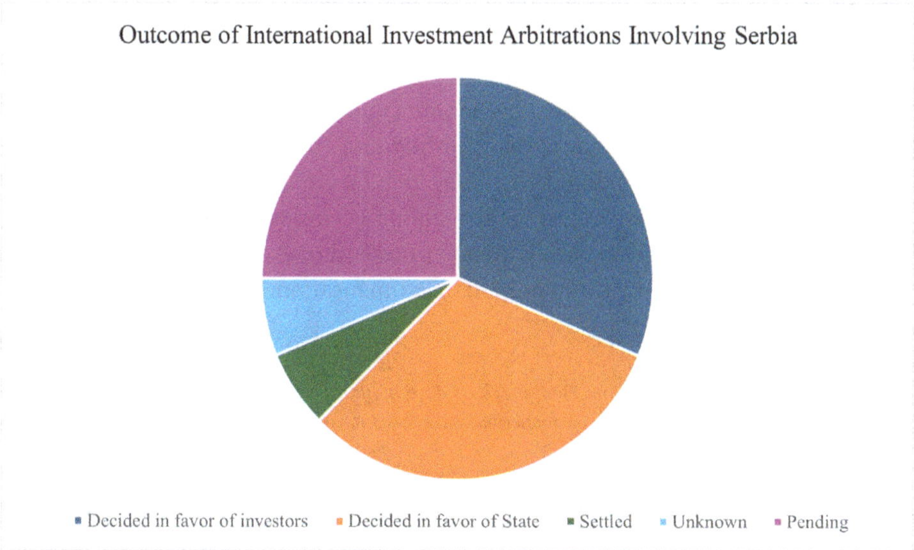

FIGURE 17.5 Outcomes of International Investment Arbitrations involving Serbia

Claimants have invoked 12 different BITs in their cases against Serbia. The BITs with Greece and Cyprus have been invoked most frequently, each three times, followed by those with Austria, Canada, and the BLEU, each invoked twice. Most of these BITs are treaties with EU countries, with the exceptions being those with Canada, Switzerland, and Turkey.

Most of the claimants have been companies, including six Serbian subsidiaries involved in five ICSID cases.[76] In fact, the only individuals who have sued Serbia have been five Canadian citizens in two different arbitrations.[77]

The disputes concerned arose in relation to the mining, construction, information and communication, agricultural, financial, food manufacturing, waste management, transportation, and entertainment sectors.

6.1 *ICSID Arbitrations*

Serbia has been a respondent in 12 cases before ICSID tribunals. There have been 10 cases since 2014, averaging about one case per year. Three of them have reached the annulment stage, with one still pending. Case materials and information regarding outcomes and the enforcement are predominantly confidential. A summary of these cases, based on publicly available information, is provided below.

6.1.1 UAB 'ARVI' ir ko and UAB 'SANITEX' v Serbia (2009)

This case was the first arbitration initiated against Serbia under the ICSID Convention. It concerned a dispute over a fertilizer plant privatized by a pair of Lithuanian investors. They brought the claim under the Lithuania-Serbia BIT.[78]

According to publicly available information, the claimants alleged that Serbia illegally expropriated their shares in a fertilizer company when its privatization was cancelled.[79] The subsequent proceedings before the Lithuanian courts have revealed that the claimants prevailed in the arbitration, but that they were awarded only EUR 1 million in compensation.[80]

---

76 See below *Zelena N.V. and Energo-Zelena d.o.o Inđija v Serbia, Kunsttrans Holding GmbH and Kunsttrans d.o.o. Beograd v Serbia, BRIF TRES d.o.o. Beograd and BRIF-TC d.o.o. Beograd v Serbia, United Group B.V. et al. v Serbia, APG SGA SA and D.O.O. za promet i usluge Alma Quattro Beograd v Serbia.*

77 See below *Rand Investments Ltd. et al. v Serbia, Coropi Holdings Limited et al. v Serbia.*

78 ICSID, *Case Details – ICSID Case No. ARB/09/21* <https://icsid.worldbank.org/cases/case-database/case-detail?CaseNo=ARB/09/21> accessed 11 May 2024.

79 *Global Arbitration Review*, 'Serbia and El Salvador Panels Formed, Yemen Case Settled' (7 July 2010).

80 *Investment Arbitration Reporter*, 'Result of Investment Treaty Claim Finally Comes to Light in "ARVI" ir ko and UAB "SANITEX" v. Serbia Case' (10 June 2019).

The tribunal was composed of Thomas Buergenthal (president), Charles N Brower (appointed by the claimants), and Tibor Várady (appointed by the respondent). Mr Brower provided a separate opinion attached to the award.

Club Hotel Loutraki S.A. and Casinos Austria International Holding GMBH v Serbia (2011)

This arbitration, related to the operation of gaming and entertainment facilities, commenced by Greek and Austrian companies under the BITs that Serbia has with Greece and Austria.[81]

The claims stemmed from a partnership between the claimants, who are gaming and entertainment companies, and the Serbian national lottery, which involved the development of a casino in Belgrade.[82] The proceedings were discontinued in 2012 after the parties reached a friendly settlement of their dispute.

Members of the tribunal were Francisco Orrego Vicuña (president), Horacio Grigera Naón (appointed by the claimants), and Jernej Sekolec (appointed by the respondent).

Zelena N.V. and Energo-Zelena d.o.o Inđija v Serbia (2014)

This dispute arose under the BLEU-Serbia BIT concerning the waste management services.[83] The claimants were a Belgian waste management company and its Serbian subsidiary who built in northern Serbia the state-of-the-art facility intended to process animal-by-products. However, they alleged that their animal-rendering facility could not operate due to the failure of Serbian authorities to enforce laws on veterinary practices, public health and environmental protection. Furthermore, they claimed discriminatory treatment compared to other market players who were allowed to dispose of waste more inexpensively.[84]

While the award remains unpublished, it is known that the tribunal found Serbia liable for infringing the fair and equitable treatment. The details of any compensation ordered have remained confidential.[85] The tribunal was

81 ICSID, *Case Details – ICSID Case No. ARB/11/4* <https://icsid.worldbank.org/cases/case-database/case-detail?CaseNo=ARB/11/4> accessed 11 May 2024.

82 *Global Arbitration Review*, 'Dice Rolled Against Kazakhstan and Serbia' (11 February 2011).

83 ICSID, *Case Details – ICSID Case No. ARB/14/27* <https://icsid.worldbank.org/cases/case-database/case-detail?CaseNo=ARB/14/27> accessed 11 May 2024.

84 *Investment Arbitration Reporter*, 'As Serbia Is Sued at ICSID Over Regulation of Animal-Rendering Industry, a Tribunal in UNCITRAL Case Is Finalized After Arbitrator Disqualification' (25 November 2014).

85 *Investment Arbitration Reporter*, 'Serbia Held Liable at ICSID in Case Alleging Failure to Enforce Environmental Regulations' (10 November 2018).

composed of Bruno Simma (president), Karl-Heinz Böckstiegel (appointed by the claimants), and Vaughan Lowe (appointed by the respondent).

Kunsttrans Holding GmbH and Kunsttrans d.o.o. Beograd v Serbia (2016)

This is another dispute brought under the Austria-Serbia BIT, concerning an art storage facility.[86]

In 2006, the Austrian logistics company Kunsttrans and its Serbian subsidiary signed a contract with the Serbian Government to transport and store over 300,000 pieces of the National Museum of Serbia's art collection in a tailor-made depot during the museum's refurbishment. However, the Serbian authorities contested the enforceability of the contract under Serbian law and failed to honor its terms.[87]

The tribunal reportedly found that Serbia breached the claimants' legitimate expectations by failing to adhere to the agreed terms. Nevertheless, it is alleged that the tribunal granted the claimants only a small portion of the damages claimed.[88] The tribunal consisted of John Townsend (president), Stanimir Alexandrov (appointed by the claimants), and Toby Landau (appointed by the respondent).

Mera Investment Fund Limited v Serbia (2017)

Mera Investment was involved in a financial dispute with Serbia under Cyprus-Serbia BIT.[89]

The holding company Mera Investment claimed that Serbia had implemented several hostile measures against its Serbian subsidiary. These included freezing of all its assets, fabricating a tax claim, and blocking the subsidiary's bank accounts, accounts receivables from related companies, and the bank accounts and accounts receivables of certain affiliated companies. As a result, the claimant's subsidiary ceased trading, abandoned ongoing projects, lost term deposits, and became over-indebted, thereby depriving Mera Investment of its investment.[90]

Among others, Serbia argued that the claimant did not qualify as a 'foreign investor' due to the Serbian origin of its ultimate owner and the absence of its

---

86 ICSID, *Case Details – ICSID Case No. ARB/16/10* <https://icsid.worldbank.org/cases/case-database/case-detail?CaseNo=ARB/16/10> accessed 11 May 2024.

87 *Global Arbitration Review*, 'New Treaty Claims Registered Against Serbia and Côte d'Ivoire' (30 March 2016).

88 *Global Arbitration Review*, 'Austrian Art Storage Company Secures Damages Against Serbia' (22 November 2018).

89 ICSID, *Case Details – ICSID Case No. ARB/17/2* <https://icsid.worldbank.org/cases/case-database/case-detail?CaseNo=ARB/17/2> accessed 11 May 2024.

90 Decision on Jurisdiction dated 30 November 2018, *Mera Investment Fund Limited v Serbia* (ICSID Case No. ARB/17/2) paras 13–14.

seat in Cyprus. Serbia also contended that granting jurisdiction in this case would contradict the object and purpose of both the BIT and the ICSID Convention.[91] The tribunal dismissed Serbia's jurisdictional objections and issued the final award on the merits in 2021. Serbia subsequently sought to annul this award. The annulment proceedings concluded in 2023, but the outcome has not been publicly disclosed.[92] The tribunal was composed of Georg von Segesser (president), Yves Fortier (appointed by the claimant) and Bernardo Cremades (appointed by respondent), who attached his dissenting opinion. The *ad hoc* committee consisted of Michael Nolan (president), Jacomijn Van Haersolte-Van Hof, and Githu Muigai.

Rand Investments Ltd. et al. v Serbia (2018)

Mr. William Rand, his family, and their associated Canadian and Cypriot companies invested in a Serbian agricultural enterprise through the privatization process. Given that one of the applicable BITs was the Canadian one, along with the Cyprus-Serbia BIT, the proceedings in this case were conducted publicly.[93] Mr. Rand acquired a 70% stake in BD Agro ad, a formerly state-owned dairy farm, under the privatization contract with the Serbian Privatization Agency. The corporate structure he established included his three children, one Canadian company, and a Cypriot shelf company. The Privatization Agency conducted periodic controls to ensure compliance with the contract, ultimately terminating it due to non-compliance, despite the claimants' efforts to implement a reorganization plan. Following the termination, the shares were transferred back to the Privatization Agency, and BD Agro was declared bankrupt.

The claimants initiated a single arbitration dispute under the two BITs, arguing that Serbia breached the fair and equitable treatment standard and seeking compensation of at least EUR 67 million. The tribunal accepted jurisdiction over Mr. Rand's claims under the Canada-Serbia BIT concerning his interest in the shares but denied jurisdiction over all other claims under this and the Cyprus-Serbia BIT. The arbitrators found that Serbia breached the fair and equitable standard, awarding Mr. Rand approx. EUR 15 million in compensation.[94]

91 *Ibid.* para 59.

92 ICSID, *Case Details – ICSID Case No. ARB/17/2* <https://icsid.worldbank.org/cases/case-database/case-detail?CaseNo=ARB/17/2> accessed 11 May 2024.

93 ICSID, *Case Details – ICSID Case No. ARB/18/8* <https://icsid.worldbank.org/cases/case-database/case-detail?CaseNo=ARB/18/8> accessed 11 May 2024.

94 *See* Award dated 29 June 2023, *Rand Investments Ltd. et al. v Serbia* (ICSID Case No. ARB/18/8).

This was followed by supplementary decision proceedings initiated by the claimants concerning the date from which interest would accrue. Subsequent proceedings for partial annulment of the award were initiated by the claimants in March 2024.[95]

The tribunal was composed of Gabrielle Kaufmann-Kohler (president), Baiju Vasani (appointed by the claimants), and Marcelo Kohen (appointed by the respondent). Marcelo Kohen submitted his dissenting opinion. Members of the *ad hoc* committee are Claudia Annacker (president), Lawrence Boo, and Colm Ó Hoisín.

Kornikom EOOD v Serbia (2019)

This dispute arose under the Bulgaria-Serbia BIT concerning the termination of a privatization contract. It has been classified by ICSID as pertaining to the oil, gas and mining sector.[96] In 2010, the Serbian Privatization Agency terminated a privatization contract that had been concluded in 2007, under which the Bulgarian company Kornikom had acquired a 70% stake in the Serbian company Rudnik Kovin, running an underwater coal mine located on the banks of the Danube River in the northeastern part of Serbia. The termination of the contract was justified by Kornikom's failure to maintain the mine's business continuity and to fulfil its obligations towards employees as stipulated in the privatization contract.

Kornikom initiated arbitration in 2019, seeking compensation of approximately EUR 35 million. It argued that Serbia had expropriated its investment illegally, by wrongfully terminating the contract pursuant to which it acquired its shareholding and by transferring these shares without compensation.

The tribunal in this case, composed of Bernard Hanotiau (president), William Rowley (appointed by the claimant) and Pierre Mayer (appointed by the respondent), unanimously dismissed all claims on the merits and ruled in favor of Serbia. The tribunal found that the privatization contract was validly terminated, as the investor failed to fulfil its contractual obligations. Furthermore, it established that Serbia did not privatize Rudnik Kovin in such a manner that it made Kornikom's performance of its contractual obligations unduly burdensome. The award dated 20 September 2023 is publicly available.[97]

BRIF TRES d.o.o. Beograd and BRIF-TC d.o.o. Beograd v Serbia (2020)

95 ICSID, *Case Details – ICSID Case No. ARB/18/8* <https://icsid.worldbank.org/cases/case-database/case-detail?CaseNo=ARB/18/8> accessed 11 May 2024.

96 ICSID, *Case Details – ICSID Case No. ARB/19/12* <https://icsid.worldbank.org/cases/case-database/case-detail?CaseNo=ARB/19/12> accessed 11 May 2024.

97 *See* Award dated 20 September 2023, *Kornikom EOOD v Serbia* (ICSID Case No. ARB/19/12).

This is another arbitration initiated under the BLEU-Serbia BIT. It is classified by ICSID as a construction dispute.[98]

In 2004, BRIF-TC won a tender and signed a long-term lease contract with the Serbian Government to develop a former dump on the Danube River into a shopping mall located in the attractive area near the city center. However, the mall was never built because a competing claim for one of the land parcels led to the loss of development funding. Claimants alleged that the acts and omissions of Serbian authorities deprived them of their investment, quantifying the claims of no less than EUR 140 million.

The tribunal dismissed the case on grounds of abuse of process, after determining that the claims were fore*See*able before the Serbian entities were acquired by a Luxembourg company during a corporate reorganization.[99] Following this outcome, the claimants commenced annulment proceedings, which were discontinued in December 2023.[100] The tribunal was composed of Yves Derains (president), Samaa Haridi (appointed by the claimants), and Brigitte Stern (appointed by the respondent). Samaa Haridi disagreed with the majority's findings. The *ad hoc* committee included Monica Pinto (president), Yoshimi Ohara, and Jakob Ragnaldh.

United Group B.V. et al. v Serbia (2021)

This arbitration involves a telecommunications enterprise within the information and communication sector, initiated under the Netherlands-Serbia BIT in 2021.[101] The Dutch company, United Group, and its subsidiaries, which provide broadband and television services, allege that they have been subjected to arbitrary and discriminatory measures by various Serbian authorities and entities since 2014. According to the company, these measures are part of a widespread and orchestrated campaign aimed at reducing the market presence of SBB, United Group's operator in the country, to the benefit of the state-owned competitor.[102]

The tribunal is composed of Juan Fernández-Armesto (president), Stanimir Alexandrov (appointed by the claimants), and Raúl Vinuesa (appointed by the respondent). The tribunal has not issued its final award.

---

98 ICSID, *Case Details – ICSID Case No. ARB/20/12* <https://icsid.worldbank.org/cases/case-database/case-detail?CaseNo=ARB/20/12> accessed 11 May 2024.

99 *See* Award dated 30 January 2023, *BRIF TRES d.o.o. Beograd and BRIF-TC d.o.o. Beograd v Serbia* (ICSID Case No. ARB/20/12).

100 ICSID, *Case Details – ICSID Case No. ARB/20/12* <https://icsid.worldbank.org/cases/case-database/case-detail?CaseNo=ARB/20/12> accessed 11 May 2024.

101 ICSID, *Case Details – ICSID Case No. ARB/21/5* <https://icsid.worldbank.org/cases/case-database/case-detail?CaseNo=ARB/21/5> accessed 11 May 2024.

102 *N1 Belgrade*, 'United Group Files Arbitration Claim Against Serbia' (9 March 2021).

APG SGA SA and D.O.O. za promet i usluge Alma Quattro Beograd v Serbia (2021)

This dispute pertains to an advertising enterprise within the information and communication sector, governed by the Switzerland-Serbia BIT.[103] The claimants are Alma Quattro, an outdoor advertising company in Serbia, and its owner APG, a Swiss company specializing in outdoor advertising. According to APG's annual report for 2022, Alma Quattro's local competitor was granted a concession by the City of Belgrade to operate advertising panels, despite Alma Quattro's existing long-term exclusive contract that Alma Quattro has with the city.[104]

The tribunal handling this case consists of Wendy Miles (president), John Townsend (appointed by the claimants), and Maxi Scherer (appointed by the respondent). As of April 2024, the proceedings are still ongoing.

Coropi Holdings Limited et al. v Serbia (2022)

This proceeding, concerning a real estate project, was initiated by Canadian citizen Mr Broshko, along with one Cypriot and one Canadian company.[105] The claimants assert ownership of the Serbian company Obnova, which has held a permanent right to use land at two locations in the center of Belgrade for decades. However, in 2013, Serbia allegedly decided arbitrarily to use Obnova's premises for the construction of a bus loop and its access roads, refusing to compensate Obnova and thereby violating both domestic and international laws. As a result, the claimants have initiated arbitration to seek compensation for their EUR 30 million share in the value of the expropriated land. One of the claimants is entirely controlled by Mr Rand.[106]

Serbia, on the other hand, contends that Obnova had no property rights over the disputed land and buildings, and argues that the City of Belgrade's decision to use the land for its own purposes was Serbia has challenged the tribunal's jurisdiction too.[107] The tribunal comprises Daniel Bethlehem (president), with Andrés Jana Linetzky and Zachary Douglas, appointed by the claimants and

103 ICSID, *Case Details – ICSID Case No. ARB/21/13* <https://icsid.worldbank.org/cases/case-database/case-detail?CaseNo=ARB/21/13> accessed 11 May 2024.

104 APG, *Annual Report 2022* 18.

105 ICSID, *Case Details – ICSID Case No. ARB/22/14* <https://icsid.worldbank.org/cases/case-database/case-detail?CaseNo=ARB/22/14> accessed 11 May 2024.

106 Claimants' Memorial dated 31 March 2023, *Coropi Holdings Limited et al. v Serbia* (ICSID Case No. ARB/22/14).

107 Respondent's Counter-Memorial dated 29 March 2023, *Coropi Holdings Limited et al. v Serbia* (ICSID Case No. ARB/22/14).

the respondent, respectively. The arbitrators have bifurcated the arbitration proceedings into separate phases for liability and damages.[108]

Kent Kart Anadolu Elektronik Sanayi ve Ticaret Anonim Şirketi et al. v Serbia (2024)

On 1 April 2024, three Turkish companies filed a claim against Serbia because the city of Belgrade terminated their public-private partnership contract to provide ticketing services in public transport. These services were subsequently transferred to a public company.[109] The parties agreed to suspend the proceedings until 30 June 2024.[110]

6.2 *Other Arbitrations*

Since non-ICSID cases are typically confidential, including details about their existence, it is challenging to determine the exact number of such cases. According to publicly available information, Serbia has acted as respondent in at least four investment arbitrations. These include three cases under UNCITRAL arbitration rules and one under ICC arbitration rules. Two of these cases pertain to the same dispute in the mining sector, with the second resulting in a finding of Serbia's breach of international law. Another case concerned privatization in the agricultural sector, while the fourth case involved an export ban imposed by the Serbian government, also within the agricultural sector.

Mytilineos Holdings SA v The State Union of Serbia and Montenegro and Republic of Serbia (I) (2005)

This case marked the first arbitration initiated by the Greek metallurgy company Mytilineos against Serbia.[111] According to publicly available information, the dispute centered on mineral extraction and metallurgy operations involving the Serbian public company RTB Bor, which reportedly failed to fulfil its contractual obligations. Impeded by Serbia's new privatization and restructuring regime, Mytilineos was unable to recover the sums owed. Therefore, Mytilineos initiated arbitration under the Greece-Serbia BIT, alleging expropriation, full protection and security, and fair and equitable treatment.

---

108 Procedural Order No. 4 dated 21 August 2023, *Coropi Holdings Limited et al. v Serbia* (ICSID Case No. ARB/22/14).

109 *Global Arbitration Review*, 'Turkish E-Tickets Investor Brings ICSID Claim Against Serbia' (5 April 2024).

110 ICSID, *Case Details – ICSID Case No. ARB/24/10* <https://icsid.worldbank.org/cases/case-database/case-detail?CaseNo=ARB/24/10> accessed 11 May 2024.

111 UNCTAD Investment Policy Hub, *Mytilineos v. Serbia (I)* <https://investmentpolicy.unctad.org/investment-dispute-settlement/cases/200/mytilineos-v-serbia-i> accessed 11 May 2024.

It sought USD 30 million from Serbia. While the tribunal affirmed its jurisdiction, it found no breaches, citing the ongoing status of local proceedings as the main reason for rejection. However, the tribunal expressly left the door open for potential future treaty claims.[112] The tribunal rendering the award was composed of August Reinisch (president), Anna Mantakou (appointed by the claimant), and Gašo Knežević (appointed by the respondent).

Civis-Ing Kft v Serbia (2007)

The details of the case remain confidential. It is known that it was resolved under the Hungary-Serbia BIT in accordance with the UNCITRAL arbitration rules.[113] Reportedly, it pertained to privatization in the agricultural sector. The claimant sought approximately EUR 10 million, but the claim was unsuccessful. The tribunal consisted of Andreas Bucher (president), Claudia Kalin-Nauer (appointed by the claimant), and Maja Stanivuković (appointed by the respondent).[114]

Mytilineos Holdings v Serbia (II) (2013)

In 2013, Mytilineos initiated a second arbitration against Serbia under the same Greece-Serbia BIT, again concerning its contractual relationship with RTB Bor.[115] Mytilineos again claimed that Serbia intentionally shielded RTB Bor through alleged restructuring for privatization. This time, the tribunal found that Serbia committed indirect expropriation without proper compensation and breached the standard of fair and equitable treatment. Consequently, Serbia was ordered to pay USD 40 million, including interest.[116] The tribunal was composed of Klaus Sachs (president), Doak Bishop (appointed by the claimant), and Mirko Vasiljević (appointed by the respondent).

Tvornica Šećera Osijek d.o.o. v Serbia (2013)

112 *Investment Arbitration Reporter*, 'In Final UNCITRAL Award, Door Left Open for Greek Company Mytilineos Holdings, to Bring Another BIT Claim Against Serbia' (26 April 2013); Partial Award on Jurisdiction, 8 September 2006, *Mytilineos Holdings SA v The State Union of Serbia and Montenegro and Republic of Serbia (I)* (UNCITRAL case).

113 UNCTAD Investment Policy Hub, *Civis-Ing v. Serbia* <https://investmentpolicy.unctad.org/investment-dispute-settlement/cases/1029/civis-ing-v-serbia> accessed 11 May 2024.

114 *Investment Arbitration Reporter*, 'Balkans Update: Unpublicized Treaty Cases Come to Light – Medusa v. Montenegro and Civis v. Serbia – and an Arbitrator Challenge to Jernej Sekolec Shakes up an Ad-Hoc Tribunal' (19 April 2016).

115 UNCTAD Investment Policy Hub, *Mytilineos v. Serbia (II)* <https://investmentpolicy.unctad.org/investment-dispute-settlement/cases/560/mytilineos-v-serbia-ii-> accessed 11 May 2024; PCA, *Case Information – PCA Case No. 2014-30* <https://pca-cpa.org/en/cases/114/> accessed 11 May 2024.

116 *Aceris Law*, 'Mytilineos v. The Republic of Serbia: Serbia Held Liable in Investment Arbitration' (3 October 2017).

This ICC case, initiated under the Croatia-Serbia BIT, concerned the purchase of sugar beets from Serbian companies by a Croatian sugar manufacturer that were essential for sugar production in its factories in Croatia. The claimant argued that Serbia breached the protection standards of the BIT by prohibiting sugar beet exports to Croatia. A key issue in this case was whether the claimant had made investments in Serbia as defined under the applicable BIT. The tribunal concluded it had not, determining those simple commercial transactions, not resulting in asset acquisition, should be considered trading contracts rather than investments.[117] The tribunal was composed of Juan Fernández-Armesto (president), Andreas Reiner (appointed by the claimant), and Jernej Sekolec (appointed by the respondent).

7 Ongoing Reforms

Currently, there are no ongoing or announced legal reforms in Serbia that may be relevant to investor-state dispute resolution. As mentioned earlier, if Serbia progresses towards EU membership, it will be required to align its network of BITs with EU policies, likely leading to the termination of BITs concluded with EU members.[118] Similarly, since Serbia currently lacks a legal framework for screening of FDI comparable to those recently adopted by EU members, it may be expected such a framework in the future, depending on Serbia's European integration progress and the EU's future stance on the FDI screening regime.

8 Special Features

In terms of division of competence between state institutions, the Ministry of Economy is designated as a competent ministry for government administration tasks related to proposing measures to encourage investments and coordinating tasks related to investments (except in the field of the food industry); coordinating the work of the public agency responsible for promoting exports and encouraging investments; and regulations in the field of investments. Its Rapid Response Administration performs government and professional tasks

117 *Investment Arbitration Reporter*, 'Revealed: In Previously-Unseen ICC Investment Treaty Award, Serbia Prevailed as Majority Ruled that Croatian Investor's Interest in a Series of Commercial Agreements Did Not Constitute a Protected Investment' (14 April 2020).

118 *See* also Maja Stanivuković, 'Bilateral Treaties on Protection and Promotion of Investments Between Serbia and Member States of the European Union' [2011] 12 PŽ 311.

related to improving conditions for attracting foreign investments.[119] This ministry also negotiates BITs and prepares laws on their confirmation.[120] Up until 2020, the designated body for negotiating BITs was the Ministry of Trade, Tourism and Telecommunications.[121]

The State Attorney represents Serbia before foreign and international courts and arbitrations and before other competent authorities abroad when Serbia is a party or intervenor whose rights and obligations are being decided in that proceeding.[122] The State Attorney's Office usually cooperates with external counsel when representing Serbia in investment arbitrations.

Additionally, the Commission for the Examination of Disputable Relations that May Be Subject to International Arbitrations was established in 2017 (Examination Commission).[123] Its tasks are to examine disputable relations that may be subject to international arbitrations in which Serbia could be the respondent; to analyze the legal and factual situation in order to assess the position of Serbia in a potential dispute before an international arbitration; and to provide proposals to the Government for the amicable resolution of disputable relations before a lawsuit is filed in international arbitration if this solution is justified and expedient. The Examination Commission consists of eight members, including the ministers of justice, finance, internal affairs and economy; the State Attorney; the Governor of the National Bank of Serbia; the representative of the Security Information Agency; and the assistant minister of justice.

9 Conclusion

Serbia is an attractive market for foreign investors from diverse backgrounds, including those from the EU, China, the United States, and Russia. These and other foreign investors are active in various industries, ranging from automotive to textiles. Additionally, it is anticipated that FDI will especially surge in the energy, mining, and ICT sectors in the future. Potential investors can

119 Law on Ministries (*Official Gazette of RS*, Nos. 128/2020, 116/2022 and 92/2023 – other law), Article 4.

120 *Ibid.*

121 Former Law on Ministries (*Official Gazette of RS*, Nos. 44/2014, 14/2015, 54/2015, 96/2015 – other law and 62/2017), Article 8(2).

122 Law on the State Attorney (*Official Gazette of RS*, No. 55/2014), Articles 11 and 12.

123 Decision on the Establishment of a Commission for Examination of Disputable Relations that May Be Subject to International Arbitrations (*Official Gazette of RS*, Nos. 83/2017 and 14/2020).

expect government support, which is reflected in various incentives, benefits, and guarantees provided under the Law on Investments and other legislation.

Further protection for foreign investors is available under the ICSID and New York Conventions, as well as a plethora of applicable BITs. To date, investors have invoked at least 12 of these BITs in 16 arbitrations, alleging breaches by Serbia. Serbia has prevailed in half of publicly known concluded cases, with several more cases still pending. Serbia's future approach to FDI and investor-state dispute resolution mechanisms is closely tied to its EU accession, which could influence the status of existing BITs and potentially lead to the introduction of a screening regime currently absent in Serbia.

CHAPTER 18

Investment Protection and Investor-State Dispute Resolution in Slovenia

Peter Rižnik and Maja Menard

1 FDI Trends

The stock of inward foreign investment in Slovenia has ranged, over the past several years (2012–2022), from EUR 8.9 billion to EUR 20.2 billion, averaging around EUR 13.5 billion. The volume of the foreign investment is equivalent to a share ranging from 18% to 35.4% of the gross domestic product, or a ten-year average of 32,06%.[1] According to most recent available data, the current level of foreign direct investment volume is approximately EUR 21 billion, representing the equivalent of approximately 34% of the gross domestic product.[2]

1 Bank of Slovenia, *Neposredne naložbe – Direct Investment 2012*. Year 17, No. 1, October 2013. <Neposredne_nalozbe_2012.pdf (windows.net)>; Bank of Slovenia, *Neposredne naložbe – Direct Investment 2013*. Year 18, No. 1, November 2014. <Neposredne_nalozbe_2013.pdf (windows.net)>; Bank of Slovenia, *Neposredne naložbe – Direct Investment 2014*. Year 19, No. 1, October 2015. <Neposredne_nalozbe_2014.pdf (windows.net)>; Bank of Slovenia, *Neposredne naložbe – Direct Investment, 2015*. Year 20, No. 1, October 2016. <Neposredne_nalozbe_2015.pdf (windows.net)>; Bank of Slovenia, *Neposredne naložbe – Direct Investment, 2016*. Year 21, No. 1, November 2017. <gdgehbqhggfBGU_neposredne_nalozbe_2016.pdf (windows.net)>; Bank of Slovenia, *Neposredne naložbe – Direct Investment, 2017*. Year 22, No. 1, October 2018. <gdghffXvRggjcW_neposredne-nalozbe-2017.pdf (windows.net)>; Bank of Slovenia, *Neposredne naložbe – Direct Investment, 2018*. Year 23, No. 1, October 2019. <https://bankaslovenije.blob.core.windows.net/publication-files/gdhajcRQjbBfhfi_neposredne_nalozbe-2018.pdf>; Bank of Slovenia, *Neposredne naložbe – Direct Investment, 2019*. Year 24, No. 1, November 2020. <neposrednenalozbe_2019.pdf (windows.net)>; Bank of Slovenia, *Neposredne naložbe – Direct Investment, 2020*. Year 25, No. 1, October 2021. <neposredne-nalozbe-2020_slo.pdf (windows.net)>; Bank of Slovenia, *Neposredne naložbe – Direct Investment 2021*. 2022. <https://bankaslovenije.blob.core.windows.net/publication-files/direct_investment-2021.pdf>; Bank of Slovenia, *Neposredne naložbe – Direct investment 2022*. 2023. <neposredne-nalozbe-2022.pdf (windows.net)> (all websites accessed on 29 May 2024).

2 Bank of Slovenia, *Neposredne naložbe – Direct investment 2022*. 2023. <neposredne-nalozbe-2022.pdf (windows.net)> (accessed on 29 May 2024), p. 8; Bank of Slovenia, Ekonomski odnosi Slovenije s tujino – november 2023. January 2024. <https://bankaslovenije.blob.core.windows.net/publication-files/pb_2023_11.pdf>, p. 6.

 | DOI:10.1163/9789004729889_019

According to the classification of foreign direct investment as new, existing and other investments – whereby only direct capital affiliation is taken into account – there are twice as many new investments as existing investments. However, in terms of value, the proportion is reverse, as the value of existing investments is between 3 and 3.5 times larger than the value of new investments.[3]

The share of Slovenian companies with foreign direct investments has decreased in recent years, going from 4–5%, to less than 2% during the past decade. However, such companies overall account for between 20 and 30% of capital, assets and employees of the entire Slovenian corporate sector, throughout the past decade to the present day.[4]

EU Member States prevail as countries of origin of foreign investors, with an average combined share of over 80% of all foreign direct investment in Slovenia over the past decade. Austria remains most prominent throughout this period, followed by, *inter alia*, Switzerland, Italy, Germany, France, the Netherlands, Croatia, the United Kingdom, Belgium, Luxembourg, Sweden, Cyprus and Hungary. However, in terms of the ultimate funders, the Russian Federation, the United States of America, Mexico, Japan and China also come to the forefront as countries of origin of investment funding.[5]

---

3 Bank of Slovenia, *Neposredne naložbe – Direct Investment 2012*. Year 17, No. 1, October 2013. <Neposredne_nalozbe_2012.pdf (windows.net)>; Bank of Slovenia, *Neposredne naložbe – Direct Investment 2013*. Year 18, No. 1, November 2014. <Neposredne_nalozbe_2013.pdf (windows.net)>; Bank of Slovenia, *Neposredne naložbe – Direct Investment 2014*. Year 19, No. 1, October 2015. <Neposredne_nalozbe_2014.pdf (windows.net)>; Bank of Slovenia, *Neposredne naložbe – Direct Investment, 2015*. Year 20, No. 1, October 2016. <Neposredne_nalozbe_2015.pdf (windows.net)>; Bank of Slovenia, *Neposredne naložbe – Direct Investment, 2016*. Year 21, No. 1, November 2017. <gdgehbqhggfBGU_neposredne_nalozbe_2016.pdf (windows.net)>; Bank of Slovenia, *Neposredne naložbe – Direct Investment, 2017*. Year 22, No. 1, October 2018. <gdghffXv RggjcW_neposredne-nalozbe-2017.pdf (windows.net)>; Bank of Slovenia, *Neposredne naložbe – Direct Investment, 2018*. Year 23, No. 1, October 2019. <https://bankaslovenije.blob.core.windows.net/publication-files/gdhajcRQjbBfhfi_neposredne_nalozbe-2018.pdf>; Bank of Slovenia, *Neposredne naložbe – Direct Investment, 2019*. Year 24, No. 1, November 2020. <neposrednenalozbe_2019.pdf (windows.net)>; Bank of Slovenia, *Neposredne naložbe – Direct Investment, 2020*. Year 25, No. 1, October 2021. <neposredne-nalozbe-2020_slo.pdf (windows.net)>; Bank of Slovenia, *Neposredne naložbe – Direct Investment 2021*. 2022. <https://bankaslovenije.blob.core.windows.net/publication-files/direct_investment-2021.pdf>; Bank of Slovenia, *Neposredne naložbe – Direct investment 2022*. 2023. <neposredne-nalozbe-2022.pdf (windows.net)> (all websites accessed on 29 May 2024).

4 *Ibid.*

5 *Ibid.*

Slovenia became a full member of the EU on 1 May 2004 and as such, a part of the EU internal market, adopting the common trade policy.[6] The choice for Slovenia to join the EU and subsequently to adopt the Euro in 2007 secured both the opening of the Slovenian services markets and improved access to external finance.

Following a trend of strengthening of the economic growth since the beginning of the millennium, due *inter alia* to the positive effects of joining the EU, and more importantly foreign demand and strong investment activity,[7] the negative effects of the financial crisis remained until 2016. Thereafter, total investment rebounded and exceeded the 2006 investment levels by 2019, only to drop again with the outbreak of the COVID-19 pandemic in 2020.[8] Since 2008, the gap between inward and outward foreign direct investment stocks has been growing so that Slovenian investment is rather inward-oriented.[9]

During the COVID-19 pandemic, flows of inward foreign investment decreased significantly and more generally, the value of foreign investment has gradually increased since 2015, mainly in the form of inflows of equity capital and partly in the form of debt instruments. Foreign investments were mainly a result of accelerated privatization, overall higher sales of shareholdings in Slovenian companies, as well as increased expansion of existing companies with foreign capital and new (greenfield) investments.[10] While the region of Eastern and Central Europe recorded a smaller decline than Western Europe during

6 Barbara Ferk, Marjan Hafner, et al. *Učinki vstopa Slovenije v EU na gospodarska gibanja v letu 2004*. Urad RS za makroekonomske analize in razvoj. Ljubljana, 2005. <https://www.umar.gov.si/fileadmin/user_upload/publikacije/dz/2005/dz05-06-05.pdf>, p. 14 (accessed on 29 May 2024).

7 Branka Tavčar, Ivanka Zakotnik, Igor Strmšnik, Tomaž Kraigher. *Scenariji gospodarskega razvoja Slovenije do leta 2030. Markoekonomska analiza obdobja po letu 2000*. Delovni zvezek štev. 8/2007, let. XVI. Urad RS za makroekonomske analize in razvoj, Ljubljana, August 2007. <https://umar.si/fileadmin/user_upload/publikacije/dz/2007/dz08-07.pdf> p. 1 (accessed on 29 May 2024).

8 Jože Damijan, Jozef Konings, Črt Kostevc, Katja Zajc Kejžar. Explaining the Low Level of Investment in Slovenia, July 2022. <https://economy-finance.ec.europa.eu/system/files/2022-07/dp169_en.pdf> p. 20 (accessed on 29 May 2024).

9 International trade, foreign direct investment and global value chains. Slovenia trade and investment statistical note. 2017. <https://www.oecd.org/investment/SLOVENIA-trade-investment-statistical-country-note.pdf> p. 2 (accessed on 29 May 2024).

10 mag. Barbara Bratuž Ferk, Urška Brodar, mag. Tanja Čelebič et al. Poročilo o razvoju, UMAR, Ljubljana, July 2022. <https://www.umar.gov.si/fileadmin/user_upload/razvoj_slovenije/2022/slovenski/POR2022_splet2.pdf> p. 145 (accessed on 29 May 2024).

the pandemic period, Slovenia even recorded a relatively smaller decline than other countries of the region.[11]

At the end of 2020, the stock of inward foreign investment had increased by over two percent compared to the end of 2019, but the reticence to invest following the COVID-19 pandemic continued, as there were no major notable transactions in 2020. However, the investment restraint had subsided by 2021. From 2020 onwards, Slovenia's economy has thus been growing faster than the EU average, despite the difficult external environment, driven by the increases in consumer spending as well as investment.[12]

2 Key Sectors for Foreign Investments

Foreign investment in Slovenia is mainly concentrated on services, with generally over sixty percent of the annual stock of foreign investment pertaining to service activities. In more recent years, foreign investors have invested significantly in the Slovenian corporate sector.

The highest concentration of foreign investment has, over the past decade at least, regularly been in the financial services (including insurance) sector, followed by retail and wholesale trade (both excluding and including motor vehicles), real estate activities, energy (various types of activities), pharmaceuticals and general manufacturing.[13]

11 SPIRIT Slovenija. Izhodne investicije: Trendi po pandemiji Covid-19 in po začetku vojne v Ukrajini. <https://www.izvoznookno.si/mednarodno-trgovanje/izhodne-investicije> (accessed on 29 May 2024).

12 Bank of Slovenia. Neposredne naložbe 2021. October 2022 <https://bankaslovenije.blob.core.windows.net/publication-files/neposredne_nalozbe_2021.pdf> 7; Commission staff working document: 2023 Country Report – Slovenia. <https://economy-finance.ec.europa.eu/system/files/2023-05/SI_SWD_2023_624_en.pdf> p. 2 (both accessed on 29 May 2024).

13 Bank of Slovenia, *Neposredne naložbe – Direct Investment 2012*. Year 17, No. 1, October 2013. <https://bankaslovenije.blob.core.windows.net/publication-files/Neposredne_nalozbe_2012.pdf>; Bank of Slovenia, *Neposredne naložbe – Direct Investment 2013*. Year 18, No. 1, November 2014. <https://bankaslovenije.blob.core.windows.net/publication-files/Neposredne_nalozbe_2013.pdf>; Bank of Slovenia, *Neposredne naložbe – Direct Investment 2014*. Year 19, No. 1, October 2015. <Neposredne_nalozbe_2014.pdf (windows.net)>; Bank of Slovenia, *Neposredne naložbe – Direct Investment, 2015*. Year 20, No. 1, October 2016. <Neposredne_nalozbe_2015.pdf (windows.net)>; Bank of Slovenia, *Neposredne naložbe – Direct Investment, 2016*. Year 21, No. 1, November 2017. <gdgehbqhggfBGU_neposredne_nalozbe_2016.pdf (windows.net)>; Bank of Slovenia, *Neposredne naložbe – Direct Investment, 2017*. Year 22, No. 1, October 2018. <gdghffXvRggjcW_neposredne-nalozbe-2017.pdf (windows.net)>; Bank of Slovenia, *Neposredne naložbe – Direct Investment, 2018*. Year 23, No. 1, October 2019. <https://bankaslovenije.blob.core.windows.net

3 Legal Framework for Foreign Investment Protection

In addition to sector-specific legislation and regulations that may apply to various categories of foreign investments, the relevant legal framework for the protection of foreign investment consists of, on the one hand, applicable investment agreements and other international treaties,[14] and on the other, of a set of general laws governing the different dimensions of foreign investment within the internal legal order, the most important ones of which are briefly described in the following sections.

The most prominent among such laws is the Investment Promotion Act,[15] which defines the forms of investment incentives, the conditions, criteria and procedure for granting investment incentives, the activities for investment promotion and the internationalization of companies, the procedure for notification and review of foreign direct investment and the competent authorities pursuant to the applicable EU regulations.[16]

Based on the aforementioned law, the Regulation on the method of determining conditions and criteria for the allocation of investment incentives and conditions for strategic investment[17] provides the method of determining the fulfillment of the conditions and evaluation of the criteria for the allocation of investment incentives, and the method of determining the fulfillment of the conditions for a strategic investment.

/publication-files/gdhajcRQjbBfhfi_neposredne_nalozbe-2018.pdf>; Bank of Slovenia, *Neposredne naložbe – Direct Investment, 2019*. Year 24, No. 1, November 2020. <neposred-nenalozbe_2019.pdf (windows.net)>; Bank of Slovenia, *Neposredne naložbe – Direct Investment, 2020*. Year 25, No. 1, October 2021. <neposredne-nalozbe-2020_slo.pdf (windows.net)>; Bank of Slovenia, *Neposredne naložbe – Direct Investment 2021*. 2022. <https://bankaslovenije.blob.core.windows.net/publication-files/direct_investment-2021.pdf>; Bank of Slovenia, *Neposredne naložbe – Direct investment 2022*. 2023. <neposredne-nalozbe-2022.pdf (windows.net)> (all websites accessed on 29 May 2024).

14 *See* Section 4 *below*.

15 *Zakon o spodbujanju investicij* (ZSInv), Official Gazette of the Republic of Slovenia, nos. 13/18, 204/21, 29/22, 65/23 and 31/24.

16 Regulation (EU) 2019/452 of the European Parliament and of the Council of 19 March 2019 establishing a framework for the screening of foreign direct investment in the Union (OJ L 79I, 21.3.2019, p. 1), as last amended by Commission Delegated Regulation (EU) 2021/2126 of 29 September 2021 amending the Annex to Regulation (EU) 2019/452 of the European Parliament and of the Council establishing a framework for the screening of foreign direct investment in the Union (OJ L 432, 3.12.2021, p. 1). See Article 1 of ZSInv.

17 *Uredba o načinu ugotavljanja pogojev in meril za dodelitev investicijskih spodbud ter pogojev za strateško investicijo*, Official Gazette of the Republic of Slovenia, No 34/24.

On the corporate front, the Companies Act[18] provides for a comprehensive legal framework governing corporate status, including the establishment and operation of companies and sole proprietorships, associated persons, business interest groups, branches of foreign companies and their status transformation.

In case of financial difficulties, the Act on Financial Operations, Insolvency Procedures and Compulsory Termination[19] governs the financial management of legal persons, insolvency proceedings against legal and natural persons, and compulsory winding-up proceedings against legal persons.

In the domain of taxes, the Corporate Income Tax Act[20] regulates the system of corporate income tax, payable on the profit achieved by a taxable person in the pursuit of their activities, consisting of the surplus of income over expenditure.

In the context of employment and other labor matters, the Labor Relations Act[21] regulates employment relationships based on an employment contract between an employee and an employer. The law pursues the objectives of inclusion of workers in the work process, ensuring the coordinated flow of the work process and the prevention of unemployment, taking into account the right of workers to freedom of work, dignity at work and protecting the interests of workers in the employment relationship. The law applies to employment relationships between employers incorporated in Slovenia, as well as foreign employers, and employees based on employment contracts concluded in Slovenia, and to workers sent by foreign employers to work in Slovenia based on foreign employment contracts.[22]

18 *Zakon o gospodarskih družbah* (ZGD-1), Official Gazette of the Republic of Slovenia, No 65/09 – official consolidated text, 33/11, 91/11, 32/12, 57/12, 44/13 – Sec. US, 82/13, 55/15, 15/17, 22/19 – ZPosS, 158/20 – ZIntPK-C, 18/21, 18/23 – ZDU-1O and 75/23.

19 *Zakon o finančnem poslovanju, postopkih zaradi insolventnosti in prisilnem prenehanju* (ZFPPIPP), Official Gazette of the Republic of Slovenia, No 176/21 – official consolidated text, 178/21 – corr., 196/21 – sec. US, 157/22 – sec. US, 35/23 – sec. US, 57/23 – sec. US and 102/23.

20 *Zakon o davku od dohodkov pravnih oseb* (ZDDPO-2), Official Gazette of the Republic of Slovenia, No 117/06, 56/08, 76/08, 5/09, 96/09, 110/09 – ZDavP-2B, 43/10, 59/11, 24/12, 30/12, 94/12, 81/13, 50/14, 23/15, 82/15, 68/16, 69/17, 79/18, 66/19, 172/21, 105/22 – ZZNŠPP and 12/24.

21 *Zakon o delovnih razmerjih* (ZDR-1), Official Gazette of the Republic of Slovenia, No 21/13, 78/13 – comp., 47/15 – ZZSDT, 33/16 – PZ-F, 52/16, 15/17 – dec. US, 22/19 – ZPosS, 81/19, 203/20 – ZIUPOPDVE, 119/21 – ZČmIS-A, 202/21 – sec. US, 15/22, 54/22 – ZUPŠ-1, 114/23 and 136/23 – ZIUZDS.

22 Articles 1 and 3 of ZDR-1.

Competition on the Slovenian market is regulated by the Act on Prevention of Restriction of Competition,[23] which governs restrictive practices, concentrations of companies, unfair competition, official restrictions on competition and measures to prevent restrictive practices, as well as the powers of the Public Agency of the Republic of Slovenia for the Protection of Competition and the procedures before it.

With regard to public companies, the Takeover Act[24] governs the manner, the conditions and the procedure in relation to takeover offers, aimed essentially at the protection of all shareholders, in particular minority shareholders.

4 International Investment Treaty Framework

Slovenia has entered into a number of treaties governing investment protection, including dozens of bilateral investment treaties (BITs) as well as the Energy Charter Treaty (ECT). We will begin this chapter by providing an overview of the BITs and then move on to the ECT, a multilateral investment treaty from which Slovenia has recently withdrawn.

In recent decades, the number of BITs has significantly increased, with the Investment Policy Hub of the United Nations Conference on Trade and Development (UNCTAD) listing 2835 BITs as of May 2024, with 2222 currently in force.[25] No exception to this trend, Slovenia has concluded a number of BITs with its trade partners, but it has also taken part in the more recent general backlash against ISDS, in particular in the EU context. In 2020, Slovenia joined the Agreement for the termination of Bilateral Investment Treaties between the Member States of the European Union (Termination Agreement) and has, as a result, thereby terminated most of its Intra-EU BITs. This substantially changes the investment protection framework in Slovenia, as most of its BITs had been concluded with other EU Member States. We will cover this development in the sub-chapters below.

---

23 *Zakon o preprečevanju omejevanja konkurence* (ZPOmK-2), Official Gazette of the Republic of Slovenia, No 130/22 and 12/24.

24 *Zakon o prevzemih* (ZPre-1), Official Gazette of the Republic of Slovenia, No 79/06, 67/07 – ZTFI, 1/08, 68/08, 35/11 – ORZPre75, 105/11 – dec. US, 10/12, 38/12, 56/13, 63/13 – ZS-K, 25/14 and 75/15. See also, Agencija za trg vrednostnih papirjev. Zakonska ureditev prevzemov in vloga ATVP. May, 2021. <https://www.atvp.si/storage/app/media/Documents/nadzor/nadzorovani-subjekti/javne%20dru%C5%BEbe/zakonska-ureditev-prevzemov-in-vloga-atvp-final-002.pdf> (accessed on 29 May 2024).

25 UN Trade and Development (UNCTAD) Investment Policy Hub <https://investmentpolicy.unctad.org/international-investment-agreements> (accessed on 29 May 2024).

Finally, under the Lisbon Treaty, the EU's "exclusive competence" over direct investment as part of the common commercial policy includes the conclusion of international investment agreements with non-member States. Slovenia, as an EU member State, is bound by such treaties concluded by the EU, which it has ratified.[26]

4.1 *Intra-EU BITs and the Intra-EU BIT Termination Agreement* (2020)

Since 2020, Slovenia has terminated, through bilateral negotiations and consent, all of its BITs concluded with other EU Member States (Intra-EU BITs). The EU-wide termination of Intra EU-BITs has been primarily driven by the legal consequences of the judgment of the Court of Justice of the European Union in *Case C-284/16 Achmea,*[27] which found that investor-State arbitration clauses in Intra-EU BITs are contrary to the EU Treaties.

4.1.1 Intra-EU BIT Termination Agreement (2020)

On 5 May 2020, 23 EU Member States adopted the Termination Agreement.[28] The Termination Agreement was ratified by the Republic of Slovenia on 20 November 2020 by way of the Act ratifying the Agreement for the termination of Bilateral Investment Treaties between the member States of the European Union.[29]

The Termination Agreement provides for the termination of all intra-EU BITs,[30] and mandates the termination of all sunset clauses included in those BITs, stating that those clauses will have no legal effects.[31] The Termination Agreement further addresses the individual arbitration agreements contained in the BITs, declaring that they shall not serve as legal bases for new arbitration proceedings, commenced after its entry into force.[32] However, any arbitration

26 *See e.g.* EU – Singapore Investment Protection Agreement (2018). Ratified by Slovenia by way of: *Zakon o ratifikaciji Sporazuma o partnerstvu in sodelovanju med Evropsko unijo in njenimi državami* članicami *na eni strani ter Republiko Singapur na drugi strani* (MPSEUSG). Official Gazette 14/22. <https://pisrs.si/pregledPredpisa?id=ZAKO8719> (accessed on 29 May 2024).

27 Case C-284/16 *Slowakische Republik v Achmea BV* of 6 March 2018.

28 Official Journal of the EU OJ L 169/1 of 29 May 2020. As of writing this contribution, the Termination Agreement has not been joined by Austria, Finland, Ireland and Sweden.

29 *Zakon o ratifikaciji Sporazuma o prenehanju veljavnosti bilateralnih investicijskih pogodb med državami* članicami *Evropske unije* (MPVBIP), Official Gazette of the Republic of Slovenia, No 179/20 <https://pisrs.si/pregledPredpisa?id=ZAKO8247> (accessed on 29 May 2024).

30 Article 2 of the Termination Agreement.

31 *Ibid.,* Article 3.

32 *Ibid.,* Article 5.

proceedings concluded prior to the entry into force of the Termination Agreement (and any agreements on amicable settlement of disputes, subject to arbitration proceedings initiated prior to 6 March 2018) are not affected.[33] Parties to pending arbitration proceedings are, however, under a duty to inform arbitral tribunals about the legal consequences of the *Achmea* judgment and, moreover, to initiate setting aside proceedings of arbitral awards issued on the basis of Intra-EU BITs before the competent national courts, or to refrain from recognizing and enforcing such awards.[34] Needless to say, this may bring EU Member States into breach of their other international obligations, such as those under the New York and ICSID Conventions.

When it comes to pending arbitration proceedings, the Termination Agreement provides for "transitional measures" and a "structured dialogue". This conveys the right to request the commencement of a special settlement procedure by the investor or the State, subject to certain conditions provided in the Termination Agreement.[35]

Additionally, the Termination Agreement entitles investors to seek redress regarding the contested measures before national courts, even if the limitation periods for such claims have lapsed, under the condition that the investor withdraw any pending arbitration proceeding, waive all rights pursuant to the relevant BIT (or renounce the execution of an already issued award), and commit to refrain from instituting new arbitration proceedings. Such a claim could be lodged with national courts within six months from the termination of the BIT (provided the settlement procedure referred to in the paragraph above was not used) or from the State's rejection of the request to enter the settlement procedure. However, it is not possible to rely on the provisions of the BIT in proceedings so commenced in front of national courts.[36]

4.1.2 Intra-EU BITs Entered into by Slovenia No Longer in Force

We provide below a chronological list of Intra-EU BITs, which have all been terminated either pursuant or prior to the Termination Agreement:

a. **Austria–Slovenia BIT (2001):** concluded on 7 March 2001, entered into force on 1 February 2002. Terminated by consent on 1 May 2022.
b. **Belgium–Luxembourg Economic Union–Slovenia BIT (1999):** concluded on 1 February 1999, entered into force on 14 January 2002.

33 *Ibid.*, Article 6.
34 *Ibid.*, Article 7.
35 *Ibid.*, Article 9.
36 *Ibid.*, Article 10.

Terminated by consent on 26 August 2022 as a consequence of the Termination Agreement.

c. **Bulgaria–Slovenia BIT (1998):** concluded on 30 June 1998, entered into force on 26 November 2000. Terminated by consent on 10 March 2021 as a consequence of the Termination Agreement.

d. **Croatia–Slovenia BIT (1997):** concluded on 12 December 1997, entered into force on 8 July 2004. Terminated by consent on 10 March 2021 as a consequence of the Termination Agreement.

e. **Czech Republic–Slovenia BIT (1993):** concluded on 4 May 1993, entered into force on 21 May 1994. Terminated on 12 August 2010.

f. **Denmark–Slovenia BIT (1999):** concluded on 11 May 1999, entered into force on 30 March 2002. Terminated by consent on 10 March 2021 as a consequence of the Termination Agreement.

g. **Finland–Slovenia BIT (1998):** concluded on 1 June 1998, entered into force on 3 June 2000. Terminated by consent on 22 October 2021 as a consequence of the Termination Agreement.

h. **France–Slovenia BIT (1998):** concluded on 11 February 1998, entered into force on 5 August 2000. Terminated by consent on 28 August 2021 as a consequence of the Termination Agreement.

i. **Germany–Slovenia BIT (1993):** concluded on 28 October 1993, entered into force on 18 July 1998. Terminated by consent on 9 June 2021 as a consequence of the Termination Agreement.

j. **Greece–Slovenia BIT (1997):** concluded on 29 May 1997, entered into force on 11 February 2000. Terminated by consent on 29 October 2021 as a consequence of the Termination Agreement.

k. **Hungary–Slovenia BIT (1996):** concluded on 15 October 1996, entered into force on 9 June 2000. Terminated by consent on 10 March 2021 as a consequence of the Termination Agreement.

l. **Italy–Slovenia BIT (2000):** concluded on 8 March 2000, entered into force on 11 August 2003. Terminated by consent on 1 September 2008.

m. **Lithuania–Slovenia BIT (1998):** concluded on 13 October 1998, entered into force on 15 May 2002. Terminated by consent on 4 September 2021 as a consequence of the Termination Agreement.

n. **Malta–Slovenia BIT (2001):** concluded on 15 March 2001, entered into force on 6 November 2001. Terminated by consent on 10 March 2021 as a consequence of the Termination Agreement.

o. **Netherlands–Slovenia BIT (1996):** concluded on 24 September 1996, entered into force on 1 August 1998. Terminated by consent on 31 March 2021 as a consequence of the Termination Agreement.

p. **Poland–Slovenia BIT (1996):** concluded on 28 June 1996, entered into force on 31 March 2000. Terminated by consent on 31 March 2020 as a consequence of the Termination Agreement.

q. **Portugal–Slovenia BIT (1997):** concluded on 14 March 1997, entered into force on 4 May 2000. Terminated by consent on 14 October 2022 as a consequence of the Termination Agreement.

r. **Portugal–Slovenia BIT (2000):** concluded on 14 May 1997, entered into force on 4 May 2000. Terminated by consent on 14 October 2022 as a consequence of the Termination Agreement.

s. **Romania–Slovenia BIT (1996):** concluded on 24 January 1996, entered into force on 24 November 1996. Terminated by consent on 24 March 2022 as a consequence of the Termination Agreement.

t. **Slovakia–Slovenia BIT (1993):** concluded on 28 July 1993, entered into force on 28 March 1996. Amended on 14 May 2003. Terminated by consent on 10 March 2021 as a consequence of the Termination Agreement.

u. **Spain–Slovenia BIT (1998):** concluded on 15 July 1998, entered into force on 3 April 2000. Terminated by consent on 10 March 2021 as a consequence of the Termination Agreement.

v. (v) **Sweden–Slovenia BIT (1978):** concluded on 10 November 1978, entered into force on 21 November 1979. Terminated on 12 May 2001 and replaced with the 1999 Slovenia–Sweden BIT (see below)

w. **Sweden–Slovenia BIT (1999):** concluded on 5 October 1999, entered into force on 12 May 2001. Terminated by consent on 21 September 2021 as a consequence of the Termination Agreement.

4.2 *BITs with Western Balkans Nations, Excluding Croatia, which Remain in Force*

Several BITs that Slovenia has concluded with other Western Balkans nations remain in force. We are providing short summaries of these BITs below.

a. **Albania–Slovenia BIT (1997):** concluded on 23 October 1997, entered into force on 22 March 2000.[37]

The BIT encompasses an asset-based, open-ended definition of investment. It does not exclude portfolio investments or any other specific assets and does

37 Agreement between the Republic of Albania and the Republic of Slovenia on Reciprocal Promotion and Protection of Investments. <https://investmentpolicy.unctad.org/international-investment-agreements/treaty-files/31/download>. Ratified by Slovenia by way of: *Zakon o ratifikaciji Sporazuma med Republiko Slovenijo in Republiko Albanijo o vzajemnem spodbujanju in zaščiti vlaganj* (BALSZV), Official Gazette of the Republic of Slovenia, No 19/00. <https://pisrs.si/pregledPredpisa?id=ZAKO2109> (all websites accessed on 29 May 2024).

not list the required characteristics of an investment. It does, however, contain a clean hands requirement requiring an investment to be made "in accordance with the laws and regulations" to qualify as an investment under the BIT.[38]

The BIT's definition of investor covers nationals of the State parties, without explicitly excluding dual nationals. However, with regard to Albania, the term "natural person" includes an additional requirement for the natural person having the nationality of Albania in accordance with its laws.[39] It also provides different definitions for Slovene and Albanian legal persons. The definition of a Slovene "legal person" applies to entities[40] which are constituted or otherwise duly organized under Slovenian law and have their seat, together with economic activities, in the territory the Republic of Slovenia. On the other hand, the definition for an Albanian legal person provides merely that an entity is incorporated or constituted and recognized as a legal person under its laws, with a permanent residence in the territory of Albania. The BIT does not, however, define ownership and control of legal entities.[41]

The substantive scope of the BIT is unrestricted, and it is applicable to investments made prior to and after its entry into force, provided they have been made after 1 January 1992.[42] The BIT includes a post-establishment national treatment clause[43] and a post-establishment most-favoured nation clause,[44] which, however, does not apply in case of economic integration agreements, customs unions and taxation treaties. The BIT further includes an unqualified fair and equitable treatment (FET) clause and a standard full protection and security clause.[45] It covers direct as well as indirect expropriation, without further definitions for the latter.[46] The BIT also covers the transfer of funds, with no specifically listed exceptions.[47]

In terms of dispute resolution between investors and one of the Contracting States, the BIT initially requires a six-month mandatory negotiation period. Should such negotiations not yield results, either party may submit the dispute

38 Article 1(1) of the Albania–Slovenia BIT.

39 The definition for Slovenia, on the other hand, states merely: »*natural persons having the nationality of the Contracting Party*«, without including the adage »*in accordance with its laws*«.

40 »*legal entities, including companies, corporations, business associations and other organizations*«.

41 *Ibid,* Article 1(3).

42 *Ibid,* Article 10.

43 *Ibid,* Article 3(2).

44 *Ibid,* Article 3(3).

45 *Ibid,* Article 3(1), 3(2).

46 The BIT simply refers to "*any other measures*". *See Ibid,* Article 4(1).

47 *Ibid,* Article 6.

to: (i) the competent court of the host State; (ii) ICSID arbitration; or (iii) an arbitrator or an international *ad hoc* arbitral tribunal pursuant to the UNCITRAL rules, which may be modified when agreed so by the parties in writing.[48]

The BIT has a term of ten years which renews automatically. It can be unilaterally terminated by each Contracting party with a written notice lodged at least one year before the expiry of the original or each subsequent period. It includes a ten-year sunset clause.[49]

b. **Bosnia and Herzegovina–Slovenia BIT (2001)**: concluded on 30 May 2001, entered into force on 1 July 2002.[50]

The BIT encompasses an asset-based, open-ended definition of investment. It does not exclude portfolio investments or any other specific assets and does not list the required characteristics of an investment. It does, however, contain a clean hands requirement requiring an investment to be made "in accordance with the laws and regulations" to qualify as an investment under the BIT.[51]

The BIT's definition of investor covers nationals of the State parties, without explicitly excluding dual nationals. However, the definition of "natural person" differs between the two. Unlike its Slovene counterpart, a Bosnian natural person is required to derive their status from the law in force in Bosnia and have his permanent residence (or main place of business) in Bosnia.[52] It also provides different definitions for Slovene and Bosnian legal persons. While the Slovene "legal person" must have its seat in the Republic of Slovenia and be incorporated in accordance with its laws, the definition of a Bosnian "legal person" applies to legal persons which are established in accordance with Bosnian law and have their seat, central management or main place of business in the territory of Bosnia and Herzegovina.[53]

The substantive scope of the BIT is unrestricted, and it is applicable to both existing and post-BIT investments. However, it is limited to *disputes* that arose

48 *Ibid,* Article 10.

49 *Ibid,* Article 13.

50 Agreement between Bosnia and Herzegovina and the Republic of Slovenia for the Reciprocal Promotion and Protection of Investments. <https://investmentpolicy.unctad.org/international-investment-agreements/treaty-files/492/download>. Ratified by Slovenia by way of: *Zakon o ratifikaciji Sporazuma med Republiko Slovenijo in Bosno in Hercegovino o vzajemnem spodbujanju in zaščiti naložb* (BBHSZN). Official Gazette 90/01. <https://pisrs.si/pregledPredpisa?id=ZAKO3244> (all websites accessed on 29 May 2024).

51 Article 1(1) of the Bosnia–Slovenia BIT.

52 The definition for Slovenia, on the other hand, states merely: »*natural persons having the nationality of the Republic of Slovenia in accordance with its laws*«, without including the permanent place of business/main place of residence requirement.

53 *Ibid,* Article 1(2).

following its entry into force.[54] The BIT includes a post-establishment national treatment clause[55] and a post-establishment most-favoured nation clause,[56] which, however, does not apply in case of economic integration agreements, customs unions and taxation treaties.[57] The BIT further includes an unqualified fair and equitable treatment (FET) clause.[58] It covers direct as well as indirect expropriation, without further defining the latter.[59] The BIT also covers the transfer of funds, with no specifically listed exceptions.[60]

In terms of dispute resolution between investors and one of the Contracting States, the BIT initially requires a three-month mandatory negotiation period. Should such negotiations not yield results, either party may submit the dispute to: (i) the competent court of the host State; (ii) an *ad hoc* arbitral tribunal pursuant to the UNCITRAL rules; or (iii) ICSID arbitration or conciliation.[61]

The BIT has a term of ten years which renews automatically. It can be unilaterally terminated by each Contracting party with a written notice, lodged at least six months before the date of expiry of the original or each subsequent period. It includes a ten-year sunset clause.[62]

c. **Serbia–Slovenia BIT (2002)** (original parties Federal Republic of Yugoslavia–Slovenia): concluded on 18 June 2002, entered into force on 1 May 2004.[63]

The BIT encompasses an asset-based, open-ended definition of investment. It does not exclude portfolio investments or any other specific assets and does not list the required characteristics of an investment. It does, however, contain

54 *Ibid,* Article 11.
55 *Ibid,* Article 3(2).
56 *Ibid,* Article 3(2).
57 *Ibid,* Article 3(3).
58 *Ibid,* Article 3(1).
59 The BIT simply refers to "*measures having an effect equivalent to nationalisation or expropriation*". *See Ibid,* Article 5(1).
60 *Ibid,* Article 6.
61 *Ibid,* Article 8.
62 *Ibid,* Article 12.
63 Agreement between the Government of the Republic of Slovenia and the Federal Government of the Federal Republic of Yugoslavia on the Mutual Promotion and Protection of Investments. <https://investmentpolicy.unctad.org/international-investment-agreements/treaty-files/5209/download>. Ratified by Slovenia by way of: *Zakon o ratifikaciji Sporazuma med Vlado Republike Slovenije in Zvezno vlado Zvezne republike Jugoslavije o vzajemnem spodbujanju in zaščiti naložb* (BYUSZN). Official Gazette of the Republic of Slovenia, No 112/02. <https://pisrs.si/pregledPredpisa?id=ZAKO3492> (all websites accessed on 29 May 2024).

a clean hands requirement requiring an investment to be made "in accordance with the laws and regulations" to qualify as an investment under the BIT.[64]

The BIT's definition of investor covers nationals of the State parties, without explicitly excluding dual nationals. Its definition of a "legal person" requires a legal person, incorporated, constituted, or otherwise duly organized in accordance with the laws of the relevant Contracting Party to also have its seat in the relevant Contracting Party.[65]

The substantive scope of the BIT is unrestricted, and it is applicable to both existing and post-BIT investments. However, it is limited to *disputes* that arose following its entry into force.[66] The BIT includes a post-establishment national treatment clause[67] and a post-establishment most-favoured nation clause,[68] which, however, does not apply in case of economic integration agreements, customs unions and taxation treaties.[69] The BIT further includes an unqualified fair and equitable treatment (FET) clause[70] and a standard full protection and security clause.[71] It covers direct as well as indirect expropriation, without further defining the latter.[72] The BIT also covers the transfer of funds, with no specifically listed exceptions.[73]

In terms of dispute resolution between investors and one of the Contracting States, the BIT initially requires a six-month mandatory negotiation period. Should such negotiations not yield results, either party may submit the dispute to: (i) the competent court of the host State; (ii) an *ad hoc* arbitral tribunal pursuant to UNCITRAL Rules (unless otherwise agreed upon by the parties); (iii) ICSID arbitration or conciliation; or (iv) ICSID under the Additional Facility Rules.[74]

The BIT has a term of ten years which renews automatically for a period of five years. It can be unilaterally terminated by each Contracting party with a written notice, lodged at least a year before the date of expiry of the original or each subsequent period. It includes a ten-year sunset clause.[75]

---

64 Article 1(1) of the Serbia–Slovenia BIT.
65 *Ibid*, Article 1(2).
66 *Ibid*, Article 12.
67 *Ibid*, Article 3(2).
68 *Ibid*, Article 3(2).
69 *Ibid*, Article 3(3).
70 *Ibid*, Article 3(1).
71 *Ibid*, Article 2(3).
72 The BIT simply refers to "*measures having an effect equivalent to nationalisation or expropriation*". *See Ibid*, Article 4(1).
73 *Ibid*, Article 6.
74 *Ibid*, Article 10.
75 *Ibid*, Article 15.

d. **North Macedonia–Slovenia BIT (1996):** concluded on 5 June 1996, entered into force on 21 September 1999.[76]

The BIT encompasses an asset-based, open-ended definition of investment. It does not exclude portfolio investments or any other specific assets and does not list the required characteristics of an investment. It does, however, contain a clean hands requirement requiring an investment to be made "in accordance with the laws and regulations" to qualify as an investment under the BIT.[77]

The BIT's definition of investor covers nationals of the State parties, without explicitly excluding dual nationals. Its definition of a "legal person" covers legal persons incorporated, constituted, or otherwise duly organized in accordance with the laws of the relevant Contracting Party, with its seat in the relevant Contracting Party.[78]

The substantive scope of the BIT is unrestricted, and it is applicable to both existing and post-BIT investments.[79] The BIT includes a post-establishment national treatment clause[80] and a post-establishment most-favoured nation clause,[81] which, however, does not apply in case of economic integration agreements, customs unions and taxation treaties.[82] The BIT further includes an unqualified fair and equitable treatment (FET) clause[83] and a standard full protection and security clause.[84] It covers direct as well as indirect expropriation, without further defining the latter.[85] The BIT also covers the transfer of funds, with no specifically listed exceptions.[86]

In terms of dispute resolution between investors and one of the Contracting States, the BIT initially requires a six-month mandatory negotiation period. Should such negotiations not yield results, either party may submit the dispute

---

76 Agreement between the Republic of Slovenia and the Republic of Macedonia on the Reciprocal Protection and Promotion of Investments. <https://investmentpolicy.unctad.org/international-investment-agreements/treaty-files/3038/download>. Ratified by Slovenia by way of: *Zakon o ratifikaciji Sporazuma med Republiko Slovenijo in Republiko Makedonijo o vzajemni zaščiti in spodbujanju investicij* (BMKZSI). Official Gazette of the Republic of Slovenia, No 27/99. <https://pisrs.si/pregledPredpisa?id=ZAKO1960> (all websites accessed on 29 May 2024).

77 Article 1(1) of the North Macedonia–Slovenia BIT.

78 *Ibid,* Article 1(2).

79 *Ibid,* Article 11.

80 *Ibid,* Article 3(2).

81 *Ibid,* Article 3(2).

82 *Ibid,* Article 3(3).

83 *Ibid,* Article 3(2).

84 *Ibid,* Article 3(1).

85 The BIT simply refers to "*measures having an effect equivalent to nationalisation or expropriation*". *See Ibid,* Article 4(1).

86 *Ibid,* Article 5.

to: (i) the competent court of the host State; (ii) an *ad hoc* arbitral tribunal pursuant to UNCITRAL rules; or (iii) ICSID arbitration or conciliation.[87]
The BIT has a term of ten years which renews automatically. It can be unilaterally terminated by each Contracting party with a written notice, lodged at least a year before the date of expiry of the original or each subsequent period. It includes a ten-year sunset clause.[88]

4.3 *Other BITs Currently in Force*

We are providing below a list of BITs that Slovenia has concluded with other countries which are currently in force:

a. **China–Slovenia BIT (1993):** concluded on 13 September 1993, entered into force on 1 January 1995.[89]
b. **Egypt–Slovenia BIT (1998):** concluded on 28 October 1998, entered into force on 7 February 2000.[90]
c. **Israel–Slovenia BIT (1998):** concluded on 13 May 1998, entered into force on 2 October 1999.[91]

---

87 *Ibid,* Article 7.

88 *Ibid,* Article 13.

89 Agreement between the Government of the People's Republic of China and the Government of the Republic of Slovenia concerning the encouragement and reciprocal protection of investments. <https://investmentpolicy.unctad.org/international-investment-agreements/treaty-files/779/download>. Ratified by Slovenia by way of: *Zakon o ratifikaciji sporazuma med Vlado Republike Slovenije in Vlado Ljudske republike Kitajske o spodbujanju in vzajemni zaščiti investicij* (BCNSZI). Official Gazette of the Republic of Slovenia, No 11/94. <https://pisrs.si/pregledPredpisa?id=ZAKO750> (all websites accessed on 29 May 2024).

90 Agreement between the Government of the Arab Republic of Egypt and the Government of the Republic of Slovenia on the Mutual Promotion and Protection of Investments. <https://investmentpolicy.unctad.org/international-investment-agreements/treaty-files/5351/download>. Ratified by Slovenia by way of: *Zakon o ratifikaciji Sporazuma med Vlado Republike Slovenije in Vlado Arabske republike Egipt o medsebojnem pospeševanju in zaščiti naložb* (BEGPZN). Official Gazette of the Republic of Slovenia, No 27/99. <https://pisrs.si/pregledPredpisa?id=ZAKO1961> (all websites accessed on 29 May 2024).

91 Agreement between the Government of the State of Israel and the Government of the REpublic of Slovenia for the Reciprocal Promotion and Protection of Investments <https://investmentpolicy.unctad.org/international-investment-agreements/treaty-files/1674/download>. Ratified by Slovenia by way of: *Zakon o ratifikaciji Sporazuma med Vlado Republike Slovenije in Vlado Države Izrael o vzajemnem spodbujanju in zaščiti naložb* (BILSZN), Official Gazette of the Republic of Slovenia, No 27/99. <https://pisrs.si/pregledPredpisa?id=ZAKO1908>.

d. **Kuwait–Slovenia BIT (2002):** concluded on 26 April 2002, entered into force on 28 July 2004.[92]
e. **Republic of Moldova BIT (2003):** concluded on 10 April 2003, entered into force on 1 June 2004.[93]
f. **Singapore–Slovenia BIT (1999):** concluded on 25 January 1999, entered into force on 8 September 2000.[94]
g. **Switzerland–Slovenia BIT (1995):** concluded on 9 November 1995, entered into force on 20 March 1997.[95]
h. **Thailand–Slovenia BIT (2000):** concluded on 18 February 2000, entered into force on 20 October 2002.[96]

---

92 Agreement between the Government of the Republic of Slovenia and the Governement of the State of Kuwait on the Mutual Promotion and Protection of Investments. <https://investmentpolicy.unctad.org/international-investment-agreements/treaty-files/6659/download>. Ratified by Slovenia by way of: *Zakon o ratifikaciji Sporazuma med Vlado Republike Slovenije in Vlado Države Kuvajt o spodbujanju in medsebojni zaščiti naložb* (BKWSZN). Official Gazette of the Republic of Slovenia, No 89/02. <https://pisrs.si/preglegPredpisa?id=ZAKO3466> (all websites accessed on 29 May 2024).

93 Agreement between the Government of the Republic of Moldova and the Government of the Republic of Slovenia on the Mutual Promotion and Protection of Investments. <https://investmentpolicy.unctad.org/international-investment-agreements/treaty-files/6316/download>. Ratified by Slovenia by way of: *Zakon o ratifikaciji Sporazuma med Vlado Republike Slovenije in Vlado Republike Moldove o vzajemnem spodbujanju in zaščiti naložb* (BMDVSN). Official Gazette of the Republic of Slovenia, No 40/04). <https://pisrs.si/pregledPredpisa?id=ZAKO4012> (all websites accessed on 29 May 2024).

94 Agreement between the Government of the Republic of Singapore and the Government of the Republic of Slovenia on the Mutual Promotion and Protection of Investments. <https://investmentpolicy.unctad.org/international-investment-agreements/treaty-files/3535/download>. Ratified by Slovenia by way of: *Zakon o ratifikaciji Sporazuma med Vlado Republike Slovenije in Vlado Republike Singapur o medsebojnem spodbujanju in zaščiti naložb* (BSGSZN), Official Gazette of the Republic of Slovenia, No 69/00). <https://pisrs.si/pregledPredpisa?id=ZAKO2664> (all websites accessed on 29 May 2024).

95 Agreement between the Republic of Slovenia and the Swiss Confederation on the Promotion and Reciprocal Protection of Investments. <https://investmentpolicy.unctad.org/international-investment-agreements/treaty-files/2271/download>. Ratified by Slovenia by way of: *Zakon o ratifikaciji Sporazuma med Republiko Slovenijo in* Švicarsko *konfederacijo o vzpodbujanju in vzajemni zaščiti investicij* (BCHSVZI). Official Gazette of the Republic of Slovenia, No 16/97. <https://pisrs.si/pregledPredpisa?id=ZAKO1143> (all websites accessed on 29 May 2024).

96 Agreement between the Government of the Kingdom of Thailand and the Government of the Republic of Slovenia on the Promotion and Protection of Investments. <https://investmentpolicy.unctad.org/international-investment-agreements/treaty-files/2273/download>. Ratified by Slovenia by way of: *Zakon o ratifikaciji Sporazuma med Vlado Republike Slovenije in Vlado Kraljevine Tajske o spodbujanju in zaščiti naložb s Protokolom* (BTHSZN). Official Gazette of the Republic of Slovenia, No 69/00. <https://pisrs.si/pregledPredpisa?id=ZAKO2651> (all websites accessed on 29 May 2024).

i. **Turkey (now Türkiye)–Slovenia BIT (2004):** concluded on 23 March 2004, entered into force on 19 June 2006.[97]
j. **Ukraine– Slovenia BIT (1999):** concluded on 30 March 1999, entered into force on 1 June 2000.[98]
k. **United Kingdom–Slovenia BIT (1996):** concluded on 3 July 1996, entered into force on 27 March 1999.[99] According to reports by the Slovenian government, this BIT is in the process of termination.[100]
l. **Uzbekistan–Slovenia BIT (2003):** concluded on 7 October 2003, entered into force on 18 May 2004.[101]

---

97 Agreement between the Republic of Turkey and the Republic of Slovenia on the Promotion and Protection of Investments.<https://investmentpolicy.unctad.org/international-investment-agreements/treaty-files/2274/download>. Ratified by Slovenia by way of: *Zakon o ratifikaciji Sporazuma med Republiko Slovenijo in Republiko Turčijo o spodbujanju in zaščiti naložb* (BTUSZN), Official Gazette of the Republic of Slovenia, No 45/06. <https://pisrs.si/pregledPredpisa?id=ZAKO4788> (all websites accessed on 29 May 2024).

98 Agreement between Ukraine and the Republic of Slovenia on the Mutual Promotion and Protection of Investments. <https://investmentpolicy.unctad.org/international-investment-agreements/treaty-files/6250/download>. Ratified by Slovenia by way of: *Zakon o ratifikaciji Sporazuma med Republiko Slovenijo in Ukrajino o medsebojnem pospeševanju in zaščiti naložb* (BUKSZN), Official Gazette of the Republic of Slovenia, No 24/00. <https://pisrs.si/pregledPredpisa?id=ZAKO2163> (all websites accessed on 29 May 2024).

99 Agreement between the Government of the United Kingdom of Great Britain and Northern Ireland and the Government of the Republic of Slovenia for the Promotion and Protection of Investments. <https://investmentpolicy.unctad.org/international-investment-agreements/treaty-files/2275/download>. Ratified by Slovenia by way of: *Zakon o ratifikaciji Sporazuma med Vlado Republike Slovenije in Vlado Združenega kraljestva Velike Britanije in Severne Irske o zaščiti in spodbujanju vlaganj* (BGBZSV). Official Gazette of the Republic of Slovenia, No 20/99. <https://pisrs.si/pregledPredpisa?id=ZAKO1941> (all websites accessed on 29 May 2024).

100 Prenehanje veljavnosti bilateralnih naložbenih sporazumov, sklenjenih med državami članicami EU ter učinki sodbe Achmea na naložbene spore med vlagateljem in državo na podlagi teh sporazumov. Ministrstvo za gospodarski razvoj in tehnologijo. 4 April 2022. <https://www.gov.si/novice/2022-04-01-prenehanje-veljavnosti-bilateralnih-nalozbenih-sporazumov-sklenjenih-med-drzavami-clanicami-eu-ter-ucinki-sodbe-achmea-na-nalozbene-spore-med-vlagateljem-in-drzavo-na-podlagi-teh-sporazumov/> (accessed on 29 Mary 2024).

101 Agreement between the Republic of Uzbekistan and the Republic of Slovenia on the Mutual Promotion and Protection of Investments. <https://investmentpolicy.unctad.org/international-investment-agreements/treaty-files/6291/download>. Ratified by Slovenia by way of: *Zakon o ratifikaciji Sporazuma med Republiko Slovenijo in Republiko Uzbekistan o vzajemnem spodbujanju in zaščiti naložb* (BUZVSN). Official Gazette of the Republic of Slovenia, No 40/04. <https://pisrs.si/pregledPredpisa?id=ZAKO4010> (all websites accessed on 29 May 2024).

4.4 *Other BITs Which Have Been Terminated or Have Not Entered into Force*

a. **Belarus–Slovenia BIT (2006):** concluded on 18 October 2006. Not ratified by the Republic of Slovenia (no information on ratification by Belarus) and consequently not in force.[102]

b. **India–Slovenia BIT (2011):** concluded on 14 June 2011, never ratified. Unilaterally terminated by India on 22 March 2017.[103]

c. **Russian Federation–Slovenia BIT (2000):** concluded on 8 April 2000. Ratified by the Republic of Slovenia on 20 December 2000. Not ratified by the Russian Federation and consequently not in force.[104]

4.5 *Energy Charter Treaty (ECT)*

Slovenia has not remained immune to the recent wave of criticism against the ECT and the failed attempts for its modernization, particularly among the members of the EU. Consequently, on 11 November 2022 Slovenia announced its intention to withdraw from the ECT. This decision was ostensibly driven by the fact that the enlargement of the EU and further European integration have opened new opportunities for investment cooperation in the energy field and for ensuring legal certainty for energy sector players. At the same time, Slovenia expressed its dissatisfaction with the pace of progress in the modernization of the ECT. In its view, one of the most significant indicators of the ECT's alleged obsolescence is ISDS. However, it is noteworthy that this stance may have been influenced by the filing of the notice of dispute in the case of

102 Agreement between the Government of the Republic of Belarus and the Government of the Republic of Slovenia on the Mutual Promotion and Protection of Investments. <https://investmentpolicy.unctad.org/international-investment-agreements/treaty-files/5296/download> (accessed on 29 May 2024).

103 Agreement between the Government of the Republic of India and the Government of the Republic of Slovenia on the Mutual Promotion and Protection of Investments <https://investmentpolicy.unctad.org/international-investment-agreements/treaty-files/1598/download> (accessed on 29 May 2024).

104 Agreement between the Government of the Republic of Slovenia and the Government of the Russian Federation on the Promotion and Reciprocal Protection of Investments. <https://investmentpolicy.unctad.org/international-investment-agreements/treaty-files/3435/download>. Ratified by Slovenia by way of: *Zakon o ratifikaciji Sporazuma med Vlado Republike Slovenije in Vlado Ruske federacije o spodbujanju in medsebojni zaščiti naložb* (BRUSZN), Official Gazette of the Republic of Slovenia, No 1/01. <https://pisrs.si/pregledPredpisa?id=ZAKO3067> (all websites accessed on 29 May 2024).

Ascent v Slovenia[105] on 5 May 2022 and the notice of intent in the case of *Towra v Slovenia,*[106] both based on the ECT.

The Government's Initiative for the Withdrawal from the ECT received a positive opinion of the Commission for International Relations and European Affairs of the National Council on 15 November 2022. On 16 November 2022 the Initiative was approved by the Foreign Affairs Committee of the Slovenian Parliament and on 13 October 2023, Slovenia deposited its withdrawal with the ECT Depositary, the Government of Portugal. The withdrawal will take effect on 14 October 2024. According to the sunset clause included in Article 47(3) of the ECT, the investments covered by the ECT at the time the withdrawal takes effect will continue to be covered for a period of 20 years. This may effectively prolong the existing regime under the ECT, as opposed to its modernized version. No information is available on whether Slovenia plans to negotiate any agreements with other former ECT members providing for a different application of the sunset clause.

5 ISDS Cases and Outcomes

For a country of its size, Slovenia, rather unsurprisingly, does not frequently feature as a host State in ISDS proceedings. Since 2004, Slovenia has participated as a respondent in six arbitrations under the auspices of International Centre for Settlement of Investment Disputes (ICSID). Two of those disputes have been settled, one was been resolved following complex proceedings and one withdrawn by the investor. Two arbitrations are currently pending.

In terms of outgoing investments, publicly available data indicates that Slovenian investors have acted as claimants in two ICSID arbitrations, one of which has been decided in favor of the investor and one is still pending. Another (pending) arbitration is conducted under the auspices of the Permanent Court of Arbitration (PCA). Given the general trajectory of investments by Slovenian investors, it is not surprising that all three claims pertain to investments made in host States that were part of the former Yugoslavia. As is clearly evident from an overview of cases involving Slovenia and its investors, , the ECT remains the principal legal instrument under which proceedings are brought.

105 *Ascent Resources Plc and Ascent Slovenia Ltd v. Republic of Slovenia* (ICSID Case No. ARB/22/21). See below, Sub-Chapter 5.1.5.

106 *Towra SA-SPF v. Republic of Slovenia* (ICSID Case No. ARB/22/33). See below, Sub-Chapter 5.1.6.

5.1 *Cases Concerning Incoming Investments*

5.1.1 Interbrew Central European Holding BV v. Republic of Slovenia – Settled

Slovenia faced its first investment treaty arbitration in the case of *Interbrew Central European Holding BV v. Republic of Slovenia.*[107] At the time there was limited knowledge or experience with the field of international investment law internally within the Government. The claims of the investor, based in the Netherlands, arose out of the alleged role of the Slovenian government in the contemplated acquisition of equity interests by Interbrew in the second-largest Slovenian brewer, Pivovarna Union.

The case was lodged with ICSID and concerned alleged violations of the 1996 Slovenia–Netherlands BIT, which has since been terminated pursuant to the provisions of the Termination Agreement (see Chapter 4.1.2 above). The proceedings were conducted under the ICSID Arbitration Rules, and the tribunal was composed of Charles N. Brower (appointed by the claimant), Florentino P. Feliciano (appointed by the respondent) and the tribunal President, Francisco Orrego Vicuña. The case settled at an early stage of the proceedings and the arbitration was discontinued.

5.1.2 Hrvatska Elektroprivreda d.d. v. Republic of Slovenia – Concluded in Favor of the Investor

The second case, *Hrvatska Elektroprivreda d.d. v. Republic of Slovenia,*[108] concerned the dispute between the Croatian national electricity company as investor and Slovenia concerning the ownership and operation of the Krško nuclear power plant located in Slovenia. The power plant, which commenced operation in 1981 as a joint venture between the two (at the time) Yugoslav republics, is governed by an international treaty concluded between the two States (NEK Treaty).[109] In 1998, following alleged breaches of HEP's financial obligations towards the power plant, the delivery of electricity to HEP was

107 *Interbrew Central European Holding BV v. Republic of Slovenia* (ICSID Case No ARB/04/17), discontinued on 18 July 2005.

108 *Hrvatska Elektroprivreda dd v. Republic of Slovenia* (ICSID Case No ARB/05/24), award rendered on 17 December 2015.

109 Agreement between the Government of the Republic of Croatia and the Government of the Republic of Slovenia on Regulation of Status and Other Legal Relations Regarding the Investment, Use and Dismantling of Nuclear Power Plant Krško (attached to Decision on the Treaty Interpretation Issue, *Hrvatska Elektroprivreda dd v. Republic of Slovenia* (ICSID Case No ARB/05/24, 12 June 2009)).

suspended.[110] The investor alleged losses resulting from Slovenia's alleged failure to resume electricity deliveries and claimed a violation both of the NEK Treaty and the ECT. The tribunal was composed of Charles Brower (appointed by the claimant), Jan Paulsson (appointed by the respondent), and the tribunal President, David A.R. Williams KC. The arbitration was conducted pursuant to the ICSID Arbitration Rules.

The case, however, gained notoriety primarily due to the tribunal's decision to disqualify Slovenia's counsel. Three years into the proceedings, the claimant raised a request to remove one of Slovenia's counsel, Mr David Mildon KC of Essex Court Chambers.[111] It argued that Mr Mildon KC belonged to the same Chambers of which the tribunal president of the tribunal was a door tenant and that this raised questions of impartiality of the tribunal. In its decision the tribunal thus addressed the conflict between the general rule in international arbitration allowing parties freely to select their own legal representatives, juxtaposing it with the principle of immutability of properly constituted tribunals under Article 56(1) of the ICSID Convention. The tribunal concluded that, when changes to the parties' legal team take place after the tribunal had been constituted, the principle of immutability prevails where such changes could imperil a tribunal's status or legitimacy.[112]

Moreover, the tribunal adopted an unconventional definition of justifiable doubt as to the impartiality or independence of tribunal members. It stated that the perspective of a reasonable independent observer could be construed in such a manner that the lack of understanding of the English chambers system could lead a reasonable independent observer to doubt the impartiality of a tribunal member.[113]

A year later the tribunal rendered a decision pertaining to the interpretation of the NEK Treaty. Slovenia was found liable to the claimant for the financial value of the undelivered electricity during the relevant timeframe under the NEK Treaty. However, the arbitral tribunal did not find any breaches by

110 For a more detailed summary *see* Inaê Siqueira de Oliveira. Slovenia is condemned to pay €20 million in damages and US$10 million in costs to Croatian national electric company. Investment Treaty News, International Institute for Sustainable Development (IISD). 16 May 2016. <https://www.iisd.org/itn/en/2016/05/16/slovenia-is-condemned-to-pay-e20-million-in-damages-and-us10-million-in-costs-to-croatian-national-electric-company-hrvatska-elektroprivrieda-dd-v-republic-of-slovenia-icsid-case-no-arb-05-24-inae-siq/> (accessed on 29 May 2024).

111 Order Concerning the Participation of Counsel, *Hrvatska Elektroprivreda dd v. Republic of Slovenia* (ICSID Case No ARB/05/24, 6 May 2008).

112 *Ibid* at 4, §§ 24–26.

113 *Ibid* § 31.

Slovenia of the ECT.[114] Jan Paulsson authored an extensive dissenting opinion on the matter. His primary disagreement was with the majority's conclusion that a treaty which does not establish an obligation of delivery, can nonetheless create liability for non-delivery.[115]

After nine years of arbitration proceedings, which were characterized by intricate procedural and document production issues, as well as expert witness testimony, the arbitral tribunal issued an award in 2015, awarding damages, interest and costs to the Croatian investor.[116]

5.1.3 Impresa Grassetto SpA, in Liquidation v. Republic of Slovenia – Settled

The third investment arbitration lodged against Slovenia was initiated in 2013 by the Italian investor Impresa Grassetto SpA, in liquidation.[117] The claims were filed under the (now terminated) 2000 Italy–Slovenia BIT. The dispute arose from disagreements over the execution of a construction contract awarded to the investor for a motorway tunnel project.

The case was settled on 29 January 2020 at a fairly advanced procedural stage, after the parties had already filed their statements of costs, but before any award had been rendered.[118] The discontinuation appeared to coincide with the claimant's settlement of a dispute with the Slovenian roads authority. This had followed a reported first instance win in national courts by the claimant, in which it was awarded approximately EUR ten million, out of more than EUR fifty million that it had requested.[119] As this was the third ISDS claim that Slovenia had encountered, it had already learned lessons regarding the

---

114 Decision on the Treaty Interpretation Issue, *Hrvatska Elektroprivreda dd v. Republic of Slovenia* (ICSID Case No ARB/05/24, 12 June 2009).

115 Individual Opinion of Jan Paulsson, *Hrvatska Elektroprivreda dd v. Republic of Slovenia* (ICSID Case No ARB/05/24, 12 June 2009) § 3.

116 Award, *Hrvatska Elektropriveda dd v. Republic of Slovenia* (ICSID Case No ARB/05/24, 17 December 2015).

117 *Impresa Grassetto SpA, in liquidation v. Republic of Slovenia* (ICSID Case No ARB/13/10).

118 The proceedings were discontinued in accordance with Rule 43(1) of the ICSID Rules on 29 January 2020: see 'Case Details: *Impresa Grassetto SpA, in liquidation v Republic of Slovenia*'. International Centre for Settlement of Investment Disputes 2020. <https://icsid.worldbank.org/en/Pages/cases/casedetail.aspx?CaseNo=ARB/13/10> (accessed on 29 May 2024).

119 Vladislav Djanic. Balkans round-up: Slovenian and Macedonian cases are discontinued. Bulgaria case moves to the merits, and awards loom in a quartet of other cases in the region. IA Reporter, 3 February 2020. <https://www.iareporter.com/articles/balkans-round-up-slovenian-and-macedonian-cases-are-discontinued-bulgaria-case-moves-to-the-merits-and-awards-loom-in-a-quartet-of-other-cases-in-the-region/> (accessed on 29 May 2024).

management of its participation in the proceedings. The recognition of a lack of adequate domestic capacity and expertise to handle such cases prompted the engagement of external counsel from the very outset of the case. Additionally, the realization of the need for organized, intersectoral support for counsel led to the latter collaborating closely with multidisciplinary expert teams. The proceedings were conducted under the ICSID Arbitration Rules, and the tribunal was constituted of Pierre-Yves Tschanz (appointed by the claimant), Brigitte Stern (appointed by the respondent) and the tribunal President, William W. Park.

5.1.4 Addiko Bank AG v. Republic of Slovenia – Discontinued

The fourth ICSID case, *Addiko Bank AG v. Republic of Slovenia*, was initiated under the 2001 Austria–Slovenia BIT.[120] The case pertained to claims arising from legislation adopted by the Slovenian Parliament in 2022, which limited and distributed currency risk among creditors and borrowers of loans in Swiss francs, and which mandated lenders to adjust CHF loan agreements concluded between 2004 and 2010.

The dispute has since become moot, as the Slovenian Constitutional court deemed the legislation incompatible with the Slovenian constitution and consequently repealed it.[121] On 2 February 2024 the Secretary-General of ICSID issued an order taking note of the discontinuance of the proceedings pursuant to ICSID Arbitration Rule 43(1).

5.1.5 Ascent Resources Plc and Ascent Slovenia Ltd. v Republic of Slovenia – Pending

The first of the two currently pending ICSID investment arbitration cases filed against Slovenia, *Ascent Resources Plc and Ascent Slovenia Ltd v. Republic of Slovenia*,[122] has been brought on the basis of both the ECT and the 1996 Slovenia–UK BIT. It concerns allegations of breaches of the fair and equitable treatment standard, the prohibition of unlawful expropriation, and the guarantee that the management, maintenance, use, enjoyment, or disposal of the

---

120 *Addiko Bank AG v. Republic of Slovenia* (ICSID Case No. ARB/22/9).

121 See the Constitutional Court of Slovenia's decision No U-I-64/22-21, U-I-65/22-23, dated 17 November 2022 <https://www.us-rs.si/documents/18/ef/u-i-64-22-u-i-65-22-decision-en5.pdf> (accessed on 29 May 2024).

122 *Ascent Resources Plc and Ascent Slovenia Ltd v Republic of Slovenia* (ICSID Case No. ARB/22/21).

investments would not be impaired by arbitrary, unreasonable, or discriminatory measures.[123]

The claims substantially relate to the rights granted to the investor for the exploration and exploitation of hydrocarbons, by means of any hydraulic stimulation ("fracking"), which Slovenia allegedly infringed when the environmental regulator failed to grant an approval without an environmental impact assessment. Furthermore, they relate to the later amendments to the Slovenian Mining Law, which have banned fracking. The proceedings are governed by the ICSID Arbitration Rules.

5.1.6 Towra SA-SPF v. Republic of Slovenia – Pending

The latest ICSID case against Slovenia, *Towra SA-SPF v. Republic of Slovenia*,[124] has also been lodged under the protections granted by the ECT. It concerns an alleged expropriation of minority shareholders in Slovenia's only coal mine, Premogovnik Velenje, in 2012. As the notice of intent in this case has been lodged in December 2022, the proceedings are currently in their initial stages, however, their initiation may have had quite an important consequence – following the filing of the notice of intent in these proceedings the Slovenian government announced Slovenia's withdrawal from the ECT.[125]

These proceedings are anticipated to bring forth intriguing admissibility issues. Among these are questions relating to the doctrine of (un)clean hands, given that Towra's director has been accused in criminal proceedings of assisting in the draining of Premogovnik Velenje and its principal buyer, Termoelektrarna Šoštanj. The proceedings are governed by the ICSID Arbitration Rules and the tribunal consists of Charles Poncet (appointed by the claimant), Albert Jan van den Berg (appointed by the respondent) and the tribunal President, Juliet Blanch.

5.2 *Cases Concerning Outgoing Investments*

5.2.1 Boris Goljevšček, Viaduct d.o.o. Portorož and Vladimir Zevnik v. Bosnia and Herzegovina – Concluded

The case of *Viaduct d.o.o. Portorož, Vladimir Zevnik and Boris Goljevšček v Bosnia and Herzegovina*[126] has been so far the only concluded ISDS arbitration

123 See Notice of Dispute, *Ascent Resources v Slovenia Plc. and Ascent Slovenia Ltd. v. Republic of Slovenia* (ICSID Case No. ARB/22/21) § 1.3.

124 *Towra SA-SPF v. Republic of Slovenia* (ICSID Case No. ARB/22/33).

125 See Chapter 4.3 above.

126 *Viaduct d.o.o. Portorož, Vladimir Zevnik and Boris Goljevšček v Bosnia and Herzegovina* (ICSID Case No. ARB/16/36), award rendered on 18 April 2022.

dealing with an outgoing investment by Slovenian investors. It was initiated on 15 November 2016 and concerned alleged acts and omissions of the Government of Republika Srpska, one of the two entities constituting Bosnia and Herzegovina. These actions and omissions had reportedly frustrated the claimants' two hydroelectric power plant projects on the Vrbas River.

In 2004, the claimants' subsidiary HES Vrbas entered into concession agreements to build and operate the power plants. However, the facilities were never built, ostensibly due to Republika Srpska's failure to issue the requisite permits or to approve an updated conceptual project design. Additionally, the claimants contended that Republika Srpska had granted concession rights to the State-owned company ZP Hidroelektrane, to construct a competing power plant on the river, bypassing a public tender process.

The proceedings were conducted under the ICSID Arbitration Rules and the tribunal consisted of Ian Laird (appointed by the claimants), Horacio A. Grigera Naón (appointed by the respondent) and the tribunal President, William W. Park.

The claimants alleged violations of the substantive protections accorded by the ECT and the 2001 Bosnia and Herzegovina–Slovenia BIT. In its final award, issued on 18 April 2022, the tribunal unanimously determined that Bosnia and Herzegovina had violated its obligation of fair and equitable treatment under both the ECT and the Bosnia and Herzegovina–Slovenia BIT.

While the tribunal also considered a claim of indirect expropriation, it did not deal with it in detail in the award, stating that the outcome of the arbitration would not be affected by a finding of an additional breach.[127] It awarded the claimants about 40 million EUR in damages, in addition to their costs and fees.

On 5 August 2022, Bosnia and Herzegovina filed an application for annulment of the award. On 1 May 2024, the *ad hoc* committee rejected the annulment request in its entirety as unfounded.

5.2.2 Elektrogospodarstvo Slovenije – razvoj in inženiring d.o.o. v Bosnia and Herzegovina – Pending

In the case of *Elektrogospodarstvo Slovenije – razvoj in inženiring d.o.o. v. Bosnia and Herzegovina*[128] the claimant, a State-owned Slovenian company, has

127 Vladislav Djanic, ICSID ad hoc committee grants conditional stay of enforcement in dispute with Bosnia, as additional information surfaces regarding the underlying award, IAReporter, 7 December 2022, Available at: https://www.iareporter.com/articles/icsid-ad-hoc-committee-conditionally-grants-stay-of-enforcement-of-award-against-bosnia-as-additional-information-surfaces-regarding-the-underlying-award/.

128 *Elektrogospodarstvo Slovenije – razvoj in inzeniring d.o.o. v. Bosnia and Herzegovina* (ICSID Case No. ARB/14/13).

initiated claims before the ICSID arising out of alleged outstanding payments for the claimant's contribution of funds towards the construction of a thermal power plant in Bosnia and Herzegovina. In addition, the claimant requests compensation due for undelivered electricity.

The thermal plant is presently fully owned by the Government of Republika Srpska. The claims are based on the substantive protections afforded by the ECT and the 2001 Bosnia and Herzegovina – Slovenia BIT and the proceedings are governed by the ICSID Arbitration Rules. The arbitral tribunal consists of Jan Paulsson (appointed by the claimant), Maja Stanivuković (appointed by the respondent) and the tribunal President, Christopher Greenwood KC.

Since 29 March 2024 the proceedings have been suspended pursuant to the parties' agreement.[129]

5.2.3 Blažo Tasev v. Republic of North Macedonia

The case of *Blažo Tasev v. Republic of North Macedonia*[130] is the only ISDS case involving either a Slovenian investor or Slovenia as a host State which has not been lodged with ICSID. Rather, it has been filed under the 1976 UNCITRAL Rules and administered by the PCA. The tribunal consists of Vera van Houtte (appointed by the claimant), J. Christopher Thomas (appointed by the respondent), and the tribunal President, Melanie Van Leeuwen.

The claims concern alleged breaches of the 1996 Former Yugoslav Republic of Macedonia–Slovenia BIT, related to a lead and zinc mine, acquired by Mr Tasev, a Slovenian national, in 2004. No further details regarding this ongoing case are in the public domain.

6 Special Features

Since its independence, Slovenia has neither established a formal strategy for the resolution of disputes involving the State, nor has it established a clear allocation of responsibilities among the potentially relevant State authorities.

The main responsibility for the representation of the State in disputes is formally with the State Attorney's Office (*Državno odvetništvo Republike Slovenije*), an independent representative and advisory body. Its existence and setup are to a large extent a legacy of the former Yugoslav system, and in certain regards comparable to its counterparts in France, Spain, Greece, Germany, Austria, Norway, and other countries. The primary responsibility of the State

129 The proceedings have been suspended for the most part of the period since May 2020.

130 *Blažo Tasev v. Republic of North Macedonia* (PCA Case No. 2019-09).

Attorney's Office is the defence of the patrimonial rights and benefits of the State through *ex lege* representation, but it also has an advisory function.

With approximately 100 State attorneys (and a similar number of additional staff), the State Attorney's Office annually handles around 90,000 cases, of which around 2% are international, *i.e.* involving representation before foreign or international courts and other dispute settlement bodies.[131]

In specific cases, the law allows the State Attorney's Office to delegate its representation powers to external agents, with the consent of the Government. This provision allows the State Attorney's Office to organize the representation of the State in the most optimal way, especially in more complex cases where its internal capacity may not be sufficient, whether on quantitative or on substantive grounds.

In addition, advisory and support teams are regularly set up to support the State Attorney's Office, often at its initiative, involving experts from relevant State authorities, but also industry experts and academic professionals.

The practical experience thus far shows, on the one hand, that the engagement of foreign counsel and experts allows the State to access the expertise and experience that a small country like Slovenia may not necessarily have at home. On the other hand, the internal, less public, multidisciplinary support teams and consultation with academia have proven to be beneficial as they allow for productive interaction, knowledge and experience sharing and access to information relating to the pre-contentious events (i.e. developments predating the occurrence of the dispute, evolution of relevant legislation, etc.). Moreover, such interaction enables involvement and a sense of commitment across the relevant levels of State authority.

7 Conclusion

In conclusion, Slovenia has established itself as a desirable destination for foreign direct investment, underpinned by its political stability, modern infrastructure, a highly educated workforce and a comprehensive legal framework governing various aspects of foreign direct investment. Furthermore, Slovenian courts enjoy a comparatively high degree of trust and independence.

131 See, *e.g.*, the annual report of the State Attorney's Office for 2022: Letno poročilo o delu Državnega odvetništva Republike Slovenije za leto 2022. February 2023 <https://www.dodv-rs.si/fileadmin/datoteke/dokumenti/LETNO_POROCILO/Letno_porocilo_o_delu_Drzavnega_odvetnistva_RS_za_leto_2022.docx> (accessed on 29 May 2024).

Recent developments have, however, seen a notable shift in Slovenia's position on ISDS and a resulting significant transformation in its investment protection framework. This is particularly evident in the termination of its Intra-EU BITs, following the adoption of the Termination Agreement, and the alignment of its international investment policies with those of the EU. This is further reflected in Slovenia's recent withdrawal from the ECT.

Despite these changes, several investment agreements that Slovenia has concluded with non-EU countries remain in force. Moreover, the sunset clause contained in the ECT as it stands provides for the application of the ECT to existing investments until 2044. Against this background, Slovenia may therefore not yet have seen the last of its investment arbitrations.

CHAPTER 19

Conclusions

Fahira Brodlija and Armela Ramić

While it is tempting to close this book with a set of conclusions tying up the robust analysis in the preceding chapters, the Western Balkans region and the field of investment law and dispute resolution are on a steady course of change and reform. The latter has been subject to intensive scrutiny, with multiple tracks of substantive and procedural reforms running in parallel, to address the identified concerns with the existing system. The growing body of reform solutions include everything from the abandonment of the system of bilateral investment treaties and the establishment of a standing investment court, to a gradual reform of the existing framework to enhance the time and cost efficiency, consistency and integrity of the process. Although all the proposed solutions are touted as significant improvements to the existing system, none of them have been tested yet in practice.

At the same time, the Western Balkans governments are on a forward-looking path which requires a more agile and adaptable reform package which will propel their progress towards sustainable economic development and EU integration, while protecting them from legal exposure and liability in investment disputes. Therefore, the Western Balkans region has carved out a reform path which allows each economy to remain on track towards EU accession, while addressing more immediate needs to improve their frameworks for investment protection and dispute resolution.

In light of this undeniable forward-looking movement of the subject and field of focus in this book, its chapters analyze and assess the current stage of reform and development, highlighting the milestones for each economy, and placing them in the context of the global reform dynamics, as well as those from other regions.

1 Navigating the Dynamic Tracks of Reform

Most of the compiling international reform proposals, including those from the EU, have not been tested in practice to date, pending the ratification of the relevant treaties (such as the CETA, EU SIPA, the modernized ECT provisions, etc.) or the establishment of the novel institutional mechanisms (such as the

 | DOI:10.1163/9789004729889_020

multilateral investment court or the Advisory Centre for States). Therefore, as detailed in the Section II chapters, the Western Balkans governments have carved out their own reform space, tailoring the best practices proposed at the international level, to their own set of priorities and structures, in light of the lessons drawn from their ISDS experiences.

In this sense, some governments have modernized their model bilateral investment treaties (including both substantive and procedural provisions), seeking to balance the rights and obligations of the sovereign state and the foreign investors and to reduce the frequency and scope of potential investment disputes. Other governments have recently enacted legislation exclusively dedicated to investment law and dispute resolution, or reformed existing legislation addressing these issues. These developments affirm the level of attention these issues have captured among policy makers in the Western Balkans, which may improve the standing of the respective economies in investment arbitration or help prevent or mitigate such disputes.

Along with the treaty and legislative reforms, the region has expressed increasing interest in institutional mechanisms for the early identification and prevention of investment disputes, as well as coordination bodies for the amicable settlement of investment disputes, before and during the cooling-off period. Considering the fact that a large number of investor grievance escalate into investment arbitration in the region due to the lack of communication and coordination among the competent institutions and with the investors, the Western Balkans governments are seeking to create robust structures which will enable a seamless flow of information and a timely reaction of the competent institutions to the initial notices of problems and potential disputes submitted by foreign investors. Some structures are already in place at the national level in several Western Balkans economies, while others are deliberating proposals developed with the support of international and regional experts. The multi-tiered framework in Bosnia and Herzegovina is already considered as a best practice for the region and beyond.

In order to strengthen and expand institutional knowledge and effectiveness of the implemented and deliberated reforms, the Western Balkans governments are engaging in continuous capacity development activities supported by international organizations, such as GIZ, the Regional Cooperation Council (RCC) and the World Bank Group (including ICSID). In addition, competent institutions from the region attentively follow and contribute to the ongoing reform discussions in international fora, including UNCITRAL WGIII and OECD (joint submissions to the WGIII)

With the systemic integration of modernized treaty standards into domestic legislation and investment contracts, along with the growing regional and international partnerships, the Western Balkans region will be in a better position to make steady progress towards attracting the investment necessary for a sustained economic development and a sustainable future. In addition, the timely adaptation to existing and emerging EU investment protection and dispute resolution policies will also streamline the EU integration process for the aspiring EU Member States in the region.

2 International Perspectives on Investment Law and Dispute Resolution in the Western Balkans

The discussion opens with an outline of concrete regional movements for investment and trade integration with the EU market, and how they have impacted the investment policies and reforms in the region. Samira Sulejmanovic and Ivana Gardasevic provided first-hand insights on the policy background of the regional initiatives and their practical realities. An area of particular focus was the regional effort to establish a harmonized set of standards and principles for the negotiation of investment treaties, which would be compatible with the EU requirements and support the progress made towards opening the markets towards the EU. The authors paint a positive picture of recent regional initiatives and attempts to form cohesive and mutually reinforcing economic and investment structures, emphasizing that the approach to investment law and dispute resolution will determine whether the progress made in the region can be cemented.

Setting the stage for the broader policy and practical analysis, Diana Rosert provided a clear-eyed empirical primer on the investor-State disputes against the Western Balkans economies and their outcomes to date. The statistics diligently compiled by UNCTAD showed that the Western Balkans economies as respondents in investor-State disputes have been fairly successful in defending against investor claims, although some of the largest claims remain pending as of the date of writing. Western Balkans respondents prevailed in large part either on the merits or jurisdiction, while claimant investors prevailed on the merits in full or in part in 19% of the cases. In this sense, the practical reality of investment jurisprudence involving the Western Balkans is in line with the international trends. However, the high costs of investment arbitration and difficulties in enforcing adverse costs awards against the investors continue to present significant challenges.

Recent investor-State disputes against EU Member States for changes in their regulatory changes in the renewable energy sector have demonstrated the risks and enormous financial consequences of the energy transition process.

As the Western Balkans region is seeking to attract renewable investors in compliance with the Paris Agreement and the Western Balkans Green Agenda, the quality of the regulatory framework and the treatment of the incoming investors will open the doors for immense opportunities, but also serious risks of new and consequential investment disputes in the renewable energy sector. Ilija Mitrev Penushliski analyzed in detail the policy, institutional and legal implications of the energy transition process, drawing from the experiences from Italy, the Czech Republic and Spain, transposing them into the Western Balkans context. The author provided a cutting-edge and thought-provoking analysis of the rich (an still unfolding) investor-state saga in Spain, highlighting how States may not be able to escape liability in renewable energy cases under investment treaties (particularly the Energy Charter Treaty) even for regulatory changes introduced in the public interest. This is particularly pertinent for governments in the Western Balkans whose complex institutional frameworks often operate without consideration of the consequences of their measures under international law. In this sense, effective treaty provisions protecting the State's right to regulate in the public interest become even more important.

EU policies and reform packages are already the highest priorities for the aspiring EU Member States in the Western Balkans region, and international investment agreements are no exception. Nikos Lavranos and Marialena Komi unpacked the "non-paper" recently published by the EU Commission, which provides the model provisions for EU Member State BITs with third countries (including candidate States). Although the Member States have agreed in 2020 to terminate all their mutual BITs following the *Achmea* decision of the CJEU, they are still allowed to renegotiate or conclude new treaties with third countries. Following an in-depth and meticulous analysis of the key provisions of the model clauses, the authors succinctly lay out possible implications for Western Balkans governments should they opt for the adoption of the specific substantive and procedural provisions. Their analysis showed that, despite the clear course of the EU investment protection policies in the field of investment protection and dispute resolution, aspiring EU Member States (including those from the Western Balkans) may have some space to calibrate and adapt the model provisions in their own prospective treaties, while maintaining the spirit and principles of the EU policies reflected in the Model Provisions. This is particularly true in the realm of environmental and corporate social responsibility standards, as well as the dispute resolution clauses, while providing for a transition to the EU framework upon accession.

Staying on the topic of treaty design, Kabir Duggal, Kevin W. Gray and Samiha Gopal zoom into the recent Model BITs, comparing three generations of treaties adopted by North Macedonia, Serbia and Bosnia and Herzegovina.

The provisions of these treaties, drafted at different stages of EU approximation and ISDS reform, also reflect their responses to their direct and indirect experiences in investor-state disputes, which the respective governments sought to address and refine. The BiH Model BIT, as the most recent and most robust model, shows how WB governments can take the best from the international and regional proposals and good practices, while tailoring the mosaic of substantive and procedural protections to their own economic and strategic priorities.

In reforming their existing network of investment treaties, Western Balkans policy treaty negotiators are particularly interested in the investment protection clauses which have either expanded the coverage of the treaties beyond their intended scope or allowed for broad tribunal interpretations in favor of foreign investors. Chief among such provisions are the definition of investor and investment and the fair and equitable treatment standard – each of which were analyzed in detail in the book.

Vlora Maxhuni explored the origins, development and current manifestations of the threshold definition of investor and investment as they appear in bilateral investment treaties, including those in force in the Western Balkans. In her thorough analysis, the author outlined how arbitral tribunals have dealt with determining personal and subject-matter jurisdiction in cases where the respondent States contested the status of the claimant as an investor under the treaty, or the coverage of their alleged investment. Western Balkans economies, deriving from their ISDS experiences, are particularly wary of the possibility of investment claims by dual nationals, or so-called "mailbox" enterprises with no substantial business activities in their alleged home State. This chapter offers examples of treaty language which may mitigate such risks and ensure that only covered investors and investments can take advantage of the applicable treaty protections.

The Fair and Equitable treatment standard has also been a constant presence in investor-State jurisprudence and the most successful claim for foreign investors. The broad formulations of this standard provided in old-generation investment treaties (including most Western Balkans bilateral investment treaties) have enabled claimant investors to put forth a wide spectrum of claims under its umbrella, with a high degree of success. A particularly problematic element of the FET standard is the violation of the investor's legitimate expectations, which could have a chilling effect on the State's ability to regulate for fear of facing investment claims.

Filip Balcerzak masterfully presents the many faces of the FET standard in its various formulations in investment treaties, and its diverse interpretations by arbitral tribunals. Since FET claims featured in all of the known investment disputes against Western Balkans governments, the author draws from the regional experiences and indicates the factual and legal issues which enabled such claims to arise. Importantly, this chapter also presents several options for the modernization of the FET standard, i.e. the new FET models featured in recent EU treaty practices (e.g. CETA), the proposed modernized ECT, and the USMCA. Each of these models seeks to set clearer parameters for the FET standard, thus balancing the expectations of investors and the right of the state to regulate in the public interest.

Although the effectiveness of the new models of the FET clause has not yet been tested in investment disputes, the more detailed provisions provide clear roadmaps to guide arbitral tribunals through their interpretive endeavors in future cases.

In addition to reforms to the most prevalent issues emerging from investor state disputes (i.e. calibrating investment protection standards and improving the investment arbitration process), States are also increasingly considering and creating space for a path less taken in investor-state disputes – dispute prevention mechanisms and investor-State mediation. Although investment arbitration is the primary association with ISDS, there is a much broader investor-State conflict continuum with opportunities to address problems and grievances without recourse to any adversarial procedures. In addition, the vast majority of investment treaties also provide space in the "cooling-off period" for good faith attempts to settle disputes through amicable methods, such as mediation. Both of these opportunities are largely neglected or simply underutilized in the Western Balkans ISDS context, for a variety of reasons, including fear of political exposure, public scrutiny, lack of capacities or lack of designated settlement authority.

In her chapter on dispute prevention mechanisms, Fahira Brodlija explored how improved communication and coordination between the competent institutions and with foreign investors could help prevent investor grievances from escalating to disputes. Dispute prevention mechanisms can be established as separate institutions within the government, or they could function through a single focal point connected to a coordination body of competent institutions which can jointly deliberate and propose solutions for the relevant grievance or emerging dispute. Such mechanisms could help maintain existing investments, but also demonstrate to potential investors that the government disposes of transparent and agile mechanisms to respond to their issues in their mutual interest. The author highlighted some models proposed by international organizations or established in specific countries, including those in the Western Balkans.

Investment mediation is becoming increasingly interesting as a dispute resolution mechanism in cases where early, direct interventions are insufficient to resolve the possible investment dispute. Although mediation, as a form of facilitated negotiation is available to the disputing parties at any time before, during and even after the initiation of arbitral proceedings, it has only recently captured the attention of policy makers, prompted by the deliberations at the UNCITRAL WGIII and the adoption of the standalone ICSID Mediation Rules. Frauke Nitschke laid out the key features of the mediation process under the new ICSID Rules, as well as the robust supporting services ICSID could offer the parties to mediation. Importantly, the chapter provided some key points of consideration which may help governments decide whether mediation is an appropriate mechanism for the resolution of a particular dispute. The author offered unique insights into the known settlement rates based on the ICSID caseload data, which show that Western Balkans economies have already settled or discontinued dozens of cases, although the means of amicable settlement are unclear from the available data. In addition, the author emphasized the important initiatives taking place in the region, indicating the interest of the competent institutions to foster the practice of mediation in investment disputes.

3 Regional Perspectives on Investment Law and Dispute Resolution

The Section 2 chapters, focusing on individual Western Balkans economies, provide granular data, national perspectives and most recent legal and institutional developments from each economy, mapping their evolving legal and institutional frameworks, as well as some lingering challenges in effectively implementing the modern reform solutions. Chief among the remaining roadblocks are complex governmental structures and outdated bureaucratic procedures which are difficult to reform or navigate.

In addition, the competent institutions are often understaffed and lack the requisite capacities to follow and implement the reform proposals, especially those that would add responsibilities to their portfolio. None of the economies in the Western Balkans have specialized agencies or departments dealing exclusively with issues of international investment law and dispute resolution, but such competences are dispersed through the governmental structures, often with little coordination.

With the ongoing efforts to design institutional coordination bodies and focal points, and the rich offering of training and capacity development measures (including the possible establishment of the UNCITRAL Advisory Centre for States), the Western Balkans economies are addressing an important factor which will determine the rate and effectiveness of their progress. In addition to the aspiring EU-member States from the Western Balkans, Section 2 includes inputs from Croatia and Slovenia, providing a regional experience with an EU flavor. These chapters shed light on the effect of EU membership on their legal and institutional frameworks for investment law and dispute resolution, and the level of control (or lack thereof) they have over opting for particular reform paths. Importantly, the authors reflect on the realities of facing and navigating intra-EU disputes, and how they unfold before arbitral tribunals and enforcement courts, in light of the *Achmea* and *Komstroy* judgments of the CJEU.

4 Outlooks Instead of a Conclusion

In light of the numerous moving parts in the realm of investment law and dispute resolution reform, this book could not, nor did it seek to, provide any definitive answers or predictions as to the final contours of the reform solutions which will shape the future of the Western Balkans region and each of its constituent parts.

The book and each of its chapters provide a timestamp at a crucial point for the evolution of the international investment law and dispute resolution systems in the Western Balkans, comprehensively laying out the status quo from the regional and international perspectives. It also provides, in one place, a compass for decision makers and treaty negotiators in their policy decisions, as well as dispute resolution lawyers seeking guidance on the key issues underpinning their approach to concrete investor-State disputes. It is also a unique point of reference for scholars, researchers and others interested in the development of international investment law and dispute resolution in the Western Balkans, which can open new avenues for research and a continuous discourse on these crucial topics for the region.

Index